HEADS OF FAMILIES

AT THE FIRST CENSUS OF THE
UNITED STATES TAKEN
IN THE YEAR
1790

RECORDS OF THE STATE ENUMERATIONS: 1782 TO 1785

VIRGINIA

GENEALOGICAL PUBLISHING CO., INC.
BALTIMORE   1976

Originally Published
Government Printing Office
Washington, 1908

Reprinted
Southern Book Company
Baltimore, 1952

Genealogical Publishing Co., Inc.
Baltimore, 1966
Baltimore, 1970
Baltimore, 1976

Library of Congress Catalogue Card Number 77-111630
International Standard Book Number 0-8063-0344-1

FIRST CENSUS
OF THE UNITED STATES
1790
RECORDS OF THE STATE ENUMERATIONS: 1782 TO 1785

VIRGINIA

HEADS OF FAMILIES AT THE FIRST CENSUS
1790

RECORDS OF THE STATE ENUMERATIONS: 1782 TO 1785

INTRODUCTION.

The First Census of the United States (1790) comprised an enumeration of the inhabitants of the present states of Connecticut, Delaware, Georgia, Kentucky, Maine, Maryland, Massachusetts, New Hampshire, New Jersey, New York, North Carolina, Pennsylvania, Rhode Island, South Carolina, Tennessee, Vermont, and Virginia.

A complete set of the schedules for each state, with a summary for the counties, and in many cases for towns, was filed in the State Department, but unfortunately they are not now complete, the returns for the states of Delaware, Georgia, Kentucky, New Jersey, Tennessee, and Virginia having been destroyed when the British burned the Capitol at Washington during the War of 1812. For several of the states for which schedules are lacking it is probable that the Director of the Census could obtain lists which would present the names of most of the heads of families at the date of the First Census. At the census of 1790 the state of Virginia was returned with a population of 747,160, leading, by more than 300,000, Pennsylvania, the second state of the Union in point of population at the First Census. The loss of Virginia's original schedules for the First and Second censuses is so unfortunate that every endeavor has been made to secure data that would in some measure fill the vacancy. The only records that could be secured were some manuscript lists of state enumerations made in the years 1782, 1783, 1784, and 1785; also the tax lists of Greenbrier county from 1783 to 1786. These documents were on file in the State Library and could not be removed therefrom. Through the courtesy of the State Librarian and the members of the Library Board, an act was passed by the legislature allowing the Census Office to withdraw the lists for the purpose of making copies and publishing the names, in lieu of the Federal census returns. The counties for which the names of the heads of families are returned on the state census lists are 39 in number, and contained in 1790 a population of 370,000; 41 counties with 377,000 population are lacking; this publication covers, therefore, only about one-half of the state. A copy of the enumerator's list for the city of Richmond has been obtained, and the data are presented on page 111.

The schedules of 1790 form a unique inheritance for the Nation, since they represent for each of the states concerned a complete list of the heads of families in the United States at the time of the adoption of the Constitution. The framers were the statesmen and leaders of thought, but those whose names appear upon the schedules of the First Census were in general the plain citizens who by their conduct in war and peace made the Constitution possible and by their intelligence and self-restraint put it into successful operation.

The total population of the United States in 1790, exclusive of slaves, as derived from the schedules was 3,231,533. The only names appearing upon the schedules, however, were those of heads of families, and as at that period the families averaged 6 persons, the total number was approximately 540,000, or slightly more than half a million. The number of names which is now lacking because of the destruction of the schedules is approximately 140,000, thus leaving schedules containing about 400,000 names.

The information contained in the published report of the First Census of the United States, a small volume of 56 pages, was not uniform for the several states and territories. For New England and one or two of the other states the population was presented by counties and towns; that of New Jersey appeared partly by counties and towns and partly by counties only; in other cases the returns were given by counties only. Thus the complete transcript of the names of heads of families, with accompanying information, presents for the first time detailed information as to the number of inhabitants—males, females, etc.—for each minor civil division in all those states for which such information was not originally published.

In response to repeated requests from patriotic societies and persons interested in genealogy, or desirous of studying the early history of the United States, Congress added to the sundry civil appropriation bill for the fiscal year 1907 the following paragraph:

The Director of the Census is hereby authorized and directed to publish, in a permanent form, by counties and minor civil divisions, the names of the heads of families returned at the First Census of the United States in seventeen hundred and ninety; and the Director of the Census is authorized, in his discretion, to sell said publications, the proceeds thereof to be covered into the Treasury of the United States, to be deposited to the credit of miscellaneous receipts on account of "Proceeds of sales of Government property:"

Provided, That no expense shall be incurred hereunder additional to appropriations for the Census Office for printing therefor made for the fiscal year nineteen hundred and seven; and the Director of the Census is hereby directed to report to Congress at its next session the cost incurred hereunder and the price fixed for said publications and the total received therefor.

The urgent deficiency bill, approved February 15, 1908, contained the following provision:

That the Director of the Census is hereby authorized and directed to expend so much of the appropriation for printing for the Department of Commerce and Labor allotted by law to the Census Office for the fiscal year ending June thirtieth, nineteen hundred and eight, as may be necessary to continue and complete the publication of the names of the heads of families returned at the First Census of the United States, as authorized by the sundry civil appropriation act approved June thirtieth, nineteen hundred and six.

In accordance with the authority given in the paragraphs quoted above, the names returned at the First Census in the states of Connecticut, Maine, Maryland, Massachusetts, New Hampshire, New York, North Carolina, Pennsylvania, Rhode Island, South Carolina, and Vermont have been published, thus completing the roster of the heads of families in 1790 so far as they can be shown from the records of the Census Office. As the Federal census schedules of the state of Virginia for 1790 are missing, the lists of the state enumerations made in 1782, 1783, 1784, and 1785, while not complete, have been substituted.

THE FIRST CENSUS.

The First Census act was passed at the second session of the First Congress, and was signed by President Washington on March 1, 1790. The task of making the first enumeration of inhabitants was placed upon the President. Under this law the marshals of the several judicial districts were required to ascertain the number of inhabitants within their respective districts, omitting Indians not taxed, and distinguishing free persons (including those bound to service for a term of years) from all others; the sex and color of free persons; and the number of free males 16 years of age and over.

The object of the inquiry last mentioned was, undoubtedly, to obtain definite knowledge as to the military and industrial strength of the country. This fact possesses special interest, because the Constitution directs merely an enumeration of inhabitants. Thus the demand for increasingly extensive information, which has been so marked a characteristic of census legislation, began with the First Congress that dealt with the subject.

The method followed by the President in putting into operation the First Census law, although the object of extended investigation, is not definitely known. It is supposed that the President or the Secretary of State dispatched copies of the law, and perhaps of instructions also, to the marshals. There is, however, some ground for disputing this conclusion. At least one of the reports in the census volume of 1790 was furnished by a governor. This, together with the fact that there is no record of correspondence with the marshals on the subject of the census, but that there is a record of such correspondence with the governors, makes very strong the inference that the marshals received their instructions through the governors of the states. This inference is strengthened by the fact that in 1790 the state of Massachusetts furnished the printed blanks, and also by the fact that the law relating to the Second Census specifically charged the Secretary of State to superintend the enumeration and to communicate directly with the marshals.

By the terms of the First Census law nine months were allowed in which to complete the enumeration. The census taking was supervised by the marshals of the several judicial districts, who employed assistant marshals to act as enumerators. There were 17 marshals. The records showing the number of assistant marshals employed in 1790, 1800, and 1810 were destroyed by fire, but the number employed in 1790 has been estimated at 650.

The schedules which these officials prepared consist of lists of names of heads of families; each name appears in a stub, or first column, which is followed by five columns, giving details of the family. These columns are headed as follows:

Free white males of 16 years and upward, including heads of families.
Free white males under 16 years.
Free white females, including heads of families.
All other free persons.
Slaves.

The assistant marshals made two copies of the returns; in accordance with the law one copy was posted in the immediate neighborhood for the information of the public, and the other was transmitted to the marshal in charge, to be forwarded to the President. The schedules were turned over by the President to the Secretary of State. Little or no tabulation was required, and the report of the First Census, as also the reports of the Second, Third, and Fourth, was produced without the employment of any clerical force, the summaries being transmitted directly to the printer. The total population as returned in 1790 was 3,929,214, and the entire cost of the census was $44,377.

A summary of the results of the First Census, not including the returns for South Carolina, was transmitted to Congress by President Washington on October 27, 1791. The legal period for enumeration, nine months, had been extended, the longest time consumed being eighteen months in South Carolina. The report of October 27 was printed in full, and published in what is now a very rare little volume; afterwards the report for South Carolina was "tipped in." To contain the results of the Twelfth Census, ten large quarto volumes, comprising in all 10,400 pages, were required. No illustration of the expansion of census inquiry can be more striking.

The original schedules of the First Census are now contained in 26 bound volumes, preserved in the Census Office. For the most part the headings of the schedules were written in by hand. Indeed, up to and including 1820, the assistant marshals generally used for the schedules such paper as they happened to have, ruling it, writing in the headings, and binding the sheets together themselves. In some cases merchants' account paper was used, and now and then the schedules were bound in wall paper.

As a consequence of requiring marshals to supply their own blanks, the volumes containing the schedules vary in size from about 7 inches long, 3 inches wide, and ½ inch thick to 21 inches long, 14 inches wide, and 6 inches thick. Some of the sheets in these volumes are only 4 inches long, but a few are 3 feet in length, necessitating several folds. In some cases leaves burned at the edges have been covered with transparent silk to preserve them.

THE UNITED STATES IN 1790.

In March, 1790, the Union consisted of twelve states—Rhode Island, the last of the original thirteen to enter the Union, being admitted May 29 of the same year. Vermont, the first addition, was admitted in the following year, before the results of the First Census were announced. Maine was a part of Massachusetts, Kentucky was a part of Virginia, and the present states of Alabama and Mississippi were parts of Georgia. The present states of Ohio, Indiana, Illinois, Michigan, and Wisconsin, with part of Minnesota, were known as the Northwest Territory, and the present state of Tennessee, then a part of North Carolina, was soon to be organized as the Southwest Territory.

The United States was bounded on the west by the Mississippi river, beyond which stretched that vast and unexplored wilderness belonging to the Spanish King, which was afterwards ceded to the United States by France as the Louisiana Purchase, and now comprises the great and populous states of South Dakota, Iowa, Nebraska, Missouri, Kansas, Arkansas, and Oklahoma, and portions of Minnesota, North Dakota, Montana, Wyoming, Colorado, New Mexico, Texas, and Louisiana. The Louisiana Purchase was not consummated for more than a decade after the First Census was taken. On the south was another Spanish colony known as the Floridas. The greater part of Texas, then a part of the colony of Mexico, belonged to Spain; and California, Nevada, Utah, Arizona, and a portion of New Mexico, also the property of Spain, although penetrated here and there by venturesome explorers and missionaries, were, for the most part, an undiscovered wilderness.

The gross area of the United States was 827,844 square miles, but the settled area was only 239,935 square miles, or about 29 per cent of the total. Though the area covered by the enumeration in 1790 seems very small when compared with the present area of the United States, the difficulties which confronted the census taker were vastly greater than in 1900. In many localities there were no roads, and where these did exist they were poor and frequently impassable; bridges were almost unknown. Transportation was entirely by horseback, stage, or private coach. A journey as long as that from New York to Washington was a serious undertaking, requiring eight days under the most favorable conditions. Western New York was a wilderness, Elmira and Binghamton being but detached hamlets. The territory west of the Allegheny mountains, with the exception of a portion of Kentucky, was unsettled and scarcely penetrated. Detroit and Vincennes were too small and isolated to merit consideration. Philadelphia was the capital of the United States. Washington was a mere Government project, not even named, but known as the Federal City. Indeed, by the spring of 1793, only one wall of the White House had been constructed, and the site for the Capitol had been merely surveyed. New York city in 1790 possessed a population of only 33,131, although it was the largest city in the United States; Philadelphia was second, with 28,522; and Boston third, with 18,320. Mails were transported in very irregular fashion, and correspondence was expensive and uncertain.

There were, moreover, other difficulties which were of serious moment in 1790, but which long ago ceased to be problems in census taking. The inhabitants, having no experience with census taking, imagined that some scheme for increasing taxation was involved, and were inclined to be cautious lest they should reveal too much of their own affairs. There was also opposition to enumeration on religious grounds, a count of inhabitants being regarded by many as a cause for divine displeasure. The boundaries of towns and other minor divisions, and even those of counties, were in many cases unknown or not defined at all. The hitherto semi-independent states had been under the control of the Federal Government for so short a time that the different sections had not yet been welded into an harmonious nationality in which the Federal authority should be unquestioned and instructions promptly and fully obeyed.

AN ACT PROVIDING FOR THE ENUMERATION OF THE INHABITANTS OF THE UNITED STATES

APPROVED MARCH 1, 1790

SECTION 1. Be it enacted by the Senate and House of Representatives of the United States of America in Congress assembled, That the marshals of the several districts of the United States shall be, and they are hereby authorized and required to cause the number of the inhabitants within their respective districts to be taken; omitting in such enumeration Indians not taxed, and distinguishing free persons, including those bound to service for a term of years, from all others; distinguishing also the sexes and colours of free persons, and the free males of sixteen years and upwards from those under that age; for effecting which purpose the marshals shall have power to appoint as many assistants within their respective districts as to them shall appear necessary; assigning to each assistant a certain division of his district, which division shall consist of one or more counties, cities, towns, townships, hundreds or parishes, or of a territory plainly and distinctly bounded by water courses, mountains, or public roads. The marshals and their assistants shall respectively take an oath or affirmation, before some judge or justice of the peace, resident within their respective districts, previous to their entering on the discharge of the duties by this act required. The oath or affirmation of the marshal shall be, "I, A. B., Marshal of the district of ———, do solemnly swear (or affirm) that I will well and truly cause to be made a just and perfect enumeration and description of all persons resident within my district, and return the same to the President of the United States, agreeably to the directions of an act of Congress, intituled 'An act providing for the enumeration of the inhabitants of the United States,' according to the best of my ability." The oath or affirmation of an assistant shall be "I, A. B., do solemnly swear (or affirm) that I will make a just and perfect enumeration and description of all persons resident within the division assigned to me by the marshal of the district of ———, and make due return thereof to the said marshal, agreeably to the directions of an act of Congress, intituled 'An act providing for the enumeration of the inhabitants of the United States,' according to the best of my ability." The enumeration shall commence on the first Monday in August next, and shall close within nine calendar months thereafter. The several assistants shall, within the said nine months, transmit to the marshals by whom they shall be respectively appointed, accurate returns of all persons, except Indians not taxed, within their respective divisions, which returns shall be made in a schedule, distinguishing the several families by the names of their master, mistress, steward, overseer, or other principal person therein, in manner following, that is to say:

The number of persons within my division, consisting of ———, appears in a schedule hereto annexed, subscribed by me this —— day of ———, 179-. A. B. *Assistant to the marshal of ———.*

Schedule of the whole number of persons within the division allotted to A. B.

Names of heads of families.	Free white males of 16 years and upwards, including heads of families.	Free white males under 16 years.	Free white females, including heads of families.	All other free persons.	Slaves.

SECTION 2. And be it further enacted, That every assistant failing to make return, or making a false return of the enumeration to the marshal, within the time by this act limited, shall forfeit the sum of two hundred dollars.

SECTION 3. And be it further enacted, That the marshals shall file the several returns aforesaid, with the clerks of their respective district courts, who are hereby directed to receive and carefully preserve the same: And the marshals respectively shall, on or before the first day of September, one thousand seven hundred and ninety-one, transmit to the President of the United States, the aggregate amount of each description of persons within their respective districts. And every marshal failing to file the returns of his assistants, or any of them, with the clerks of their respective district courts, or failing to return the aggregate amount of each description of persons in their respective districts, as the same shall appear from said returns, to the President of the United States within the time limited by this act, shall, for every such offense, forfeit the sum of eight hundred dollars; all which forfeitures shall be recoverable in the courts of the districts where the offenses shall be committed, or in the circuit courts to be held within the same, by action of debt, information or indictment; the one-half thereof to the use of the United States, and the other half to the informer; but where the prosecution shall be first instituted on the behalf of the United States, the whole shall accrue to their use. And for the more effectual discovery of offenses, the judges of the several district courts, at their next sessions, to be held after the expiration of the time allowed for making the returns of the enumeration hereby directed, to the President of the United States, shall give this act in charge to the grand juries, in their respective courts, and shall cause the returns of the several assistants to be laid before them for their inspection.

SECTION 4. And be it further enacted, That every assistant shall receive at the rate of one dollar for every one hundred and fifty persons by him returned, where such persons reside in the country; and where such persons reside in a city, or town, containing more than five thousand persons, such assistants shall receive at the rate of one dollar for every three hundred persons; but where, from the dispersed situation of the inhabitants in some divisions, one dollar for every one hundred and fifty persons shall be insufficient, the marshals, with the approbation of the judges of their respective districts, may make such further allowance to the assistants in such divisions as shall be deemed an adequate compensation, provided the same does not exceed one dollar for every fifty persons by them returned. The several marshals shall receive as follows: The marshal of the district of Maine, two hundred dollars; the marshal of the district of New Hampshire, two hundred dollars; the marshal of the district of Massachusetts, three hundred dollars; the marshal of the district of Connecticut, two hundred dollars; the marshal of the district of New York, three hundred dollars; the marshal of the district of New Jersey, two hundred dollars; the marshal of the district of Pennsylvania, three hundred dollars; the marshal of the district of Delaware, one hundred dollars; the marshal of the district of Maryland, three hundred dollars; the marshal of the district of Virginia, five hundred dollars; the marshal of the district of Kentucky, two hundred and fifty dollars; the marshal of the district of North Carolina, three hundred and fifty dollars; the marshal of the district of South Carolina, three hundred dollars; the marshal of the district of Georgia, two hundred and fifty dollars. And to obviate all doubts which may arise respecting the persons to be returned, and the manner of making the returns.

SECTION 5. Be it enacted, That every person whose usual place of abode shall be in any family on the aforesaid first Monday in August next, shall be returned as of such family; the name of every person, who shall be an inhabitant of any district, but without a settled place of residence, shall be inserted in the column of the aforesaid schedule, which is allotted for the heads of families, in that division where he or she shall be on the said first Monday in August next, and every person occasionally absent at the time of the enumeration, as belonging to that place in which he usually resides in the United States.

SECTION 6. And be it further enacted, That each and every person more than 16 years of age, whether heads of families or not, belonging to any family within any division of a district made or established within the United States, shall be, and hereby is, obliged to render to such assistant of the division, a true account, if required, to the best of his or her knowledge, of all and every person belonging to such family, respectively, according to the several descriptions aforesaid, on pain of forfeiting twenty dollars, to be sued for and recovered by such assistant, the one-half for his own use, and the other half for the use of the United States.

SECTION 7. And be it further enacted, That each assistant shall, previous to making his return to the marshal, cause a correct copy, signed by himself, of the schedule containing the number of inhabitants within his division, to be set up at two of the most public places within the same, there to remain for the inspection of all concerned; for each of which copies the said assistant shall be entitled to receive two dollars, provided proof of a copy of the schedule having been so set up and suffered to remain, shall be transmitted to the marshal, with the return of the number of persons; and in case any assistant shall fail to make such proof to the marshal, he shall forfeit the compensation by this act allowed him.

Approved March 1, 1790.

FIRST CENSUS OF THE UNITED STATES.

Population of the United States as returned at the First Census, by states: 1790.

DISTRICT.	Free white males of 16 years and upward, including heads of families.	Free white males under 16 years.	Free white females, including heads of families.	All other free persons.	Slaves.	Total.
Vermont	22,435	22,328	40,505	255	[1] 16	[2] 85,539
New Hampshire	36,086	34,851	70,160	630	158	141,885
Maine	24,384	24,748	46,870	538	None.	96,540
Massachusetts	95,453	87,289	190,582	5,463	None.	378,787
Rhode Island	16,019	15,799	32,652	3,407	948	68,825
Connecticut	60,523	54,403	117,448	2,808	2,764	237,946
New York	83,700	78,122	152,320	4,654	21,324	340,120
New Jersey	45,251	41,416	83,287	2,762	11,423	184,139
Pennsylvania	110,788	106,948	206,363	6,537	3,737	434,373
Delaware	11,783	12,143	22,384	3,899	8,887	[3] 59,094
Maryland	55,915	51,339	101,395	8,043	103,036	319,728
Virginia	110,936	116,135	215,046	12,866	292,627	747,610
Kentucky	15,154	17,057	28,922	114	12,430	73,677
North Carolina	69,988	77,506	140,710	4,975	100,572	393,751
South Carolina	35,576	37,722	66,880	1,801	107,094	249,073
Georgia	13,103	14,044	25,739	398	29,264	82,548
Total number of inhabitants of the United States exclusive of S. Western and N. territory	807,094	791,850	1,541,263	59,150	694,280	3,893,635

	Free white males of 21 years and upward.	Free males under 21 years of age.	Free white females.	All other persons.	Slaves.	Total.
S. W. territory	6,271	10,277	15,365	361	3,417	35,691
N. "						

[1] The census of 1790, published in 1791, reports 16 slaves in Vermont. Subsequently, and up to 1860, the number is given as 17. An examination of the original manuscript returns shows that there never were any slaves in Vermont. The original error occurred in preparing the results for publication, when 16 persons, returned as "Free colored," were classified as "Slave."

[2] Corrected figures are 85,425, or 114 less than figures published in 1790, due to an error of addition in the returns for each of the towns of Fairfield, Milton, Shelburne, and Williston, in the county of Chittenden; Brookfield, Newbury, Randolph, and Strafford, in the county of Orange; Castleton, Clarendon, Hubbardton, Poultney, Rutland, Shrewsbury, and Wallingford, in the county of Rutland; Dummerston, Guilford, Halifax, and Westminster, in the county of Windham; and Woodstock, in the county of Windsor.

[3] Corrected figures are 59,096, or 2 more than figures published in 1790, due to error in addition.

Summary of population of Virginia, by counties: 1790.

COUNTY.	Name of assistant.	Free white males of 16 years and upward.	Free white males under 16 years.	Free white females.	All other free persons.	Slaves.	Total.
Augusta, the part east of the north mountain	R. Porterfield	2,048	1,665	3,438	40	1,222	} 10,886
Part west of ditto	C. Cameron	551	572	986	19	345	
Albemarle	James Kerr	1,703	1,790	3,342	171	5,579	12,585
Accomack	R. Tunford	2,297	2,177	4,502	721	4,262	13,959
Amherst	C. Kenny	2,056	2,235	3,995	121	5,296	13,703
Amelia, including Nottoway, a new county	Charles Jones	1,709	1,697	3,278	106	11,307	18,097
Botetourt, as it stood previous to the formation of Wythe from it & Montgomery.	Joseph Paxton	2,247	2,562	4,432	24	1,259	10,524
Buckingham	G. Bernard	1,274	1,537	2,685	115	4,168	9,779
Berkley	N. Orrick	4,253	4,547	7,850	131	2,932	19,713
Brunswick	John Stith	1,472	1,529	2,918	132	6,776	12,827
Bedford	D. Sanders	1,785	2,266	3,674	52	2,754	10,531
Cumberland	P. I. Carrington	885	914	1,778	142	4,434	8,153
Chesterfield	A. Graves	1,652	1,557	3,149	369	7,487	14,214
Charlotte	Jacob Morton	1,285	1,379	2,535	63	4,816	10,078
Culpeper	T. C. Fletcher	3,372	3,755	6,682	70	8,226	22,105
Charles City	R. Goodrich	532	509	1,043	363	3,141	5,588
Caroline	Henry Chiles	1,799	1,731	3,464	203	10,292	17,489
Campbell	R. Hunter	1,236	1,347	2,363	251	2,488	7,685
Dinwiddie	J. R. Davis	1,790	1,396	2,853	561	7,334	13,934
Essex	T. Banks	908	869	1,766	139	5,440	9,122
Elizabeth City	R. Saunders	390	388	778	18	1,876	3,450
Fauquier	S. Morgan	2,674	2,983	5,500	93	6,642	17,892
Fairfax	T. Pollard	2,138	1,872	3,601	135	4,574	12,320
Franklin	Thomas Hale	1,266	1,629	2,840	34	1,073	6,842
Fluvanna	J. Johnston	589	654	1,187	25	1,466	3,921
Frederick Division	Edward Smith	1,757	1,653	3,041	49	1,319	} 19,681
Ditto	John Smith	2,078	2,517	4,269	67	2,931	
Gloucester	W. Camp	1,597	1,523	3,105	210	7,063	13,498
Goochland	R. H. Saunders	1,028	1,059	2,053	257	4,656	9,053
Greensville	J. Peterson	669	627	1,234	212	3,620	6,362
Greenbrier, including Kanawa, a new county	W. Johnson	1,463	1,574	2,639	20	319	6,015
Henrico	Z. Rowland	1,823	1,170	2,607	581	5,819	12,000
Hanover	J. M. Walker	1,637	1,412	3,242	240	8,223	14,754
Hampshire	F. Taggart	1,662	1,956	3,261	13	454	7,346
Harrison	W. Martin	487	579	947	....	67	2,080
Hardy	W. Bullet	1,108	2,256	3,192	411	369	7,336
Halifax	W. M'Craw	2,214	2,320	4,397	226	5,565	14,722
Henry	R. Payne	1,523	1,963	3,277	165	1,551	8,479
Isle of Wight	T. Fearn	1,208	1,163	2,415	375	3,867	9,028
James City	R. Saunders	395	359	765	146	2,495	4,070
King William	W. Winston	723	732	1,438	84	5,151	8,128
King and Queen	John Bagby	995	1,026	2,138	75	5,143	9,377
King George	W. H. Parker	757	781	1,585	86	4,157	7,366
Lunenburg	John Ballard	1,110	1,185	2,252	80	4,332	8,959
Loudon	S. D. Hariman	3,677	3,992	7,080	183	4,030	18,962
Lancaster	Joseph Carter	535	542	1,182	143	3,236	5,638
Louisa	C. Yancey, junior	957	1,024	1,899	14	4,573	8,467
Mecklenburg	John Ballard	1,857	2,015	3,683	416	6,762	14,733
Middlesex	T. Churchill	407	370	754	51	2,558	4,140
Monongalia	J. Dougherty	1,089	1,345	2,168	12	154	4,768
Montgomery, as it stood previous to the formation of Wythe from it and Botetourt.	James Newell	2,846	3,744	5,804	6	828	13,228
Norfolk	John Ingram	2,650	1,987	4,291	251	5,345	14,524
Northampton	James Palmer	857	743	1,581	464	3,244	6,889
New Kent	W. Graves	605	587	1,199	148	3,700	6,239
Northumberland	Joseph Locke	1,046	1,137	2,323	197	4,460	9,103
Nansemond	John Best	1,215	1,167	2,331	480	3,817	9,010
Orange	J. Wood, junior	1,317	1,426	2,693	64	4,421	9,921
Ohio	R. Woods	1,222	1,377	2,308	24	281	5,212
Prince Edward	Charles Jones	1,044	1,077	1,961	32	3,986	8,100
Prince William	W. Grayson	1,644	1,797	3,303	167	4,704	11,615
Prince George	J. R. Davis	965	822	1,600	267	4,519	8,173
Powhatan	P. I. Carrington	623	548	1,115	211	4,325	6,822
Pendleton	C. Cameron	568	686	1,124	1	73	2,452
Pittsylvania	W. M'Craw	2,008	2,447	4,083	62	2,979	11,579
Princess Anne	J. Ingram	1,169	1,151	2,207	64	3,202	7,793
Richmond	W. H. Parker	704	697	1,517	83	3,984	6,985
Randolph	John Elliott	221	270	441	....	19	951
Rockingham	L. Yauncey	1,816	1,652	3,209	....	772	7,449
Russell	C. Carter	734	969	1,440	5	190	3,338
Rockbridge	John M'Kee	1,517	1,532	2,756	41	682	6,548
Spotsylvania	John Fox	1,361	1,278	2,532	148	5,933	11,252
Stafford	S. Payton	1,341	1,355	2,769	87	4,036	9,588
Southampton	James Gee	1,632	1,546	3,134	559	5,993	12,864
Surry	I. C. Adkins	732	651	1,379	368	3,097	6,227
Shenandoah	W. Jennings	2,409	2,779	4,791	19	512	10,510
Sussex	David Mason	1,215	1,174	2,382	391	5,387	10,554
Warwick	R. Saunders	176	158	333	33	990	1,690
Washington	W. Preston	1,287	1,440	2,440	8	450	5,625
Westmoreland	W. H. Parker	815	754	1,614	114	4,425	7,722
York	R. Saunders	530	461	1,124	358	2,760	5,233
Total		110,936	116,135	215,046	12,866	292,627	747,610

Summary of population of Virginia, by principal towns, the inhabitants whereof being included in the general return: 1790.

TOWN.	County.	Free white males of 16 years and upward.	Free white males under 16 years.	Free white females.	All other free persons.	Slaves.	Total.
Alexandria	Fairfax	734	480	939	52	543	2,748
Fredericksburg	Spotsylvania	318	187	354	59	567	1,485
Richmond	Henrico	878	353	786	265	1,479	3,761
Petersburg in Dinwiddie comprehending Blandford in Prince George & Pocahuntas in Chesterfield.		583	205	465	310	1,265	2,828
Williamsburg	James City & York	186	108	368	46	636	1,344
Borough of Norfolk	Norfolk	599	312	693	61	1,294	2,959
Portsmouth	do	294	209	536	47	616	1,702
Winchester	Frederick	464	341	664	12	170	1,651
York	York	68	56	148	17	372	61

Amounting to one hundred and ten thousand nine hundred and thirty-six free white males of 16 years and upwards, one hundred and sixteen thousand one hundred and thirty-five free white males under 16 years, two hundred and fifteen thousand and forty-six free white females, twelve thousand eight hundred and fifty-six other free persons, and two hundred and ninety-two thousand six hundred and twenty-seven slaves. Total, seven hundred and forty-seven thousand six hundred and ten.

EDWARD CARRINGTON,
Marshal of the District of Virginia.

Summary of population and buildings: 1782 to 1785.

COUNTY.	1782 White.	1782 Black.	1783 White.	1783 Black.	1784 White souls.	1784 Dwellings.	1784 Other buildings.	1785 White souls.	1785 Dwellings.	1785 Other buildings.
Albemarle								4,341	673	2,317
Amelia	5,549	8,749						3,941	1,185	2,899
Amherst			5,964	3,852				4,530	406	1,133
Charlotte	3,790	3,442								
Chesterfield			4,885	5,961						
Cumberland	2,670	3,882			2,415	459	1,514			
Essex			2,489	2,817						
Fairfax	5,154	3,609						3,687	594	1,652
Fluvanna	1,985	1,330								
Frederick	4,786	767								
Gloucester			3,151	2,764	3,348	573	1,919			
Greenbrier								1,029[1]		
Greensville			1,845	2,691						
Halifax	5,335	3,290						6,486	963	2,176
Hampshire	7,469	513			7,182	1,066	1,783			
Hanover	3,707	5,184								
Harrison								1,507	209	121
Isle of Wight	3,760	2,948								
Lancaster			1,541	2,567				1,726	319	1,142
Mecklenburg	6,397	4,927								
Middlesex			1,167	2,282						
Monongalia	2,302	81								
Nansemond			2,842	2,567	730	166	456	357	92	257
New Kent	1,617	2,957						1,621	671	1,853
Norfolk								5,273	980	2,289
Northumberland	3,809	3,925			3,370	686	2,071			
Orange	3,410	2,848						4,020	603	1,809
Pittsylvania	5,304	1,835						5,851	469	2,491
Powhatan			1,468	2,669						
Prince Edward			1,552	1,468				3,425	538	1,710
Princess Anne			3,999	2,656				3,995	785	2,214
Richmond			2,947	3,885						
Rockingham					3,657	475	782			
Shenandoah			7,908	347				6,460	930	1,186
Stafford								2,483	428	783
Surry	2,389	2,729			2,667	427	1,358			
Sussex	2,923	3,696								
Warwick	569	776			597	116	485			
Williamsburg, city of	722	702								
Total	73,647	58,190	41,758	36,526	23,966	3,968	10,368	60,732	9,845	26,032

[1] List of names returned on tax lists of 1783 to 1786.

HEADS OF FAMILIES—VIRGINIA, 1782.

AMELIA COUNTY.[1]

NAME OF HEAD OF FAMILY.	White.	Black.	NAME OF HEAD OF FAMILY.	White.	Black.	NAME OF HEAD OF FAMILY.	White.	Black.	NAME OF HEAD OF FAMILY.	White.	Black.
LIST OF LAU. WILLS.			**LIST OF LAU. WILLS—con.**			**LIST OF WM. FINNEY.**			**LIST OF WILLIAM CROSS CRADDOCK—con.**		
Allen, Daniel	7	5	Tucker, Wm, sr	4	13	Booker, John, Senr	3	28	Farley, Stephen	2	3
Allen, Richd	3	1	Tucker, Daniel	4	3	Booker, John, Junr	7	19	Farley, Wm	3	10
Adams, David	6	3	Tucker, John	10	11	Bottom, William	3	8	Jackson, Wm, Senr	6	2
Beavers, Mary	4		Williams, David	5		Bott, Miles	10	23	Howell, John	4	....
Boulton, John	5		Tucker, Robt	4	2	Bass, William, Junr	6	15	Frazer, Wm	2	....
Bolling, Mary	15	98	Tucker, Wm	7	3	Bailey, Thomas	8		Farley, Nathl	4	2
Brooking, Vivion	11	82	Wilkerson, Thos	6	10	Coleman, Sutten	6		Farley, Steud	6	13
Bevill, James, sr	3	6	Bennitt, John	6		Ragsdale, George	2	19	Perkerson, Mathw	4	6
Bevill, James, jr	6	4	Bennitt, Wm	5		Mann, Samuel, Jr	9	2	Allen, Richd	4	
Bevill, Thomas (Este)	8	3	Weeks, Emanuel	10	3	Howlett, William	5	19	Baldwin, Phebe	4	....
Bevill, Robt	6		Weeks, Wm	4		Webster, William	8	4	Chumbley, Martha	7	4
Cousins, Rosamond	1	4	Hawks, John	6	14	Worsham, William	6	5	Roberts, Alex	4	2
Cousins, Phebe	2		Hawks, Richd	11	3	Elam, John	7		Lunsford, Sarah	1	10
Coleman, Isaac	3		Hawks, Judith	4	2	Reams, Frederick	7	1	Mays, Wm	2	1
Cousins, John	6	20	Pitchford, Daniel	5		Jackson, Mathew	7	3	Worsham, Ellin	4	15
Cousins, Robt (Este)	12	19				Morgan, William	5	3	McCann, Jno	7	....
Cousins, William	8	6	**LIST OF WILLIAM CRYER.**			Morgan, Simon	6	8	Smith, Corgn	8	5
Coleman, Burwell	2	1				Neal, Ann	6	13	Baldwin, George	11	4
Coleman, Francis	5	1	Cryer, William	1	29	Neal, John	6	7	Wingo, Jams	5	....
Coleman, Daniel, jr	13	7	Hood, Robert	12	4	Webster, Edward	4	9	Hill, Jno	1	2
Chandler, Martin	10	5	Clardy, Benjamin	8	15	Risen, Elery	5		Hill, Eliza	1	9
Coleman, Peter	8	2	Clardy, John	9	2	Webster, Peter	10	8	Hill, Sarah	2	4
Coleman, Abraham	7	4	Crawley, William	4	27	Dyer, Thomas	5		Hill, Jams	3	12
Coleman, Jesse	8	13	Beavell, Joseph	4	6	Willson, Thos B	5	62	Fagg, Wm	2	1
Caudle, John	3		Wills, Thomas T	7	7	Wallthall, Henry	1	22	Mitchell, John	1	
Davenport, Saml	3		Graves, Ceman	6		Worsham, Daniel	4	22	Mitchell, James C	1	....
Dicken, Richd	7		Hood, Solomon	3		Ford, Mary	15	36	Whitlow, Francis	3	10
Drake, William	3		Hood, Abraham	7		Rowlett, George	8	3	Foster, Rich	7	2
Dunnivant, Clemt	6	1	Tucker, John	4	1	Childress, John	2	31	Forster, Ann	2	7
Drake, Thos	9	2	Tucker, John	2		Towns, James	4	32	Craddock, Richd	9	12
Dodson, John	11	3	Clardy, William	4	1	Johnson, Elizabeth	9	11	Adkerson, Joshua	3	6
Ellington, Jesse	7		Tucker, Absalom	8		Webster, John	7	6	Stott, James		5
Foster, Wm	4	2	Tucker, Francis	3	3	Gibbs, William	8	10	Walton, Sherwood	5	15
Ford, Fredk	4	6	King, Henry	10	3	Gibbs, Miles	1		Forster, John	7	7
Green, Thos	4	6	Wilson, William	8	28	Walthall, John	2	20	Motley, Joell	4	17
Green, Wm	4	9	Bevill, Joseph	5		Walthall, Thomas	5	14	Mitchell, Jno	1	
Green, Abraham	8	55	Tucker, Mathew	11	2	Perkinson, Isham	7		Vaughan, Bartholomew	6	4
Herndon, Humphrey	5		Thomas, William	3	1	Dunnavant, Mary	4	9	Craddock, Charles	7	8
Hood, Wm	5		Spain, Joshua	12	1	Mann, Cain	8	12	Hubard, Benjamin	6	4
Hasings, Wm	3		Jones, Peter	9	25	Royall, Joseph	9	39	Vaughan, Jeen	1	1
Hastings, Sutten	3		Munford, Edward	13	16	Vasser, Richd	8	11	Geter, Ambrous		5
Hamlin, Stephen	4	19				Vasser, John	5	5	Vaughan, Wm	7	2
Hood, Tucker	8	2	**LIST OF HENRY ANDERSON.**			Finney, John	4		Roberson, Matthew	11	16
Hawkins, David	3	4				Dunnavant, Hodge	12	15	Mayes, Daniel	7	2
Hawkins, William	5	2	Beasley, Peter	6	41	Murry, Richard	6	1	Mayes, Phebey	5	1
Hastins, Zachariah	6		Forster, Robert	2	14	Robertson, Bridgewater	6		Mayes, Gardner	1	2
Hood, Thomas	6		Hays, Richard	8	36	Coates, John	5	7	Vaughan, Lewis	2	2
Hood, John	6	10	Hays, Mary	1	10	Perkinson, Ralph	9	1	Vaughan, Zedekiah	4	1
Kidd, George	10		Walthal, William	10	13	Cashen, David	5		Scott, Geo	7	2
Kennon, Richard	7	43	Jones, Daniel	8	41	Perkinson, Field	9	1	Thomson, Roger	2	10
Munford, Ann	7	15	Jones, Capt Dan, Decd (Estate)		11	Robertson, George	4	4	Mann, Wm	4	....
Mitchell, Evans	11	3	Holt, John	4	1	Finney, William	7	29	Roberson, John	1	....
Newman, Rice	9	15	Munford, Capt Bowling (Decd)	7	33	Finney, Mary	4	22	Cobbs, Jno C	12	31
Newman, Richard	3	12	Parish, Abram	8	12	Crittenton, Henry	9		Booker, Edmd	4	27
Neal, John	4	4	Ward, Rowland, Senr	6	43	Mann, Samuel, Senr	5		Childers, Robt	2	....
Perkinson, Jeremiah	5	1	Ward, Rowland, junr	3	14	Brooks, William	13	19	Archer, Jno (Chesto)		15
Perkinson, Elizabeth	2	2	Neal, Stephen	8	11	Bevell, Archer	7		Murry, Lenord	6	....
Pitchford, Samuel	9	4	Neal, Roger	6	4	Belcher, Jacob	5		Hudson, Jeen	3	24
Pitchford, Jno	3		Hardaway, Daniel	3	34	Davis, Henry	5		Berry, Peter	6	9
Roach, Millinton	5	5	Royall, Wm	1	11	Leigh, William	3	12	Booker, Richd	1	....
Roach, Wm	6	1	Marshall, John		5	Buttler, John	3		Lockett, Benja	1	10
Southall, James	9	7	Marshall, Mary	2	11				Booker, Saml	1	7
Stern, Frances	4	14	Marshall, Abram	1	3	**LIST OF WILLIAM CROSS CRADDOCK.**			Ward, Matthew	6	1
Southerland, Findal	10	35	Osborne, Jos	6	27				Harrison, Nathal		30
Smith, Wm	5	2	Jones, Margaret	1	5	Craddock, William Cross	12	15	Pride, Francis	6	12
Southall, Jno	5		Marshall, Robert	5	11	Ward, Benjamin, Senr	2	29	Forster, Booker	6	8
Stondfield, Robert	4		Jones, Richd	5	22	Claybrook, John	8		Ford, Wm, Senr	8	22
Spinner, Jno	3		Avory, Wm	10	11	Anderson, Francis	8	34	Smithey, Joshua	5	1
Talley, Wm, junr	8		Thompson, Peter	3	20	Roberts, Jacob	3	3	Friend, Thos (Estate)		14
Talley, Tucker (Esta)	7	8	Night, Wm	5		Branch, Benjamin		12	Pride, John	6	21
Talley, Jessey	6	1	Akin, Charles	5		Farley, John	4	2	Marshall, John	3	10
Talley, Lodwick, junr	3	5	Bradbys, James R. (on plantation)	8	39	Scott, Roger	10	8	Lockett, Abraham	6	11
Tucker, Godfrey	8	3	Anderson, Henry (R. P.)	9	132	Burton, John	2	1	Osborne, Branch	4	12
Talley, Lodwick, Senr	4	1	Bass, Edward	3	40	Powell, Abraham	2		Hudson, Peter	6	2
Tabb, Jno		11	Booker, Ann	3	21	Jackson, Francis	5	7	Truit, Jno	8	....
Talley, Wm	6	14	Booker, Edward	11	28	Maddra, Micajah	8	7	Bradshaw, Wm	4	1
Talley, Daniel	6	1	Osborne, Wm, Senr	2	21	Hatchett, Archer	1		Hardaway, Daniel		10
Tucker, Mary	4		Thompson, Robert	3	6	Truley, John	4	9			
Tucker, Thomas	7	1	Marshall, Judith	1	5	Jackson, John C	3	1	**LIST OF MACK GOODE.**		
Vadin, Henry	2	15				Craddock, Wm, Junr	2	1	Foster, James	2	7
Wills, Edmd	12	18				Piles, Conradus	3	3	Foster, Robert	7	8
Wills, Laurence	7	18									

[1] No attempt has been made in this publication to correct mistakes in spelling made by the assistants, and the names have been reproduced as they appear upon the state lists.

AMELIA COUNTY—Continued.

Name of Head of Family	White	Black	Name of Head of Family	White	Black	Name of Head of Family	White	Black	Name of Head of Family	White	Black
LIST OF MACK GOODE—continued.			LIST OF CHRISTO'R FORD—continued.			LIST OF SAM'L SHERWIN—continued.			LIST OF STITH BOLLING—continued.		
Allen, Sam¹	8	....	Ham, Mary	5	4	Pincham, Mrs Eliza	6	37	Fagg, John	3	....
James, John	4	6	Ham, George	4	2	Cutt, Majr	8	....	Mayes, Ricd	4	....
Foster, Jno	6	1	Robinson, John	1	....	Williams, Billington	6	1	Maddax, Robt	4	....
Foster, Thos	6	14	Walthall, Daniel	10	7	Osborne, Capt Abner	2	36	Williamson, Lew	9	27
Foster, Wm, jr	4	6	Deaton, Geo	3	2	Fletcher, Nathan	6	20	Williams, Phillip	8	4
Lovern, Richd	1	....	Deaton, Levi	6	3	Byassee, John	6	1	Dupuy, Peter, Senr	9	9
Lovern, Adam	1	....	Whitworth, John	8	....	Nicholson, James	4	10	Harper, John	9	11
Lovern, Moses	3	....	Hughs, John, Senr	10	40	Featherston, Richd	7	5	Oliver, James	4	16
Foster, Wm	6	....	Whitworth, Thomas	7	1	Featherston, Charles H.	2	8	Jackson, John	3	8
Anderson, Richd	10	20				Burrough, Peter	6	6	Jackson, Isaiah	2	....
Anderson, Fran	4	29	LIST OF PETER LAMKIN.			Smith, Henry	7	6	Woodson, Joseph	6	15
Stern, Tabitha	3	6				Clarke, John	9	9	Foster, James	7	4
Anderson, Churchill	4	5	Anderson, John	5	11	Couzins, William	3	4	Dupuy, Peter, jr	1	6
McGlasson, James	4	2	Anyon, John	6	....	Jones, Peter, Senr	9	60	Dupuy, John B	2	18
Foster, Geo	7	1	Brumer, William	3	....	McLacklen, John	8	13	Dupuy, Judith	4	7
Foster, Geo. P	5	....	Beasley, John	12	18	Vaughan, John	6	10	Dupuy, James, Jr	2	10
Foster, Anthony	2	1	Brown, Larence	2	4	Featherston, Burwell	4	3	Jinnings, Wm	7	4
Seay, Jesse	5	12	Brown, Thomas	8	1	Featherston, William	2	9	Jinnings, John	3	11
Seay, Gideon	7	....	Beasley, Robert	2	2	Beasley, Benjª (Estaᵉ)	4	6	Forrist, Abr, Sr	3	6
Seay, Sergus	1	....	Bradshaw, Jeremiah	1	1	Still, George (Estate)	1	4	Dickerson, Barnard	4	3
Eggleston, Richard	1	26	Bruce, Alexander	7	18	Bass, Elizabeth (quartr)	6	15	Foster, Mary	5	12
Arms, Edward	8	....	Cock, Colo John (Surry)	....	24	Cabaniss, George	7	19	Hurt, Wm, Sr	6	17
Booker, Geo	6	37	Craddock, William, Senr	8	2	Gilliam, William (quatr)	2	52	Beasley, Wm	5	7
Booker, Richeson	1	4	Cabaness, Henry	3	....	Jones, Letticia	3	25	Cook, Rains	1	4
Whites, Jno	7	2	Crute, Robert	3	....	Greenhill, William	3	19	Thompson, Robt	8	7
Hudson, Burton	5	6	Davis, Hezekiah	2	....	Short, Colo Thomas	15	39	Harriss, James	8	3
Seay, Moses	5	9	Davis, James	4	4	Pryor, John, Senr	10	19	Jinnings, Joseph	9	15
Hilsman, Joseph	3	1	Davis, William	3	6	Greenhill, Mrs Cathrine	6	24	Cook, James	8	8
Clements, Isham	10	10	Dyson, William	6	1	Bennit, Benjª	3	....	Mann, James	9	1
Walker, Alex	11	2	Davenport, William	3	4	Sturdavant, James, Jr	1	4	Farley, Henry	6	2
Tabb, Edward	9	9	Davenport, George	1	1	Sturdavant, James	1	2	Farley, James	7	9
Allin, David	8	....	Elliott, John	5	20	Sherwin, Sam¹	7	35	Blankinship, David	7	....
Cox, Henry	10	21	Farley, Daniel Stwart	1	....				Blankinship, John	7	....
Chaffin, Joshua	9	12	Farguson, Henry	3	13	LIST OF STITH BOLLING.			Grigg, Peter	1	....
Phillips, Richard	10	10	Gooch, John	10	13				Motley, Isaac	1	....
Seay, Jacob	6	11	Green, John	9	11	Bennet, Richd	12	26	Hundley, Josiah	7	17
Wingo, Jno	12	5	Gooch, William	7	6	Zackry, David	4	8	Craddock, David	3	6
Wingo, Thomas	2	....	Henderson, James	2	26	Zackry, Jonathan	1	....	Harper, Wm	9	1
Foster, Jno (son of Wm)	11	....	Hall, Bowler	12	19	Fowlkes, Gabriel, Junr	6	10	Thompson, Ann	5	4
Overton, Thos	2	6	Hazalwood, Benjª	3	....	Fowlkes, Henry	2	6	Jackson, Arther	8	6
Clement, Jno	3	23	Harriss, William (Surry)	6	24	Craddock, Moses	8	2	Harper, Anner	6	8
Eggleston, Judith	5	13	Jinnings, John	5	5	Robertson, Edward	2	3	Jinnings, Dickerson	8	8
Moulson, Mary	4	18	Jones, Richd, Jun	5	25	Fowlkes, James	2	2	Purkinson, Seth	8	2
Mumford, Thos	8	33	Johns, Judith	8	5	Hatchett, Abraham	5	3			
Brown, Daniel	2	4	Jones, John	1	....	Borum, James	7	8	LIST OF RALEIGH CARTER.		
Jinkins, James	11	7	Jones, Colo Richd (Estate)	4	23	Jinnings, Henry	2	3			
Ford, Wm, jr	7	13	Jones, Lewelling	1	....	Fowlkes, Jinnings	7	17	Anderson, Charles	1	1
Wright, Thomas	4	2	Jones, Thomas & Wm	2	8	Hatchett, William	2	6	Ball, Thomas	9	22
Clements, Edmd	2	2	Lamkin, Peter	8	39	Fowlkes, John, Senr	4	10	Billups, John	5	....
Clements, Sarah	3	4	Lipscomb, Uriah	12	14	Robertson, Maryann	4	8	Brain, Robt	1	....
Sadler, Wm	8	....	Lipscomb, Richd L	9	5	Fowlkes, William	5	3	Beuford, Henry	3	12
Overton, Sam¹	1	....	May, William	2	4	Ligon, Richd	8	6	Blakely, William, Sr	3	8
Sadler, Jno	3	....	Mann, Robert (Estate)	3	8	Anderson, Worsham	8	10	Blakely, William	5	2
			Mann, John	1	....	Berkeley, Alexander	9	....	Bruse, Elezabeth	6	3
LIST OF CHRISTO'R FORD.			Muse, William	8	4	Fowlkes, Gabriel, Senr	9	13	Crenshaw, William	7	18
			Nance, Giles	10	2	Jeter, Winnifred	3	7	Carter, Rawleigh	8	21
Wright, John	7	12	Nicholas, Zachariah	1	....	Watson, William	2	28	Crenshaw, Wm, Senr	3	17
Liggon, Wm, Senr	5	8	Porter, Susanah	4	10	Smith, Richard	5	2	Crenshaw, David	3	5
Asselin, David	7	12	Peachy, Thos G	4	73	Smith, Susanna	2	1	Crenshaw, James	6	6
Gills, John	7	8	Royal, Littlebury	3	20	Borum, Edmund	10	12	Crawley, William	9	12
Jeter, Ambrose	8	21	Ramsey, Richard	4	5	Bailey, Charles	5	3	Cross, William	....	....
Ford, Christor	9	24	Robertson, Nathaniel	5	11	Harrison, Christopher	6	1	Cross, Charles	....	....
Gray, Wm	5	6	Robertson, Elizabeth	1	4	Fowlkes, John, Junr	6	8	Crute, Hannah	4	1
Anderson, Paulin	3	14	Robertson, James	6	2	Jeter, Oliver	9	5	Dudley, Thomas	3	14
Wood, William, Senr	6	29	Robertson, Henry (Estate)	8	16	Jinnings, Wm, Senr	9	8	Doswell, John	2	11
Covendar, Hugh	10	7	Spain, Thomas	7	3	Fowlkes, John (son of Jos)	2	3	Davis, Jacob	3	8
Hurt, Wm (Caroline)	9	6	Thompson, John	4	....	Fowlkes, Thomas	....	4	Doswell, William	6	13
Lockett, John	8	....	Tanner, Joel, Senr	4	9	Pace, Newsom	7	1	Davis, Thomas	4	4
Booth, John	6	9	Wilkinson, Revd Thos	2	19	Robertson, John	8	5	Dixon, William	8	....
Whitworth, Abram	8	8	Ward, Richd	8	5	Gray, Joseph	5	2	Davis, Robert	5	....
Whitworth, Claiborne	5	1	Winfrey, Robert	3	3	Bass, John	'10	10	Ellis, Ambrose	7	8
Morriss, Tabitha	5	1	Winfrey, Charles	3	4	Foster, John	4	5	Ellis, William	8	5
Morriss, Moses	13	9	Walker, William	3	3	Hubbard, Joseph	7	2	Evens, William (Estate)	4	10
Butler, William	9	2	Winfrey, Gideon (Estate)	5	9	Walton, Simeon	13	20	Evens, John	3	6
Burton, William	10	4	Winn, John & Charles	4	17	Clay, John	1	....	Ellis, Thomas	4	7
Meador, Isaac	3	....	Williams, John	8	....	Foster, Mary	5	12	Epes, Francis (Quarter)	....	24
Jackson, Wm	6	2	Ward, Mark	3	....	Borum, Richd	3	4	Green, Maston	4	22
Hendrick, Benjª	7	4	Vasser, Daniel	1	....	Bennet, Richd, Junr	1	....	Gunn, Thomas	11	18
Dillen, John	10	....	Vaughan, Samuel (Dinwª)	5	2	Dobson, Thomas	2	10	Hollondsworth, James	7	7
Hendrick, Zachary	1	....				Shelton, James	4	19	Harrison, Richard	9	10
Morriss, Sylvanus	3	1	LIST OF SAM'L SHERWIN.			Gray, Joseph	5	2	Hurt, Absolum	5	3
Jones, Martha, & Jaˢ League	14	1				Dupuey, Barthw	13	28	Huddleston, Robert	3	....
Bell, John	8	....	Jones, Batt	7	23	Walton, Jessey	8	6	Hurt, Zacharias	7	9
Wingo, Thomas	2	....	Staw, William	6	....	Bell, Wm	4	25	Horskins, Thomas	7	2
Blake, William	5	....	Pavory, Mary	3	3	Baldwing, John	11	4	Horskins, John	1	....
Lovern, Wm	6	....	Osborne, William, Jr	6	15	Howson, John	9	11	Holland, George	1	1
Liggon, Thomas	8	12	Parham, Daniel	1	2	Cook, Thomas	1	1	Holland, Phebe	4	3
Hendrick, John	5	2	Westbrook, Henry	6	....	Forrist, Abrahm	5	6	Hundley, Joel	9	3
Hendrick, Prudence	5	10	Clarke, Lew	5	1	Stewart, Charles	5	5	Hurt, Moses	4	19
Hendrick, Obediah	4	1	Westbrook, Phebe	6	3	Nash, Thomas	7	....	Jackson, Josiah	4	....
Hendrick, Daniel	4	....	Westbrook, Lucy	3	1	Anderson, Henry	8	5	Jeffress, Thomas	12	26
Smith, James	3	....	Parham, William	9	10	Roberts, Step	9	10	Jordan, William	4	19
Winston, William	9	11	Parham, James	7	5	Jinnings, Robt	10	15	Irby, William	8	16
Harper, Henry	7	....	Grig, Josiah	10	10	Gray, Alexr	4	1	Jones, Adam	3	16
Hendrick, Stephen	1	....	Thornton, Sterling C.	6	14	Fleming, Wm	6	....	Irby, John	5	4
Chapman, John	10	8	Moore, John, Jr	4	....	Stewart, Mary	2	2	Jordan, Samuel	4	34
Cobb, Sam¹ (Carpenter)	7	14	Moore, John	3	....	Gray, Joseph	5	2	Jordan, Thomas	5	13
Ham, Sarah	7	2	West, Sam¹	5	4	Ward, Ben (Estate)	6	30	Jinnings, William	4	2
Hughs, John, Jr	11	9	Moore, Mark	6	....	Worsham, William	5	10	Knight, John	10	7
Ham, Wm	2	5	Radford, Andrew	11	15	Mitchell, Thos	13	17	Loafman, John	6	....
Jolly, Susanna	5	....				Stewart, Berry	7	2	Lipscomb, Luke	5	1

AMELIA COUNTY—Continued.

NAME OF HEAD OF FAMILY.	White.	Black.	NAME OF HEAD OF FAMILY.	White.	Black.	NAME OF HEAD OF FAMILY.	White.	Black.	NAME OF HEAD OF FAMILY.	White.	Black.
LIST OF RALEIGH CARTER—continued.			**LIST OF EDM'D BOOKER—continued.**			**LIST OF CHRISTOPHER HUDSON—continued.**			**LIST OF ROBERT BOLLING—continued.**		
Lewis, John	3	9	Jeater, Samuel	7	20	Robertson, John	4	22	Ford, George	6	8
Lewis, William	7	1	Johnson, Noham	3	1	Jones, Robert	1	9	Tudar, John	1	13
Mills, John	4	5	Jackson, Josiah	6	7	Robertson, William	5	9	Davis, John	3	....
Morgan, Samuel	11	14	Johnson, Nicholas	8	1	Walke, Thomas	4	1	Blanton, Richd	10	....
Oliver, Isaac	6	9	Howell, Sarah	11	....	Robertson, George	5	4	Bently, Saml, Senr	7	....
Overstreight, Thomas	7	....	League, Benjamin	1	....	Worsham, Henry	10	6	Bently, Saml, junr	8	....
Pace, John	6	2	League, James	11	....	Featherstone, Charles	3	18	West, Drury	4	....
Phillups, Thomas	5	....	League, Joab	1	....	Robertson, James	6	31	Draper, James	2	....
Phillups, Rhody	2	....	League, Aaron	8	....	Lamb, Anthony	7	5	May, John	2	3
Smith, Samuel	6	15	Jones, Hannah	8	....	Hutchinson, Charles	7	1	Powell, John	8	1
Smith, Griffin	9	9	Meader, Benje	10	2	Gibbs, Edward	3	....	Grig, James	5	....
Sneed, William	13	3	Moore, William	9	....	Worsham, Charles	8	1	Moore, James	5	....
Swinney, Elizabith	2	3	Mitchell, John	11	5	Lorton, Thomas	9	7	Leath, Arthur	5	6
Stephens, Joseph	5	1	Noble, Joseph	12	....	Booker, William M	8	33	Green, Geo	2	5
Stewart, William	4	1	Flood, John	3	....	Burton, Allen	1	2	Green, Lucy	2	5
Shelton, William	1	....	Overton, Benjamin	5	8	Dunnavant, Hezekiah	7	2	Clarke, Aldr	4	4
Smith, Burwell	3	4	Osborn, Thomas, Jr	5	6	Cocke, Chastain	4	40	Clarke, Wm	5	1
Shelton, Joel	2	....	O Neal, Jemima	4	....	Brackett, Ludwell	3	17	Damron, Joseph (Bk)	....	2
Thomas, Samuel	8	5	Pollard, William	5	5	Murray, William	1	23	Holloway, Wm	5	8
Thompson, Medkip	7	6	Pillow, Jasper	5	....	Southall, William	9	4	Sammons, Thos	8	3
Thomas, Joseph	3	1	Palmore, Elijah	1	....	Broadnax, Sarah	1	3	Grammar, Joseph	8	5
Thrveets, John (Quarter)	....	7	Pillow, Mary	4	....	Suddbury, John	4	5	James, Rose Ann	7	....
Trotter, James	11	4	Roberts, Plesant	8	10	Tabb, John	13	257	Bonner, Ann	2	....
Williams, Thomas (Quartr)	....	19	Rucker, William	3	4	Scott, Sarah	5	20	Bland, Theodk, Junr	....	10
White, Joseph	9	3	Rucker, Mordica	7	....	Scott, Joseph, Junr	4	11	Amos, James	8	....
White, Moses	3	3	Seay, James	11	4	Dunnavant, Philip	2	1	Barker, Charles	3	10
Wommock, Josiah	6	4	Vaughn, Nicholas	7	2	Weatherford, David	8	....	Ward, Wiley	2	3
Wilkirson, Jean	1	1	Vaughn, James	7	6	Baker, William	7	....	Willson, Charles	6	12
Wilkerson, Stephen	2	5	Rucker, Joshua	9	1	Bentley, Samuel	6	16	Woodward, Jesse	10	15
Walker, Henry	9	3	Wray, Thomas	8	....				Bevil, Robt	9	4
Wallar, Major	8	10	Wright, Thomas	6	3	**LIST OF STEPHEN COCKE.**			Stoe, Jacob	1	1
Walker, Thomas	7	12	Waters, Nicholas	7	9	Fitz Gerrald, Wm	8	61	Roach, James	3	2
Wood, William	4	1	Williams, Phillip	8	14	Tucker, Jno	8	....	Clay, Isham	8	....
Wollis, Matthew	3	....	Webster, Anthony	....	3	Gunn, James	11	27	Allgood, Mary	10	....
Wilkerson, Benjamin	2	5	Major, Phillip	7	3	Fitz Gerrald, Frans	1	22	Harper, Drury	3	2
Davis, Matthew	7	....	Vaughn, Robert	9	19	Crute, Robert	4	....	Clement, Stephen	5	2
Quinn, William	2	....				Cross, Richd	8	15	Bently, Jeremiah	4	7
			LIST OF JOHN OGILBY.			Jones, Repps	9	5	Jackson, Thos	6	1
LIST OF EDM'D BOOKER.			Meade, Colo Everard	4	56	Spain, Wm	8	4	Jackson, Charles	10	2
Atkinson, Thomas	6	17	Booth, William	11	10	Anderson, Jno	11	2	Yates, Edwd R.	....	13
Atkinson, Musco	6	7	French, Robert	6	1	Jackson, Edwd	9	8	Hames, Edmund	9	....
Beadle, Augustin	7	4	Tanner, Robert	7	5	Crenshaw, Sanders	4	3	Foord, Abraham	12	1
Beadle, Abraham	3	5	Burton, Able	7	8	Thomas, Woodlieff	2	4	Hightower, Charnel, Senr	1	4
Ballow, Thomas	7	....	Waller, John Tucker	9	10	White, Frans	7	6	Hightower, Charnel, Jur	5	....
Beadle, John	10	6	Walthall, Robert	3	6	Crenshaw, Wm, Sr (Haricane)	6	2	Hightower, Susanna	1	6
Baugh, Bartley	7	11	Tanner, Field	6	1	Wallace, Theodk	8	....	Foard, Albry	7	....
Brooks, William	1	....	Wills, Thos Tabb	7	7	Wilks, Jno	5	11	Wills, Abraham	3	....
Booker, Edmund, Ju	1	8	Coleman, Joseph	7	....	Lock, Eliza	9	14	Hardy, Isack	10	....
Cannon, William	6	1	Coleman, John	11	....	Irby, Wm	2	17	Anderson, Charles	6	15
Compton, Zachariah	9	7	Wilson, John	9	6	Foster, Richd	7	1	Randolph	5	....
Cheatham, James	4	6	Powell, Mary	1	3	Levesil, Shaderick	3	....	Bevel, Hezekiah	5	2
Cardwell, Thomas	6	....	Crawley, David	1	38	Batte, Thos	8	11	Eppes, Francis	6	66
Dearen, William	7	....	Crawley, John	1	33	Lewis, John	10	10	Thomas, David	11	1
Dearen, Richd	4	....	Crawley, Benja	1	27	Cocke, Stephen	10	21	Baley, Jonathan	7	4
Dalby, John	10	6	Wilson, Capt Daniel	2	25	Caleham, Sherod	1	....	Woodward, Francis	7	16
Duypuy, James	2	10	Wilson, Daniel (Esta)	3	16	Caleham, David	1	....	Thomas, Athanatius	3	1
Elmore, Thomas	3	15	Ogilby, John	7	26	Justis, Daniel	6	....	Walthel, Richd	1	3
Foster, Clayborne	5	....	Clay, Thomas	6	....	Cocke, Thos	3	20	Dudley, Edwd (Est)	....	9
Farley, William, Jun	5	1	Old, William	5	8	Cocke, Jno	1	7	May, Mathew (Est)	7	12
Farley, Sarah	5	....	Cheatham, Archer	13	3	Hood, Wm	10	2	Bland, Theodk, Senr	14	70
Foster, John	3	....	Belsher, George	2	1	Jackson, Wm P.	6	3	Haskins, Christopher	....	7
Foster, William	6	....	Wilkinson, Daniel	2	1	Hardaway, Stith	1	33	Connally, George	5	4
Farley, William	5	4	Powell, Robert	9	5	Westbrook, Amos	2	....	Robertson, James	5	....
Flemming, Beverley	12	2	Powell, John	7	2	Comer, Thomas	2	3	Jackson, Wm P.	6	3
Foster, James	8	....	Walthall, William, Junr	2	8	Farguson, Peleg	9	11	Leonard, Joseph	3	....
Forrest, John	2	1	Walthall, William, Senr	5	17				Jackson, Amey	4	....
Green, Thomas	6	3	Clay, John, Jr	3	9	**LIST OF ROBERT BOLLING.**			Stuart, Thos	5	....
Holt, Shadrick	6	6	Clay, John, Senr	7	12	Watkins, Saml	7	17	West, Robt, jr	8	10
Holt, Thomas	2	10	Cocke, Stephen	....	44	Bolling, Robt	8	23	Powell, Angilica	9	....
Hundley, Anthony	6	8	Tanner, Branch	6	75	Clarke, George	5	2	Hightower, Thos	9	....
Hudson, John	3	1	Bolling, Robt	8	23	Ford, Tady	6	4	Hobbs, Samuel	1	13
Hudson, Edward	6	....	Pearson, David	4	1	Ford, John	5	2	Brackett, Benjamin	6	12
Hundley, Anthony, Jun	1	....	Chappel, William	1	....	James, John P.	5	1	Compton, John	4	13
Johnson, Stephen	8	2	Johnston, Archer	12	25	Draper, Wm	7	....	Compton, Micajah	6	1
Jackson, Obediah	4	1	Morgain, John	5	12	Bennet, Wm	5	....	Hutchinson, William	2	6
Jackson, John	5	8	Freeman, Anderson	3	....	Leonard, Fredk	7	1	Eggleston, Joseph	14	63
Johnson, Garrard	10	3	Rogers, William	5	....	Tucker, John	4	1	Gibbs, Thos (for German Baker)	4	25
Johnson, John	8	3				Wynne, John	12	3	Hudson, Christopher	9	56
Johnson, Ashley	9	4	**LIST OF CHRISTOPHER HUDSON.**			Leath, John	2	4	Archer, John	1	43
Johnson, John	9	5	Giles, William	4	29	Lewis, Henry	12	2	Royall, John	5	12
Johnson, Richd	8	1	Royall, John, Senr	3	21	Mays, Daniel	3	4	Clay, Charles	6	12
Johnson, Isham	8	3									

CHARLOTTE COUNTY.

NAME OF HEAD OF FAMILY.	White.	Black.	NAME OF HEAD OF FAMILY.	White.	Black.	NAME OF HEAD OF FAMILY.	White.	Black.	NAME OF HEAD OF FAMILY.	White.	Black.
Spencer, John	6	10	Muckelroy, John	2	....	Cardwell, John	9	6	Gordins, John (Estate)	8	26
Russell, Edward	5	8	Berry, William	2	1	Morton, John	8	....	Farguson, Bryant	11	14
Buchley, Butlar	12	....	Bryant, Jane	1	....	Bowman, Royal	8	1	Smith, John F.	12	9
Mullins, David	9	....	McGehee, Samuel	4	4	Wood, Joseph	8	3	Scott, Thomas	6	49
Morris, John	8	....	Gray, Elizabeth	5	....	Cardwell, George	5	10	Vernon, Richard	2	....
Hatchett, John	8	10	Spencer, Gedion	1	3	Fowler, Bullard	9	9	Brown, William	8	....
Foster, James	5	10	King, Phillip	10	13	Simmons, John	7	7	Brown, William	8	....
Canaday, John, jr	3	1	Morton, Agnes	3	21	Nixon, William	3	2	Brown, George	7	....
Canaday, John, Senr	6	1	Morton, Jacob	6	12	Claybrook, Obadiah	9	6	Burt, Matthew	9	13
Hood, William	2	1	Mullins, Thomas	7	....	Dabbs, William	8	7	Postwood, Thomas	9	3
Ewing, Samuel	4	1	Venable, James	13	12	Dabbs, Richard	12	5	Brown, Burwell	11	7
Russell, James	6	2	Morton, Josiah	4	20	Berry, William	3	1	Belcher, Edmd	6	3
Bowman, Robert	2	1	Epperson, Francis	7	8	Roberts, Thomas	10	2	Blanks, Shadrack	2	....
Foster, Joshua	2	1	Russell, William	6	8	Bowman, Thomas	2	....	Bridges, John	6	5

CHARLOTTE COUNTY—Continued.

NAME OF HEAD OF FAMILY.	White.	Black.	NAME OF HEAD OF FAMILY.	White.	Black.	NAME OF HEAD OF FAMILY.	White.	Black.	NAME OF HEAD OF FAMILY.	White.	Black.
Bullard, Joel	4	1	Woodall, Sampson	9	....	Mann, Turner	3	....	Terry, George	10	3
Bullard, George	4	8	Roberson, Jesse	4	1	Mann, Millington	2	....	Clements, Benjamin	12	....
Burt, Francis	1	....	Barksdale, Joseph	10	2	Gausling, John	1	....	Belcher, Robert	9	1
Burt, Robert	1	....	Barksdale, John	5	8	Johnston, William	7	12	Elmore, James	10	....
Brook, Dudley	1	3	Bunkley, Jesse	3	5	Burge, Drury	10	20	Smith, Thomas	3	....
Collier, Thomas	9	10	Burnley, Henry	8	5	Caldwell, Mary	4	7	Eudailey, Moses	4	....
Cheatham, Benjamin	3	2	Clayton, John, Senr	5	7	Williamson, Cutbirth	7	6	Eudailey, John	5	....
Chaffin, Joshua, Senr	5	....	Clark, Isaac	4	1	Keersey, John	4	6	Hailey, John	6	3
Collier, John	9	11	Clark, Thomas	6	7	Nunley, Alexander	4	....	Hendrick, Gustavus	9	6
Craig, Alexander	2	....	Clayton, John, jr	8	6	Fuqua, Joseph, Senr	11	26	Bedford, Thomas	9	49
Colier, Joseph	6	7	Clark, John, jr	3	3	Fuqua, Joseph, jr	6	10	Hammock, Lewis	6	....
Crenshaw, Charles	3	6	Clark, Francis	8	1	Fuqua, Samuel	7	21	Bedford, Thomas, jr	3	9
Collins, Richard	8	1	Davenport, William	7	5	Fuqua, John	4	5	Friend, Joseph	6	12
Cocke, Chasteen	....	18	Davenport, Richard	7	6	Mailer, George	7	....	Vaugh, Abraham	12	3
Clay, Henry	18	21	Evans, Griffith	5	....	Rading, George	5	....	Cammel, William	2	....
Dunning, Thomas	1	....	Ford, Culverain	8	11	Mayhew, Samuel	4	....	Tarpley, James	10	2
Gill, Michal	5	....	Harvey, Thomas, Senr	7	7	Hunt, James	3	20	Lee, William	6	....
Green, Henry	5	....	Harvey, Thomas, jr (son of Jno.)	4	....	Booker, Richard	9	30	Lee, John	10	5
Goare, Chatharine	3	4	Howard, John	7	....	Coles, Walter (Esta & overseers)	10	43	Arnold, James	9	....
Hatchett, Thomas	6	2	Hunter, John	6	....	Phelps, John	9	8	Hundley, George	3	4
Hamblen, Macka	8	....	Harvey, William (G. C.)	4	5	Brewer, William	10	2	Shorter, James	6	....
Hamlet, James	8	7	Harvey, Charles	9	2	Barnes, Henry	10	6	Pettus, Thomas	5	2
Johnston, Sias	8	....	Jenings, Robert	6	29	Oliver, Joseph	4	14	Gillam, James	12	13
Lain, James	8	....	Knady, Eleanor	3	....	Olliver, Thomas	5	13	Bedford, Robert	1	7
Lain, Elizabeth	3	....	Mckenny, Charles, jr	3	4	Fletcher, James	8	13	Chaffin, Thomas	8	1
Loggins, James	9	....	Moore, Samuel	10	....	Womack, William	2	10	Pettus, John	10	10
Leggon, Thomas, Senr	5	6	Overton, Mildred	4	11	Eans, Henry	7	5	Shelton, Josiah	9	1
Mullins, John	8	....	Parsons, Thomas	5	2	Totty, William	6	....	Mullins, James	7	1
Mullins, Mary	4	....	Parsons, William	3	....	Franklin, Peter	5	....	Sullivant, John, jr	3	....
Mosby, Jacob	3	11	Paulett, Thomas	12	5	Lowe, Jesse	3	3	Chaffin, Joshua, jr	8	....
Mullins, William	10	....	Rowten, William, Senr	5	5	McCraw, Stephen	6	....	Chaffin, Joseph	3	1
Martin, Henry	3	2	Rowten, William, jr	3	1	Dudgeon, William	5	....	Breedlove, Robert	3	6
Matthews, William	3	....	Ross, Peter	3	....	Dudgeon, John	5	....	Lee, Joseph	7	3
May, Abner	5	7	Spencer, Eleanor	8	....	Tomkies, Francis (& overseer)	5	27	Taylor, John	7	....
May, John	8	....	Seawell, Thomas	9	1	Hubard, William	4	30	Chaffin, Mary	8	....
May, Alce	6	....	Wallace, Andrew	7	5	Smith, John, jr	6	2	Townes, Joel	5	7
Malone, Mary	6	....	Watson, Douglas	9	13	Manns, Page & Ezekiel	8	15	Carter, John	6	....
May, Precilla	4	6	Wilson, Mary	7	....	Turner, Edmund	6	....	Read, Jonathan	4	25
McIntosh, Mrs	6	13	Wheeler, John	9	....	Barnes, Henry, jr	2	....	Colvert, Nelson	3	9
Northcut, William	8	....	Weatherford, John	5	....	Bell, Daniel	3	1	Bedford, Stephen	4	7
Osborne, Claiborne	2	....	Wood, William	7	....	Turner, John	10	3	Crews, Richard	8	....
Perrin, Josephus	10	8	Wood, Richard	5	....	Spencer, Ahimaaz	2	....	Lambert, Hugh	4	2
Perrin, George	7	5	Tackett, Francis	12	....	Skates, William	7	....	Mckenny, William	6	....
Roberts, William	6	....	Wilson, John	2	....	Maddox, Wilson	7	....	Kirk, William	3	3
Roberts, Francis	9	10	Mckenny, Charles	7	8	Maddox, Dan	4	....	Inge, James	5	....
Redman, Thomas	9	4	Cardwell, John	6	....	Singleton, William	6	....	Williams, William	6	....
Redd, John	3	9	Glazebrook, Julius	8	....	Ward, John	2	10	Goare, John	3	....
Redd, George	5	12	Vernon, Ebenezer	5	....	Ward, Richard	2	16	Middleton, James	4	3
Randolphs, John (Estate)	4	45	Sadler, Thomas	7	....	Cage, Benjamin	8	....	Lambert, Leroy	1	....
Rawlins, John	5	1	Pugh, Willoughby	11	....	Edmunds, Thomas (& overseer)	4	9	Dickerson, Jean	5	1
Smelt, Robert	13	5	Gaines, Richard, Senr	10	20	Bottom, William (& overseer)	6	3	Bouldin, James	7	15
Skelton, William	6	....	Timberlake, William	8	13	Rawlings, Peter	7	13	Middleton, John	3	3
Standish, John	3	....	Payne, Thomas	8	11	Badget, Edmund	2	....	Crews, John	3	....
Sullivant, Owen	4	2	Reynolds, William	6	2	Hughs, John	10	8	Gwin, George	3	15
Sullivant, Pleasant	1	1	Hannah, Andrew	6	6	Smith, Valentine	8	2	Mckenny, Peter	6	1
Worsham, Robert	8	....	Henry, Jane	6	5	Smith, Rachel	5	....	Brumfield, William	7	....
Williams, Thomas	10	7	Brent, Margaret	10	11	Dickerson, John	5	7	Farmer, Stephen	5	7
Worthy, Martin	6	....	Gaines, Richard, jr	6	8	Owen, Jessee	3	1	Crews, William	7	....
Williams, Redman	1	....	Cook, Benjamin	4	5	Hughs, William	4	1	Worthy, Thomas	8	7
Pearson, Sherwood	7	8	Jones, Publius	6	....	Ward, Joseph	5	2	Goare, Isaac	2	....
Abernatha, James	7	2	Sublet, William	6	....	Ward, Seth	3	15	Daniel, John	8	16
Adkins, Ann	4	3	Ayres, Edward	7	1	Hines, Caleb	9	1	Mullins, James	8	....
Bryant, Robert	4	....	George, William	10	3	Jenings, David	8	....	Luster, John	6	....
Butlar, George	7	....	Barksdale, Dudley	9	8	Wood, John, Senr	7	....	Prewit, Joseph	5	....
Brown, Russell	8	10	Nelson, John	7	3	Franklin, Robert	3	7	Cheatham, Bernard	4	10
Baker, Martin	9	10	Cheatham, Epps	5	1	Saddler, Edward	8	....	Reynolds, Joseph	8	1
Brown, James	3	2	Greenwood, William	8	4	Taquet, Francis	10	....	Beasley, William	4	1
Clark, Samuel	7	17	Slayden, Arthur	12	1	Marshall, William	6	2	Morton, George	11	....
Coleson, David	4	....	Jordan, Matthew	7	1	Copeland, John	3	....	Morton, Little Joe	5	20
Cuninghame, James	9	....	Kay, Henry	6	5	Richardson, John	5	4	Nash, William	8	....
Cardwell, Susanna	3	5	Hazlewood, William	9	....	Scott, Samuel	8	....	Overton, Judith	6	1
Epperson, Thomas	2	7	Pattilo, George	12	....	Davis, Temple	8	5	Lawson, Nathan	5	....
Epperson, Francis	2	5	Rodgers, Thomas	11	6	Davis, William	2	5	Lawson, George	6	....
Epperson, William	10	8	Smith, William	4	7	Jordan, Charles	2	4	Traynum, William	8	....
Griffith, William	6	2	Thomas, John	7	....	Fore, Peter	11	....	Cardwell, Frances	4	2
Garrett, James	11	7	Smith, Robert	9	13	Baulding, Caleb	6	4	Carrington, Paul	4	62
Harris, John	9	....	Miller, Smith	2	1	Bunkley, Mildred	2	9	Whitess, Thomas	5	6
Huntsman, Jacob	5	2	Criddington, Henry	6	1	Fore, John	5	4	Pollard, Thomas	4	....
Huntsman, John	5	1	Rawlins, Peter	7	10	Fore, George	3	....	Watkins, Joel	8	26
Handcock, Anthony	9	9	Armstead, William	8	21	Farrow, Charles	3	1	White, James	7	....
Huntsman, Adam	9	6	Harroway, Charles	13	2	Sublet, Benjamin	9	2	Downey, James	8	....
Jackson, John	3	....	Madison, Henry	11	10	Townsln, John	12	1	Adams, James	9	4
Jackson, Thomas	5	....	Morris, Joshua	4	4	Hines, Henry	7	1	Hailey, James	9	....
Parsons, Samuel	3	2	Brewer, Phillip	7	3	Ferguson, Thomas	8	3	Mitchel, Richard	4	....
Ramsey, John	6	....	Jude, George	6	15	Marshall, Benjamin	4	1	Randolphs, John (Estate)	....	37
Robertson, James	1	....	Brewer, Sackville	11	14	Palmer, Luke	5	8	Pugh, Samuel	5	....
Rice, William	5	3	North, Thomas	9	16	Copland, William	10	....	Buttar, John	2	....
Ruffin, Edward (P. George)	....	41	Scott, Thomas	....	10	Chaffin, Nathaniel	6	15	Lunderman, Samuel	4	....
Randolph, Bettey (Williamsburg)	....	42	Young, Samuel	7	1	Mckenny, William	1	4	Love, James	2	3
Smith, Joseph, Senr	8	....	Rice, John	1	3	Thornton, Francis	6	9	Love, John	6	4
Smith, Joseph, jr	5	....	Barksdale, Clayborne	9	18	Moore, Robert	4	....	Clayton, Charles	8	2
Smith, Thomas	4	5	Jones, John	10	4	Hendrick, John	4	4	Ward, William	7	11
Sims, Agnes	5	....	Jones, Wood	7	36	Pollett, John	1	2	Butridge, Henry	6	....
Samson, Frances	5	1	Holland, Moses	6	....	Price, William	9	30	Worthy, Richard	6	....
Samson, William	6	3	Cheatham, Joel	7	6	Whorley, Joseph	9	....	Toombs, William	7	....
Smith, George (P. E.)	2	5	Smith, William	4	1	Price, Daniel	3	6	Owen, Thomas	3	....
Scott, Thomas	8	1	Hundley, Charles	7	4	Harvey, John	5	9	Hart, Caleb	6	4
Vernom, Thomas	5	1	Farmer, Joel	4	4	Leghorn, Thomas	5	14	Williams, Robert	7	....
White, Matthew	3	12	Scott, Francis	6	18	Johnston, The Reverend Thomas	11	20	Hundley, Anthony	11	5
White, Daniel	2	4	Pugh, Thomas	6	....	Hailey, Ambrose	2	3	Dean, Richard	2	4
White, William	5	7	Barten, James	2	....				Herndon, Jacob	8	....
Wilson, Joseph	4	3	Holt, Joseph	7	28				Lesslie, George	7	3
Williams, Hubard	4	7	Allen, James	6	....				Clayton, Britton	6	6
			Greenhill, Paschal	2	26				Beasley, John	8	5
									Haimes, William	8	....

CHARLOTTE COUNTY—Continued.

NAME OF HEAD OF FAMILY.	White.	Black.	NAME OF HEAD OF FAMILY.	White.	Black.	NAME OF HEAD OF FAMILY.	White.	Black.	NAME OF HEAD OF FAMILY.	White.	Black.
Fowler, Mary	4		Nixon, John	6		Ashworth, Harrison	3		Blanks, John	5	
Firth, Samuel		4	Nevill, George	1		Bouldin, Thomas	8	6	Callicoat, James	1	5
Morton, William	11	20	Almond, Elisha	3		Word, Peter	5	1	Finch, Adam	8	19
Sexton, Agnes	2		Bouldin, Richard	7	14	Jackson, William	2		Farley, Mary	7	12
Wilson, Daniel	2		Bouldin, Wood	4	8	Jackson, William, jr	2		Griffin, Richard	10	
Williams, Robert, Senr	3		Clark, William	1	1	Moore, John	10		Hord, Thomas	11	19
Williams, Jonathan	9	1	Carter, George	5	1	Thompson, John	8		Holloway, George	7	3
Read, Thomas	4	35	Dabbs, William	8	7	Hughs, Thomas	3		Hamblin, Peter	9	
Spencer, Thomas, jr	3	8	Greenhill, William		14	Hughs, Joseph	9		Herndon, Joseph	10	13
Watkins, John	4	17	Holt, William	10	3	Rawlins, William	4	5	Hudson, Agnes	4	
Watkins, Benjamin	7	11	Hannah, George, Senr	6	4	Callicoat, William	7	4	Hamblin, Mary	2	
Mitchell, John	8	13	Harris, John	7		Callicoat, Beverly	8	1	Holland, James	8	
Foster, Josiah, Senr	9	3	Jackson, Lewis	12	11	Bibb, John	9	16	Haskins, Thomas	10	22
Foster, John	5	3	Jones, Godfrey, jr	3	1	Sibley, Robert	6		Hudson, Daniel	10	4
Foster, Francis	5	2	Jones, Cadwallader	7	4	Elam, William	7	11	Herbert, John	8	2
Handkins, John	8	1	Jones, Lewelling	6	28	Elam, Edward	9	1	Lucas, John	6	
Page, Richard	4	1	Johnston, Samuel	5	4	Northcut, Nathaniel	5		Moseley, George, Senr	3	
Allderson, John	3		Johnston, James (Son of Wm)	6	2	Barnes, James	13	6	Moseley, George, jr	3	
Childrey, Benjamin	10		Jetar, William	7	1	Brizendine, William	11	1	Monday, Isaac	11	
Legrand, William	2		Kennedy, William	4	3	Watkins, William	1	5	Moseley, Edward, jr	5	7
Foster, Thomas	6	4	Moore, John	2	1	Watkins, James, Senr	10	24	Moseley, Edward, Senr	7	30
Foster, Josiah, jr	6	2	Read, Mary, Senr	1	26	Chisolm, William	10	12	Mimms, Thomas	10	
Tankersley, John	3	8	Read, Edmund	1	24	Watkins, James	4	11	Newton, Giles		6
Spencer, Thomas, Senr	4	19	Sullivan, John, Senr	7	5	Petty, John	12	3	Roberson, Henry	8	21
Spencer, Mary	5	9	Sullivant, James	9	8	Malcum, James	7		Ryon, William	6	1
Read, Mary	4	35	Sutton, Robert	5	6	Newcomb, John	8		Staples, William	9	2
Foster, William	6	9	Thorp, William	3	2	Toombs, Emanuel	4		Sansum, William	8	
Foster, George	1	18	Thorp, James	1		Harrison, Moses	9	4	Toombs, William	4	
Haney, John	7		Thorp, Theotho	5		Owen, James	8		Vaughan, William	3	
Harllee, Peter	6	1	Jameson, William	6	31	Davis, James	8	5	Webb, Thomas	7	1
White, Sarah	5		Prewit, Joseph	5	4	Almond, Edward	5	6	Wilmott, Joseph	5	
Buckner, Mary	3		Sullivant, Menoah	8		Almond, John	4	3	Wilmott, Thomas	2	3
Johnston, Reuben	7	5	Marable, Christopher	4		Goode, Mack	8	13	Wilmot, George	1	
Watkins, William	6	16	London, Isaiah	6		Ail, Mary	3		Whitlow, Darby	6	
Breedlove, John	8	8	Morton, Quinn	6	7	Adkins, John	10		Whitlow, John	6	4
Breedlove, Benjamin	10	6	Hight, John	4	4	Allin, Muke	8		Zachery, John	7	1
Comer, Samuel	2	8	Fuqua, John	7	5	Bacon, Langston	9	11	Bibb, Richard	7	11
Whitlock, Charles	7	3	Pritchett, Nicholas	3		Bardin, William	10		Bond, Phillip	6	
Hines, James	6	5	Griffin, William	4		Blanks, Thomas	5		Cuninghame, John	6	2
Toombs, Gabriel	3	3	Osborne, Reps	10	11	Burton, Thomas	7	1	Marable, Mathew	14	42
Williamson, John	6		Ashworth, Samuel	10	4	Burton, James	3				
Page, Nathaniel	6	8	Osborne, John	7		Barnes, Francis	11	8			
White, Alexander	1					Bailey, Roger Cock	6	4			

CUMBERLAND COUNTY.

NAME OF HEAD OF FAMILY.	White.	Black.	NAME OF HEAD OF FAMILY.	White.	Black.	NAME OF HEAD OF FAMILY.	White.	Black.	NAME OF HEAD OF FAMILY.	White.	Black.
Amos, Ann	5		Bond, Wright	3	1	Cary, Archibald:			Farmer, James	4	
Armistead, Thaddeus	7	8	Brown, Clement	13	3	In Cumberland	19	189	Ford, John	6	25
Armistead, Francis	5	4	Boatwright, Jesse	6		In Buckingham	5	41	Francis, John	8	4
Armistead, John	9	6	Burton, William	3		Cayee, Shadrack	11	2	Findley, David	1	
Armistead, William	10	13	Bradley, John, junr	6	2	Chalton, John	4		Fretwell, William	3	9
Austin, James	7	12	Barker, Charles	5	7	Chalton, Abraham	7	1	Fretwell, Thomas	5	
Alderson, Richard	5	4	Bradley, Hezekiah	5	1	Colquet, John	7	3	Fretwell, James	4	3
Alderson, John	5		Brown, Robert	9	10	Calland, Joseph	2	19	Fretwell, Richard	8	5
Anderson, Robert (of Hanr)	11	8	Burton, John	8	16	Caldwell, Thomas	10	1	Farmer, John	4	
Anderson, Robert, junr	9	13	Burton, Allen	4	11	Cock, Anderson	2	10	Glover, Phinehas, junr	7	4
Adams, Thomas	9		Burton, William Allen	2	5	Cobbs, Sarah	1	7	Glover, Phinehas	3	18
Anderson, William	9	4	Beacham, Isaac	7	5	Cook, Stephen	2	8	Glover, Samuel	4	1
Anderson, Rhoda	5		Bowles, Hannah	7	1	Coleman, William	5	13	Gilliam, James	9	9
Allen, Archer	7	26	Beck, Judith	8		Cunningham, Elizabeth	4		Gilliam, Catharine	3	6
Arnold, Moses	9	8	Baskerville, John	8	13	Cox, Francis	8	2	Glover, Robert	6	2
Amos, William	8		Baskerville, George	5	1	Davidson, Hezekiah	5	2	Gentry, Simon	2	8
Allen, William, senr	2	4	Brown, Robert (Meed)	8		Davidson, Charles	2		Gordon, Solomon	7	6
Allen, Benjamin	7	12	Bond, William	4	2	Douglass, James	5	4	Gaines, Bernard	5	14
Anderson, Jesse	5	3	Burton, John	3	3	Daniel, Abraham	11	21	Guttery, Thomas	2	2
Allen, Daniel	11	15	Bolling, Archibald	6	38	Douglass, Robert	3	9	Guttery, Alexander	10	12
Allen, Benjamin, junr	4	2	Blanton, James	5	1	Dowdy, William	11		Guttery, Henry	3	4
Allen, Martha	1	11	Bowker, Byrd	5	15	Dowdy, James	1		Guttery, William	4	6
Armstrong, Elizabeth	3	6	Brown, Frederick	5		Duncomb, John	9		Guttery, Bernard	10	2
Angela, William	10	8	Brown, John (Camph)	4		Dean, Richard	5		Glenn, James Coleman	3	
Angela, Bartlett	9	6	Butler, John	5	1	Daniel, William	7	14	Glenn, James	9	5
Anderson, Thomas	4	5	Brown, James	8		Davenport, Henry	12	10	Glenn, William	9	3
Anderson, James	5	17	Carrington, Nathaniel	4	16	Davenport, David	9	3	Glenn, Nathan	6	21
Anderson, Charles	1	12	Creary, John	10		Davenport, William	8	12	Hudgens, Drury	9	1
Anderson, William	7	7	Cunningham, Valentine	4	2	Doss, James	7	3	Harris, Richard		
Allen, Charles	5	5	Carrington, George	9	34	Doss, Joshua	7	1	Harrison, Carter H	20	136
Allen, Benjamin	5	5	Carrington, Joseph	9	35	Daniel, John	2	18	Hughes, Simon	6	3
Anderson, John	6		Craine, John	9		Degraffenreid, Sarah	4	2	Haskins, Creed	9	15
Allen, Richard	11	7	Carter, Isham	6	2	Donaho, James	1		Hatcher, Drury	7	7
Adams, James	3		Cobbs, Jesse	6	4	Davis, John	8		Hobson, Caleb	7	6
Bryant, Isaac	5	13	Cunningham, William	7	5	Dillon, William	4		Hobson, Joanna	4	17
Bolling, Thomas	4		Cunningham, James	4	5	Edwards, Andrew	5		Hatcher, Frederick	10	12
Bailey, James	4		Carrington, George, junr	5	34	Edwards, William	7		Hobson, John	4	8
Bagby, William	5	4	Colquet, Hezekiah	4	10	Eppes, Francis		55	Hatcher, John	3	5
Brown, Armistead	4		Carter, David	6	2	Ellyson, Gerrard	3	6	Hill, William C	4	20
Brown, John	6	9	Cohan, Jacob	5	2	Edwards, Flemstead	1		Hubbard, Joseph	8	
Boatwright, Daniel	13	5	Carter, Thomas	10	7	Edwards, William	7	5	Hudgens, James	8	6
Boatwright, James	10		Chapman, John	8		Elliot, Richard	6		Hudson, William	10	1
Baskerville, Richard	9	12	Cock, William	9	23	Fouling, Robert	5	1	Hobson, William, sen	5	19
Boatwright, William	5		Cobbs, John	5	40	Ferguson, William	6	10	Hobson, John (est.)	4	16
Baltimore, Christopher	6		Chamberlayne, Edward Pye	2	36	Faulkner, Nicholas	8		Hobson, Sarah	4	10
Baughn, Tucker	12	3	Coleman, Patience	5	13	Faris, Benjamin	10		Hobson, William, jun	6	6
Bartee, Thomas	7	4	Coleman, Daniel	1		Flippen, Francis	9	4	Hobson, Thomas	7	5
Booker, Richard	3	16	Cuisack, Robert	3	16	Flippen, Philip	4	7	Hudgens, Holloway	1	2
Ballou, Charles	5	13	Clements, Edward	6	3	Flippen, Jacob	1	1	Holland, Thomas	9	5
Ballou, Thomas	3	3	Creedle, John	5	4	Flippen, John	12	11	Holloway, Billy	3	
Ballou, William	2	2	Coleman, Thomas	3	4	Flippen, Martha	1	6	Holloway, Samuel	13	4
Bowles, John	4		Coleman, Elizabeth	6		Fuqua, Joseph, senr	2	16	Hunnibus, Henry	4	
Bowles, Benjamin	3		Carter, Theoderick	3	8	Fuqua, Joseph, junr	10	7	Hubbard, Moses	9	1
Bradley, John	3	14	Carter, William	4		Frazer, William	6	1	Hill, Elizabeth	14	27
Bradley, William	5	2	Clapton, Robert	1	9	Folks, John	5	3	Hammondier, Sally	4	
Brown, William	4	1	Cauthon, Thomas	8		Flippen, Robert	2	3	Hudgens, James	11	4

CUMBERLAND COUNTY—Continued.

NAME OF HEAD OF FAMILY.	White.	Black.	NAME OF HEAD OF FAMILY.	White.	Black.	NAME OF HEAD OF FAMILY.	White.	Black.	NAME OF HEAD OF FAMILY.	White.	Black.
Harrison, Precilla	6	36	Minton, William	6	7	Russell, William	7	3	Tapscott, Henry	7	6
Harrison, Cary	1	12	Moore, John	10	....	Robertson, John	4	3	Thompson, Bartlett	14	25
Hix, John	7	....	McCormack, Hugh	7	....	Robertson, David	8	....	Thompson, Benajah	6	13
Hendrick, William	1	....	Maddox, William	11	8	Richardson, Robert	2	....	Thomas, Job	10	15
Hill, —— (est.)	....	13	Meader, Jesse	9	5	Randolph, Thomas:			Thomas, Phinehas	5	3
Harman, Henry	1	....	Montague, John	5	4	In Goochland	6	31	Trent, Alexander	24	123
Hill, Dennet	4	1	Minton, John	4	1	In Powhatan	4	6	Trent, Peterfield	9	22
Hill, John	10	....	Merryman, John	3	17	In Buckingham	3	20	Taylor, Peter	1	3
Hendrick, Zachariah	12	10	Martin, Henry	11	1	In Chesterfield	....	7	Turner, John	6	....
Hendrick, Obadiah	4	3	Melton, Samuel	9	....	In Cumberland	5	3	Thompson, Josiah	8	27
Hall, Thomas	2	1	Melton, Nathan	7	....	Richardson, William	4	2	Tucker, Sᵗ George	5	32
Hughes, Powell	8	9	Moon, Stephen	5	....	Richardson, John	5	3	Trent, Peter Field	4	18
Hughes, Stephen	6	2	Minter, John	7	....	Richardson, Isham	9	12	Vauter, Samuel	10	4
Holeman, John	10	3	Meggs, Joel	4	3	Randolph, David M	4	21	Venable, Elizabeth	3	8
Holeman, John, junr	1	....	Mason, William	5	....	Randolph, Richard, junr	1	22	Walton, Edward	9	20
Holland, James	6	2	Macon, Henry	7	83	Randolph, Beverly	5	16	Woodson, Charles	3	5
Holland, Meader	1	....	McCrae, Christopher	11	16	Scruggs, William	7	2	Woodson, Drury	8	16
Johnson, Daniel	5	11	Macon, William Hartwell	2	18	Spears, William	8	10	Woodson, Jesse	5	5
Jennings, John	5	....	Moore, Thomas	7	....	Smith, Robert	5	....	Woodson, Joseph	4	16
Johnson, David	2	....	Martin, Benjamin	8	....	Scruggs, Tabitha	7	15	Woodson, John	7	30
James, Richard	13	35	McGlapon, James	5	....	Southall, John	5	....	Walton, Robert	6	13
Johnson, Obadiah	1	....	McCann, John	5	....	Sandy, Vincent	2	....	Walton, Martha	2	11
Jones, Judith	9	8	Muse, John	3	2	Scruggs, Thomas	5	....	Winnefred, Margarett	4	2
Johnson, Isaac	6	4	Micheaux, Joseph	11	20	Sanderson, William	6	5	Winfree, Charles	12	4
Johnson, Mary	3	2	Miles, William	3	1	Scruggs, Edward	10	....	Walton, George	8	4
Johnson, Job	7	4	Meadors, John	12	11	Sanderson, John	9	8	Weatherford, Joseph	6	....
Jones, Harrison, senr	2	7	Newton, John	9	1	Scruggs, Drury	8	8	Winfree, John	3	7
Jones, John	7	29	Norris, Thomas	6	9	Scruggs, Mary	3	11	Womack, William	1	10
Jones, Harrison, jun	2	5	Nash, Thomas	3	13	Stone, Prudence	4	10	Walker, John	6	....
Jones, John, junr	2	....	Noel, John	5	7	Sims, John	6	3	Winniford, David	2	2
Jenkins, John	2	....	Noel, Robert	9	6	Smith, Catherine	6	4	Winfree, William	6	....
Johns, Jefferson	8	17	Nelson, Mary	5	11	Sims, Benjamin	6	4	Wilson, Benjamin	14	26
Jenkins, Joseph	9	3	Oakley, Erasmus	4	....	Slaughter, John	10	10	Wilson, Benjamin, junr	2	4
Johns, Thomas, senr	4	20	Orange, Joshua	4	....	Skipwith, Henry	6	96	Weatherford, Richard	9	2
Johns, Thomas	7	6	Orange, Lewis	4	....	Smith, Robert	9	7	Woodson, Stephen	6	22
Keeble, Walter	6	2	Page, James	8	....	Smith, Betty	3	9	Wilson, Richard	6	4
Keeble, Dorathy	2	1	Palmore, William	7	....	Sims, Mary	7	11	Woodson, John	5	10
Keville, Thomas	5	....	Price, Joseph	8	21	Scruggs, Henry	2	5	Womack, Massinello	6	8
Keeling, George	9	40	Parker, Jeremiah	2	2	Scruggs, Littleberry	2	1	Woodfen, George	5	3
Keeble, Humphry	1	31	Prince, John	6	....	Seay, John, senr	8	....	Wright, Seymore	2	7
Lawless, William	5	....	Philips, James	5	2	Stinson, Joseph	9	1	Walker, Warren	5	39
Ligon, William	9	....	Pollard, Isaac	5	11	Starkey, Joseph	6	1	Woodson, Anderson	4	3
Loyal, Bathsheba	2	1	Pierce, Edmund	6	5	Sharp, Betty	4	....	Woodson, John (D. W.)	6	13
Langhorne, John	7	32	Price, John	3	4	Sharp, Joseph	8	....	Walker, William	1	17
Langhorne, Maurice	9	47	Price, Mary	4	7	Shepherd, William	11	10	Womack, Nathan	7	8
Lorton, Robert	5	8	Robinson, James	3	....	Sandifer, Abraham	7	24	Wright, Griffin	4	9
Lee, John	12	9	Robinson, Samuel	8	....	Scott, Seymore	9	17	Williams, Jane	6	....
Lee, Charles	4	10	Richardson, Richard	4	8	Swann, Thomas Thompson	4	12	Williams, Matthias	5	....
Lee, William	8	5	Robinson, Joseph, junr	7	1	Scruggs, Edward, junr	4	3	Woodson, John (Pit.)	9	10
Lee, Joseph	8	10	Robinson, John	4	2	Taylor, Joseph	6	4	Woodson, Miller	10	22
Lee, Richard	2	7	Robinson, Hezekiah	6	12	Taylor, Richard	3	....	Williams, Samuel	9	11
Moore, Joseph	8	1	Robinson, Field, junr	6	2	Turpin, William	4	27	Williams, Roger	11	7
Mosby, Nicholas	11	6	Robinson, Josiah	4	10	Taylor, Samuel, junr	4	....	Wright, George	4	9
Martin, Orson	8	4	Robinson, Edward	2	1	Thomas, James	10	4	Webber, Richard	5	11
Mayo, Joseph	7	39	Robinson, Stephen	5	3	Taylor, Samuel	7	8	Webber, Philip	8	31
Murry, John	8	8	Robertson, Jeffrey	6	8	Thomas, Jesse, junr	3	....	Womack, William, jr	....	5
Montague, Thomas	4	1	Richardson, Martin	7	10	Thompson, Neil	4	7	Woodson, Joseph	6	16
Montague, Peter	2	2				Taylor, Elizabeth	8	....			

FAIRFAX COUNTY.

LIST OF WILLIAM RAMSAY.	White.	Black.	LIST OF WILLIAM RAMSAY—continued.	White.	Black.	LIST OF WILLIAM RAMSAY—continued.	White.	Black.	LIST OF WILLIAM RAMSAY—continued.	White.	Black.
Ramsay, William	10	20	Skidmore, Ann	2	....	Short, John	6	....	Donaldson, William	9	....
Lawrason, James	8	....	Con, Gerrard T	4	4	Price, Oliver	8	1	Harding, Hall	7	1
Watson, Josiah	12	9	Skidmore, Elizabeth	2	....	Anderson, William	5	....	Avery, John	8	....
Evans, John	4	....	Hartshorne, William	10	2	Richards, John	2	....	Talbutt, Henry	5	2
Lyles, William	8	14	Skidmore, Edward	2	....	McCrea, Robert	8	7	Bolling, Martha	4	15
Shreeve, Benjamin	11	....	Hay, Robert	6	1	Mills, John	1	9	Reedy, William	3	....
Ramsay, Edward	7	6	Hannah, Alex	3	....	Gabbard, John	4	....	Bowling, John	8	....
Henenger, Frederick	3	....	Wilson, Joseph	7	7	Frond, James	4	....	Talbutt, Levy	2	....
Tayler, Jesse	13	7	Adam, Robert	7	15	Reed, Thomas	7	....	Lake, Ann	7	1
Allison, Robert	5	9	Simms, Charles	7	8	Doyle, Conrod	6	1	Bell, Charles	4	....
Allison, & Ramsay	3	1	Bolling, William	9	6	Arnold, Thomas	6	....	Roch, William	7	....
Lyle, Robert	3	2	Richards, George	1	....	Gollatt, John	8	1	Carlyle, John (Estate)	6	49
Hughes, Aaron	9	....	Ward, William	8	2	Graham, John	1	2	Lomax, John	7	6
Zimmerman, Lewis	2	1	Hannah, Nicholas	4	....	Bright, Windle	4	1	Duvall, William	5	7
Williams, John	6	....	Moxley, Thomas	7	6	Grymes, William	3	1	Ferguson, Cumb	3	....
Hess, Jacob	3	1	Weston, Lewis	7	3	Humphreys, Thomas	7	6	Walles, Andrew	8	5
Merry, Philip	2	1	Cooper, Joel	9	2	Conway, Richard	4	15	Wise, John	7	6
Zimmerman, Tobias	6	....	Bromley, William	3	....	Gretter, Michael	9	2	Harding, Edward	10	....
Chapman, Geo	6	21	Gretter, Michael	5	3	Adam, James	2	....	Harding, Elisha	4	....
Fitzgerald, John	5	12	Curtis, Charles	7	....	Graham, Thomas	5	....	Griffin, William	5	13
McKnight, Willm	3	1	McIver, Colin	1	....	Marr, Charles	4	....	Marle, Joseph	5	....
Keith, James	8	8	Hepburn, William	3	4	Merchant, John	4	1	Custis, Eleanor	6	65
Hendricks, James	4	4	Wise, Peter	5	4	Hays, Andrew	3	2	Kenneday, Uner	5	....
Hendricks, John	3	6	Ryan, Michael	6	....	Spurling, Jere	11	3	Daniel, Thomas	6	....
Hooe, Rob. P	3	14	Cox, Jacob	8	2	Read, James	3	....	Kirkpatrick, Thomas	2	1
Broders, Joseph	3	....	Oyenbread, William	3	....	Salmon, George	2	....	Longdon, John	8	1
Massey, John	7	....	Heald, John	3	....	Vanpelt, Benjamin	6	....	Almond, Mary	2	1
Lynn, Adam	10	3	Lott, John	4	....	Munday, Elizabeth	2	3	Muir, John	2	6
Zenever, Lewis	2	1	Herbert, William	5	6	Jones, Charles	4	8	Nicholson, Joseph	10	....
Craig, Charles	10	....	Hooff, Lawrance	5	2	Alexander, Charles	5	16	Earp, Mary	5	....
Ray, Thomas	7	1	Webster, Philip	3	1	Talbutt, Osborn	4	....	Reed, Nelson	10	....
Rollings, John	4	....	Longdon, Ralph	4	3	Burch, Joseph	8	....	Butcher, John	7	....
Rollings, Winifred	3	....	Bonts, Jacob	4	1	Jaco, William	5	....	Earp, Matthew	14	1
Harden, Anastatia	3	7	Blunt, Washer	5	1	Scott, John	8	....	Chew, John	5	....
Duncan, George	4	4	Yoest, John	10	....	payne, Annanias	12	....	Mason, George	4	1
Hunter, William, Jun	2	3	Muir, Robert	1	....	Scott, Zacha	3	....	Bryan, William	4	3
Harper, John	5	1	Holliday, James	6	1	Nelson, William	3	....	West, Thos	5	10
Machey, John	1	....	Smith, John	4	....	Ball, Moses, Junr	7	1	Bladen, William	10	....
Skidmore, Melinda	2	....	Evans, Whilothan	4	....	Thrift, Jere	8	....	Bladen. William, Jr	4	....

FAIRFAX COUNTY—Continued.

NAME OF HEAD OF FAMILY.	White.	Black.
LIST OF WILLIAM RAMSAY—continued.		
pendall, Thomas	11	
Harding, Moses	7	
Hoskins, John	5	
Johnson, Lancelot	6	2
Johnson, John	7	
Ballenger, Joseph	3	
McLean, Samuel	2	
Robinson, Joseph	6	2
Hunter, William	5	7
Hunter, Alex	2	
Copper, Cyrus	4	2
Arell, Samuel	4	1
Arell, Richard	4	6
Sanford, John	5	3
Winterberry, John	5	1
Slimer, Christopher	10	
Smith, James	3	
Orr, Elizabeth	2	
Stewart, Doctr D.	3	1
parsons, James	9	5
Wilkenson, Thomas	8	
Bird, William	3	7
Thompson, Wm	8	
Goodrich, Benje	9	
Nelson, Richard	7	
Simmond, Samuel	6	
Dade, Baldwin	4	14
Peers, Valentine	3	8
Lemasten, John	4	
Chew, Roger	8	4
Myler, James	2	2
Bryce, John	3	3
Uler, Valentine	3	2
Harrison, Jo W	2	1
Thorn, Michael	1	2
Chapin, Margarett	4	1
Thomas, William	5	
Thompson, Joseph	7	
Thompson, John	4	
Money, Neil	3	1
Sanford, Cath.	5	2
Fleming, Thomas	6	3
Ball, Moses	5	
Williams, John	7	
Ball, Jas	5	
Calverley, Joseph	8	9
Mcfarling, Ignatius	11	
Sanford, Edward	7	4
Harper, Col. John	7	3
Alexander, philip	6	22
LIST OF HENRY DARN.		
Adams, John	5	1
Anderson, John	8	
Ball, John	6	2
Blake, George	7	
Bowling, Ann	7	1
Baker, James	7	
Bradley, Dennis	3	
Bradley, Mathew	5	
Baker, Thomas	6	
Darne, John	5	2
Donaldson, Andrew	5	
Dulin, Thadeus	10	1
Darne, Thomas	5	1
Darne, William	4	3
Darne, Henry	9	8
Earp, James	5	
Edwards, Mary	7	
Earp, Caleb	1	
Earp, Abedneza	5	
Frizell, Luke	3	1
Frizell, Mary	9	
Follen, William	8	2
Gunnell, William	7	19
Goldup, John	7	
Harle, John	7	1
Hollinsberry, Richard	5	
Hurst, James	11	10
Hunter, George	6	10
Hipkins, Lewis	2	13
Hunter, John	9	16
Hurst, John	1	10
Jenkins, James	3	
Jenkins, Daniel	5	
Self, John	1	
Jenkins, Simon	3	1
Jenkins, Charles	4	
Jenkins, Thomas	9	10
Jenkins, William	13	
Jackson, John	10	13
Jenkins, Samuel	7	3
Walker, John	6	
Lee, phil L., Esq. (Estate)		82
Mattenley, James	8	
Mattenley, John	3	
Magruder, Thomas	1	11
Minor, George	6	4
Moxley, Thomas	8	3
Moxley, Jobe	5	1

NAME OF HEAD OF FAMILY.	White.	Black.
LIST OF HENRY DARN—continued.		
Minor, Ann	4	11
Owens, John	8	1
piper, William	2	
payne, Jacob	7	
Robertson, James	11	
Richards, Calib	7	
Robertson, John	6	
Rucksby, Edward	6	1
Sand, James	6	
Shortridge, John	6	4
Swain, Archibald	5	
Scott, Sebret	6	
Sutton, John	3	
Simpson, Joseph	8	3
Swink, William	11	
Smith, George	9	7
Scott, William	1	11
Simpson, James	4	1
Tramell, Gerrard, Junr	10	2
Tramell, Gerrard	2	3
Thrift, Charles	5	2
Thrift, George	7	8
Turberville, John		31
Thrift, Charles	5	10
Thomas, James	7	2
Wren, William	8	6
Williams, William	7	
Whittle, Richard	4	
Huzy, Henry	1	
Adams, Samuel, Junr	5	6
Adams, Simon	2	3
Adams, Samuel	1	1
Jenkins, Wm, Junr	1	
Adams, William	8	20
LIST OF THOMAS LEWIS.		
Monroe, John	11	8
Monroe, William	3	
Williams, George	7	6
Carrington, Timothy	7	
Garrett, Nicholas	7	1
Lester, John	7	
Obriant, William	2	
Daly, Thomas	11	
Ball, George	4	
Keith, John	13	2
Lindsay, Robert	6	6
Fernister, John	5	
Beach, Thomas	7	
Lindsay, Thomas	5	2
Wheeler, Drummond	8	4
Tailer, Thomas	7	1
Sears, William	7	
Sheperd, John	5	
Gunnell, John	4	4
Davis, Allan	8	
Gunnell, William	10	3
Talbrett, Benja	1	8
Cotton, John	11	4
Stone, William	7	5
Winn, George	14	18
Moore, Jeremiah	10	1
Scutt, William	7	3
Chun, Mary	4	
Bates, Edward	12	
Henderson, John	5	
Hardy, William	7	
Cotton, Nathaniel	3	10
Ferguson, Joshua	9	3
Wren, James	6	25
Davis, Nehemiah	4	10
Thompson, Samuel	10	
Hoskins, Ralph	12	2
Bennett, William	4	
Oliver, Joseph	12	
Oliver, Eli	3	
Alexon, James	2	7
Rose, Francis	5	
Bennett, Joseph	7	5
Kidwell, Hezekiah	9	1
Tunnell, William	6	
Monroe, Spencer	7	
Talbott, Demoville	4	3
poston, Francis	9	3
Blackburn, Edward	8	2
Garrett, Henry	7	
Harden, Martha	5	
Garrett, Henry, Junr	3	
Palmer, Thomas	2	8
Smith, Alex	6	
Beedle, Andrew	6	
Simms, William	12	
Offutt, Rezin	9	10
Sewell, Mary	2	
Hurst, John	4	12
Broadwater, Chas	6	25
Lewis, Thomas	6	12
McCarty, Thomas	7	
McCarty, James	5	
Broadwater, Chas (Quarter)	2	14

NAME OF HEAD OF FAMILY.	White.	Black.
LIST OF THOMAS LEWIS—continued.		
Gunnell, Henry	5	19
Edmond, John	7	
Gunnell, Thomas	10	10
Hunter, Elizabeth	3	14
Crump, Turner	10	1
Hally, Richard	6	2
LIST OF GEO. GILPIN.		
Jefferson, Jeremiah	9	
Senior, John	8	
Johnson, Samuel	7	
Richard, James	7	3
Frazier, William	2	2
Boswell, William	3	
Smith, Joseph	3	
Summers, Francis	14	
Ratcliff, John	4	7
Potter, Edward	9	
Cook, Giles	6	8
Crump, William	5	
Doughlas, Thomas	7	
powell, Elisha	9	3
Davis, Edward, Senr	7	
Mills, Daniel	9	8
Burges, Charles	7	
payne, John	4	
Morris, Zachariah	7	
Ratcliff, John, Senr	3	5
Gibson, Sybil	2	1
Spinks, Chandler	3	2
price, David	9	3
Crump, William, Senr	9	
Popejoy, Nathl	7	
Perrett, William H. G.	4	16
Kirby, Thomas	5	
Moss, John	11	8
Roe, Absolom	7	3
Beach, Thomas	9	1
French, penelope & B. Dulany	9	102
West, Margaret	13	30
Smith, Charity	9	
Williams, Jere	10	7
Summers, William	4	
Summers, Daniel	7	
Burges, Thomas	3	
Dulin, Sarah	5	15
Cockerill, Joseph	6	8
Cockerill, Sampson	4	3
Ballenger, Martha	6	
Ballenger, John	4	
Burgess, Joseph	3	
Horseman, John	8	
Horseman, William	5	
Sisson, William	7	
Thomas, priscilla	3	
pearson, Simon	11	4
Graffort, Thomas	4	
Minor, Jemima	1	10
Curry, Charles	7	
popejoy, Edward	7	
Elliott, John	6	
Fitzhugh, William (B. G.)	7	122
Dove, Thomas	7	
West, John	1	6
Williams, Ann	3	
Heagons, Joseph	7	
Jones, Thomas	6	
Yoest, William	8	
Pettit, James	4	
Hawkins, William	5	1
Murry, John	6	
Gilpin, George	9	11
Lightfoot, William	9	2
Boswell, Alex	5	
LIST OF RICHARD CHICHESTER.		
Alliston, Bryan	2	
Armstrong, William	8	
Ashford, Michael	6	
Alliston, John	13	
Alliston, Thomas	7	
Boswell, Benjamin	7	
Boswell, George	2	
Ballenger, Joseph	4	
Beach, Charles	4	
Baylis, Thomas	6	1
Burton, Benjamin	2	1
Compton, John	10	8
Clark, Josias	7	4
Chichester, Richard	9	32
Davis, Bartin	7	
Dodson, Charles	10	7
Devaugh, John	8	
Devaugh, Elizabeth	6	
Darrell, Sarah	8	16
Dawson, George	7	

NAME OF HEAD OF FAMILY.	White.	Black.
LIST OF RICHARD CHICHESTER—continued.		
Dorsey, John Samuel	9	
Freeman, Richard	4	
Freeman, William	3	
Frazier, John	5	
Ferrell, Hezekiah	7	
Ferrell, James	3	3
Gregsby, Sarah	7	
Grace, Patrick	2	
Glocester, James	5	
Gordon, Sarah	7	
Hopkins, Richard	7	
Hagon, John	7	
Hill, Bennett	8	
Hill, Walter	3	
Hammilton, Dennis B	8	
Hornbuckle, Solomon	10	
Hally, Nathaniel	7	10
Hagon, Henry	3	1
Javins, Joseph	6	
Jones, John	10	7
Johnson, William, Junr	7	
Johnson, Ann	4	
Johnson, James	4	
Keaton, William	8	2
Knowles, John	2	
Kirk, Grafton	5	
Kent, Daniel	5	
Kent, John	8	
Kent, Jane	6	
Mcfarlane, John B	7	
Mills, Sarah	4	
McDonald, Alex	1	3
Moore, John	4	
McDonald, James	3	
Morton, Jane	6	23
Ogden, William	9	
Oneale, Charles	5	
Rigg, John	7	
Rogers, William	4	1
Reed, John	7	
Stone, Jonathan	1	
Scrivener, Richard	9	
Sanford, Elizabeth	5	8
Smith, Charles	9	4
Swallow, Zepheniah	6	
Stone, Daniel	8	3
Tyler, William	9	
Talbutt, William	6	
Thompson, James	9	1
Violett, William	8	2
Underwood, John	4	
Williams, Alor	7	
Warner, Joseph	5	
Worthen, Edward	6	
Worthen, Henry	3	
West, Benjamin H	7	
Wingate, Henry	5	
Wiggs, Ann	4	
Young, Henry	1	
Payne, Jane	5	
Potter, William	4	
LIST OF CHARLES LITTLE.		
Peake, Humphrey	6	20
Washington, General	2	188
Washington, Lund	2	16
Bishop, Thomas	3	
Fairfax, Hezekiah	5	
Alton, John	4	
Roberts, William	2	3
Evans, John	6	
Adams, Abednego	7	12
Summers, George	5	8
Boswell, Henry	2	1
Flatford, Thomas	4	
Darrell, Mary	6	18
Darrell, philip	5	9
Eaton, John	4	
Robertson, John	7	13
Alexander, Robert	4	8
Simpson, William	8	7
Little, Charles	8	13
Dow, Peter	4	8
Cox, Mrs	1	16
Going, Joseph	7	
Bennett, Henry, Esqr		32
Allen, Thomas	3	
Ferguson, Zacharia	7	
Judge, Andrew	6	1
McKenzy, John	3	
Boyd, William	4	
Williams, Edward	12	
Buchannan, Arthur	7	
Triplett, William	7	13
French, penelope		20
West, Colo John (Estate)	13	36
Mason, Colo Geo	6	38
Dowdale, John	7	2
McLaughlin, Thos	9	
Sanford, Robert	8	2

FAIRFAX COUNTY—Continued.

NAME OF HEAD OF FAMILY.	White.	Black.	NAME OF HEAD OF FAMILY.	White.	Black.	NAME OF HEAD OF FAMILY.	White.	Black.	NAME OF HEAD OF FAMILY.	White.	Black.
LIST OF CHARLES LITTLE—continued.			**LIST OF JOSIAH WATSON.**			**LIST OF JOHN GIBSON—continued.**			**LIST OF JOHN GIBSON—continued.**		
Brook, Walter	4	9	Grymes, philip	7	14	pollard, Thomas	12	22	Beckwith, Marma	16	27
Slaughter, Ann	7	27	Grymes, John	6	3	payne, Edward	8	26	Boggess, Robert	5	8
Bird, William	1	14	Richards, William	5	2	Sangster, Thomas	12	10	Hedgman, John	4	10
Sanford, Richard, Senr	7	3	Hammond, Jervis	4	18	Reardon, Yelverton	4	2	Fallen, Elizabeth	4	2
Gates, Samuel	6	....	Lawrance. Moses	4	....	Langfett, philip	4	5	Abrahams, Susanna	3	....
Pool, William	12	....	Moxley, James	7	....	Deneale, James	5	20	Coombs, Walter	3	....
Pool, Thomas	6	....	payne, Clark	5	4	Deneale, William	3	9	Green, William	4	....
Javins, John	6	....	Johnson, Thomas	3	....	Harrison, John	10	....	Hampton, John	7	10
Gates, Isaac	6	....	Skinner, William	8	4	Clarke, John	4	9	Gossom, Thos	8	....
Linton, Elizabeth	3	....	Dove, Leonard	4	....	Ferguson, Josiah	11	7	Spragg, John	7	....
Violett, Harry	6	....	Emmerson, Richard	6	....	posey, John	9	1	Hiple, William	3	....
Wyley, George	8	....	Dove, William	4	....	powell, William	7	2	Kerrick, James	4	....
Stone, Samuel	4	....	Woolbright, Barnabas	5	....	Wood, Joseph	6	....	Dyer, Edward	5	....
Vioty, John	2	....	Hally, Richard	7	2	Middleton, Lutner	7	1	Simmons, William	4	....
Barry, William	2	2	Love, Thomas	6	....	Harroway, Merryman	12	....	King, John	6	2
parker, Lawson	6	....	Woodward, Thomas	7	....	West, Sarah	9	....	Bayly, William	4	....
Carter, Henry	2	....	Gooding, William	7	....	Coe, William	5	7	Conner, Terrence	5	....
Parker, Mashal R	6	....	Martin, Joseph	9	....	Halbert, Isaac	5	2	Conner, Terrence, Junr	3	....
Evans, John	6	1	Johnson, Thomas	7	....	King, Margaret	5	....	Hally, James, Junr	11	....
West, Mrs. Sibyl	1	7	Chichester, Richard	7	14	Tayler, Edward	10	....	Harris, William	7	....
Middleton, Hugh	7	4	Sanders, Lewis	9	....	Tayler, James	5	....	Harris, Thomas	9	....
			Allan, Andrew	8	....	West, John	4	....	Bayly, Henry	6	....
LIST OF DANIEL M'CARTY.			Noaling, Charles	9	....	Clark, Richard	11	5	Brown, Doctr William	8	8
Arrington, Thomas	3	....	pearson, Nicholas	6	....	Gilpin, Jane	2	....	Wagener, Peter	7	15
Baylis, William payne	10	....	Ashton, John	8	5	Skinner, John	5	....			
Barker, William	9	....	Wheeler, Ignatius	8	5	Gill, James	8	....	**LIST OF MARTIN COCKBURN.**		
Barker, William, Junr	7	....	Raley, Mathias	5	....	Martin, James	6	....	Athy, Sarah	5	1
Barker, Moses	7	....	Wren, John	11	6	Coffer, Francis	8	28	Athy, Thomas	4	....
Barker, John	6	3	Gray, John	4	1	King, William	11	....	Athy, Samuel	8	....
Barnes, Sarah	1	11	Davis, William	5	....	powell, John	5	....	Armstrong, John	9	....
Bryan, philip	3	....	Oneil, John	11	....	Blansett, Joseph	9	....	Allason, William	8	....
Clark, Samuel	10	....	Stone, William	2	2	Tillett, John	3	1	Bayly, Samuel	8	2
Compton, Zebede	7	....	Davis, John	5	....	Tillett, George	7	....	Bayly, Wm, Decd (The Estate of)	2	7
Devers, Gilbert	7	....	Woodward, Jane	6	7	Hally, William	2	14	Barnes, Abraham	3	19
Denty, Jonathant	7	....	Orendore, Henry	3	....	Simpson, Moses	1	37	Boggess, John	8	....
Ellzey, Thomazin	1	1	Johnson, William	5	....	Nichols, George	8	....	Bussy, Hezekiah	5	....
Fowler, John	5	14	Dove, Joseph	6	....	King, Hargis	4	1	Church, Thomas	10	....
Gilmore, Jeremiah	5	....	Hall, parmer	4	....	Stone, Caleb	6	2	Church, Robert	5	....
Gray, Sarah	8	....	Davis, James	9	....	Halbert, Aaron	6	....	Church, Mary	4	....
Hornbuckle, Thomas	8	10	McDougal, Robert	5	1	Reed, Sarah	8	....	Cranford, John	5	....
Hornbuckle, William	6	1	Dulin, John	3	6	Hammond, Jacob	5	2	Chambers, Ann	6	....
Holden, Charles Gardner	4	....	Ashford, John	3	....	Wheeler, Richard	2	7	Culleson, Jere	5	2
Harper, Leonard	7	....	Gray, Drakeford	10	1	Roe, John	2	....	Cockburn, Martin	2	18
Hall, Jacob	6	....	Johnson, Thomas	8	....	Turner, William	7	4	Clark, John	4	....
Hall, William	5	....	Hall, Michael	8	....	Hopwood, Moses	5	1	Coulter, Peter	8	....
Harley, Rachel	9	....	Lewis, Thomas	12	6	Turner, William, Junr	3	13	Clements, Jacob	3	....
Johnson, Aaron	7	....	Wisden, Samuel	6	....	Simpson, John	13	1	Culleson, William	4	....
Keen, William	11	12	Ratcliff, Richard	6	4	Jacobs, Joseph, Junr	11	2	Compton, Houson	3	....
Keen, Francis	2	1	Steel, William	5	....	Hollyman, William	8	1	Donaldson, William	10	13
McCarty, Daniel	3	38	Stone, Eli	9	7	Reed, John	3	....	Doughlas, Robert	4	....
peacock, John	6	....	Summers, John	6	3	Lucas, Thomas	6	7	Finley, Sarah Ann	5	4
powell, John	5	....	powell, Joseph	9	4	Dogan, Henry	1	5	Green, William	4	....
Robertson, George	5	2	McLoughlen, Jesse	4	....	Walden, James	3	....	Harris, John	4	1
Ryley, Benjamin	7	1	Middleton, Thomas	5	....	McIntosh, John	1	2	Hutcheson, John	5	4
Rogers, Mary	4	....	Fitzhugh, Thos, for Colo Hy Fitzhugh	3	91	philips, John	4	....	Linton, Mary	2	1
Ratcliff, Thomas	6	....	Barret, John	11	....	Baylis, James	5	....	Little, Webster	2	....
Rigg, Benjamin	4	....	Davis, Isaac	11	....	Johnson, John	7	....	Hutcheson, Leonard	7	....
Rigg, Benedictus	5	....	Summers, John, Jun	9	7	Ellzey, Lewis	7	16	Little, Sarah	3	....
Ryley, peter	12	....	Summers, Simon	3	3	Turley, Sampson	9	19	Moreland, Jacob	5	....
Simpson, George	7	14	Moore, James	3	6	Simpson, William, Junr	8	1	Mason, Geo. (Pohic)	7	1
Simpson, Richard	7	3	Moore, William	8	1	Evans, James	1	....	McCarty, Daniel, Junr	4	20
Simpson, William	7	3	Richards, John	11	....	Waldon, Nathan	4	....	Massey, Lee	4	15
Stone, Samuel	9	1	Smith, Samuel	6	6	Payne, Sanford	9	8	Moore, Cleon	4	4
Suddath, Benjamin	6	6	payne, William	4	14	Pritchard, Lewis	6	....	Mason, George	9	90
Simpson, Thomas	7	....	Buash, Charles	10	....	Gray, Richard	5	....	Mason, George, Junr	1	24
Spinks, Gerrard	9	1	Johnson, William	5	....	Gibson, John	1	30	Payne, Virlinda	4	5
Smitherman, Samuel	7	....	Mills, William	7	5	McKey, Ann	3	....	Regan, John	9	....
Smitherman, William	4	....	Fieldar, Samuel	11	7	Eaton, William	9	....	Reardon, William	2	7
Smitherman, Samuel, Junr	6	....	Dauson, John	9	....	Edwards, Jacob	6	1	Simpson, William	5	....
Stone, Caleb	6	2	Martin, John	5	....	Owens, Samuel	1	6	Scott, John	5	8
Tayler, Thomas	3	....	Dove, Leonard	4	....	Rolland, Gilbert	8	....	Simpson, Gilbert	4	12
Tayler, Sarah	7	2	Johnson, Bennett	3	....	Kay, Joshua	8	....	Smith, Mary	10	1
Tasker, James	4	....	Hall, Sarah	5	....	Ross, Hector	1	1	Stone, Francis	2	2
Windsor, Thomas	5	8	Woolbright, Samuel	2	....	Edward, James	8	1	Saxon, John	6	....
Windsor, Thomas, Junr	6	1	Williams, Bazel	9	....	Edward, William	5	2	Shakespear, William	3	....
Williamson, William	11	....	Geoghegans, Michael	7	....	Tillett, John	10	....	Speake, Robert	8	....
Ward, John	4	11	presgraves, William	10	....	Morris, Nehemiah	7	....	Simpson, John	6	3
Wakefield, Abel	12	....				Loofburrow, David	4	....	Triplett, Sarah	7	20
Woolbright, Jacob	4	....	**LIST OF JOHN GIBSON.**			Athy, Robert	5	....	Tayler, Samuel	8	....
White, Sarah	6	....	Russaw, Henry	7	3	Athy, Ann	3	....	Vernon, John	7	1
Harris, Thomas	9	....	Mauzy, peter	10	13	Pomeroy, John	6	....	Ward, John	10	....
Ryley, John	3	....	Waugh, John	7	9	Stone, John	4	3	Washington, Lawrence	2	22
Jacobs, Mordecai	8	....	McDonald, John	6	....	Ford, Edward	14	16	Weston, William	9	....
patterson, Susanna	4	7	Doughlas, Daniel	1	....	West, Thomas	4	....	Warden, Nathan	3	....
Dyer, Thomas	8	....	Wade, Daniel	4	1	Hally, James	2	6	Thompson, William	1	1
Hunt, priscilla	7	2	Henderson, Alex	10	72	Hally, Francis	2	....	Reardon, Henry	5	2
Wright, Thomas	5	....				Wren, James	5	4	Moreland, Jacob, Junr	6	....
						Bond, Zachariah	7	....			
						Washington, Edward	3	15			

FLUVANNA COUNTY.

NAME OF HEAD OF FAMILY.	White.	Black.	NAME OF HEAD OF FAMILY.	White.	Black.	NAME OF HEAD OF FAMILY.	White.	Black.	NAME OF HEAD OF FAMILY.	White.	Black.
Lisle, Sophia	6	....	Grant, Alexander	4	....	Busley, James	4	....	Robinson, John	7	4
Kidd, Moses	7	....	Parish, Abraham	8	18	Rogers, John	8	....	Stone, Caleb	5	8
Lowry, Aaron	10	....	Stanley, Solomon	4	3	Webber, Philip	4	5	Bryant, Elizabeth	8	2
Lowry, Moses	4	....	Johnson, John	4	2	Sadler, John	8	....	Ashlin, John	7	13
Clark, Jonathan	6	....	Laine, Jacob	6	....	Richardson, Robert	2	9	Venable, Wm, Decd, (Estate)	4	5
Clark, John	3	....	Stanley, Jonathan	3	....	Richardson, Jno	2	....	Grant, Alexander, Junr	6	....
Overstreet, William	4	....	Toney, Alexander	4	....	Lee, Benjamin	4	4	Hughes, William	6	5
Rice, Charles	6	1	Richardson, Green	10	....	Lilley, Thomas	8	2	Clark, Jacob	3	....

FLUVANNA COUNTY—Continued.

NAME OF HEAD OF FAMILY.	White.	Black.	NAME OF HEAD OF FAMILY.	White.	Black.	NAME OF HEAD OF FAMILY.	White.	Black.	NAME OF HEAD OF FAMILY.	White.	Black.
Richardson, Capt	4	6	Haden, John			Wills, Willis, (decd)	1	10	Tindale, Thomas	1	8
Furburk, Robert	5	4	Haden, Benjamin			Kidd, Benjamin	2		Tilman, Thomas	8	9
Richardson, William	5		Strange, John A	6	11	Seay, Austin	3	1	Morris, John	6	1
Kidd, John	7		Moore, John	5		Kidd, Saml	3	1	Haislep, Robert	6	
Allen, Richard	3	3	Askew, Anthony	8		Chandler, Elizabeth	8	1	Moore, Warren	6	
Perkins, Stephen	2	3	Pace, John	5		Ross, David	13	52	Stone, Marbel	7	2
Rice, Tandy	10	3	Bellomy, John	5		Cox, George	8	1	Napier, Champion	5	3
Lilley, Armiger	10	10	Bellomy, Benjamin	7		King, Jackville	7	5	Scott, William	2	3
Pace, Murry	4		Tuggle, Joshua	3		Wade, David	10		Kneaves, William	1	9
Adams, Richard	7	41	Thacker, Benjamin	10		Cawthorn, Robt			Murry, Richard	9	6
Clarkson, David	10	9	Thacker, Ambrose	5		Anderson, George, Senr	4	4	Perry, George	3	7
Martin, Elizabeth	7	8	Thacker, William	4		Anderson, George, Junr	8	2	Ladd, Jehoshaphat	4	
Haden, Jos	8	8	Bethel, Valentine	7		Anderson, Nathl	1	1	Ladd, John	2	1
Ross, Peter	8	4	Crewson, James	6	7	Martin, John, Senr	8		Perkins, Richard	8	5
Humphrey David	8		Southerland, Sanders	7		Martin, William	4		Pettice, Jno	4	3
Linthecum, Thomas	4	6	Timberlake, John	6	3	Rice, John	4	1	Johnson, Dilmus	7	
Jenkins, James	6		Moore, William	3	4	Anderson, Benjamin	8	3	Henry, William	3	19
Cole, William	5	5	Barnet, John	5	2	Sanders, Julias, Senr	6	2	Appleberry, Absalom	6	
Quarles, Tunstal	7	8	Cary, Wilson M	22	200	Hughes, Jesse	2		Hammonds, Ephraim	3	
Bentley, Danl	9		Barnet, William	5		Kirby, Francis	4		Brookes, Benjamin	4	
Kent, Robert	8	3	Foster, James	7		Hughes, Rees	6	4	Hammonds, Thomas	2	
Richardson, Saml	5	4	Foster, John	2		Hughes, Johns	4		Haislep, Jane	1	1
Eadson, Ann	5	1	Johnson, William	5	4	Williams, William	11		Price, Abraham	8	
White, William	7		Thacker, Nathl	4		Manley, John	6	1	Pucket, Robert	7	
White, John	5		Paine, William, Esq	11	18	Stone, Hezekiah	7	8	Sprouce, John	9	
Stodgill, Ambrose	9		Thompson, Roger	9	26	Stone, Francis T	1	3	Key, Tandy	5	20
May, Ambrose	6	1	Davis, John	6		Napier, John	7	5	Cocke, Jno Hartwel (The Estate)		45
Shepherd, John	11	9	Adams, James	9	13	Williamson, John	6	7	Cocke, Allen, decd, (Estate)		42
Hollond, Hezekiah	9	3	Adams, Robert	4	5	Williamson, Jacob	2	4	Ware, John	10	41
Humphrey, Elijah	4		Adams, William	4	2	Williamson, Patrick	4	2	Henley, William	12	10
Humphrey, Edward	5		Barnard, Peter	9	1	Napier, Patrick	5	8	Woolling, Joseph	2	17
Loveing, William	10		Stephens, James	3	1	Frazier, Donald	3	7	Winn, Thomas	3	4
Taylor, Henry	5		King, Danl	8		Woodson, Rene	4	4	Bugg, William	7	2
Clarke, Charles	7		Paine, Danl	7		Melton, John	10		Kirby, William	6	1
Frances, Reuben	8		Bibeo, John	5		Bennit, F. R.	7	1	Amohundro, Richard	9	1
Clubb, William	9		Glasby, John	7		Bashaw, Mary	6		Kidd, Samuel	2	1
Baine, Edwin	6		Smithson, Drummond	6	1	Mayo, Jos	10	9	Kidd, Benjamin	3	
Johnson, Walter	6	4	Howard, William	8	1	Sneed, Holmon	8	10	Tilman, Danl	5	3
Basket, William	14		Haggard, George	5		Mayo, Thomas	4	1	Seay, Stephen	10	
Clark, William	7		Haggard, James	4		Jiles, William	8		Mullis, Willoughby	8	
Allford, Ancil	6	2	Denton, William	3	1	Woodson, Benjamin	6	10	Sadler, William	10	
Perkins, Michael	6		Allen, Mary	1	3	Wright, Robert	7	2	Kirby, Francis	4	
Humphrey, Merry	3		Kent, John	5	4	Fitzpatrick, Joseph	1	2	Cawthorn, Thomas	4	
Askew, Charles	5		Martin, John	13	2	Fitzpatrick, William	1	1	Creasy, William	7	
Davis, James	11		Lilley, William	10	1	Fitzpatrick, Mary	3	5	Butler, George	7	
Sparks, Edward	5		Baber, John	6		Fitzpatrick, Benjamin	6	3	Hunt, John	8	
Bentley, Danl, Junr	4		Baber, Thos	6		Handcock, John	10		Perry, John	4	
Bentley, James	4		Baber, Elizabeth	3		Haislep, Henry	9		Woody, Austin	8	
Weldy, William	3		King, Jos	5		Haislep, Spencer	5		England, John	8	
Bailey, Thomas	6	7	Bibee, David	11		Allen, Robert	5	8	Hughes, Anthony	5	4
Bailey, Elizabeth	6		Thacker, Benjamin, Jr	4		Mayo, Joseph	8	9	Shores, Thomas, Senr	6	
Bryant, Silvanus	11		Pace, William	6		May, Thos	4	1	Lightfoot, Danl	6	9
Bryant, Susanna	2		Priddy, William	7	1	Champion, Cutt	5	4	Sandrige, John	5	1
Bryant, William	3		Priddy, Robert	4		Parish, Jesse	10		Farror, Mary	3	4
Carter, William	7		Alligree, Danl	7	7	Mawyer, John	6		Moody, John	11	
Wood, Thomas	8		Harlow, William	9		Rodes, George	3		Farrer, Thomas	2	2
Sanders, George	7	1	Abbney, Paul	2		Rodes, George, Junr	4		Sanders, Julias	3	1
Wood, Martha	5		Bell, John	10		Rodes, Henry	5		Eads, James	5	
Martin, William	7	8	Harlow, John, Junr	4		Napier, Richard	9	22	Barnard, John	12	
Brag, John	10	1	Gadberry, John	2	2	Napier, Rene	1	3	Richardson, Turner	7	13
Appleberry, William	10	9	Denton, Thomas	9		Herndon, Reuben	9	2	Harden, John M	8	4
Ashley, William	8	2	Parish, Jollah	6		Herndon, Jos	9	1	Jones, David	9	4
Moss, Alexander	13	5	Roundtree, Thos	9		Hall, Richard	9	5	Paisley, Robt	6	2
Thurmond, Benjamin	7	8	Shermond, Rebeckah	6	5	Dawson, Thomas	4	11	Ford, Tandy	10	
Bruce, Benjamin	3	1	Baber, Abadiah	2		Duncan, John	6	1	Linthicum, Thos	6	1
Bentley, Danl	8		Norton, Christopher	6		Handcock, Lewis	6	3	Logan, Anthony	10	
Bentley, Gilbert, Junr	3		Gilbert, Nathl	7		Duncan, George	8	14	Evans, Thos	4	1
Lindsey, Landy	7	4	Forsith, John	2		Oglesby, William	7	11	Haden, William	6	5
Cole, James	5	3	Priddy, Elizabeth	3		Stone, Elijah	9	8	Thomas, John	8	
Wells, Elias	8	17	Priddy, William			Wilson, Jonathan	6		Ford, Bartlet	5	
Napier, Thomas	8	24	Ray, William	1		Woolce, Christopher	9		Hayes, Ann	3	
Hensley, Witham	3		Appleberry, Thomas	10	4	Burgess, John	9	1	Robinson, Sarah	4	
Thompson, George	3	17	Webb, James	6	1	Burgess, William	8	1	Martin, Henry	5	4
Thompson, John	5	12	Seay, John	6	2	Moore, John	3	1	Haden, Anthony	11	19
Thompson, Leonard	5	11	Weaver, Benjamin	10	5	Tilman, Thomas	8				

FREDERICK COUNTY.

LIST OF ISAAC LANE.	White.	Black.	LIST OF ISAAC LANE—con.	White.	Black.	LIST OF ISAAC LANE—con.	White.	Black.	LIST OF ISAAC LANE—con.	White.	Black.
Willson, William	5		Keller, George	12		Gorse, John	1		Brenner, Peter	1	
McKenny, John	3		Hannah, Henry	5	1	Goose, George	8		Paschcall, John	4	
Smith, David	8		Wier, Peter	5		Larrick, John	9		Ashby, Henry	8	8
Pierce, George	8		McDonals, Hugh	5		Larrick, George	9		Ashby, George	6	1
Harrell, John	13		Barnes, Charles	4		Miers, John	1		Jones, Mason	8	4
Buck, Thomas	5	13	Barnes, John	9		Miers, Charles	3		Bean, John	9	
McPherson, Nathaniel	5	1	Gardiner, Michl	8		Delong, Nichs	4		Ringel, George	9	
Toor, William	7		Step, Michl	8		Nisewanger, David	5		McFarling, John	7	
Wingfield, Sam	5		Guffin, George	7		Chrieser, Christo	5		Carrol, Danl	5	
Wethers, Ralph	8		Cline, Jacob	13		Stein, Michl	11		Nisewanger, John	6	
Wethers, Alex	4		Campbell, Danl	8		Dush, Josha	3		Brinker, George	10	4
Wethers, Robt	3		Stump, Danl	7		Sutherland, David	6		Murphy, Robt	6	
Darst, Danl	4		Stump, Joshua	3		Goodeconse, George	11		Harrell, William	11	
Harrell, Jacob	3		Miers, Casper, Sen	8		Warth, George	8		Snider, Henry	13	
Jones, John	5		Miers, Casper, Jun	7		Sperry, Peter	3		Hearse, Abram	4	
McCann, Danl	4		Bradley, William	1		Rowzel, Ruben	9	2	Reading, Benjn	3	
Wiley, Allen	6		McNally, Michl	6		Clavenger, Saml	3		Romine, Thos	11	
Fotheringill, John	8		Baker, Josh	9	9	Clavenger, Joshua	3		Ellzey, Jno	6	
Lehue, William	11		Barron, William	5		Hite, Isaac, Esq	8	38	Reynolds, Thomas	4	1
Train, John	4		Jackson, Jno	9		Willson, John	6		Foley, Leah	5	1
Sperry, Nichs	7	1	Scholl, Nichl	9	1				Cartmill, Edwd	9	1

FREDERICK COUNTY—Continued.

NAME OF HEAD OF FAMILY.	White.	Black.	NAME OF HEAD OF FAMILY.	White.	Black.	NAME OF HEAD OF FAMILY.	White.	Black.	NAME OF HEAD OF FAMILY.	White.	Black.
LIST OF ISAAC LANE—continued.			LIST OF ROBERT WHITE—continued.			LIST OF COLO. HOLMES—continued.			LIST OF COLO. DOWDALL—continued.		
Brown, Hugh	13	....	Marple, Enoch, Sen	5	....	Loy, Dan¹	7	....	Smith, Thomas	5	....
Willson, Hugh	1	....	Lockart, Robert	8	....	Hatt, Sam¹	7	....	Hamilton, John	2	....
Willson, James	7	5	Boyd, Sam¹	7	1	Snap, Adam	5	....	McGuire, Edwᵈ	12	....
Nisewanger, Colᵒ John	7	1	White, Robert	9	....	Bridges, Joseph	6	....	Dowdall, J. Gamul	9	1
Bush, Vance	5	3	Perry, Ignˢ	8	30	Mounts, Sam¹	4	....	Cochran, William	9	....
Clanton, Philip	5	6				Holt, John	6	....	Glover, William	3	....
Dixon, Lucy	2	19	LIST OF COLO. HOLMES.			Holt, Henry	7	....	Kean, William	10	....
Hummick, Rudolph	5	....				Holt, George	6	....	Anderson, James	2	....
Cunnard, Joseph	7	....	Mooney, Joseph	18	....	Bailey, Joseph	3	....	Lane, Larkins	1	....
Sailor, Peter	7	....	White, Alexʳ	2	9	Babble, John	4	....	Moredat, Anthony	5	....
Rakestraw, Joshua	8	....	Evans, Moses	5	....	McDonald, Benjᵃ	8	....	Anderson, Jeremiah	9	....
			Taylor, Abraham	6	....	Pool, John	4	....	Deadrich, David	5	2
LIST OF COL. SMITH.			Baldwin, Thomas	9	....	Dilor, Henry	7	....	Beatty, Henry	1	....
			Johnston, Topper, Sʳ	8	....	Smith, Sam	1	....	Simpson, John	7	....
Nelson, James	6	....	Johnston, Topper, Jʳ	2	....	Coopstick, Thomas	2	....	Miller, Godfried	8	....
Smith, John	3	34	Johnston, Moses	6	....	Lohry, John	7	....	Curts, Frederick	4	....
Likens, John	12	....	Brown, Jotham	10	....	Brewer, John	6	....	Wolfe, Lewis	7	....
Grapes, Jacob	9	....	Roof, Jacob	5	1	Holt, George	2	....	Overdere, George	5	....
Lemon, John	3	....	Legate, William	5	....	Ruble, George	8	....	Huff, John	6	....
Taylor, Benjᵃ	8	....	Berry, John	8	....	Crumbley, Catharine	1	3	Linn, George	10	....
Bailey, John	11	....	Handshaw, John	13	....	Loy, John	7	....	Raycraft, Thomas	4	....
Parrell, Joseph	13	....	Handshaw, William	5	....	McCooly, John	7	....	Windle, Samuel	5	....
Hill, John	9	....	Young, Robert	1	....	Lewis, Mary	3	....	Porty, Christʳ	4	....
Dawson, Jacob	7	....	Piper, Wᵐ	5	....	Adams, William	7	....	Huff, Lewis	9	....
Huff, John	8	....	Adams, John	3	....	Rigg, Richard	1	....	Sperry, Nicholas	6	....
Hiland, John	3	....	Light, Frederick	19	....	Strowbridge, Samuel	6	....	Cusler, Michˡ	8	....
Sidwell, James	6	....	Burwell, Nathaniel	1	14	Martin, Thomas	3	....	Otho, Catharine	2	....
Huff, Mathias	7	....	Wiser, Henry	8	....	Bonsill, Joseph	4	....	Grim, John	6	....
Hickman, William	5	18	Waggoner, Andrew	11	28	McGinnis, James	7	....	Glazier, Christian	3	....
Hickman, John	1	4	Waggoner, Thomas	2	....	Barrett, John	5	....	McCoy, Alex	3	....
Edmondson, Will	4	1	Carson, Sam¹	4	....	Foot, Joseph	5	....	Crush, Peter	8	....
Fleming, Alex	9	2	Long, Cookeon	9	....	Alexander, John	4	....	Witzell, Christopher	12	....
Fryer, William	7	....	Cole, John	5	....	Blackford, Peter	4	....	Settler, Isaac	6	1
Power, Edwᵈ	3	....	Cole, Dan¹	3	....	Purtle, Nicholas	5	....	Heiskell, Christopher	6	....
Egan, Thomas	3	2	Abernathy, Wᵐ	4	....	Humber, Sam¹	11	....	Pancoast, David	4	1
Reynolds, Anthʸ	6	....	Setter, John	10	....	House, William	12	....	Butler, Jnᵒ Michˡ	4	....
Williams, John S	6	3	Babb, Peter	12	....	Pugh, Thomas	5	....	Crockwell, John Collin	11	....
Washington, Colᵒ Warner	12	134	Glover, John	6	....	Denny, Walter	3	....	Grim, Jacob	5	....
Rutherford, Benjᵃ	4	....	Gosney, William	5	6	Wright, John	3	....	Lindsay, James	1	....
Rutherford, Robᵗ	6	2	Clerk, Abner	6	....	Kiles, William	7	....	Walker, James	5	....
Rutherford, James	1	....	Edwards, John	5	....	Kiles, Joshua	5	....	Power, Edwᵈ	3	....
Rutherford, Benjᵃ, Jun	1	....	Weber, Robert	3	....	Stonebridge, John	6	....	Bower, Philip	3	....
James, David	4	....	Barton, Sam¹	7	....	Hart, Adam	6	....	Seizenup, Adam	5	....
Duffield, John	6	....	Folks, Jacob	5	....	Hog, William, Sen	2	....	Finley, Henry	8	....
Bowham, Hezekiah	10	....	Ronamas, Conrad	10	....	Rogers, John	1	....	Carlton, Hugh	6	....
Throckmorton, Robᵗ	7	18	Shaver, Elizabeth	6	....	Rogers, Evan, Sen	5	....	Kirk, Patrick	8	....
Willis, Francis, Senʳ	10	36	Hunter, Henry	6	3	Rogers, Evan, Jun	5	....	Richardson, Joseph	8	....
Hoober, Henry	6	....	Eason, Sam¹	2	....	Pickering, John	7	....	Philips, William	4	....
Carmer, Christian	5	....	Barton, Roger	7	1	Pickering, Jacob	4	....	Rutter, Jacob	6	1
Neff, Martin	7	....	Fulton, John	9	....	Dillen, James	5	....	Sovain, Abraham	7	1
Cochran, James	6	1	Coghill, Elisha	9	....	Barrell, Arthur	8	....	Shoemaker, George	2	....
Grove, Jacob	5	....	Thomas, Evan	2	1	Harrison, James	7	....	Wood, John	6	....
Grove, Abraham	5	....	Kennon, Robert	9	....	Mackey, Robert	9	....	Keger, Andrew	6	....
Rogers, James	5	....	Steel, John	4	....	Gossell, William	14	....	Magill, John	4	....
Kerfoot, Rebecca	6	2	Stockdon, George	10	10	Pickering, William	6	....	Holliday, William	9	2
Reeley, William	4	....	Connel, Arthur	3	8	McCool, James	7	....	May, Samuel	8	4
Rekle, George	10	....	Davies, Elisha	4	....	Jackson, Josiah	9	....	Moneysmith, Daniel	3	....
Loyer, Peggy	2	....	Barton, Undrie	4	....	Dillin, John	8	....	Albert, Adam	6	....
Graves, John	7	....	Renker, Casper	9	....	Wright, Nathan	1	....	Haymaker, Adam	11	....
Peters, Henry	6	....	Allemong, Jacob	4	....	Darlington, Meredith	11	1	Hunderbrome, Thoˢ	2	....
Hukle, Tawalt	9	....	Mercer, Aron	5	....	Davis, David	7	2	Kurts, James	5	....
			Babb, Philip	14	....	Merret, Michael	2	....	Shultz, John	1	....
LIST OF ROBERT WHITE.			Adams, Henry	6	....	Adams, John, Jun	5	....	Holliday, James	4	....
			Taylor, Edwᵈ	7	....	Thompson, William	9	....	Hutcheson, James	7	....
Miller, Ann	5	....	Crumbley, Catharine	1	3	Fenton, John	4	....	Huntsbury, Henry	4	....
Dillophane, Ben	6	....	Johnston, David	4	....	Adams, John	6	....	Cromoett, Margᵗ	2	....
Hickman, Jacob	7	....	Ross, Jonᵃ	4	....	Fenton, Enoch, Sen	4	3	Sexton, Mesheck	10	....
Hickman, Adam	7	....	Yarnall, Mordecai	3	1	Adams, Joseph	1	....	Nichols, William	4	....
Perkins, Isaac	9	....	Martin, Thomas	3	....	Fenton, Enoch, Jun	1	....	Williams, Barnet	7	7
Whaler, Martin	6	....	Jolliff, Elizabeth	5	1	Gossell, Richard	2	....	Williams, Peter	4	....
Lupton, John	13	....	Smith, Sarah	5	....	Stip, George	3	....	Brinker, Catharine	8	....
Pickering, Sam	12	....	Brown, Thomas	10	....	Keern, Thomas	9	....	Piles, Joshua	4	....
Snipe, George	8	....	Pew, Job	2	....	Frease, Martin	6	....	Wood, Thomas	5	....
Steepleton, Wᵐ	3	....	Pew, Jesse	2	....	Washington, John	3	....	Miller, Michˡ	11	....
Denny, Robᵗ	4	....	Dick, Peter, Jun	7	....	Bond, George	10	....	Allen, Robert	10	3
Denny, Sam	3	....	Wills, Lewis	6	....	Steerly, Jacob	2	....	Harman, Jacob	5	....
Denny, John	2	....	Dick, Peter, Sen	6	....	Ruble, George	7	....	Kiger, Adam	3	....
Pickin, Sam	10	....	Dick, John	1	....	Bowen, Henry	7	5	Sowers, Jacob	6	2
Philips, Elizabeth	5	....	Lewis, Sam	6	....	Holmes, Joseph	9	8	Bailey, Abraham	7	....
Hamilton, John	6	....	Catlett, William	6	1	Hickman, William	12	7	Helverstine, Catharine	6	....
Stewart, Thomas	7	....	Dorvis, Henry	4	....				Helverstine, Philip	6	....
Hoik, Andrew	11	....	Hingle, Leonard	5	....	LIST OF COLO. DOWDALL.			Creamer, Conrad	3	....
Hiet, Charles	7	....	Carnes, John	9	....				Sowers, Daniel	6	....
Johnston, Charles	5	....	Trotter, Mathew	5	....	Prince, Henry	8	....	Perston, John	4	6
Stafford, Ralph	5	....	McBride, Stephen	3	....	Baker, Henry	10	2			
Boston, John	10	....	Crummey, Robert	2	....	Lantz, John	10	....	LIST OF JOSEPH LONGACRE.		
Scott, James	....	3	Garner, Henry	6	3	Murray, Patrick	8	4			
Johnston, Sam	5	....	Ross, James	4	....	Grim, Charles	7	....	Brill, Herman	5	....
Carter, Sam	6	....	Johnson, George	5	....	Keger, Jacob	3	....	Piles, Franies	5	....
Hodgson, Elizabeth	14	....	Day, Joseph	10	1	Hoover, Philip	4	....	Peher, P. Peter	3	....
Davis, Ben	6	....	Joyer, John	6	....	Donaldson, John	9	1	Cooper, John	9	....
Chambers, Mary	2	....	Sutherland, Isaac	6	....	Sperry, John	3	....	Humble, Michael	3	....
Saunders, George	6	....	Strowbridge, Sam¹	6	....	Willkes, Isaac	2	....	White, Jacob	3	....
Coffman, George	7	....	Ewen, Tristram	9	....	Taylor, Edmond	10	17	Brown, Jacob	4	....
Wolf, Chrl	8	....	Williams, John	8	....	Elkins, John	9	8	Heekley, Elias	8	....
Davidson, George	7	....	Bowman, Lewis	6	....	Drumgoole, Alex	6	....	Renner, George	11	....
Taylor, Har	14	....	Hoge, William	8	....	Extine, Leonard	3	....	Shriver, Adam	11	....
Smith, Josiah	11	....	Wright, Edward	4	....	Smith, Edwᵈ	4	25	Jorden, Peter	6	....
Pugh, Jesse	4	....	Whiteman, Edward	8	....	Loyers, Michˡ	10	....	Whiteman, Rudolph	8	....
Marple, Enoch, Jun	4	....	Cather, Casper	7	....	Kise, George	3	....	Hasbough, Peter	8	....
Milton, John	2	5	Antrem, Godfrey	7	....	Bougher, Jacob	8	....	Orndorf, Lewis	5	....
									Bachelor, John	4	....

FREDERICK COUNTY—Continued.

Name of head of family.	White.	Black.
LIST OF JOSEPH LONGACRE—continued.		
Bachelor, Margt	6	
Poker, Michl	4	
Tole, Henry	5	
Sibert, Jacob	9	
Hoffman, Jacob	10	
Wolfe, Jacob	5	
Brill, Henry	8	
Longau, Richard	4	1
Longau, John	5	
Longau, Joseph	11	
Strawshnider, Frederick	9	
Wissant, Catharine	6	
Richards, Henry	8	4
Redd, Mordecai	11	13
Allan, John	12	1
Livergall, Peter	7	
Snapp, John	4	
Snapp, Jacob	4	
Fry, Jacob	8	
Fry, Benjamin	10	
Gillham, Peter	8	3
Scholl, Henry	11	
Hozenpeler, George	11	
Vance, Joseph	3	
French, William	5	
Vance, Samuel	8	
Russell, Joseph	4	
Shultz, Henry	7	
Orndorff, John	13	
Collings, David	7	
Russell, Moses	2	1
Desponet, Bernard	6	
Richard, Henry	3	
Jones, Joseph	3	1
Moore, Henry	5	
Rudolph, Adam	6	
Cartmill, Nathaniel, Jr	2	
Havely, Jacob	3	
Livergalt, Jacob	9	
Marquis, James	6	
McCaulley, Danl	6	
Lupton, Jona	8	
Fawcett, Richard	4	
Fawcett, Richard, Jr	8	
Faucett, John	2	
Fawcett, John, Jr	3	
Fawcett, Joseph	1	
Redd, George	3	
Antrim, John	7	
Cartmill, Thomas	8	6
Cartmill, Nathan, Jr	3	1
Cartmill, Nat	8	11
Smith, David	8	
Cochran, James	8	
Cochran, Robert	5	
Gregory, Richard	4	
Colvin, Joseph	8	
Glass, Samuel	4	
Marquis, William	10	
Hamilton, James	5	
McFilleys, Edward	7	
Wallice, John	2	
Glass, Joseph	13	7
Laney, Samuel	9	
Meloney, Augustine	4	
Glass, Robert	13	3
Briscoe, Gerard	7	18
Hammon, Absalom	6	
Cowley, James	1	
Waller, Benjamin	4	
Lawrence, James	3	1
Bean, Mordecai	8	1
Snapp, George	4	
Bower, Henry	5	
Lamp, John	3	
Tomlin, Michael	8	
Snapp, John	8	
McBeth, Andrew	9	
Dunbar, Andrew	3	
Douglass, William	8	
Wisegarter, John	9	
Sicrest, Frederick	4	
Sicrest, Henry	7	
Benegar, John	9	
Hall, James	9	
Carter, Richard	9	
Cachley, John	8	
Cachley, Jacob	7	
Ireson, William	2	
LIST OF GEORGE NOBLE.		
Ashby, David	10	2
Lansford, Swanson	6	7
Neil, John	5	
Johnston, Stephen	13	2
Johnston, Mary	3	4
Kanagy, Andrew	6	1
Williams, John	9	2
Heckman, Joseph	2	5
Smallwood, James	8	
Smallwood, William	3	
LIST OF GEORGE NOBLE—continued.		
Munroe, Daniel	5	
Smallwood, Hebbern	2	
Romine, Rebecca	4	
Smallwood, Bean	3	
Stonestreet, Butler	3	2
Calmes, Lucy	5	12
Colson, Thomas	2	12
Neilson, Hugh (Estate)		64
Ball, William	6	
Morgan, William	7	
Garrison, Nehemiah	3	2
Graves, John	8	
Strechberry, Jacob	2	
Houseman, John	2	
Brown, George	3	2
Loyd, Joseph	5	
Patrick, Thomas	3	
Lancaster, Jeremiah	7	
Loyd, Thomas	10	
Taylor, Wasters	8	
Taylor, George	10	
Johnston, Richard	12	
Bowling (Widow)	5	
Smith, John	7	
Peck, Samuel	11	
Lewis, Fielding, De'd (Estate)	5	47
King, Joseph	3	3
McGuire, John	4	7
Vize, Robert	13	
Southwood, John	11	
Lipscomb, Richard	7	
Mardes, William	4	
Berry, Thomas	12	10
Gassway, James, Jr	3	
Barlow, Benja	5	
Berry, Ben	12	16
Vize, Nathaniel	8	
Lewis, George	6	22
Noble, George	6	15
Kechwall, William	8	2
Summers, John	7	
Herrald, Hugh	5	
Havins, John	8	
Havins, John, Jr	3	
Dean, Michl	6	
Craig, Josuf	8	
Chambling, Aaron	14	
Price, Samuel	13	10
Sedwick, Benjamin	9	16
Johnston, Josius	9	
Williams, Haziel	4	
Riggs, Greenberry	2	
Custus, Conrad	6	
Thrulkel, Benjamin	4	7
Obanning, John	3	2
McCartney, Andrew	10	
Castleman, David	10	5
Hampton, Thomas	6	5
Hampton, Mary	8	6
Micham, Barnet	7	
Smith, Michael	8	
Smith, Bartholomew	9	
Fry, Christian	6	
Carman, Joseph	9	
McCabe, William	9	
Lindsay, Abram	1	
McCluse, William	7	
Larue, Isaac	12	6
Hodgen, Robert	11	2
Dorsey, Leakin	5	4
Helm, William	8	10
Snickers, Edwd	6	51
Aldridge, William	6	
Gassway, James	9	
LIST OF THOMAS THROCKMORTON.		
Throckmorton, Thomas	8	19
Ellis, Leonard	2	1
Wemstead, Thomas	2	
Throckmorton, William	3	12
Rice, John	9	
Barnett, John	7	4
Shaver, Gasper	7	1
Abernathy, James	6	
Neil, Samuel	7	3
Chapman, Thos	10	
Roling, Gorden	3	5
Stean, James	4	
Brown, Alex	10	1
Thompson, James	2	
Carter, George	8	
Bishop, John	5	
Douglass, George	6	
Bishop, John	10	
Bonham, Aaron	16	
Crum, Henry	5	
Crum, Christian	6	
Syms, Henry	8	
Crumb, Anthony	4	
LIST OF THOMAS THROCKMORTON—continued.		
Heckerton, Danl	5	
McCormack, Francis	16	3
Brooks, Thomas	10	
Crumb, Anthony, Jr	8	
Hite, Jacob	7	
Fealey, Alex	8	
Colvill, Thomas	4	3
Harvey, Patrick	5	
McGinnis, John	4	
Herbert, Josiah	3	
Stove, Jacob	4	
Shrake, Andrew	9	
Shaver, Martin	4	
Springs, Rachiel	5	
Mouser, Jacob	7	
Mouser, John	11	
Hover, Mathias	7	
Wisely, Arthur	4	
Iterss, James	8	
Regerway, Richard	8	
Cougle, John	7	
Allerway, Wm	8	
Shepherd, Mercer	5	
Johnson, Ellenor	7	
Carter, Josiah	6	
Neil, Lewis	9	
Neil, John	7	
Chalfan, Joseph	6	
Neil, Abraham	1	
Neil, Joseph	1	
Neil, Thomas	1	
West, George	6	
Throckmorton, Gabl	11	20
Cope, Joshua	10	
Settlemoer, George	10	
Carter, James	5	7
Huntsiker, Danl	9	
Slusher, John	4	
Cook, John	3	
Ash, Thomas	9	
Summerville, John	4	
Barnett, Mille	9	5
Booth, William	1	37
Marr, John	4	
Helm, Henry	1	
Blackmore, Thomas	8	10
Calmes, George	1	2
Bragg, Thomas	3	2
Bulger, James	6	
Tolin, Elias	9	1
Johnson, Moses	5	
Ross, Francis	4	3
Jones, John	3	
Magill, John	4	1
Taylor, Benjamin	8	
Chapman, James	4	9
Stripling, Francis	2	12
Helm, Meredy	8	10
LIST OF ELISHA WILLIAMS.		
Horseley, Richard	13	
Leatt, John	3	
Baker, Isaac	4	1
Shadle, Danl	3	
Cartmill, John	3	
Keys, William	9	
Simons, John	5	
Genens, Edward	1	
Williams, Simon	5	
Chick, George	8	
Conner, Thomas	8	
Grubb, Humphrey	9	2
Vaughown, Thomas	9	
Potts, Aquetta	4	2
Seaburn, George	3	5
Seaburn, James	6	6
Gilkerson, John	10	1
Dedale, Elias	8	
Bryerly, Thomas	6	8
Williams, Catharine	8	4
Nichols, John	10	2
Hampton, Henry	5	
Hampton, Henry, Jr	6	
Nicholas, Jno. Fielding	3	
Beks, Christopher	2	
Chropleys, William	11	6
Hotspeler, Jacob	6	
Clevenger, Edwin	3	
Cooper, Thomas	5	
Ashby, John	4	
Ashby, Nathl	3	
Mires, Jacob	6	1
Clyne, Anthony	7	
Marcher, George	4	
Marcher, George, Jr	4	
Pifman, Anthony	8	
McCloud, William	5	
Davis, Alse	3	
Motborough, John	3	
Neil, Charles	2	
LIST OF ELISHA WILLIAMS—continued.		
Berry, Francis	6	2
Henning, James	3	
Burwell, Nathl	3	31
Baker, Saml	4	2
Cordill, Nicholas	6	2
Bell, John	2	1
Bell, Ann	8	10
Bell, George	4	1
Catlett, Mary	2	4
Wood, John	9	
Tabb, William	9	
Jacobs, Eliza	7	
Jacobs, Rowly	3	
Morgan, John	4	
Winderson, Alexander		42
Davis, William	6	2
Clark, Joseph	1	
Campbell, Collin	4	6
Thurston, Charles Mynn	12	80
Ireson, Thomas		4
Hobday, William	1	1
Hite, John, Jun	7	6
Poker, John	9	
Willson, David	1	
Shivertaker, Philip	5	
Stephens, Mary	6	10
Myers, Stephen	4	
Trout, Philip	5	
Linard, Jacob	4	
Hawkins, Jane	8	
Kemp, John	7	
Gromes, Philip	5	
Weathers, Ralph	4	
Lee, John	9	
Reed, James	9	
Carver, Gasper	4	
Groves, John	8	
Hooper, Stephen	2	
Catlett, James	4	10
Cordill, John	6	9
Greenway, George	4	1
Vance, William	6	
Upp, Peter	7	
Roots, John	4	13
Wright, David	6	
Cline, Adam	8	
Ewing, Elize	7	
Weaver, Leonard	7	
Philips, Solomon	5	
Miller, Henry	2	
Miller, Peter	5	
Farrow, George	20	7
Fairfax, Lord (Estate)	2	51
Martin, Byan	5	91
Levingston, Cornelius	5	20
Usher, Robert	5	
Slucher, Fredk	11	
Taylor, John	5	2
Plumb, Cosciner	8	
Crider, Jacob	7	
Laney, John	2	
Taylor, William	8	5
McQueaken, Archa	5	
Page, John		10
Page, Mathew		36
Walter, Benja C. & Robert Page		36
Womach, William	9	6
Thomas, James	4	4
Prichard, Stephen	8	4
Stephens, Joseph	7	
Mobberger, John	3	
Maginnis, John	7	
Kendrick, Abraham	7	
Kendrick, Jacob	7	
Kendrick, Christopher	5	
Kendrick, Benja	1	
Moore, Joseph	4	
Lepue, David	5	
Lepue, Imy	3	
Taylor, Argele	8	
Brown, Francis	3	
Chuck, James	3	
Shain, John	6	
Grubb, ——	7	
Ashby, John	5	17
Grubbs, Uriah	7	
Medinger, Danl	1	
Earl, Saml	10	3
Stokes, William	8	
Haines, Adam	12	
Karns, Mary	7	
Erehart, Nicholas	12	
Carter, Thomas	4	
Robinson, John	4	
Freehold, William	4	
Milbert, Andrew	1	
Ashby, Lewis	4	11
Catlett, James	8	
Stokes, Samuel	7	
Wrought, Peter	7	

FREDERICK COUNTY—Continued.

NAME OF HEAD OF FAMILY.	White.	Black.	NAME OF HEAD OF FAMILY.	White.	Black.	NAME OF HEAD OF FAMILY.	White.	Black.	NAME OF HEAD OF FAMILY.	White.	Black.
LIST OF ELISHA WILLIAMS—continued.			LIST OF COLO. KENNEDAY—continued.			LIST OF COLO. KENNEDAY—continued.			LIST OF COLO. KENNEDAY—continued.		
Redman, Mrs.	8		Louder, Henry	3		Green, William	6		Wilson, Robert	10	2
Prichard, John	8		Ball, Edwd	7		Shiner, George	9		Albert, Michl	9	
Kennentson, Francis	4		Rutter, John	7		Robert, Eliza	3	3	Louck, Peter	5	
Emison, Thomas	16		Trimble, Christn	4		Halam, Jacob	3		Tiftet, Michl	8	
Clevenger, Asa	12		Striker, John	4		Horough, John	5		Simrell, James	7	1
Clevenger, Absalom	5		Wisson (Widow)	7		Seflett, Lawrence	3		Edmondson, Thomas	6	10
Draker, Thomas	7		McDougall, Thomas	4		Knight, William	4		Mesmore, Nicholas	8	
Postgate, Honis	3		Donaldson, Francis	3		Loyer, Adam	4		Kean, John	2	2
Honeck, Simon	4		Rilland, James	4		Campbell, William	3		Parmer, Edwd	8	
Shepherd, Thomas	3		Groves, John	9		Somerville, George	6		Cunningham, John	7	1
Kemp, James	8		Helm, George	7		March, Michl	5		Dunlap, Robert	1	8
Breton, Benja	8		Betty, Margt	4		Swords, William	4		Curry, Danl	7	
Thorp, Isaac	5		McGolan, Catharine	4		Fry, Christr	5		Cockran, Robert	4	1
Bash, Danl	5		Lydy, Benja	2		Anderson, Adam	7		Carter, John	3	
Glasscock, William	6		Beamer, George	4		Anderson, Peter	3		Calvert, Joseph	7	
Shipe, Christo	9		Craigen, Robert	4		Anderson, Jacob	3		Wilson, Robt	5	
Sharp, John	6		Louckleker, Peter	1		Haymaker, John	8		Piles, William	5	
Evans, Henry	10		Cooper, Philip	7		McCord, Arthur	4		McCoy, Alex.	3	
Williams, Elisha	6	2	Cooper, Philip, Ju	3		Post, George	3		Gibbins, Jacob	8	
			McMullen, Wm	7		Lounder, James	11		Haas, Fredk	12	
LIST OF COLO. KENNEDAY.			Kengore, Robt	2		Woolwine, Philip	10	1	Harding, George	5	
Bush, Philip	6	8	Carper, John	2		Conrad, Fredk	14	6	Kercheval, John	13	
Kenneday, David	6		Jenkins, Tob.	4		Gardner, James	5		Helm, Meredith	10	4
Rutter, Mathias	3		Pikestaff, Christr	6		Dent, Arthur	2		Wright, George	6	
Pierce (Widow)	6		Spears, Robt	10		Kizer, George	9	2	Hoffman, Henry	4	
Hammond, Job	4		Mackey, Robt	2	5	Stilson, George	7		Vance, James David	7	3
Bishop, John	5		Poland, Stephen	15		Pierce, Joseph	5				
Pappor, James	7		Waters, John	5		Smith, John	5				
			Mason, Robt	9		Earkam, Martin	9				

HALIFAX COUNTY.

NAME OF HEAD OF FAMILY.	White.	Black.	NAME OF HEAD OF FAMILY.	White.	Black.	NAME OF HEAD OF FAMILY.	White.	Black.	NAME OF HEAD OF FAMILY.	White.	Black.
Irvine, John	10	9	Adkins, William	6	5	Throckmorton, Josiah	5		Clardy, Michael	10	4
Grant, Burwell	7		Hudson, Peter	6		Pass, John	1		Cole, James	9	
Traylor, William	12	6	Johnson, Isaac	7	2	Brewis, John, Jr.	2	1	Townes, Henry	3	8
Carson, Thomas	10	3	Austell, Isaac	10		Nelson, George	9		Martin, Frances	1	
Hatter, Richard	9		Mellins, Charles	2	1	Carrington, Paul		16	Comer, John	7	
Chapman, John	5	5	Turner, William	3	1	Poore, Moses	4	1	Wooding, John	8	5
Marten, John	8		Malone, Drury	8	2	Fitts, Robt W	1		Stegall, William	10	1
Glass, John	10	1	Perrey, John	4		Bond, Wright	13		Purcell, James	11	11
Gholston, Mary	3	13	Salmon, William	8		Pass, Thomas	9		Mannin, Nathaniel	2	5
Peterson, James	6	5	Ford, David	4		Hughes, John	8	1	Mannin, Samuel	1	16
Day, Philip	8	4	Graves, John	7		Wattington, John	2	1	Irby, Anthony	4	13
Edwards, Richard	6	11	Link, Thomas	6		Comer, Archd	1		Williams, William	1	8
Caison, John	9	1	Link, Jno A	3	3	Thompson, John	3	18	Liggon, Joseph	6	6
Lawson, Frances	8	1	Watkins, William	5		Cocke, Nathaniel	7	36	Liggon, Judith	5	7
Turner, Anne	7		Holt, Robert	5	3	Cocke, John		21	Pointer, Samuel	6	9
Hunt, Thomas	3		Holt, Robt, Jr	3	1	Cain, Howard	2		Burwell, Mary		12
Hopson, William	4	5	Holt, William	1		Norris, John, Jr	3	10	Liggon, John	1	1
Edwards, Elizabeth	12	15	Rogers, Armestead	3	1	Norris, John, Senr	2	3	Thompson, William	11	56
Shackelford, John	7	14	Turner, John	7		Irby, Jno	4	5	Hoskins, Dolly	4	12
Whitlock, Elizabeth	3	1	Thomas, Robbard	2	1	Powell, William	8	2	Hoskins, James	3	8
Guthrey, Thomas	7		Poiner, Francis	6		Garrott, Thomas	5	1	Combs, George	9	15
Dukie, John	5	11	Wood, William	6	1	Lammonds, William	2	7	Wattington, Armistead	6	25
Peterson, George	6		Chappell, Robert	3		Allen, Joseph	5		Welsh, James	4	
Morris, William	5		Sells, John	7		Dunkly, Martha	8	1	Estes, Abram	4	
Brooks, Rachael	6		Salmon, William	8		Haynes, Jos. N	7	12	Robertson, Walter (Est.)		7
Taylor, George	3		Brasher, Richard	8		Prider, William	7	6	Hope, Thomas	1	13
Richardson, James	3	10	Gilson, Jonathan	2	1	Bond, Jno	3		Chandler, Robert	8	21
Turner, Francis	2		Kidd, James	7		Ashlock, John	9		Yates, John	4	
Banks, John	10		Sullens, John	10	2	Watkins, Thomas	4	3	Rowlett, William	8	8
Tinney, William	3	2	Rogers, John	7	13	Stevens, Jeremiah	10		Palmer, Jefrey	9	1
Stanfield, Robert	11	10	Pravitt, Field	7		Hall, Benjamin	9	12	Abbott, Joseph	14	3
Salmon, John	10	1	Gordon, William	4		Roberts, Moses	6	1	Palmer, Elias	4	
Taylor, William	3		Hawkens, William	9	7	Wooding, Robert	3	11	Palmer, Thomas	6	6
Turner, James	9	4	Brooks, John	9		Hill, Elizabeth	4	7	Prewitt, Byrd	2	
Powell, Charles	10	3	Stanfield, Thos	10	10	Roberts, Francis	1		Mann, Beverly	7	1
Watkins, James	6	2	Stanfield, Marmaduke	10	10	Roberts, Jane	6	6	Wood, John	5	
Boyd, Sarah	4	6	Watkins, James	6	2	Cole, Joseph	7	3	Abbott, Joseph, Jr	3	
Miller, Elizabeth	4	5	Boyd, Sarah	4	6	Holt, Simon	19	12	Williard, Henry	5	
Lawson, William	10	19	Miller, Elizabeth	4	5	Camp, Mary	8	8	Wooton, John	3	
Wily, George	4	2	Wiley, William	4	11	Camp, William, Jr	1	3	Palmer, Thomas, Jr	6	
Link, John	9	1	Coleman, John	4	58	Camp, William, Senr	3		Harden, Thomas	1	
Link, William	9	1	Moss, Fredk	10	4	Camp, George	5	8	Morton, Samuel	8	3
Mitchell, Charles	2	10	Williams, John	4	18	Anderton, George	4	2	Lax, John	8	
Hunter, John	13		Hill, Sarah	4	15	Brewis, John, Senr	9	1	Lax, Benjamin	3	
Chambers, William	6	1	Owen, William (Barr)	7	6	Chandler, William	14	4	Hunt, Ambrose	6	5
Wray, James	4	6	Owen, Hateker	1	1	Tuck, Thomas	10	3	Carmady, William	8	
Chambers, John	11	2	Brewis, Michael	8		Davis, William	11	8	Jackson, Simon	2	11
Spencer, Margaret	6	1	Maskill, James	4		Echols, John	11	8	Chandler, John	6	4
Thaxtor, William	7	22	Maskill, Mary	4		Moore, William	1	4	McKenner, James	7	
Carmichael, John	7		Perkins, John	5		Powell, Luke	1		Ashby, Joseph	4	1
Hepson, William	4	7	Cumbo, Charles	7		Jones, Reuben	7		Theveatt, Giles	5	6
Hughes, Gabriel	7		Johnson, Smith	11	16	Scoggan, John	6	1	Brown, James	9	
Gravett, Tatom	6		Arnold, James	11	1	Lewis, John (Mo)	3	74	Cassdy, James	2	
Hughes, Thomas	6		Bell, James	10		Lewis, John, Jr	4	37	Smallman, John	8	
Dyall, James	5		Ragland, Evan	4	20	Clay, Marston	7	9	Bowman, William	7	2
Buchanan, James	6		Terry, Sarah	7	22	Robbins, Thomas	8	7	Brumfield, Jno	8	
Hix, Joseph	6		Nocle, Thomas	11	4	Morefield, John	10		Estes, Ambrose	2	6
Bragg, William	7	1	Owen, Jno (Barrister)	10	6	McGinnis, Alex.	5	1	Stanley, Richard	8	
Parrott, Ruth	11	1	Powell, Edward	5	4	Morefield, Edward	3		Wright, Thomas	4	
Salmon, Joel	11		Pass, Thomas, Jr	1		Arnold, William	7	4	LeGrand, John	5	
Smith, Rebekah	7		Powell, David	10	3	Osborne, William	7		Palmer, Elisha	2	
Carmichael, Archd	5		Conner, John	5		Estes, George	3		Perkins, Robert	7	
Turner, William	13	4	Prindle, Parro H.	5		Wall, David	7	6	Funstall, Jno O	4	2
Cleft, Henry	9	1	Throckmorton, Robt	8		Hall, William	7	10	Campbell, Mosses	8	
Colman, Benedictus	6		Bott, Jno Arnold	7		Parrott, Lewis	4		LeGrand, Abraham	7	4
Gentry, Michael	5		Bott, Jno Arnold, Jr.	1		Jennett, James	6		Knox, Hugh	2	
Rogers, Peter	11	12	Throckmorton, Robt, Jr	2		Comer, Thomas	8	9	Francis, Nathaniel	1	

HALIFAX COUNTY—Continued.

NAME OF HEAD OF FAMILY.	White.	Black.	NAME OF HEAD OF FAMILY.	White.	Black.	NAME OF HEAD OF FAMILY.	White.	Black.	NAME OF HEAD OF FAMILY.	White.	Black.
Hudson, Charles	5		Lawson, Thomas	7	1	Walker, Richard	6		Booker, Parham	6	27
Jennett, Samuel	4		Chatham, Robert	7	2	Hawkins, Zachariah	12	1	Overton, Moses	7	5
Rice, Jno.	6	4	Kirby, Joseph	6		Willis, Meshack	6		Richardson, Thomas	8	
Cocke, Chasteen		21	Kirby, Joseph	6		Spraggins, Thomas	9	14	Thompson, George	13	4
Stokes, Elizabeth	4	6	Watkins, William	5	4	Abney, Reuben	4	11	Harris, Reuben	3	
Hunt, William	5	2	Woddell, Noell	6	5	Clay, Caleb	7		Harper, James	6	
Barksdill, Claiborne		5	Johns, John	5	2	Petty, Francis M	7	6	Yuelle, Thomas	3	34
Sneed, James	6		Woddell, William	5	5	Petty, Frances	2	2	Gettington, Susannah	6	1
Covington, Mary	2	2	Bates, Fluming	1	1	Petty, Davis	5	3	Richardson, John	5	1
Harris, William	9		Carter, Richard (G. S.)	11	3	Light, John, Jr.	7	4	Murphy, Edward	9	
Harris, James	5		Dodson, Elisha	5	8	Light, John, Senr.	2		Petty, Joseph	10	2
Shange, Richard	3		Hopson, Joseph	3	6	Hunt, Nathaniel	6	24	Carter, Richard	10	1
Rickman, Robert	4		Goare, Henry	2	1	Rowden, Abraham	4		Cox, Harry	2	
Hudson, Peter	7		Baker, Martin	6	2	Trebble, James	4		Jackson, Ephraim	6	
Irby, Harrison	5	12	Moore, George	3	3	Crews, Joseph	8		Williams, Luke	8	5
Wattington, Paul	5	4	Stewart, Jonn	5		Handcock, Joseph	9		Price, William	11	10
Vaughn, Nicholas	5	8	Pearman, William	3		Cox, Henry	6	3	Tucker, Edmund	5	2
Ferrell, William	13	8	Jones, John	7	1	Guthrey, Travis	10	2	Deavenport, Cathrine	4	7
Jenkins, John	6		Pairott, Rhodman	3	4	Martin, William	2		Deavenport, Bedford	8	2
Jenkins, Rob	9		Glasscock, William (Est.)		22	Martin, James	9		Royster, Nathaniel	6	3
Parker, William	11	2	Clardy, John	5		Prewitt, Michael	6	3	Shaw, Gardner	5	
Parker, Frances	4	3	Cuningham, Samuel	7	5	Brumfield, Major	7		Powell, Mary	8	14
Stanley, John	12	1	Stone, John	6	7	Richardson, John	3		Lipscomb, Thomas	4	7
Womack, Abraham	2	8	Compton, Meredith	7	2	Handcock, Benja	4		Hurt, Moza	14	19
Vaughan, Frederik	3	1	Kesee, John	4	5	Handcock, Absalom	2		Melner, Mark	9	
Wade, Stephen	6	4	Douglass, William	7		Forrest, Richard	7	8	Collins, Joseph	6	
Covington, Edmund	6		Welch, John	7		Martin, John	5		Powell, William	7	
Jones, Stephen	5		Grant, Jasper	5		Chick, William	3		Watkins, Susannah	1	17
Boulware, Starke	9	3	Preston, James	1	1	Handcock, Thomas	5		Kelly, Jacob	7	
Sims, Matthew	8	26	Farmer, Thomas	10		Handcock, Benja, Jr	2		McCraw, James	14	19
Wall, Charles	9	5	Fambrough, Anderson	4		Handcock, Jno	1		Brown, James	5	
Moore, Alexander	2	12	Glass, William	7	1	Martin, Jacob	5		Ferguson, Thomas	6	2
Wall, Henry	1		Caldwell, David	2	2	Cope, John	5		Beazly, John	9	5
Wall, Edward	3		Martin, Warren	1		Bostick, William	6		Carr, Thomas	4	9
Matthews, Samuel	6		Clardy, Joseph	4		Bostick, John	1		Hampton, Micajah	7	
Moore, John	7	4	Hall, William, Sr	6		Nunally, Edward	8	8	Green, William	6	
Wall, Jno.	9	1	Bowman, Thomas	6	1	Ourly, Thomas	10		Brown, John	3	
Miller, Jno F.	5	5	Pearman, William, Sr.	6		Ourly, William	3		Newbell, George	3	
Miller, Harman	9	3	Echols, James	8	5	Francis, Jno	6		Carr, William	6	
Gaines, Thomas	11		Wilson, Isaac	1		Bostick, Elizabeth	5	2	Robertson, George	4	1
Bonner, Thomas	9		McDaniel, William	1	6	Taylor, James	5	3	Robertson, Christopher	5	6
Gaines, Richard	4	4	Pinder, John	4		Mallecott, John	9		Silf, Thomas	2	
Chilton, Charles	7		Walrons, Benja	5	5	Jones, John	6		Carr, John	5	3
Martin, William P.	5	16	Going, Daniel	2		Handcock, Thomas, Sr	7		Hall, John	6	
Walters, Jno.	9		Hall, William, Jr	7	2	Worthy, William	4		Hall, William	6	
Lumkin, Joseph	8	13	Sims, Micajah	4	1	Richardson, Skip	3	2	McGriggor, John	8	
Wilson, Daniel	3	10	Freeman, Jno	8	1	McCraw, Samuel	6	4	Glass, James	4	1
Cheatham, Abra.	2	3	Glass, William, Senr	2	10	Stott, Solomon	9		Phelps, John	7	9
Ozbrook, Michael	5		Lansdown, George	6		Fisher, William	6		Byrns, John	6	1
Edmunds, Sterling		8	Glass, John	4	2	Fisher, John	3		James, Enoch	8	
Harper, Banister	5	3	Logan, John	7	14	Rowden, John	7		Milan, Dudley	2	
Akin, Joseph	6	3	Logan, David	1	4	Drinkard, John	10	5	Younger, William	6	
Irbell, Peyton	3		Chappell, James	4	6	Thompson, Martha	7		Gates, William	6	9
Dunn, John	7		Wilson, Robert	1		Bates, William	7	4	Dixon, Stephen	4	1
Fomby, Nicholas	10		Williams, John	6	4	Rice, James	4	2	Finney, Thomas	1	7
Akin, Robert	6	4	Yates, Richard	7		Cheatham, David	8	2	Farmer, Frederick	5	1
Akin, Edward	6	2	Wyatt, John	7		Black, Thomas	4	1	Gwinn, Bartlett	4	
Farmer, Elizabeth	6		Levenney, Benjamin	6		Oliver, William	8	6	Glass, Dudley	8	8
Harris, Richard	1		Logan, William	1	1	Carter, Drury	4		Hall, Nathaniel	9	
Nobles, John	3	1	Weakly, Robert	7	11	Martin, William	11	4	Bass, Henry	6	12
Dixon, Anne	1		Fambrough, James	5		Dean, Joshua	2		Edmunds, John	5	
Douglass, Alexr	10		Miller, Luke	5		Chandler, Timothy	8	1	Milam, John	4	
Russell, George	3	1	Martin, Nathan	5		Nance, Zachariah	5		Fambrough, Thomas	4	
Hopson, Henry (S. H.)	4	8	Barnes, Henry	5		Nance, William	4	8	Preddy, Richard	2	2
Dodson, Elish.	5	8	George, Jonadab	6	3	Barksdill, Nathaniel	5	16	Glass, David	4	2
Feaus, James	6		Childress, Abraham	10		Vaughan, Drury	7	8	Hall, Robert	7	1
Dodson, Thomas	7	1	Wilkerson, William	5		Brown, John	9	2	Milam, Benjamin	1	
Hopson, Henry, Senr.	3	12	Pollard, William	6	3	Hall, Fenton	9		Barksdill, Jeffrey	2	1
Douglass, Mary	7	6	Raimey, John	5	3	Royall, William	2	4	Milam, John, Senr	4	
Groce, Jairo H.	9	3	Johnson, Juham	1		Franklin, Frances	6		Baber, John	6	
Groce, John	5	1	Haygood, John	6	1	Pucket, Thomas	1		Hunt, Reuben	6	
Watson, James	4		Burnley, Candace	4		Pucket, Stephen	7		Hunt, Molly	5	4
Sheppard, James		5	Waller, Richard	5		Royall, John	4	9	Burchfield, John	9	
Rice, William	6		Maddison, Roger	4	10	Jones, Richard	4		Thomas, Thomas	5	
Rose, Thomas	2	6	Tomkins, Samuel	10	8	Black, William	8	17	Cooper, William	6	2
Smith, James (W. W.)	7		Kursey, Thomas	6		Crews, John (Sadler)	4		Sparrow, John	7	
Echols, Moses	12	8	Hambrick, Charles	6		Scates, Thomas	8		Gray, Anne	5	
Hopson, Benjamin	2	4	Collins, John	8	1	Hurt, Philemon	4	4	Tribble, Peter	7	
Hopson, Henry (S. W.)	1	1	Raimey, Absalom	3		Crews, Peter	7		Adams, John	7	1
Hopson, William	1	1	Braughill, James	5		Chissum, James	11		Johnson, David	8	
Boyd, William	5	15	East, Thomas	10		Hodges, Thomas	8		Martin, Isaac	1	
Carter, Daniel	1		Dillon, Henry	7		Seemore, George	11		Blackwell, James	13	13
Horsley, James	9		Dillon, Thomas	1		Seemore, William	9		Hardwick, James	8	12
Horsley, Richard	2		Glass, Zachariah	5	6	Dunaway, Samuel	5	1	Finch, Richard	9	2
Edwards, Benjamin	10	3	Murphy, James	6		Sparrow, Thomas	6		Lee, Andrew	7	3
Dodson, Thomas	10	7	Farmer, Enoch	1		Jones, William	5		Terry, Moses	9	5
Wright, William	8	3	Adams, Nipper	5	1	Mullins, John	6	2	McCool, Andrew	3	8
Thompson, William	6		Hunt, William	6	2	Piles, William	4	1	Torian, Peter	8	5
Dejernett, Elias	12	17	Dixon, Thomas	1		Seemore, Burgess	1		Farmer, David	4	1
Pankey, John	8		Dixon, Stephen	1		Wimbish, John	5	12	Going, John	2	
Jordan, Benjamin	5	5	Finney, Thomas	1	2	Crews, David	7		Parker, Benajah	8	
Johnson, Joseph	10	4	Ridgway, James	7	6	East, William	7	3	Parker, Mary	2	1
Medley, James	7	2	Adams, Joshua	9	8	Hunt, Benjamin	4	1	Epps, Elizabeth	11	
Stevens, James	2	4	Slaughter, Ezekial	7	14	Bates, James	6	2	Clay, Abra.	3	4
Walten, Spencer	10		Adams, William	7		Cox, Elisha	7	3	Slaughter, Samuel	2	3
Walten, William	6		Sydnor, William	12	21	Bates, Stephen	2		Slaughter, John	5	
Harris, Bartho	6		Sydnor, Epa	7	3	Bates, Samuel	8	2	Going, Shadrack	12	
Wilson, William	2		Beach, William	1		Snelson, Charles	10	3	Evans, George	4	
Bowman, Bibby	3		King, Edmund	7	10	Barksdill, Peter	4	7	Younger, William	7	
McDaniel, Anne	5	13	Hunt, Elijah	12	22	Lax, William	6		Daniel, Agnes	4	12
Murphy, John	6	13	Pairott, Nathaniel	12		Childress, Susannah	5		Dixon, Thomas	7	6
Kennon, Charles	4	20	Keeling, Thomas	10		Jones, Daniel	9		Mays, William	12	1
Taylor, Philip	3	20	Street, Jane	6	5	Crews, John	5		Young, James	7	
Caldwell, John	7	2	Seates, Peggy	8		Jarvis, Aaron	6		Wamack, Charles	9	17
Scott, Robert	6		Hankly, James	8	6	Booker, John		14	Hailey, Lewis	8	
									Hailey, Benjamin	6	

HALIFAX COUNTY—Continued.

NAME OF HEAD OF FAMILY.	White.	Black.	NAME OF HEAD OF FAMILY.	White.	Black.	NAME OF HEAD OF FAMILY.	White.	Black.	NAME OF HEAD OF FAMILY.	White.	Black.
James, David	7	....	Hodges, William	6	....	Marten, Benjamin	5	2	Ballindine, William	3	....
Boyd, William	12	1	Butler, Barsha	7	....	Morehead, John	1	....	Purreyer, Thomas	4	....
Estes, Moses	11	1	Hudleston, Benja	10	1	Marten, John	4	....	White, Charles	2	....
Parker, Richard	12	....	Ferguson, Hugh	3	....	Maxey, John	3	7	Smith, John P	5	7
Boram, John	6	8	Slone, John	4	....	Morehead, James	1	....	Wall, Robert	9	1
Scurlock, Thomas	6	....	Ferguson, Jane	7	....	Nichols, David	7	2	Hackney, John	6	....
Morrison, Joseph	5	....	Prewett, Hannah	4	....	Nichols, Mary	2	5	Wilson, William	4	....
Bently, Samuel	7	....	Smith, Thomas, Sr	9	....	Nichols, William	9	4	Arrington, Richard	1	....
Matlock, John	4	....	Smith, Thomas, Jr	3	....	Nichols, John	9	3	Arrington, John	5	....
Matlock, Jane	6	1	Thompson, James	2	....	Nichols, Byrd	7	1	Jones, Reuben	6	....
Osborne, Skearn	4	....	Lambs, Richard	7	....	Nichols, Jessie	6	7	Elliott, Bartlett	2	....
Hudson, John	8	....	Tindall, Samuel	8	....	Owen, Abraham	7	....	Elliott, Anne	7	....
Day, Thomas	4	1	Yates, Francis	7	....	Organ, William	3	....	Hite, Stanley	5	....
Townes, Henry	11	....	Lovelace, Thos	12	....	Owen, James	6	6	Wilson, Thomas	8	7
Daniel, William	10	....	Jeffries, Thomas	2	....	Owen, Ralph, Senr	10	....	Pettyfool, William	7	7
Boyd, Wilmoth	6	30	Poindexter, Jno	2	....	Owen, Ralph, Jr	7	1	Jones, Robert	....	11
Boyd, David	6	5	Tolar, Jno	8	....	Owen, Richard, Jr	3	....	Loftes, Archibald	3	....
August, John	7	....	Ferguson, Isaac	4	....	Owen, Jessie	5	....	Williams, John	7	....
Estes, Moses, Senr	2	....	Yates, William	1	....	Owen, Daker	3	....	Wade, Hampton	4	5
Bennett, Anne	6	1	Moore, William	6	....	Owen, William	8	....	Wall, David	7	6
Boyd, John	10	....	Cumbo, Thomas	12	....	Owen, James	6	....	Fontaine, Joseph	7	3
Gill, Daniel	4	12	Ferguson, Nimrod	10	4	Owen, William	6	....	Tally, Peyton	4	....
Smith, Charles	9	1	Harris, William	4	4	Owen, Thomas	7	....	Pucket, Henry	3	....
Parker, William	5	3	Sullins, Nathan	10	....	Owen, John	4	....	Wilson, William, Senr	2	....
Strange, Littlebury	9	....	Moore, James	6	....	Parker, Edward	12	14	Wall, Elizabeth	1	....
Hendrick, John	3	2	Henderson, Edward	5	....	Pleasants, Jessie	7	18	Wilson, Wallace	1	....
Irby, Joshua	7	....	Going, David	2	....	Roberts, Michael	10	33	Griffin, John	7	....
Crunshaw, Bartlett	5	3	Wilson, Mary	2	....	Rickman, John	2	....	Wright, Jarrott	3	....
Whittworth, John	5	2	Wilson, Milly	5	....	Roberts, Betty	3	20	Griffin, Richard, Senr	3	2
Parker, Daniel	4	6	Colguett, Jonathan	6	1	Sims, David	5	29	Dearden, George	11	7
Gill, John	9	3	Camp, George	5	9	Stovall, Bartholmew	9	....	Faulkner, Benjamin	10	11
Crunshaw, Cornelius	9	2	Follis, John	4	....	Sims, William (Estate)	5	18	Faulkner, Jacob	7	3
Easly, Worham	9	....	Spradling, Jessie	2	....	Sevillivant, Charles	4	....	Isbell, George	6	9
Easly, Robert	4	3	Anderson, Jno	8	1	Shelton, Frances	4	....	Collins, William	6	4
Evans, Nancy	5	....	Anderson, Mede	8	2	Sherwood, Robert	6	....	Rogers, Peter	11	12
Davenport, Thomas	....	8	Smith, James	10	9	Thureatt, William	5	4	Carmichael, Rhoderick	4	....
Kent, William	7	2	Pankey, Stephen	9	2	Watkins, Joel	....	12	Rogers, Armstead	2	1
Arnold, John	8	5	Adkins, Stephen	9	....	Watts, Samuel	7	....	Thomas, Jno, Senr	11	15
Nance, Tavner	6	1	Buckner, Amey	10	3	Clark, Thomas	9	13	Gill, Joseph, Jr	6	6
Wellinghame, Gerrald	9	2	Bretton, William	6	17	Gresham, William	8	6	Gill, Joseph, Senr	3	4
Fitzjairald, Christr	4	....	Cobbs, Samuel	10	7	McCarty, Jarrard	10	10	Hodges, William	9	....
Chavus, Betty	2	....	Cassady, John	5	....	Overby, Meshack	8	....	Boran, William	7	7
Kent, Robt, Senr	5	4	Cassady, William	4	....	Childress, Nicholas	8	....	Wade, Jne	9	20
Holt, Peter	10	....	Cobbs, James	6	35	Legon, Blackman	3	5	Adkins, William	9	....
Echols, William	13	1	Dyernett, Thomas	7	1	Wright, Jairott	3	....	Hopson, William	4	9
Brady, Elizabeth	6	1	Dobson, Thomas	7	5	Roach, Thomas	6	....	Whitt, William	2	....
Chumbly, Francis	3	....	Eastham, Robert	8	4	Griffin, Susannah	8	....	Glass, Thomas	8	....
Ragland, John	5	5	Frances, Milichi	1	....	Faulkner, John	7	3	Pricket, Reuben	7	5
Wilson, Peter	4	....	Frances, Vincent	4	....	Jordan, Robert	6	19	Roach, Samuel	3	....
Pound, John	4	....	Fulker, John	3	....	Overby, Shadrack	7	....	Boyd, George	9	7
Carly, William, Jr	4	1	Graves, Edmund	3	....	Erskine, Robert	6	11	Boyd, James	12	2
Lacy, Thomas	6	4	Hillard, John	3	....	Overby, Obadiah	7	5	Wade, Richard	5	....
Carly, William, Sr	9	....	Hill, Ephraim	1	3	Hooper, Obadiah	2	1	Gill, Jacob	6	....
Murphy, William	15	16	Keen, Jeremiah	3	5	Harrison, Samuel	3	....	Whitt, John	9	....
Matlock, Zachariah	3	....	Lacy, Lyner	7	....	Pinson, John	9	5	Hurst, Howard	4	....
Donathan, Nelson	1	....	Lee, William	9	....	Siximore, John	9	....			
Early, Daniel	4	13	LeGrand, John, Senr	3	9	Seat, Robert	8	....			

HAMPSHIRE COUNTY.

LIST OF JOHN WILSON, GT.	White.	Black.	LIST OF JOHN WILSON, GT.—continued.	White.	Black.	LIST OF JOHN WILSON, GT.—continued.	White.	Black.	LIST OF ABEL RANDALL, GENT.—continued.	White.	Black.
Rosecrantz, Hesekiah	4	....	Wood, Joseph	3	....	Henkle (widow)	7	....	Kimble, John	10	....
Pickle, Jacob	9	....	Hier, John	5	....	Henkle, Moses	5	....	Kimble, Lambert	5	....
Wease, Adam, Senr	13	....	Hier, Leonard, Junr	4	....	Ligget, John	4	....	Hite, Casper	6	....
Wease, Adam, Junr	5	....	Coons, Joseph	4	....	Crites, Philip, Junr	3	....	Harness, Michael, Sr	3	12
Cantrill, Christopher	6	....	Shobe, Martin	6	....	Crites, Philip, Senr	4	....	Harness, George	6	2
Buzzard, Henry	11	....	Shobe, Rudolph	3	....	Regan, Jacob	9	....	Richardson, Daniel	6	1
King, Henry	2	....	Shobe, Jacob	8	....	Weaze, John	6	....	Cuningham, Wm, Senr	2	4
Cuningham, James	8	3	Shobe, Ridely	6	....	Yeazle, Jacob	3	....	Harness, Michael, Jur	5	....
Hicks, Thomas	3	....	Stinglee, Jacob	5	....	Borrer, Charles	3	....	Miller, John	7	....
Carpender, Jacob	7	....	Powers, Martin	9	....	Crites, Jacob	6	....	Ward, Israel	2	....
Poague, Robert	2	....	Bailey, William	7	....	Weaze, Jacob	5	....	Powell, Caleb	7	....
Moses, Adam	7	....	Strader, Christopher	9	....	Westfall, Daniel	11	....	Cuningham, Robert	9	10
Mallow, Henry	3	....	Sleith, Alexander	3	....	Weaze, Michael	2	....	Cuningham, Wm, Jur	5	8
Mallow, Adam	6	....	Porter, Robert	5	....	Pendleton, John	5	....	Parsons, Thomas	11	7
Rule, Henry, Senr	11	....	Mace, Nicholace	7	....	Kersman, John	6	....	Maxwell, Robert	5	....
Rule, Henry, Junr	5	....	Haun, Michael	7	....	Thorn, Valentine	7	....	Sea, Michael	9	1
Peterson, Michael	6	....	Ermintrout, Christopher	9	....	Butcher, Eve	3	....	Shanklin, Robert	5	....
Petro, Leonard	5	....	Stookey, Magdalan	4	....	Woolf, John	8	....	Fisher, Adam, Junr	9	2
Straley, Christian	6	....	Stookey, Abram	6	....	Reel, David	7	....	Fisher, Adam, Senr	9	2
Butcher, Paulser	7	....	Swank, Philip	5	....				Brinks, Ursulla	9	....
Algier, John	7	....	Post, Valentine	6	....	**LIST OF ABEL RANDALL, GENT.**			Boggard, Esekial	9	....
Algier, Michael	6	....	Whetstone, George	7	....	Inskeep, Abram	11	....	Westfall, John, Senr	8	2
Fisher, George	10	....	Shultz, Andrew	4	1	Sadouskie, Jacob	4	....	Westfall, Cornelius	2	....
Judy, Nicholas	7	....	McIlhaney, Felix	5	1	March, Henry	12	2	Petty, Joseph	13	....
Wise, John, Senr	8	....	Wilson, John	9	9	Hutton, Moses	9	12	Hornback, Isaac	10	3
Judy, Henry	7	....	White, Ebenezer	7	....	Baker, Anthony	8	....	Jenny, William	7	3
Wise, John, Junr	5	....	Rodebaugh, Henry	8	....	Miles, David	6	....	Welton, David	7	....
Wise, Jacob	5	....	Hier, Leonard, Senr	7	....	Thomas, Morris	10	....	Hutton, Isaac	2	....
Davis, John	8	....	Schoonover, Benjamin	5	....	Weaver, George	5	....	Cutright, Samuel	6	1
Harpole, Adam, Junr	4	....	Atchison, Wm, Junr	12	....	Hite, Matthias	5	....	Hornback, Samuel	6	....
Likens, John	7	....	Atchison, Wm, Senr	8	....	Yoakum, Jacob	6	2	Hornback, Abram	4	....
Sims, John, Junr	2	....	Hagler, Bastian	9	....	Worley, Michael	6	....	Hornback, James	4	....
Peterson, Martin	8	....	Caplinger, John	7	....	Brown, Thomas	10	....	Hornback, Simon	12	....
Peterson, Jacob, Senr	6	....	Whitecotton, James	5	....	Buzzard, John	5	....	Hornback, James	3	....
Peterson, Jacob, Junr	8	....	Berry, Joel	5	....	Yoakum, Philip P	6	1	Leary, Dennis	4	....
Morrow, Ralph	2	....	Horst, William, Senr	7	....	Yoakum, John	4	....	Marrs, Henry M	6	1
Ours, Sithman	4	....	Cooper, Valentine	7	....	Hainess, John	14	2	Shanklin, Richard	4	....
Cutrack, John	5	....	Sites, George	7	....	Steel, Henry	8	....	Steel, John	2	....
Cutrack, Henry	7	....	Coones, Peter	5	....				Helmick, Jacob	7	....

NAME OF HEAD OF FAMILY.	White.	Black.	NAME OF HEAD OF FAMILY.	White.	Black.	NAME OF HEAD OF FAMILY.	White.	Black.	NAME OF HEAD OF FAMILY.	White.	Black.
LIST OF ABEL RANDALL, GENT.—continued.			LIST OF MICHL. STUMP, GENT.—continued.			LIST OF ABRM. HITE, GENT.—continued.			LIST OF LEVI ASHBROOK, GENT.—continued.		
Borrer (Widow)	4		Combs, Francis, Igª	6	1	Fowler, John	7		Powell, Samuel	1	
Stotts, Abram	6		Huffman, Cathrine	6		Higgins, John	10	4	Hill, William	4	
Pancake, Joseph	4		Jefferson, Luke	4		Higgins, Robert	11	10	Devear, John	10	
Westfall, Jacob	6		Naaff, Michael	8		Hite, Abraham	5	7	Park, Andrew	5	
Longwith, Thomas	3		Reel, Nicholas	5		Vanmeter, Joseph	6	10	Perrill, John	8	
Mace, Isaac	4		Hedger, John	7		Thorn, Peter	3		Starkey, Frederick	6	
Thursbay, Hannah	6		Moor, Anthony	9		Yoakum, Michael	3		Martin, John	6	
Heath, Jonathan	4	7	Naaff, Henry	6		Foley, John	8		Martin, George	10	
Heath, Asahel	6		Hornback, Anthony	8		Weidner, Jacob	5		Hubbard, John, Senʳ	3	
Starr, Catherine	8		Eldridge, David	2		Snyder, Christopher	8		Pugh, Bethuel	8	
Anderson, John	8		Row, William	5		Renick, Elizabeth	5		Morehead, George	5	
Wells, Phineas	6		Jordan, Katherine	3		Delozea, John	8		Bell, George	5	
Shadd, George	7		Funk, Adam	5		Green, Henry	7		Pugh, Jonathan	11	2
Moak, Henry	3		Shadd, George	9		Harris, John	10		Ashbrook, Aaron	9	1
Smith, Jacob	9		Hog, Aaron	9		Canter, Henry	8		Carruthers, James	6	
Westfall, John, Juʳ	7		Lyon, Charles	4					Emmet, Jacob	8	
Kittle, Abram	10		Stackhouse, Isaac	4		LIST OF LEVI ASHBROOK, GENT.			Person, Alexander	4	
Timmons, Samuel	10		Kent, Isabel	3					Harsher, Thomas	7	
Johnson, Elisha	6		Wilson, John	2		Lineger, William	4		Clutter, Jacob	11	
Goff, Thomas	3	6	Shook, William	12		Asberry, Joseph	2	2	Prunty, John	8	2
Westfall, Henry	8		Shook, John	3		Howard, Resin	6		Johns, Isaac	8	
Smith, David	7		Lynch, Charles	4		Corbin, Ann	6		Emmry, John	8	
Randall, Abel	10		Hays, John	3		Thomas, Ezekial	10		Swisher, Nicholas	5	
Westfall, Eleanor	2		Trumbo, George	7	1	Chinoweth, John, Senʳ	13		Hubbert, Jacob	5	1
Westfall, Isaac	2		Carter, William	5		Chinoweth, Arthur	7		Thomson, Wᵐ, Senʳ	2	
Blair, William	6		Bullitt, William	6	2	Smith, James	9		Thomson, John	6	
			Stump, Michael	7	1	Hubbard, John, Juʳ	4	1	Thomson, Joseph	4	
LIST OF MICHL. STUMP, GENT.						Powell, Abram	4		Millslagle, Andʷ	7	
			LIST OF ABRM. HITE, GENT.			Moor, James	12		Millslagle, George	3	
Harness, Peter	6	1	Radcliff, Benjamin	5		Harris, John	6		Pritchard, Rees	7	
Shepler, Henry	5		McKenny, John	3		Millburn, Andrew	5		Davis, Thomas	3	
Harness, Leonard	6		Bailey, Ann	2		Hammory, John	5		Brody, James	4	
Trumbow, Andrew	8		Lorrentz, John	12		Monroe, Alexander	2		McIver, Paul	9	
Simon, Leonard	3		Waggoner, John	4		Arnold, John	9		Pugh, Robert	11	
Cauffman, Adam	3		Murphy, William	8	1	Hiett, Evan	8		Cotrall, Elizabeth	5	
Simon, George	9		Rennick, William	12	1	Largent, James	7		Reid, Jeremiah	8	
Regar, Jacob	11		Davis, Thomas	3		Pugh, Samuel	3		Reed, George	4	
Mitchar, Nicholas	9		Roby, Peter	9		Nixon, Marcy	5		Shannon, Hugh	4	
Mace, John	7		Batson, Mordecai	5		Hook, William	2		Lander, Henry	9	
George, Susanna	7	6	Batson, Mordecai, Juʳ	3		Swisher, Valentine	5		Lander, Jacob	4	
Roy, Thomas	5		Ashby, Stephen	9	3	Nixon, George	3	2	Clayton, Thomas	8	
Marrs, Barnabas	4		Rennick, John	10		Wickam, Matthew	6		Sommett, Jacob	2	
Smith, Michael	3		Cade, Major	10		Kail, George	6		Ohaver, Cornˢ	2	
Simond, Christian	4		Oneal, Edward	11		Kail, John	3		Ohaver, Chrisº	9	
Trace, Jacob	7		Conner, Daniel	8		Kail, Peter	5		Keys, James	5	
Doyal, Francis	6		Casey, Peter	8	2	Sloan, John	6		Wood, Bethia	3	
Hall, Thomas	7		Smith, John	2		Pugh, Thomas	6		Stackhouse, Isaac	4	
Cowger, George	4		Tucker, Jacob	11		McCormick, John	3		Horn, George	7	
Stephenson, James	7		Blackburn, William	3		McCord, John	6		Ashbrook, Levi	13	
Dickison, Jacob	8		Snale, William	2		Magraw, Morris	8		Poston, Elias	5	3
Smith, Charles	12		Shephard, John	10		Hayden, William	5		Chesshire, Ann	3	
Bible, Christian	6		Talbot, Thomas	5		Barnhouse, John	8		Cheshire, Samuel	5	
Mitchell, John	4		Lilly, David	5		Leaphart, Augusteen	8		Revnals, William	4	
Mahuran, Ebenezer	3		Berry, George	4	2	Chinoweth, John, Junʳ	5		Glass, Samuel	6	
Regar, Anthony	1		Nevill, Joseph	2	9	Bright, John	8		Wilson, Willᵐ, Senʳ	6	3
Rorebaugh, John	11		Nevill, Joseph, Juʳ	13	7	Kenneday, Thomas	7		Wilson, Willᵐ, Juʳ	3	
Ozburn, Jeremiah	10		Kayser, Joseph	7		Lyon, Michael	5	1	Hughs, Jonathan	4	
Brake, Jacob, Senʳ	8		Balthas, George	7		Donelly, Elizabeth	4		Park, John	11	
Scott, Joseph	1		Shipley, Richard	4		Carlyle, Ann	5		Rose, John	5	
Stump, George	8	2	McCarty, Thomas	5	1	Miars, George	8		Edwards, Sarah	5	
Roads, Henry	5		Shares, Michael	4		Engle, Wᵐ, Senʳ	5		Dixson, Thomas	7	
Yoakum, George	4		Bradford, John	5		McBride, James	7		Moonie, Bryan	4	
Dasher, Christian	7		Shrote, Peter	8		Park, Samuel	6				
Wilson, Charles	5		Logan, David	6		Downing, Dillon	3		LIST OF STEPHEN RUDDELL, GENT.		
Regar, John	4		Fiddler, Edward	3		Engle, William, Juʳ	5				
Rogers, James	8		McNeal, John	6	1	Edwards, Samuel	6		Ruddell, Stephen	6	
Spore, John Ul	10		Hider, Adam	10	2	Belford, Barnet	4		Baker, Samuel	10	1
Lewis, John	5		Horebaugh, Philip	8		Buttler, Richard	6		Baker, William	8	
Shinear, George	8		Green, Lewis	4		Forman, David	9		Baker, James	8	
Calahan, Charles	8		Pancake, Andrew	10		Pugh, Jacob	9		Robinson, Joel	8	
Sears, William	10		Parsons, James	8	13	Orton, Robert	10		Baker, Jacob	5	
Sears, James	3		Dugan, Alexander	4		Bumgarner, Rudy	10		Nailor, William	6	
Naaff, George	6	1	Cudding, John	3		Hoover, Jacob	13		Quehen, Paul	3	
Mace, Ann	5		McNeal, Daniel	9	4	Tivault, John	11		Viney, Susanna	4	
Mace, Nicholas	3		Neil, John	7		Little, Thomas	9		Taaff, Elizabeth	3	
Cowfelt, Philip	9		Berry, Reuben	7		Hawk, Isaac	9		Wardin, William	7	
Spillman, John	6		Vanmeter, Garret	8	16	Crawford, William	3		Lewis, George	7	
Morrow, James	7		Wood, Ebenezer	3		Swisher, John	8		Kidner, George	7	
Shook, Herman	6		Thomas, Enoch David	8		Hawk, John	5		Hill, Joseph	9	
House, Jacob	5		Suffolk, John	4		Cherry, Andrew	6		Oneal, Benjamin	5	
Shook, Peter	7		Long, Rosanna	6		Sharp, Andrew	3		Wilson, David	4	
Willowby, Benjamin	10		Broughton, William	8		Richardson, Richᵈ	6		Claypoole, George	3	
Lacewell, Elias	6		Ashby, Thomas	7		Tivault, Andrew	7		Fitzpatrick, Anthº	6	
Stump, Leonard	7		Ashby, Jesse	6		Fry, Henry	8	1	Chilcott, Mary	4	
Wertmiller, Jacob	6		Ashby, Peter	5		Michael, George	9		Chilcott, Eber	2	
Goodwine, Solomon	2		Miller, Catharine	5		Shoemaker, Peter	4		McFarlane, Thomas	8	
Wilson, David	7		Carr, John	5		Oldacre, Isaac	5		Thomas, James	8	
Rodebaugh, Adam	9		Hardin, Vangelist	5		Schried, Charity	4		Wilson, John	5	
Brake, John	3		Vanmeter, Jacob	8	1	Hughs, James	8		Ellis, Philip	10	
Brake, Jacob, Junʳ	4		Hawk, Henry	7		Hughs, Susanna	4		Rounsivell, Benjamin	6	
Sea, George	8	3	Suttles, Henry	6		Thompson, Wᵐ, Juʳ	8		Thomas, David	6	
Sears, John	8		Godfry, William	4		Dugan, Wᵐ	4		Taaff, James	1	1
Tivebaugh, Daniel	8	2	Godfry, Edward	10		Williams, Thomas	6		Roberts, Thomas	4	
Coutzman, Adam	3		Obannion, Joseph	2		Millburn, Willᵐ	6		Payne, John	6	
Leonard, Martin	7		Hunter, William	3		Smith, Thomas	7		Vandivender, Jacob	7	
Barger, Jacob	4		Monks, John	4		Salts, Thomas	3		Harris, John	8	
Sellers, John	5		Lynch, Patrick	2	2	Steward, James	10		Claypool, Jesse	7	
Algier, William	3		Gibbony, Robert	5		Caudy, David	9		Miller, Jacob	5	2
Algier, Hermonus	12		White, Charles	3		Gard, Cornelius	9		Wilkins, Matthias	9	
Watts, Thomas	6		Branson, Amos	7		Hamilton, Henry	3		Payne, David	7	
Marshall, Benjamin	3	1	Sibley, John	4		Young, John	3		Lewis, Amos	8	

HAMPSHIRE COUNTY—Continued.

NAME OF HEAD OF FAMILY.	White.	Black.	NAME OF HEAD OF FAMILY.	White.	Black.	NAME OF HEAD OF FAMILY.	White.	Black.	NAME OF HEAD OF FAMILY.	White.	Black.
LIST OF STEPHEN RUDDELL, GENT.—continued.			LIST OF MICHL. CRESAP, GENT.—continued.			LIST OF JOB WELTON, GENT.—continued.			LIST OF SIMON TAYLOR, GENT.—continued.		
Ozburn, Josiah	4		Walker, John	7		Hock, Catherine	6		Neale, William	4	
Vantinvender, Janety	7	3	Walker, James	5		Scott, Alexr	3		Friback, George	2	
Denton, Jacob	11	1	Kimberly, Michael	7		Clark, Watson	4		Short, Jacob	2	
Claypole, James	11		Murphy, William	4		Richardson, Joseph	5		Taylor, Simon	6	21
Metcalf, James	5		McDonald, Daniel	4		Scott, Benjn, Senr	6	1	Newman, Isaac	4	
Lowrie, Adam	8		Taylor, Simon	5		Byrns, Philip	8		Newman, George	11	
Wilkins, George	6		Hargis, William	7		Shevelear, Anthony	5		Newman, David	4	
Elswick, Thomas	6		Scott, John	7		Hornback, Michael	8		Broom, John	3	
Homan, Jacob	8		Dobson, William	3		Thickstone, Thomas	8		Newman, John	2	
Redsleevs, George M	3		Key, Sarah	3		Childers, William	9		Peterson, Peter	5	
Alman, John	9		Roy, Abram	3	2	Shook, Lawrence	8		Williams, Richard, Senr	10	
Roberts, David, Senr	7		Roy, James	6	3	Shook, Jacob	3		Laird, Michael	7	
Dean, Susanna	10		Rhodes, John	2		Powell, Caleb	8		Ball, James	6	
Roberts, David, Jur	3		Walker, Thomas	8		Eaton, Thomas	8		Humbler, Adam	6	
McBride, Francis	3		Wilson, Robert	4		Eaton, Benjamin	3		Lockart, Bird	5	
Ozburn, George	10		Long, Jacob	9		Eaton, Joseph	4		Short, Isaac	10	
McHendry, Wm	10		Glaze, Andrew	1		Radcliff, Richard	7		Chapman, William	5	
Claypoole, John	15		Glaze, Erhart	1		Smith, William	7		Williamson, John	3	
Denton, Thomas	8		Buckridge, James	8		Watts, Jonathan	4		Williamson, Thomas	2	
Denton, Jane	2	2	Myers, Francis	4		Boulger, John	4		Williamson, Samuel	9	
Wise, Christopher	10		Glaze, Conrod	6		Hutson, John	3		Ealy, Isaac	2	
Garrison, John	7		Sisler, William	5		Hutson, David	7		Alexander, Robert	5	
Chrisman, Jacob	8	1	Miller, Philip	8		Curle, Jeremiah	8		Ely, Benjamin	8	
Dunbar, John	6		Long, Christian	8		Majors, John	9		Corbin, David	6	
McNees, John	6		Allen, Eliza	2		Jordan, Julius	3		Williamson, William	10	
Chesterson, John	5		Pierse, Daniel	2		Clark, Abram	7		Calmees, Marquis	2	12
Davis, Samuel	9		Martin, James	7		Clark, Henry	7		Williams, Remembrance	2	
Stone, James	8		Read, Mrs	2	4	Norman, William	6		Blue, John, Junr	10	
Leg, Ambrose	6		Pierse, Benjamin	3		Badgley, Anthony	7		Blue, John, Senr	12	
Oldacre, Isaac	6		Martin, Uriah	5		Richardson, Jonathan	7		Blue, Michael	6	1
Hill, Daniel	1		Ward, Stephen	8		Little, Josiah	7		McLintock, Alexander	8	
			Buck, Anthony	2		Everman, Michael	12		Kearen, Patrick	9	
LIST OF WILLIAM VAUSE, GENT.			Buck, Robert	6		Judy, Margaret	8				
			Buck, William	4		Hole, Daniel	5		LIST OF VINCT. WILLIAMS, GENT.		
Vause, William	10	1	Sulivan, Jeremy	4		Miller, Thomas	5				
Gibbony, Alexr, Senr	3	1	Donaldson, Jas	9		Miller, George	5		Terry, George, Senr	3	
Savage, John	7		Walker, Robert	8		Miller, Michael	7		Terry, George, Junr	5	
Tivult, Nicholas	6		Casselman, Jacob	8		Welton, Job	10	6	Jacobs, Samuel	3	
Lander, Michael	7		Denham, John	9					Ross, Stephen	9	
Neel, Jacob	8		Maid, John	2		LIST OF SIMON TAYLOR, GENT.			Williams, Edward	3	
Reed, James	3		Doe, John	4					Barnard, Edward	4	
McCarty, Edward	5		Cresap, Michael	6	3	Parker, Robert	7	10	Douthait, John	14	
Dewit, Peter	5		Murphy, James	6	2	Anderson, William	3		Ryan, John	8	
Williams, James	7		Carline, Andrew	3		Hagarty, John	5		Douthait, Thomas	3	
Miller, Henry	5					McBride, John	6		Arnold, Moses	10	
Myers, Francis	8		LIST OF JOB WELTON, GENT.			Stoker, John	6		George, Joseph	3	
Kyger, George	9					Stocker, Bolser	2		Purcell, Edward	5	
Ashby, Benja	4	2	Mouse, Daniel	8		Critton, John	5		Purcell, William	6	
Gibbony, Alexr, Jur	6	1	Harpole, Adam	8		Critton, John, Senr	11		Lee, William	9	
Ravenscroft, John	7		Boulger, Michael	8		Carline, Andrew	6		Hanks, Joseph	11	
Champ, Thomas	12		Coberly, James	9		Johnson, Joseph	4		Sage, William	13	
Nut, John	4		Huffman, Christopher	9		Johnson, John, Senr	3		Doran, Felix	11	
Oddle, Willm	11		Carr, Henry, Senr	9		Newcomb, Daniel	8		Purcell, Jonathan	6	
Rawls, John	6		Carr, Conrad	6		Henwood, William	3		Wood, Richard	4	
Miers, John, Senr	2		McKave, Ross	5		Enochs, Enoch	13		Johnson, John	12	
Miers, John, Junr	4		Carr, Joseph	6		Batten, Henry	6		Ryan, James	12	
Bush, Lewis	3		Gilmore, Sarah	6	3	Bills, William	6		Kelly, Samuel	10	
Parker, John	4		Fleming, James	3		Bills, John	3		Smith, David	10	
Baker, John	8		Stacey, Thomas	3		Largent, William	7		Koon, John	15	
Bruce, Charles	7		Shook, Jonas	5		Enochs, Henry	2		Lewis, John	9	1
Hiss, Henry	10		Whitman, George	7		Leason, Richard	5		Coon, David	4	
Moor, John	6		Chinoth, Jonathan	4		Largent, John, Junr	8		Cross, Christian	11	
Whitman, John	3		Yeazle, David	3		Porter, William	8		Tucker, William	8	
Bond, Thomas	2		Lansisko, Henry	12		Porter, Elias	4		Vanmeter, Abram	4	3
Acton, Richard	9		Horse, Peter	3		Morgan, William	7		Williams, Vincent	10	2
Robison, Roger	4		Little, Job	6		Daniels, William	9		Alfree, Joseph	3	
Kite, Samuel	4		Cubberly, Thomas	3		Blue, James	10	3	Lewis, Samuel	7	2
Doyle, Tarrance	3		Buffinberry, Peter	5		Crack, George	6		Sturman, John	6	
Seavers, Nichs	2		Sadouskie, Samuel	8		Black, John	4				
McDade, James	4		Peck, George	7		Taylor, Tarpley	6		LIST OF ABRM. JOHNSON, GENT.		
Barnet, Mainy	7		Bonner, William	6		Rannells, William	6	4			
Seavers, Nicho, Jur	4	1	Miller, Henry	2		Notman, James	6		Howell, William	6	1
Bogle, James	7		Finlay, Patrick	3		Rannells, John	4		Redman, William	4	
Popejoy, John	2		Fearis, James	7		Humes, Andrew	3		Lighter, Henry	7	
Waterman, James	11		Clark, Robert	8		House, John	3		Rogers, William	10	
Painter, Benjn	6		Clark, Daniel	4		Hamilton, Thos	6		Reasoner, Garret	2	2
Kiger, John	8		Stroud, Adam	7		Glaze, George	5		Paugh, John	7	
Plumb, John	6		Clark, John	4		Taylor, Richard	2		Hansom, Thomas	5	
			Clark, William	5		Taylor, Margret	9		Umstat, Peter	7	
LIST OF MICHL. CRESAP, GENT.			Simson, Alexander	6	1	Humphrys, Ralph	7	10	Queen, Charles	7	
			Welton, Jesse	8	2	Pritchard, Rees	4		Spencer, John	7	
Dudley, William	4		Simson, Jonathan	8		Male, Wilmer	11		Thomson, John	6	
Fields, Simon	3		Statts, Elijah	1		Trouten, Richard	3		Coulson, John	3	7
Reaves, Benjn	15		Sims, John, Senr	7		Flougherty, James	5		Beverley, John	5	
Tarpley, James	4		Curle, William	5		Deaton, Isaac	5		Parker, Benjamin	7	
Haines, Joseph	5		Thomson, Jethro	6		Norman, George	4		Wise, Adam	6	
Young, William	12		Orr, James	6		Earsom, John	8		Woolf, George	8	
Fryback, John	4		Robey, Prior	9		Earsom, Simon	2		Blackburn, Willm	11	
McGloughlan, Danl	2		Seymour, Thomas	2		Earsom, Jacob	7		Cannon, Thomas	7	
McGloughlan, Danl, Jur	5		Jane, Joseph	7		Pancake, John	8		Jones, Peter	11	
Aughney, Darby	4	3	Scott, Benjn	6		Long, David	8		McBride, John	7	
Rector, Daniel	9		Seymour, Felix	12	3	Ross, Robert, Senr	4		Beeler, Charles	3	2
Rector, Charles	2		Bodkin, Charles	2		Ross, Robert	8		Cuningham, John	5	
Kiser, John	10		Bodkin, Richard	7		Spillman, John	6		New, Peter	7	
Muse, George	3		Orahood, Alexander	10		Spillman, William	4		Thomson, David	5	
Rhodes, Thomas	5		Ward, Sylvester	11	3	Hubs, Thomas	3		Powell, William	8	
Chapman, Luke	7	1	Robinson, John	6		Wiggins, Philip	2		Kent, John	11	
Kearen, Barnard	3		Smith, Robert	9		Milaw, James	4		Price, Arjalon	8	6
Carter, Henry	9		Wamsley, David	4	1	McLintock, John	5		Dobbins, Thomas	5	
Twilley, William	5		Craig, David	3	1	Andrews, George	10				
			Radcliff, Stephen	6							

LIST OF ABRM. JOHNSON, GENT.—continued.

NAME OF HEAD OF FAMILY.	White.	Black.
Thomson, Francis	1	....
Benkit, Jacob	7	....
Buffington, Thos	4	1
Parker, Benjn	6	....
Cooper, Joel	11	....
Parker, George	6	....
Parker, James	3	....
Hirsman, Casper	8	....
Good, Isaac	6	....
Good, Peter	3	....
Casselman, Lewis	9	....
Huffman, Henry	6	....
Cooper, Thomas	10	....
Miller, George	8	....
Hazle, Henry	8	2
Johnson, Wm	9	....
Reasoner, Jacob	9	1
Johnson, Wm, Junr	2	1
Boggard, Jacob	5	....
Holland, Thomas	2	....
Kimberlin, Abrm	6	....
Capell, Littleton	9	....
Thompson, Samuel	4	....
Holloback, Thomas	11	....
Jones, John	10	....
Jones, David	5	....
Jones, Peter	4	....
Jones, Solomon	2	....
Taylor, John	1	....
Kimberline, John	5	....
Totton, Esekial	9	....
Titzord, Isaac	3	....
Corn, Andrew	4	....
Timmons, John	7	....
Vandivear, Willm	12	5
Fearend, Isaac	8	....
Pigman, Moses	7	....
Vandivear, John	2	....
Hartley, Hugh	5	....
Brandenburg, Maths	12	....
Johnson, Okey	6	....
Piersall, John	3	5
Beaver, Matthias	6	....
Beaver, Michael	6	....
Beaver, Peter	4	....
Nave, Henry	10	....
Miller, Michael	6	....
Riding, Joseph	8	....
Stagg, John	8	....
Putman, Peter	12	....
Clark, Stephen	9	....
Hendrick, Abrm	3	....
Bacorn, Job	3	....
Martin, Thomas	3	....
Martin, Samuel	3	....
Johnson, Abrm, Senr	2	....
Johnson, Abrm, Junr	6	....
Wright, Gabriel	8	....
Taylor, George	4	....
Hiersman, Matthias	2	....
Hiersman, George	2	....
Noel, Peter	5	....
Cory, Joseph	5	....
Blue, Abram	6	....
Parker, Nathaniel	10	5
Ross, Lawrence	10	12

LIST OF OKEY JOHNSON, GENT.

NAME OF HEAD OF FAMILY.	White.	Black.
Parker, Nathl, Senr	3	3
Johnson, William	7	....
Fairley, John	3	....
Vincent, John	4	....
Reily, Patrick	3	....
Williams, Ebenezer	2	....

LIST OF OKEY JOHNSON, GENT.—continued.

NAME OF HEAD OF FAMILY.	White.	Black.
Scritchfield, Joshua	3	....
Baker, John	2	....
Archer, John	5	....
Collens, Elisha	5	....
Ray, Joseph	3	....
Critchlow, William	8	....
Hardin, Mark	11	....
Durgan, John	6	....
Fairley, David	9	....
Vandivere, George	7	....
Slagle, Jacob	8	3
Heater, Michael	9	....
Lawson, Thomas	12	15
Lyon, Esekial	6	....
Jordan, Mark	5	....
Archer, Benjamin	3	....
Newell, Joseph	1	....
Ronnells, Jeremiah	5	....
Early, Thomas	9	....
Kimberline, Jacob	8	....
Mahen, James	8	....
Mahen, William	10	....
Denham, John	9	....
Anderson, Thomas	10	....
Anderson, William	5	....
Forshey, John	8	3
House, John	6	....
Martin, Edmund	8	....
Johnson, Okey	8	....
Hogeland, Cornels	10	....
Lee, Peter	7	....
House, Joseph	3	....
Dougherty, James	1	....
Hartley, John	8	....

LIST OF WM. BUFFINGTON, GENT'N.

NAME OF HEAD OF FAMILY.	White.	Black.
Barber, James	11	....
Ferguson, Robert	8	4
Brookes, James	3	....
Fiddler, George	3	....
Hiersman, Chriso	4	....
Dew, Samuel	9	2
Miller, John	11	....
Scott, James	8	....
Campbell, John, Jur	2	....
Devore, William	5	....
Bush, John	5	....
Carder, William	9	....
Lard, Michael	5	....
Dixon, John	4	....
Hathaway, Eliezer	10	....
Williams, Richard	9	....
Buffington, Joel	7	....
Burns, John	3	....
Berry, Joel	4	....
Berry, William	4	....
Murphy, Hugh	4	....
Collins, Thomas	6	3
Berry, Enoch	4	....
Decker, John	5	1
Haff, Peter	5	....
Miller, Isaac	5	2
Huffman, Conrod	12	1
Plough, Jacob	5	....
Watters, John	8	....
Kuykendall, Cathrn	2	1
Miller, John, Junr	4	....
Devore, John	2	....
Kuykendall, Henry	7	3
Beatty, Robert	3	....
Bierly, John	5	....
Bean, John	2	....
Beattis, George	9	....
Plow, Aldert	8	....

LIST OF WM. BUFFINGTON, GENT'N—continued.

NAME OF HEAD OF FAMILY.	White.	Black.
Kuykendall, Nathl	7	7
Kuykendall, John	6	6
Dayley, William	2	....
Price, William	7	....
Crossly, Abel	6	....
Bonham, Hesekiah	8	....
Miller, Abram	6	....
Vanmeter, Isaac	9	4
Atchison, William	5	1
Harness, Adam	7	....
Keran, Peter	1	....
Anderson, James	3	....
Smook, Jacob	1	....
O'Bryan, Tallent	5	....
Claypole, Jeremiah	3	1
Forman, John	7	6
Forman, William	4	1
Fox, Gabriel	4	....
Allan, David	4	....
Herriott, Ephraim	8	....
Blue, Uriah	7	1
Colvin, Robert	4	....
Buzby, John	9	....
Forman, Benjn	6	....
Forman, John, Junr	8	9
Lander, Charles	3	1
Calvin, Stephen	8	1
Parsons, Isaac	4	6
Means, Isaac	9	....
Byrns, John	1	....
Miller, John Henry	9	....
McGuire, William	9	3
Huffman, Benjn	4	....
Roby, Thomas	8	....
Taylor, Robert	8	....
Roby, Benjamin	4	....
Parker, Job	7	....
Cuppy, John	7	....
Norman, John	9	....
Norman, Benjn	2	....
Bordman, Joseph	4	....
Glaze, John	4	....
Cuppy, John, Junr	4	....
Henry, Michael	8	1
Yeater, Peter	6	....
Hartman, Henry	5	....
High, John	9	....
Burkit, Henry	3	....
Smalley, And	6	....
Campbell, John	7	....
Buffington, Wm	12	....
Casey, Nicholas	7	1

LIST OF DAVID MITCHELL, GENT.

NAME OF HEAD OF FAMILY.	White.	Black.
Bickerstaff, William, Sr	3	....
Bickerstaff, Willm, Junr	6	....
Bickerstaff, John	8	....
Hartly, Thomas	6	....
Tervin, George	10	....
Dawson, Isaac	4	....
Constant, John	8	....
Morgan, John	9	....
Jackson, William	11	....
Morgan, Jonathan	5	....
Richards, Isaac	6	....
Haff, Cornelius	7	....
Demoss, John	6	....
Pervin, Thomas	9	....
Lock, Jacob	7	....
Swim, John	3	....
Flora, Thomas	13	....
Hughs, Thomas	5	....
Throgmorton, Lewis	10	....
Hartly, John	7	....

LIST OF DAVID MITCHELL, GENT.—continued.

NAME OF HEAD OF FAMILY.	White.	Black.
Malcolm, James	6	....
Dawson, David	12	....
Duffill, William	4	....
Martin, John	8	....
Craycraft, Joseph	9	....
Dawson, Abraham	4	1
McMahen, William	7	....
Williams, Thomas	9	....
Marquis, Andrew	6	....
Marquis, Richard	10	....
Belew, John	10	....
Risley, Daniel	5	....
Rose, John	4	....
Gustin, Alpheus	8	....
Beagle, Jonathan	2	....
Worthington, John	8	....
Haff, Lawrence	7	1
Haines, Rudolph	4	....
Chrisman, Philip, Senr	4	....
Chrisman, Adam	6	....
Chrisman, Jacob	3	....
Chrisman, Conrad	3	....
Macdonald, Archd	8	1
Chrisman, Philip	2	....
Jenkins, Evan	4	....
Butcher, John	7	....
Connard, James, Senr	4	....
Connard, James, Junr	5	....
Mathews, Levi	6	....
Hughs, John	4	....
Stevenson, Edward	2	....
Steed, Aaron	4	....
McDonald, Neil	8	....
Demoss, William	7	....
Haff, Richard	6	....
Demoss, Mary	8	....
Largent, John, Senr	10	....
Gordon, George	6	....
Swim, Lasler	4	....
Creacraft, Thomas	7	....
Dutty, Thomas	5	....
Demoss, Thomas	9	....
Larue, Jacob	5	....
Larue, Peter	9	....
Larue, John	6	....
Smith, Richard	6	....
Smith, John	3	....
Casler, Michael	4	....
Higgins, John	9	....
Bruce, Joseph	5	....
Beale, Benjamin	6	....
Scoals, John	6	....
McCabe, Tarrance	3	....
Mecrakin, Ann	2	....
Johnson, Wm, Sen	8	....
Blith, Wm	6	....
Mecrakin, Ovid	11	....
Flora, William	7	....
Wiggins, Archd	11	....
Lamaster, Isaac	5	....
Lamaster, Joseph	4	....
Wiggins, Philip	11	....
Ferrall, Patrick	4	1
Bigam, Hugh	5	....
Williams, William	12	....
Ozmund, Samuel	3	....
Ozmund, Isaac	4	....
Ozmund, Jabez	10	....
Martin, David	5	....
Kelly, Patrick	3	....
Morgan, Thomas	8	....
Reeves, Richard	5	....
Mitchell, David	1	6

HANOVER COUNTY.

PRECINCT NO. 1—LIST OF WM. JONES, GENT'N.

NAME OF HEAD OF FAMILY.	White.	Black.
Pearsons, Samuel (Family)	7	16
Beal, John	5	6
Blacknells, James	10	16
Cockburn, John	9	6
Goodman, Benjamin	8	5
McDougle, Ann	6	9
Peace, Joseph	4	3
McDougle, John	7	11
Jordan, Robert	7	10
Lemay, Susannah	6	18
Turner, Jedediah	6	9
Turner, Nathaniel	9	5
Clopton, William, Senr	6	25
Ragland, Samuel	9	1
Burnett, John	12	....
Burnett, William R	5	....
Thacker, Nathan	7	2
Anderson, John	10	....

PRECINCT NO. 1—LIST OF WM. JONES, GENT'N—con.

NAME OF HEAD OF FAMILY.	White.	Black.
Barker, John	12	1
Wade, Edmund, Junr	9	9
Charles, Mourning	3	3
Jones, William	8	23
Thompson, Nathaniel	1	10
Cobbs, Nathaniel	4	3
Cobbs, Judith	8	17

PRECINCT NO. 5—LIST OF THOS. TREVILIAN, GENT'N.

NAME OF HEAD OF FAMILY.	White.	Black.
Trevilian, Thomas	9	17
Seay, William	5	....
Seay, Hezekiah	6	1
Thomson, Charles	4	9
Owen, Richard	8	....
Walton, Mary	3	13
Jones, Jane	2	6

PRECINCT NO. 5—LIST OF THOS. TREVILIAN, GENT'N—continued.

NAME OF HEAD OF FAMILY.	White.	Black.
Spicer, Wm	8	....
Crawford, James	1	....
Duggin, Wm	2	1
Hancock, Benjamin	5	....
Terrell, Timothy	7	20
Terrell, Wm	4	4
Harris, Tyree	6	....
Wingfield, John	2	6
Smith, Bartlett	11	18
Winston, Isaac	9	36
Whitman, Wm	5	....
Bullock, James	11	17
Duke, Burnley	6	20
Anderson, Garland	9	32
Gillam, Peter	3	2
Farmer, Obediah	7	....
Sims, John	5	1
Anthony, John	6	7

PRECINCT NO. 5—LIST OF THOS. TREVILIAN, GENT'N—continued.

NAME OF HEAD OF FAMILY.	White.	Black.
Going, Henry	8	....
Overstreat, James	8	6
Fontain, Mrs Elizabeth (at Beverdam)	....	10
Butler, Anderson	5	....
Matthews, James	7	3
Liveley, Edmond	1	....
Smith, Thomas	6	1
Smith, Francis	1	14
Brown, Susanna	10	15
Smith, George	8	8
Hall, Henry	5	....
Spicer, Benjamin	6	6
Sims, David	7	....
Seay, John	8	1
Hall, James	7	....
Fontaine, Wm (at Beverdam quarter)	....	7

HANOVER COUNTY—Continued.

NAME OF HEAD OF FAMILY.	White.	Black.	NAME OF HEAD OF FAMILY.	White.	Black.	NAME OF HEAD OF FAMILY.	White.	Black.	NAME OF HEAD OF FAMILY.	White.	Black.
PRECINCT NO. 5—LIST OF THOS. TREVILIAN, GENT'N—continued.			**ST. PAUL'S PARISH—LIST OF WILLIAM ANDERSON, JUN'R—continued.**			**ST. PAUL'S PARISH—LIST OF BARTELOT ANDERSON—continued.**			**ST. PAUL'S PARISH—LIST OF BARTELOT ANDERSON—continued.**		
Gillom, Wᵐ	5	16	Tomkins, Sarah	10	14	Earnest, George	5	14	Via, Littleberry	9	....
Brown, Dudley	8	9	Snead, Jnᵒ, Senʳ	6	16	Foster, Thomas	6	10	Via, Abigal	6	4
Dickerson, Nelson	6	....	Lumkin, Wᵐ	1	....	Fox, Samuel	10	6	Whitlock, James	6	18
Daves, Richard	2	....	Green, Macon	3	5	Francis, Elijah	8	....	Warren, Elijah	5	....
Jones, Wᵐ	11	9	Walker, Jnᵒ	3	....	Gathright, Joseph	10	10	White, James	6	10
Luck, John	4	1	Cross, Joˢ, Junʳ	3	22	Gardner, John	5	7	Wade, Littleberry, Junʳ	7	8
Phillips, John	4	14	Grimes, Jnᵒ	7	15	Gardner, William	3	6	Wheeler, Robert	3	....
Terrell, Joseph	11	11	Norvel, Wᵐ	9	14	Gooch, Lucy	4	....	Woody, John	10	3
Still, John A.	7	....	Markes, Thˢ	2	18	Gooch, Wade	4	....	Woody, Samuel	7	4
Davis, Henry	2	1	Ragland, Pettus	9	19	Gauldin, John	5	....	Woody, Micajah	4	....
Davis, Lewis C.	1	3	Oliver, Beⁿ	10	23	Grantland, Walter	5	2	Woody, Lucy	4	1
Duddleston, Thoˢ	8	....	Cock, Elizabeth	7	7	Harris, Blandina	5	5	Wade, Jeremiah	6	2
Anderson, Thomas	8	17	Walker, Mary	5	14	Hundley, Jane	6	17	Wright, William	7	....
Bradley, Anderson	4	6	Tinsley, Martha	4	14	Hill, Samuel	6	....	Wood, Leighton, Junʳ	6	7
Wingfield, Thomas	9	27	Tinsley, Natᵗ	1	1	Hazelgrove, Joshua	9	....	Wade, David	9	....
Abbott, Elizabeth	5	4	Bow, Catharine	6	15	Hooper, Thomas	5	13	Wade, Littleberry	3	10
Claybrook, Wᵐ	7	6	Wingfield, Thˢ	7	10	Hooper, William	3	2	Whitlock, David	7	9
Goodwin, John	9	19	Dixon, Holbendy	4	28	Hughes, Henry	5	3	White, Chillion	5	7
Brown, Wᵐ	2	....	Street, John	9	13	Hood, Nathˡ	4	3	Warren, Benjᵃ	5	....
Mason, Thomas	4	17	Davis, Supry	4	7	Haw, Elizabeth	5	3	White, Robert	7	1
Watts, Sheverick	4	8	Tinsley, Cornelius, Senʳ	9	14	Hooper, Elizabeth	7	9	Wood, Henry	7	5
Hanes, Thomas	3	5	Davis, George, Junʳ	6	3	Howard, Benjamin	1	....	Wade, John	5	1
Hogan, James	4	....	Wingfield, John, junʳ	9	11	Hogg, Micajah	5	2	Wade, Zachʰ	4	....
Hanes, John	5	....	King, Mary	11	3	Hollings, John	5	....			
Nelson, Wᵐ (at his Quarter)	....	2	Youland, Thomas	1	1	Hughes, William	5	....	**CAPT. OWEN DABNEY DISTRICT—LIST OF GEO. CLOUGH.**		
Roberts, Thomas	7	....	Alsup, William	2	2	Hughes, Kemuel	6	1			
Brown, Joseph	6	....	Hundley, Jacob	2	2	Holliday, John	9	....			
Hall, John	7	....	King, Susannah	4	....	Holliday, William	3	2	Dabney, Capᵗ Owen	6	26
Goodwin, Reubin	6	13	Carter, Charles (Estate)	....	67	Johnson, Thomas	8	9	Anderson, Capᵗ John	3	12
Goodwin, James	6	1	Ragland, Gidion	7	2	Johnson, Richard	5	9	Atkerson, lewis	4	....
Terry, John	8	....	Davis, John	10	15	Ingram, Soloman	5	....	Atkerson, Henry, Senʳ	2	....
Brown, Sarah	10	10	Burnley, Elizabeth	5	35	Jones, William	8	14	Harris, William (Wolfˢ)	5	14
Corley, Austin	4	1	Brooks, James, Junʳ	7	....	Kent, Lucy	5	2	Harris, George	4	4
Lowery, Soloman	8	....	Brooks, James, Senʳ	3	....	Kendrick, Nathan	5	....	Jennings, Dannul	8	....
Sacra, Sabrey	8	....	Turner, Lewis	4	13	Killingham, Benjamin	4	....	Atkerson, Henry, Junʳ	4	5
Matthews, Berry	5	....	Glazebrook, Richard	5	4	Lipscomb, Ambrose	3	17	Huges, William, Senʳ	4	16
Tulloah, David	9	12	England, John	12	7	Lane, Julius	3	....	Colley, Charles	8	12
Epperson, John	10	5	Butler, Christopher	3	....	Lipscomb, Menoah	5	1	Bullock, John, Senʳ	7	14
Hanes, Christopher	9	....	Glenn, Nathaniel	3	2	Lyons, Peter	12	55	Higgason, John, Senʳ	3	10
Hanes, Thomas, Junʳ	7	1	Priddy, Thomas	5	2	Lindsay, Jeremiah	11	....	Higgason, Richard	5	1
Goodman, Timothy	1	14	King, William	7	2	Lemay, William	3	6	Alvis, Forester	7	....
Lane, Peggey	3	....	Tinsley, Cornelius, junʳ	7	1	Meredith, Elisha	4	12	Matlock, George	4	2
Brakenridge, George	6	12	Hargrove, Thomas	7	....	Martin, William	5	....	Matlock, John	2	....
Mallory, Thomson	7	1	Rowland, Cuthbert H.	3	1	Macon, William	11	91	Chisholm, David	7	8
Nelson, General Thoˢ (at Bridg. Qʳ)	....	55	Shepherd, Jaˢ	11	5	May, Nicholas	3	5	Devonport, Martin	7	....
			Clarke, Wᵐ, Junʳ	4	1	Mᶜfall, Samuel	3	1	Mitchell, John	4	1
Nelson, General Thoˢ (at Offley)	15	73	Hooper, Wᵐ	3	8	Meredith, George	4	4	Williamson, Joseph	2	2
			Smithey, Robert	1	....	Mills, Mary	3	9	Glenn, John, Junʳ	10	8
Nelson, General Thoˢ (at Bullfield)	....	49	Perrin, Isaac	9	12	Mills, Nicholas	4	....	Richardson, Richard	6	2
Anderson, David	6	22	Perren, Sam	1	....	Melton, Joel	4	5	Simes, James	9	20
Trevilian, Wilson	2	8	Perren, Henry	3	3	Matthews, Richard	10	....	Hughes, James	1	....
Goodwin, Rebekah	10	14	Davis, Jaˢ, Junʳ	1	1	More, Thomas	7	2	Austin, Francis	7	18
Harris, Overton	12	24	Garland, Thˢ	6	33	Nelson, Thomas, Esqʳ	3	31	Hagges, William	2	....
Doswell, Rebekah	2	17				Pate, William	8	3	Coles, Lucy	1	15
Hamlett, Mary	11	9	**ST. PAUL'S PARISH—LIST OF BARTELOT ANDERSON.**			Powers, Thomas	8	....	Sharp, John	5	3
Nelson, Wᵐ (overʳ at Bull Field)	5	....				Pasley, John	6	5	Gentry, Watson	4	6
Watkins, John	6	3	Acre, William	4	1	Roach, Oansy	3	....	Dickerson, Benjamin	6	6
Doswell, James	5	7	Adams, John	11	....	Reddick, Constantine	4	2	Sims, David	3	1
Cosby, James	10	11	Acre, Rebecca	8	7	Richardson, William	5	11	Sims, Nathan	7	7
Anderson, John	9	4	Anderson, Bartt	8	25	Richardson, Thomas	5	11	Glenn, John, Senʳ	3	4
Williams, John, Junʳ	2	....	Abbott, Matthias	8	6	Richardson, Richard	1	1	Henderson, Thomas	1	4
Garrot, John	3	2	Bailey, Mary	6	1	Richardson, Turner	2	14	Mayo, John	7	2
Hargrove, John	5	2	Braeme, William	8	4	Robertson, Samuel	10	4	Ginnings, Maiden	2	18
Austin, John	4	1	Brim, John	1	....	Rowe, William	3	2	Pullom, William	4	5
Williams, Jacob	7	5	Bailey, John	3	....	Stanley, John	5	10	Henderson, David	8	4
Harris, William	2	5	Barnes, William	11	3	Slaughter, George	3	....	Berryman, Martha	2	12
Farmer, Mary	3	....	Burnett, Alexʳ C.	12	3	Spears, James	7	....	Cogil, John	3	....
			Barker, John	11	1	Stanley, Samuel	7	1	Payne, John (Quaker)	9	5
ST. PAUL'S PARISH—LIST OF WILLIAM ANDERSON, JUN'R.			Badkins, John	3	....	Steward, Alexander	7	5	Turner, James	8	14
			Barker, Charles	7	8	Shepperson, Elisha	5	....	Smith, Geo.	11	5
			Barker, William	4	1	Slaughter, Turner	5	1	Hix, John	5	23
Anderson, Wᵐ, Junʳ	7	15	Barker, Margaret	5	5	Talley, Nathaniel, Junʳ	4	3	Jones, David	10	14
Burnley, Harden, Junʳ (Estate)	....	8	Burnett, Isaac	9	(*)	Talley, Nathˡ, Inspʳ	6	7	Bowles, John	6	7
Smith, John	3	....	Beale, John	5	6	Talley, Mary	3	3	Bowles, Thoˢ	3	13
Smith, Christopher (Estate)	....	44	Boatwright, Daniel	8	3	Thurmon, Sarah	1	2	Chisholm, Walter	11	2
Thomson, Francis	3	....	Burnett, John	4	1	Talley, Micajah	6	5	Doswell, Capᵗ Thomas	1	7
Hollings, George	3	....	Barker, Lankford	8	....	Talley, Zebulon	5	1	Clough, George	10	12
Starke, John, Senʳ	2	10	Boatwright, Anne	4	3	Turner, George	6	....	Powell, Doctᵗ John	1	18
Starke, Joˢ	2	3	Boatwright, James	3	2	Tucker, Michael	6	....	Gentry, John	8	....
Jones, Jnᵒ (Estate)	1	24	Boatwright, John	7	....	Tucker, Littleberry	10	....	Martin, John	4	3
Smith, Elizabeth	3	11	Bowbes, Kezia	3	....	Tucker, Stephen	8	....	Mallory, Mary	6	....
Thilman, Capᵗ Paul	8	37	Boatwright, Benjamin	3	....	Tate, Jesse	3	11	Faris, John, Senʳ	11	....
Clay, Elizabeth	9	18	Bailey, William	3	1	Talley, Kitty	5	5	Shelbern, John	5	....
Bow, Natᵗ	7	29	Badkins, William	6	....	Talley, Elisha	10	4	Jones, William	4	....
Cooper, Wᵐ	3	....	Bumpass, William	7	14	Talley, Bartlet	5	3	Sims, Benjamin	5	....
Gist, Samuel (Estate)	11	80	Brown, James	7	16	Talley, Charles	2	3	Anderson, Henry	6	5
Hanes, David	8	1	Cockrane, David	6	14	Talley, Mary	4	2	Anderson, Robert	10	....
Hix, Jnᵒ, Senʳ	12	2	Chappell, John	1	....	Tucker, Gideon	9	....	Woolfolk, Paul	1	....
Hix, Wᵐ	4	1	Clarke, Thomas	11	12	Tucker, Obadiah	3	....	Hawes, James	1	....
Snead, Jnᵒ, Junʳ	3	3	Castlin, Andrew	6	5	Talley, David	6	1	Syme, Colᵒ John	7	88
Priddy, Jnᵒ, Junʳ	5	4	Clarke, David	7	....	Talley, Nocholas	8	4	Pryor, John	9	....
England, Wᵐ	10	....	Carter, John	4	16	Talley, William	7	5	Hughes, John	9	15
Hix, Joˢ	10	....	Carter, Mary	13	15	Talley, Jack	2	3	Grinstead, Richard	5	....
Hix, Henry	2	....	Durham, Abraham	4	....	Talley, Billey	1	....	Black, Jonathan	7	....
Cross, Joˢ, Senʳ	6	20	Daniel, James	4	....	Talley, Joseph	4	....	Hawes, Daniel	5	15
			Durham, Samuel	4	....	Tucker, Thomas	8	....	Bartlett, William	6	....
			Durham, Jacob	5	....	Tucker, Jesse	4	7	Faris, Richard	6	....
			Earnest, Samuel	5	8	Via, Robert	4	7	Harris, Partrick	5	....
						Via, Gideon	10	8			

*Illegible.

HANOVER COUNTY—Continued.

NAME OF HEAD OF FAMILY.	White.	Black.	NAME OF HEAD OF FAMILY.	White.	Black.	NAME OF HEAD OF FAMILY.	White.	Black.	NAME OF HEAD OF FAMILY.	White.	Black.
CAPT. OWEN DABNEY DISTRICT—LIST OF GEO. CLOUGH—continued.			CAPT. JOHN THOMSON'S AND THOMAS PRICE'S COMPANIES OF MILITIA—LIST OF JOHN LAWRENCE, GENT'N—continued.			CAPT. JOHN THOMSON'S AND THOMAS PRICE'S COMPANIES OF MILITIA—LIST OF JOHN LAWRENCE, GENT'N—continued.			LIST OF GEDDES WINSTON, GENT.—continued.		
Childress, Joseph	3		Swift, Thomas, jr	2	2	Blunt, Page	10	7	Pasley, Solomon	8	
Childress, William, Senr	13		Hopkins, Charles	9	2	Mallory, Thomas	8	11	Ellis, Francis	3	7
Childress, William, jr	7	4	Mills, Charles	9	6	Pollard, Sarah	5	1	White, Elisha	6	7
Childress, John	8		Sanders, George	7	11	Wright, Margret	5	2	Green, Elijah	7	4
Lacy, Charles	5	2	Huckstep, John	1	5	Dickenson, William	8		Sims, Matthew	7	2
Anderson, Robert (Gold mine)	3	21	Thomson, Elizabeth	6	9	Duke, John	13	8	Kersey, Julius	9	
Sims, John	1		Rice, Jessey	8		Grubbs, Richard	9		Green, Thomas	10	2
Sims, David	7	2	Higgason, John	8		Dickinson, Zack	3	1	Smith, Nathaniel	8	4
Elliott, Robert	12	12	Hall, Timothy	7		Plant, John	11		Tinsley, David	3	
Tyler, Thomas	7		Higgason, Benjamin	8		Richardson, David	7	16	Tinsley, Philip	1	
Denton, John	7	1	Sims, John, jr	0	2	Thornton, John	9	20	Pollard, William	8	23
Meeks, Martin	5		Higgason, Charles	5	1	Miller, Robert	1		Tinsley, William	3	18
Bryers, Edward	9	4	Smith, Henry (for Jno Winston)	5	21	Alvis, Stanley	2		Whitlock, Matthew	10	20
Hines, John	4	4	Anderson, David, jr	8	15	Harris, James	3	1	Tinsley, Thomas	5	16
Martin, John, Senr	3		Hall, John	5	3	Hope, John	9	16	Brand, Joseph	4	6
Anderson, John	7		Stanley, William	4	1	Arnold, Joshua	9	3	Tylor, Skelton	4	
Draper, David	5		Thomas, David	5		Arnold, Henry	7	2	Gentry, David	8	18
Anderson, Betty	2	1	Baker, Martin	3	6	Arnold, William	4	2	Hundley, Charles	1	9
Harlow, James (his mother, &c)	8	3	Baker, Martin, Junr	6	4	Goodwin, Rebekah	10	14	Archer, Elisha	4	
Harris, Mourning	9		Swift, Clessears	6	11	Eggleston, Elizabeth	3	5	McClara, William	5	2
Harris, John	7		Walton, William	5	6	Winston, James (Estate)			Waxley, William	3	
Dabney, George			Sharp, Robert	7	13	Overton, Samuel (Estate)	7	69	Sims, William	7	15
Crenshaw, Charles, Senr	8	39	Mills, Robert	6	4	Overton, Wm (Estate)	1	29	Lewis, Charles	7	
Duval, Claiborne	2	9	Chewning, Geo. (for Genl Nels)	6	45	Furgusson, John	3	12	Nailor, Elizabeth	8	24
Ambler, John			Minor, John (for Do)	8	62	Hinde, Thomas	8	24	Gentry, William	1	
Askew, John	5		Dickinson, Thomas (Do)	8	46	Robinson, John			Wingfield, John	7	17
Harris, Robert	3	5	Oliver, Robert (Do)	2	40	Longan, Beverley	5	1	Butler, Edward	8	18
Crenshaw, Nicholas			Spencer, John (Do)	3	31	Overton, Mildred	4	3	Priddy, John	8	7
Camron, Wm	6		Watkins, James	6		Southward, Robert	7		Keyser, William	3	
Harris, David	10	13	Hawkins, Mary	8	32	Richardson, John		9	Hughes, Reuben	3	9
Harris, John (Quaker)	13		Hawkins, James	3	6	Hadon, Isaiah	14	15	Tyree, Sarah	9	7
Cary, Colo W. M. (at Scotch Town)	12	80	Walton, Robert	7	6	Alvis, George	5		Basset, William	1	14
Crew, Micajah	5	1	Hawkins, Edmund	3	9	Mallory, Thomas, jr	8	2	Thomson, Nathaniel	8	18
Harris, Moses	5		Barret, Revd Robert	6	43	Mallory, John	5	3	Tylor, Maggy	4	
Sydnor, Robert	5	16	Goodman, Joseph	11	20	Berkeley, Nelson	17	146	Tylor, William	9	
Sheton, Capt John (Hanover Estd)	1	24	Yeamons, Charles	6		Lawrence, John	8	37	Tylor, Henry	7	
Perkins, Wm	8		Wheeler, Robert		1	Hinchey, Bartelot	5		Tylor, Charles	5	
Bingham, Josias	7	1	Sims, Fenton	8		Lively, John	7		Francis, Nelly	4	5
Mallory, Henry H.	2		Dandridge, William	8	31	Hinchey, John	4		Gentry, Joseph	5	
Bingham, Thomas	6		Goodman, Samuel	1	13	Spencer, Lucy	6	5	Tylor, Lucy	5	
Bingham, George	2		Byarse, James	2	8				Blair, John, President of Washington Henry Academy & Walter Davis & their Students	33	
Crenshaw, Joseph	1	21	Brooks, Richeson	6	2	LIST OF GEDDES WINSTON, GENT.			Elmore, William	4	
Crenshaw, Charles	1	3	Day, John	9	25	Timberlake, Burnet	11	19	Scherer, Samuel	3	
Crenshaw, Wm	4	3	Jones, John	7	1	Timberlake, Richard	9	16	Winston, Geddes	7	27
Crenshaw, James	8	2	Dickenson, Henry	5		Ellis, William	9	6	Tylor, John	2	
			Byarse, Jeremiah	4	4	Hughes, Nathan	3	6	Winston, Thomas	9	15
CAPT. JOHN THOMSON'S AND THOMAS PRICE'S COMPANIES OF MILITIA—LIST OF JOHN LAWRENCE, GENT'N.			Price, Thomas	13	21	Austin, Chapman	1	8	Radford, William	3	6
			Hendrich, John	7	22	Winston, William	8	14	Spradley, Agness	2	4
Thomson, Capt. John	6	11	Dalby, Mary	5	9	Timberlake, Francis	7	16	Tinsley, John	5	25
Mells, Nicholas	3	10	Dickenson, Margaret	6		Timberlake, Henry	4	13	Bowe, Sarah	5	13
Mells, Ann	2	13	Taylor, Edmund	8	12	Browning, John	6		Picket, George		11
Walton, Edward	6	10	Davis, Sarah	10	1	Browning, Sarah	5		Armstrong, Ellis	6	4
Mills, Francis	3	8	Duke, Thomas	6	8	Jones, Ben	8		Jones, Absalom	3	
Thomson, Richard	2	3	Dickinson, Ann	4	2	Shelton, Joseph	4	10	Austin, Thomas	6	44
Thomson, William	7	18	Bumpass, Nathan	5	5	Toler, William		8	Anderson, Nelson, jr	7	24
Thomson, William, jr	7	4	Sandige, Martin	5	8	Jinkins, James	8		Sydnor, Ann		
Sims, William	5	15	Mallory, Charles	9		Tylor, Frederick	7	2	Richardson, Turner		
			McNemar, Wm	2	4	Tylor, Charles	5		Austen, John	8	52
			Mallory, Liddia	8	14	Richardson, John	6	16	Welman, Ann	1	12
			Loyall, John	4		Burnley, William	8		Bell, Nathan	6	17
			Grubbs, Benjamin	5		Kendrick, Robert	6		Bell, More	5	10
			Grubbs, William	5		Kersey, Edward	6				
			Mallory, Lactitia	4		Timberlake, John	7	27			
						Glass, Thomas	4				

ISLE OF WIGHT COUNTY.

NAME OF HEAD OF FAMILY.	White.	Black.	NAME OF HEAD OF FAMILY.	White.	Black.	NAME OF HEAD OF FAMILY.	White.	Black.	NAME OF HEAD OF FAMILY.	White.	Black.
Applewhaite, Elizabeth	4	8	Bowzer, Phillip	1		Babb, Ann	10	2	Brewer, Joseph	1	
Ash, Chloe	3		Bowzer, Giles	1		Bullock, Samuel	1		Bradshaw, Richard	3	2
Applewhaite, Josiah	4	4	Best, Martha	2		Briggs, David	6		Bridger, James Allen	4	14
Ash, Sarah	7		Bunkley, Joshua	4	2	Benn, John	5	14	Beal, Dempsey	8	
Allmond, John	6	2	Barlow, James	2	8	Butler, John	6		Butler, James	3	
Allmond, William	8	2	Bennett, John	6	1	Butler, James	7		Bowden, Lemuel	4	2
Applewhaite, Arthur	4	12	Barlow, Thomas	1		Bracey, John	10		Bowden, Richard	1	1
Atkinson, Jesse	8	6	Brantley, Wilson	5		Bracey, Campion	5	2	Bagnal, William	3	
Armstrong, John	5	3	Betts, William	4		Britt, Jordan	10	2	Butler, Charles	6	2
Allen, Jesse	5	1	Betts, Elverton	3		Bowden, John	8		Bridger, Joseph	4	1
Atkinson, Simon	7		Betts, Sally	7		Bowden, Thomas	7	2	Butler, John	6	
Atkinson, Christopher	1		Braddy, Patrick	5		Bridger, Mrs. Susanna	4	10	Brantley, Joseph	8	2
Atkinson, Harwood	1		Braddy, Mason	2	6	Bridger, William	4	12	Baker, Henry	5	5
Askew, Jonathan	5		Bidgood, Ann	3		Butler, Ephraim	5		Bullock, Thomas	6	
Averitt, John	8	2	Brantley, Thomas	1		Barrott, Rauleigh	6	3	Bullock, William	2	1
Averitt, Samuel	5	8	Britt, Elizabeth	5		Butler, Stephen	7	9	Bullock, Obediah	3	
Averitt, Samuel, Junr	6	6	Blunt, Elizabeth	2	3	Boon, Ratcliff	6	6	Bullock, Joseph	5	
Askew, Thomas	10	1	Braswell, James	8		Butler, Epaphroditus	3		Beal, Benjamin, Jr	5	7
Allen, Randall	3	1	Braswell, William	1		Butler, Eleazer	7		Beal, Benjamin	9	5
Atkinson, Benjamin	4	1	Barlow, William	2	1	Bracey, William	4		Brown, John	6	
Atkinson, Owen	4	1	Baker, Lawrence, Gent	2	37	Butler, Peter	4		Bullock, Joel	6	
Addison, Wm	6		Blunt, William	6	12	Bradshaw, Benjamin	7	1	Channell, Arthur	10	2
Addison, Thomas	4		Bell, Elisha	8		Beal, Jacob	1		Cook, Sarah	3	
Brown, John	3	1	Bushy, Adam	6	1	Beal, Honour	8		Casey, Thomas	4	6
Barlow, Harwood	4		Brown, Adam	1	14	Beal, Absalom	2		Copher, Benjamin	3	
Bagnal, William	7	9	Bracey, Solomon	6		Beal, Mary	1		Copher, James	10	1
Brown, Sophia	5	3	Baldwin, John	9	3	Brewer, John	5		Copher, Jesse	7	
Bagnal, Nathan	1	2	Butler, Stephen	2	1	Ballard, Elisha Lawrence	5	10	Crocker, Samuel	4	
Bridger, William	2	1	Babb, William	1	4	Bradshaw, Jonas	6	6	Carroll, James	4	

ISLE OF WIGHT COUNTY—Continued.

NAME OF HEAD OF FAMILY.	White.	Black.	NAME OF HEAD OF FAMILY.	White.	Black.	NAME OF HEAD OF FAMILY.	White.	Black.	NAME OF HEAD OF FAMILY.	White.	Black.
Copher, Thomas	4	1	English, Thomas	5	6	Hartwell, John	1	....	Marshall, Cap. John	9	33
Crocker, Anthony	6	....	Eley, Mills	4	6	Harriss, Thomas	4	....	Marshall, Dempsey	4	10
Cole, Betty	2	....	Eley, Cap. William	7	6	Harriss, Burwell	2	....	Mountford, Wade	10	4
Chapman, William	4	....	Eley, Benjamin, Gent	6	17	Haile, John	5	1	McKintosh, Alexander	6	....
Chapman, John	8	2	Edmunds, Solomon	7	4	Herring, Daniel, Junr	2	6	McCoy, Jesse	5	7
Chapman Charles	6	....	Eley, David	8	2	Hampton, Benjamin	10	1	Moseley, Francis	4	....
Chapman, Benjamin	5	6	Easson, Mary	2	6	Hutchings, Jesse	12	....	Matthews, William	3	2
Clark, Henry	5	....	Frizzell, Joshua	3	4	Hudson, Leven	3	1	Matthews, Jesse	1	....
Clayton, Priscilla	5	1	Floyd, Francis	1	....	Hutchings, Moses	3	1	Minton, Elisha	6	....
Casey, Thomas	4	3	Frizzell, Ralph	3	4	Hatchell, Peter	2	2	Matthews, Richard	3	....
Casey, Richard	4	5	Fones, John	5	4	Hall, George	5	1	Matthews, William	6	....
Clark, James	5	1	Fones, Shelly	3	....	Herring, Jesse	1	4	Matthews, Samuel	1	....
Crocker, John	9	6	Flake, Samson	7	....	Herring, Daniel	4	21	Matthews, Joseph	1	....
Crocker, Sarah	3	11	Flake, William	4	....	Hough, James	7	1	Murphey, George	3	....
Clark, John	3	1	Foster, Ransom	7	....	Holland, James	8	3	Matthews, James	6	....
Clark, Joseph	1	....	Fulgham, Charles	6	13	Holland, Robert	6	14	Norsworthy, Katharine	3	7
Coggin, John	6	9	Fearn, Thomas	7	15	Holland, Benjamin	7	....	Norsworthy, Tristram	5	15
Cowper, Robert	5	7	Fearn, John	3	19	Holland, William	5	....	Norsworthy, Tristram	8	11
Coggin, Robert	12	1	Fulgham, Edmund	6	....	Hedgepeth, Willoughby	7	1	Norsworthy, Tristram	9	11
Coggin, John (son of Robert)	4	3	Fulgham, Mary	4	....	Holland, Aaron	3	4	Norsworthy, Michael	3	....
Carr, Nathan	11	16	Fatheree, Ebenezor	10	....	Holland, Job	6	15	Newby, Thomas	5	5
Cook, Nathan	4	....	Fletcher, Charles	7	5	Hunter, Seth	8	3	Norsworthy, John	7	9
Chalmer, David	1	10	Flemyng, Nathaniel, Gent	1	9	Hamford, Lewis & Robert Taylor	12	18	Norsworthy, Ann	3	1
Carr, Hardy	3	....	Fulgham, Jesse	5	1	Hall, James	10	2	Newman, Thomas	6	1
Carr, Abraham	6	....	Fulgham, Hezekiah	7	3	Holliday, John	3	....	Newman, John	6	....
Council, Joshua	1	....	Fulgham, Michael	5	2	Jones, David	8	3	Newell, Thomas	7	....
Council, Cutchin	7	3	Fulgham, Rebecca	3	....	Jones, Benjamin	9	....	Outland, Marina	4	7
Council, Miles	1	2	Fowler, James	7	....	Jones, Jacob	5	....	Outland, Jeremiah	7	3
Council, Joshua	5	11	Fowler, Samuel	5	....	Jones, Solomon	6	....	Outland, Thomas	2	7
Carr, Andrew	4	....	Fowler, Joseph	6	....	James, Abel	4	6	Owen, John	8	....
Carr, William	6	....	Fowler, Thomas	9	....	Jones, Abraham	2	2	Parker, Nicholas	6	12
Carr, John	5	....	Fowler, Molly	2	....	Jones, Sally	5	1	Pitt, Willis	7	7
Council, James	5	....	Fowler, Arthur	7	....	Jones, Thomas	7	....	Pitt, Henry	3	9
Corbett, Samuel	9	....	Godwin, Brewer, Gent	9	29	Jones, Willis	3	....	Parker, Elias	5	....
Council, John	1	....	Godwin, Edmund	6	12	Jones, William, Sen	3	....	Pitts, Tamer	8	....
Council, Robert	1	....	Goodwin, Margaret	4	4	Jones, Unity	6	....	Pitt, James	3	....
Carr, John	8	....	Godwin, Joseph	6	5	Jordan, William	1	26	Parker, Thomas	8	31
Collins, James	4	....	Gibbs, Ralph	9	15	Jordan, Joseph	3	20	Pyland, James	3	8
Clayton, William	3	....	Gray, Ann	6	....	Johnston, Doctr Robert	4	17	Pittman, John	7	1
Cowlding, Thomas	8	12	Groce, Isham	2	1	Johnson, Samuel	4	1	Pinhorn, John	2	1
Daniel, Giles	7	6	Godwin, Martha	4	4	Jackson, William	5	....	Pittman, Benjamin	9	....
Driver, Rebecca	3	2	Girton, William	4	7	Jordan, Josiah	10	23	Parnall, Joseph	4	....
Devenport, William	4	3	Goodson, Thomas	7	6	Johnson, Capt James	8	5	Pittman, Joseph	4	1
Dering, James	5	16	Glover, Jesse	7	5	Johnson, Robert, Sen	2	4	Pleasant, William	2	....
Dunn, William	4	2	Glover, Robert	2	....	Johnson, Elijah	7	2	Pittman, John	4	....
Dews, Edward	5	3	Gibbs, Gabriel	9	10	Johnson, Joseph	6	1	Pittman, James	5	2
Delk, Moreland	4	7	Gray, John	6	....	Johnson, Obediah	9	....	Parnall, John	4	....
Deloach, Michael	2	....	Gray, William	3	....	Johnson, Willis	1	....	Powell, John	6	5
Deford, John	7	....	Gray, Sarah	4	....	Johnson, Thomas	9	1	Purdie, George, Gent	6	33
Davis, John	8	1	Gay, William	5	....	Johnson, Samuel	2	....	Powell, Godfrey	4	....
Davis, Robert	1	....	Gwaltney, Patrick	8	1	Johnson, Abraham	8	....	Peirce, Bennitt	3	....
Davis, Isham	6	2	Gwaltney, James	5	4	Johnson, Henry	6	12	Powell, Nathan	7	....
Davis, John	4	3	Gwaltney, Sarah	5	3	Johnson, Nathan	6	....	Peirce, Peter	6	....
Davis, James	2	3	Goodrich, Sarah	3	....	Johnson, Eley	7	2	Pope, Richard	5	5
Dardon, Jacob	5	6	Goodson, William	5	2	Johnson, Aaron	7	....	Pope, John	6	5
Deford, John	12	4	Green, James	1	....	Johnson, Henry, jun	7	....	Parkinson, John	7	....
Dunston, Thomas	5	....	Goodson, Thomas	6	1	Johnson, William	7	....	Ponsonby, William	9	....
Denson, John	4	2	Gale, Thomas	4	....	Johnson, Samuel	2	....	Pretlow, John	4	6
Deford, James	6	1	Garner, John	1	....	Johnson, Lazarus	7	7	Powell, Jethro	3	1
Daniel, Joshua	1	....	Goodrich, Joseph	6	....	Johnson, Robert, junr	6	1	Peirce, William, Jun	8	1
Dardon, Hardy	3	10	Gale, John	5	3	Johnson, Michael	8	14	Peirce, William	4	4
Duck, John	9	....	Gale, Jethro	8	8	Inglish, William	3	....	Powell, Joshua	10	....
Dardon, Willis	1	7	Gale, Thomas	4	4	Joyner, Thomas	6	8	Powell, Thomas	9	1
Doughlass, Jesse	6	....	Gale, Thomas W	2	3	Joyner, John	4	9	Powell, Mary	4	....
Duck, William	7	....	Gay, John	6	....	Jordan, William	3	9	Powell, Benjamin	8	....
Dardon, John, jun	3	3	Gay, John	1	....	Jordan, John	3	1	Powell, Arnold	2	....
Dardon, Cap. John	4	11	Gay, Joshua	3	5	Jolliff, John	6	....	Powell, Joseph	3	....
Duck, Robert	9	....	Gay, William (Son of Ann)	5	1	Jolliff, Ann	6	....	Pope, Joseph	6	....
Duck, Jacob	2	6	Gay, William	9	....	Jordan, Richard	6	4	Powell, William	6	....
Dardon, Benjamin	1	....	Gay, William, Junr	9	....	Jordan, Edward	5	....	Parker, William	3	1
Daughtry, Matthew	5	....	Gwynne, William	5	....	Jordan, James	4	3	Parker, William, Jun	5	....
Daughtry, Joshua	4	4	Griffin, Lott	3	....	Jordan, Patience	1	4	Pope, Ephraim	8	1
Daughtry, Theophilus	5	....	Gordon, Stephen	3	1	King, Martha	3	11	Philips, John	11	....
Dardon, John	1	8	Garner, Jesse	7	....	Lawrance, Joseph	7	11	Pope, John	8	....
Dardon, Sarah	3	....	Garner, John	5	....	Lawrance, Mary	8	....	Pope, Mary	4	....
Daughtry, John	5	10	Godfrey, Lemuel	9	11	Laylor, Luke	7	....	Parnal, Henry	8	2
Daughtry, Thomas	3	1	Goodson, George	7	7	Lancaster, Henry	7	....	Pitt, Thomas	7	1
Daughtry, Moses	4	....	Goodson, John	4	1	Little, John	3	2	Parr, William	8	3
Davis, Edward	6	2	Goodson, James	5	....	Little, Ann	4	1	Pinner, John	9	5
Daniel, John	4	4	Hawkins, Benjamin	7	1	Lawrance, Colo John	8	17	Peirce, Thomas	3	22
Davis, Thomas	3	4	Holliday, Samuel, Junr	4	2	Lankford, Jesse	2	8	Pruden, Nathaniel	1	....
Driver, Charles	11	16	Holliday, Samuel	4	2	Lawrance, Hardy	8	11	Pruden, Flora	3	....
Dick, David	5	8	Holliday, Josiah	6	....	Lawrance, Cap. Mills	2	12	Powell, Mary	4	4
Dixon, John R	7	3	Hawkins, John	5	1	Lightfoot, Lemuel	4	6	Quay, Samuel	4	....
Dickson, Thomas	12	4	Hunt, Dempsey	6	4	Murry, Thomas	5	....	Randolph, Jacob	6	8
Driver, Robert	11	18	Holliday, Mary	5	5	Morgan, Samuel	5	....	Roberts, John	7	12
Dixon, John	2	1	Hawkins, Samuel	1	....	Mallicote, George	6	4	Roberts, John, Jun	6	1
Durley, Mary	9	16	Holliday, Hezekiah	4	6	Mangam, Josiah	5	....	Roberts, William	7	....
Edward, Shelton	1	3	Hardy, Richard, Junr	4	8	Mackie, Andrew	11	26	Robertson, Arculus	4	....
Edward, Richard	6	3	Heath, William	8	3	Mangam, Henry	7	2	Robertson, Jonathan	7	1
Ellis, Joseph	8	....	Haynes, William	3	22	Mintz, John	3	....	Reynolds, Sharp	5	14
Edward, James	5	....	Harrison, Peggy	3	1	Muntford, John	6	....	Robertson, George	4	25
Edward, Benjamin	6	....	Harmonson, John	....	5	Mangam, Micajah	8	....	Royall, Thomas	5	....
Edward, Britain	6	....	Harriss, Matthew	4	....	Mintz, Thomas	5	....	Smelly, James	6	2
Edward, William	4	....	Hazzard, Thomas	6	....	Maddery, Joseph	6	....	Shelly, John	5	1
Edward, Elias	2	....	Hicks, Charles	5	....	Maddery, James	4	....	Shelly, Mary	3	....
Edward, John	7	....	Hicks, Benjamin	6	....	Matthew, Richard	2	....	Stringfield, John	7	....
Edward, Robert	7	....	Hicks, Lemuel	3	....	Morrison, William	11	5	Shelly, Lucy	10	3
Eley, Sarah	2	5	Holliman, Jesse	9	....	Moody, Phillip	8	13	Savage, Thomas	1	....
English, Mary	4	....	Holliman, Christopher	2	....	Moody, Isaac	11	6	Stringfield, Benjamin	8	....
English, Thomas (Mill dam)	4	....	Hunter, Emanuel	9	4	Murphy, William	7	....	Stringfield, John	3	....
Eley, Robert	9	7	Harriss, William	1	3	Murphy, John	4	1	Stallings, John	5	7
Eley, Gale	3	15	Harvey, Barnitt	2	1	Murphey, John, Junr	3	3	Smith, Susanna	4	....
English, Patience	7	....	Harriss, John	8	3	Matthews, Benjamin	2	....	Smith, Thomas	5	....
			Hail, Thomas	3	....	Morriss, Conyous	11	11			

ISLE OF WIGHT COUNTY—Continued.

NAME OF HEAD OF FAMILY.	White.	Black.
Stevens, John	1	
Stagg, Josiah	3	
Simmons, Samuel	3	11
Stevens, Jacob	5	
Stagg, Sarah	2	
Segar, Mildred	3	
Sykes, Andrew	6	3
Sykes, John	5	3
Saunders, Henry	4	13
Spencer, Ezekiel	6	
Smelly, William	5	3
Smelly, Thomas	7	5
Saunders, Joseph	4	
Saunders, Thomas	5	9
Saunders, Robert	4	6
Saunders, Henry	10	
Saunders, John	2	1
Saunders, Lieutenant Henry	4	11
Scott, William	5	16
Strickland, Thomas	5	
Smith, Virgis	10	
Stevens, William	7	
Stevens, Edmund	6	1
Stevens, John	7	1
Sykes, Mary	3	5
Spivey, Joseph	3	1
Stevens, John, jun	7	
Stevens, Nathan	4	
Spivey, Jacob, Jun	4	
Spivey, John	3	
Spivey, Jacob	4	
Smelly, Moses	3	
Smith, Thomas	8	28
Smith, Nicholas	3	
Stevenson, Walter	3	2
Sinclair, John	9	32
Shivers, William	9	10
Shivers, Joseph	2	1
Tynes, Timothy	1	15
Taylor, Mary	4	1
Turner, John	7	
Turner, John	4	1
Turner, George	5	
Turner, Lewis	5	
Thomas, John	7	12
Tynes, Benjamin	4	8
Turner, William	4	
Turner, William, jun	4	
Turner, William, Sen	7	
Turner, Pass	5	
Turner, Joshua	10	3
Turner, Kinchin	6	
Turner, Martha	6	
Tomlin, Matthew	4	
Turner, Joseph	9	
Turner, Henry	7	
Turner, William	8	
Tallough, Robert	5	
Tallough, Absalom	5	
Tallough, William	1	3
Tallough, William, jun	2	
Taylor, John	3	7
Todd, Mallory	6	12
Tait, James	2	
Toler, John	5	1
Toler, James	5	
Toler, Jesse	5	
Vellines, Armistead	5	3
Vellines, Twaites	4	8
Vellines, Nathaniel	1	
Vaughan, Francis	3	2
Vaughan, Uriah	4	4
Vaughan, Thomas	4	
Vaughan, Timothy	4	1
Underwood, Sampson	7	
Underwood, Theophilus	6	2
Uzzell, James	5	2
Uzzell, Thomas	9	4
Uzzell, Mary	2	
Waile, Josiah	5	5
Williams, John	4	4
Williams, Sarah	6	1
Williams, Richard	6	14
Williams, David	5	
West, Ralph	6	16
Wheadon, John Jenings	6	34
Wilson, Josiah	10	16
Ward, William	1	
Ward, Benjamin	6	1
Wilson, Samuel	2	20
Wilson, Goodrich, Gent	8	18
Wall, Robert	1	
Wrenn, Richard	1	2
Wombwell, Joseph	3	1
Wombwell, John	9	
Wombwell, Matthew	7	
Wombwell, Thomas	2	
Ward, Britain	7	
Ward, Ann	3	
Wombwell, Henry	7	
Wrenn, Josiah	6	8
Whitley, William	8	
Whitley, John	5	
Wombwell, Josiah	3	

NAME OF HEAD OF FAMILY.	White.	Black.
Westray, Sarah	3	
Wombwell, Thomas	3	
Wombwell, William	7	
Wooton, William	5	3
Wooton, John	1	
Wooton, Thomas	1	
Wombwell, Thomas	6	
Wrenn, Richard	1	2
West, Silvia	3	
Whitley, Elisha	6	
Whitley, Nathan	6	
Williams, John	4	
Westray, Edmund	8	
Westray, Joseph	6	
Westray, Lucy	7	1
Woodward, William	6	3
Woodhouse, Charles	5	1
Wright, Henry	1	1
Wills, Thomas	8	5
West, Randolph	4	
Watkins, William	4	20
Watkins, Robert	2	5
Watkins, Priscilla	7	10
Watkins, John	10	4
Westray, Robert	7	
Walkinson, Peter	1	
Watson, Michael	2	1
Whitfield, William	10	10
Wills, Josiah	7	9
Webb, Samuel	6	9
Wills, Miles	4	8
Wills, James	6	15
Wills, John Sek, Gent	12	42
Wills, Mary	4	6
Whitfield, Abraham	2	1
Wills, Miles	7	18
Wills, Miles, Jun	2	11
Wills, Emanuel	6	10
Wrench, John	8	2
Younger, George	5	
Young, Francis	13	9

LIST OF WILLIAM HODSDEN, GENT.

White males.

NAME OF HEAD OF FAMILY.	White.	Black.
Applewhaite, Henry		
Barlow, Benjamin		
Barlow, James		
Barlow, John		
Brantley, Willis		
Brantley, Thomas		
Brantley, Thomas, Jun		
Brantley, Valintine		
Brantley, Francis		
Brantley, James		
Brantley, Willis		
Bidgood, Jesse		
Bidgood, William		
Bidgood, William, Jun		
Bidgood, James		
Bidgood, John		
Barlow, Nathaniel		
Casey, William		
Casey, James		
Casey, John		
Carroll, William		
Carroll, William, jr		
Carroll, Samuel		
Carroll, Thomas		
Chapman, Lewis		
Davis, William		
Davis, John		
Day, James Bennett		
Dews, Dolphin		
Davis, William		
Davis, Josiah		
Davis, James		
Davis, William		
Barlow, George		
Barlow, Elisha		
Barlow, Harwood		
Barlow, Cary		
Bidgood, Samuel		
Hodges, John		
Hodges, Henry		
Harvey, Wm Mallory		
Harrison, Benjamin		
Harrison, Nathaniel		
Harrison, Benjamin, jun		
Hodsden, William		
Hodsden, William, jun		
Hodsden, Joseph		
Jenkins, William		
Goodrich, John		
Hatton, Robert		
Hatton, Robert, jr		
Lupo, James		
Lupo, Laban		
Lupo, Philip		
Brantley, Carey		
Mallory, John		
Mallory, William		

LIST OF WILLIAM HODSDEN, GENT.—continued.

White males—Continued.

NAME OF HEAD OF FAMILY.	White.	Black.
Brown, John		
Day, John		
Nelson, Thomas		
Pasture, John		
Pasture, Charles		
Pasture, Charles, Junr		
Wilson, Willis		
Wilson, John		
Bidgood, Micajah		
Lupo, James, Jun		
Lupo, Zachariah		
Whitfield, Thomas		
Whitfield, Wilson		
Miller, James, Miller, John		
Miller, Wm, Miller, Robert		
Whitfield, Mattw, Wrenn, John		
Wrenn, John, jr., Wrenn, James		
Wrenn, Joseph, Williams, Walter		

White females.

NAME	White.	Black.
Applewhaite, Sarah		
Applewhaite, Martha		
Applewhaite, Sally		
Barlow, Isabell		
Barlow, Martha		
Brantley, Mary		
Brantley, Frances		
Patterson, Betsey		
Bidgood, Jane		
Bidgood, Sally		
Barlow, Constant		
Barlow, Jenny		
Casey, Celia		
Casey, Celia, junr		
Carroll, Mary		
Carroll, Molly		
Carroll, Patience		
Davis, Sally		
Davis, Mary		
Davis, Holland		
Bridger, Hester		
Fones, Priscilla		
Dews, Elizabeth		
Dews, Sarah		
Davis, Celia		
Barlow, Elizabeth		
Barlow, Lucy		
Hodges, Mary		
Hodges, Ann		
Hodges, Rebecca		
Hodges, Comfort		
Hodges, Betsey		
Harvey, Keziah		
Harrison, Mary		
Hodsden, Mary		
Hodsden, Mary		
Hodsden, Sarah		
Goodrich, Mary		
Hatton, Keziah		
Nelson, Sophia		
Nelson, Elizabeth		
Lupo, Mary		
Lupo, Mary, Junr		
Lupo, Milly		
Gray, Betsey		
Mallory, Mary		
Brown, Frances		
Berryman, Elizabeth		
Nelson, Sophia		
Nelson, Elizabeth		
Pasture, Honour		
Pasture, Molly		
Cutchin, Mary		
Smith, Ann		
Lupo, Ann		
Whitfield, Catey		
Whitfield, Mary		
Whitfield, Frances		
Whitfield, Molly		
Wrenn, Tabitha		
Wrenn, Martha		
Bidgood, Martha		
Williams, Elizabeth		

Black males.

Name	White.	Black.
Cuffy		
Ben		
Ben		
Davey		
Abraham		
Jacob		
London		
Manuel		
Tim		
Aaron		

LIST OF WILLIAM HODSDEN, GENT.—continued.

Black males—Continued.

Name	White.	Black.
Bob		
Sam		
Peter		
James		
Dick		
Dick		
Andrew		
George		
Davie		
Sam		
Bob		
Barton		
Ben		
Cornish		
Toby		
Abraham		
Sharper		
Pompy		
Sussex		
Mial		
Jacob		
Will		
Joe		
Isaac		
Mial		
John		
Peter		
Toby		
Sam		
Tom		
Peter		
Kitt		
Tim		
Aberdeen		
Stephen		
Tom		
Lewis		
York		
Dick		
Peter		
Abraham		
Joe		
Dick		
Pompy		
Battis		
Tom		
Mountain		
Liberty		
Moses		
Joshua		
Charles		
Bob		
Pompy		
Joseph		
Sam		
Jim		
Mial		
Bob		
Charles		
Tom		
Bob		
Prince		
Ned		
Peter		
Ben		
Fredrick		
Jem		
Poladore		
Cyrus		
Donpedro		
Davie		
Tom		
Aaron		
Bob		
Sam		
Jack		
Portroyal		
Mingo		
Will		
Isle of Wight		
Abraham		
Jack		
Tom		
Peter		
Frank		
Bob		
Davie		
Jacob		
Charles		
York		
Davie		
Sam		
Marlow		
Peter		
Joe		
Poladore		
Jacob		
Will		
Daniel		
Godfrey		

FIRST CENSUS OF THE UNITED STATES.

ISLE OF WIGHT COUNTY—Continued.

NAME OF HEAD OF FAMILY.	White.	Black.	NAME OF HEAD OF FAMILY.	White.	Black.	NAME OF HEAD OF FAMILY.	White.	Black.	NAME OF HEAD OF FAMILY.	White.	Black.
LIST OF WILLIAM HODSDEN, GENT.—continued.			LIST OF WILLIAM HODSDEN, GENT.—continued.			LIST OF WILLIAM HODSDEN, GENT.—continued.			LIST OF WILLIAM HODSDEN, GENT.—continued.		
Black males—Continued.			*Black females*—Continued.			*Black females*—Continued.			*Black females*—Continued.		
Daniel			Jane			Siller			Bett		....
Davie			Aggy			Mary			Nan		....
Dennis			Lucy			Rachel			Sall		....
Bob			Moll			Bett			Tinah		....
Frank			Pegg			Pegg			Dinah		....
Jack			Pheby			Nan			Bett		....
Davie			Bett			Siller			Nell		....
George			Nanny			Cate			Rachell		....
Sam			Flora			Silvia			Charlotte		....
Davie			Patience			Rose					
Barton			Sall			Bek			LIST OF JAMES PEDEN, GENT.		
Bob			Milly			Sarah					
Ben			Zenith			Hannah			Godwin, Shamuel	8	8
Sam			Hannah			Tilly			Powell, Godfrey	6	2
Peter			Pegg			Nelly			Jordan, Billingsley	5	4
Sam			Comfort			Clemantine			Smelly, Mary	5	9
Peter			Rose			Rachel			Godwin, Jeremiah (Nansem^d)	....	17
James			Molly			Jude			Stuckey, Edmund	5	1
Phill			Patience			Pegg			Godwin, John	7	15
Bob			Philis			Moll			Hall, Thomas	8	4
Cain			Fanny			Judy			Maneyard, Joseph	1	....
John			Patience			Pink			Cuthchin, Josiah	1	7
Charles			Conny			Christian			Dardon, John	8	2
			Courtney			Philis			Smelly, Giles	4	6
Black females.			Abigail			Judy			Green, William	5	2
			Molly			Sarah			Daniel, John	4	....
Nan			Philis			Pegg			House, John	7	....
Tamer			Jenny			Jenny			Godwin, Jonathan	3	18
Eady			Hannah			Patt			Wail, John	4	3
Dinah			Philis			Rose			Grow, Charles	3	5
Aggy			Milly			Nan			Dickinson, Mary	4	2
Hannah			Sue			Molly			Dardon, John	6	9
Treasie			Patience			Eady			Godwin, Samuel, Sen.	3	8
Dinah			Sarah			Dice			Godwin, Samuel, Jun.	4	5
Annie			Bess			Philis			Pitt, Joseph	8	16
Pegg			Dido			Sibb			Whitfield, Copeland	6	4
Hannah			Maggy			Pinky			Whitfield, Samuel	7	9
Ply			Bett			Nan			Bowzer, James	1	....
Nancey			Milly			Nan			Whitfield, John	7	3
Patience			Dinah			Jane			Wilkinson, Mills	6	28
Rachel			Nan			Aggy			Cutchin, Priscilla	7	19
Keziah			Pink			Conney			Peden, James	9	19
Patt			Viney			Lucy			King, Thomas	3	26
Pink			Bett			Manzey			Reynolds, Rowland	8	7
Hannah		....	Sall			Mercer					
Nancey			Hester			Nan					

MECKLENBURG COUNTY.

NAME OF HEAD OF FAMILY.	White.	Black.	NAME OF HEAD OF FAMILY.	White.	Black.	NAME OF HEAD OF FAMILY.	White.	Black.	NAME OF HEAD OF FAMILY.	White.	Black.
LIST OF CLUVERIUS COLEMAN.			LIST OF CLUVERIUS COLEMAN—continued.			LIST OF CLUVERIUS COLEMAN—continued.			LIST OF CLUVERIUS COLEMAN—continued.		
Allen, John	7	....	Crowder, Elizabeth	6	....	Clark, James	5	6	Smith, Augustin	10	2
Adams, Thomas	5	....	Crowder, Robert	9	....	Lipford, John	9	....	Simmons, Samuel	11	29
Arnold, John	4	5	Crook, John	6	1	Lett, Joseph	7	2	Salley, Isaac	15	9
Allgood, Moses	7	1	Crook, James	8	5	Matthews, Laban	3	....	Smith, Jeremiah	8	1
Andrews, Varn	3	1	Daley, Josiah	8	8	Matthews, Enos	2	....	Smith, William	2	8
Andrews, John	5	1	Dardin, David	5	1	Moore, Joel	8	....	Smith, John	6	8
Allen, William	11	7	Day, James	5	....	Minor, William	3	....	Ship, Thomas	8	12
Andrews, Ephraim	5	15	Ezell, John	5	....	Mallett, Stephen	4	2	Stuart, Martha	7	....
Allen. Robert	8	....	Ezell, Mich¹	9	....	McDaniel, Edward	4	4	Tucker, Daniel	19	....
Adams, John	2	....	Edmundson, Richard	7	2	McDaniel, John	1	....	Thompson, John	9	3
Allen, William, jr	3	6	Farrar, John	10	12	McDaniel, Drury	9	6	Tisdale, Edward	7	....
Allen, Turner	7	3	Greer, Catherine	9	....	Thomason, George	7	....	Tisdale, Cuthbert	3	....
Arnold, Elisha	3	3	Gregory, Richard	9	16	McDaniel, John	11	....	Turner, James	12	....
Arnold, Mary	8	....	Gregory, Roger	6	35	Mason, John	3	....	Taylor, Mary	3	....
Burnett, John	5	4	Goode, Edward	6	16	Moore, William	8	....	Talley, Jean	6	....
Bing, John	4	....	Goode, Thomas	4	2	Moore, Gideon	6	....	Thompson, Richard	8	2
Bacon, George	9	....	Goode, Richard	3	5	Mason, William	5	1	Turner, Matthew	5	5
Burnett, Nath'l	7	3	Hutchison, Richard	9	10	Mason, Jean	7	1	Tucker, Abram	7	....
Bevers, Zach	4	1	Hutchison, Elizabeth	11	10	Marey, Thomas	7	....	Traylor, Mary	5	....
Burnett, James	5	3	Hutchison, Charles	11	19	Merrymoone, Stephen	2	....	Vaughan, Reuben	10	12
Brooks, David	4	2	Hightower, Thomas	6	6	Mitchel, Abram	4	5	Willson, John	3	3
Burnett, Elizabeth	11	8	Hastey, James	7	....	Mitchel, Thomas	....	2	Walker, Tandy	9	7
Brown, James	8	1	Hazlewood, Daniel	10	6	Merrymoone, Archer	2	....	Waller, Edward	4	5
Brown, Thomas	9	5	Huson, Edward	5	30	Matthews, Nehemiah	5	....	Walker, Silvanus	4	10
Burnett, Godfrey	3	....	Hudson, William	10	....	Massay, Thomas	7	....	Whitemore, John	7	....
Beasley, William	5	....	Harper, John	6	11	Nowel, William	6	10	Whitemore, Buckner	9	4
Brown, Henry	4	1	Hightower, William	8	1	Ogburn, John	5	6	Willson, James	8	1
Brown, Mordecai	9	3	Harrish, John	8	1	Ormby, Matthew	4	....	Walker, Willam	4	3
Brown, Aries	3	....	Insco, William	3	....	Powers, Sampson	6	3	Young, John	6	1
Bradley, John	5	3	Insco, James	9	....	Powers, William	7	....			
Cardin, John, jr	5	....	Ingram, Pines	8	8	Powers, Joseph	8	....	LIST OF WM. RANDOLPH.		
Crowder, George	9	4	Johnson, James	6	1	Parish, Peter	3	....			
Cardin, Leonard	5	1	Johnson, Philip	10	....	Parish, Wm	3	....	Randolph, William	8	48
Cardin, John	8	....	Johnson, John	5	1	Phillips, John	7	....	Wooten, Samuel	5	6
Crutchfield, William	8	....	Johnson, Ellis	6	....	Pennington, John	9	7	Jones, Tegnal, Sen	6	40
Curtis, Churchwell	9	1	Johnson, Randolph	4	....	Pennington, William	4	3	Anderson, James	3	13
Croxton, Thomas	7	1	Johnson, Howel	1	....	Page, Lewis	5	....	Rising, Richard	6	....
Crowder, Batt	6	9	Johnson, Zach	2	....	Pennington, Howell	4	9	Thompson, James	2	....
Colley, Edward	16	....	Johnson, James, jr	4	....	Pistole, Charles	8	2	Willis, Sherwood	5	....
Crowder, John	9	2	Johnson, Pleasant	5	....	Ricks, Philip	7	10	Anderson, Sarah	3	28
Crowder, David	7	....	Johnson, Isaac	5	4	Ryland, Thomas	11	11	Hawkins, Matthew	1	9
Crowder, Jeremiah	7	....	Jones, Tabitha	3	....	Russell, Jeffry	7	2	Walton, Edward	6	12
Credle, Hannah	5	....	Kirkland, Richard	6	....	Russell, John	7	....	Hughes, James	9	7
Cooper, William	5	5	Keeton, Joseph	9	....	Roffe, William	8	4	Edmundson, Samuel	8	4
Coleman, Cluverius	10	16	Cook, William	3	....	Roach, Joseph	3	7	Sparrow, James B	8	....

MECKLENBURG COUNTY—Continued.

NAME OF HEAD OF FAMILY.	White.	Black.	NAME OF HEAD OF FAMILY.	White.	Black.	NAME OF HEAD OF FAMILY.	White.	Black.	NAME OF HEAD OF FAMILY.	White.	Black.
LIST OF WM. RANDOLPH—continued.			**LIST OF JESSE SANDERS**—continued.			**LIST OF JESSE SANDERS**—continued.			**LIST OF LEWIS PARHAM**—continued.		
Hutchison, Peter	3	7	Hunley, William	7	6	Yancey, Thomas	8	6	Clench, Jeremiah	6	....
Swepson, Richard, jr	4	8	Harris, Matthew	11	....	Yancey, Robert	15	3	Kitchen, John	3	....
Daniel, William	3	4	Hendrick, William	12	....	Yancey, Zachariah	3	....	Sage, John	7	....
McLin, James	2	11	Hailey, Thomas	7	8	Yancey, Richard	5	2	Talley, David	12	....
Allen, William	8	....	Hamlin, Thomas	11	1	Bugg, Jacob	3	18	Munford, Robert	5	91
Easter, John	10	1	Hardy, John	5	....				Hester, James	9	10
Hatsell, Lewis	8	....	Hailey, Richard	9	....	**LIST OF LEWIS PARHAM.**			Hubbard, John	5	12
Toone, James	9	....	Jones, James	8	5				Jones, Richard	8	21
Boyd, Alexander	11	21	Jones, Richard	7	7	Malone, Isham	14	9	Hyde, John, Senr	6	14
Jones, Tignal, jr	6	24	Jones, Capt. Thomas	7	5	Roberts, William	8	....	Overton, Moses	8	3
Talley, Hardaway	2	....	Jones, Robert	8	9	Malone, Jones	3	5	Hyde, Robert	3	4
Cradock, Edmund	8	4	Jones, John	9	....	Malone, Drury, Secd	1	15	Fanning, Laughlin	9	....
Hunt, William	6	3	Johnson, James	2	....	Nanney, William	7	....	Dodson, Edward	8	11
Decker, William	8	....	Johnson, George	6	....	Roberts, Ann	6	....	Allgood, John, Junr	8	....
Coleman, Richard	7	7	Kelley, William	11	....	Morgan, Betty	3	....	Jones, Peter	....	31
Stone, Benjamin	6	4	Davis, Lewis	5	....	Cleaton, John	8	8	Holloway, Edward	7	....
Hutt, Daniel	9	1	Lewis, Jane	1	....	Burton, James	8	....	Davis, William	3	....
Decker, John	6	....	Moore, Field	4	2	Wright, Austin	8	8	Hester, Ann	7	8
Young, Allen	4	18	Moore, George	4	2	Hatsel, John	5	1	Lewis, John	2	1
Davis, John	7	23	Mayes, John	6	6	Muscheon, Jesse	5	....	Oliver, John	11	19
Caltharp, John	7	3	Murray, Richard	3	....	Ellis, Stephen	10	....	Pritchett, Thomas	5	....
Decker, Joseph	6	....	Maynard, Nicholas	11	25	McKenney, Munford	1	....	Adams, James	6	....
Wilkins, John	8	....	Mealer, Philip	7	3	Jones, Richard	2	....	Royal, Sarah	2	1
Thomas, Daniel	4	4	Munro, John	4	2	Bartlett, Thomas	1	....	Greenwood, Thomas	12	16
Puryear, Sam'l, Senr	5	9	Matthews, Bartlett	4	....	Lambert, John	4	9	Jones, Benjamin	10	....
Thomas, Hannah	4	....	McLachlin, Nathaniel	3	1	Lambert, John, Jr	1	....	Finch, William	5	4
Clark, Edwd	4	....	Neal, William	13	21	Floyd, Charles	10	15	Robertson, John	4	....
Hayes, Elizabeth	5	5	Newton, Henry	4	....	Crook, Frederick	7	5	Allgood, William	6	....
Hayes, Wenkfield	5	....	Newton, Robert	4	....	Rottenberry, Ann	4	....	Allgood, John	6	....
Hester, Barbary	5	17	Nunn, Carleton	8	....	Worsham, Ludwell	6	24	Allgood, Manley	2	....
Drew, Ephraim	4	2	Newton, George	11	....	Hudson, William	6	....	Royal, John, Junr	3	....
Stuart, Francis	2	....	Newton, Henry	2	....	Jones, William	7	6	Allgood, Ishmael	7	....
Puryear, Seymour	7	7	Overbee, Drury	5	....	Jones, John	1	....	Robertson, John, jr	9	....
Draper, Joshua	10	1	Overbee, Zach	8	....	King, William	3	....	Thompson, John	7	7
Royster, Joseph	11	22	Overbee, Alexander	4	....	King, James	4	2	Blake, Robert	6	....
Taylor, William	5	25	Owen, William	6	....	Thomas, Peter	8	8	Wagstaff, Britain	4	3
Carroll, Ellis	10	....	Overbee, Peter	12	14	Williams, Lewis	5	1	Moss, Joshua	8	5
			Overbee, Nicholas	5	4	Lambert, Joseph	7	1	Blackburne, Thomas	5	10
LIST OF JESSE SANDERS.			Pulliam, James	12	1	Lambert, Jervis	8	....	Coleman, James	1	5
			Purkins, David	6	....	Ellis, Abigal	10	....	Finch, Edward	7	8
Apperson, Davis	8	4	Pace, Josiah	2	....	Hargrove, James	7	....	Burrus, Wm I	5	8
Akin, Thomas	17	2	Pettey, George	10	....	Parham, Lewis	9	14	Call, William	....	29
Akin, John	3	....	Parish, James	7	....	Worthen, Anne	3	....	Millender, William	7	1
Allen, William	5	2	Pitchford, Daniel	3	....	Hix, Robert	6	....	Chamberlaine, Thomas	10	7
Baynes, John	11	1	Parish, John	10	1	Jones, Carrel	1	....	Butler, Zachariah	9	....
Butler, John	4	....	Phillips, Thomas	6	....	Muscheon, Thomas	2	....	Royal, John	7	....
Butler, John	7	2	Pinson, Thomas	7	6	Cleaton, Poythress	7	1	Moore, Jeremiah	1	....
Boyd, Thomas	3	4	Royster, William	6	11	Muscheon, John	3	....	Butler, James	4	....
Boswell, John	4	....	Royster, John	6	1	Edwards, Nathaniel	5	....	Hanson, Job	9	1
Butright, Sarah	2	....	Royster, Jacob	9	8	Brooks, Robert	7	17	Jether, Nicholas	6	....
Cockerham, Lettice	4	1	Ransey, Guilbert	7	....	Evans, Archer	2	7	Kendrick, William	3	....
Clark, Archibald	11	1	Royster, David	5	3	Bass, Dennis	3	....	Puryear, John	10	8
Christopher, Ambrose	7	....	Randolph, Joseph	4	....	Wilkerson, William	8	....	Lewis, Francis	1	2
Chandler, David	4	1	Stovall, George	6	2	Yeargan, Sebrant	4	....	Puryear, Samuel	1	2
Chandler, David, jr	3	....	Stone, Hezekiah	5	....	Cradle, John	6	....	Puryear, Sarah	2	7
Carter, Alexander	9	2	Stone, Stephen	7	1	Starling, William	7	24	Lewis, Edward	10	15
Crafford, Peter	2	....	Shotwell, John	12	2	Archer, William	8	....	Armisted, John	3	12
Cockerham, John	7	....	Stone, Eucibius	4	....	Brooks, William	6	2	Reamey, James	6	1
Culbreath, William	3	15	Sizemour, John	4	....	Patello, Austin	5	8	Crews, John	2	....
Chandler, John	8	....	Sanderlain, James	2	....	Douglass, Senior	6	....	Rudd, Elijah	1	3
Carter, Joseph	6	22	Stone, Nancey	3	....	Smith, John	7	8	Crowder, Darcas	8	2
Culbreath, Priscilla	6	....	Southern, William	10	....	Muscheon, John, Jr	3	....	Hudson, William	4	5
Clark, John	4	8	Moore, Thomas	6	5	Coppage, Charles	9	7	Hopkins, Benjamin	7	....
Clark, John, Jr	7	....	Stroud, William	3	2	Douglass, John	4	1	Cox, Thomas	8	1
Cockerham, Matthew	1	....	Stone, John	6	1	Booth, Thomas	11	25	Stuart, William	6	2
Caveness, Henry	9	....	Sanders, Jesse	11	4	Hudson, Ephraim	5	....	Hood, Robert	8	....
Culbreath, Mary	5	....	Tarry, George	3	39	Hudson, Robert	4	1	Winn, Richard	3	3
Culbreath, Joseph	6	....	Twisdale, James	9	....	Petillo, Solomon	6	2	Waggstaff, Basel	2	10
Culbreath, John	3	....	Tureman, Martin	10	2	Epps, Edward	6	13	Clark, Bolling	7	....
Culbreath, Thomas	7	2	Thompson, Steth	8	6	Suggett, Edgcomb	4	12	Hudson, Stephen	6	....
Chandler, Joel	5	13	Tilletson, Thomas	11	....	Holmes, John	3	2	Hudson, Cuthbert	1	....
Culbreath, Daniel	2	....	Talley, Frederick	7	....	Brown, John	7	11	Avory, Henry	10	2
Cockerham, Henry	4	....	Tureman, Thomas	8	1	Mitchel, Reuben	1	....	Chavous, Anthony	3	....
Cockerham, Benj	3	....	Vaughan, Peter	7	....	Wright, Laban	8	1	Sparrow, James R	10	....
Christopher, David	7	....	Vaughan, Richard	8	....	Poole, William	4	....	Puryear, John, Sen	8	22
Caveness, Matthew	8	....	Vaughan, Joshua	5	3	Fox, William	11	4	Vaughan, Thomas	6	7
Caveness, John	3	....	Vowel, William	11	....	Watson, Burrell	8	1	Kendrick, James	6	....
Chandler, John	3	....	Vaughan, James	6	5	Lark, Robert	2	19	Rudd, Harwood	5	....
Camp, John	2	9	Vaughan, John	9	1	Nance, Robert	7	3	Hearwood, William	9	1
Duncan, George	5	....	Vaughan, Samuel	10	....	Wall, Henry	7	....	Edmundson, Benjamin	1	....
Davis, Baxter	9	21	Vaughan, William	3	8	Ladd, William	6	....	Clausel, Clausel	7	14
Davis, William	5	4	Wiles, Luke	5	....	Allen, Turner	7	3	Feild, Thomas	3	50
Farrar, Thos	11	10	Willson, Lemuel	8	....	Thompson, Edward	4	1	Hinton, Wood	4	1
Feagan, Henry	4	....	Wright, John	7	....	Thompson, Amey	4	10	Marrow, Daniel	4	1
Floyd, Maryan	3	....	Winn, John	9	3	Chavous, James	3	....	Baker, Jane	7	19
Floyd, Sarah	3	....	Wiles, Elizabeth	10	....	Chavous, Henry	8	....	Puryear, Samuel, jr	4	....
Franklin, Thomas	6	....	Wade, Isbella	5	28	Wall, Hannah	5	....	Puryear, Obadiah	6	10
Floyd, Richard	5	....	Williamson, John	11	1	Webb, John	6	4	Johnson, Caleb	7	....
Fowler, Israel	7	....	Wilkerson, William	9	7	Webb, John	6	4	Hayes, John	9	....
Franklin, Owen	3	16	Wilkins, Charles	6	9	Crowder, Batte	8	....	Merrell, Andrew	3	....
Ford, Frederick	4	....	Wadkins, Thomas	9	5	Crowder, Keziah	4	....	Pitchford, William	7	....
Gold, Daniel	10	4	White, George	9	11	Handserd, Richard	8	5	Gordon, Henry	....	26
Green, William	11	....	White, William	5	3	Crowder, Richard	9	....	Christopher, David	6	19
Graves, Elijah	8	11	Winn, James	4	3	Homes, William	1	6	Hale, Thomas	9	1
Grinage, Joshua	3	5	Wood, Archerbald	4	....	Adams, David	11	1	Hayes, Henry	1	....
Greenwood, Jene	5	4	Williamson, Robert	4	....	Crowder, William	3	....	Lamkin, James	4	4
Gladden, Richard	3	....	Westmourland, Jesse	4	....	Poole, Walter	7	3	Epperson, Richard	10	1
Gunn, Thos	12	....	Westmourland, Martha	10	....	Hoobry, Jacob	8	....	Meader, Nicholas	5	....
Glasscock, Zach	8	1	Wallace, Richard W	7	....	Sage, Henry	2	....	Ragsdale, Richard	3	2
Hester, Henry	5	7	Wilkins, James	4	....	Blackelter, William	11	....	Mealer, William	1	....
Hailey, William	3	1	Wilkins, Thomas	2	....	Biswell, Mary Ann	7	....	Harris, William	8	1
Hill, Matthew	9	....	Yancy, Mary	2	9	Wells, Jesse	5	....	Bruce, John	6	4

MECKLENBURG COUNTY—Continued.

LIST OF LEWIS PARHAM—continued.

NAME OF HEAD OF FAMILY.	White.	Black.
Lamkin, Jeremiah	11	9
Mealer, Matt	11	1
Clay, Charles	11	4
Wilson, John	8	21
Barnes, James	6	1
Hurt, Philemon	7	5
Berry, Thomas	2	1
Ross, David		5
Pulliam, William	5	
Burt, John	8	1
Tucker, Daniel	9	3
Cox, Samuel	5	8
Cox, John	6	10
Gregory, Joseph	11	1
Gregory, Andrew	10	7
Jones, Edward	1	29
Brown, Jeremiah	6	5
Evans, Stephen	12	5
Bragg, John	3	
Williams, Joseph	3	6
Williams, Matt	7	9
Evans, William	6	
Daniel, Martin	7	2
Smith, Robert	2	1
Evans, Ludwell	2	
Evans, Stephen	4	
Neal, Thomas	10	21
Bevers, John	8	
Smith, Andrew	1	
Jones, John	1	
Milner, Richard	6	1
Lamkin, Jeremiah	4	4
Ivey, Frederick	6	
Street, Richard	9	3
Skipwith, Sir Peyton		82
Marshall, John	8	5
Marrow, Daniel	4	9
Marshall, William	3	5
Crowder, Godfrey	9	2
Evans, Thomas	7	
Lester, P.	6	1
Guoden, Peter	8	8
Ragsdale, John	10	
Burton, Hutchins	5	
Weathers, Thomas	1	
Hasting, Absolom	1	
Christopher, Robert	4	
Royster, Charles	9	18
Normant, William	8	8
Brame, John	9	5
Cheatham, James	1	2
Cheatham, Elizabeth	1	6
Murray, Sukey	8	36
Thompson, Hermon	15	4
Hogan, Edward	5	14
Foulks, Thompson	7	8
Allen, Thomas	10	
Chavous, Samuel	7	
Hunt, James	5	4
Hudson, John	9	7
Hudson, William	8	1
Chavous, Jacob	13	2
Willis, William	10	6
Elam, Joel	11	1
Rowland, Christopher	6	6
Crowder, Philip	3	
Hall, James	9	15
Hall, Miles	3	6
Marshall, Francis	7	11
Clay, John	3	4
Whitlow, Nicholas	6	3
Whiles, John	8	2
Walker, Henry	7	32
Doggett, John	13	5
Hunt, William	10	4
Doggett, Benjamin	11	4
Garner, James	8	4
Evans, Richard	9	
Cook, John	2	2
McLen, Thomas	11	
Lucas, William	6	18
Morgan, John	5	4
Evans, Anthony	9	4
Fox, Jacob	6	7
Collier, Howell	11	14
Lark, Samuel	9	7
Watson, Jacob	9	5
Dortch, Anne	3	20
Nance, Daniel	4	7
Morgain, Mary	7	5
Cheatham, Daniel	9	4
Drumright, William	9	1
Bowen, David	2	
Chavous, Milden	7	
Pennington, Henry	3	4
Ingram, John	4	3
Bowen, Littleberry	7	
Brown, John	3	6
Short, Jacob	6	6
Noblen, Thomas	9	

LIST OF LEWIS PARHAM—continued.

NAME OF HEAD OF FAMILY.	White.	Black.
Taylor, David	4	8
Taylor, Jones	4	9
Taylor, James	12	8
Whitehead, Richard	6	5
Cook, Nath¹	5	
Bowen, Jesse	3	1
Evans, Mark	10	
Bowen, David	11	
Pegram, William	6	4
Brogdon, William	4	
Bowen, Charles	8	1
Evans, Ludwell	4	
Evans, Mark	1	
Bowen, Robert	3	
Williams, James	4	1
Bugg, John	12	10
Kirk, Samuel	10	
Thompson, Peter	7	4
Fowler, Thomas	11	
Merrymoone, James	8	
Bowen, James	9	
Bowen, Hicks	2	
Pennington, James	8	9
Bowen, William	6	
Bowen, Isham	5	
Merrymoone, Stephen	2	
Merrymoone, Abram	8	
Wall, Meall	8	
Adams, William	8	
Vaughan, James	8	
Ladd, James	1	
Ladd, Urcilla	3	1
Davis, Randolph	6	5
Thompson, John	6	
Goode, Samuel	7	34
Speed, Sarah	3	5
Bartlett, William	8	
Sullivant, Hannah	5	6
Jones, Stephen	7	5
Epps, Ishams	5	
Archer, Roger	8	
Holmes, Lucy	7	7
Pointer, Alexander	3	
Nash, John	7	
Tanner, Ludwell	2	
Rainey, Buckner	3	1
Rainey, Williamson	3	5
Rainey, Francis	3	8
Pennington, Benjamin	7	2
Hall, John	6	
Standley, James	11	6
Bennett, Joseph, Senr	9	18
Smith, Benjamin	5	
Pennington, Benjamin	6	2
Tanner, Thomas	10	2
Bennett, Anthony	3	9
Malone, Nath¹	4	10
Cleaton, William	11	1
Hilton, John	5	
Dickery, John	6	
Tanner, Mary	5	1
Baugh, James	8	20
Earle, James	7	
Baugh, Daniel	7	3
Harris, Benjamin		11
Guy, William	4	
Collier, Frederick	2	11
Johnson, Robert	7	
Sanders, John	5	4
Blanton, James	2	11
Burrus (or Walker), Delphe.	5	
Rottenberry, Prudence	5	
Rottenberry, Henry	13	
Guy, Daniel	8	
Mabry, Stephen	9	4
Pennington, Edward	8	2
Jones, Hardy	7	7
Malone, Thomas	3	1
Northington, Jabys	3	6
Lambert, Joseph (war)	7	
Nipper, James	11	
Deacon, William	4	
Nance, Isham	7	6
Taylor, Goodwin	10	11
Lightfoot, Francis	7	4
Malone, Daniel	5	
Taylor, William (F. C.)	4	6
Ladd, Jacob	7	1
Wright, Lucy	9	
Holmes, Samuel	9	6
Wattson, Isaac	9	5
Cook, John	5	1
Cook, Nathaniel	5	
Holmes, Samuel, jr	9	6
Watson, Elizabeth	9	2
Gee, Jones	4	1
Pennington, James, jr	4	1
Thomerson, William	7	
Edwards, Isaac	8	
Connell, Robert	3	1
Connell, Robert	6	1

LIST OF LEWIS PARHAM—continued.

NAME OF HEAD OF FAMILY.	White.	Black.
Winkfield, Peter	7	5
Meanly, Richard	4	4
Osling, Jesse	9	11
Bowen, Drury	8	
Bowen, Sterling	2	

LIST OF SAMUEL DEDMAN.

NAME OF HEAD OF FAMILY.	White.	Black.
Brooke, Dudley	9	10
Bragg, Newman	7	
Belbo, Joseph	3	
Burton, Charles	5	4
Burton, Benjamin	6	1
Bevil, Edward	6	8
Bevil, Edward, jr	1	
Bevil, John	5	3
Burton, Thomas	6	3
Bragg, John	3	
Burton, Peter	12	6
Burton, Abram	3	12
Berry, Andrew	4	1
Burton, Robert	9	8
Burton, Archer	2	
Boswell, Joseph	4	26
Berry, Margaret	8	
Coley, David	10	5
Cox, Bartley	7	24
Carleton, Thomas, jr	6	4
Carleton, Thomas, Senr	6	11
Dedman, Samuel	9	11
Draper, Solomon	5	5
Draper, William	3	
Edwards, John	10	17
Goode, Edward, jr	9	7
Graves, Thomas	6	
Green, Matthew	6	19
Goode, Joseph	6	9
Green, William	13	34
Hyde, Sarah	6	7
Hyde, John, jr	1	
Humphress, John	8	8
Hudson, Thomas	9	3
Keeton, John	11	1
McGuire, John	9	10
McGuire, William	1	4
Nethry, Thomas	5	1
Neil, Francis Moore	7	5
Poole, Mitchell	1	
Pettus, Samuel	5	7
Pettus, Thomas	10	22
Poindexter, Philip	7	10
Poindexter, Philip, jr	5	9
Ragsdale, Peter	6	1
Southerlin, Gibson	1	
Tucker, Isham	4	
Tucker, Elizabeth	4	2
Tucker, Catharine	4	1
Roberts, Thomas (Mulatto)	5	
Whilworth, Thomas	7	5
Wilton, Richard	2	17
Wills, William	1	9
Wilkins, Clement	5	
Westbroke, Thomas	8	
Weatherford, William	8	1
Weaver, William		
Westbroke, James	11	1
Whitehead, Elisabeth	10	16
Willis, Ann	5	
Worsham, John	9	5

LIST OF WM. DAVIS.

NAME OF HEAD OF FAMILY.	White.	Black.
Davis, Edward	4	13
Davis, Joshua	7	13
McKinney, James	9	
Alexander, Robert	8	32
Davis, Hardaway	8	31
Kennon, James	6	
Vaughan, John	5	
Richardson, Thomas	10	11
Palmour, Amasa	6	13
Smith, John	5	
Garrott, Thomas	9	
King, Charles	9	6
Willson, George	7	
Kendrick, John	6	10
Evans, Charles	6	
Fox, Richard	9	9
Johnson, John	10	2
Stephens, Thomas	10	
Stephens, John	6	
Johnson, Mich¹	7	
Freeman, George	9	4
Kidd, James	8	5
Belbo, James	7	14
Belbo, John	8	7
Henderson, Henry	4	
Langley, Thomas	7	17
Kennon, John	7	10
Perry, William	8	
Carter, Thomas	4	8

LIST OF WM. DAVIS—continued.

NAME OF HEAD OF FAMILY.	White.	Black.
Reives, Thomas	9	13
Newton, Robert B.	11	2
Carter, Robert, Senr	5	
Carter, Benjamin	5	
Bottom, John	2	
Wood, Michael	5	
Wood, Henry	5	
Parbrick, John	4	
Pound, William	4	
Cunningham, Jonathan	8	
Spurlock, Zachariah	2	
Spurlock, Agnes	4	
Harris, Solomon	4	
Brandom, William	5	
Andrews, Rowlen	6	
Clemonds, Edmund	5	
Matthews, Mary	3	
Bugg, Samuel	1	1
Ballard, Devereux	3	6
Kidd, William	2	
Carter, Charles	2	
Hopkins, Samuel	8	21
Hopkins, Samuel, jr	1	8
Price, William	10	7
Johnson, Mary	5	15
Price, Joseph	2	
Davis, Charles	1	11
Allen, Rober J.	2	
Fowler, Alexander	9	
Rottenberry, Winney	6	
King, Susannah	5	
Raiborne, George	2	
Davis, William	9	45
Cradle, Henry	3	
Gobor, John	3	
Taylor, Richard	5	21
Lewis, Charles	4	20
McKenney, James	1	
Harriss, Philip	2	

LIST OF HENRY WALKER.

NAME OF HEAD OF FAMILY.	White.	Black.
Burwell, Mary	4	88
Burwell, Lewis	11	61
Oliver, Asa	4	19
Dennis, William	6	1
Clark, Stephen	6	
Gordon, Charles	4	
Pottom, Obadiah	3	6
Normand, Thomas	1	1
Marshall, Robert	5	9
Johnson, John	9	2
Jeffries, John	4	20
Cheatham, Leonard	8	16
Berry, Thomas	5	11
Berry, John	7	3
Glaspy, Martin	5	1
Harris, Samuel	1	
Nash, John	7	
Ragsdale, Peter	9	
Harrison, James	7	
Baptist, William	7	7
Clay, Samuel	1	3
Robertson, William	8	8
Harrison, John	4	7
Smith, John	10	9
Smith, Robert	3	2
Christopher, William	2	3
Avory, John	7	5
Davis, William	3	
Crowder, Abram	7	4
Crowder, William	12	
Harris, James	5	1
Carter, Matthew	8	
Carter, William	8	
Lockett, Abner	8	6
White, William	13	2
Cox, John	3	9
Culbreath, Priscilla	4	
Fagan, Keziah	5	
Hunt, James	5	3
Pulliam, Benjamin	3	12
McNiel, John	1	10
Call, William	8	9
Franklin, Hugh	3	10

LIST OF WILLIAM JOHNSON.

NAME OF HEAD OF FAMILY.	White.	Black.
Ruffin, Francis	12	92
Roffe, William, Senr	4	14
Roffe, Lewis	3	6
Johns, John	10	4
Bugg, Jesse	9	2
Pulley, Isaac	5	1
Holloway, Bennett	10	1
Cox, James	7	
Taylor, Howel	5	17
Mayo, Joseph	6	33
Bilbo, William	6	1
Robertson, James	4	
Robertson, Alexander	6	1

MECKLENBURG COUNTY—Continued.

NAME OF HEAD OF FAMILY.	White.	Black.	NAME OF HEAD OF FAMILY.	White.	Black.	NAME OF HEAD OF FAMILY.	White.	Black.	NAME OF HEAD OF FAMILY.	White.	Black.
LIST OF WILLIAM JOHNSON—continued.			LIST OF WILLIAM JOHNSON—continued.			LIST OF WILLIAM JOHNSON—continued.			LIST OF WILLIAM JOHNSON—continued.		
Durham, Samuel	8	5	Eaton, Col. John	3	....	Cameron, The Rev. John	10	9	Harris, William	5	....
Morten, James	3	3	Daws, John	4	2	Carroll, Dennis	9	....	Pulley, Spettle	11	3
Cradle, Joseph	4	....	Poole, James	12	....	Maheares, Thomas	6	....	Dorch, James	9	1
Dortcher, David (est.)	8	20	Nowell, Thomas	12	3	Delony, Henry, senr	10	24	Andrews, George	4	8
Phillips, Dabney	8	10	Hix, James	8	9	Holliers, Simon (est.)	....	7	Ballard, William	10	6
Baskerville, William	1	6	Hamner, James	8	3	Farrar, William	11	7	Mitchel, Edward	2	7
Sandifer, William	6	1	Hamner, Henry	4	....	Farrar, Judith	1	4	Nicholas, Elizabeth	9	34
Ferguson, Benjamin	10	3	Roberts, Thomas	12	....	Speed, John	2	9	Pettus, Phillips	1	7
Bailey, George	6	4	Roberts, William	2	....	Smith, Zach	5	2	Toone, William	3	....
Bailey, William	8	8	Holmes, William	14	16	Eaton, John	3	....	Small, James	6	2
Winkler, John	6	....	Clack, Sterling	2	....	Lawrence, Catharine	1	2	Johnson, William	8	22
Speed, James	6	2	Taylor, Robert	2	2	Roberts, William	2	1	Bing, George	1	1
Holloway, William	8	2	Goode, John	4	38	Forroll, Benjamin	6	10	Goode, Bennett	4	24
Rhodes, John	11	4	Ballard, John	4	20	Sandefer, James	3	7	Burton, John	8	18
Brame, Richens, Senr	6	15	Parks, James	5	7	Sandefer, James, jr	3	1	Young, Samuel	5	31
Brame, Thomas	5	4	Mallett, Zach	6	1	Hix, Amos	5	12	Levepson, Richard, senr	10	41
Daley, John	11	4	Jones, Mary	7	....	Buggs, Saml (est.)	12	16	Whitlow, James	4	....
Mallet, Stephen, jr	8	....	McCarter, James	2	....	Bottom, William	7	....	McHarg, Mrs. Elizabeth	4	27
Bottom, Wilkerson	3	4	Stuart, John	6	....	Ferrell, James	9	4	Baskerville, John	8	17
Ren, William	2	....	Moss, Nathl	4	5	Ferrell, Hubbard	4	5			

MONONGALIA COUNTY.

NAME OF HEAD OF FAMILY.	White.	Black.	NAME OF HEAD OF FAMILY.	White.	Black.	NAME OF HEAD OF FAMILY.	White.	Black.	NAME OF HEAD OF FAMILY.	White.	Black.
Evans, John	10	2	Strait, Jacob	10	....	Woolf, Samuel	2	....	Stoots, Elijah	2	....
Morgan, Morgan	10	....	Rodgers, Lewis	8	....	Ward, Peter	5	....	Crouch, John	4	....
Smith, Henry	6	....	Stuart, John	4	....	Worley, Anthoney	11	....	Crouch, John, Junr	4	....
Morgan, Evan	2	....	Samuel, John	1	....	Robsenet, Joseph	7	....	Allexander, John	7	....
Bush, John	6	....	Thomas, John	6	....	Meneer, Jonathan	5	....	Detay, Henry	9	1
Miller, Ann	5	....	Donnay, James	9	....	Meneer, David	8	....	Currance, John	8	....
Ratcliff, John	7	....	Hall, Zwidon	6	....	Cooper, Hannah	2	....	Smith, Jonathan	3	....
Zornes, Martin	4	....	Mason, Isaac	5	....	Hadden, William	4	....	Maxwell, Alexander	7	....
Croll, David	6	....	Wheeler, John	3	....	Goof, Salathial	7	4	Jones, Benjamin	6	....
Smith, William	7	....	Balla, Augustus	6	....	Stackpole, John	2	....	Breeding, George	8	....
Bonar, Ruben	3	....	Griggs, Thomas	7	....	Goof, James	5	....	Breeding, Peter	4	....
Haymond, William	9	....	Barnes, William	6	....	Cameron, Elisabeth	3	....	Cassaty, Peter, Junr	6	....
Dent, John	4	....	Bennet, Charles	7	....	Johnson, Michael	8	3	Cassaty, David	10	....
Johnson, James	8	....	Baines, Thomas	6	....	Johnson, Edward	3	....	Cassaty, John	8	....
Gifford, John	5	....	John, William	6	....	Craycroft, Samuel	11	....	Mchenry, Samuel	8	....
Smith, John	2	....	Stuart, William	8	....	Bozard, Cornelious	5	....	Clam, Phillip	4	....
Kain, Michael	6	....	Cain, Richard	10	....	Parsons, Charles	7	....	Pauley, John	6	....
Harp, Abner	6	....	Davis, Owen	4	....	Worlf, Jacob	2	....	Yocham, John	6	....
Tucker, Henry	4	....	Dunaway, William	7	....	Eberman, Samuel	6	....	Carpenter, Daniel	7	....
Sisco, Abraham	7	....	Hall, Esau	5	....	Pringle, Samuel	4	....	Shavours, George	4	....
Wilson, George	8	....	Mills, Thomas	12	....	Casaty, William	6	....	Riffle, Elenor	7	....
Wilson, Benjamin	6	....	Ridgeway, Lot	11	....	Parsons, George	6	....	Shavours, Elisabeth	5	....
Cochran, James	4	....	Stafford, James	4	....	Parsons, Joseph	5	....	Parsons, Charles	6	....
Youngman, Jacob	8	....	Meriwether, David	3	14	Stalnaker, Jacob, Junr	6	....	Parsons, George	6	....
Dunn, James	6	....	Croll, Henry	2	....	Springstone, Elisabeth	6	....	Parsons, Joseph	4	....
Prichet, Isaac	1	....	Scott, David	8	6	Phillips, Thomas	9	....	Johnson, Edward	9	....
Joseph, William	9	....	Pendell, Phillip	3	....	Kittle, Jacob	5	....	Pearce, Elias	6	....
Morgan, Zachqtt	10	....	Currant, James	6	....	Wilson, Benjamin	9	2	Scott, John, Senr	6	....
Morgan, Zachqtt, Junr	1	....	Boydstone, George	7	....	Isenor, Michael	6	....	Lowe, Richard	5	....
Morgan, James	1	....	Snyther, Margret	2	....	Westfall, Jacob, Junr	5	....	Lewellin, Samuel	9	....
Morgan, David	4	....	Stephens, Daniel	2	....	Levit, William	7	....	Simpson, Jeremiah	2	1
Prichet, Jacob	5	....	Norriss, William	7	8	Stalnaker, Jacob, Senr	6	....	Lowe, Nathan	4	....
Lowe, Abraham	6	....	Butler, Ignatiaus	5	....	Stalnaker, Valentine	5	....	Helmeck, Adam	6	....
Jacobs, Jacob	9	....	Warman, Francis	8	6	Ratcliff, William	10	....	Johnson, Patrick	5	....
Burrell, Francis	6	....	Holt, John	9	2	Cutright, John	7	....	Dorothy, John	7	....
Burrows, John	4	....	James, William	5	....	Smith, Nicholas	5	....	Hamilton, William	8	....
Fray, Simon	7	....	Lowe, Joshua	5	....	Westfall, Jacob, Sen	4	....	Taunahill, Jeremiah	3	....
Wilson, Josiah	1	....	Scott, John, Junr	2	....	Whitman, Matthias	6	....	Layton, Elias	6	....
Wilson, James	3	....	Ramsey, John, Senr	3	4	Ryon, Solomon	6	....	Martin, Joseph	6	....
Scott, Elisabeth	5	2	Ramsey, John, Junr	3	1	Smith, William	9	....	Downard, Joseph	8	....
Burrows, Elijah	3	....	Cozad, Jacob	6	....	Crouch, Judith	5	....	PettyJohn, William	4	....
Haymond, Calder	8	2	Ruble, Samuel	6	....	Westfall, William	13	....	Trader, Aurther, Senr	2	....
Cobun, James	7	....	Lewellin, Francis	6	....	Stalnaker, Margaret	2	....	Hastings, Joseph	2	....
Haymond, Edward	3	....	Jones, John	5	....	Richason, Aaron	8	....	Jackson, George	5	....
Robanson, William	8	....	Grigsbey, Charles	4	....	Booth, Daniel	7	....	Barkley, Thomas	5	....
Fenell, Robert	9	....	Jenkins, George	2	1	Smith, Anthoney	3	....	Davis, William	9	....
Finch, John	9	....	Jenkins, Bartholamew	7	7	Woolf, Nicholas	5	....	Davison, Obediah	5	....
Ashcraft, Richard	7	....	Drago, John	7	....	Cutright, Benjamin	5	....	Davison, Josiah	2	....
Mahon, James	4	4	Lee, Frederick	7	....	Trubey, John	3	....	Nutter, Thomas	8	....
Robe, William	7	....	Ross, James	5	....	Shaver, Jacob	2	....	Nutter, Christopher	1	....
King, Cornelious	2	....	Lewellin, John	6	....	Warwick, John	11	3	Hughes, Thomas	6	....
King, Peter	7	....	Jones, Jacob	12	....	Hamilton, Patrick	8	....	Hannaman, Christopher	6	....
Peirpoint, John	6	....	Davison, David	4	....	Lackey, Thomas	2	....	McColley, John	3	....
Hanway, Samuel	1	....	Spingin, James	8	....	Lackey, James, Senr	2	....	Davison, Isaac	4	....
Freeman, Edmond	8	....	Hogue, Zebulon	7	....	Hamilton, William	2	....	Reed, John	1	....
Whitelock, Michael	3	....	Morris, John	4	....	Moore, James	5	....	Hickman, Suth	7	....
Tibbs, Francis	8	....	Craft, Thomas	6	....	Henderson, Rober	8	....	Fomash, Charles	1	....
langston, Jacob	8	....	Robenet, John	4	....	McDonald, Francis	6	....	Davison, Daniel	7	....
Jenkins, Joseph	5	1	Henrey, John	6	....	Abbet, Benjamin	5	....	Runyon, John	6	....
Jenkins, James	1	....	Horten, Elihu	5	....	Collens, Edmond	8	....	Jackson, John	9	....
Bozarth, John	6	....	Tomlinson, Joseph	2	4	Rifle, Jacob	10	....	Beard, Samuel	9	....
Brumegin, Garvis	2	....	Morris, Richard	3	....	Westfall, George, Senr	12	....	Washbun, Rebekah	4	....
Brumegin, Honor	2	....	Morris, Morris	2	....	Westfall, George, Junr	2	....	Richards, John	8	....
Goodferrey, John	4	....	Arskins, Edward	9	....	Petty, Ebenezer	9	....	Steeth, John	4	....
Johnson, John	6	....	Conner, John	4	....	Trubey, Christopher	4	....	Hacker, John	10	....
Peters, John	3	....	Conner, James	5	....	McClean, Charles	7	....	Schoolcraft, John	1	....
Ridgway, Lot	3	....	Trader, Moses	3	....	Holder, Thomas	7	....	Schoolcraft, Christian	2	....
Park, Robert	6	....	Trader, Aurther, Junr	3	....	Fornalon, Joseph	11	....	Reed, Thomas	1	....
Cleland, James	7	....	Wolleson, Richard	5	....	Stoots, Joseph	8	....	Carpenter, Nicholas	8	....
litle, Mary	5	....	Morris, John	11	....	Crouch, Joseph	10	....	Powers, Major	5	....
Evans, Thomas	9	....	Parker, James	4	....	Shavor, Peter	5	....	Arnold, James	2	....
Hamilton, John	5	....	Fraze, David	5	....	Fornelson, Charles	6	....	Goodwin, John	4	....
Brumegin, Elias	4	....	Fraze, Samuel	7	....	Henderson, David	2	....	Webb, Elisabeth	10	....
									Edwards, David	8	....

MONONGALIA COUNTY—Continued.

NAME OF HEAD OF FAMILY.	White.	Black.	NAME OF HEAD OF FAMILY.	White.	Black.	NAME OF HEAD OF FAMILY.	White.	Black.	NAME OF HEAD OF FAMILY.	White.	Black.
Stout, Thomas	3		Runyon, William	7		Douglass, Levy	4		Green, John (kild by the Indians)	10	
Plummer, Robert	8		Richards, Jacob	6		Husted, Moses	5		Lemon, George (Refuses)		
Stout, Jonathan	6		Lowther, Joel	3		Nutter, Matthew	4		Woolf, Jacob (Refuses)		
Lambert, Jonathan	7		Cain, John	8		Davison, Andrew	4		Cheney, Thomas	8	
Wilkenson, Samuel	4		Runyon, Henry	8		Murphey, Denis	5		Judey, Martin, Junr	5	
Wilkenson, Joseph	7		Hughes, Elias	5		Thomas, Evan	5		Warner, John	5	
Wilkenson, Joseph, Junr	3		Obryan, Adam	7		Pike, Robert	3		Lane, Joseph	5	
Nutter, John	5		Tanner, William	2		Davison, Josiah	5		Hers, Martin	5	
Davison, Ann	7	1	Flesher, Henry	9		Shinn, Benjamin	8		Severens, Daniel	7	
Stout, Daniel	6		Tanner, Edward	6		Davison, Amaziah	7		Severens, Joseph	1	
Edwards, Isaac	7		Richards, Martha	5		Anderson, James	5		Judey, Martin	9	
Abben, John	7		West, Alexander	3		Chips, Thomas	8		McCollums, James	5	
Harbour, Esabel	5		Wood, John	8		Grayham, John	4		Linser, George	3	
Smith, Aaron	8		Webb, Thomas	4		Roberts, Amos	3		Donaldson, Charles	9	
Owens, John	6		Gregorsy, Josep	6		Kirkpatrick, William	3		Welch, John	2	
Everett, Walter	5		Robenson, Benjamin	3		Kirkpatrick, Andrew	2		Conner, John	6	
Husted, Gilbert	8		Copelan, Benjamin	5		Jones, Ezekiel	9		Kelley, John	6	
Powers, John	8		West, Edmond	7		Stiles, John	6		Sims, John	6	
Robenson, William	10		Murphey, John	3		Butler, Joseph	12		Worl, Attewill	6	
Knots, Edward	2		Cunningham, Edward	7		Butler, Thomas	10	2	Spurgin, William	12	
McKinney, James	4		Shinn, Levy	7		Biggs, William	4		Robenet, Samuel	5	
Harris, Charles	1		Moore, Ann	3		London, Barth	7		Worl, Samuel	5	
Lowther, William	8		Wolf, John	6		Daugherty, John	4				
Cobun, Jonathan	6		Davison, John	4		Morgan, William	7				

NEW KENT COUNTY.

LIST OF BURWELL BASSETT.	White.	Black.	LIST OF BURWELL BASSETT—continued.	White.	Black.	LIST OF LYDALL BACON—continued.	White.	Black.	LIST OF ARMISTEAD RUSSELL—continued.	White.	Black.
Ammons, William	6	5	Rawson, Thomas	4	3	Higins, Joseph	8	5	Roper, Lucy	5	10
Allens, Richd (Estate)		22	Brooker, John	8		Thomson, John	4		Pasley, Susanna	5	1
Allen, Richmond	7	14	Taylor, William	3	17	Martin, Robert	10		Peasley, Polly	3	1
Allen, Daniel	4	3	Taylor, Richard	8	10	Martin, Tarlton	8		Moss, William	11	11
Armistead, Mary	3	14				Turner, John	6	1	Gaulling, Jacob	9	
Allen, James	5	17	LIST OF LYDALL BACON.			Johnson, Michael	4	1	Armistead, Mary	8	30
Bradenham, John	8	13	Mannin, Samuel	5	10	Peace, William	6	4	Meekins, Chritmass		5
Ball, Betty	6	3	Hewlett, William	8	3	Ellyson, Gerrard R.	3		Apperson, Peter	6	
Breeding, John	6	2	Apperson, Samuel	3	18	Cloptoh, Waldegrave, Senr	8	15	Waddill, Edwin	8	30
Bennett, Mary	3	2	Crump, John P.	2	2	Sneed, John	3		Bailey, Ann	4	11
Breeding, Julius	4	1	Crump, Jessee	2	5	Turner, Robert	11	1	Cox, Pressley	4	2
Bennett, Elisha	6	1	Gathright, Milos	8	17	Martin, John	7		Perkins, David	8	8
Baker, George	6	15	Wilkinson, Nathl, Junr	4	14	Elliot, Thomas	5	10	Miller, Patty	4	5
Boswell, John	6	5	Wilkinson, Sarah	6	18	Gathright, Theod	7	9	Harfield, Michael	1	20
Bassett, Burwell	33	133	Baily, John	2	2	Ellyson, Gerrard	2	12	Webb, Lewis	5	42
Curle, Henry	8	9	Wilkinson, Nathl, Senr (Henrico)	4	8	Barkwell, John	11	2	Webb, Foster	6	20
Curle, William	5	3	Parke, Edmund	1	4	Mason, Wm. H.	8	34	Bacon, John	10	6
Christian, Isham	8	12	Chappel, Samuel	10		Clayton, William	4	28	Davis, James	8	1
Davies, Price	6	35	Dudley, William	6	7	Wilsford, Mary	3	5	Adams, Richd	4	18
Daingerfield, Hannah	2	33	Howle, Gideon	4	20	Pike, Richard	7		Perkins, Ann	10	16
Dillard, Thomas	9	6	Jenkins, Joseph	4	15	Lindsey, John	4		Sharpe, Robert	6	1
Dillard, George	4	5	Giles, Nicholas	4	6	Johnson, Thomas	4		Word, Charles	9	6
Eames, John	6	2	Thilman, Paul (Hanover)	5	15				Minitree, Isham	3	7
Franks, John	6	5	Crew, John	2		LIST OF ARMISTEAD RUSSELL.			Clopton, William	5	5
Flack, George	2	2	Howle, Susanna	7	5	Graves, Richd C.	9	27	Freeman, Barnet	5	
Garland, Andrew	1		Massie, William	5	44	Tyree, Richard	7	13	Atkinson, Henry	3	14
Godding, Elizabeth	6	17	Wilkinson, Lyddall	5	15	Firth, Samuel	8	11	Richardson, Edward	2	7
Gillam, Jacob	9		Wilkinson, Mary	2	8	Morris, John	8	3	Richardson, George	7	2
Hockaday, Edmund	6	9	Wilkinson, Parke	4	6	Martin, Susanna	6		Martin, Daniel	7	2
Hockaday, Rebecca	4	21	Chowning, Jessee	4		Cox, Charles	5		Firbush, George	5	
Harman, William	7	2	Clopton, Waldegrave, Junr	6	6	Lacy, John	5	6	Joseph, Susanna	2	
Holt, Samuel	4	10	Parish, Mary	10	3	Christian, Richard	1		Roper, Thomas	4	1
Hockaday, James	9	13	Duval, Daniel	3	7	Daniel, Ann	5		Glenn, John	6	6
Jolidon, ——	3	1	Hall, John	7	23	Dixon, Mellenton	10	2	Vaughan, Timothy	5	6
James, Edward	2	3	Crump, David	5	7	Parkinson, Jacob	10	10	Thomson, William	6	2
Jones, James	4	2	Harris, John	7		Lad, William	7	3	Baker, Phebe	2	1
Lorial, John B.	2		Johnson, David	8		Orey, James	8	3	Waddill, Charles	7	14
Langley, John	6	20	Cooper, John	1	20	Meekins, David		4	Pearson, Charles	6	2
Lacy, Henry	5	11	Cunningham, John (Hanover)		6	Meekins, Joseph		7	Bailey, Parke	7	1
Meridith, John	3	17	Massie, Peter	5	7	Clarke, Edward G	6	8	Pollard, James	4	1
Moore, Benjamin	5	3	Elmore, Turner	7	1	Clopton, John	2	8	Poindexter, Nimrod	6	7
Ratcliffe, William	4	4	Slaughter, Elias	9		Dandridge, William	3	20	Wilkins, Robert	8	
Richardson, Sarah	8	16	Ellyson, Mary	5	13	Crump, Sarah	5	5	Pearson, Rebecca	6	4
Russell, Armistead		41	Moss, Samuel	6	3	Vaiden, John	3	8	Graves, Richard	6	4
Slater, John	8	6	Sneed, Reubin	6	1	Holt, Josiah	5	20	Poindexter, Geo. B	12	21
Slater, William, Senr	4	7	Crump, Robert	9	7	Stiff, Jacob	8	9	Christian, William	4	13
Smith, William	2	11	Bassett, Burwell		23	Hillard, Benskin	4	15	Scruggs, Hannah	1	10
Sweeny, Moses	6		Bosman, James (mulattoes)	8		Walls, Thomas	2	2	Hopkins, Walter	4	15
Slater, William, Junr	3	3	Bowis, Robert	9	26	Vaughan, Stanhope	10	14	Herbert, Henry	1	5
Sweney, William	3		Finch, James	3	8	Crump, Sarah	4	8	Howle, Epaphraditus, Senr	8	15
Tyree, William	9	4	Dews, John	4	7	Pollard, Elisha	3	4	Howle, Epaphraditus, Junr	4	1
Taylor, James	7	6	Howle, Richard	8		Barnes, Thomas	1		Hollings, Elizabeth	5	5
Timberlake, John	6	14	Howle, James	7		Hopkins, William	4	16	Nance, James	7	3
Taylor, John	6	8	Howle, John	5		Pearson, John	3	9	Burch, Samuel	8	3
Temple, Alexander	6	1	Horsley, George	4		Apperson, William	7	1	Burch, John	2	
Taylor, Timothy	4	6	Smether, Thomas	10	11	Ragland, Jacob	3	7	Sherman, William	11	12
Volentine, John	3	3	Keingham, Wm	8	1	Poindexter, Jacob	1	12	Tallman, William	6	6
Woodward, Joseph	6	11	Smether, John	2		Apperson, John	9	20	Madeiras, Henry	3	7
Warren, Edward	4	11	Savage, Nathl L.	11	36	Cook, William	5	4	Volentine, Joseph	2	4
Williams, Bartlet	5	31	Clopton, Wm (Hanover)		11	Webb, William	4	2	Sinker, Charles	4	
Woodward, Jane	5	10	Howle, Absolem	5	14	Harvey, Charles	2	3	Douglass, William	3	62
Williams, David	6	14	Morgan, Ann	7	9	Pearson, William	5	1	Heath, George	8	4
Wily, Robert	2		Morgan, Thomas	1		Watkins, John	5	34	Godding, David	4	15
Williams, Dudley	10	5	Finch, Henry	10	12	Woodward, John	5	2	Doncastles, Thomas (Estate)	5	11
Woodward, Philemon	8	20	Waddy, John	1	2	Crump, William	3	3	Warren, James	4	22
Williams, Edward	6	3	Wilkinson, George, Senr	6	34	Hewlett, Austin	8	8	Poindexter, Jonathan	3	13
Williams, Dudley, Junr	7	9	Ammons, Christopher	4	15	Cook, Fanny	3		Austin, Richard	3	1
Willis, Stephen	7	15	Gaulling, Samuel	3		Martin, Julius	7	3	Hopkins, John	4	15
Yates, John	6	6				Porter, John	7		Crump, John	9	
Lewis, David	6	24				Russell, Armistead	4	17	Bacon, Lyddall	6	9
Roper, John	7	3									

NEW KENT COUNTY—Continued.

NAME OF HEAD OF FAMILY.	White.	Black.	NAME OF HEAD OF FAMILY.	White.	Black.	NAME OF HEAD OF FAMILY.	White.	Black.	NAME OF HEAD OF FAMILY.	White.	Black.
LIST OF ARMISTEAD RUSSELL—continued.			LIST OF ARMISTEAD RUSSELL—continued.			LIST OF ARMISTEAD RUSSELL—continued.			LIST OF ARMISTEAD RUSSELL—continued.		
Word, William	5	2	Sherman, Henry D	1	12	Wilkinson, Thomas	5	13	Barkwell, Thomas	8	3
Poindexter, Henry	3	17	Hays, Robert	6	2	Mitchell, Thomas	9	10	Green, Ithamer	6	2
Perkins, James	5	2	Shard, Julius	4	1	Sherman, Michael	3	16	Custis, John Parke (Estate)	..	115
Redwood, Ann	5	4	Lacy, Edmund	8	7	Lewis, Benjamin	6	22	Harfield, Eliza C	1	23
Marston, John	4	16	Wilkins, Edward	6	18	Foster, Joseph	6	30	Posey, John P	4	16
Vaiden, Elizabeth	5	17	Christian, John	7	21	Mucx, Thomas	4	22	Chamberlayne, Mary	1	18
Allen, Matthew	4	4	Crump, Benedict	12	20	Pears, Elisha	1	2	Armistead, William	..	5
Lacy, William	11	11	Semple, Revd James	9	32	Morris, Elizabeth	6	11	Condon, Henrietta	2	..

NORTHUMBERLAND COUNTY.

NAME OF HEAD OF FAMILY.	White.	Black.	NAME OF HEAD OF FAMILY.	White.	Black.	NAME OF HEAD OF FAMILY.	White.	Black.	NAME OF HEAD OF FAMILY.	White.	Black.
LOWER DISTRICT OF WICCOMICO PARISH—LIST OF CHARLES LEE.			LIST OF JOHN HEATH—con.			LIST OF JOHN HEATH—con.			ST. STEPHEN'S PARISH—LIST OF SAM'L BLACKWELL—continued.		
Gaskins, Thomas, Junr	7	25	Taylor, William (Estate)	6	29	Pitman, Mitchell	4	1	Blackwell, Samuel	2	17
Wheeler, John, Junr	3	..	Waddey, James	9	13	Palmer, Joshua	6	..	Blackwell, Nancy	..	16
Gaskins, Isaac	3	4	Haydon, Ezekiel	5	7	Swanson, Benjamin	3	..	Beatley, Joseph	10	..
Hurst, Thomas	8	13	Haydon, Thomas, Junr	5	7	Weaver, Aaron (free)	..	9	Beatley, Jesse	5	..
Hurst, Isaac	6	12	Parrott, William	6	10	Pinn, John (free)	..	3	Blundall, John	3	4
Snow, Elisha	2	1	Swanson, Stephen	4	..				Carpenter, Sarah	..	5
Hughlett, Samuel	10	5	Swanson, Asa	4	1	LIST OF WILLIAM NUTT.			Creddick, Thomas	1	4
Oliver, Tapscott	5	..	Swain, Joseph	8	..	Goodrich, George	6	9	Causey, Judith	..	5
McAdam, Joseph	..	8	Brown, Sarah	7	..	Lamkin, Lewis	4	5	Coles, William	4	12
Jones, Judith	5	15	Dulan, Betty	3	..	Fallin, William	8	7	Causey, William	..	5
Angell, John	4	1	Lume, Nancy	4	..	Fallin, Sarah	4	16	Corbell, William	4	8
Sydnor, Elizabeth	8	21	George, John	6	4	Kirk, John	10	2	Conway, Robert	2	8
Watts, William	4	1	Hudnall, Richard	6	12	Griffis, George	3	1	Coles, Winifred	4	16
Weaver, Joseph	..	8	Nutt, Richard	6	12	James, Thomas	10	..	Coles, Edward	4	23
Hurst, Henry	6	6	George, Nehemiah	3	6	Potts, Thomas	8	3	Coles, Richard	1	13
Carter, Robert Wormley	..	42	Gaskins, John (Estate)	12	22	Potts, Enoch	6	1	Conway, Francinah (Dece'd)	..	11
Davis, William	10	..	Lunsford, Moses, Junr	6	7	Hazzard, Rawleigh	7	3	Covington, Elizabeth	5	12
Billins, Soloman	3	1	Hurst, John	2	..	Potts, Francis Anne	5	1	Cockarill, William	8	..
Lee, Charles	11	31	Hurst, Joseph	8	14	Sutton, Moses	8	7	Corbell, John	6	4
Haydon, Thomas	6	..	Payne, Richard H	1	13	Gibbons, John	9	11	Cockarill, John	5	10
Haydon, Elizabeth	4	..	Hurst, Susanna	8	13	Cundiff, Benjamin	7	10	Cockarill, Littleton	3	..
Ingram, George	12	18	Barrett, William	4	6	Moore, William	5	..	Downing, John	8	20
Waddey, Margaret	4	12	Harvey, Onisiphouis	9	8	Davis, Sarah	2	..	Dudley, Ransom	4	..
Taylor, Dorothy	7	1	Hurst, Mary	4	..	Leland, Lucy	4	19	Daughity, James	3	7
Harding, Mary	4	..	Hester, Joseph	7	1	Hunt, George	5	9	Daughity, John	8	5
Remm, Jemime	5	..	Rawson, Joseph	4	1	Ball, George	1	10	Edwards, Robert	5	10
Ball, David, Junr	3	12	Champion, James & his mother	7	8	Gaskins, Jesse	3	..	Edwards, Thomas	5	10
Phillips, George	5	13	Adams, Lot	6	..	Beane, Peter	6	3	Edwards, Elisha	4	3
Gill, Thomas	12	..	Bussell, Benjamin & Mays Est's	6	5	Basye, Isaac	6	11	Evans, Mark	..	8
Dameron, Bartholomew	7	9	Dameron, Winifred	4	..	Denny, William	8	1	Edwards, Rodham	3	1
Ball, David	14	35	Mahanes, Mary Anne	6	..	Hornsby, John	10	7	Fontaine, William	6	..
Patridge, John	7	..	Potts, Robert	5	..	Marsh, Richard	8	..	Gill, Taylor	3	11
Pinckard, John	4	1	George, Eleanor	3	..	Marsh, Cuthbert	5	..	Gill, William	7	11
Waddey, Thomas	5	17	Crosley, William	3	1	Marsh, Benjamin	7	..	Harcum, Thomas	6	6
Hester, Moses	6	2	Sebree, John	6	..	Walker, Frances	7	..	Haynie, William	5	9
Kent, Daniel	3	4	Wheeler, Moses	4	..	Hughlett, Ephraim	6	..	Harcum, Elisha	3	10
Percivall, Ephaphroditus A.	6	1	Harvey, Sinah	5	3	Walker, Risden	3	3	Hague, Joseph	6	..
Dameron, Jesse	4	1	Lattimore, Charles, Junr	2	12	Christian, Rawleigh C	5	13	Harcum, Cuthbert	6	3
Dameron, Mary	2	2	Hudnall, Ezekiel	9	14	Pope, Sarah	4	14	Hayes, Peter	5	9
Kellum, William	5	1	Ledford, James	6	7	Sampson, Joseph	4	..	Harcum, Millicent	4	4
Snow, Spencer	1	..	Sutton, James	7	6	Sullivan, Dennis	9	..	Hughlett, Yarrett	1	..
Pope, Josias	1	..	Sutton, John	6	4	Moore, Thomas	9	..	Hill, John	3	..
Hutson, George	7	2	Haynie, James	5	1	Webb, Homer	8	2	Harcum, William	10	10
Gaskins, Thomas	2	2	Garlington, John	6	4	Palmer, David	4	-2	Hosey, Immanuel	5	1
Nicken, Richard	..	4	Barrett, Sarah	5	9	Palmer, Robert	3	4	Harcum, Joseph	6	13
Davis, Joseph	6	..	Marsh, Charles	7	..	Pitman, Mitchell	4	..	Harcum, William W	4	2
Gaskins, William	5	..	Sebree, William	7	..	Sampson, William	6	3	Jacques, William H	6	5
Snow, Elisha	2	1	Copedge, Augustine	5	6	Lunsford, Elias	4	..	Jones, Anne	2	1
Pool, Peter	8	..	Barrett, George	1	3	Dudley, Richard	6	1	Keeve, John	1	1
Gaskins, Thomas, Senr	3	35	Wheeler, John	4	9	Marsh, Thomas	3	..	Kenner, Winder	8	37
Eustace, John	4	50	Lunee, Joseph	4	..	Cornish, John	6	..	Kesterson, William	9	2
Conway, Peter	5	46	Lunee, Tarpley	3	..	Dudley, Joseph	4	1	Kesterson, George	7	..
Mott, William	3	5	Angell, Mrs	6	6	Webb, John	6	1	Keeve, Elizabeth W	4	7
Robuck, Robert	3	8	Sebree, John	8	..	Sampson, William, Jr	4	..	Kenner, Rodham	9	1
Robuck, William	1	2	Harding, Hopkins	5	5	Sebree, Moses	10	2	Loe, Charles	5	3
Dameron, George	6	31	Leland, Lucy	4	16	Lunsford, Ezekiel	7	..	Mason, Josiah	6	2
Lee, Betty	8	25	Jeffries, Joseph	6	..	Everitt, Thomas	4	5	Pasquett, John	8	..
Lee, William	3	9	Fletcher, John	3	..	Garner, Moses	7	..	Phillips, James	5	..
Edwards, Thomas	7	9	Everitt, Thomas	4	5	Garner, Edward	2	..	Popplewell, Richard	5	1
			Garner, Moses	8	..	Dameron, Mary	2	1	Parker, Toulson	7	7
LIST OF JOHN HEATH.			Garner, Edward	2	..	Davenport, William	6	28	Pickren, Judith	4	6
Heath, John	9	27	Palmer, Robert	4	3	Smee, Robert	1	..	Pickren, John	4	2
Lattimore, Charles	8	14	Tally (Widow)	5	..	Knight, Hannah	5	3	Robertson, William	8	..
Copedge, Charles	5	5	Barns, Henry	2	4	Webb, Aaron	3	..	Soorell, James	..	5
Smith, Samuel	10	9	Gibbons, John	8	9	Aspray, John Faldo	4	1	Soorell, Jesse	..	4
Nelms, Meredith	3	1	Cooke, Nathaniel		8	Nutt, William	5	25	Shepherd, Thomas	3	1
Marsh, Gideon	8	2	Walker, Robert	4	1	Ball, Richard	8	18	Shepherd, George	3	11
Cox, William	5	..	Webb, Leannah	3	7	Beane, George	6	5	Smith, John	8	..
Spriggs, Joseph	6	..	Webb, Lazarus	7	..	Carter, Anne	7	2	Smith, Edward	4	6
Barr, Zachariah	5	11	Craine, John	3	..				Throp, Aaron	5	..
Easton, John	5	2	Smee, Robert	1	..	ST. STEPHEN'S PARISH—LIST OF SAM'L BLACKWELL.			Tolston, Patrick	..	8
Nicken, Limas	..	5	Riley, William	5	..	Avis, Thomas	8	7	Tolston, Thomas	..	9
Pitman, George	3	..	Lunee, Ellis	4	..	Betts, Thomas	1	1	Tolston, Thomas, Jr	5	3
Rawson, William	6	1	Palmer, David	4	1	Beatley, John	7	1	Tignor, Phillip	7	4
Angell, Rodham	4	2	Mott, Thomas	6	3	Bluford, Elijah	5	..	Taylor, Moses	7	12
Curtice, Hillary	7	11	Aspray, John F	4	1	Beatley, William	4	1	Tignor, James	9	1
Lunsford, Moses	4	26	Nutt, Moseley	3	27	Blundall, William	4	..	Thomas, John	5	16
Fletcher, Mays	2	3	Nicken, Amos (free)	..	4	Blackwell, George	8	14	Webb, John S	4	9
Yerby, Thomas	3	18							Webb, Isaac	7	..
									Webb, John	7	..
									Webb, John, Junr	5	..

NORTHUMBERLAND COUNTY—Continued.

NAME OF HEAD OF FAMILY.	White.	Black.	NAME OF HEAD OF FAMILY.	White.	Black.	NAME OF HEAD OF FAMILY.	White.	Black.	NAME OF HEAD OF FAMILY.	White.	Black.
ST. STEPHEN'S PARISH—LIST OF SAM'L BLACKWELL—continued.			ST. STEPHEN'S PARISH—LIST OF WILLIAM DOWNING—continued.			ST. STEPHEN'S PARISH—LIST OF KENNER CRALLE—continued.			ST. STEPHEN'S PARISH—LIST OF JOHN CRALLE—continued.		
Wornom, Thomas	4	4	Rogers, John	11	10	Haynie, Maxamillan	8	....	Christopher, John	4	6
Walker, Richard	5	....	Bramdell, John	5	....	Hogan, John	4	....	Wall, Edward	5	5
Williams, Thomas	4	....	Corbell, Peter	1	5	Lansdell, Benjamin	8	8	Astin, George	11	1
Williams, John	8	....	Power, Joseph	7	....	Lansdell, William	4	6	Clark, William	7	....
White, Simon	5	....	Morison, John	3	4	Fossitt, Richard	3	1	Menzies, Samuel	2	16
Wornam, William	7	4	Morison, William	6	2	Hughlett, Winter	4	....	Harrison, George	1	1
Yopp, Jeremiah	3	1	Conway, Thomas	1	7	Walker, William	6	8	Middleton, William	....	4
ST. STEPHEN'S PARISH—LIST OF WILLIAM DOWNING.			Brown, Sarah	4	....	Pullin, Nathan	2	4	Norris, William	3	5
			Walker, Joseph	7	....	Boyds, David (Estate)	....	24	Brown, Richard	6	1
Coleman, Joseph	6	....	Ball, Joseph	2	10	Haynie, Bridgar	10	14	Skinner, Charles	3	1
Welch, Sylvester	4	....	Ball, Hannah	6	12	Cralle, Kenner	1	25	Williams, Rawleigh	6	5
Pickren, William	7	2	Wheeler, James	3	2	Thomas, Robert	7	....	Barns, William	8	....
Pickren, George	7	1	Webb, John	5	15	Thornton, Presly (Estate)	1	56	Mason, James	3	2
Pickren, John	8	6	Wood, Joseph	4	2	Pullin, Leroy	5	1	Winstead, Francis	5	1
Haynie, John	4	2	Lucas, William	4	....	Owens, Richard	5	....	Haynie, Charles	4	2
Humphris, Anne	5	1	Simms, Ellis	4	1	Haynie, Spencer	2	....	Graham, John	7	18
Townsend, Haynie	7	7	Simms, James	3	....	Haynie, Thomas	8	....	Winstead, John	8	1
Conway, Walker	5	22	Jones, Robert	3	....	Haynie, John, Senr	9	....	Hudson, Jeremiah	6	....
Cottrell, John	6	12	Palmer, Jesse	4	....	Rice, William, Junr	4	1	Webb, William	4	....
Leland, Peter	6	....	Jones, John	2	....	Dawkins, Moses	4	....	Webb, Thomas	7	8
Ryon, Judith	5	....	Haynie, Daniel	3	10	Luttrell, Moses	7	....	Eskridge, Mary	4	4
Humphris, John, Senr	7	....	Robertson, Elisha	6	7	Rice, John	5	1	Foushee, Mary	4	....
Betts, Daniel	2	1	Haynie, William	4	12	Christopher, Henry	10	7	Foushee, John	8	2
Anderson, John	8	....	Gill, Thomas	2	4	Rice, Isaac, Senr	9	8	Eskridge, John	8	....
Hudnall, Judith	7	15	Humphris, Joseph	5	10	Mott, Randall	12	9	Vanlandingham, Henry	7	....
Smoot, Charles	6	1	Sebree, James	11	....	Appleby, Norman	6	....	Jones, Thomas	8	27
Humphris, Jane	1	5	Walker, George, Jr	3	1	Patridge, Hannah	2	....	Opie, Lindsy	9	29
Hays, William	1	5	Elliston, Cuthbert	7	8	Wilkins, William	7	1	Hendrick, William	7	....
Palmer, Isaac	5	2	Blundall, Seth	2	3	Rice, Charles	9	1	Lewis, Charles	7	....
Barecroft, John	6	1	Waddey, Shapleigh	2	3	Smoot, William	1	....	Eskridge, George	5	13
Nelms, Aaron	6	1	Brown, Joseph	3	1	Rice, William P.	7	....	Williams, William	3	....
Downing, John	3	8	Elliston, John S	7	3	Palmer, Joseph	4	....	Harding, William	9	14
Bridgman, Thomas	6	....	Dyches, John	1	....	Everitt, William	3	....	Bussell, John	2	....
Downing, Charles	2	6	Gill, Sarah	6	9	Hughlett, John, Jr	5	3	Power, William	6	1
Smithers, George	10	8	Nelms, William	6	13	Alexander, Rawleigh	10	4	Barns, Mary	3	2
Edwards, George	7	....	Harford, John	7	1	Alexander, William	6	1	Harrison, Jesse	5	1
Wildey, William	10	28	Cundiff, John	3	6	Ball, George	10	14	Blenise, Mary	9	6
Dunway, John	3	....	Edwards, Jonathan	5	....	Haynie, Samuel	4	....	Griffis, George	7	....
Edwards, Sarah	6	....	Hughs, William	5	2	Humphris, John, Jr	4	2	Winstead, Jemiah	6	1
Carter, Richard	3	....	Blackwell, Samuel	6	14	Denny, Samuel	4	5	Dawson, William	3	1
Haynie, David	3	....	Fallin, Elisha	8	1	Moxley, Daniel	8	15	Greenstreet, Grace	3	5
Chilton, John	3	....	Hobson, Thomas	6	16	Ball, James	6	29	Vanlandingham, Thomas	4	....
Schofield, Thomas	7	2	Downing, William	5	40	Daughity, James	3	....	Russell, Thomas	4	....
Wilson, Nathaniel	4	1	Lansdell, John	5	2	Daughity, John	6	....	Boggess, Henry	5	9
Humphris, George	6	....	Opie, Lindsy	....	15	Betts, William	4	....	Crutcher, Jane	6	....
Gill, John	5	....	Clarke, Robert	4	....	Campbell, Winifred	4	....	Garner, William P.	9	21
Almond, John	4	....	ST. STEPHEN'S PARISH—LIST OF KENNER CRALLE.			Alexander, William	6	1	Short, William	6	....
Ball, Richard	8	18				Avis, William	6	....	Crosfield, Margaret	2	....
Shepherd, William	4	....	McCave, Blackman	3	....	Avis, James	8	....	Jenkins, John	3	1
Parker, William	2	....	Cole, Samuel	8	1	Edwards, Letty	3	....	Lewis, John	4	....
Hull, John	7	25	Haynie, Jeduthan	2	1	France, James	2	....	France, Judith	4	....
Hull, Edward (Dece'd)	....	15	Haynie, Richard	10	....	France, George	4	....	Doran, Margaret	7	....
Owens, William	5	2	Burrows, Charles	7	....	Edwards, William	5	....	Ashburne, William	4	....
Haynie, John	4	3	Haynie, William	4	....	Muse, Daniel	6	16	Barecroft, Samuel	7	....
Harding, Samuel	12	12	Walker, Richard	6	2	McAdam, Joseph	8	19	Tillory, James	3	4
Nutt, Richard	7	1	Meath, William	1	....	Landerkin, Thomas	3	1	Anderson, William	2	....
Haynie, Anne	1	12	Dawkins, Penley	4	2	Booth, John	8	4	Oldham, William	7	7
Haynie, John	3	9	Richardson, Peggy	6	1	Headley, Luke	6	....	Eidson, Joseph	5	3
Nelms, Eben	8	22	Haynie, Jacob	3	....	Welch, Isaac	1	....	Lewis, William	8	8
Hardom, John	5	....	Alexander, Jesse	7	10	Iles, Absolom	3	....	Davis, Thomas	5	83
Jones, William	1	....	Layland, Ellis	3	....	Hill, Joseph	3	1	Davis, Mary	3	4
Jones, Sarah	4	....	Davis, Samuel	3	4	Butler, Mary	3	....	Steel, Jane	3	5
Hays, George	7	....	Thomas, Richard	1	....	Gordon, John	11	44	Clarke, Robert	5	5
Swan, Alexander	4	....	Nicholas, Nancy	3	....	Hughlett, John	8	36	Clarke, Charles	6	1
Smoot, Charles	2	....	Davis, Judith	6	....	Muse, Hudson	5	15	ST. STEPHEN'S PARISH—LIST OF ABRAM BRACKHAM.		
Smith, Thomas	4	....	Davis, Isaac	2	....	ST. STEPHEN'S PARISH—LIST OF JOHN CRALLE.					
Welch, Benjamin	7	3	Simmons, Aaron	5	....				Beacham, Abraham	10	6
Welch, Benja, Jr	3	....	Boush, Elizabeth	3	1	Cralle, John	6	26	Barecroft, Anne	2	....
Pickren, George	4	4	Way, Winifred	6	3	Neale, John	9	....	Singer, William	4	....
Walker, James	2	....	Routt, George	6	9	Hartley, John	7	....	Knott, Eleanor	4	5
Jones, Morris	2	....	Walker, Thomas	7	3	Cox, Peter	4	12	Claughton, Magdalane	1	5
Sullivan, John	7	....	Routt, Thomas	3	....	Hudson, Rawleigh	4	....	Turner, John	5	7
Davis, Robert	4	....	Blackorby, Hetha	3	....	Betty (Free)	1	....	Shiverall, Allan L.	3	6
Chapman, Mary	3	....	Luttrell, Richard	3	....	France, John	4	....	Hall, Anne	4	....
Welch, Elizabeth	4	....	Sebree, Jane	3	....	Menzies, George	2	8	Walker, Henry	8	....
Simms, Job	5	....	Ashburne, Thomas	8	....	Ashburne, George	5	2	McClanahan, James	7	1
Harris, George	7	....	Magoone, Hannah	1	....	Haynie, Hezekiah	4	7	Knott, Richard	7	6
Hudnall, Thomas	7	65	Abbay, John	8	4	Efford, Catharine	6	2	Claughton, John	7	7
Betts, William	8	3	France, William	4	....	Hill, George	4	....	Thomas, Thomas	6	....
Downing, Elizabeth	1	9	Thornton, Peter P. (Estate)	1	54	Routt, Richard	2	12	Frasee, John	12	3
Downing, Betty	1	2	Carter, Landon	....	19	Neale, Presly	3	8	Bell, Thomas	7	1
Mott, Anne	3	3	Haynie, Elisha	4	1	Forrester, Robert	4	1	Knott, James	3	4
Jones, Elizabeth	3	....	Nash, John	5	....	Garner, Jesse	8	3	Lewis, William	3	4
Beckham, Catharine	4	....	Burton, William	5	2	Dawson, George	6	2	Hall, Stephen	9	8
Rich, David	1	....	Burton, Richard	8	....	Thomas, John	6	....	Self, William	7	....
Haynie, Elizabeth	4	....	Stephens, John	3	....	Garner, Winifred	1	3	Lutterall, Leroy	3	....
Rogers, Sarah	4	1	Tycer, Judith	3	....	Tillory, Samuel	5	....	Self, John	3	3
Corbell, John	1	1	Watts, Mary	2	....	Brumley, Daniel	5	4	Douglass, Edward	7	1
Flint, John	8	1	Keene, William	5	11	Barns, Neddy	7	1	Douglass, William	6	....
Morison, Richard	7	8	Christopher, John, Senr	9	12	Barns, Neddy, Jr	3	1	Hale, John	5	....
Cornish, William	10	....	Crowther, John	7	....	Hall, Peter	4	....	Harrison, John R.	3	1
Weaver, Lucy	1	3	Haynie, Henry, Senr	6	....	Oldham, William	3	7	Roberts, John	3	....
Walker, George	4	3	Conway, Edwin	1	3	Dawson, William	6	....	Walker, Daniel	5	....
Mott, Moseley	4	5	Ball, Spencer M.	20	83	Oldham, George	2	....	Jones, Charles, Junr	3	1
Doxey, John	3	3	Crowther, Thomas	6	....	Neale, Jane	5	14	Straughan, Samuel L.	3	3
Williams, Mary Anne	5	4	Rice, William, Senr	10	16	Boush, Bennett	5	....	Hall, John	10	....
Cockarill, Elizabeth	2	3	Rice, Elizabeth	4	4	Mealey, James	6	1	Bailey, Stephen	8	....
Newsome, Robert	4	2	Todd, Cornelius	3	....	Thomas, William	6	3	Lewis, James	4	5
			Downing, Thomas	8	53	Baylis, John	4	....			

NORTHUMBERLAND COUNTY—Continued.

ST. STEPHEN'S PARISH—LIST OF ABRAM BRACKHAM—continued.

NAME OF HEAD OF FAMILY.	White.	Black.
Sharley, Arjalon	7	
Beacham, Thomas	5	
Hudson, Robuck	7	
Maskill, Thomas	5	
Winstead, James	7	
Brumley, Samuel	3	1
Greenstreet, Richard	8	
Vanlandingham, Benjamin, Jr	4	
Vanlandingham, James	7	
Vanlandingham, Geo. A	7	
Efford, Zachariah	5	8
Butler, James	3	
Harper, Joshua	4	
Lathrom, William	7	
Standley, Thomas	3	1
Winstead, Winifred	5	7
Eidson, Creaton	4	
Winstead, Daniel	6	
Jenkins, John	3	1
Beacham, Parker	8	
Cookman, Rice	12	6
Dawson, John	10	
Dawson, George	4	
Self, Matthias	8	
Claughton, Thomas	4	5
Brown, Jeremiah	3	
Folks, William	3	2
Norwood, Anne	5	
Self, William	6	6
Dameron, Roger	4	1
Oldham, Leroy, Junr	2	4
Oldham, Thomas	6	1
Stuckey, James	5	
Beacham, John, Senr	5	
Williams, George	4	
Cralle, Samuel	4	14
Hughs, John	7	
White, George	10	
Leader, Samuel	10	
Self, Thomas	3	
Short, Benedict	7	
Lewis, William, Junr	3	
Hale, Anne	3	
Claughton, Pemberton	6	15
Lewis, John	6	
Jones, Walter	10	26
Davis, John	9	11
Lamkin, Anne	9	1
Self, Henry	4	2
Claughton, James	10	10
Hardwich, John	6	8
Dale, John	5	3
Vanlandingham, Benjamin, Jr	4	
Yates, Amey	3	
Neale, William	2	6
Brin, Joshua	8	
King, Henry	6	
Keene, Sarah	9	20
Keene, Newton (Estate)		14
Beman, William	4	3
Larkin, Patrick	2	
Fulks, John	6	7
Dameron, William	7	4
Cox, Anne	6	18
Jones, Joshua	5	
Jones, Joshua, Jr	1	
Beacham, Daniel	4	

ORANGE COUNTY.

LIST OF ZACH'Y BURNLEY.

NAME OF HEAD OF FAMILY.	White.	Black.
Powell, Benjamin	7	5
Sullivan, William	4	10
Miller, Robert	11	2
Fortson, Thomas	8	6
Kee, Simon	9	
Jarrell, Solomon	5	
Taylor, Charles	8	
Roach, David	4	
Furnis, Eliza	3	
Walker, Charles	9	6
Taylor, James (son of Charles)	5	
Collins, William	6	13
Powell, Mary	7	1
Sheflett, Eliza	5	
Cross, Abner	8	
Bush, James	4	
Jarrell, James	11	
Bryant, Edward	5	
Kendall, John	7	
Crow, Daniel	7	
White, John	9	17
Beadles, John	3	2
Coffer, Jacob	5	4
Powell, Thomas	9	
Underwood, Reuben	9	
Thornton, George	6	19
Walker, Thomas	1	6
Underwood, Margaret	8	
Taylor, James	5	
Taylor, William	1	
Powell, Francis	8	4
Duncan, James	8	
Furnis, Eliza	7	
Eddens, Joseph	3	18
Rucker, John	2	
Stanards, Wm		52
Pickett, Mace	3	3
Plunkett, Jesse	6	6
Simpson, James	8	5
Scott, Wm	3	7
Page, John	10	3
Neal, Macajah	2	
Burnley, Zach	9	60

LIST OF JAMES MADISON.

NAME OF HEAD OF FAMILY.	White.	Black.
Baylor, John		84
Bell, Mary	10	32
Barnett, Henry	7	
Bickers, Robert	8	
Bickers, William	6	
Boston, Yowell	6	
Blair, James	3	
Brown, William	8	
Beale, William	1	19
Burnley, Garland	7	12
Coleman, Thomas	7	6
Brown, William, Junr	7	
Coleman, James	4	
Clark, Joseph	6	
Chew, Martha	4	9
Carlton, Richard	5	
Edwards, William	8	
Finnell, William	11	
Gaston, Zachy	8	
Graves, John	2	
Glassell, Andrew	1	5
Herndon, Zachy	7	18
Hancock, William	7	
James, Nicholas	5	2
Leathers, John	14	
Leak, William	5	2
Mozingo, Spence	6	
Madison, James	6	88
Madison, Ambrose	3	30
Mallory, Thomas	12	1
Newman, James	7	19
Newman, William	8	1
Newman, George	6	3
Noell, John	4	
Petty, John	5	
Porter, Benjamin	5	11
Roman, Philip	6	
Stevenson, Thomas	9	3
Sutton, Samuel	6	
Sutton, William	7	
Sanford, Pearce	8	
Stockdell, John	4	16
Shepherd, Andrew	8	13
Self, Vincent	5	2
Smith, Jeremiah	6	
Taliaferro, Hay	1	21
Taylor, James	2	40
Taylor, James, Junr	6	22
Taylor, Erasmus	12	34
Taylor, Francis	1	1
Taylor, George		21
Taylor, Charles	4	14
Taylor, Chapman	2	5
Terrell, Robert	4	21
Thomas, Sarah	2	12
Vaughn, James	5	
Winslow, Benjamin	8	6
Willis, Lewis	4	6
Watson, Samuel	5	
Rice, Michael	9	3
Bickers, Thomas	3	

LIST OF AND'W SHEPHERD.

NAME OF HEAD OF FAMILY.	White.	Black.
Banner, Joseph	3	
Bourn, Henry	11	
Bourn, William	6	
Beckham, James	10	5
Bramham, Spencer	10	
Bohan, Benjamin	5	
Bohan, Benjamin, Junr	3	
Bohan, John	4	
Booth, John	7	
Bryant, Thomas	6	1
Cartie, william	4	6
Cockran, Patrick	4	5
Clark, John	8	7
Dale, Alexander	6	
Davis, Thomas	3	6
Foster, Anthony	5	2
Foster, Thomas, Junr	5	2
George, Catherine	11	8
Gillett, Lawrence	4	1
Herring, William	4	
Jones, George	10	1
Jones, Hugh	3	
Jameson, James	6	2
Jameson, Margaret	1	4
Jameson, William	3	2
Kendall, John	8	
Lantor, Thomas	5	
Moore, Francis	3	14
Moore, Francis, Junr	12	10
Moore, Reuben	7	10
Mothershead, Nathl	2	3
Minor, Jeremiah	9	2
Minor, William	4	
Morton, Richard	7	
Moores, Lucy (Estate)		5
Newman, Alexander	8	3
Newman, Abner	3	1
Porter, Charles	14	20
Price, John	6	5
Price, Richard	4	3
Ransdell, Jessee	5	
Ransdell, John	8	
Ransdell, William	11	
Spencer, Joseph	11	10
Thornton, William	7	
Thornton, John	3	
Thornton, James	10	
Thornton, Daniel	11	
Terrell, John	9	
Tweesdell, William	4	
Thomas, Joseph	9	7
Waugh, Alexander	2	16
Waugh, George	2	7

LIST OF CATLETT CONWAY.

NAME OF HEAD OF FAMILY.	White.	Black.
Hunter, William	7	39
Mothershead, Mary	9	9
Bruce, Charles	11	30
Morton, William	3	30
Clark, Jesse F	8	
Strother, William	3	4
Thornton, William	7	
Reynolds, Richard	7	6
Morrison, Thomas	6	4
Barker, James	5	
Hansford, John	10	
Hilman, Joseph	8	
Pannell, William	11	19
Chambers, John	11	2
Gibson, Jonathan	5	8
Bramham, John	5	
Martin, Benjamin	11	2
King, John	2	1
Graves, Richard	10	11
Stubblefield, George	5	3
Robb, James	13	17
Conway, Catlett	7	27
Hughs, Francis	8	2
Mallory, Uriel	9	17
Cooke, John	5	2
Cooke, Henry	9	
Long, Richard	3	
Long, John	3	
Bradley, Robert	7	
Coghill, Zachy	9	
Lancestor, William	7	4
Miller, John	7	4
Tinder, James	10	
Scott, Ann	4	
Scott, Reuben	3	
Summers, Thomas	6	
Welch, Thomas	6	6
Wotherspoon, James	6	
Goodlet, Adam	21	6
Faulconer, John	6	6
Dawson, John	10	
Chisham, John	8	1
Perry, Lewis	4	3
Abell, Richard	8	1
Abell, Caleb	4	1

LIST OF THOMAS BARBOUR.

NAME OF HEAD OF FAMILY.	White.	Black.
Barbour, Thomas	10	30
Brookes's, John		24
Burton, May, Junr	5	7
Burton, John	8	4
Burton, Ambrose	9	1
Burton, James	9	
Bruce, David	9	
Ballard, Thomas, Junr	7	
Beadler, Robert	4	3
Ballard, Philip	10	3
Ballard, Philip, Junr	5	
Ballard, Philip, the younger	1	
Ballard, Elijah	6	
Beazley, James, Junr	3	1
Ballard, William	8	
Burton, May	4	7
Bruce, Mordicai	3	
Collins, William	5	1
Carters, John, 2n	16	30
Connoley, James	6	6
Chapman, Joseph	7	3
Carrell, John	5	6
Belfield, Cave	4	5
Coffer, James	12	
Creel, Charles	5	1
Daughoney, Thomas	11	13
Daughoney, James	5	
Ehart, Jacob	4	
Gulley, Enoch	5	
Gan, Lewis	3	7
Head, Benjamin	8	11
Haney, Benjamin	5	
Hening, Thomas	4	
Johnson, Benjamin	5	18
Johnson, Martin	3	7
Jones, William	7	
Lucas, John	10	
Lucas, William	8	17
Mallory, Nathan	9	3
Oliver, Tabitha	6	5
Pearson, Robert	8	2
Payne, John	10	3
Patterson, Joseph	6	
Payne, Richard	6	5
Rucker, John	10	6
Rucker, Peter	4	4
Rucker, Ephraim; Junr	4	
Rogers, John	7	
Smith, Thomas	4	3
Sanford, Robert	11	14
Snell, John, Junr	11	10
Stapp, Joshua	1	7
Stapp, Joshua, Junr	9	3
Stapp, Thomas	5	
Stapp, Achilles	1	
Stodghell, Isell	4	
Sebree, Richard	2	1
Sebree, Richard, Junr	7	
Sebree, William	6	1
Underwood, Joshua	8	
Wayt, James	13	2
Wilhoit, John	8	
Lucas, William, Junr	5	

LIST OF JOHNNY SCOTT.

NAME OF HEAD OF FAMILY.	White.	Black.
Acre, William	9	1
Acre, John	6	2
Bush, Francis	6	2
Boswells, John	13	16
Bell, John	8	20
Buckner, William	11	11
Craig, Elijah	9	20
Cowherd, Jonathan	8	14
Davis, Joseph	9	7
Dearing, Robert, Junr	5	2
Davis, Jonathan	10	5
Dearing, John	4	1
Dearing, Edward	4	11
Davis, James	4	1
Daniel, John	3	8
Eastin, Elizabeth	6	10
Eve, Hancy	6	1
Gellaspy, David	11	9

ORANGE COUNTY—Continued.

NAME OF HEAD OF FAMILY.	White.	Black.	NAME OF HEAD OF FAMILY.	White.	Black.	NAME OF HEAD OF FAMILY.	White.	Black.	NAME OF HEAD OF FAMILY.	White.	Black.
LIST OF JOHNNY SCOTT—continued.			**LIST OF JEREMIAH WHITE—continued.**			**LIST OF WILLIAM MOORE—continued.**			**LIST OF ROWLAND THOMAS—continued.**		
Gaines, Richard	2	5	Harvey, Joseph	4	....	Atkins, Benjamin	4	....	Daniel, Robert	4	5
Hill, David	12	....	Brook, Thomas	3	16	Atkins, John	4	....	Brown, John	4	....
Harrod, Moses	8	....	White, Jeremiah	12	16	Alcock, John	6	10	Loyd, John	9	....
Hamilton, John T	7	24	Bell, William	2	17	Atkins, James, Junr	8	....	Knowles, Noah	8	....
Jones, Thomas	12	9	Simmons, Ephraim	4	5	Atkins, John	4	....	Moore, George	6	....
Martin, Robert	10	9				Atkins, William	5	....	Peacher, William	10	2
Martin, Ann	1	7	**LIST OF BENJA. GRYMES.**			Brockman, Lewis	11	5	Collins, John	11	....
Merry, Prittyman	7	7				Boling, Ann	3	....	Allen, David	3	1
Marr, Alexander	8	5	Grymes, Benjamin	5	40	Boling, John	12	....	Reynolds, Joseph	4	5
Mallory, Roger	10	2	Gaines, Robert	9	2	Bullock, Richard	10	....	Mountague, Peter	7	....
Morris, John	6	....	Spotswood, John	8	39	Bell, Thomas	8	2	Stevens, Benjamin	4	1
Martin, Ann	8	3	Jacobs, Robert C	2	13	Burrus, Thomas	5	12	Smith, Stephen	3	3
Smith, George	7	8	Jones, Churchill	2	23	Brockman, Samuel, Junr	4	6	Fisher, Nicha	4	....
Smith, Joseph	12	27	Hume, William	6	4	Brockman, William	3	2	Proctor, Uriah	5	....
Sutton, John, Junr	3	2	Woolford, John	4	....	Brockman, Samuel	3	13	Lancestor, Robert	3	....
Scott, Johnny	5	20	Wells, George	4	....	Brockman, John	8	4	Proctor, John	8	....
Silvester, Joseph	3	1	Rossan, Joseph	2	....	Burrus, Mary	9	1	Lancestor, Richard	4	....
Taylor, Zachary	5	15	Hawkens, Elisha	2	....	Bledsoe, John	4	....	Daniel, Eliza	3	13
Taylor, Alexander	7	....	Martin, Henry	7	8	Chiles, Henry	7	2	Coleman, James	9	14
Winslow, Harry	5	5	Chapman, George	3	1	Chandler, Jeremiah	10	....	Barrett, David	4	....
Webb, William	10	18	Smith, Stephen	8	4	Crosthwait, Jacob	12	4	Morton, Elijah	5	12
Willis, John	4	24	Sanders, Nathl	13	2	Cooper, James	12	....	Arnold, Elisha	4	....
White, Jonathan	4	....	Parish, Joseph	9	....	Duncan, Joseph	6	7	Herndon, William	1	....
Young, John	6	17	Bledsoe, George	2	....	Daniel, Vivian	6	3	Clayton, Henry	7	1
Young, William	5	12	Sullivan, William	7	....	Embre, John	4	6	Wright, John	8	2
Hawkins, John	8	2	Smith, James	5	1	Freeman, Isaac	7	....	Grady, James	4	1
			Morris, Reuben	1	....	Graves, Isaac	7	10	Hiatt, Stephen	4	4
LIST OF JEREMIAH WHITE.			Morris, Thomas	5	....	Garton, Uriah	7	....	Hudson, Rush	8	2
Riddle, Lewis	3	6	Webb, Richd	6	3	Gaines, James	7	2	Dear, John	5	1
Shackleford, Edmund	7	4	Webb, John C	9	....	Groom, William	10	....	Reynolds, William	8	7
Ansill, Edward	6	3	Overton, Obediah	6	....	Goodrich, John	8	....	Dear, Catherine	4	....
Riddle, James	9	10	Overton, George	7	....	Harris, Lindsay	5	....	Chandler, Robert	5	1
Ham, Samuel	6	....	Oakes, Major	12	....	Henderson, John	4	17	Bradley, William	9	....
Lamb, Thomas	7	....	Lucas, Thomas	8	....	Harris, Thomas	6	6	Bradley, Richard	3	....
Hainey, James	1	....	Conner, Timothy	9	1	Lendrum, Thomas	5	....	Dear, Charles	2	....
Collier, William	3	....	Rhodes, John	4	....	Lindsay, Caleb	1	3	Chandler, Joseph	7	11
Collier, Martin	5	....	Jennings, John	10	....	Lendrum, Reuben	7	....	Hiatt, Sarah	6	....
Rogers, William	8	....	Jones, John	1	....	Moore, William	15	53	Dear, Thomas	6	1
Ogg, Alexander	9	2	Bradley, Benjamin	4	1	Manspoil, Michael	8	4	Wright, William	7	2
Estis, Samuel	6	2	Richards, Joseph	5	....	Manning, Andrew	2	13	Herndon, James	8	3
Goodall, John	9	11	Robinson, John	9	1	Morton, George	8	13			
Cox, William	9	4	Head, Benjamin	3	1	Oakes, John	7	....	**LIST OF THOS. BELL.**		
Lamb, John	11	....	Singleton, Daniel	1	5	Payne, William	8	2	Allen, Richard	6	8
Stodghell, John	12	....	Bledsoe, John	2	9	Pollock, William	9	16	Atkens, Joseph	5	12
Lamb, Richard	11	....	Humphreys, William	4	....	Payne, Judy	1	2	Boston, Joseph	10	5
Lamb, William	7	....	Smith, Jesse	8	....	Page, John	5	....	Cockburn, Robert	6	....
Ogg, John	4	4	Gorden, James	1	15	Payne, Thomas	10	5	Campbell, Rosanna	9	2
Earley, James	10	33	Hawkins, William	7	3	Quisenberry, Aaron	4	14	Davis, James	3	1
Williams, David	6	....	Lancestor, John	7	....	Quisenberry, Aaron, Junr	8	5	Finnell, John	7	5
Haney, John	3	....	Perry, Peirce	8	....	Quisenberry, William	4	10	Finnell, Simon	9	1
Ham, Samuel, jr	5	....	Hawkins, Reubin	5	....	Quisenberry, Moses	9	1	Grace, George	4	1
Petties, Martin	3	....	Wood, John	4	....	Quisenberry, John	7	1	Hawkins, James	2	4
Smith, Wm	10	....	Wood, James	3	....	Quisenberry, James	5	1	Ingram, William	2	....
Raines, Richard	2	....	Procter, John	3	3	Richards, William	9	1	Jacksons, John	....	18
Lane, Edward	6	4	Pigg, Mourning	7	....	Smith, Ann	3	....	Lee, John	9	....
White, John, Junr	12	4	Jones, Elijah	7	....	Smith, James	9	6	Lee, William	8	....
Davis, Henry	7	....	Richards, Philimon	5	....	Smith, Stephen J. K	2	1	Marsh, Edward	2	3
Lane, Littleberry	8	1	Richards, Ambrose	4	....	Shackleford, Zachy	10	2	Porter, Abner	7	12
Shiflett, John	3	....	Jones, Thomas	5	....	Tandy, Henry	12	17	Ransdell, Sanford	4	3
Shackleford, Henry	6	....	Perry, Henry	2	....	Thomas, Edward	9	3	Samuel, John	7	7
Snow, Thomas	13	....	Bledsoe, Moses	4	....	Thomas, William	4	4	Sleet, James	8	6
Bryson, John	7	....	Row, Edmund	8	4	Wright, John	7	3	Thompson, Samuel	5	2
Eastis, William	....	2	Row, Thomas	6	....	Williams, Jacob	11	1	Taliaferro, Francis	6	33
Harvey, Thomas	4	....	Wharton, George	9	....				Bell, Thomas	10	30
Simmons, Ephraim	7	....	Faulconer, Thomas	11	1	**LIST OF ROWLAND THOMAS.**			Taliaferro, Lawrence	10	61
Douglass, Margaret	2	....				Thomas, Rowland	10	13	Dade, Francis	2	12
Herring, Francis	4	....	**LIST OF WILLIAM MOORE.**			Thomas, Rowland, Junr	3	3			
Bruce, Eliza	4	2	Atkins, Edward	4	....	Stubblefield, Robert	7	9			
Slater, Agnes	6	....	Atkins, James	6	....	Sharpe, Thomas	10	4			
Head, James	5	8									

PITTSYLVANIA COUNTY.

NAME OF HEAD OF FAMILY.	White.	Black.	NAME OF HEAD OF FAMILY.	White.	Black.	NAME OF HEAD OF FAMILY.	White.	Black.	NAME OF HEAD OF FAMILY.	White.	Black.
Shelton, Crispin	3	37	Todd, William	8	15	Keatts, John	8	6	Greggory, William	3	6
Shelton, Abraham	12	6	Roberts, Joseph	15	9	Crenshaw, Joseph	2	3	Tunstall, Thomas, jr	3	6
Shelton, Gabriel	13	6	Bruce, James, Senr	3	3	Hamblett, Tilletha	3	....	Short, Joshua	4	....
Shelton, Beaverley	8	4	Terrell, Richd	5	....	Lankford, Ben	8	12	Farris, Charles	8	....
Shelton, Vincent	5	2	Rowland, John	7	....	Vaughan, Thomas	5	3	Buckley, John	1	1
Hurt, Moses	9	4	Rowland, Simon	7	....	Vaughan, Wm	8	6	Turner, Mesheck	8	10
Fambraugh, Ben	7	....	Shelton, Daniel	11	9	Vaughan, Wm, jr	2	....	Turner, Shadrick	8	2
Barber, David	10	....	McBryant, John	5	....	Vaughan, Thomas, jr	3	....	Vaughan, Alexander	7	....
Stark, Turner	4	6	Parham, James	....	1	Irby, Francis	6	3	Hodges, Jesse	5	....
Cleaven, John	4	....	Swinney, Joseph	1	....	Farris, Joseph, Senr	12	1	Solomon, John	8	....
Davis, Thomas	8	1	Pace, William	9	2	Allen, George	4	....	George, John	9	10
Lattamore, Samuel	8	1	Thurston, John	5	....	Stone, Joshua	7	7	Cheek, Richd	3	2
Farris, Jacob	9	....	Taylor, Edmund	6	....	Doss, William	9	....	Dix, John	5	21
Keezee, Richard	2	2	Payne, Thomas	3	....	Sanders, William	5	....	Dix, William	2	2
Keezee, Jeremiah	5	1	Payne, William	7	....	Allen, William	5	....	Wynne, Thomas	10	5
Keezee, Charles	8	....	King, James	10	....	Todd, Richard	3	2	Farguson, Joseph	12	....
Bruce, James, jr	2	....	Shelton, John	10	....	George, James	5	3	Fearn, Thomas	1	15
Mitchell, Henry	10	....	Poore, Adam	11	....	Griggory, John	3	6	Hands, Richd	3	....
Bates, Daniel	2	....	Brown, Janson	4	....	Betterton, William	10	....	Jones, Samuel	5	....
Nicholes, Jacob	10	....	Clark, Martha	5	2	Vasan, William	4	....	Gossett, James	5	....
Doss, John	6	....	Waller, John	6	2	Mcbee, James	6	2	Brown, Thomas	4	....
Bird, John	8	....	Keatts, Charles	3	1	Henderson, James	4	2	Wynne, John	8	10
Musteen, Thomas	7	....	Keatts, William	6	1	Allen, William, Senr	5	....	Hendrick, Absalum	2	....
Musteen, Jesse	8	....	Lewis, Charles, senr	8	8	Farris, Joseph, jr	5	....	Thomas, William	9	13
Brown, James	6	....	Lewis, Charles, jr	1	5	Perkins, John	3	....	Wynne, Robert	12	4
Irby, Peter	10	3	Shelton, Ben	7	8	Tunstall, Thomas, Senr	6	13	Binnion, William	4	10

PITTSYLVANIA COUNTY—Continued.

NAME OF HEAD OF FAMILY.	White.	Black.	NAME OF HEAD OF FAMILY.	White.	Black.	NAME OF HEAD OF FAMILY.	White.	Black.	NAME OF HEAD OF FAMILY.	White.	Black.
Everett, Daniel	9	8	Luck, Sarah	7	2	Brown, Richd	5	9	Mullins, John	4	1
Cook, George, jr	4		Baber, James	2		Mottley, Joseph	9	12	Roberson, James	5	
Pistole, Thomas	10		Childries, Major	9		Mottley, Danl	1		Burton, Charles	9	4
Warsham, John	4	12	Cheek, William	8	1	Meadows, Joal	8	1	Payne, Robert	13	21
Warsham, Daniel	6	2	West, Joseph	7		Willard, Beaverley	4		Barker, Sarah	4	
Nelson, James	7		West, George	3		Murphey, George	7		McLane, John	8	
Wier, John	4	2	Templeton, Robt	6		Dickinson, Thos C	1		McLane, Thomas	2	
Wier, Bazeal	3	8	Hubbard, Eliza	8		Bayes, Joseph	8	3	Yates, John	7	
Cantrill, James	2		East, John	3		Bayes, Joseph, Senr	3		Bynum, Samuel	9	8
Dix, James	6	11	East, Thomas	7	3	Greggory, Wm	3	8	Lynch, William	10	1
Chapman, Hannah	21		Burton, Edward	3		Burton, James	11		Harris, Samuel	7	21
Cook, George, Senr	7		Pryor, Edwd	6	4	Burton, Wm	3	1	Wilson, Bazel	2	3
Cook, Elijah	4		Vaughan, Thomas	4		Markham, John	5	9	Ashworth, John	2	2
Combs, Betsey	5		Vaughan, John	9		Cantrill, Joshua	6	1	Smith, Randolph	2	
Woody, James	5	6	Burns, Jeremiah	6	2	Johnson, Ann	7		Givins, John	7	
Thrasher, Benja	2	2	Lester, Thomas	11		McGeehee, Matthew	2		Cook, Josiah	7	
Glasley, Joseph	3		Brown, Henry	7		McGeehee, James	2		Elliott, Richd	5	
Owen, John	9		Craddock, John	6	7	Duncan, Thomas	4		Thomas, Margret	8	
Worfe, Thomas	6		Mitchell, James	6	2	Gibson, Julius	4		Elliott, William	5	
Going, Seth	11	8	Hunt, Joel	7	7	Gibson, Richd	8		Vincient, William	4	
Hudson, Amey	5		Glass, Thomas	5	1	Yates, George	4		Elliott, John	2	
Stillwell, Jacob, jr	3		Clifton, Thomas	4		Yates, Elizabeth	4	9	Ross, James	7	
Twiddle, William	8		Ward, Majr John		16	Lumkins, George, jr	8	3	Dyer, John	10	3
Brown, Goram	3		Childries, Matthew	6		Gwinn, George H	10	9	Worsham, Jeremiah	7	3
Asher, Samuel	6		Gilbert, Preston	5	3	Southerland, John	5	9	Holder, William	10	
Owen, Uriah	3		Clements, Isaac	9	1	Ware, Samuel	5		Dennis, John	5	
Colley, James, Senr	9		Bruce, James, jr	2		Ardin, Richd	8		Holder, Davis	4	
Prewett, Samuel	6		Bruce, Robert	11		Lay, John	6		Hardin, Mark	6	
Wynne, William	3		Lester, William	3	1	Wilson, Colo John	10	32	Witcher, William	6	8
Roberson, James	2		Parrott, Tyree	1		Wilson, Peter	6	11	Witcher, William	3	
Gossett, Shadrick	5		Barrett, John	6	1	Wilson, William	3	3	Ward, Jeremiah	8	3
Glassco, John	8	1	Barnett, William	1		Duncan, William	12		Vaughan, Hundley	6	
May, Gabriel	7		Doss, James	6		McMillion, John	9		Polley, David	9	
Stillwell, Jacob, jr	6		Doss, John	2		McMillion, Andrew	2		Hundley, Caleb	4	1
Jones, Nathan	4		Doss, James, Senr	8		Dean, Jacob	7		Witcher, James	3	
Lumkins, George, jr	8	3	Patey, Jesse	8		Whiteworth, Jacob	6		Witcher, John, senr	4	
Hendrick, Humphrey	8	5	West, Sarah	4		Travis, Wm	9		Dalton, David, jr	8	
Waller, John	10	8	McGeehee, John	4	2	Mahoon, Hugh	2		Terry, Thomas, jr	1	
Walters, John	9	3	Adams, Cha L	3	13	Southerland, George	12	15	Keezee, Jesse	7	
Walters, Thomas, Senr	9	3	Hunt, Gilbert	2	10	Lay, David	12		Dalton, Solomon	1	
Watkins, John	6	4	Hunt, David	4	10	Lay, David, jr	7		Ellis, William	7	
Sheilds, Pleasant	4		Moody, Blanks	4	1	McDaniel, James	12		Bobbitt, John	6	1
Hall, John, jr	2		Wilson, George	7		Vandeavour, John	4		Dalton, Samuel	4	
Hall, Joseph	5		Saunders, Daniel	4		Whiteby, Richd	8		Dalton, John	6	
Hall, John, Senr	7	3	Patrick, John F		13	Fallin, Redmond	2		Hudson, John	11	
Richards, Gabriel	9	3	Collins, Mary	3		Fallin, Edmd	9		Nowling, Bryant W	13	2
Durnett, William	7	5	Hunt, James	1	1	Quinn, John	4		Wade, Peyton	4	
Scott, Nimrod	6		West, Joseph	3		Quinn, William	12		Goad, John	3	
Hill, Jonathan	13		Coleman, Stephen	10	12	Quinn, Joseph	9		Hensley, John	1	
Lumkins, John	3	3	Terry, Stephen	5	7	Stone, John	4		Bobbitt, Randolph	4	
Ayres, Moses	13		Bayes, John	6		Stone, John, jr	7		Walker, James	1	7
Yark, Wm	2		Bayes, John	10		Harrison, William	10	27	Hensley, Ben	6	
Murray, Nathl	11		Short, Cornelius	4		Legg, Edward	4		Henson, Ben	1	
Matthews, Chechester	3		Singleton, James	7		Hammon, Abraham	4		Henson, William	6	
Slayton, Joseph	8	2	Brooks, John	9		Tinsley, John	3		Parker, William	7	
Walters, Robert	7	2	McDaniel, Clement	4	7	Tinsley, Thomas	8		Barger, Jacob	6	
Slayton, Daniel	8		Coleman, James	8		Hammonds, Wm	6		Mitchell, James	6	
King, Benjamin	4		Barker, Richd	5		Hammonds, Edwin	6		Terry, Thomas, senr	9	3
Burgass, Edwd	11		Walrond, William	10	14	Owen, Wm	9	1	Phillips, Jonathan	8	
Hillberry, Lemuel	7		White, Daniel	3	1	Owen, John	7	2	Witcher, John, Jr	5	
Seal, Solomon	4		Maberry, Braxton	5	6	Dix, Larkin	4	1	Reice, John	4	
Seal, James	4		White, Reubin	9		Mickleberry, Henry	10	5	Herndon, George	2	33
Harrison, Sarah	5	8	Shackleford, John	8	1	Anglin, John	9		King, Joseph, senr	6	3
Stimpson, Jeremiah	4		Kidd, Webb	9	1	Connar, Wm	7		Lovell, Daniel	9	15
Stimpson, Rachel	3		Ragsdale, Wm	10		Ragan, Timothy	5		Tuggle, Ludiwick	10	11
Stimpson, Rawsey	2		Williams, Lewis	4	1	Tomblin, Joseph	6		Black, Thomas	10	
Stimpson, Benja	10		Williams, Lucy	6	6	Cato, Sterling	5	2	Laskey, William	2	
Walters, Robert	8	6	Williams, John	3		Ramsey, James	9		Kirby, John	6	
Maslone, Reaney	4	3	Crafford, David	6		Wright, Thomas	8		Taylor, George	3	
Phleping, Joseph	6		Terry, Champ	2		Bolling, John	5		Henry, Francis	6	
Lee, Alexr	4		Terry, William	10		Tuckner, Lewis	7		Dyer, Joseph	5	
Bennett, Thomas	4		Leak, Joseph	5		Ashworth, Nathan	6		Leprade, Ben	7	
Bennett, John	6		Farmer, Isham	7	2	Prewett, John	7		Smith, Peyton	10	12
Morris, Samuel	7		Shields, Thomas	5		Shelton, Wm	10		Thompson, William	7	
Dennerson, James	5		Corbin, Thomas	3		Booth, John	8		Cook, Harmon	7	12
Echolles, Joseph	9		Corbin, Rawley	5	1	Wheeland, Thomas	5		Razan, Paul	5	
Stamps, John	9	6	Hammonds, John	5		Sparks, Matthew	4		Calland, Samuel	4	9
Hall, John	2	3	Corbin, Ambrose	12		Wright, Edward	7		Gorman, Joseph	6	
Harris, John	7		Woodson, Tucker	8		Scott, Bazel	6		Ellis, John	6	
McMunday, James	10		Allen, David	6		Scott, John	2		Mitchell, William	3	
Maddin, William	8	7	Miller, John	3		Booth, William	4		Hubbard, Matthew	4	
Maddin, John	8		Yates, John	3		Scott, Simon	10		Walker, Joseph	6	6
Adams, James	9		Farmer, James	9	8	Tenneson, Ignatius	8		Killionsen, Killion	9	
Wilson, Mary	9		Russell, William	9		Gossett, James	9		Peak, William	7	
Slayton, William	4		Irby, Charles	5	5	Ward, George	6		Atkinson, William	2	6
Mann, Jesse	4		Mayes, Joseph	6		Wells, John	3		Atkinson, William, jr	4	
Clapton, Robt	3	3	Mayes, Mattox	4		Beard, Martin	9		Atkinson, Jesse	3	
Dodson, Fortunatus	4		Blanks, Henry	6		Billings, Jasper	8		Atkinson, Nathl	6	
Anderson, Matthew	1	3	Watkins, Benja	3		Drake, Thomas	5		Walker, Elisha	5	1
McDaniel, Rhoderick	4		Brooks, Samuel	9		Justice, John	7		Campbell, John	8	
Raglin, Gideon	3	6	Johnson, Archd	9		Muncas, William	7		Burdet, William	8	
Dodson, Joshua	3		Wimbish, John	8	32	Rose, Francis	3		Peak, George	5	
Dodson, George, Senr	11	7	Basdale, Beaverley	3	3	Ware, James	1	12	Dale, Mary	6	
Cole, Tunas	8		White, Rawley	6	7	Astin, William, jr	4	4	Shockley, David	2	
Martin, Peter	9		Terry, Joseph	8	10	Williams, Charles	5	10	Shockley, James	3	
Owen, William	10		Brawner, Ben	6	1	Cornwell, Stephen	3		Justice, William	11	
Holloway, James	12	1	Ellington, Jeremiah	13	11	Lumkins, Robert	10	4	Atkinson, Henry	2	
Pratley, Francis	3		Martin, John	7	6	Astin, William	12	4	Ramsey, Thomas	12	
Lewis, Colo John	5	46	James, Thomas	7		McDaniel, Ann		10	Ramsey, Thomas, jr	3	
Hendrick, Nathl	5	3	Owen, John	8		May, John	5	1	Wray, David	3	
Hendrick, Obediah	1	9	Stewart, John	4	2	Williams, William	1		Easley, Pyrant	4	1
Pemberton, William	6		Stewart, Martha	7	5	Tomlin, Jasper	1		Allen, James	6	
Pemberton, Joseph	5		Howard Francis	4	5	Smith, Hezekiah	8	4	Meade, James	4	
Pemberton, John	5		Watkins, John	5		White, Ben	4		Burton, Elisha	8	
						Horton, Townsend	11		Wade, Edward	5	

PITTSYLVANIA COUNTY—Continued.

NAME OF HEAD OF FAMILY.	White.	Black.	NAME OF HEAD OF FAMILY.	White.	Black.	NAME OF HEAD OF FAMILY.	White.	Black.	NAME OF HEAD OF FAMILY.	White.	Black.
Hutchings, Moses	3	2	Payne, Edmund	1	....	Oakes, William	6	....	Begerley, John	9	....
Carter, Jesse	10	17	Fitzgarald, Edm^d	5	1	Oakes, James	6	4	Sparks, Matthew	10	....
Dyer, George	7	....	Medcalf, John, jr	2	....	Prewett, John	4	....	Sparks, Thos	4	....
Ferguson, Joseph	5	....	Medcalf, John, Senr	6	....	Brim, Richard	5	....	Armstrong, John	7	....
Pynor, William	3	....	Willis, Major	3	4	Emmers, Mark	1	....	Boaz, James	3	....
Lawyers, James	4	....	Adams, Cain	5	2	Nance, William	7	....	Boaze, Shadrick	4	2
Ricketts, William	6	....	Parsons, Samuel	3	....	Nance, Clement	2	....	Beck, William	7	....
Rogers, Joseph	7	....	Williams, John	5	....	Nance Martha	1	1	Beagerley, John	9	....
Nelson, Ambrose	3	....	Swinney, John	9	....	Cahill, Edward	8	....	Smith, John	12	7
Dillard, Samuel	7	1	Mayes, Joseph	9	....	Bullington, Robt	9	2	Nelson, John	10	....
Lawson, John	5	....	Swinney, James	5	....	Stephens, David	16	....	Watts, Rich^d	10	....
Lawson, Jonas	10	1	Swinney, Moses	2	....	Shores, David	3	....	Terry, Ben	10	9
Allen, Welcom	7	....	Parsons, Rich^d	5	....	Shores, Rich^d	1	....	Williams, Robt	11	39
Prosize, George	4	....	Parsons, George	3	....	Wilson, Ignatious	6	1	Wisdom, Francis	3	13
Ragsdale, Daniel	7	3	O'Neal, Bryant	3	....	Conn, Joseph	8	5	White, Jeremiah	11	17
Adams, Thomas	5	....	Willis, William	8	....	Scales, David	8	3	Lacy, Batt	8	13
Burks, James	5	....	Goodman, William	8	1	Barkshear, Henry	4	....	Terry, David	9	8
Hutchings, Aaron	3	3	Haymes, William	8	5	Norton, Ellinor	10	....	Handey, William	8	....
Payner, John	8	6	Tucker, William	5	5	Hampton, John	7	....	Handey, Ben	10	....
Adams, John	6	2	Earley, William	9	2	Dodson, Daniel	9	....	Hill, Thomas	16	....
Short, John	8	....	Tuckner, Elizabeth	5	....	Sullivan, Daniel	5	....	Chaney, Jacob	10	....
Hall, John	3	....	Farthing, Rich^d	10	....	McMillion, William	3	....	Dodson, David	8	....
Hall, Henry	7	....	Bucknall, Francis	3	....	Durham, John	10	....	Dodson, Rawley	5	....
Adams, Robert	7	3	Parsons, Joseph	8	....	Lewis, Wm	8	....	Shaw, Thomas	12	....
Freeman, Moses	7	....	Payne, Phill	1	....	Brim, Joseph	16	....	McLaughland, Ch^s	5	....
Nicholes, Josiah	2	....	Adams, Nathan	7	....	Wright, Randolph	8	....	Anderson, Mat	1	2
Prosize, Daniel	4	....	Dowell, Charles	1	....	Broadass, Rich^d	9	....	Walters, William	5	....
Hutchings, Ann	4	7	Thompson, John	4	....	Watkins, William	2	....	Herring, William	8	10
Bailey, Peter	8	....	Yates, Stephen	7	....	Brown, John	8	1	Tanner, Matthew	10	8
Hutchings, Christopher	7	9	Watson, William	9	....	Streetman, John	8	....	Terry, Joseph	1	14
Cammell, Abra	12	....	Watson, John, jr	2	....	Williams, James	4	....	Price, William	7	2
Echolles, Joshua	6	1	Watson, Thomas	8	....	Haggard, James	1	....	Wright, John	5	4
Carter, Jeduthan	6	1	Watson, John, sen^r	2	1	Perkins, William	1	....	Lawless, James	6	....
Adams, John	5	1	Parsons, John	5	....	Hampton, Henry	7	1	Reynolds, John	6	....
Vadin, Burwell	9	....	Meade, Mary	3	....	Hampton, James	4	....	Kerby, John	15	....
Ashlock, Rich^d	2	3	Caldwell, Seth	6	....	Hampton, Thomas	6	5	Harvey, John	4	....
Welch, Joshua	8	....	Caldwell, Mrs	2	....	Roberson, Thomas	6	....	Lewis, Charles	3	3
Yates, Stephen	9	....	Lackey, Thomas	7	....	Garner, James	7	1	Handey, George, jr	5	....
Handy, Thomas	12	1	Lackey, Alex^r	3	....	Read, James	2	....	Ryburn, William	6	5
Handy, William	4	....	Polley, John	1	....	Shields, Samuel	9	....	Gray, James	4	8
Pigg, John	3	10	Davis, Thomas	7	....	Burnett, James	9	....	Hughes, Nathl	11	1
Miller, Jacob	6	....	Martin, John	7	6	Cunningham, Thomas	11	....	Creel, John	8	5
Pigg, Hezekiah	8	10	Jones, Thomas	5	11	Hawkins, George	4	....	Farguson, John	8	....
Davis, William	10	9	Pain, Reubin	6	2	Read, William	10	....	Dodson, George	4	....
Davis, John	6	1	Maples, William	12	....	Deason, Enoch	6	....	Creel, Thos	4	....
Miers, George	9	1	Hammock, John	4	....	Roberson, Thomas	6	....	Dodson, Jesse	10	....
Meade, Thomas	2	....	Prosize, William	7	....	Burnett, Henry	9	9	Dodson, Thomas	5	....
Richards, Joseph	9	1	Cammeron, Uriah	7	....	Burnett, Gilbert	3	....	Prestage, John	2	....
Parks, John	12	17	Collins, Thomas	3	....	Shields, William	8	1	Smith, Orlando	13	....
Martin, John	7	....	Wilson, George	8	....	Shields, Joseph	6	....	Terry, Henry	5	....
Thacker, Nathl	10	....	Templeton, Robt	6	....	Cunningham, Elizabeth	9	....	Terry, Barton	6	....
Thacker, Joseph	8	....	Morton, Joseph	7	9	Cunningham, Joseph	9	3	Ragland, Gedion	3	4
Chambers, Thomas	8	....	Alsup, Joseph	6	....	Nash, Arthur	3	6	Terry, Henry	11	....
Chattin, John	8	2	Hawkins, Daniel	1	9	Brown, John	4	....	Hanks, Moses	8	....
Davis, Samuel	6	3	Goad, Thomas	3	....	Mosley, Saml	3	2	Walters, Elijah	4	....
Adams, Allen	7	2	Hawkins, William	10	....	Perrey, Thomas	9	....	Pond, John	6	....
Stokes, Silvanus	7	12	Reynolds, Rich^d	9	....	Richardson, Thos	5	2	Bennett, William	5	....
Hamlin, Job	2	....	Thornton, Presley	10	....	Sheilds, John	10	4	Burgas, John	6	3
Davis, George	8	....	Lansford, Henry	7	3	Grisham, Thomas	7	....	Tanner, Matthew	4	....
Davis, William	2	....	Barnett, Zadock	10	....	King, James	5	....	Wilson, John	9	2
Davis, John	8	....	Lansford, Isham	6	2	Roberson, John	19	....	Chelton, Mark	9	....
Wright, George	3	....	Mitchell, William	5	....	Grisham, James	2	....	Jackson, Joseph	9	10
Lewis, Samuel	6	....	Fullerharris, George	11	....	Shields, Thos	6	....	Kerby, Francis	3	....
Anglin, John	10	....	Perkins, Peter	7	25	Fulton, James	7	....	Hardin, Mark	6	....
Conn, George	7	6	Perkins, Nicholas	11	26	Fulton, John	8	....	Stratton, Thos	4	....
Pullim, Drury	7	....	Smith, Lemuel	4	11	Harris, John	6	....	Stratton, Ben	4	....
Watson, Nathan	4	2	Murry, Thomas	8	....	McCullock, Barnett	6	....	Daverson, Abra	3	....
Shelton, Armstead	6	....	Musgrove, Harrison	2	1	Graveley, James	7	....	Lewis, John	7	....
Jones, Elisha	3	....	Warren, Edward	6	13	Cox, John	6	....	Gardner, Nathl	5	....
Rigney, Charles	5	....	Briscoe, John	6	13	Perkins, Volentine	6	....	Hodnett, Mary	9	3
Rigney, John	6	....	Perkins, Constant	5	18	Crowley, Benj^a	15	2	King, Elijah	10	3
Bransom, Absalum	9	....	Spencer, Abra	2	1	Reynolds, Spencer	8	2	Henry, James (quarter)	....	13
Rigney, Jonathan	5	....	Toney, Sherwood	5	....	Wright, Rand	6	....	Hendrick, John H	6	1
Johnson, James	8	11	Jinkins, Phillip	4	5	Young, John	5	....	Dodson, Zachariah	10	6
Shelton, Spencer	7	....	Harris, David	10	....	Weatherford, Harden	3	....	Chelton, Thos	7	....
Moore, William	10	....	Harris, Rich^d	6	....	Farrow, Rich^d	3	....	Kelley, Hugh	4	....
Portor, William	5	....	Oakes, Charles	5	1	Alsup, Joseph	3	....	Chelton, William	5	....
Bucknall, William	7	....	Minter, Joseph	7	3	Weatherford, John	5	....	Fitzgerald, John	9	....
Jones, William	5	2	Southerland, William	8	....	Young, James	7	....	Slate, Samuel	12	....
Parks, William	3	1	Southerlin, Jesse	8	....	Riger, Jacob	8	3	Chaney, Ezekial	8	....
Parsons, William	3	....	Stephens, Thomas	7	....	Fauntane, Jos	4	3	Dodson, Joshua	5	....
Wareham, John	8	....	Farrow, Stephen	5	....	Young, George	5	5	Dyer, James	8	....
Willis, John	3	1	Rickles, John F	10	....	Grooms, Zachariah	6	....			
			Watkins, Isaiah	10	1	Denton, James	6	....			

SURRY COUNTY.

NAME OF HEAD OF FAMILY.	White.	Black.	NAME OF HEAD OF FAMILY.	White.	Black.	NAME OF HEAD OF FAMILY.	White.	Black.	NAME OF HEAD OF FAMILY.	White.	Black.
Adams, William	5	2	Bailey, William, j^r	5	4	Bishop, James, jun^r	2	1	Bedingfield, Ann	8	7
Anthony, William	5	....	Burt, Elizabeth	2	6	Bishop, John	7	....	Bailey, Anselm	5	28
Adamson, Andrew	2	2	Buchanan, Susanna	1	10	Bishop, Thomas	8	....	Burgiss, Thomas	1	10
Allen, William, Esqr	9	83	Bailey, William	4	3	Barker, Elizabeth	2	....	Bryant, Jesse	5	....
Avoris, John	7	5	Barradall, Robert	5	3	Byrd, Joseph	6	....	Brown, James	10	....
Andrews, Nathaniel	8	2	Bishop, Joshua	6	....	Browne, William, Esqr	10	54	Batts, John	11	9
Andrews, John, Senr	3	1	Bishop, James, Senr	1	6	Bage, Thomas, Senr	2	7	Bailey, John	2	11
Andrews, William	9	3	Bagley, Hannah	3	1	Bartle, John	3	3	Bailey, Lemuel	5	15
Andrews, William	11	7	Bilbro, Benj^a	1	1	Bailey, William	10	7	Bailey, Benj^a	5	15
Adams, William	1	5	Bishop, Benj^a	5	....	Bartle, Thomas	2	2	Bailey, Samuel	6	45
Adams, Martha	3	7	Barker, Elizabeth	5	1	Browne, Benj^a E	2	8	Bell, Stephen	6	....
Allen, John	7	....	Barker, Lucy	1	1	Bailey, Mary	3	6	Briggs, Benj^a	3	7
Alexander, James	5	7	Bishop, David	10	....	Browne, William, jr	4	23	Bland, Thomas	6	5
Belsches, James	3	21	Burgiss, John	6	7	Brock, William	3	1	Barham, Joseph	7	4
Badgett, John	3	....	Barker, Lemuel	5	3	Bryant, John	3	....	Berriman, Mary	4	....

SURRY COUNTY—Continued.

NAME OF HEAD OF FAMILY.	White.	Black.
Bennett, William	7	3
Binns, Elizabeth	4	14
Barham, Faith	5	1
Bell, Benjᵃ	7	4
Bell, Silviah	10	7
Brown, John	2	....
Bryant, James	4	....
Barlow, James	6	....
Bell, Robert	7	2
Bell, Jacob	5	....
Bruce, James	8	....
Browne, Edward	6	7
Browne, Ann	3	....
Bennett, Ann	7	....
Blow, William	2	6
Banks, John	7	....
Barham, John	6	....
Brown, James	7	9
Berriman, Nathaniel	8	2
Barlow, George	4	....
Barlow, James	4	4
Brown, Richard D	6	32
Cocke, John, Esqʳ	6	30
Cheatham, John	8	16
Coman, John	2	2
Collier, Benjᵃ	4	3
Cunninghame, Robert	2	3
Cocke, Catharine	5	15
Cheatham, Rebecca	2	5
Charity, David	4	....
Cary, Martha	6	2
Cocke, John	4	10
Cocke, William	2	19
Collins, William	2	29
Campbell, Archibald	7	36
Caseley, Edmund	1	....
Cooper, Frederick	4	....
Caseley, Michael	5	4
Charity, Sarah	7	....
Caseley, John	2	1
Cooper, John	6	2
Cocke, Lemuel	4	30
Clinch, William, jr	5	10
Clinch, William, Senʳ	9	26
Clarke, James	3	10
Cryer, Nicholas	3	2
Carrell, Mary	7	1
Charity, Henry	9	....
Collier, John	5	7
Cocke, Ann	2	17
Collier, Lucy	2	2
Cocke, Richard	8	21
Cocke, John H	8	27
Coggin, Micajah	8	1
Clarke, Etheldred	9	....
Clarke, William	3	1
Cocks, Jesse	4	6
Cocks, William, jr	2	....
Cocke, Thomas	7	45
Cocks, William	7	17
Clarke, Martha	6	3
Cofer, Thomas	10	5
Carter, William	8	....
Cocks, Mary	5	....
Clarke, Jesse	6	....
Cornwell, Joseph	4	5
Crafford, Henry	9	24
Colcote, Harwood	3	4
Crafford, Carter	6	25
Crafford, Mary	1	11
Dunlop, Archibald	1	34
Dewell, Mary	2	....
Dewell, Thomas	6	....
Dewell, Jesse	1	....
Dewell, Littleberry	7	....
Dewell, Drury	1	....
Deleereaux, John	13	....
Dewell, Richard	1	....
Dowden, Thomas	1	....
Dewell, James	6	....
Deleereaux, David	11	....
Davis, Martha	8	3
Davis, James	1	8
Dicken, William	2	....
Degge, Anthony	6	3
Drewry, Richard	3	5
Davis, Thomas	9	5
Davis, John, Senʳ	1	5
Davis, James	11	....
Davis, Thomas	4	3
Delk, Lucy	3	2
Davidson, Thomas	6	6
Derring, William	2	6
Degge, Anthony, junʳ	11	32
Davis, Dolphin	3	....
Davis, Francis	7	....
Emery, Charles	8	....
Ellis, Thomas	2	1
Emery, John, Sen	8	....
Emery, Sarah	4	....
Emery, Howell	5	....
Ellis, Benjᵃ	4	7
Emery, James	4	....
Ellis, Jonathan	5	9
Evans, William	6	21
Emery, Ruth	6	1
Edwards, Etheldred	8	7
Edwards, James	7	2
Edwards, Hartwell	2	....
Edwards, J'Anson	7	11
Eaton, Rebecca	7	11
Ingram, Patience	6	....
Edwards, Wm Phil	6	5
Edwards, Lewis	....	2
Edwards, William	10	....
Fugler, Mary	4	1
Fletcher, Thomas	2	11
Faulcon, Nicholas, Sen	4	17
Faulcon, Jacob	8	16
Faulcon, Nicholas, jr	10	35
Foster, Richard	4	6
Grantham, Stephen	6	....
Grantham, Thomas	5	7
Gilchrist, James	3	8
Gilbert, Henry	6	10
Gardner, George	4	4
Gwaltney, Joseph	4	....
Gwaltney, William	4	....
Gwaltney, Benjᵃ	6	....
Gwaltney, John	7	....
Green, William	4	....
Gwaltney, Thomas	6	17
Goodrich, Charles	6	3
Gray, Henry	5	3
Gray, John	7	....
Gray, James	10	10
Harrison, Nathaniel, jr	5	41
Harriss, Thomas	5	10
Harriss, William	6	26
Howard, Henry, jr	4	13
Hill, Mary	1	3
Howard, Henry, Sen	4	12
Howard, Thomas	9	20
Hill, Stirling	6	4
Hamlin, William	5	5
Holdsworth, Rebecca	5	11
Holdsworth, John W	4	16
Hargrave, Hinchea	4	....
Holt, William	5	2
Holleman, Joseph, Sen	10	13
Hargrave, Lucy	6	....
Hargrave, John	1	1
Holleman, Joseph, jr	4	5
Hart, Joseph	4	3
Harris, Chapman	9	1
Hargrave, Robert	4	20
Hargrave, Anselm	6	6
Hart, Hartwell	5	10
Holt, Joseph	6	2
Hutchings, John	11	43
Holt, Thomas	8	1
Holleway, Lazarus	11	....
Holleway, Jesse	7	....
Holleway, Job	5	1
Hart, Bramley	2	4
Harrison, William	7	....
Hartwell, James	8	....
Hart, William	9	35
Hunnicutt, Hartwell	5	....
Harrison, John	4	10
Holt, Archer	5	....
Holt, Elizabeth	6	6
Hunnicutt, Robert	1	10
Hunnicutt, John	3	15
Hunnicutt, Augustine	3	1
Holt, William	6	11
Holt, James	4	3
J'Anson, Thomas	1	10
Jarratt, John	9	12
Jimm, Rice	5	2
Johnson, Peter, Junʳ	9	....
Johnson, Thomas	3	1
Justiss, William	5	6
Johnson, Levy	5	....
Johnson, William	7	....
Johnson, Mary	1	1
Johnson, Peter, Senʳ	3	....
Jones, Jane	4	....
Justiss, Elizabeth	4	....
Jones, Nathan	5	30
Jones, Hamilton (Estᵃ)	5	18
Johnson, Hartwell	6	....
Jordan, Stephen	7	....
Jordan, Perry	3	....
Inman, Ann	2	5
Judkins, John	1	1
James, Jeremiah	6	4
Judkins, James	4	7
Inman, Isham	4	8
Judkins, Jacob	5	2
Judkins, Elizabeth	2	3
Jordan, Ann	3	1
Judkins, Samuel	9	10
Judkins, Charles	6	25
James, Enos	6	18
Judkins, Martha	6	18
Judkins, Mark	1	....
Judkins, John	5	2
Judkins, John, Junʳ	8	....
Judkins, Jesse	2	....
Judkins, Mary	6	2
Jordan, Ann	4	....
King, Randolph	6	2
King, Mary	3	4
Kee, Robert	4	1
Kee, William	4	5
Kee, James	11	19
Kee, Sarah	3	2
Kee, Charles	9	....
Laughton, William	1	8
Lucas, John	12	27
Lunsford, Swann, Junʳ	1	....
Lunsford, Swann, Senʳ	5	6
Lane, John	10	6
Little, John, jr	4	1
Lane, Micajah	3	1
Lane, William	9	4
Little, Jesse	6	....
Little, John	8	....
Lane, Frederick	4	6
Logan, John	4	4
Lane, Thomas	6	4
Lane, Lucy	6	....
Long, Hartwell	5	....
Long, David	3	....
Long, Lewis	3	2
Little, John	5	1
Milby, William	5	2
Moring, Christopher	1	....
Moring, John	6	5
Munro, Joseph	6	....
Moring, Benjᵃ	6	7
Marks, John	4	5
Marriott, Elizabeth	3	12
Macintosh, Robert	7	6
Maddera, Joel	4	6
Moody, Archibald	5	2
Moring, Henry, Jun	8	9
Maddera, Joanna	1	2
Maddera, Elizabeth	5	6
Maget, William	4	13
Moreland, Mary	2	....
Moore, Jesse	6	....
Moring, Henry	7	10
Mitchell, William	5	1
Mitchell, Mary	1	3
Norsworthy, John	6	4
Newsom, Littleberry	4	10
Nimmo, Andrew	7	2
Newton, Thomas	8	25
Nelson, William	9	26
Partin, William C	1	....
Peterson, Peter	8	3
Putney, Benjᵃ	9	12
Putney, David	9	4
Peters, Armistead	15	....
Peter, Thomas	5	20
Peter, Robert	2	4
Putney, Lewis	1	12
Parker, Elizabeth	2	2
Porter, Edward	10	....
Phillps, Hannah	2	2
Pleasants, Thomas	6	....
Presson, John	8	7
Puily, Lewis	9	6
Price, Lucy	4	6
Pettway, John	8	4
Pyland, Robert	8	4
Pyland, Mary	1	....
Pyland, Thomas	1	....
Pyland, John	1	....
Pyland, Ann	6	....
Pyland, Obediah	4	1
Presson, Toomer	6	....
Person, Mary	12	4
Pitt, John	8	7
Pretlow, Samuel	3	29
Pierce, Jeremiah	9	24
Price, William	10	3
Rae, James	4	2
Rigan, William	10	....
Rigan, Benjᵃ	4	....
Rispess, Robert	8	....
Rae, William	5	3
Rose, William	9	....
Rigan, Jesse	8	....
Rogers, William	5	....
Rhoads, Benjᵃ	2	....
Rhoads, John	5	....
Rowell, Richard	6	4
Roberts, Joseph	8	....
Sorsby, Stephen	12	16
Simon, Thomas	6	....
Stewart, William	3	2
Sorsby, Thomas	5	11
Slade, Benjᵃ	1	....
Simmons, William	10	17
Scott, Nicholas	9	....
Stewart, James	6	....
Short, William	7	49
Shuffield, Jesse	5	11
Shuffield, Elizabeth	5	3
Saunders, John	4	6
Shuffield, James	8	....
Scarbrough, Mary	2	....
Sledge, Ann	5	6
Stephens, William	5	1
Shuffield, Hardy	6	....
Sherman, Mary	4	....
Smith, Michael	5	10
Savidge, Joel	4	....
Smith, Lucy	7	10
Smith, Nicholas	4	1
Smith, Henry	1	....
Spratley, Benjamin	4	10
Spratley, John	1	8
Sharp, Burwell	4	13
Sebrell, Nathaniel	10	12
Smith, William	1	5
Spratley, William	6	19
Steward, John	8	....
Seward's, Wm Cofill (Estᵃ)	4	11
Seward, Britain	7	1
Seward, James	3	....
Sinclair, Arthur	4	6
Savidge, Henry	3	....
Slade, John	6	....
Savidge, Michael	3	....
Savidge, John	3	....
Savidge, Sarah	7	....
Slade, William	8	....
Skipwith, Peyton	4	26
Smalley, John	4	5
Smith, Benjᵃ (for Allen Cockes Estᵃ)	3	75
Shelley, James	3	1
Scammell, Richard	7	10
Salter, William	4	8
Smith, Mary	5	5
Tucker, Jane	4	....
Tillot, John	5	6
Thompson, Ann	3	4
Thorp, Joseph	4	5
Thompson, William	3	....
Thompson, William	7	2
Thompson, Joel	10	12
Thompson, Philip	5	6
Taylor, John	7	....
Thompson, John	7	3
Taylor, James, junʳ	8	1
Taylor, James	6	....
Thomas, John	7	....
Turner, Thomas	7	....
Valentine, Peter	10	....
Verell, John	1	....
Wyatt's, Hubbard (Estᵃ)	....	6
Walden, Stephen	1	....
Wall, Thomas	6	6
Walden, Sarah	3	2
Warren, John	6	....
West, Philip	3	17
Watkins, John, Senʳ	9	32
Wrenn, Thomas	6	2
Wall, Aaron	4	3
White, Benjᵃ	3	2
Wilson, Elizabeth	2	14
Wilson, John	8	....
White, Henry	12	....
White, John	4	35
Wrenn, John	10	4
Warren, John, Senʳ	2	10
Warren, John, junʳ	2	2
Waller, Benjᵃ	6	11
Warren, Joseph	8	3
Ward, Wm (for John Paradise)	4	27
Wesson, John	3	5
Warren, Hannah	7	14
Warren, Jesse	5	13
Warren, William	7	6
Warren, John	8	1
White, Thomas	6	15
Warren, Arthur	7	4
Wilson, Willis	7	36
Wright, John	2	....
Wildair, John	7	1
Wright, William	1	3
Williams, Jeremiah	3	....
Wilson, Thomas	6	....
Williams, Thomas	3	17
Wills, Thomas	11	4
Wills, Mary	3	13

SUSSEX COUNTY.

LIST OF NATH'L DUNN.

NAME OF HEAD OF FAMILY.	White.	Black.
Allen, William	14	241
Adkins, Lucy		25
Cullom, Thomas	3	1
Clark, Eve	6	2
Cotton, William	7	1
Cotton, Nathaniel	2	9
Cotton, Harris	5	2
Cotton, Richard	6	6
Cook, Richard	6	10
Caton, Henry	1	9
Chappel, John	12	16
Chappel, James	8	11
Chappel, Mary	2	12
Collier, Jesse	8	2
Cosby, William	7	2
Clemons, Thomas	6	36
Claiborne, William	6	35
Baird, William	9	8
Baird, Benjamin	4	2
Boiseau, James	3	4
Belsches, Alexander	4	30
Berryman, John	6	11
Baird, Stephen	7	4
Dobie, Nathaniel	2	8
Dunn, Nathaniel	7	20
Glover, Mary	3	1
Harrison, Alexander	2	7
Hall, Willis	6	13
Hight, Ann	7	1
Hines, Frederick	4	6
Hines, Hartwell	11	12
Hines, Sarah	2	11
Heath, Henry	3	8
Heath, Peggy	4	9
Hunnicutt, Pleasants	5	23
Harrison, William	1	34
Heath, Nathan	2	9
Heath, Adam	6	5
Hall, Solomon	9	7
Harden, Frances	5	7
Ivey, Daniel	6	4
Jones, David	7	15
Jones, John	1	4
Jones, Rebecca	3	14
Jones, Samuel	1	5
Ivey, Hugh	3	11
Jarrat, Fadde	6	6
Jarrat, Howell	4	....
Johnson, Elizabeth	6	5
Land, Robert	4	9
Lanier, Benjamin	11	27
McKinish, John	3	3
Moss, Thomas	8	3
Mason, Jno, junr	7	36
Mason, John	4	18
Ozburn, Nicholas	6	14
Partridge, Jesse	4	6
Parkham, Lewis	5	6
Parkham, Robert	4	8
Peters, Matthew	1	9
Parker, Mary	5	14
Parker, Richard	7	22
Parsons, Henry	7	7
Peete, Thomas	7	23
Underhill, Giles	5	....
Underhill, Howell	7	4
Weaver, Henry	6	11
Weaver, Jno	4	2
Weaver, Jane	4	3

LIST OF THOS. SAUNDERS.

NAME OF HEAD OF FAMILY.	White.	Black.
Bonner, John	10	7
Hall, Dixon	6	9
Cain, Peter	8	5
Malone, Jno	8	13
Robinson, Nathl	8	....
Sturdivant, Henry	2	12
Vaughn, Thos, jr	6	17
Parkam, Wm	7	6
Jones, Henry	2	5
Harwell, Richard	9	23
Robinson, James	3	24
Parkam, Geo	8	7
Tucker, Mary	7	2
Coman, Jno, senr	3	....
Vaughn, Thos, senr	4	12
Mitchell, Jno	7	8
Wilkins, Jeremiah	5	....
Harwell, Gardiner	1	2
Fires, Jno	3	....
Harwell, Sterling	7	14
Huson, Thos	7	4
Chappel, Thos	5	7
Winfield, Jno	4	12
Huson, Jno	6	5
Kelley, Jno	8	1
Winfield, Peter	4	10
Porch, Solomon	4	6
Rainey, Will	8	3
Rachell, Richard	6	....

LIST OF THOS. SAUNDERS—continued.

NAME OF HEAD OF FAMILY.	White.	Black.
Spratley, Wm	5	15
Brent, Wm	5	7
Cain, Isham	8	4
Powell, Edward, senr	6	9
Robinson, Elizabeth	3	1
Powell, Seymour	8	8
Powell, Jno	7	4
Winfield, Robert	9	14
Saunders, Thomas	8	11
Cain, James, senr	6	2
Cain, Micajah	4	4
Butler, Thos, junr	5	6
Randall, Peter, junr	8	10
Cain, Wm	5	4
Randall, Peter, Senr	10	3
Mitchell, Saml	6	3
Wilkinson, Nathan	7	4
Powell, Edward (Church)	5	6
Mitchell, Jacob	9	6
Hitchcock, Russell	3	5
Gilliam, Charles	3	20
Smith, Isham	12	16
Burrough, Jarrell	9	....
Harper, Wilkins	6	2
Raney, Peter	4	8
Cain, James, junr	3	....
King, Fathey	6	2
Freeman, Jno	4	2
Hill, Thos	6	25
Hill, Margaret	4	31
Winfield, Wm	8	5
Robinson, Isaac	5	4

LIST OF GEORGE RIVES.

NAME OF HEAD OF FAMILY.	White.	Black.
Chambliss, James	7	20
Chambliss, Wm, jr	3	3
Rives, Timothy, senr	1	3
Rives, Lucy		6
Rives, Timothy	4	21
Mitchell, Thomas	3	13
Rives, Elizabeth	5	17
Mitchell, Scott	2	11
Parham, Stith	6	12
Leath, William	7	....
Morris, Lewis	4	....
Heath, Wood	6	1
Hill, Joshua	4	3
Tomlinson, William	6	2
Hobbs, William	4	2
Duff, Abdon	3	3
Eppes, Joel	....	9
King, Ephraim	4	....
Jones, David	3	2
Hawthorn, Joshua	4	2
Willis, Elizabeth	1	6
Adkins, Sarah	2	4
Weeks, Thomas	3	....
Williams, David	4	2
Lessenberry, Eliza	3	4
Sykes, Wm	4	8
Mason, John, jr	....	13
Potts, John	4	2
Moss, Ephraim	6	5
Anderson, Mack	6	2
Mitchell, Branch	6	2
Adkins, Lucy	....	23
Adkins, Thomas	9	17
Roythress, Peter (Esta)	4	16
Hawthorn, Isham	7	5
Dunn, Wm, jr	6	10
Ambrose, Thomas	8	....
Dunn, Lewis	4	16
Dobie, Mary	1	....
Harwell, Peter	6	....
Young, Joshua	3	2
Young, Drury	1	4
Pittway, Sterling	4	2
Pittway, Robert	1	29
Biggins, Sarah	1	11
Dunn, William, jr	2	31
Eppes, James	6	6
Bell, James	2	1
Ashwell, Ann	5	1
Moss, Edmund	3	10
Gilbert, William	3	9
Barker, Nathan	5	1
Barker, Benjamin	4	4
Rives, George	9	43
Worthington, Priscilla	4	12
Meachan, Banks	8	....
Parham, James		2
Leath, John	5	2
Parham, Abram, senr	2	1
Parham, Abram, junr	5	6
Tucker, Robert	6	12
Wilkerson, Wm	5	....
Parham, John	3	....
Belsches, Hugh	8	40
Wilkerson, Richard	9	1
Cooks, Joseph	2	....

LIST OF GEORGE RIVES—continued.

NAME OF HEAD OF FAMILY.	White.	Black.
Smith, Edward	5	3
Claiborne, Augustine	9	31
Cocks, John	3	12

LIST OF LAWRENCE SMITH.

NAME OF HEAD OF FAMILY.	White.	Black.
Maggot, Samuel	3	11
Wilson, Capt Nicholas	7	4
Cole, John	5	1
Cross, Sarah	5	6
Cross, Wm	3	3
Rogers, Mary	7	1
Holdsworth, Charles	4	4
Clary, Eliza	3	3
Judkins, William, senr	5	....
Judkins, William, junr	5	1
Pepper, Stephen	7	1
Smith, Arthur	8	5
Blow, Col. Michael	9	20
Freeman, Lucy	6	1
Rogers, Rebecca	5	....
Turner, James, junr	8	....
Massengale, Thomas	4	....
Bailey, Thomas	5	1
Carrel, Wm, junr	10	2
Carrel, Wm, senr	3	2
Hancock, Jno	4	5
Hancock, Thomas	1	1
Smith, Joseph	11	....
Kee, John	5	4
Clary, James	3	4
Owen, Hannah	4	....
Nicholson, John	9	14
White, John	9	4
Holloway, James	6	....
Blizzard, Samuel	8	....
Fason, Henry	8	4
Nichols, Elizabeth	5	5
Hancock, Nicholas	6	2
Bailey, Joshua	7	4
Bailey, Joseph	6	....
Clarey, Capt Benja	3	9
Freeman, Henry	7	1
Owen, Elizabeth	5	....
Freeman, John	7	2
Pritlow, Thomas	1	3
Bradley, Eliza	2	....
Wells, Samuel	11	....
Carrell, Mark	5	3
Carrell, Nathan	7	....
Atkins, Benja	3	1
Andrews, Richard	9	18
Ellis, Isaac	3	6
Jordan, Jno	2	....
Alsbrook, Jno	4	4
Nichols, Harris	7	19
Watkins, Joseph	1	....
Phillips, Thomas	6	2
Blow, Henry	3	5
Bailey, Edmund	10	....
Bailey, Abidan	9	....
Bailey, William	4	1
Bailey, Elijah	4	1
Edmunds, Nicholas	....	3
Nicholson, Wm	4	14
Ellis, Wm	10	7
Ellis, Benja	8	4
Ellis, Jno	3	....
Wootton, Edward	7	7
Murpy, Charles	7	4
Judkins, Robert	4	5
Blunt, Collins	2	10
Tomlinson, Thomas	5	19
Mason, Capt David	2	10
Lamb, Jno, junr	5	4
Stacey, Simon	6	9
Smith, Lawrence	5	17
Kerr, George	3	15
Kitchin, Benja	3	....
Clary, Mary	6	1

LIST OF JOHN MASON.

NAME OF HEAD OF FAMILY.	White.	Black.
Oliver, William	8	14
Sturdivant, Jno, senr	4	5
Weathers, Benja	6	3
Wynne, Jno, senr	4	9
Wynne, Will, senr	2	6
Wynne, Matthew	4	1
Hawthorn, Jno	4	7
Threewits, Joel	3	7
Redding, Wm	7	4
Horn, James	2	....
Horn, Thos	9	....
Athens, Lewis	11	....
Horn, Wm	8	....
Whitehead, Isham	7	....
Loyd, Kimmin	3	....
Newman, Joel	2	....
Whitehead, Robert	9	....

LIST OF JOHN MASON—continued.

NAME OF HEAD OF FAMILY.	White.	Black.
Knight, Moses	12	5
Wynne, Matthew (son of M.)	5	....
Lilley, Fredk	6	2
Cocks, Wm	12	6
Cocks, James	10	....
Byshop, Nathan	10	3
Byshop, Stephen	5	....
Zills, Morris	5	3
Zills, Ann	3	....
Zills, Susanna	3	....
Dunn, Thos	4	1
Jones, Jno	5	2
Marrable, Hartrocle	7	17
Hill, Jno	5	1
Hill, Mildred	4	4
Tyus, Benja	7	8
Sturdivant, William, sr	11	15
Hood, Henry	6	....
Hood, Jno	5	....
Sturdivant, Anderson	6	4
Stewart, Jno	4	2
Hardy, William	5	....
Wynne, Robert	10	9
Lilley, Ann	3	2
Partin, Drury	7	....
Wynne, Wm, jr	7	5
Partin, Wm	6	3
Pare, Jno	9	....
Renn, Ann	5	1
Porch, Henry	11	1
Bailey, James	4	10
Wynne, Matthew, sr	4	3
Hobbs, Thomas	10	8
Renn, Thomas	3	9
Bendall, Isaac	8	2
Lanier, Drury	4	....
Moody, Henry	3	2
Massenburg, Jno	7	16
Booth, Michael	4	1
Sturdivant, Thomas	8	9
Hill, Green	6	25
Sturdivant, Rachel	4	16
Sturdivant, Ann	6	3
Sturdivant, Wm, jr	4	3
Sturdivant, Jno, jr	5	1
Miscall, Jeremy	2	2
Bailey, Thos, senr	8	....
Mason, Col. David	7	38
Wynne, Sarah	6	2
Ozburne, Augt	2	6
Parham, Stith, senr	7	30
Hobbs, Joseph	8	2
Glover, James, Senr	2	6
Glover, James	7	5
Tomlinson, Alex	7	2
Carter, Jno	3	9
Hobbs, Mary	3	....
Whitfield, Thos	8	3
Pennington, Frederick	5	9
Moss, Henry, jr	7	12
Moss, Joshua	8	9
Sturdivant, Hollorn	21	13
Sledge, Thomas	6	1
Lightfoot, Wm	....	79
Hancock, Rebecca	6	7
Mason, Jno	6	12
Land, Webb	1	....
Soot, Samuel	1	3
Cocks, Lucy	1	....
Mason, Capt Jno	....	10
Baird, Benja	5	2
Harrison, Jones	5	5
Lewis, Capt Wm	....	6
Hite, Thos	9	....

LIST OF PETER JONES.

NAME OF HEAD OF FAMILY.	White.	Black.
Blunt, Colin	2	10
Barker, Nathaniel	2	2
Bain, James	5	....
Byshop, Averis	4	3
Byshop, Harmon	3	2
Barker, Joanna	8	3
Blunt, William	5	35
Bain, John	3	....
Briggs, Nathaniel	6	11
Brier, John	3	1
Barker, Henry	6	2
Cooper, James	6	1
Chappel, Howell	9	14
Davis, Charles	2	2
Ellis, Edwin	8	5
Gilliam, Wm	1	....
Heath, Durham	6	4
Harrison, Wm	9	9
Judkins, Jno	4	2
Jarrate, Henry	8	13
Irby, Jno	8	25
Jones, James B	5	1
Jarrate, Nicholas, jr	6	5

SUSSEX COUNTY—Continued.

NAME OF HEAD OF FAMILY.	White.	Black.	NAME OF HEAD OF FAMILY.	White.	Black.	NAME OF HEAD OF FAMILY.	White.	Black.	NAME OF HEAD OF FAMILY.	White.	Black.
LIST OF PETER JONES—con.			LIST OF LEWIS THORP—con.			LIST OF LEWIS THORP—con.			LIST OF LEWIS THORP—con.		
Lashley, Wm	3	5	Stewart, Richard	8	24	Sammons, James	9	....	Wyche, Mary	8	14
Lamb, Jno	4	10	Ezell, Thos	7	....	Hay, Richard, junr	7	2	Thorp, Lewis	5	17
Lamb, Wm	11	4	Ezell, Balaam	5	....	Weaver, Wm	3	2	Knight, Jno, senr	9	12
Lewis, Enoch	2	5	Whitehorn, Edward	4	2	Underwood, Mark	7	....	Hay, Richard, senr	4	5
Massingale, Thomas	4	....	Worthington, Nathan	2	7	Rawlings, Isaac	5	1	Walpole, Thos	11	30
Mangum, Samuel	4	11	Sledge, Jno	6	....	Bottom, Saml	9	....	Whitehorn, Thos	4	5
Partridge, Nicholas	4	8	Grizzard, Wm	3	6	Harwood, Daniel	9	2	Williamson, Mary	9	2
Presson, Thos	2	1	Magee, Wm	5	2	Newsum, Wm	11	5	Barham, Wm	5	13
Pope, Stephen	6	5	Barham, Thos	3	2	Prince, Wm	7	4	Sands, Jno	6	12
Roberts, Benja	3	15	Roland, Susanna	5	....	Johnson, Jno	8	2	Hail, Micajah	4	....
Roberts, Sarah	4	8	Magee, Harmon	3	....	Linn, Robert	6	....	Mclemore, Burwell	8	2
Rosser, Joseph	7	2	Whitehorn, Jno	8	1	Munns, Jno	6	....	Hail, Benja	6	1
White, James	10	5	Fort, Frederick	10	2	Stokes, Saml	4	....	Atkins, Jno	6	4
Wallis, Jesse	10	9	Whitehorn, Philip	7	7	Stokes, Christopher	3	....	Armstrong, Robert	10	1
Turner, Daniel	1	3	Hail, Benja	2	1	Sammons, Thos	8	....	Newsum, Nathaniel	8	6
Tomlinson, Jno	1	....	Seat, Nathaniel	3	2	Adams, James	7	....	Parham, Eliza	3	19
Turner, James	5	8	Seat, Robert	3	11	Freeman, Arthur	6	1	Gilliam, Wm	1	....
Turner, Edmund	1	7	Ivy, Aaron	5	....	Godwin, Christopher	4	9	Hay, Balaam	1	....
Hix, James	7	1	Ivy, Peebles	4	....	Richardson, Wm	4	27	Hay, Jno	4	1
Hix, Robert	9	1	Ivy, Adam	7	....	Woodland, Wm	6	11	Tyler, Wm	1	15
Hix, Mary	3	2	Rose, Wm	2	....	Weathers, Michael	6	....	Myrick, Wm	10	29
Hix, Wm	4	....	Glover, Jones	8	9	Rowland, Jno	10	....	Mason, Littleberry	1	17
Jones, Peter	4	15	Harwood, Saml	2	8	Harrison, Hannah	5	4	Bullock, Joel	6	2
			Felts, Nathl	8	....	Ross, Wm	11	....	Hood, Wm	4	....
LIST OF LEWIS THORP.			Hearn, Frederick	6	....	Smith, Drury	9	11	Clifton, Saml	8	5
Tillar, Major	5	11	Sammons, Wm	6	....	Walker, James	10	6	Bullock, Benja	5	1
Bass, Arthur	9	3	Linn, Curtis	4	....	Bell, Silvanus	9	4	Mabry, Abel	9	5
Seaburn, Wm	8	....	Phipps, Benja	8	3	Barham, Charles	8	6	Sammons, Benja	1	....
Dunn, Morris	11	....	Maury, Henry	5	....	Davis, Wm	6	....	Ivy, David	8	1
Tuder, Henry	6	1	Cornet, Jones	8	....	Mason, Richard	8	4	Newsum, Peter	4	....
Pate, Thos	11	....	Cornet, Selah	3	....	Sledge, Augustine	3	....	Avent, Jno	6	6
Pate, Edward	9	....	Jarratt, Nicholas	9	....	Underwood, Lewis	6	....	Adams, Thos	7	1
Seat, Hartwell	5	3	Ezell, Abel	3	....	Jones, Howell	1	....	Mason, Thos	5	18
Bailey, Philip	4	1	Hail, Jno	3	2	Smith, Sarah	9	5	Zills, Wm	5	....
Underwood, Absalom	9	....	Harris, Reuben	4	1	Solomon, Lewis	2	8	Sammons, Ann	3	....
Shadrack, Bailey	6	....	Harris, Lewis	4	....	Tillar, Mary	3	....	Grizzard, Lucy	5	13
Bailey, Henry	4	1	Avent, Thos	10	4	Hubbard, Olive	6	....	Ivy, Ephraim	6	....
Vaughan, James	6	6	Morgan, Matthew	8	5	Bullock, Wm	4	....			
			Prince, Nicholas	7	....	May, Allen	5	4			

WARWICK COUNTY.

NAME OF HEAD OF FAMILY.	White.	Black.	NAME OF HEAD OF FAMILY.	White.	Black.	NAME OF HEAD OF FAMILY.	White.	Black.	NAME OF HEAD OF FAMILY.	White.	Black.
Harwood, Edward	12	45	Noblin, Eliza	4	2	Loyde, Thos	4	....	Young, Richd	3	2
Ambler, Jaquelin, Esqr	....	7	Chapman, Walter	6	7	Levy, John	7	....	Chamberlayn, Thos (Amory)	8	19
Lee, Wm	7	11	Charles, Martha	7	7	Wood, Susanna	5	3	McGregor, Wm	7	12
Wood, Margaret	5	6	Lee, Francis	10	18	Wills, Mattw	10	22	Manning, John	6	2
Wood, Mattw	4	1	Harwood, Wm	7	22	Prentis, Daniel	6	14	Smith, Eliza	8	7
Wynne, Richd	8	8	Blanks, Eliza	9	....	Glanville, Thomas	5	6	Marrow, Wm	8	5
Gibbs, Mattw	9	7	Williams, Godfrey	5	....	Curtis, Edmd	3	6	Patrick, Thos	6	....
Lucas, Thos	1	6	Cary, Thomas	7	18	Curtis, Robert	2	2	Langhorne, Wm	11	19
Wood, John	11	2	Cary, Richd	10	30	Bland, Samuel	7	4	Drewry, Wm	5	6
Smith, James	5	1	Garron, Sarah	5	2	Hansford, Benja	3	5	Henderson, Wm	8	2
Smith, Wm	8	1	McKintosh, Richd	6	20	Wills, Miles	3	9	Crandol, Richd	2	2
Gibbs, John Geo	5	4	Morris, John	4	1	Fox, John	5	....	Allin, Richd	13	9
Harwood, Thos	5	5	Mallicote, Philip	5	....	Jones, Allen	5	22	Brown, Dixon	1	5
Jordan, Thos	6	....	Cary, Wilson Miles	....	1	Jones, Wm	9	11	Wood, Mattw	9	3
Wild, Thos	....	6	Noblin, Simmonds	4	....	Cofflin, John	4	1	Badget, Wm	4	2
Gibbs, Wm	8	1	Pierce, Penuel	5	....	Blow, Samuel	1	4	Russell, Hinde	11	13
Gibbs, Wm, junr	1	....	Dunn, John	10	11	Noblin, Matthew	8	2	Drewry, Jno, jr	4	....
Gibbs, Martha	2	1	Dunn, Hanah	4	7	Haynes, Christopher	6	8	Picket, John	3	....
Dowsing, Everard	1	7	Harrison, Richd	5	6	Haynes, Lucy Bassett	6	15	Mallicote, Wm	4	2
Southall, James	....	5	Harrison, Wm	4	....	Houghton, Peter	5	10	Langston, Mattw	3	6
Money, John	6	....	Pierce, Peter	6	....	Thomas, Samuel	5	13	Dubrey, Samuel	2	9
Chisman, Thomas	3	5	Digges, Wm	....	89	Burnham, John	3	6	Lively, Wm	5	2
Long, Wm	1	....	Mallicote, Thos	6	5	Drewry, Mattw	9	7	Jones, Francis	....	9
Mahone, Wm	7	....	Gray, Saml	7	4	Drewry, John	3	1	Brown, Robert	2	3
Wynne, Edmund	6	9	Young, Mary	4	2	Mallicote, Moory	6	2	Rice, Judith	4	....
Moore, Eliza	4	6	Gray, Eliza	6	3	Houghton, William	9	15	Blaston, Thomas	3	....
Nelson, Eliza	....	13	Pully, Robt	4	1	Lewelling, John	3	9	Massenburg, Josiah	5	11
Dudley, Rebecca	2	8	Gouge, Mattw	4	1	Brown, Samuel	1	7			

CITY OF WILLIAMSBURG.

NAME OF HEAD OF FAMILY.	White.	Black.	NAME OF HEAD OF FAMILY.	White.	Black.	NAME OF HEAD OF FAMILY.	White.	Black.	NAME OF HEAD OF FAMILY.	White.	Black.
Middleton, David	3	....	Curtis, Sally	2	1	Crump, John	5	4	Draper, John	7	2
Wallace, Betty (free)	....	4	Tyler, Mary	5	4	Massenburg, Alexr	6	3	Diddip, Archibald	12	4
Cardwell, Lewis	3	....	Saunders, John	10	10	Bentley, Mr	1	2	Galt, James	4	11
Lawson, Richard	1	....	Andrews, Robert	6	6	Lockley, John	1	1	Bucktrout, Ben	3	1
Digges, Miss	3	5	Holt, William	13	21	Anderson, Robert	4	13	Finnie, William	6	7
Jaram & Wray	6	6	McCarty, Michael	4	1	Durfey, Siverinus	5	2	Moyer, Peter	3	1
Abbot, Roger	6	....	Farquhaison, John	4	4	Lewis, John	5	4	Crittendon, Ephraim	4	2
Thompson, Joseph	1	....	Slavin, Catharine	4	....	Taliaferro, Chas	2	11	Bryant, Rachel	7	3
Plitt, Harman	2	....	Tazewell, Sarah	7	6	Perry, Hartwell	5	....	Carter, John H	10	5
Holt, Thomas	1	....	Bland, William	4	8	Wilson, Rosanna	2	1	Moyer, Peter, Senr	5	2
Fisher, John	4	1	Marr, Andrew	1	....	Greenhow, John	9	17	Hubard, Mrs	6	12
Carter, William	....	1	Jones, Nanny (free)	....	3	Keel, Fanny	3	1	Dudley, Mrs	1	....
Millard, Sarah	2	....	Carter, Sally (free)	....	1	Jeggitts, William	7	1	Beall, Samuel	1	1
Hyland, Sarah	4	....	Urie, William	2	....	Nichols, James	6	1	Davis, James	2	....
Allison, Francis	4	1	Pearson, Maggy	6	6	Orr, Katharine	2	10	Pine, Samuel	2	5
Dean, Mary	4	5	Carter, John	6	5	Reid, George	2	4	Gilbert, Robert	7	8
Wythe, George, esqr	5	9	Griffin, Corbin	3	15	Singleton, Mary	6	8	Vobe, Jane	6	7
Prentis, Joseph	4	9	Honey, James	4	7	Craig, Thomas	5	4	Houston, Mrs	4	2
Parker, Mr	4	....	Moyer, Peter	6	4	Russell, William	2	1	d'Sequeyra, John	3	2
Blair, John, Esqr	5	18	Pitt, William	3	4	Carter, William	6	8	Graham, Mr	2	....
Cocke, James	3	7	Lewis, William	2	8	Maupin, Gabriel	16	17	Dreuidtz, Mr	6	3
Jones, John	6	4	Dickson, Beverley	6	6	Carter, James	2	6	Low, David	1	2
Rozario, Elizabeth (free)	....	3	Anderson, Matthew	3	2	Rowsay, William	5	8	Anderson, Matt	2	2
Reynolds, John	4	2	Roadman, John	3	7	Waller, Benja	5	16	Moir, James	5	2

CITY OF WILLIAMSBURG—Continued.

NAME OF HEAD OF FAMILY.	White.	Black.	NAME OF HEAD OF FAMILY.	White.	Black.	NAME OF HEAD OF FAMILY.	White.	Black.	NAME OF HEAD OF FAMILY.	White.	Black.
Craig, James	5	5	Deforrest, Sarah	3	4	Hatton, Matthew	7	1	Waters, Sarah	1	3
Hallam, Sarah	3	1	Shiphard, John	6	8	Coke, Sarah	4	....	Charlton, Edward	2	2
Hunter, Margaret	1	5	Moody, Phil	16	2	Wharton, Thomas	2	1	LaCroix, Monsr	3	....
Russell, William	4	9	Morton, David	6	5	Flack, Alexr	5	1	Anderson, Robert	3	3
Clarkson, John	1	....	Barrom, John	3	3	Moody, Hugh	1	1	Lenox, Walter	2	....
Southall, James	10	21	Lafong, George	6	....	Watkins, Hubberd	4	....	Cloud, Mr	2	....
Galt, John M	7	9	Craig, Mary	4	5	Davis, Jas	6	1	Dutchfield, James	1	....
Carter, John	5	4	Nicolson, Robert	5	12	Chaplin, Rebecca	3	....	Blassengham, John	1	1
Nicolson, William	6	6	Davis, Augustine	3	1	Bingley, Matthew	5	3	Martin, Mrs	3	3
Taylor, James	7	1	Ross, Donald	1	....	Withers, Mary	7	1	Coke, John	4	3
Dickson, Charlotte	1	2	Young, James	1	....	Watkins, M	1	....	Reynolds, Mrs	2	....
Elson, Mary	1	2	Harwood, Humr	7	7	Napcut, James	2	1	Crawley, Samuel	6	7
Davenport, Fanny	6	5	Bond, Robert	5	1	Sance, Christo	2	1	Nicholson, Henry	3	4
Scovermort, Nicholas	4	1	Orton, Marg	3	1	Davenport, Amy	....	3	Hay, Elizabeth	4	4
Pasteur, Blovet	3	2	Brien, Morto	5	5	Cary, Polly	1	....	Simmons, George	3	....
Sclater, John	6	4	Hoy, Alexander	6	....	Cumbo, Edith	2	....	Randolph, Betty	3	15
Coke, Robey	8	10	Burns, Mrs	2	1	Sweat, Peggy	4	....	Maddison, James	4	9
Many, Peter	3	1	Hornsby, Will	2	8	Blue, Betty	5	4	Riddle, Mrs	4	16
Robinson, Patrick	2	2	Robinson, Mrs	4	1	Chambers, Sulky	4	....	Brown, Mrs	2	1
Campbell, Christ	6	19	Wood, James	2	....	Scott, Abraham	4	....	Dixon, John	4	3
Tazewell, Henry	1	1	Selby, Sally	3	....	Richards, Edith	2	....			
Abel, Samuel	3	2	Gray, John	3	....	Price, Edward	5	....			

AMHERST COUNTY.

NAME OF HEAD OF FAMILY.	White.	Black.
Allen, Samuel	10	16
Arrington, Presylla	3	
Arrington, William	3	
Alford, William	8	
Allcock, Richard	6	3
Allen, John	4	2
Brabban, William	6	
Bicknall, Thomas	9	
Bicknall, Micajah	5	
Ballew, Thomas	7	1
Burnett, James	9	
Baine, Richard	4	2
Bettisworth, Richard	1	
Burk, John	6	3
Bibb, John	9	4
Bethell, John	10	
Blain, George	5	
Ball, John	5	2
Brown, Adam	4	1
Bibee, Peter	4	
Bailey, Hezekiah	8	
Brown, John	10	2
Bibb, William	12	14
Campbell, Ambrose	8	
Campbell, Aaron	6	
Cabell, William	6	90
Cannady, Jissee	4	3
Cash, John	2	
Campbell, Moses	10	
Chisnall, Alexander	2	2
Cabell, Samuel Jordon	2	21
Cabell, William, Jun	3	17
Cockburn, George	6	
Crisp, William	10	3
Campbell, William	1	
Cartwright, John	7	3
Dillard, James	7	4
Deavour, William	10	
Dillard, Joseph	6	5
Dunnican, Daniel	3	
Davis, Isaac	7	1
Davis, William	1	
Depriest, John	11	6
Canniday, John	5	
Emond's, John (Estate)	2	3
Emonds, Charles	5	
Enniss, John	11	
Emonds, James	10	4
Emonds, Samuel	12	5
Emonds, William	1	
Freeland, Mary	3	18
Gregory, John	10	
Galaspie, George	11	6
Gatoing, Julius	7	
Griffin, Thomas	13	3
Gay, Thomas	10	
Hinsley, Leonard	3	1
Hargrove, Hezekiah	10	3
Hunter, Titus	5	1
Horsley, William	9	12
Horsley, John	4	8
Hendrixson, Peter	4	
Harper, John	3	
Horsley, Robert	5	11
Hilton, George	5	25
Hawkins, Thomas	6	11
Hollandsworth, William	3	1
Joslin, William	4	1
Joslin, John	6	7
Joslin, John, Jun	8	
Loving, William	13	16
Loving, John, Jun	11	14
Lavender, William	3	
Laine, John	1	
Landrum, Young	8	8
Laine, William	9	6
Mays, Joseph	7	11
Mays, James	6	4
Mays, John	10	2
Meggenson, Samuel	4	3
Merredith, William		18
Montgomery, John	8	6
Mays, Joseph, Jun	2	2
Proffitt, David	11	1
Perrow, Daniel	5	7
Penn, Rawley	7	
Pamplin, James	12	4
Purvis, George	6	
Pollard, William	10	9
Ray, William	1	
Ray, Moses	5	1
Robertson, Robert	4	1
Spencer, William	17	25
Staples, Joseph	3	
Seay, Abraham	9	1
Stoneham, George	4	5
Stratton, John	11	1
Smith, Augustine	2	
Staples, John	8	1
Stuart, Charles	2	3
Stevens, James	10	13
Smith, Alexander	8	
Tyrce, Nathan	5	
Thompson, Robert	7	3
Volentine, Littleberry	5	

NAME OF HEAD OF FAMILY.	White.	Black.
Via, Giddeon	10	
Vigust, James	9	
Wooddy, George	6	
Whittle, John	6	
Woods, William	9	
Warwick, Beverley	2	
Wright, Achillis	10	3
Welch, Joseph	1	
Welch, John	5	
Wright, Minor	12	
Watts, Stephen	7	8
Wingfield, Josias	1	1
Walton, Tilman	1	1
Walton, William	9	15
Walker, Jacob	2	
Warwick, Abraham	9	7
Wright, Robert	1	
Walton, James	4	
Ware, John	6	1
Wortham, George	6	2
Anderson, Samuel	5	4
Burks, Samuel	10	
Bowman, William	13	6
Blair, Allen	5	2
Bocock, John	4	1
Bryant, Thomas	3	
Burras, John	8	
Brown, James	13	
Bowman, William, Jr	2	
Bailey, Lucey	4	
Childress, Lucy	1	6
Conner, James	8	1
Cabell, Nicholas	9	53
Dickson, William	9	
Dunn, John	4	
Dawson, John	8	6
Eades, Charles	5	1
Enix, David	12	
Farguson, Samuel	8	
Forbus, Mary	2	
Fitzpatrick, William	10	2
Farrar, Thomas	9	1
Fortune, Thomas	10	
Griffin, John	5	2
Hopkins, James	10	23
Hopkins, John		3
Hooton, Thomas	4	
Harding, Edward	7	1
Howard, William		13
Harding, Groves (Est.)		7
Hopper, Thomas	10	
Hitchcock, William	8	
Jopling, Thomas	5	12
Jopling, Thomas, Jun	8	3
Johnston, William	12	7
Johnston, William (Ovr)	7	3
Jopling, Daniel	5	1
Key, Susannah	9	
Lyon, John	3	13
Lazenby, Thomas	5	
Layne, Joseph	6	
Liveley, Joseph (Wagr)	11	1
Liveley, Bethell	7	
Liveley, Joseph	6	
Lyon, Peter	3	2
Lanham, Joseph	4	
Lanham, Ben Dick	9	
Murrow, Richard	5	
Morriss, Jessee	4	
Matthews, Thomas	6	
Martin, Hudson	1	
Massey, Thomas	3	2
Montgomery, David, Jr	8	
Martin, Henry	10	7
Matthews, James	7	4
Martin, John	2	1
Montgomery, James	8	
Murrell, Cornelius	7	
Moore, Benjamin	10	22
Montgomery, David	2	4
Nevil, James	10	30
Nevil, Thomas	1	
Prichard, Richard	3	2
Phillips, Matthew		
Phillips, Leonard, Jr	10	3
Phillips, William	1	
Phillips, Leonard	1	1
Phillips, David	4	
Roberts, Henry	11	26
Raines, Ignatius	10	3
Sorrow, Henry	5	
Staples, Sarah	2	
Snider, John	4	1
Sorrell, John	2	26
Turner, James	12	11
Thomas, Cornelius (Est.)	2	13
Fail, Charles	9	
Tyler, Thomas	1	
Turner, Terisha, Jr	4	
Turner, Stephen	11	23
Turner, Terisha	5	12
Trail, Thomas	8	
Trail, James	5	
Tiller, William	9	3
Thomas, John, Junior	3	6

NAME OF HEAD OF FAMILY.	White.	Black.
Tiller, John	1	
Tuggle, Charles	4	
Ward, Nathand	5	
Ward, James	9	
Wright, William	4	1
Wright, Andrew	4	1
Watkins, Anne	2	
Wright, Robert	12	1
West, Francis	11	
West, Francis, jun	5	
Ward, Samuel		
Morrison, William	2	7
Lyon, William	11	2
Morris, John	9	
Pugh, John	10	1
Blaine, Ephraim	4	2
Scruggs, Samuel Scott	3	
Scruggs, John	2	
McAlexander, John	4	1
Woods, James	4	11
Smith, Joseph	10	
Smith, Augustine	1	1
Martin, James	9	17
Rhodes, Charles	5	24
Gilmer, John	7	20
Fry, Benjamin	5	
Merriwether, David	2	11
Talliaferro, Benjamin	3	9
Howell, Thomas	6	
Howell, William, jr	2	
Howell, Oliver	1	
Harris, William	3	
Aaron, Benjamin	3	
Harris, John	7	1
Church, Thomas	7	
Bell, James	2	3
Clark, Nathaniel	8	10
Peasley, Hugh	9	
McAlexander, James	4	4
McAlexander, James, Jr	4	5
Crawford, Jeremiah	6	
Thusler, James	4	
Willson, William	5	
Dinwiddie, Robert	6	
Herd, John	3	
Dinwiddie, James	3	
Reid, Alexander	6	2
Baber, Robert	10	
Burnett, Bond	6	
Puckett, Jacob	4	
Burnett, William	2	
Wood, John	10	
Puckett, John	7	
Allen, William	8	
Taite, Charles	4	1
Denny, Samuel	8	
Henderson, James	5	
Small, William	5	
Simpson, David	4	2
Hardy, Robert	2	3
Carpenter, Sarah	6	
Hughes, Henry	4	
Carpenter, John	4	
Clark, William	3	
Killand, Thomas	5	
Smith, Thomas	6	2
Perkins, Richard	4	4
Dawson, Henry	6	
Pratt, Thomas	4	
Ayres, Samuel	5	14
Tomes, Thomas	11	
Tomes, Joseph	1	
McCue, John	6	
Reid, Alexander, Jun	3	4
Clark, Susannah	4	
Bailey, Moses	1	
Carpenter, Thomas	6	2
Henderson, Alexander	5	
Clark, David	7	
Depriest, Langsdon	9	
Bryant, Benjamin	9	
Clark, William, Jun	1	
Morrison, Thomas	11	1
Shropshire, Semes	9	
Lobban, John	12	
Wadkins, John	5	
McClain, Henry, Jun	5	
McClain, James	1	2
McClain, Henry	3	
Boulware, James	4	
Biggs, John	6	
Pannell, William	1	
Pannell, Benjamin	4	
Pannell, Thomas	1	
Fox, Samuel	11	
Bailey, Philip	9	
Hulse, James	2	
Vines, Thomas	6	
Elliott, William	6	1
Wooddy, Thomas	5	
Cross, Cornelius	7	
Murrell, John, jun	9	1
Stanley, Nehemiah	4	
Witt, David	8	
Shields John	12	

NAME OF HEAD OF FAMILY.	White.	Black.
Shields, John, Jun	1	
Ramsey, Simon	8	1
Murrell, John	4	
Plodd, John Henry	2	
Martin, Azeriah	8	11
Martin, Sherod	9	7
Henderson, James	6	
Henderson, Robert	7	
Witt, William	4	
Witt, Littleberry	5	
Morrison, Joseph H	6	4
Martin, Stephen	8	
Staples, William	10	
Martin, Giddeon	7	
Martin, John	5	2
Evers, Thomas	9	
Morrison, John	9	11
Pope, John	9	11
McNeely, Michael	5	
Crawford, Nathan	8	17
Crawford, Ann	2	7
Wades, John	7	
Miller, Sarah	10	
Bones, William	7	
McClure, James	1	
McClure, John	8	
McCarter, James	6	
Berry, Isham	3	
Casey, Roger	12	
Johnson, John	4	
Small, Lawrence	2	
Miller, Martha	6	
Barnett, William	14	
Wood, Robert	6	
Lackey, Samuel	6	2
Roberts, Joseph	15	3
Adams, Thomas		19
Britt, William	8	
Reid, David	9	
Williams, John	6	3
McDaniel, Thomas	7	12
Witt, Lewis	2	
Witt, Abner	7	4
Luttrell, James	5	
Reid, Alexander (Min.)	6	2
Griffin, John	10	1
Jobling, Josiah	10	5
Harris, William	9	32
Childress, Ann	5	1
Merriwether, Francis	11	21
Shelton, Clough	1	13
Fitzpatrick, Thomas	1	1
Phillips, Zacharias	11	6
Thurmond, Gutridge	5	1
Bailey, John	5	5
Pryor, John	1	
Morrison, John	1	5
Cole, John	5	8
Montgomery, Joseph	3	5
Thurmond, John	6	2
Morris, Joseph	9	
Wood, James	8	4
Patton, Alexander	3	
Patton, Thomas	1	
McCloud, William	10	
Burton, James Holly	4	1
Dood, Josias	5	2
Witt, George	5	
Carpenter, Benjamin	5	
Smith, Johnson	1	
Simpson, William	7	6
Harris, Lee	10	23
Harris, Matthew	13	31
Shelton, David	8	18
Statam, Charles	9	8
Furbush, Sary	3	3
Wright, James	9	2
Depriest, William	8	2
Pullin, Joseph	6	
Diggs, John	10	21
McKnight, William	5	
McDonald, Archibald	9	
Montgomery, John	6	7
Clack, Moses	7	1
Bigge, John, Jun	5	
Biggs, Edward	9	
McAnally, John	13	
Henderson, Joseph	1	
Strange, Abraham A	8	3
Strange, Archibald A	3	1
Brooks, William	2	
Henderson, John	11	
McAnally, David	8	
Hardy, John	5	
Allen, Joseph	9	
Bradin, James	6	
Bibb, Thomas (Estate)	8	4
Bibb, Henry	1	
Barnett, Robert	7	5
Barnett, John	7	3
Brown, James	11	
Campbell, George	12	
Cammeron, Duncan	11	
Clackson, John	16	10
Coffey, Edmund	7	

AMHERST COUNTY—Continued.

NAME OF HEAD OF FAMILY.	White.	Black.	NAME OF HEAD OF FAMILY.	White.	Black.	NAME OF HEAD OF FAMILY.	White.	Black.	NAME OF HEAD OF FAMILY.	White.	Black.
Clark, David	4		Wright, John	2	1	Childress, Goolsbey	3		Goodwin, John H	3	1
Coffey, Ozburn	2		Brown, Jacob, Jun	7	1	Childress, Robert	2		Harvie, William		6
Camden, Benjamin	7		Waters, Francis	9		Edmonston, James	3		Harrison, John	9	1
Campbell, George, jun	8		Rolls, Caleb	5		Taylor, George	8		Harrison, Reubin	8	1
Campbell, John, jun	4		Hann, Elleoner	5		Clarke, William	7		Harvie, Richard		16
Campbell, John	8		Payton, Valentine	6		Clarke, George	1		Harrison, Franca	3	7
Campden, John	5		Laine, Joseph	9		Hall, William	5		Harper, Edward	5	
Campbell, James	6		Payton, John	7		Redcross, John	11		Johnston, Ann	4	8
Campbell, William	7		Galaspie, Sherod Moore	4	2	Eubank, Ambrose	6		Jones, John	6	20
Cull, James	10		Satterwhite, Francis	9	4	Davis, Jane	9	1	Key, Martin	6	
Campbell, Francis	7		Ballew, Steward	5	3	Peter, Richard	5		Lyon, Nicholas	8	
Campbell, Anthony	5		Goode, Campbell	3		Whitton, John	5		London, Larkin	2	
Coffey, William	11	6	Thurmond, Phillip	9	13	Davis, Moses	5	1	Lamaster, Ralph	13	
Cashwell, Henry	1		Ware, William	5	4	Veale, Francis	4		Magann, Joseph	7	1
Durham, Thomas	7		Davis, Richard, Jun	..	..	Davis, George	9		Morton, John	1	
Dood, Joseph	7		Goolsbey, Martha	3		Duncan, John	9		Davis, John	5	
Davis, Phillip	7		Burks, David	10	5	Goolsbey, James	4		Mitchell, Archelaus	11	17
Davis, David	9		Carter, Solomon	8	2	Adkins, Absolum	6		Mayo, Joseph	2	
Davis, Benjamin	6		Payton, William	3		Payton, Sarah	3		Mahone, Daniel	7	
Davis, Elizabeth	11		Saunders, Edward	4	3	Payton, John	8		Merritt, John	7	
Donohoe, David	4		Tooley, James	10		Payton, Henry, Jun	1		McDaniel, Henry	16	3
Eades, Isaac	6		New, David	6		Payton, James	1		McDaniel, George	3	5
Fulcher, John	1		Brown, Jacob	9		Burks, John	4	6	McDaniel, John	5	3
Fortune, Benjamin	13		Stinnett, John	7		Jones, John	1		Powell, Richard	6	2
Frazer, Micajah	6		Payton, William	8		Goodrich, Edmund	8	3	Parks, Mary	5	7
Forbes, William	4		Anderson, Charles	7		Haynes, William	12	1	Pendleton, Richard	1	2
Going, Phillip	13		Eubank, John	6	3	Byas, Larkin	5		Pendleton, Elizabeth	8	2
Hawkins, William	8		Carter, Peter	10	8	Byas, Obediah	1		Perley, Charles	5	
Hill, John	5	11	Graves, William	5		Whitton, William	1		Penn, Moses	11	5
Henderson, William	5		Eubank, George	8	2	Whitten, Ann	5	1	Pollard, Robert	4	3
Hughes, Moses	9	8	Beckley, John	4	5	Nowlin, James	10		Powell, Wiatt	9	13
Hatter, John	6		Byas, John	7		Whitten, Jeremiah	5		Pollard, William	2	6
Harper, Henry, Jun	6	5	Willson, Matthew	8		Roberds, John	9		Palmer, Pledge	2	1
Hight, Matthew	1		Hogg, John	13		Pryor, Nicholas	10		Taylor, Richard Powell	3	2
Hight, George	2		Grimes, Thomas	9		Pryor, David	1		Pendleton, James	3	2
Houchings, Edward	4		Byas, James	6		Gew, John	3		Plunket, Benjamin	5	1
Hamilton, James	5		Houching, Charles	3		Noell, Benjamin	1		Rucker, Anthony	9	7
Hamilton, William	3		Page, William	7		Carter, Landon	2		Reynolds, Charles	7	7
Hamilton, Luke	11		Burks, Charles	7	1	Goodrich, James	7	1	Rickets, Thomas	9	
Hooker, William	5		Burks, Samuel	..	7	Sandidge, William	1	1	Rucker, Isaac	8	9
Hight, John	6		Payton, Phillip	7		Sandidge, John	10	4	Rucker, Elleoner	6	6
Harper, Henry	7		Powell, John	6		Sandidge, Larkin	2		Richardson, John	5	6
Johnston, Stephen	12	4	Wright, Isaac	11	12	Higginbotham, Wm	3	4	Rucker, Ambrose	11	16
Jones, Thomas	4		Sale, John	8	6	Coleman, Benjamin	6	2	Rucker, John	8	1
Jones, Mary	8		Tooley, John	8	1	Hartless, Henry	9	1	Street, Thomas	9	
Irving, Charles		36	Roach Ashcraft	11	2	Sandidge, Pullom	5	1	Smith, William	10	
Jacobs, John	8	9	Shoemaker, Ezekiah	2		Gilbert, George	2	6	Street, Anthony	3	5
King, Jacob	7		Willson, George	2		Pendleton, James	4	2	Shelton, Richard	5	8
Levy, Solomon	1		Sledd, John	10		Swinney, Joseph	2		Staton, Lucy	8	2
Lesley, Robert	7		Morris, Thomas	4		Watson, Edward	8	16	Simmons, James	11	2
Leak, Mask	4		Ware, Mark	7		McDaniel, John	5	3	Stinnett, William	10	
Luttrell, Richard	6		Shackelford, Samuel	10	11	Wilcox, Thomas	4		Steel, William	2	
Lochard, Phillip	1		Powell, Francis	1		Stovaul, Thomas	3	3	Shelton, Joshua	2	4
Lankester, John	8		Edwards, Joseph	9	13	Wilburn, Richard	10		Symmons, James, Jr	1	
Lunsford, William	10		Milstead, Joseph	9		Crews, Joseph	9	7	Scott, William	6	1
Mays, Benjamin	4		McCulloch, Roderick	7	24	Bailey, Samuel	8		Swinney, Joseph	2	
Martin, Moses	5	1	Waugh, Thomas	8	7	Bonds, John	4		Slatten, Tyree	6	
Murrah, James	2		Carter, Edward	2	2	Crews, James	12	2	Swinney, Moses	8	2
Miller, Charles	6		Brown, John	8		Crews, Joseph	2		Taylor, Jeremiah	1	5
Masters, James	4		Brown, Moses	2		Childress, Joseph	10	9	Thomas, James	9	
Moran, Nicholas	8	5	Brown, William	..	..	Campbell, John	3		Williams, Francis	3	4
McGehee, Samuel	6		Milstead, Zeal	4		Crittendon, John	9		Tuley, John	1	
McDaniel, Daniel	4	1	Lewis, John	4	4	Dawson, John	7	1	Woodroof, John	2	
Massie, John	3		Lewis, John	4	2	Dehart, Aaron	9		Woodroof, Richard	1	
Masters, John	4		Carter, William	3		Dawson, Robert	2	2	Walker, Baylor	..	..
Nightingale, Matthew	7	4	Camden, John	3	1	Gaines, Daniel	16	55	Miles, Joseph	14	
Oglesbey, Joseph	1	1	Noell, John	6		Garland, Thomas	4		Douglass, George	6	2
Ponton, Joell	4		Jones, Nicholas	2		Goodwin, William	1		Tinsley, William	7	6
Parrock, Thomas	6	1	Tucker, Joseph	7	7	Goodrich, Thomas	12	8	Thacker, Pettkis	..	..
Patterson, Elizabeth	8		Ellis, Josiah	9	8	Guttrey, William	9		Tinsley, David	11	5
Powell, Thomas	4	2	Crawford, David	9	8	Harvey, Daniel	2	7	Tinsley, John	10	8
Powell, Lucas	9	17	Talliaferro, Richard	3	5	Harvie, Martha		11	Tinsley, Joshua	5	4
Phillips, John	10		Smith, John	3		Harris, John	3		Tinsley, Isaac	7	8
Powell, William	5	8	Wilsher, Richard	8		Hamm, Stephen	14	3	Trent, Henry	6	7
Powell, Nathaniel	3	7	Huffman, Henry	6		Jenkins, Thomas	9		Tennison, John	12	2
Patterson, John	1		Grisham, Thomas	8		Johns, Robert	3		Turner, Henry	6	7
Ramsey, James	6		Davis, Nathaniel (Est.)	7	12	Knight, John	6		Turner, John	8	3
Ryann, John	11	1	Davis, Charles	2		Lee, Richard	3	4	Wright, Thomas	8	10
Rose, Charles	6	49	Goodwin, Joseph	12	2	Lucas, Thomas	4	9	Wright, Moses	9	
Rippeto, Peter	10		Gillum, Archibald	3	2	Lee, William	8	14	Woodroof, David	11	7
Rose, John	5	111	Milstead, Aaron	5		McDaniel, George	7	11	Whitehead, John	15	3
Rose, Patrick	6	56	Veale, William	5		Morton, James	5	4	Williams, William	2	
Rose, Margaret	1	3	Hall, John	5		McDaniel, George	3	5	Ellis, E. Solomon	9	
Smith, John	3		Jones, Ambrose	8		Davies, Henry L	10	35	Bell, Henry	6	10
Shields, John	11	1	Ison, Charles	7		Rucker, Benjamin	8	18	Brannum, Edward	1	
Smith, Abraham	3	2	McDaniel, Angus	10		Adkins, John	7		Bryant, William	5	
Shields, Jane	2		Huffman, Frederick	5		Robertson, John	12	6	Bell, Samuel	3	2
Taliaferro, Zacharias	8	19	Ison, Elijah	5		Burford, Danl (Minor)	4	1	Christian, Robert	9	12
Thompson, James	1		Taylor, William	14		Burford, John B	5	2	Christian, John B	8	12
Thompson, John	9		Matthews, William	8		Boling's Robert (Estate)	9	60	Christian, Drury (Est.)	5	12
Talbert, Thomas	7	14	Staton, Thomas	6		Burden, Archa	9		Christian, Capt John	8	11
Trent, Peterfield	4	35	Staton, Benjamin	1		Brown, William	2		Christian, Charles	10	10
Tilford, James	8	1	Staton, William	6		Bailey, Allen	9		Christian, Henry	8	2
Tuggle, Henry	1		Casteel, William	2		Hughes, William	8	11	Christian, Elijah	7	2
Tankersley, Richard	7	2	Tungett, Fielding	2		Coleman, John Daniel	13	8	Christian, John Harvey	1	5
Tilford, James, Jun	4		Higgenbotham, Wm	6		Coleman, Elizabeth	8	4	Christian, George	5	14
Thompson, James	10		Ampey, William	5		Cox, Vol	8	2	Church, Mary	7	
Witt, John	8	1	Powers, Walter	4		Davis, Henry L	9	35	Dillard, William	9	2
Wren, Nicholas	10		Maxwell, James	5		Dawson, Martin	9	7	Dillard, James	5	13
Wright, Benjamin	7	3	Frazier, James	5		Dawson, Joseph	7	9	Evans, Benjamin	6	
Wilcox, Edmund	1	23	Jarvis, John	10		Evans, William	6	1	Fields, Joice	8	
Wells, James	8	8	Hartless, William	1		Gooch, Thomas	5		Goode, William		7
Witt, Elisha	3		Childress, John	9		Goodwin, Micajah	8	2	Gatewood, Larkin	4	5
Wright, Moses	7		Earchart, John	6		Ghilds, John	1		Gatewood, Ambrose	8	5
Watt, Thomas	7		Hogg, John	4		Gillenwater, Martha	7	1	Gilleland, Hugh	9	5

AMHERST COUNTY—Continued.

NAME OF HEAD OF FAMILY.	White.	Black.	NAME OF HEAD OF FAMILY.	White.	Black.	NAME OF HEAD OF FAMILY.	White.	Black.	NAME OF HEAD OF FAMILY.	White.	Black.
Gatewood, John	2		Vea, William	5		Carter's, Charles (Est.)		5	Merredith, Samuel	5	38
Gatewood, Richard	12	4	Evans, Elizabeth	6		Cottrell, James	7		Matthews, John	5	
Gillenwater, Mary	7		Evans, James	1		Cash, Tamson	6	5	Mays, Robert	8	
Gatewood, William	4		Laine, James	7		Cox, Margarett	2	4	Mays, Benjamin	8	
Gatewood, William, Jr	7	1	Largen, Thomas	11		Camden, Benjamin	9		Marr, John	5	4
Grissham, James	7	6	Welch, William	7		Duggins, Ellick	11		Marr, John, Jun	3	
Hutcheson, John	8		Laine, William	7		Fitzgarrell, George	8		Martin, Joseph	8	1
Johnson, John	4		Wright, Jessee	5		Franklin, Henry	6	2	Penn, Philip	11	12
Holloday, Tabitha	1	1	Wilsher, Thomas	8		Franklin, Maryann	7	4	Penn, John	8	25
Humbles, Martha	3		Lavender, Charles	8		Gilbert, Mary	2	16	Penn, George	8	14
Hodges, Rachel	6		Arrington, Samuel	3		Gilbert, Henry	8	4	Powell, Thomas	3	10
Johns, Mary	7	5	Page, William	8		Gilbert, Josiah	1	4	Penn, Gabriel	8	39
Joiner, Peter	8	5	Oglesbey, Richard	6	2	Gilbert, Ezekiel	3	4	Phillips, Jacob	8	
London, James, Jun	7	2	Henderson, Alexander	1		Galaspie, George, Jr	1		Powell, Amey	1	3
Lamaster, Abraham	3		Harloe, Nathaniel		10	Galt, William	1	3	Payton, Henry	2	
Mayos, Joseph	8	21	Biddlecomb, John	7		Gilbert, Thomas	1	2	Giles, Perrin	7	3
Mahon, William	9		Bond, Joseph	5		Gilbert, Richard	1	3	Pollard, Absolum	4	
Old, John	2	7	Bond, Richard	1		Gilbert, Sally	3	1	Oglisbey, Richard	11	5
Oglesbey, William	1		Burton, William	4	6	Garrett, Henry	4		Rogers, Benjamin	5	
Pagett, Edmund	8		Bowman, Drury	10	3	Gibson, Isaac	6	1	Rose, Hugh	10	64
Penn, Thomas	9	2	Ballenger, Joseph	4	12	Higgenbotham, Benjaᵃ	3	10	Smith, Philip	5	
Pemberton, James	5		Burden, Henry	7		Higgenbotham, Benjaᵃ, Jr	3	1	Sutherland, George	6	
Patterson's, James (Est.)	3	13	Burrass, Charles	8	21	Higgenbotham, Jacob	8	4	Scott, John	7	12
Phillips, John	7	5	Burton, Philip	1	5	Higgenbotham, Joseph	4	7	Smith, Jacob	9	15
Phillips, William	8	3	Baldock, Levy	8	2	Higgenbotham, Samˡ	10	6	Saunders, Elizabeth	5	9
Phillips, George	5	2	Banks, Linn	11	3	Higgenbotham, Aaron	2	15	Steel, Augustine	1	
Penn, Phillip	10	2	Banks, Anne	2	2	Higgenbotham, Aaron, Jr	4	3	Swinney, John	11	
Ridgway, Thomas	7		Banks, Reubin	1		Higgenbotham, James	4	14	Sale, Cornelius	8	2
Rowsie, John	10		Ballenger, Richard	9	8	Higgenbotham, John	11	18	Tungett, Jeremiah	8	
Rowsie, James	9		Carter, Edward, Esq	28	99	Higgenbotham, Moses	8	7	Tomlin, Ambrose	5	
Tyree, Jacob	9	8	Coleman, George	5	12	Higgenbotham, Caleb	6	3	Taliaferro, Charles	9	19
Upshaw, John	5	1	Croutcher, William	1		Hudson, Robert	3	1	Tucker, Daniel	1	1
Whittle, Joseph	10		Cash, Joseph	1		Hay, Gilbert	5	2	Tucker, William	4	4
Wilsher, Charles	6		Cash, Tabitha	7	1	Hay, Charles	3	1	Tucker, Matthew	5	13
White, Sarah	7	1	Coleman, Lindsey	5	15	Harper, Henry	6	1	Tucker, Drury	7	12
Wood, Francis	5		Cash, Bartlett	2		Hudson, Josnua	11	12	Tungett, Thomas	6	
Wood, Paul	5		Campbell's, Neill (Est.)	1	15	Hudson, Rush			Tyler, Charles	5	3
Wood, Silas	5		Cash, Stephen	7		Hix, William	6		Tandy, Smyth	5	6
Wood, Mary	5		Campbell, Joell	7	1	Hilley, Thomas	6		Wiatt, John	7	25
Warren, James	8		Cash, Howard	6		Lee, George	7	8	Wattson, James	9	10
Walker, Joell	4	8	Camden, William	11	1	Lee, Frank	1	5	West, John	12	46
Wingfield, John	5	8	Cash, Ruth	6	12	Landrum, Thomas	9	3	Wortham, Thomas	10	
Warren, Benjamin	2		Campbell, Lawrance	10	4	Landrum, Thomas, Jr	3		Ware, Edward	3	15
Barker, Edmund	4		Cashwell, Peter	10		Johnson, Noell	6	9	Whitloe, John	7	
Been, Johnston	6	6	Cameron, Duncan	1		Mays, William	11	2			
Spears, William			Clements, James	2		Manteply, Nathaniel	4	10			

CHESTERFIELD COUNTY.

NAME OF HEAD OF FAMILY.	White.	Black.	NAME OF HEAD OF FAMILY.	White.	Black.	NAME OF HEAD OF FAMILY.	White.	Black.	NAME OF HEAD OF FAMILY.	White.	Black.
Goode, Robert	10	104	Morrisett, John	4	14	Hylton, John		3	Robertson, William		9
Bingham, James	3	1	Morrisett, David	4	9	Worsham, Elizabeth	5	13	Edwards, Thosˢ	3	6
Cary, Archibald	1	36	Caulfield, William	3	1	Walthall, John	5	4	Osborne, John	5	14
Winpey, James	7	18	Hopkins, Benjamin	5	4	Jones, William	3	1	Randolph, David M.	3	24
Smith, Francis	7	18	Goode, William	6	9	Smith, Philip	7		Covington, Richard	7	9
Paul, James	6		Brumall, William	7		Featherston, Edward	3	11	Varner, Edward	7	7
Paul, Robert	6		Thurman, John	11	9	Ashbrook, Peter	7	6	Covington, John	6	3
Cheatham, Thomas	11	32	Bridgwater, Thomas	9	9	Mosely, Blackman	8	19	Williamson, Robert	4	2
Brier, Edward	2	2	Markham, Bernard	8	30	Trent, Peter F.	9	23	Hodge, James	2	
Morgan, Sarah	3		Branch, James	2	6	Perkins, John	6	1	Ligon, Judith	4	15
Crisp, John	5	6	Scherer, Nicholas	2	14	Leigh, Wᵐ	5	24	Toms, Benjamin	6	
Stevens, Robert	2	1	Howlet, Thomas	2	15	Smith, William	6		Walthall, Richard	3	9
Pankey, Stephen, jr	10	19	Blades, Francis	7		Pouland, Thomas	4	5	Walthall, Gerrard	3	16
Handcock, Simon	5	10	Fore, John	6	16	Martin's, John (Est.)	1	4	Folks, Edward	4	5
Gibson, William	5	4	Moody, John	4	1	Walthall, Eliz.	6	4	Folks, Edward, Jr	7	6
Branch, Daniel	7	6	Cox, Milner	4	1	Walthall, James	3	4	Woodson, George	1	14
Rubsamin, Jacob	3	10	Cary, Mary	11	11	Randolph, John	4	10	Bass, Archᵈ	4	3
Dunlavy, Anthony	10		Pattison, David	8	29	Marshall, Alexander	4	13	Ross, David	8	18
Branch, Ridley	3	17	Martin, Wᵐ	4	9	Walthall, Archᵈ	2	12	Bragg, William	7	7
Branch, Samuel	7	31	Upshaw, —	0	11	Nunnally, Obedient	2	8	Jones & Bragg	1	3
Baker, Martin	7	2	Goodsher, Martin	7	1	Nunnally, Nowell	1		Jones, Joseph		6
Branch, Matt	9	22	Scott, William	3	40	Dillon, Joseph	6		Bass', Wᵐ (Estate)	5	16
Trabue, John	5	18	Blankinship, Stephen	3		Dillon, John	4		Davies', Caleb (Estate)		1
Phillips, Alexander	3	2	Rigby, Henry	4	2	Smith, James	5		Hatcher, Samuel	10	28
Fowler, John, Sr	8	24	Branch, Edward	8	15	Davis, Elizabeth	1	4	Branch, Benjamin	4	16
Treadway, Moses	5	17	Branch, Edward	4		Wormack, William	8	1	Edwards', Peter (Estate)	4	16
Elam, Daniel	9	15	Dick, Stoney C.		3	Pleasants, William	8	11	Elam, Robert	4	21
Ellison, Oran	6	15	Chaulkley, David	1	3	Norris, James	6		Branch, Christopher	10	27
Brumall, John	5	2	Paul, James	5	3	Nunnally, Wᵐ Wormack	7	6	Randolph, Richard		10
Burton, John	6	8	Evans, George	1	1	Bolling, Thomas	4	34	Latchet, John	5	
Burton, Thomas	1	8	Martin, William	9	11	Baugh, Burwill	4	26	Batte, Richard	2	25
Burton, William	1	1	Clarke, Charles	4	3	Baugh, Francis	7	5	Nunnally, Joe Puckett	8	
Burton, John	4	12	Black's, William (Estate)	2	74	Baugh, Elizabeth	8	2	Wormack, Isham	5	
Burton, Thos., Sr	1	9	McKenzie, William	2	18	Batts, Thosˢ, Senʳ	2	27	Burwell, Lewis	3	34
Ellison, Enos	10	17	Logwood, Archᵈ	5	7	Batts, Thosˢ, jr	7	15	Ludsbury, Ezekiel	7	3
Lockett, Phebe	3		Logwood, William	2	3	Baugh, Richard	9	18	Horner, Daniel	7	2
Peck, John	8	3	Labouch, Sarah	5	5	Brintle, Jacob	6	4	Cogbill, George, Sr	4	5
Goode, Thomas	3	34	Gones, George	2	1	Burton, John	3	4	Cogbill, William	5	5
Sumpter, John	7	2	Marpoles, George	6	1	Bevill, Francis	5	8	Gill, Stephen	9	1
Cheatham, Christopher	5	15	North, John	2	1	Baugh, John	9	8	Wilson, William	8	
Weisegree, Daniel	4	17	McCallum, Daniel	2	15	Osborne's, Thosˢ (Estate)	10	25	Jackson, Peter	1	5
Sallee, Abram	5	67	Stratton, Henry	1	5	Desears, James	9	23	Wormack, William	1	
Nivens, Susannah	6	42	Stone, Rowland	2	5	Elam, Wᵐ	4	1	Clayton, John	8	1
Pankey, Stephen, Sr	4	12	Pointer, William	1	1	Cogbill, Thomas	11	24	Cogbill, Charles	6	11
Hill, Edward	5		Featherstone, Henry	9	20	Hill, Elizabeth	1	3	Blankinship, Matthew	9	
Hill, Olive	6		Akin, Thomas	5	5	Hardy, John	2	2	Ferquran, John	11	8
Branch, Fanny	5		Walthall, William	2	42	Archer, Henry	10	24	Hewlett, James	1	
Randolph, Henry	1	14	Belcher, Burwel	6		Pride, John	6	17	Wooldridge, Thomas	5	10
Baker, John	5	12	Walthall's, William (Est.)	4	24	Walthall, John	1	18	Wooldridge, Robert	5	11
Scott, Walter, Senʳ	8	21	Frend, Nathaniel	7	17	Cogbill, Jesse	4	29	Frend, Edward	9	20
Scott, James	1	7	Frend's, Thomas (Est.)	5	17	Cogbill, John	1	1	Watkins, Joseph	9	8
Pattison, Mary	5	21	Jesper, Henry	7		Goode, Edward	1	4	Dupee, Judith	1	8
Branch, Thosˢ	9	14	Puckett, Edy	5		Akin, James	8	5	Powell, John	5	
Elliott, Cornelius	11	13	Archer, John	9	28	Clarke, Thomas	7	1	Trent, Henry	8	6

CHESTERFIELD COUNTY—Continued.

NAME OF HEAD OF FAMILY.	White.	Black.	NAME OF HEAD OF FAMILY.	White.	Black.	NAME OF HEAD OF FAMILY.	White.	Black.	NAME OF HEAD OF FAMILY.	White.	Black.
Miles, John	5	....	Andrews, Lewis	7	....	Batford, John	5	1	Fergusson, William	2	....
Powell, James	5	....	Andrews, Claiborne	3	....	Rowlett, William	3	10	Fergusson, Bartlett	2	....
Grissell, Henry	10	....	Andrews, Rolph	3	....	Rowlett, William	10	13	Fowler, Guardnr	4	....
Short, Thomas	7	....	Andrews, Isham	15	....	Royall, John	7	10	Fowler, Abram	4	....
Martin, John	1	1	Andrews, Randolph	3	....	Royall, Joseph	4	22	Clarke, William	5	....
Bottom, Thomas	9	....	Ashbrook, William	4	16	Rowlett, John	7	26	Clarke, James	5	....
Moody, Francis	7	6	Atkins, John	10	5	Ratlif, Phillip	3	1	Crostick, Edward	4	....
Wooldridge, Edward	4	7	Archer, John	7	10	Stewart, Sarah	5	....	Patram, George	9	2
Wooldridge, William	4	7	Atkinson, James	2	....	Smith's, John (Est.)	0	4	Hencock, George	6	9
Simpson, Althea	6	....	Blankinship, Ephraim	5	....	Smith, John	5	....	Patram, Francis	11	3
Hancock, Wm	7	5	Blankinship, Ephraim, Jr	4	....	Traylor, Elizabeth	2	6	Newby, William	7	....
Flournoy, Jacob	14	21	Blankinship, Joel	8	....	Traylor, Buckner	7	....	Gibbs, Matthus	9	7
Brumall, John	7	3	Blankinship, Joseph	5	....	Traylor, Elizabeth	3	2	Whitworth, Samuel	6	....
Roberts, Ruth	3	2	Blankinship, Abram	3	....	Traylor, Littlebury	8	3	Puckett, John	2	1
Bins, Wiltshire	2	1	Bass, Thomas	7	4	Traylor, Azeker	3	....	Barron, William	5	....
Roberts, Morris	7	....	Bolton, John	7	....	Traylor, Daniel	5	....	Coshon, William	9	3
Bowman, Drury	4	....	Bott, John	6	32	Traylor, Field	5	3	Cole, Hamblin	3	....
Brooks, Alexander	4	7	Belcher, Marris	7	....	Totty, Abner	3	....	Mills, Henry	12	....
Bowman, John	4	7	Belcher, William	4	....	Totty, John	8	....	Blankinship, William	10	1
Flournoy, William	14	11	Belcher, Thomas	3	....	Totty, John, Jr	4	....	Wyatt, William	3	....
Taylor, Josiah	3	....	Burton, Thomas	5	7	Totty, Thomas	6	16	Blankinship, Abram	3	....
Liggon, William	4	11	Berry, David	10	....	Totty, Usley	6	....	Rudd, Thomas	12	13
Lacy, Archd	4	....	Blankinship, Olive	7	....	Traylor, William	3	1	Rudd's, William (Est.)	6	8
Wooldridge, William	1	....	Bragg, Joel	3	....	Taylor, Joseph	7	5	Elam, Samuel	8	8
Elam, Lodwick	4	....	Burfoot, Thomas	4	6	Traylor, Archer	7	13	Talbott, Peter	5	9
Moseley, Edward	7	18	Blankinship, Matthew	10	....	Traylor, Jesse	8	2	Hill, John	7	12
Asshurst, Ann	6	12	Bragg, Hugh	2	....	Totty, Francis	8	....	Baugh, John	7	6
Watkins, John	8	26	Brown, James	9	....	Vaden, Daniel	7	1	Baugh, John, jr	7	1
Flournay, William	5	14	Bennet, James	3	....	Vaden, Joseph	10	....	Belcher, Thomas	5	4
Sublett, Lewis	4	15	Brown, Thomas	2	....	Vaden, John	11	7	Thweat, William	7	20
Winfrey, Rubin	4	10	Brown, Daniel	5	....	Vaden, George	5	12	Bowman, Pleasant	3	7
Trabue, Olimph	7	18	Cousins, John	3	8	Vaden, Gardner	4	1	Hix, John	8	....
Leprade, Andrew	8	9	McColvin, Neill	5	....	Vaden, Lodwick	5	....	Gates, Thos	3	....
Gregory, Thomas	4	2	McClavin, John	3	....	Willson, Drury	8	....	Caster, Bidu	4	....
Railey, Thomas	2	1	McClavin, Daniel	2	....	Willson, Edward	5	....	Fergusson, Thomas	3	1
Railey, Isham	1	1	Cheatham, Samuel	4	12	Williams, John	5	3	Mann, Joseph	4	2
Railey, William	1	1	Clay, Peter	5	13	Worsham, John	2	6	Newby, John	4	....
Railey, John	7	36	Dunavant, Edward	7	....	Williams, John	5	....	Newby, John	2	1
Vest, Phill	6	....	Dance, Henry	6	7	Wells, Michael	14	11	Ammonet, Charles	1	....
Bowman, Daniel	4	3	Dance, Edward	12	....	Watkins, Joseph	8	20	Lockett, Benja	3	7
Roberts, John	9	....	Dishman, Drury	4	....	West, George	3	2	Lockett, Charles	6	8
Farrer, John	7	11	Dison, John	9	4	Walker, Gollothen	6	1	Lockett, Francis, jr	2	2
Morris, James	5	....	Dyson, Daniel	6	10	Ward, Benjamin	4	29	Lockett, Francis, Sr	11	32
Sublett, Lewis	8	11	Davis, Benja	7	....	Hardiway, Joseph	9	24	Clarke, Isham	7	....
Eppes, Francis, Esq'r	14	124	Dunavant, Abram	7	....	Hardiway, Drury	3	3	Flournoy, Gibson	13	14
Locain, Barnabas	4	....	Deaton, John	6	3	Worsham, Thomas	4	22	Akins, Isham	8	5
Durant, Rebecca	3	....	Dishman, Daniel	6	....	Blankinship, Beverly	7	1	Flournoy, James	9	3
Chiles, Samuel	1	....	Dodd, Ann	6	....	Smith, Cleyton	5	....	Cole, Joseph	2	....
Hatcher, Edward	1	13	Davis, Thomas	11	1	Mosely, William	4	6	Cheatham, Thomas	9	10
Turner, Jehu	3	2	Dyer, Francis	4	....	Cheatham, Richard	10	8	Wilkerson, Mark	4	1
Ward, Mary	10	48	Dyer, John	9	....	Snellings, Alexander	11	....	Hill, William	3	10
Boss', Joseph (Estate)	7	24	Dyer, John, Senr	4	3	Wilkinson, Wm	6	....	Moore, Daniel	8	6
Bolling, John	1	10	Dyer, Isham	4	....	Hill, John	3	8	Cole, William	4	....
Blankinship, Drury	7	....	Davis, Hezekiah	4	....	Perdue, Cleveland	6	....	Martin, Thos	6	2
Farmer, Dicy	6	....	Eams, Thomas	9	....	Archer, John	9	6	Folks, Abell	6	2
Winfrey, Henry	5	12	Evans, Isham	8	....	Worsham, John	6	....	Coshoon, Thos	3	....
Bass', Christopher (Estate)	1	6	Franklyn, Obedience	4	8	Ward, Blackman	3	1	Perkinson, Noel	1	....
Walthall, William	7	10	Franklyn, Peter	5	4	Hatcher, William	4	7	Rowlett, Peter	4	2
Newby, Joseph	3	....	Franklyn, David	5	4	Hatcher, Nathaniel	6	2	Cole, Francis	3	....
Newby, James	8	....	Fowler, William	9	....	Turner, William	5	1	Puckett, James	8	....
Howlett, Thomas	2	30	Fowler, Josiah	5	....	Towler, Luke	2	4	Coock, William	2	1
Downs, John	4	....	Ferqueron, Aaron	7	....	Spears, Mary	3	13	Scurry, Benjamin	6	....
Farmer, Francis	11	10	Folks, Joel	4	1	Anderson, Ralph C.	3	32	Casshon, Burrel	4	....
Jackson, Joseph	8	11	Gill, Joseph, Senr	5	....	Vest, James	7	5	Casshon, James	4	....
Franklyn, John	12	5	Gill, Elizabeth	1	....	Rudd, James	5	4	Puckett, Thomas	4	....
Franklyn, Jeremiah	5	8	Gill, Joseph, Jr	6	....	Rudde, Hezekiah	4	....	Hill, John	4	9
Cheatham, William	9	29	Gill, Edward	7	1	Matthis, Thos	2	....	Cole, Robert	5	1
Farmer, William	6	4	Gibbs, William	7	17	Clayton, Thos	3	4	Perry, John	9	11
Fergusson, James	8	3	Gibbs, John	1	....	Horner, Nathan	5	1	Robertson, James	6	10
Farmer, Daniel	6	4	Gill, Francis	8	1	Burton, Charles	7	9	Turpin, Henry	7	15
Woodcock, Henry	9	4	Glaskock, William	3	....	Farmer, Thomas, Sr	8	5	Turpin, Hezekiah	9	7
Woodcock, Robert	8	2	Granger, Absolom	1	....	Farmer, Thomas	5	3	Turpin, Obadiah	1	1
Atkins, Robert	3	7	Gill, Benjamin	8	8	Graves, Arther	6	22	Cheatham, Francis	3	17
Brooks, William	10	7	Handy, Daniel	6	....	Clarke, Peter	5	3	Grant, Edith	6	5
Caycey, Charles	8	....	Harding, William	4	4	Puckett, Mark	6	....	Fergusson, Moses	6	4
Caycey, Robert	7	....	Holmes, Isaac	2	16	Clarke, Ellison	4	3	Fergusson, Sarah	1	5
Woodcock, John	2	....	Jackson, Ezekiel	3	3	Nunnally, Watt	2	6	Fergusson, John	1	1
Turner, James	4	....	Johnson, David	7	....	Nunnally, Henry	5	2	Newby, William	6	3
Hudson, John	8	....	Keen, Currel	3	6	Nunnally, James	6	....	Newby, Elijah	2	....
Varner, Peter	4	1	Moore, Daniel	9	....	Clay, James	10	....	Newby, Elsha	2	7
Baker, John, Sr	9	14	More, George Hunt	4	6	Hamblin, Charles	5	10	Baker, Thomas	6	2
Cox, Hickerson	10	4	More, Elizabeth	8	....	Sadler, Thomas	5	7	Klinhoof, George	1	22
Elliott, Robt	9	12	Mann, Archer	6	1	Farmer, William, jr	3	4	Cheatham, Stephen	9	3
Beasley, Benjamin	5	17	Moore, Mathew	7	1	Nunnally, James	7	....	Flournoy, Josiah	11	8
Beasley, Thos (Estate)	1	14	Morris, John	4	....	Hatcher, Obediah	6	....	Phillips, Elizabeth	6	....
Chaulkly, Archer	5	1	Mann, Daniel	8	....	Newby, Levy	3	1	Frostt, Joshua	7	....
Martin, Thos	3	....	Mann, Branch	5	....	Rudd, John	7	10	Smith, Henry	6	1
Chaulkly, William	10	....	Man, Olive	5	....	Branch, Benja	3	27	Smith, Michajer	2	....
Atkins, Phebe	4	1	Mail, Joseph	10	....	Graves', William (Est.)	5	16	Cobs, Amboss	2	7
Farmer, Joseph	3	14	Mosely, Josiah	1	9	Graves, Charles	3	6	Roberts, Enock	6	....
Farmer, Mark	1	1	Mann, Obediance	5	....	Grissell, William	5	....	Grant, Edith	11	....
Tanner, Branch	2	17	Moore, Eleazer	10	....	Grissell, George	5	....	Walthall, William	4	....
Walthall, Archd	5	9	Moody, Henry	1	8	Gordon, Giles	10	....	Rudd, James	5	10
Walthall's, Henry (Est.)	5	10	Moody, Henry, Jr	8	11	Belcher, John	2	2	Rudd, Thomas	4	10
Beasley, William	9	7	Nobles, Mark	7	....	Graves, King	3	14	Worsham, John	3	....
Nunnally, John	10	7	Osborne, Edward	1	44	Baugh, James	8	....	Newby, Jesse	1	....
Andrews, Sylvester	7	....	Osborne, Francis	10	32	Perdue, Josiah	8	....	Wilkerson, Richard	6	20
Andrews, Benjamin	5	....	Perkerson, John	6	1	Elliott, Pilip	10	3	Graves, John	3	....
Andrews, Bullard	5	....	Perkerson, Ezekiel	5	....	Puckett, Nathaniel	3	....	Winfrey, Wm	4	6
Andrews, Simon	5	....	Perkerson, Robert	6	....	Puckett, Abram	8	....	Pardue, Richd	3	....
Andrews, Stanton	5	....	Perkerson, William	8	....	Patram, Daniel	7	11	Ware, William	10	3
Andrews, William	9	....	Perkerson, Baxter	10	....	Pardue, Thomas	8	....	Totty, Thos H.	2	....
Andrews, Francis	6	....	Fitzpatrick, Peter	11	21	Pardue, Francis	6	....	Mann, William	9	....
Andrews, Stephen	6	....	Puckett, Mary	8	....	Perdue, Ezekiel	10	4	Mann, Thos	9	7

CHESTERFIELD COUNTY—Continued.

NAME OF HEAD OF FAMILY.	White.	Black.	NAME OF HEAD OF FAMILY.	White.	Black.	NAME OF HEAD OF FAMILY.	White.	Black.	NAME OF HEAD OF FAMILY.	White.	Black.
Moore, Marke	11	....	Jackson, Hezekiah	1	....	Moore, Iham	10	....	Puckett, Mary	5	....
Blankinship, Fore	6	9	Kenny, Phebe	2	....	Robertson, George	7	....	Lopeman, Edward	9	6
West, Littlebury	5	5	Lessenbury, Thos	6	1	Elam, James	4	8	Goodwin, Collins	5	5
Willson, John	5	1	Linch, Henry	3	....	Clybern, George	10	....	Elam, Burwell	4	1
Blankinship, Mary	6	....	Lewis, William	6	....	Farmer, Hezekiah	3	4	Bass, Edward	6	6
Mann, John	6	....	Lattimore, James	6	5	Farmer, Phebe	5	10	Gordon, James	6	6
Dunavant, Dudly	6	....	McGraw, James	3	....	Bailey, James	7	....	Baugh, Peter	3	6
Andrews, Lewis	7	....	Moody, James	6	8	Elam, Branch	7	12	Anderson, Jordain	4	16
Ash, John	7	....	McNabb, Alexr	4	5	Syms, James	11	....	Flournoy, Samuel	1	6
Archer, Field	3	29	Norris, John	3	3	Williamson, William	11	....	Russell, John	6	2
Archer, Edward	7	23	Norris, James	6	6	Cole, William	4	....	Russell, Jesse	9	1
Ammonet, John	6	1	Nunnally, Joshua	5	....	Lester, Lewis	6	7	Robertson, John	8	21
Brawlon, John	1	2	Pigg, Francis	3	12	Moseley, Alexander	5	5	Moody, Arther	9	6
Brittain, William	11	1	Perkerson, James	5	5	Bass, Thomas	8	16	Robertson, Sarah	3	4
Bevill, Francis	5	8	Perkerson, John	6	....	Purdie, Aaron	8	2	Robertson, Mills	9	1
Booker, Richard	3	16	Perkerson, William	4	....	Stevens, William	6	14	Robertson, William	10	8
Baker, Jerman	4	27	Perkerson, John	8	....	Moseley, Richard	5	7	Bosbeach, Lodwick	7	....
Burrows, John	3	3	Perkerson, David	4	7	Cheatham, Leonard	8	12	Farmer, Elam	4	1
Blankinship, Gidion	6	....	Partin, William	7	....	Rucks, James	1	....	Goodwin, David	11	3
Burton, Susana	2	6	Rowlett, John	7	24	Bass, Henry	7	3	Haskins, Creed	1	21
Burton, Abram	1	9	Rowlett, William	3	11	Rucks, Josiah	5	1	Talbott, Haly	7	3
Baugh, Peter	9	22	Robertson, George	11	11	Clyborne, Jonas	11	....	Rudd, Frederick	7	....
Baugh, Peter, jr	3	6	Stewart, John	2	....	Gordon, James	7	....	Garrott, John	9	....
Barber, Thomas	4	....	Stewart, John, jr	8	....	Bass, Alexander	11	....	Gon, James	7	....
Buchannan, Niell	3	24	Stewart, Charles	4	....	Cheatham, Henry	10	12	Worsham, William	5	1
Chapple, Robert	4	1	Stewart, Thomas	2	3	Russell, Stephen	8	....	Bailey, Benjo	4	....
Coothrall, Martha	4	....	Stringer, John	17	14	Russell, Stephen	7	....	Wormack, Thomas	6	6
Carter, Littleton	4	....	Stiles, John	5	1	Wilkerson, Edward	10	1	Worsham, Kennon	5	....
Covington, John	6	3	Shore, Thomas	3	13	Howerton, Thomas	6	....	Lester, Morgin	7	....
Cousins, George	5	20	Tucker, St George	11	71	Cole, John	6	1	Robertson, Nicholas	8	8
Cousins, George, Jr	5	2	Towler, John	6	5	Lockett, William	14	....	Boles, Zack	7	....
Cousins, William	7	7	Tabb, John	....	15	Akin, William	4	9	Wilkerson, Drury	3	....
Cogbill, George	5	29	Traylor, Humphrey	4	7	Akins, Joseph	5	2	Forsse, Charles	4	2
Dance, William	14	14	Traylor, Fred	4	1	Akins, James	2	1	Bailey, Abram	1	....
Dance, Edward	8	4	Terry, Thomas	3	....	Goode, John	14	3	Rudd, Aldrige	4	....
Duncan, Charles	4	24	Tralor, Humphrey	7	6	Ashbrook, Joseph	12	9	Anderson, Edward	6	3
Downman, William	6	13	Traylor, George	6	2	Flourney, Lorence	1	10	Gordon, William	3	5
Dodson, William	3	12	Traylor, Humphrey	....	6	Farmer, John	4	8	Clarke, Jesse	8	10
Edwards, John	8	11	Walthall, Gerrard	9	19	Farmer, John	6	11	Flood, John	4	....
Evans, William	4	....	Wills, Isham	12	14	Nunnally, Sherman	8	7	Turpin, Phill	8	6
Edwards, Margrett	1	1	Wells, Joseph	5	8	Walthall, Richard	8	13	Gipson, Miles	2	5
Eanes, John	7	1	Worsham, William	4	10	Cheatham, Isham	8	7	Asshurst, Robert	6	5
Irby, William	8	....	Worsham, William, jr	2	4	Condee, William	5	....	Nowell, Eli	10	10
Falkernr, Ralph	5	4	Gates, William	8	2	Moore, John	7	....	Haskins, Aaran	2	4
Franks, William	4	....	Hickman, William	12	1	Lockett, Richard	10	5	Haskins, Robert	11	9
Franklyn, Alexander	5	....	Nunnally, Jeremiah	5	1	Lester, Jacob	3	6	Branch, Edward	11	18
Folks, Edward	4	5	Boles, Henry	10	....	Lester, Jeremiah	2	2	Tatum, Josiah	5	31
Franklyn, John	10	2	More, William	5	....	Cheatham, Josiah	7	8	Tatum, Henry	1	11
Folks, Edward, jr	7	6	More, William D	3	....	Gordan, William	3	5	Puckett, Mary	5	....
Franklyn, Joel	5	2	Moody, Blanks	6	....	Walthall, William	1	5	Ball's, James (Estate)	6	8
Gill, James	11	13	Mills, Henry	12	....	Wooldridge, Robert	1	2	Goode, Francis	10	34
Gill, Robert	1	....	Nunnally, David	9	....	Lynes, William	12	....	Osborne's, Thomas (Est.)	12	5
Gill, Thomas	5	8	Brown, John	6	....	Wooldridge, John	4	8	Randolph's, William (Est.)	1	40
Gill, John	2	5	Brown, George	6	....	Elam, Richard	7	12	Oshones, Francis	....	9
Holt, David	6	26	Condrey, John	5	....	Gates, James	9	3	Anderson, Claiborne (Est.)	5	30
Holt, Thomas	5	3	Basebeach, James	8	....	Gates, Mary	1	2	Watkins, Benjamin (Est.)	7	32
Hare, Parker	7	11	Blankinship, Archer	4	....	Wormack, Sally	12	5	Markham, George	10	19
Harris, Jack	2	....	Blankinship, William	6	....	Pilkington, Sally	6	....	Watkins, Thomas	1	6
Horton, William	3	2	Vest, Gabriel	5	....	Pilkington, Morris	5	....	Mills, Anthony	7	....
Hill, John	7	2	Lockett, Thomas	8	....	Boles, Thomas	9	....	McDowell, John	7	....
Hogans, Margrett	3	2	Russel, William	9	....	Boles, James	4	1	Smith, William	3	23
Ireland, John	4	....	Elam, Elizabeth	5	....	Asshurst, Francis	1	1	Smith, Oba	4	25
Jones, Charles	7	1	Robertson, George, Senr	2	5	Cox, Henry	7	12			
Jones, John	12	6	Robertson, James	7	2	Puckett, Jesse	7	7			

ESSEX COUNTY.

DISTRICT NO. 2—LIST OF NEWMAN BROCKENBROUGH.	White.	Black.	DISTRICT NO. 2—LIST OF NEWMAN BROCKENBROUGH—continued.	White.	Black.	DISTRICT NO. 2—LIST OF NEWMAN BROCKENBROUGH—continued.	White.	Black.	DISTRICT NO. 2—LIST OF NEWMAN BROCKENBROUGH—continued.	White.	Black.
Allen, Hannah	5	6	Campbell, John	9	....	Davis, Evan	6	5	Greenwood, William	4	5
Brockenborough, Newman	4	20	Chaney, Phillip	4	6	Davis, Reuben	1	....	Greenwood, William	3	2
Broocke, Thos Henry	5	2	Caulhorn, Richard	9	4	Durham, James	6	1	Greenwood, Twyman	5	1
Bush, John	8	....	Caulhorn, Thomas	9	1	Dunn, Edmund	7	5	Gatewood, Isaac	5	1
Broocke, George	4	4	Coats, Samuel	7	3	Dunn, Benjamin	7	3	Greenwood, James	3	1
Brizendine, Elizabeth	2	5	Coats, Mary	2	1	Dunn, Elizabeth	8	7	Good, John	5	2
Brizendine, Thomas	3	3	Crutcher, Thomas	2	7	Dunn, Dickinson	5	....	Good, Richard	5	....
Brizendine, Randolph	4	2	Coats, Thomas	9	4	Dobbins, Thomas	6	3	Griggs, Philip	7	....
Bush, Thomas	3	7	Croxton, James	9	6	Dunn, Nathan	4	2	Hodges, John	9	....
Broocke, Richard	3	5	Cauthorn, James	1	....	Dunn, William	5	9	Howerton, William	4	2
Broocke, John, Senr	3	6	Crow, Austin	4	1	Dennell, Francis	5	....	Howerton, Ambrose	2	3
Brizendine, Francis	5	....	Covington, Sarah	7	24	Dunn, Phill	3	....	Harper, John	6	....
Baughan, Francis	3	....	Covington, William	10	4	Davis, William	9	....	Howerton, John	5	5
Bohannon, Joseph	10	17	Crow, Isom	6	1	Davis, John	9	....	Howerton, Heritage	7	13
Broocke, Thomas	4	1	Crow, Susannah	1	5	Davis, Samuel	2	....	Harper, Stephen	5	....
Brown, Richard	4	10	Crow, John	12	8	Davis, John	3	....	Hayes, William	6	....
Broocke, John	10	....	Clark, Thomas	3	....	Davis, Jacob	6	....	Hundley, Mary	2	....
Brizendine, William	6	....	Covington, Thomas	4	3	Davis, Samuel	7	....	Johnson, Griffin	9	....
Breedlove, Nathan	5	....	Cauthorn, Henry	4	5	Davis, Isaac	3	....	Jeffries, Richard	9	20
Brown, Cornelius	4	....	Chaney, William	12	10	Dunn, William	9	....	Johnson, Ben	8	2
Brizendine, Isaac	1	....	Carter, Daniel	3	....	Dunn, Anthony	6	....	James, Thomas	4	....
Broocke, William	1	....	Cauloux	1	5	Dickinson, John	2	7	Johnson, Thomas	8	3
Brizendine, Bartlett	1	....	Cole, William	4	10	Dunn, Phill	5	....	Jordon, Isaac	6	9
Brizendine, Armstead	2	....	Coxe, Thomas	12	....	Edmondson, William	8	13	Jeffries, William	2	1
Brizendine, Abner	1	....	Dangerfield, Le Roy	5	23	Evans, James	4	11	Johnson, Samul	1	....
Brizendine, Reuben	3	....	Davis, Thomas	6	....	Edmondson, James	8	1	Kidd, Philip	5	2
Byrum, Fauntleroy	1	....	Dunn, Wm	5	15	Evans, Elizabeth	4	5	Mann, John	7	6
Breedlove (Widow)	5	....	Dunn, John	4	3	Flether, John	7	....	Marlow, William	8	6
Carter, Samuel	8	....	Dunn, Thomas	1	....	Fisher, Richard	5	....	Mann, Robert	8	7
Campbell, James	4	....	Dunn, William M	7	2	Fisher, James	5	3	Mann, Joseph	2	15
						Fuller, Richard	5	1			

ESSEX COUNTY—Continued.

DISTRICT NO. 2—LIST OF NEWMAN BROCKENBROUGH—continued.

NAME OF HEAD OF FAMILY.	White.	Black.
Marlow, John	7	
Marlow, Reuben	4	
Minter, John	6	3
Mitchel, Ralph	3	
Minter, Josiah	12	2
Ogleby, Ann	4	
Parron, Thomas	1	
Patterson, Elizabeth	6	1
Rodden, John	1	
Rodden, Ben	5	
Stephen, James	1	
Ship, John	6	1
St. John, Richard	8	5
Shackleford, Roger	8	11
Shepherd, Jeremiah	5	1
Shackleford, William	3	8
Shepherd, Milley	4	1
Shepherd, Reuben	2	3
Stodghill, James	8	
Spade, Mary	2	
Stewart, Charles	1	
Stewart, William	1	
Townley, James	8	6
Tureman, Gilbert	9	
Townley, John	9	6
Treble, Peter	8	12
Taylor, Edmund	1	
Turner, Eleaner	3	1
Ursey, Thomas	8	
Vass, John	1	1
Vass, William	7	
Williamson, Wm	7	
Williamson, Jno	6	1
Williamson, Vincent	3	5
Williamson, Abram	5	
Webb, Richard	5	
Williamson, Thos	7	
Williamson, Isaac	7	1
Williamson, James	7	2
Williamson, Richard	5	
Webb, James	2	
Williamson, Thomas	8	
Young, Wm (Est.)	3	21
Young, John	1	

DISTRICT NO. 3—LIST OF SAMUEL PEACHEY.

NAME OF HEAD OF FAMILY.	White.	Black.
Allen, Richard	5	2
Allen, Frankey	6	22
Burk, John	8	10
Banks, Richard	9	11
Banks, William	3	10
Banks, James	3	16
Baker, John	2	3
Broocke, Thomas	5	2
Burnell, Amey	6	11
Banks, Wm (Son of James)	6	9
Brougham, Cary	3	4
Baynham, Richard	1	
Boulware, Samuel	1	
Brockenbrough, John	9	11
Burk, Richard	9	2
Broughan, Major	6	2
Broughan, John	7	3
Bray, Charles		9
Brown, John	5	
Crow, Nathaniel S	8	6
Couie, James	2	2
Chenault, John	3	1
Dunn, John	1	1
Edmondson, John	1	40
Fosseu, Rice	7	1
Hay, Robert	6	1
Haile, Lewis	1	
Howard, William	6	1
Hall, Richard	11	6
Haile, R. Thomas	9	13
Hart, William	4	
Gatewood, Philemon	4	12
Gatewood, Docr Wm	4	5
Games, John	4	
Gregory, Abram	2	8
Games, William	6	
Jones, William	3	2
Jones, Benjamin	7	28
Jones, Richard	7	1
Keitchevelles, John	6	2
Kidd, Henry	2	6
McCall, George	1	35
Munday, Micajah	2	2
May, James	5	
Purkins, Mary	10	6
Purkins, William	9	1
Ramsey, Elizabeth	3	6

DISTRICT NO. 3—LIST OF SAMUEL PEACHEY—continued.

NAME OF HEAD OF FAMILY.	White.	Black.
Ritchie, Archibald	6	75
Roam, Thomas		
Smith, Thomas	1	10
Smith, Thomas (Engn)	7	2
Smith & Jones	2	1
Smith, Elizabeth	7	4
Smith, John	1	2
Sterman, Elliot	3	4
Shearwood, Jonathan	5	
Shearwood, Jacob	2	
Smith, Samuel	1	12
Temple, Joseph	6	9
Waggoner, Benjamin	7	
Wood, Thomas	12	27
Allen, Thomas	8	25
Banks, James, Junr	4	8
Brown, Henry		4
Bennatt, Elizabeth	2	3
Bailey, David	4	1
Boice, Mary	4	1
Bogie, John	4	1
Chamberlaine, James	5	2
Croxton, Samuel	7	7
Croxton, William	3	1
Croxton, Carter	4	5
Croxton, Thomas	1	1
Cooper, James	7	9
Dyke, Bowler	6	1
Davis, Thomas	4	2
Dike, James	2	2
Dunn, Henry	11	11
Dunn, Waters	5	8
Davis, Thomas	9	
Games, Thomas	7	3
Gatewood, James	7	1
Gatewood, Joseph	10	4
Lang, James	2	2
Landrum, John	4	6
Meadors, Vincent	3	
Moose, Austin (Esta)		20
Meadors, Thomas	2	1
Prosser, William	6	
Peachey, Samuel	9	29
Smith, Meriwether	7	67
Seayres, Francis	7	4
Smith, John (Na)	4	3
Ship, Gideon	10	7
Walker, John, Senr	4	3
Walker, John, Junr	2	
Welch, Michael	9	3
Allen, Rachael	4	1
Allen, Jeremiah	4	1
Curtis, Robert	4	2
Davis, Thomas, Junr	8	
Haile, John	1	1
Haile, Wheeler	1	
Roane, Thomas	3	22
Webb, James, decd (Est.)	3	19
Webb & Ritchie's (Mill)		4

DISTRICT NO. 5—LIST OF WILLIAM DOANE.

NAME OF HEAD OF FAMILY.	White.	Black.
Andrews, William	3	
Allen, William	1	
Atkinson, James	4	1
Brooke, B. Lydia	2	15
Boulware, Ritchie	13	
Ball, John	6	3
Brooke, Robert	3	40
Brown, Merriday	9	10
Bragg, Benjamin	3	1
Boulware, Younger	9	
Bunday, James		7
Bunday, Jno		1
Butler, Jno	7	4
Callis, Thomas	9	21
Cox, Abner	10	6
Davis, Anne	4	4
Elliott, Berriman	7	1
Elliott, Calib	3	6
Fogg, Thomas	4	7
Faulconer, Saml	9	3
Faulconer, Nicha, Sr	5	1
Faver, Thomas	9	9
Gouldman, Thos	5	19
Gray, Jno	9	20
Garnett, Mrs Ann	16	17
Greenstead, Jno	3	1
Greenstead, Thos	3	3
Halbert, James	4	2
Jones, James	6	1
Ingram, William	8	
Kay, Richard	3	3
Livingstone, Muscoe	5	19

DISTRICT NO. 5—LIST OF WILLIAM DOANE—continued.

NAME OF HEAD OF FAMILY.	White.	Black.
Loyde, Jno	6	3
Loyde, George	1	1
Loyde, Sarah	3	2
Lindsay, Calib	1	22
Longest, Joshua	1	1
Lumpkin, Isaac	4	
Munday, Stephen	10	1
Munday, Jane	2	9
Munday, James	9	6
Munday, Thomas	7	
Mitchell, Mark	6	
Noell, Calib	9	4
Noell, Lott	12	1
Noell, James, Junr	1	16
Parker, Robert	7	10
Pillilla, Jno	1	1
Rowzee, William	7	27
Sale, Thomas	5	34
Stoakes, Richard	8	
Sale, Jno	6	15
Sale, William	1	5
Stoakes, James	8	5
Smith, Elezas	3	1
Tayloe, Jno (Esta)	1	65
Taylor, Samuel	6	1
Thomas, James	4	2
Taylor, Prince		6
Thomas, William	8	13
Vawlers, Benja	5	
Waring, Thos	1	15
Whitlock, Mary	2	7
Whitlock, John	1	
Weeks, Charles	7	27
Younger, James	7	

DISTRICT NO. 6—LIST OF JNO. UPSHAW.

NAME OF HEAD OF FAMILY.	White.	Black.
Baston, John	8	
Beglere, Patty	8	1
Bransom, John	5	1
Bransom, Larkin	1	1
Clark, Leonard	9	1
Chenault, William	8	3
Colquit, Sarah	1	1
Clark, Frederick	6	
Clark, William	9	
Chenault, John	3	
Dyke, Jackson	6	5
Evans, James	5	1
Fogg, Joseph	4	13
Fortune, Wm (Mulatto)	8	
Fortune, Humphrey (Mulatto)	8	
Faulconer, Nicholas, Junr	5	4
Garnell, Augustine	8	31
Gouldman, Richard	9	9
Gibson, William	5	3
Graves, Rice	4	3
Giffin, Jonathan	4	
Griffin, James	4	
Garrett, William	5	
Hill, Richard	11	5
Hill, Sarah	4	12
Hill, William	2	4
Hill, Thomas	1	1
Hawes, James	6	3
Hawes, Isaac	4	6
Hawes, Samuel	11	10
Hambleton, James	7	
St. James, Wm	4	1
Frey, Andrew (Mulatto)	6	
Longest, Martha	6	3
Martin, Henry	7	
McGee, Joseph	8	
McGee, Joseph, Junr	7	
Marriner, James	3	
Noell, Richard	6	16
Noell, James, Junr	4	19
Noell, Edmund	5	15
Noell, Taylor	8	7
Noell, Rice	5	15
Pitts, David (Y)	9	10
Parker, Robert	3	2
Powel, Thomas	1	
Pilkington, Parmenas	3	1
Rennolds, John	5	7
Rouse, William	1	
Smither, Elizabeth	8	2
Smither, John	2	2
Sale, Mary	5	15
Sale, John, Junr	12	28
Samuel, Peter	7	11
Samuel, Judith	3	
Short, William	2	

DISTRICT NO. 6—LIST OF JNO. UPSHAW—continued.

NAME OF HEAD OF FAMILY.	White.	Black.
Samuel, James	9	13
Spindle, John	7	16
Shaddock, James	8	1
Sullivan, James	12	6
Taylor, John	10	
Thomas, Angelina	5	3
Upshaw, Tamzen	3	7
Upshaw, Thomas	1	3
Vawter, William	6	
Clark, James	1	
Watkins, William	3	11
Wayman, John	4	3
Garnett, Achilles		
Graves, Francis	3	1

LIST OF COLO. BEAL.

NAME OF HEAD OF FAMILY.	White.	Black.
Adam, Thomas	3	10
Beale, John	7	22
Broune, Bennett	7	22
Broocke, Elvzr	4	5
Broocke, Wm	6	7
Brim, Jno	8	1
Broock, Edmund	6	1
Brooche, Phill	8	6
Boughton, Thos	9	10
Boughton, Henry	6	5
Broocke, Reuben	7	6
Boughton, Jno	5	3
Byrd, George		9
Cauthorn, Vinct	6	13
Clark, Robert	5	11
Clark, John	2	4
Clark, Thomas	3	2
Clowdas, Jno	8	3
Cauthorn, Rice	6	
Crutcher, Reuben	1	4
Clowdas, Abner	6	9
Cole, Francis	4	7
Campbell, Sarah	3	23
Dunlop, James	9	39
Dobbins, Wm	8	1
Dunn, John	3	9
Dillard, Wm	2	3
Oliver, Daniel	5	
Evans, Jno	10	15
Evans, Thos	9	13
Edmondson, Kally	3	3
Edmondson, Edmd	3	4
Gatewood, Wm	10	26
Gwathmey, Richd	4	14
Good, Gleener	5	
Hundley, Ann	4	10
Hundley, Eleza	7	2
Hundley, Wm	2	
Howerton, Wm	6	2
Jones, James	2	21
Jones, Eliza	2	26
Johnson, Jno	5	
Montague, Jno	6	67
Montague, Lucy	6	17
Montague, Eliza	8	9
Mullins, Wm	9	5
Merrit, Archenus	4	
Mctyre, Josiah	5	5
Mintus, Joseph	9	
Medley, William	3	
Newbill, Henry	5	5
Newbill, Wm	5	4
Owen, John	11	2
Owen, Augustine	7	1
Phillips, Richard	5	4
Richards, Richard	2	6
Richards, Millicene	7	19
Smith, Meriwether	2	57
Smith, William	9	34
Smith, William D	3	9
Street, Henry	8	11
Street, Richard	9	7
Simco, William	10	1
Sadler, John	4	3
Singleton, Robert	4	1
Stedd, Elizabeth	4	
Southern, William	5	4
Shepherd, William	9	8
Saunders, Charles	7	2
Taff, Peter	6	2
Williams, Isaac	8	
Webb, Jno	4	33
Vass, William	1	5
Yarrington, Jno	7	3
Young, Smith	8	15
Hudson, Vincent	1	
Dejarnette, James	13	9

GLOUCESTER COUNTY.

NAME OF HEAD OF FAMILY.	White.	Black.
WARE PARISH—LIST OF FRANCIS WILLIS.		
News, John	9	15
Booths, Thomas	1	34
Buckners, Robt	2	20
Claytons, Jasper	1	8
Buckners, John	*35	....
Cookes, Thomas	*6	....
Cookes, Un	*30	....
Cookes, Merd	*4	....
Nuttells, James	3	15
Buckners, T	1	11
Gressels, James	5	1
Brickners, Jno	1	7
Baytop, Thomas	2	12
Boswells, Majr	5	23
Boswells, John	7	3
Rileas, Thomas	5	6
Cookes, F. W. (Esta)	4	16
Whitings, Beverley	4	8
Buckners, Jn	....	10
Kemps, Wm	8	11
Cookes, Jno	6	56
Hughes, Jno	1	15
Cookes, Merd	6	22
Davis, Anthony	5	5
Wilkins, Thomas	5	1
Wilson, James	3	10
Curry, Ann	3	4
Kemp, Dorothy	....	4
Tomkies, Francis	11	21
Fletcher, Nathan	5	11
Innis, Robert	1	5
Willis, Frans, jr	11	63
Pryon, Christopher	9	16
Page, Jno, Esq. (in Abingn)	19	162
Boswell, Abraham	*23	....
Boswell, John	*7	....
Foster, Peter	5	2
Ransone, Rd	5	25
PETSWORTH PARISH—LIST OF JAS. HUBARD.		
Ash, John	6	8
Anderson, Matthew	6	15
Bentley, James	5	11
Bentley, William	6	6
Browning, John	6	1
Booker, Lewis	6	18
Bristow, John	4	1
Baytop, James	3	11
Booth, George	9	39
Blassingame, William	4	....
Burton, Henry	5	9
Burwells, Lewis (Esta)	1	34
Blassingame, Jno	9	4
Baine, John	8	....
Blassingame, Jude	3	....
Baker, Elizabeth	7	....
Curtis, Ann	5	16
Collies, James	4	20
Carney, John	2	....
Duvall, William	8	13
Duvall, Samuel	4	2
Duvall, Francis	8	12
Duvall, William	2	12
Dunster, Warner	4	....
Douglass, Thomas	7	4
Freeman, James	10	....
Garland, Elizabeth	2	10
Garland, Christopher	4	7
Gardner, Zachh	4	6
Green, George	6	16
Guthrie, Samuel	4	6
Gressit, John	5	4
Grumley, Swan	3	9
Goalder, Thomas	2	4
Groome, Mary	5	....
Hubard, James	16	57
Howlet, John	3	6
Hughes, Thomas	11	9
Hibble, George	6	5
Hope, Benjamin	5	1
Jones, Richard	5	36
King, Samuel	1	....
Kemp, Peter	4	2
Lewis, John	6	6
Lawson, Anthony	3	2
Lewis, Thomas	5	1
Lawson, William	6	....
Laughlin, James	3	8
Lemmon, William	8	2
Lemmon, Richard	9	....
Laughlin, Laurence	7	....
Lemmon, William	3	....
Lemmon, John	8	2
Lawson, Charles	4	....
Morris, William	4	6
Mason, William	5	1
Menoggin, Saml	5	....
Pollard, Julius C.	5	2
Pollard, William	3	5

NAME OF HEAD OF FAMILY.	White.	Black.
PETSWORTH PARISH—LIST OF JAS. HUBARD—con.		
Pollard, Frances	1	5
Pollard, James	5	1
Proctor, James	5	....
Puller, William	4	....
Pollard, Elizabeth	4	4
Purcell, Peter	5	4
Puller, Elizabeth	5	....
Pointer, Henry, jun	5	9
Page, John	10	27
Robinson, Christopher	1	17
Rootes, John	9	18
Riter, William	6	2
Royston, Richd, W	7	8
Stubbs, Lawrence	8	4
Stubbs, John	9	7
Solds, Dawson	9	....
Solds, William	1	....
Shackelford, ——	4	1
Stubbs, Jno S	5	12
Taylor, Nathanl	6	....
Tomkies, Cap. Chr	....	14
Thrift, Thomas	3	3
Tomson, Bernard B	2	....
Thornton, Meaux	2	16
Wiatt, Sarah	7	43
West, Thomas	13	7
Walker, John	3	1
Whyte, Wm	8	7
Washer, William	3	....
Wyatt, John	7	11
Wyatt, William	5	1
Wood, Lewis	5	17
Yates, Robert	7	15
Thrift, Wm	....	....
Fox, John	....	....
Stanwood, Thomas	....	....
Scott, John	....	....
Spann, Mary	....	....
Jones, Mary	....	....
Roan, Alexander	....	....
Padget, Jno	....	....
Shaw, Eliza	....	....
Sears, Wm	....	....
Cottawn, Wm	....	....
Robinson, Jno	....	....
Dickinson, Wm	....	....
Dickinson, Elizabeth	....	....
Dame, George	....	....
KINGSTON PARISH.		
Armistead, William	15	86
Degge, William	7	8
Davis, Joseph	8	4
Morris, William	9	14
Smith, Armithad	3	18
Green, Christopher	1	....
White, James	3	3
Thomas, Johanna	3	5
Parsons, James	5	6
Green, Richard	8	....
Hudgen, George, Senr	2	5
Hudgen, Perrin	5	....
Hudgen, Geo., junr	6	....
White, William	6	....
White, John	1	....
Edwards, Jno	2	....
White, William	6	6
Elliott, Jno	12	31
Whyte, Edward	5	2
Watson, Jno	5	....
Deal, Jno	6	....
Machen, Samuel	9	....
Hurst, Richard	12	5
Sadler, Robert	7	4
Smith, Thomas	4	58
Tabb, Jno	5	21
Tompkins, Hannah	4	7
Williams, Frances	7	....
Bailey, Mary	6	5
Foster, Jno	7	21
Foster, Isaac	7	1
Foster, Jesse	4	....
Hudgen, Humphrey	6	9
Hudgen, Humphrey, junr	6	3
Allerman, John	5	4
Carithers, James	4	7
Degges, William	3	....
Degges, Mary	5	5
Gayle, Matthew	12	4
Davis, Richard H	2	4
Williams, Samuel	10	25
Magan, James	8	1
Parsons, Jno	8	4
Sadler, Robert	1	....
Whyte, James (Son of Wm)	5	4
Culley, Christopher	8	10
Davis, Isaac	4	5
Kunley, Matthew	3	3
Thomas, James	10	4
Thomas, Jno	3	1

NAME OF HEAD OF FAMILY.	White.	Black.
KINGSTON PARISH—con.		
Davis, James	10	29
Lewis, Thomas	3	2
Singleton, Jno	5	....
Hughes, Edward	10	15
Robins, Edmd	5	....
Soaper, William	4	....
Davis, Jno	3	....
Robins, William	4	1
Hudgen, William	7	....
Peasley, Charles	7	....
Steder, James	6	1
Roberts, Thomas	3	2
Billups, Jno	9	33
Billups, Richard	4	9
Minter, Jno	11	7
Brownley, Edward	6	....
Williams, Thomas	4	....
Keys, Edward	6	....
Brownley, James	7	....
Brownley, Elizabeth	4	2
Minter, William	7	....
Davis, Edward	7	5
Davis, Elizabeth	1	1
Blacknall, Mary	4	23
Davis, Humphrey	2	9
Huble, —†	5	18
Hayes, John	10	24
Davis, Ann	4	4
Davis, Thomas, Senr	4	5
Armestead, George	5	18
Adams, Zachh	6	2
Ransone, Letitia	5	12
Gwyn, John	5	5
Bernard, Jesse	2	12
Ransone, Thomas	5	6
Gwyn, Humphrey	1	4
Gwyn, Henry	5	9
Brookes, Thomas	2	....
Miller, Avarilla	4	2
Callis, Jno (son Robert)	3	....
Gayle, Sarah	4	2
Degges, Jno	5	....
Forrest, Philip	8	1
Harper, James	6	15
Jarvis, Francis	6	2
Dunbar, Leah	4	2
Christian, Martha	4	....
Hudgen, Humphrey	3	....
Callis, Ambrose	7	4
Callis, Robert	5	....
Callis, Richard	7	....
Studer, Thomas	7	....
Forrest, Philip	8	1
Callis, John	2	5
Forrest, George	2	....
Ripley, Richard	5	....
Ripley, Andrew	3	2
Decel, James	5	....
Foster, Josiah	6	17
Gayles, Robert (Estate)	5	5
Sampson, John	6	2
Hunley, James	5	4
Dudley, William	6	....
Hudgen, James, Senr	11	....
Mason, Thomas	4	....
Willis, John	6	....
Hunley, Henry	5	5
Soaper, John	5	1
Mullins, James	1	2
Davis, Tho (son of Jno)	5	3
Owen, Edmd	4	....
Willis, William	5	....
Lewis, Robert	6	1
Stuart, James	8	....
Gayle, Hunley	6	4
Gayle, Joshua & Matt	3	13
Borum, Edmd, Senr	2	17
Borum, Edmd, junr	7	7
Machen, Mary	6	11
Machen, Margaret	1	6
Borum, John	6	2
Southcomb, John	3	12
Dudley, George	3	6
Brounley, Edwd	6	....
Throckmorton, Mord	8	57
Peyton, Sir Jno	3	138
Culley, Judith & Ralph	7	11
Callis, William (deced.)	5	20
Callis, James, Senr	7	2
Davis, Isaac	6	1
Degges, Joseph	3	26
Hudgen, Jno	3	5
Robins, Peter	8	2
Degges, William	2	....
Hudgen, Albin	9	....
Hudgen, Lewis	10	....
Hudgen, John	4	....
White, John	2	....
Jones, Thomas	7	....
Anderson, John	4	4
Carney, William	5	....

NAME OF HEAD OF FAMILY.	White.	Black.
KINGSTON PARISH—con.		
Carney, William, junr	3	....
Jones, Edwd S	4	20
Brown, Robert	6	8
Forrest, George	9	....
Lewis, Christopher	8	2
Ardeston, William	10	....
Thomas, William	10	1
Hunley, William	3	1
Bohannon, William	11	7
Jarvis, John	6	....
Jarvis, William, Senr	4	1
Little, John	4	....
Brownley, Archibald, Junr	7	....
Reynolds, William	7	....
Cook, Igntious	3	....
Hall, Ann	3	2
Tomkins, William	7	2
Hunley, Caleb	5	2
Smith, Peter	12	11
Brownley, Archibald	8	....
Brownley, John	7	1
Foster, Robert	8	9
Foster, Joshua	6	2
Foster, Robert, junr	3	....
Forrest, Abraham	3	....
Morgan, Ransome	2	....
Hobday, Brookes	5	4
Buckner, William	6	11
Jarvis, Francis	8	1
Hayes, Thomas	10	28
Evans, William	8	....
Forrest, George	6	1
Hunley, Matt	2	....
Miller, Francis	6	....
Gregory, Richard	5	12
Brown, Christopher	2	13
Gayle, Thomas	6	3
Knight, Henry	9	13
Brown, George	3	9
Brown, William	9	....
Kerr, Andrew	2	8
Miller, Joseph	10	1
Miller, James	7	4
Miller, Gabriel	5	9
Hudgen, John, Senr	6	....
Basset, Richard	9	1
Basset, William, junr	6	1
Merchant, William	2	12
Merchant, Elisha	6	2
Carter, James	4	8
Respess, Richard	7	6
Powell, John	3	4
Angel, Robert	4	....
Mullins, Dorothy	6	....
Longest, Ann	6	1
Terry, Philip	9	7
Wiscom, Nicholas	3	10
Johnson, John	5	....
Bell, William	3	....
Jones, Philip E	4	7
Fitchet, Thomas	7	2
Fitchet, Daniel	8	11
Dudley, Dorothy	5	5
Hughes, Edwd	3	....
James, Walter	8	5
Gayle, George	9	4
Hudgen, Holder	8	19
Ayres, Richard	4	....
Brookes, Joseph	5	1
Huncey, John	2	1
Cray, John	5	....
Stedder, John	5	....
Jarvis, Francis	5	2
Fityoung, George	2	(†)
Cary, Robert	2	14
Booker, James	2	11
Kippens, Thomas (Estate)	....	5
Curtis, Charles	1	2
Wyatt, Margaret	6	2
Green, Richard	5	4
Lewis, George	1	6
Hudgen, John	4	4
Blake, Thomas	4	8
Hunley, James	7	....
Driver, Emanuel	5	....
Driver, Susanna	4	....
Driver, William	3	....
Jones, James	7	9
Iveson, Abraham	5	13
Iveson, Johnna	7	....
Plummer, Judith & Wm	8	20
Bell, Peter	12	....
Turner, John	4	2
Blake, William	11	....
Lucas, William	1	1
Hudgen, Robert	7	....
Hudgen, Mary	2	1
Hudgen, Hugh	8	2
Parrot, Augustine	1	....
Dudley, George A	9	9
Hodges, Richard	6	....

* Whites and blacks not reported separately.

† Illegible.

GLOUCESTER COUNTY—Continued.

KINGSTON PARISH—con.

NAME OF HEAD OF FAMILY.	White.	Black.	NAME OF HEAD OF FAMILY.	White.	Black.	NAME OF HEAD OF FAMILY.	White.	Black.	NAME OF HEAD OF FAMILY.	White.	Black.
King, Joseph	4	7	Forrest, Henry	2	1	Forrest, Mary	3	....	Shipley, John	4	1
Armestead, Dorothy	3	8	Hunley, John	7	2	Forrest, Edmund	5	1	Scott, Michael	2	1
Davis, Edward	4	2	Hudgens, William (Son Gabr)	7	....	Hudgen, Moses	3	....	Billups, Joseph, jr	3	11
Basset, William, Senr	9	....	Winder, Ann	4	1	Billups, Robert	8	17	Carter, Jane	7	33
Dunbar, Gowen	3	....	Winder, Edmd	2	....	Oliver, Graveley	4	....	Eddins, Jno, junr	2	12
Ashbury, Joseph	4	....	Hunley, Thomas	8	....	Dawson, Lenard	6	1	Gwyn, Robert	5	4
Respess, William	6	10	Powell, Henry	4	1	Dawson, Thomas	7	5	Foster, George	7	1
Pickett, Galen	5	1	Read, Lucy	3	1	Merchant, Ann	3	5	Hunley, Thomas	7	....
Avery, John	6	2	Hudgen, Eliza	5	....	Winder, Thomas	4	3	Boush, William	3	....
Peid, James (Estate)	4	7	Hudgen, Eliza	5	....	Blake, James	6	....	Glasscock, Abraham	6	....
Francis, John	6	3	Turner, Eliza	4	....	Anderson, Edwd	5	5	Singleton, Henry	3	....
Billups, John & mother	4	6	Dunlavy, Ann	7	....	Hurst, John	6	7	Billups, George	6	6
Billups, Thomas	10	13	Harriss, James	7	....	Haywood, Elikin	6	1	Gwyn, Hugh	3	9
Degges, Joshua	6	2	Harris, Matt	6	2	Merchant, Ambrose	7	18	Gwyn, James	1	....
Owens, John	3	....	Harris, Johanna	2	1	Meggs, John	7	....	Gwyn, John	1	....
Owens, George	8	....	Matthews, Robert	8	32	Foster, Robert	6	....	Jarvis, Machen	3	....
Weston, George	4	....	Matthews, Dorothy	1	7	Anderton, Jno	4	(*)	Glasscock, Isaac	6	....
Sadler, Richard	7	....	Eddins, Jno, Senr	2	17	Lane, Ezekiel	4	18	James, Matt	8	18
Peed, Lewis	9	....	Eddins, Davison	7	9	Dawson, James	7	....	Whiting, Thomas	9	1
Weston, Thomas	9	....	Eddins, Saml	6	8	Gayle, Christopher	8	5	Parrot, John	5	1
Summers, Richard	8	....	Forrest, Henry	6	13	Brookes, Richard	7	12	Atherton, John	5	....
Sadler, Thomas	7	....	Forrest, Thomas	4	1	Sadler, William	6	....	Atherton, Ann	4	....
Parrot, Ann	3	....	Lewis, John	7	5	Enos, Francis	9	2	Tinsley, David	5	9
Pallester, John	5	....	Forrest, George, Senr	3	8	Anderton, Ralph	2	....			
Parrot, Robert	5	....	Forrest, John	4	....	Bridge, Mary	2	....			
Tabb, Thomas	5	40				Shipley, Ralph	8	....			

GREENSVILLE COUNTY.

NAME OF HEAD OF FAMILY.	White.	Black.	NAME OF HEAD OF FAMILY.	White.	Black.	NAME OF HEAD OF FAMILY.	White.	Black.	NAME OF HEAD OF FAMILY.	White.	Black.
Allen, William	4	64	Maclin, Thomas	12	23	Smith, David	7	10	Rives, Hannah	5	5
Batte, William	10	38	Maclin, William	4	29	Smith, Joel	5	7	Bynum, Turner	6	19
Barlow, Celia	4	4	Major, Harwood	12	13	Smith, William	3	10	Massey, Richard	6	1
Blanks, Richard	4	11	Mason, James	13	44	Tyus, Lewis	14	30	Wommack, William	5	6
Blanks, Nicholas	4	....	Porch, James	8	3	Thrift, Drury	1	27	Parks, Major	1	....
Blanks, Ingram	3	2	Pelham, Peter	8	11	Vaughan, Pierce	10	11	Turner, James	2	8
Bilberry, Isham	4	....	Prince, John	8	3	Wilkinson, Joel	6	9	Dupree, Lewis, jun	8	10
Barlow, John	5	1	Pettway, Hinchia	1	2	Whittington, John	6	6	Lundy, William	5	6
Barlow, William	5	....	Pettway, William	4	6	Whitmore, William	7	11	Hines, William (So ham.)	....	....
Bailey, Henry	5	3	Newsum, William	1	2	Wilburn, William	4	9	Dupree, Haley, Jun	4	1
Collier, Thomas	4	8	Parham, Hannah	6	18	Watson, William	4	13	Bass, Byrd	1	6
Collier, Mihil	7	10	Redding, Timothy	6	2	Watson, James Alexr	4	14	Wasdon, Augustine	1	....
Dunn, William	9	....	Redding, William	3	4	Peterson, Batte	9	32	Rives, Benjamin	1	1
Eppes, James	3	8	Stark, William, junr	4	20	Metcalf, Andrew	7	....	Bynum, Benjamin	10	19
Grigg, Burrell	12	16	Simmons, Benjamin	8	14	Justice, Ephraim	4	....	Fennell, Isham	6	47
Grigg, Frederick	8	8	Smith, Tabitha	7	10	Vincent, John	17	32	Dupree, John	5	18
Grigg, William	1	....	Stewart, John	1	16	Clark, Peter	11	9	Jordan, Burrell	1	....
Grigg, Lewis	4	3	Stark, William	9	29	Jeter, John, jun	6	6	Pritchard, Henry	1	....
Grigg, Lewis, Junr	2	....	Slate, Robert	7	3	Binford, James	5	1	Jordan, Edmund	1	....
Harrison, Sarah	4	4	Tomlinson, William	1	....	Burt, William	4	9	Young, Ann	7	7
Hobbs, John	6	21	Tedder, William	5	1	Parks, Jeconias	5	2	Dancey, Francis	10	18
Harrison, Lucy	3	1	Turner, John	6	3	Parks, Lucy	4	2	Reams, John	5	....
Hazelwood, William	1	....	Vaughan, William	10	7	Crew, John	1	....	Tarbor, John	....	2
Hubbard, Anne	2	....	Wilkins, Edmund	4	45	Coker, James	10	....	Lundy, John	1	....
Hicks, Benjamin	7	29	Williams, Charles (for B. Waller)	4	16	Smith, Aaron	7	1	Lundy, James	3	....
Harrison, Mary	4	6	Williams, Alexr (for W. Allen)	6	47	Rowell, Edward	9	6	Wyche, Mary	5	15
Lawrence, Thomas	3	....	Jolley, Thomas	1	3	Collier, John	11	6	Sykes, William	8	20
Long, Joseph	2	1	Wilkins, Douglas	8	46	Jordan, Thomas	4	13	Going, James	7	....
Mason, William	7	19	Winn, Mary	1	10	Jordan, Jesse	3	5	Clark, Joshua	10	18
Mabry, Robert	1	7	Wager, Elizabeth	2	18	Bass, Samuel	7	7	Robinson, Littleberry	6	14
Morris, Thomas	3	4	Fisher, Daniel	12	43	Atkins, Aaron	14	....	Clark, Henry	6	6
Mabry, Nathaniel	10	19	Loftin, John	9	11	Hicks, Robert	5	24	Evans, William	10	....
Malone, Sarah	4	8	Jenkins, Thomas	3	23	Haley, Henry	6	13	Sherland, John	10	....
Melton, Peter	5	1	Atkinson, William, Sen	8	14	Morris, William	1	....	Bennitt, William	7	....
Melton, Hardy	2	....	Butts, John	7	13	Parks, Joseph	5	1	Brown, William	9	....
Mabry, Daniel	11	15	Batte, John	6	9	Dupree, John	8	5	Anderson, John	6	3
Nevison, John	3	18	Butts, Peter	1	4	Moody, Kerley	1	....	Fox, William	7	18
Northcross, Frederick	1	....	Brown, Ambrose (Dinwe)	....	3	Moody, James	1	....	Collier, Moses	10	....
Powell, Robert	10	10	Buckley, John	4	2	Thweatt's Thomas (quarter)	....	3	Prince, Nicolas	4	3
Richardson, Jordin	4	26	Cooksey, John Baptist	7	....	Davis, Frederick	8	5	Brewer, Benjamin	2	2
Stewart, Sally	1	2	Caine, George	5	4	Britt, Jesse	6	3	Fox, John	5	14
Sammonds, Newitt	1	....	Charles, Lewis	2	7	Morris, Chislon	1	8	Allen, James	9	2
Sammonds, John	3	....	Collier, Daniel	2	7	Stewart, Thomas	5	3	Jeter, Andrew	6	5
Trotter, William	5	2	Davis, Matthew	3	6	Combo, Cannon	1	....	Brown, John	9	9
Williams, Thomas	1	....	Denton, Susannah	1	1	Hicks, Daniel	1	16	Acres, James	7	....
Williams, Benjamin, junr	1	....	Goodrich, Benjamin	9	8	Jones, John	3	....	Dupree, Jacob	7	1
Wyche, Peter	9	22	Goodrum, Bennitt	4	3	Hines, David	6	13	Johnson, William	6	2
Walker, Robert (Dinwe)	....	16	Goodrum, Thomas	4	4	Jordan, Michael	3	....	Cooke, Henry	7	14
Whittington, Frederick	6	3	Hamilton, John	7	22	Turner, Simon	9	32	Thompson, Drury	5	2
Wrenn, James	6	1	Hamilton, James	1	....	Brown, Burrel	1	8	Sheehorn, Wilson	11	....
Wrenn, Thomas	9	....	Harwell, Frederick	10	10	Morris, Jabez	4	5	Ware, Thomas	5	....
Williams, Benjamin	7	6	Hunt, Judkins	9	13	Dupree, Cordy	2	4	Jeter, Edmund, sen	10	8
Wrenn, Francis	3	5	Hunt, Goodwin	1	....	Dupree, Jeremiah	4	3	Turner, Joseph	1	10
Rogers, William	5	5	Jones, Benjamin	2	15	Dupree, Lewis	5	13	Lightfoot, John	7	1
Bass, Henry	9	18	Lanier, Thomas	13	7	Dupree, Thomas, jun	4	14	Fielding, Thomas	6	1
Howse, Laurence	6	8	Lock, Thomas	9	6	Haley, James	3	14	Tomblinson, Lucas	1	1
Stewart, Elizabeth	1	1	Mitchell, Lockett	6	5	Britt, John	10	2	Tomlinson, Susanna	5	6
Atkins, Absalom	2	6	Mabry, Joel	5	15	Spikes, William	5	5	Harrison, Nathaniel	6	5
Atkins, Jesse	7	....	Mabry, Lewis	4	6	Grinstone, John	2	1	Massey, Richard	8	5
Butts, Jesse	1	4	McClennin, Philip	6	1	Reams, Hezekiah	5	....	Wrenn, William	9	2
Boush, John (Richd)	....	2	Mabry, Evans	5	15	Rives, Benjamin, Senr	7	17	Harris, James	11	....
Boush, Samuel	6	38	Maclin, James	11	24	Sturgis, William	7	2	Morris, John	11	....
Branscomb, Thomas	7	....	Pettway, Edward	7	8	Hines's William (Quarter)	....	4	Lewellin, Thomas	10	2
Barnes, John	7	2	Pettway, —	8	10	Spence, John	8	8	Dupree, Haley	7	7
Camp, John	8	12	Rivers, Robert	8	28	Rosser, David	4	6	McIndree, John	10	9
Jackson, Lewis	7	1	Rivers, Nathaniel	6	21	Rosser, Elisabeth	1	6	Tooke, Dempsey	5	4
Gibbons, Edmund	5	16	Rivers, Thomas	3	10	Rosser, Sarah	1	1	Dawson's, John (Estate)	4	17
Lucas, John, jun	1	....	Spencer, Robert	10	35	Rosser, Elizabeth, junr	1	....	Harris, Absalom	10	....
Lucas, Tabitha	3	14				Thweatt, Rebeccah	3	10	Jordan, Drury	9	5
Lucas, John	4	16							Jordan, Braxton	8	....

* Illegible.

GREENSVILLE COUNTY—Continued.

NAME OF HEAD OF FAMILY.	White.	Black.	NAME OF HEAD OF FAMILY.	White.	Black.	NAME OF HEAD OF FAMILY.	White.	Black.	NAME OF HEAD OF FAMILY.	White.	Black.
Williamson, Henry	7	....	Mitchell, Drury	6	....	Robinson, James	7	....	Hargrove, John	7	16
Robinson, William	4	8	Roddin, Phoebe	6	....	Johnson, John	3	5	Howard, Jesse	2	....
Heathcock, William	5	....	Vinson, Joseph	2	10	Knight, Joel	8	....	Davis, John	7	5
Robinson, John	1	1	Fergusson, William	4	....	Powell, William	5	6	Davis, John, jun	4	2
Catoe, Rowlin	7	4	Dillehay, Charles	10	2	Wyche, Henry	7	13	Bass, Burrell	4	10
Robinson, James	3	6	Fergusson, Francis	1	....	Wyche, William	1	1	Rowell, Isaac	2	4
Vinson, Peter, jun.	6	5	Going, Drury	4	....	Wyche, Peter	2	1	Harrison, Clifton	2	2
Murrell, Mark	8	....	Dungill, William	7	....	Byrum, Osburn	7	....	Pritchett, John	10	12
Brookes, John	9	....	Clark, Peter	7	....	Roper, Ann	7	....	Peebles, William	10	15
Murrell, Benjamin	3	....	Jones, Britton	2	....	Davis, Samuel	4	2	Turner, John	20	70
Anderson, Robin	10	....	Going, Thomas	1	....	Mitchell, Cheney	8	....	Brewer, Nicholas	5	....
Vinson, Peter	3	13	Prince, Joel	3	....	Day, John	1	....	Morris, Thomas	6	1
Nolley, Daniel	7	5	Branscomb, John	3	....	Peebles, Drury	6	2	Catoe, John	7	11
Heathcock, Charles	6	....	Brewer, William	5	1	Nolley, Nehemiah	9	3	Catoe, Daniel	8	10
Heathcock, Jesse	6	....	Mangum, Henry	3	2	Massey, John	5	6	Jeffries, ——	6	19
Jones, Thomas	6	....	Walker, William	4	7	Shelton, Thomas	11	....	Wall, James	15	45
Mitchell, Nathaniel	2	....	Harrison, Charles	1	....	Byrum, James	4	....			

LANCASTER COUNTY.

NAME OF HEAD OF FAMILY.	White.	Black.	NAME OF HEAD OF FAMILY.	White.	Black.	NAME OF HEAD OF FAMILY.	White.	Black.	NAME OF HEAD OF FAMILY.	White.	Black.
Ball, James	8	52	Robinson, Jesse	6	7	Brent, James	6	17	Cornelius, Samuel	4	....
Burwell, Nathaniel	8	48	Webb, Mary	3	1	Hill, Martin (Orphans)	....	1	Shearman, Rawʰ	8	7
Brent, William	4	6	Robinson, Rebecca	3	1	Schofield, William, Jur	7	2	Spilman, Joshua	6	....
Brumley, William	2	14	Newby, William	3	4	Fendla, Hannah	6	....	Edwards, John	6	6
Brumley, Elizabeth	3	3	Mitchell, William	9	12	Haydon, William	3	1	Hathaway, Thomas	9	14
Bailey, John	9	12	Davis, Margaret	1	2	Doggett, Elmour	1	2	Mason, William	9	9
Ball, Agatha	5	19	Riveer, John	5	2	Ellett, Jeduthun	5	....	George, William	4	5
Ball, Col. Jesse (Est.)	....	17	Newby, Ozwald	8	15	Tapscott, Ezekiel	2	4	Hinton, Henry	11	22
Ball, James, Jur	....	18	Robinson, William	2	1	Mahanes, Meridith	7	8	Cottrell, Thomas	5	....
Bush, James	6	....	Ball, Richard	5	22	Haydon, Mary	4	4	Shearman, Ann	6	16
Bailey, Hannah	5	....	Robertson, Andrew	7	22	Hubbard, Joseph	3	5	George, Judith	5	6
Bell, Thomas	9	9	Bivans, Thomas	6	2	Hammond, Sarah	6	7	Berryman, John	7	21
Chinn, John	12	97	Selden, John	2	14	West, Thomas	3	....	Hathaway, Lawson	7	10
Carpenter, William	5	6	Mᶜtyre, John	9	11	Longwith, Burges	3	2	Moore, John	3	2
Chinn, Robert	3	11	Sampson, Joseph	2	1	Longwith, John	5	8	Currell, Isaac	6	10
Chilton, Mary	3	6	Nutt, James	6	....	Hutchinson, John	3	2	Currell, Spencer	7	1
Chilton, Newman	1	9	Pitman, Thomas	7	....	Nicken, John	7	....	Webb, Jesse	1	....
Cammel, George	5	5	Webb, John	3	....	Nicken, John, Jur	1	....	Kern, Henry	1	....
Clutton, John	6	8	Palmer, Benjamin	4	....	Flowers, John	5	9	Pearson, Sarah	9	3
Downman, Rawleigh W	1	66	Norman, William	2	....	Flowers, Lucy	3	4	Degge, Isaac	4	10
Dunaway, Thomas	7	3	Norman, Daniel	4	....	Schofield, Mary	5	....	Lawson, Thomas	4	18
Dunaway, Darby	5	3	Riveers, John	3	....	Chilton, William	2	4	Dameron, Aaron	6	....
Dotson, Charles	8	....	Robinson, George	4	....	Pinckard, Thomas	1	47	Dameron, Moses	6	....
Davenport, Rawleigh	6	4	Calfry, Lewis	3	....	Simmonds, James	5	20	Hunton, Thomas, Jur	2	....
Dunaway, Samuel	5	3	Pitman, William	7	....	Baldwin, John	5	4	Angell, William	5	....
Goodridge, Richard	6	16	Cundiff, Maryann	2	....	Yerby, William	5	9	Arms, William	8	10
Hazard, Henry	6	....	Rich, William	....	5	Bowen, William	3	....	Coats, Rawleigh	6	....
Harvey, Mungo	7	26	Nickens, Nathaniel	....	3	George, Anthony	9	1	Carter, Henry	8	16
Hunt, William	1	2	Nickens, Robert	....	3	Corrie, Reverd David	6	38	Chilton, William, Jur	6	8
Jones, Robert	7	....	Nickens, James	....	9	Lawson, Eppa	4	5	Carter, George	5	21
Jones, Robert, Jur	4	....	Brown, Spencer	7	....	Gaston, Anthony	5	....	Chilton, William	2	17
Lenham, James	4	1	Robinson, Agnis	3	....	Gaston, William	4	....	Demovel, Sampson	11	....
Mason, William	3	1	Taylor, John	11	41	Pollard, James	8	5	Dunaway, William	7	7
Mason, Margaret	7	1	Carter, John H. (Est)	....	128	Thrall, John	4	2	George, Daniel	3	4
Mason, Sarah	2	....	Hill, John	7	....	George, Jesse	4	7	Gundry, John	4	1
Mitchell, Ann	4	21	Carter, Charles, Esq	....	32	Lumford, Traverse	6	6	George, Nicholas	8	10
Mᶜtyre, Robert	9	7	Pitman, Isaac	7	....	Chistien, Nicholas	1	....	Harris, John	2	9
Norris, Joseph	9	16	Brent, Judith	7	17	Doggett, George	1	....	Lunesford, Rodham	10	30
Norris, John	6	7	Cox, Thomas	7	....	Currell, Nicholas	4	25	Lowry, Gawin	4	8
Norris, James	7	8	Brown, Elenor	4	....	Currell, James	2	4	Moore, Samuel	7	4
Newby, James	6	11	Steptoe, Joannah	5	3	George, Martin	6	9	Merryman, John	6	1
Newby, John	5	6	Carter, George	6	7	Ingram, Thomas	7	13	Myars, Matt	3	15
Pullen, William	2	....	Wale, John	....	1	James, John	8	10	Myars, Thomas	2	14
Pullen, Thomas	4	1	Edwards, George	3	4	Parrott, John	5	10	Payne, Betty	1	6
Pullen, Henry	4	....	Kelly, James	4	5	Hunton, Thomas	3	13	Payne, John	7	9
Norwood, Charles	4	1	Divine, Thomas	5	....	Currell, George	3	20	Rogers, Charles	8	25
Riveer, William	1	....	Pollard, Thomas	6	6	Lightburn, Henry	6	3	Wilkinson, John	4	....
Rogers, John	7	9	Weaver, Aaron	3	1	James, Isaac	2	3	Ball, William	6	20
Rains, William	6	1	Gibson, William	7	12	James, Elizabeth	4	13	Brown, Rawleigh	6	....
Robinson, Jesse, Jur	7	5	Brent, Newton	4	9	Lee, Thomas	4	7	Biscoe, William	8	10
Riveers, Johnson	8	8	Haydon, Thomas	4	7	Campbell, Letticia	2	2	Blakemore, Edward	6	6
Riveer, Peter	11	1	Wheeler, Letty	5	....	Wilder, Jonathan	11	3	Bristow, William	8	12
Riveers, Bushrod (Est.)	....	6	Roberts, John	4	9	Carter, Thomas	13	16	Chitwood, George	4	....
Riveer, John, Senr	....		Kirk, Mary	3	4	Carter, George	3	1	Chitwood, William	4	3
Riveer, William, Jur	2	3	Robb, Judith	4	4	Hinton, Elizabeth	7	13	Carter, Edward	8	21
Riveers, ——*	6	2	Pullen, Jonathen	6	12	Wilder, Nathaniel	8	....	Chonning, William	12	17
Stott, Rawleigh	7	4	Hutchings, Leannah	6	7	Wilder, Michael	5	....	Chonning, John	6	10
Stott, Richard	6	3	Smallwood, John	3	5	Lee, Charles	8	24	Carpenter, John	1	7
Stott, Elizabeth	3	6	Doggett, William	9	8	James, William	3	....	Dye, John	8	....
Shearman, Ann	3	12	Kirk, William	1	3	Moughon, George	1	4	Dye, Richard	5	1
Shearman, Joseph	9	14	Yerby, Judith	3	14	James, Sally	6	3	Ewell, James	2	25
Stott, Thomas	6	10	Yerby's, George	....	15	Reaves, John	....	2	Ellett, Thomas	8	2
Sydnor, William	9	45	Stott, Eppa	4	....	Moore, Susannah	4	....	Flemming, James	4	....
Tapscott, Mary	11	32	Norris, William	6	4	Maughon, Matthias	4	....	George, Nicholas	8	10
Wilkinson, Joseph	5	2	Williams, Peter	8	....	Currell, Harry	4	30	George, William	3	7
Warren, William	10	16	Brent, Judith	5	....	Bridgford, Thomas	3	2	Leland, Reverd John	6	13
White, Thomas	4	....	Merideth, William	6	2	Crowther, Joshua	7	....	Luckam, William	4	1
Warwick, James	6	....	Doggett, William, Jur	6	6	Wilder, Jesse	3	2	Stephens, Joseph	3	11
Wilson, Mary	4	....	West, William	7	1	Lawson, William	5	11	Towles, Henry	8	15
Selden, Richard	5	42	Roberts, John, Jur	4	1	Lawson, Henry	9	20	Thomas, Tarpley	6	2
Cundiff, Richard	8	10	George, Bailie (Est)	10	15	Lawson, Mary	5	11	Wiblin, William	6	....
Moore, Jeduthun	5	2	Pullen, John	1	....	Hill, Thomas	8	....	Chilton, Jesse	7	15
Flint, Thomas	10	14	Hammond, Thomas	6	3	Boatman, William	6	9	George, Thomas	7	....
Jacob, Robert C.	4	12	Sherwood, Peter	4	....	Riveer, Wiatt	1	2	Kent, William	9	10
Montague, William	11	23	George, Benjamin	10	7	Gordon, Nathaniel	....	17	Kelly, Jesse	6	....
Webb, Tarpley	3	1	Kelly, William	6	....	Harris, James	5	3	Conway, Edwin	6	29
Goodridge, John	7	6	Merideth, John	5	17	Webb, Thomas	1	....	Cundiff, John	7	2
Crookhorn, John	3	17	Standard, George	9	4	Williams, Aaron	7	2	Palmer, Lott	5	1
Robinson, Epaphro	6	3	Garland, David	6	....	Fleet, John	5	34	Brent, Thomas	4	6
Mitchell, Richard	9	7	Tapscott, Mary	1	9	Martin, William	7	23	Brent, Margaret	6	7
Mᶜtyre, Elizabeth	1	10	Maxwell, Frances	2	3	Cornelious, William	7	....	Griggs, Ruth	5	10

*Illegible.

LANCASTER COUNTY—Continued.

NAME OF HEAD OF FAMILY.	White.	Black.	NAME OF HEAD OF FAMILY.	White.	Black.	NAME OF HEAD OF FAMILY.	White.	Black.	NAME OF HEAD OF FAMILY.	White.	Black.
Hubbard, Thomas	7	11	Brent, Vincent	1	6	Pinckard, James	1	15	Schofield, William	3	5
Chilton, William	2	..	Yopp, William	8	3	Norris, George	7	21	Heath, John, Jur	2	3
Hill, James	3	2	Alford, Zachariah	5	..	Yopp, Samuel	4	11	Edmonds, Elias	9	23
Hill, John	4	2	Doggett, John	3	4	Brent, William	9	10	Bell, Elizabeth	1	18
Garner, Thomas	11	..	Carter, Job	5	10	George, Spencer	8	8	Connolly, Patrick	5	3
Brent, Jedithen	4	6	Lock, Stephen	6	4	Degge, John	6	9	Carter, Harry	6	2
Saunders, Betty	7	4	Haw, Peter	..	9	Wallace, James	9	2	Mott, Betty	3	6
Brown, William	6	12	Kent, Edwin	6	1	Dameron, Rachel	4	..	Lizenby, Ellen	2	1
Yerby, John	6	30	Kirk, James (Est)	..	12	Galloway, William	5	1	Selden, Mary	3	39
Stevens, Ann	6	8	Norris, Martin	3	3	Gordon, James	7	31			
Sullivant, Judith	7	2	Miller, John	8	14	Tapscott, James	7	26			

MIDDLESEX COUNTY.

UPPER PRECINCT.	White.	Black.	UPPER PRECINCT—con.	White.	Black.	MIDDLE PRECINCT—con.	White.	Black.	LOWER PRECINCT—con.	White.	Black.
Brooks, Thomas	5	1	Daniel, Robert	9	15	Daniel, Hannah	4	2	West, Geor	7	2
Bennet, Thomas	5	4	Lee, Sarah	8	1	Pas Quett, George	1	..	Jefferson, Daniel	9	..
Beaman, John	3	2	Mickelburrough, Mary	6	6	Barzey, Wilkerson	4	2	Hopkins, Richard	7	1
Bird, Mary	4	17	Rilee, John	3	4	Denison, Jonan	4	9	Owen, John	7	6
Blakey, Churchhill	8	3				Walker, Hugh	10	26	Dudley, Charles	6	10
Crossfield, James	8	..	**MIDDLE PRECINCT.**			Neilson, Charlotte	6	44	Sole, John	4	2
Campbell, James	..	4	Steptoe, Willm	4	118	Groom, John	8	1	Powell, David	5	..
Corbin, Richard, Esqr	4	127	Spratt, Robt	6	16	Meacham, Lawrence	5	11	Grymes, Charles	2	7
Corbin, Garvin (Estate)	12	111	Churchhill, Benja	1	9	Canady, Ambrose	3	2	Deagle, William	3	..
Cloudas, Frances	5	2	Bristow, Benja	8	5	South, John	7	..	Martin, Ann	3	..
Clark, John, Senr	6	4	Robinson, Wm	6	3	Meggs, Chatharine	..	5	Deagle, John	6	..
Clark, John, Junr	3	..	Smith, Maue	5	16	Wortham, James	6	12	Barrick, John	7	..
Crittinden, Thomas	4	1	Mills, Elizabeth	6	47	Hibble, John	10	7	Barrick, Benjn	7	..
Collins, Elizabeth	6	1	Cosby, Overton	1	3	Daniel, Milley	5	29	Meckelburgh, Robt	6	29
Corbin, John T.	6	74	Jones, James	1	..	Newcomb, Bowling	3	3	Blackburn, Mary	3	18
Dejarnatt, Daniel	7	17	Chonning, Sarah	7	2	Moore, Willm	3	3	Boss, Ann	4	1
Dillard, George	5	2	Murray, Rachel	4	26	Baker, Elizabeth	3	4	Miller, Andrew	7	9
Dunn, Agrippa	8	3	George, John, Senr	5	11	Haley, James	1	..	Dudley, Mary	4	4
Greenwood, Samuel	5	2	Blake, Susannah	6	12	Lorimer, George	6	79	Wake, Joanna	6	5
Healy, John	7	7	Kidd, James	11	18	Reed, Elizabeth	2	6	Minton, Bowler	2	..
Hardee, John	5	1	Tuggle, Griffin	4	2	Klug, Revd Samuel	4	27	Powell, Jeremiah	3	1
Jefferies, William	7	5	Brooks, John	6	..	Gale, Margret	..	13	Kemp, Mary	7	29
Jackson, John, Senr	7	14	Willis, John	4	2	Chonning, Henry	7	3	Blake, John, Jur	7	17
Jackson, John, Junr	2	6	Kidd, Wm	7	..	Murray, Robert	12	12	Bayton, William	5	2
Jessee, Jane	5	..	Thuston, Wm	5	10	Miller, Christopher	4	..	Hearon, Willm	5	..
Lee, James	7	4	Swords, Benja	7	2	Wormeley, Ralph	9	220	Blake, Thos, Junr	8	1
Lee, Philip	5	6	Kidd, Benja, Junr	5	4				Stevens, Lewis	10	..
Lee, Charles, Senr	5	24	Hardy, Joseph	7	2	**LOWER PRECINCT.**			Harron, Thomas	6	1
Mountague, Lewis	6	3	Kidd, Benja, Senr	8	2	Churchhill, William	14	91	Blake, George, Senr	6	2
Maderas, John	6	..	Bristow, Alexander	4	1	Spotswood, Elizabeth	1	5	Boss, John	5	10
Mountague, Colo Philip	10	9	Bachelder, Heny	4	8	Barrick, John	2	..	Dunlavy, James	6	4
Mountague, William	1	4	Williams, Benja	6	..	Saunders, Jacob Stiff	3	..	Jackson, Geor	4	..
Mullins, John	6	1	Milby, Richd	7	..	Beard, John	6	..	Longuest, Robert	1	..
Miller, Elizabeth	6	4	Bristow, Saunders	3	1	Miller, Ann, Senr	4	1	Daniel, George	4	36
McTyre, Henry	4	2	Roane, John	6	2	Tisser, Mary	1	..	Elliott, Matthew	4	2
Maderas, Benjamin	6	2	Stamper, Rob	11	6	Berkeley, Edmond	..	21	Deagle, Willm, Junr	3	..
Mchan, Matthew	6	1	Guest, Wm	7	7	Ross, Francis	4	..	Herrin, Benja	1	2
Mchan, James	8	7	Daniel, John, Junr	2	8	Hackney, William	5	6	Elliott, Willm	4	9
Owen, William	4	8	Paterson, Thomas	3	5	Saunders, Thomas	7	15	Hudgen, Rob	3	..
Owen, Jacob	1	5	Daniel, John, Senr	6	1	Batchelder, Jos	7	1	Layton, John	10	3
Pryor, William	4	3	Roane, Wm	1	5	Dean, Frances	5	6	Layton, Renben, Senr	3	..
Segar, William (Dec'd.)	2	15	George, Meacham	6	1	Davis, Richard	7	13	Gregory, James (Estate)	..	38
Segar, Capt Thomas	8	13	Tuggle, Nicholas	6	6	Hunt, John	3	2	Ross, James	1	..
Seward, John	8	1	Mickelburough, Henry	2	8	Healy, Thomas	13	10	Blade, Currell	5	2
Sanders, George	7	2	Oliver, Francis	9	1	Davis, Andrew	8	9	Sibley, Benson	7	..
Sanders, Thos Wms	3	2	Fox, Tabatha	2	..	Matthews, William	6	..	Laughlin, Simon	*21	
Sanders, George	7	10	Roane, Thomas	3	9	Hodges, John	5	4	Daniel, George	5	..
Sears, John	6	1	George, John, jur	3	8	Anderson, Alexander	5	3	Robenson, Charles	7	17
Stevens, Mary	6	1	Thurston, Wm	9	..	Minto, John	5	..	Edwards, Thos	2	1
Thurston, John	2	2	Kidd, Chong	6	..	Jones, William	5	13	Stiff, James	5	11
Taff, Thomas	6	..	Thurston, Saml	4	..	Sutton, Ann	5	15	Boss, James	4	..
Thurston, Henry	9	..	Sewards, John	8	4	Deagle, Absolum	3	..	Hanks, George	5	..
Vass, Henry, Senr	5	12	Bachelor, Elizabeth	2	5	Dean, William	2	9	Blake, John	8	1
Vass, Henry, Junr	5	3	Mickelberry, John	1	1	Vaughn, Dudley	4	7	Edwards, Charles	2	7
Wood, Samuel	6	3	George, Wm	3	..	Hill, William	4	1	Jackson, John	10	5
Watts, Ralph	9	..	Michal, Sarah	2	4	Hackney, Elizabeth	4	13	Flemming, Charles	1	7
Woodley, Francis	6	3	Meggs, James	..	4	Atkerson, John	7	..	Mundy, Willm	3	26
Ware, Jane	4	2	Grymes, Philip L.	4	143	Humphris, John	6	7	Miller, Christopher	4	..
Yates, Harry B.	2	22	Wood, Willm	8	3	Jones, William	6	..	Curtis, Joanna	5	35
Lee, Reuben	3	1									

NANSEMOND COUNTY.

CAPT. WILLIAM ELEY'S COMPANY—LIST OF WILLIAM COWPER	White.	Black.	CAPT. WILLIAM ELEY'S COMPANY—LIST OF WILLIAM COWPER—continued.	White.	Black.	CAPT. WILLIAM ELEY'S COMPANY—LIST OF WILLIAM COWPER—continued.	White.	Black.	CAPT. WILLIAM ELEY'S COMPANY—LIST OF WILLIAM COWPER—continued.	White.	Black.
McCleuny, James	4	3	Peirce, Mildred	6	..	Hines, Hardy	3	6	Butler, Nathan	5	..
McCleuny, John	6	5	Wright, William	8	1	Hines, Willis	1	..	Boon, Daniel (negro)	..	1
Mintz, Edward	7	1	Tayler, Jethro	5	1	Roades, James	6	..	Beaman, Trease	4	1
Redman, Martin	2	..	Wright, John	6	..	McCleuney, Mial	6	..	Copeland, John	6	..
Tayler, Pruden	3	..	King, William	7	17	McCleuney, Wm	10	8	Hedgpeth, Holladay	2	..
Butler, Peter	5	..	Callis, George	6	13	Taylor, James	3	..	Parker, James	6	1
Gay, James	5	..	Peirce, James	6	..	Gay, William	6	1	Cowper, William	6	32
Barns, Johnson	3	1	Beasley, Benjamin	5	..	Pruden, William	9	..			
Butler, John	6	..	Johnson, Josiah	5	..	Ballard, Ann	2	13	**CAPT. KING'S COMP'Y.**		
Peirce, Stephen	2	1	Johnson, Stephen	5	1	Webb, Honour	2	5	King, Capt. Michl	2	5
Parker, Joseph	4	..	McCleuney, Thos	4	..	Powell, Francis	2	8	Jossey, Wm	4	1
Simons, John	4	2	Daughtery, John	3	4	Pinner, Thos	6	1	Campbell, John	6	7
Willis, Robert	7	2	Henderson, Jacob	8	..	Pruden, Jethro	7	..	Pugh, Theops	4	..
Tayler, Edward	5	..	Parker, John	5	..	Wright, James	6	..			

* Whites and blacks not reported separately.

NANSEMOND COUNTY—Continued.

NAME OF HEAD OF FAMILY.	White.	Black.	NAME OF HEAD OF FAMILY.	White.	Black.	NAME OF HEAD OF FAMILY.	White.	Black.	NAME OF HEAD OF FAMILY.	White.	Black.
CAPT. KING'S COMP'Y— continued.			**LIEUT. BUXTON'S COMP'Y—** continued.			**CAPT. ROBT. M. RIDDICK'S DISTRICT—LIST OF JOHN RIDDICK—continued.**			**SUMNER'S & DARDEN'S COMPANIES OF MILITIA—LIST OF ELISHA DARDEN—con.**		
Pugh, Mary	1	5	Creack, Wm	6	....	Spivy, Joshua	9	4	Cutchins, Bartholw	4	....
Moore, John, Jur	4	9	Brown, Christr	1	1	Jones, James	4	....	Cutchins, Adam	5	1
Alphin, James	6	4	Ridgaway, Thos	7	....	Treavathan, William	5	....	Whitfield, Ivy	4	1
Pugh, John	1	5	Ash, James	5	....	Raby, Jacob	6	8	Daughtery, Lewis	11	....
Howard, Stephen	5	3	Boswell, Wm	2	....	Raby, Kadah	4	8	Daughtery, Robert	7	....
Smith, Wm	1	....	Conaway, James	2	6	Ellis, Josiah	7	1	Lawrence, Robert	7	8
Tallonton, James	2	....	Churchwell, Mary	4	....	Wilkins, Wm (of Thos)	5	....	Heirs, John	5	....
Wright, Miles	5	5	Streater, Wm	2	2	Ellis, James	5	....	Gardner, Joseph	6	....
Streater, Edwd	1	....	Powell, Sarah	4	1	Brinkly, James	6	1	Glover, John	6	2
Mansfield, Mills	1	2	Deans, Matthew	5	2	Wilkins, James	5	....	Bowers, John	8	7
Brumeger, John	8	3	Dilburg, Peter	8	....	Brinkly, Kadah	8	3	Pebworth, Robert	6	....
Brumeger, James	3	1	Heffeton, James	5	....	Lassiter, Robert	9	1	Parker, Hardy	8	7
Mansfield, Wm	3	1	Jackson, Christopher	6	2	Booth, Jethro	2	....	Parker, Kader	11	6
Roberts, Wm	1	19	Lee, Sherwood	3	....	Booth, Mosses	6	1	Holland, Thomas	6	....
Evans, John	5	7	Pitt, Thos	6	14	Wilkins, Shadrack	5	3	Warren, Etheldred	5	9
Wright, Stephen	2	13	Higembotham, Wm	6	6	Lassiter, Enos	5	....	Harrod, William	7	....
Murdaugh, James	7	27	Shepherd, Lidey	6	12	Harrell, John (of Thos)	8	....	Britt, Joseph	5	....
Slatter, Sol	9	4	Streater, Willis	5	16	Harrell, Isball	3	3	Cary, Anna	2	5
Allmand, Thos	5	5				Harrell, John (of John)	8	....	Cary, Edward	3	6
Stone, Demsey	4	2	**LIST OF JEREMIAH GODWIN.**			Lassiter, Jesse	4	6	Crosland, Edward	5	3
Reddick, Mosses	5	4				Wilkins, Wm (of Shadr)	3	1	Hart, William	8	15
Beaman, Jethro	5	3	Godwin, Jeremiah	8	27	Sceater, Farraby	7	....	Rochell, John	3	7
Baker, Daniel	2	....	Green, Peter	1	6	Lassiter, Daniel	9	3	Gardner, Matthew	5	7
Cowper, James	4	5	Barkley, Samuel	9	....	Spivy, George	4	6	Barker, Benjamin	4	....
Bass, Wm	3	....	Nelms, Archer	12	1	Barr, John	7	7	Bigelow, William	3	3
Young, Isaac	5	1	Norflet, Nathl	5	6	Ellis, Joseph (of Mary)	4	....	Johnson, Nathan	7	4
Young, Jacob	3	....	Bryant, John	7	5	Brinkly, John (of Eli)	6	6	Vaughn, Charles	7	4
Young, Aaron	1	....	Norfleet, Sarah	6	8	Price, John	3	....	Vaughn, Elizabeth	1	2
Jordan, Edward	4	3	Marshall, Mills	6	4	Spivy, James	4	4	Vaughn, Mary	1	2
Smith, Eliza	4	1	Eskridge, Joseph	2	2	Harrell, James	7	....	Vaughn, Grace	1	3
Jordan, John	2	4	Green, Thos	3	15	Harrell, Thos (of Sarah)	8	1	Johnson, Jesse	8	8
Robinson, Sarah	5	15	Pinner, Francis	9	....	Davice, William	4	....	Darden, Robert	6	8
Barns, John	1	....	Nelms, William	9	....	Sivils, William	6	....	Brown, Anthony	1	1
Channel, Eliza	5	7	Smith, Arther	4	18	Harrell, Amos	3	....	Fisher, Mary	2	2
Trotter, Eliza	4	12	Campbell, Eliza	4	2	Brinkly, Aaron	5	1	Webb, Daniel	1	3
Swilivant, Judah	5	3	Stakes, William	8	....	Brinkly, Henry, Senr	5	....	Hacket, Redmond	1	3
Wakefield, Thomas	4	3	King, Mary	7	20	Franklin, Josiah	6	....	Carr, John	9	9
Heffeton, Wm	4	6	Hill, Benjamin	5	16	Franklin, Daniel	7	1	Williams, George	4	13
Jordain, Robt	5	9	Pinner, William	5	....	Booth, Abraham	6	....	Everitt, Etheldred	4	9
Deans, Thos	8	1	Godwin, Richd W	8	16	Raby, William	7	....	Hedghpeth, James	4	1
Curtis, Jonathan	3	....	Archer, Mary	5	10	Boyce, James	4	8	Crosland, John	10	....
Spencer, Abraham	6	9	Sanders, Thomas	3	....	Brinkly, Micajah	7	1	Carr, James	3	2
Hargroves, Willis	5	8	Holland, Alexander	4	....	Jones, Demsey	4	....	Gardner, Henry	4	4
Turner, Pasco	7	36	Wimmer, John	3	1	Lassiter, Mosses	6	....	Williams, John	2	6
Shepherd, Sol	1	15	Villine, Hezekiah	6	17	Melteare, John	7	....	Williams, Richard	5	2
Fasting, John	5	....	Lawrence, George	2	....	Jones, Matthew	5	....	Daughtery, Jacob	8	11
Moore, John	9	6	Stakes, Leven	6	....	Brantom, Jacob	5	....	Pender, John	3	8
Keal, Capt. R	5	17	Monk, William	6	....	Brantom, Jesse	3	....	Hines, Howell	5	5
			Baker, Joseph	7	2	Brantom, Timothy	1	....	Cobb, John	13	....
LIEUT. BUXTON'S COMP'Y.			Bateman, John	7	2	Jones, David	1	....	Vaughn, James	10	3
			Archer, Stephen	8	....	Raby, Lemuel	3	....	Hare, Henry	9	5
Buxton, James	7	10	Best, John	4	4	Brinkly, John (of Mic.)	1	4	Glover, William	7	10
Jinkins, Charles	5	6	Cahoon, Samuel	7	15	Jones, Abraham	1	....	Carr, Molly	4	13
Lattimore, Wm	5	10	Ashburn, John	6	3	Brinkly, Henry, Jur	7	....	Darden, Carr	3	1
Arthur, James	2	5	Nelms, Stephen	4	4	Griffin, Henry	10	1	Sanders, Sarah	3	4
Howard, Thos	7	....	Sumner, William	1	5	Brothers, John	7	8	Turner, Lidia	2	....
Aswell, Daniel	5	2	Whitlock, William	3	21	Brothers, William	7	3	Birdsong, Bennet	1	....
Graham, John	5	....	Nelms, Ezehel	6	1	Brinkly, David	4	3	Hamilton, John	3	1
Brewer, Josiah	4	1	Sanders, Daniel	7	1	Knight, John	9	2	Howell, Archibald	5	....
Catton, Jonathan	7	2	Richards, John	2	3	Griffin, Eli	7	1	Lawrence, John	4	23
Marshall, Jesse	7	1	Nelms, Thomas	5	7	Riddick, John	7	14	Lawrence, Eliza	4	4
Woodward, John	7	1	Norfleet, Elisha	1	5				Wren, John	3	....
Vainwright, John	5	....	Hedghpeth, Dompecy	8	....	**SUMNER'S & DARDEN'S COMPANIES OF MILITIA—LIST OF ELISHA DARDEN.**					
Aswell, James	4	3	Nelms, George	3	2				**CAPT. WILLIAM RIDDICK'S COMPANY OF MILITIA—LIST OF WILLIS RIDDICK.**		
Deans, John	3	....	Oliver, Joseph	5	....						
Frost, Noah	7	....	Roberts, Christopher	5	39	Darden, Elisha	....	....			
Powell, Cadar	8	5	Mason, Peter	5	10	Sumner, Demsey	7	33			
Ward, James	5	2	Godwin, Samuel	1	1	Gardner, William	5	....	Riddick, Josiah	8	14
Wright, Wm	6	8	Bateman, Jethro	5	1	Boyt, Timothy	6	....	Cowling, Willis	6	9
Hoffler, Thomas	7	....	Granbery, John	4	2	Riddick, Abram	7	24	Cockell, John	4	1
Thomas, Charles	7	14	Nelms, Samuel	10	13	Boyt, Thomas	4	....	Carwick, John	5	....
Hail, John	6	3	Burkit, Paggy	....	5	Howell, David	7	8	Miles, John	4	2
Creach, Charles	3	1	George, Frederick	6	7	Howell, Stephen	6	....	Lassiter, Mary	6	....
Deans, Willis	7	14	Godwin, Elisha	2	16	Howell, Michl	2	7	Nichols, Elisha	1	....
Hail, Edwd	4	1	Nelms, Mary	5	....	Howell, Hopkin	5	....	Lassiter, Sarah	8	15
Cowper, Thos	5	1	Gwin, Thomas	9	1	Howell, Eli	10	....	Baker, Christian	3	1
Miars, Charity	6	....	Palmer, Samuel	6	4	Howell, Rebecca	5	2	Tayler, Joseph	6	....
Powell, John	7	2	Henderson, John	4	1	Howell, William	1	5	Williams, Jesse	4	1
Wilder, James	2	3				Howell, Lydia	6	6	Hufton, John	8	1
Jordain, Wm	4	8	**CAPT. ROBT. M. RIDDICK'S DISTRICT—LIST OF JOHN RIDDICK.**			Jones, Thomas	4	1	Riddick, Henry	4	26
Robinson, George	7	5				Ballard, Willis	2	3	Stallings, William	4	1
Fulgham, Jesse	5	....				Jones, Ivey	8	1	Stalings, James	8	5
Hays, Wm	11	....	Riddick, Capt. Robt. M	8	18	Howell, Edward	7	21	Stalings, Uriah	6	....
Mornow, Matthias	7	2	Brinkley, John (of Peter)	7	6	Sanders, James	2	2	Stalings, Abram	6	9
Hoffler, Samuel	6	....	Franklin, Elaner	1	....	Johnson, Hezekiah	6	1	Reade, Isack	6	....
Miars, Thos	3	....	Jones, William	7	....	Rodgers, David	5	....	Reade, Ruben	3	....
Cowper, Mary	4	8	Brinkley, Wm (Fifer)	1	4	Boyt, William	3	1	Baker, Demsey	6	7
Thompson, Joseph	8	....	Ellis, William	4	....	Journigan, William	5	4	Harrison, Henry	5	24
Cordain, Thomas	3	....	Ellis, Joseph (of Thos)	13	....	Rawls, Hardy	10	....	Lassiter, Elisha	3	....
Edwards, James	3	1	Riddick, Solomon	9	16	Cross, Jonathan	4	5	Reade, Jonathan	3	....
Northam, Zorobabel	9	1	Griffin, Humphery, Senr	3	4	Jones, Hardy	11	3	Collue, Jacob	9	22
Benn, Thos	2	8	Lassiter, Abraham	6	7	Ealey, John	4	5	Brewer, James	5	....
Radwell, Thos	3	....	Ellis, Joseph (of Sarah)	8	....	Darden, Elizabeth	3	13	Cowper, Mary	1	7
Tayler, Joseph	6	....	Knight, James, Senr	5	4	Darden, Elisha	9	7	Lassiter, Kedah	5	....
Wells, Henry	6	4	Wilkins, Thomas	8	....	Spain, Absalem	7	1	Riddick, Daniel	5	20
Hays, David	4	6	Ellis, Micajah	8	....	Gardner, Joshua	10	11	Brewer, John	9	16
White, Anthony	4	10	Sumner, Jacob, Senr	5	4	Obery, Thomas	1	22	Hollowell, Eliza	6	....
Corbin, John	6	....	Sumner, Jacob, Jur	1	4	McCabe, John	6	6	Ross, John	7	....
Corbin, Joseph	3	....	Norfleet, Hezekiah	9	4	Darden, Holland	12	8	Thomas, John	8	....
Minton, James	4	....	Parker, John	4	2	Hill, Charles	3	4	Sparling, George	1	6
Tompson, John	4	....	Lassiter, Jethro	5	....	Scogin, James	3	....			
Newton, Benja	7	....									

NANSEMOND COUNTY—Continued.

NAME OF HEAD OF FAMILY.	White.	Black.	NAME OF HEAD OF FAMILY.	White.	Black.	NAME OF HEAD OF FAMILY.	White.	Black.	NAME OF HEAD OF FAMILY.	White.	Black.
CAPT. WILLIAM RIDDICK'S COMPANY OF MILITIA—LIST OF WILLIS RIDDICK—continued.			**CAPT. WILLIS PARKER'S DISTRICT OF MILITIA—continued.**			**DISTRICT OF MILITIA FORMERLY COMMANDED BY CAPT. HOLLAND—LIST OF WILLIS COWLING—con.**			**LIST OF JOS. HOLLADAY—continued.**		
Williams, John	7	1	Peele, Jeremiah	3	....	Baker, Richd	2	13	Cowper, John	5	12
Briggs, James	6	....	Ross, Babel	4	....	Darden, Eliza	5	13	Holladay, Joseph	9	23
Turlington, Peggy	6	....	Goff, Hugh	6	1	Darden, Stephen	4	8	Shivers, Thos	6	2
Terry, Richard	4	....	Harrell, James	9	....	Hedghpeth, Henry	5	....	Vessey, John	8	6
Sears, Liah	2	1	Russel, Mary	7	....	Holland, John	4	1	Ross, John	6	3
Burkett, Charles	5	....	Goodman, James	4	3	Holland, Joseph	6	....	Holladay, Brewer	4	27
Medcalf, William	4	2	Gomer, Rebecca	7	....	Johnson, Mason	9	....	Jones, Mary	6	7
Bates, James	8	6	Davidson, William	5	3	Holland, Charity	4	3	Wilkinson, William	6	27
Newiney, John	7	1	Collins, William	3	....	Hedghpeth, Cutbert	1	....	Cowling, Benja	6	11
Soiril, John	5	3	Tarlinton, John	4	....	Holland, Benjamin	5	....	Driver, Daniel	5	....
Besong, Lewis	3	....	Nearney, Nicholas	5	....	Hedghpeth, Comfort	5	....	Godwin, Anthony	10	19
John, John Fore	1	....	Hughes, William	4	....	Holland, Titus	4	6	Richardson, Archibald	3	5
Driver, John	5	12	Byrd, Daniel	6	....	Holland, Esther	3	10	Tankard, Charity	6	4
Lawson, John	4	2	Byrd, Martha	2	....	Everitt, John	8	13	Lawrence, Mary	6	2
Jones, Nicholas	3	2	Smith, Isaac	8	....	Holland, Absalem	8	....			
Jones, Eliza	3	9	Rawls, James	8	6	Denson, Martha	3	....	**CAPT. BEMBRIDGE GODWIN'S MILITARY COMPANY—LIST OF JAS. GODWIN.**		
Loney, William	4	2	Faulks, William	2	9	Holland, William	6	....			
Holland, Joseph	5	14	March, Daniel	6	13	Harrell, Lewis	7	1	Godwin, James, Senr	6	13
Granbery, Mary	3	5	Hare, Elizabeth	8	13	Rawls, Eliza	6	3	Godwin, Kinchen	7	24
Pugh, James	5	8	Rawls, Ann	4	3	Tarlington, Benja	4	....	Godwin, Joseph, Junr	4	22
Riddick, Mosses	5	12	Rawls, Uriah	7	2	Rawls, John	11	5	Godwin, Eliza	6	14
Ried, Mary	6	13	Rawls, Hardy (of Solo)	5	....	Keen, Saml	6	....	Minton, Mills	....	11
Riddick, Ezekias	7	4	Goff, Lemuel	1	....	Hines, Mourning	6	....	Fare, John	4	13
Lester, John	8	....	Crofford, Solomon	7	....	Collins, Saml	5	....	Godwin, Col. Thos	7	22
Campbell, David	3	1	Odam, William	4	1	Copeland, Zacs	7	17	Bridger, James	7	....
Parker, Christian	6	....	Cross, Jonathan	4	5	Winborn, James	5	14	Denson, John	4	14
Woodward, Richard	6	9	Dilday, William	5	....	Harrison, William	5	4	Marshall, Thos	2	3
Groves, John	4	1	Barfield, John	2	....	Valentine, James	3	5	Howell, John	7	4
Lassiter, Aaron	5	6	Austen, Richard	8	....	Butler, Saml	3	....	Campbell, Thos, Junr	3	5
Wilson, John	6	1	Rutter, Thomas	2	....	Elsbery, Joseph	8	....	Wilkinson, Thos, Senr	8	2
Skinner, Henry	2	8	Parker, David	5	2				Corbell, John	4	1
Lawrence, Jacob	5	....	Rogers, Drury	4	1	**LIST OF JOS. HOLLADAY.**			Holladay, Ann	5	15
Livingston, Thomas	2	2	Langston, Isaac	8	6				Eley, Willis	4	11
Pugh, William	6	9	Keene, Joseph	4	....	Roberts, Thos	3	9	Fulgham, John	5	15
Brewer, Jesse	6	3	King, John	7	1	Allmand, Harrison	6	10	Smith, Edward	7	5
Willis, Thomas	7	....	Tarlinton, Levin	10	....	Everitt, Willis	7	19	Godwin, Charlot	9	11
Riddick, William	1	7	Wiggins, Jesse	8	....	Farrow, Jacob	6	1	Mitchell, James	3	5
			Smith, Samuel	2	....	Milner, Thos	3	6	Coffield, Wm, Senr	6	....
CAPT. WILLIS PARKER'S DISTRICT OF MILITIA.			Ellimore, Thomas	1	....	Milner, Joseph	7	5	Corbell, Joseph	7	18
			Reide, Shad	6	....	Hodges, Jesse	7	4	Jordan, William	5	10
Langston, John	5	2	Jones, Arther, Senr	8	4	Coffield, Willis	5	8	Corbell, Thomas	5	4
Lamb, Rhady	4	....	Jones, Arther, Jur	9	7	Coffield, Wm	9	15	Mitchell, Joseph	3	6
Savage, William	4	....	Howard, Eliza	3	2	Coffield, Slatter	6	2	Godwin, Mills	2	27
Cole, Mourning	3	6	Smith, Richd	2	4	Cowling, Eliza	2	4	Godwin, Joseph, Senr	5	7
Savage, Caleb	9	6	Collins, Thomas	4	....	Rogers, Richd	7	1	Godwin, James, Junr	6	5
Parker, Jonathan	3	....	Purvis, James	12	....	Cowling, Thos	10	3	Pitt, Patience	4	8
Parker, Capt. Willis	9	20	Cross, William	5	....	Poole, Thos	4	2	Cutchin, Mary	4	16
Horton, James	6	2	Riddick, Col. Edwd	8	40	Eley, Mosses	4	7	Cutchin, Thomas	5	8
Cross, Hardy	9	3				Mackie, John	10	17	Whitley, Absalem	5	....
Smith, Thomas	10	3	**DISTRICT OF MILITIA FORMERLY COMMANDED BY CAPT. HOLLAND—LIST OF WILLIS COWLING.**			Pinner, Thos	4	1	Fry, Robert	4	4
Smith, Arther	11	8				Medcalf, Wm	2	....	Raybourn, John	7	6
Parker, Abraham	11	19	Norflet, John	7	3	Johnson, John	5	3	Meloney, Thomas	5	7
Harrell, Adam	2	....	Holland, Henry (of Henry)	7	14	Bullard, John	7	....	Pitt, Edmond	6	1
Staples, John	8	1	Holland, Henry (of John)	9	7	Bound, John	2	3	Hunt, Ralph	8	1
Horton, Mosses	3	....	Holland, Henry (of Danl)	4	2	Everitt, Saml	8	1	House, Richard	4	....
Cross, David	1	1	Holland, Joseph (of Kingsale)	6	6	Powell, Thos	3	2	Wilkinson, Arnold	1	10
Cross, Susannah	5	....	Holland, Jethro	3	....	Everitt, Josiah	5	1	Godwin, Ann	5	21
Bab, John	7	....	Winborn, Sarah	6	....	Everitt, Mary	1	1	Moore, Josiah	8	5
Peele, Jesse	7	1	Norflet, Joseph	3	10	Cowling, Josiah	12	18	Campbell, Thos, Senr	6	8
Russel, James	6	....	Holland, Solo	10	12	Light, Jesse	9	....	Foster, Coffield	2	1
Smith, James	6	1	Holland, Joshua	6	....	Cowling, Wm	6	10	Barrett, Beetley	4	2
Pierce, Edwd	4	....	Holland, Joseph (of Jo)	7	....	Powell, Wm	3	3	Jones, James	3	....
Pierce, William	7	....	Holland, Barnibi	6	1	Godwin, Jos. M.	4	14	Thomson, Alexander	4	....
Byrd, Jacob, Senr	5	....	Holland, James (of Jas)	4	3	Perrott, Nicholas	2	....	Weatherly, Sarah	4	2
Harrell, John	7	6	Holland, Job	2	....	Wilkinson, Wm, Senr	7	28	Keeley, George	6	1
Parker, Mosses	7	1	Winborn, Henry	6	....	Burton, Thos A	3	11	Godwin, Leah	3	5
Byrd, Levy	3	....	Holland, Henry (of Jo.)	4	....	Powell, Benja	10	22	Weatherly, Wm	5	2
Cross, Sarah	8	1				Bradley, John	2	5			
Penny, James	8	....				Bradley, Mary	6	7			
Byrd, Jacob, Junr	6	....				Pinner, Thos, Junr	2	1			
						Cowper, Wills	4	33			

POWHATAN COUNTY.

NAME OF HEAD OF FAMILY.	White.	Black.	NAME OF HEAD OF FAMILY.	White.	Black.	NAME OF HEAD OF FAMILY.	White.	Black.	NAME OF HEAD OF FAMILY.	White.	Black.
Barnes, John	5	9	Forsee, Mary	3	12	Banton, William	7	13	Moss, Henry	3	....
Smith, Thomas	4	20	Street, William, Senr	6	7	Porter, Capt Isaac	6	9	Cooper, Jane	4	....
Clarke, Charles	4	12	Bryant, James, Junr	9	18	Branch, Daniel	5	19	Bingley, Judith	1	12
Chastain, Charlotte I	2	6	Bryant, James, Senr	2	9	Banton, Mary	1	11	Howard, John	1	4
Woodson, John I	5	6	Chaudoin, Lewis	1	....	Drake, Joel	4	1	Mosley, William	4	2
Harris, Benjamin (Estate)	1	18	Howard, James	5	1	Bellamy, Samuel	9	2	Mosley, Robert	5	5
Porter, Magdalen	5	7	Wooldridge, William	8	2	Harris, Francis	1	10	Harris, John	6	51
Lezeure, Martel	3	....	Mansfield, Samuel	9	....	Harris, Thomas	6	27	Pleasants, Isaac	....	2
Lezeure, Fell	5	1	Trabus, William	1	3	Harris, William	4	34	Mosley, John, Senr	2	7
Gatch, Philip	5	4	Wooldridge, Edmund	6	10	Sublett, Peter, Senr	2	17	Mosley, John, Junr	1	7
Watkins, Benjamin	6	3	Depp, Peter	5	11	Lookado, Isaac	6	2	Lewis, Joseph	....	15
Porter, John	8	18	Johnson, William	7	2	Pemberton, Francis	4	....	Ready, Isham	6	....
Sublett, Peter, Junr	4	4	Jennings, Benjamin	9	....	Moss, Richard	8	....	Harrison, William	2	....
Roper, Shadrach	4	7	Salle, Joseph	12	1	Langsdon, William	4	1	Watkins, Edward, Senr	7	25
Smith, George	6	9	Street, William, Junr	1	4	Holeman, Henry	3	7	Watkins, Edward, Junr	8	19
Guerrant, Daniel	3	10	Pankey, Samuel	4	7	Jude, Benjamin	2	10	Fuqua, Giles	5	15
Smith, James	4	3	Hudnal, James	9	5	Pointer, John	9	....	Povall, John	5	19
Sublett, John	1	2	Jackson, Daniel	2	5	Moss, John	4	....	Povall, Charles	1	8
Merriman, Fracis	4	1	Pemberton, William	8	....	Moss, Benjamin	2	....	Trent, Alexander	....	7
Dupuy, James	5	13	Howard, William	7	....	Hall, Thomas	12	12	Crumpton, David	6	....
Dupuy, John	7	5	Oronett, Charles	7	....	Martin, Anthony	6	31	Cox, Richard	3	3
Forsee, Francis	5	2	Harris, Robert	6	34	Flournoy, Samuel (Estate)	5	33	Farley, Matthew, Junr	9	11
Forsee, Stephen	6	3	Harris, Ann H. W	1	5	Flournoy, David	1	6	Bailey, Ishmael	3	....

POWHATAN COUNTY—Continued.

NAME OF HEAD OF FAMILY.	White.	Black.	NAME OF HEAD OF FAMILY.	White.	Black.	NAME OF HEAD OF FAMILY.	White.	Black.	NAME OF HEAD OF FAMILY.	White.	Black.
Trent, Benjamin	6	....	Self, Robert	1	....	Strobier, John	2	2	Spiears, Nicholas	8	4
Pankey, John	2	9	Watkins, John	....	10	Turpin, Thomas, Junr	1	23	Hughes, Ann	4	12
Sudsberry, David	6	....	Carter, Thomas	2	....	Goode, John	5	28	Williams, John	11	11
Randolph, Henry	....	24	Baugh, Abraham	11	11	Turpin, Horatio	1	16	Stratton, William	9	13
Hall, Thomas	10	15	Langsdon, John	8	3	Flournoy, John	1	8	Tucker, Thomas, Junr	4	1
Mosley, Thomas	6	18	Mosley, Benjamin	2	10	Turpin, Thomas	8	41	Tucker, Jesse	6	1
Goode, Thomas	6	4	Barnett, James	6	3	Watson, William	7	....	Smith, Mary	....	....
Ligon, John (Estate)	....	11	Pelkinton, William	7	....	Salle, Joseph	10	1	Steward, John	....	1
Dean, John	6	7	Low, James	4	1	Woodfin, Samuel	9	6	Brown, Wm	....	....
Randolph, Brett	....	39	Haskins, Edward	10	20	Bradby, J. R. (Est.)	6	61	Stratton, Richard	2	3
Pitman, John	6	1	Trabue, Daniel	2	2	Biscow, Robert	5	13	Mosby, Jesse	5	3
Hatcher, Charles	11	13	Mosley, Richard (Estate)	5	21	Brechin, George	11	....	Murray, Robert	1	10
Blackburn, William	2	4	Cosby, Wingfield	5	1	Bradley, John	3	1	Steger, Samuel	2	7
Clay, Elijah	4	5	Williamson, George	5	12	Cox, Henry, Senr	3	16	Moss, William	6	3
Pool, Dudley	5	....	Drake, James	12	8	Cox, William	4	9	Hix, Daniel	6	7
Landsdon, William	5	1	Owen, James	3	....	Clay, Charles	4	10	Scott, Genl Charles	9	20
Bailey, Jane	6	....	Woodson, Charles	1	30	Clarke, John	3	4	Poor, William	7	5
Cheatwood, John	1	1	Woodson, Hughes	4	5	Cox, George	9	8	Tucker, William	8	7
Mosley, Arthur, Junr	12	15	Eans, Henry	8	....	Cardin, John	6	....	Tucker, Thomas, Senr	5	4
Mosley, Arthur (Estate of)	4	17	Strange, Thomas	7	....	Crump, Richard	6	29	Hix, Archibald	8	9
Smith, William	5	....	Lepner, Henry	3	5	Dannel, William	6	9	Duguid, Alexander	3	6
Hobson, Samuel	10	23	Amoss, John	7	....	Gordon, Robert	10	5	Hurt, James	9	....
Davis, George	8	5	Owen, George	10	17	Harris, Ann	6	24	Mosby, George	2	3
Baugh, Racheal	3	17	Toney, Edmund	14	18	Harris, Francis E.	4	16	Moss, John	10	8
Lockett, Gideon	10	5	Taylor, Robert	11	3	Harris, Edward	1	3	Wilbourn, John	7	2
Gowdy, John	2	....	Ligon, John	5	21	Hatcher, Elizabeth	3	3	Carden, Robert	6	....
Carpenter, Joseph	1	....	Smith, William	8	33	Harris, Joseph	12	19	Cocke, Charles	....	28
Moore, Henry	6	....	Smith, Robert	14	26	Logan, Charles, (Wm Ray, Overseer)	6	21	Swann, John	8	19
Chastain, Anthony	5	3	Toney, Edmund	8	4	McCraw, Mary	7	12	Moss, James	8	11
Jennings, Benjamin	7	....	Mayo, Joseph	16	34	McGehee, Jacob	9	5	Bondurant, John P	7	4
Rice, Charles	4	....	Drake, John	6	6	Mosby, Benjamin	2	10	Hix, Jesse	3	4
Marshall, Mary	8	23	Mallory, John	6	8	Moore, Robert	9	23	Mosby, Hezekiah	2	11
Maxy, John	7	13	Fitzsimmons, Patrick	11	....	Mosby, Poindexter	9	17	Stratton, Edward	3	5
Bransford, Sarah	7	9	Markham, Vincent	4	17	Montiord, Edward	5	9	Mosby, Robert	3	8
Cheatwood, William	8	1	Mayo, William, Junr	7	22	Nunnelly, Archelaus	8	7	Stratton, John	6	5
McGruder, William Miles	10	1	McLaurine, Elizabeth	5	25	Netherland, John	18	36	Brydon, Barbary	5	3
Marshall, Lucy	4	4	Povall, John	6	6	Steger, John P.	14	8	Miller, Jesse	7	15
Porter, William, Senr	7	3	Randolph, Peyton	11	125	Steger, Francis	10	6	Stratton, Martha	3	5
Smith, Childers	8	2	Radford, George	4	1	Skipwith, Colo Henry	8	58	Stratton, Peter	1	2
Burton, Charles	4	6	Radford, Richard	10	6	Tabb, Langhorn	7	13	Deavenport, Absalom	8	7
Bass, Christopher	1	8	Bagby, James	4	14	Woodson, Joseph	4	13	Carter, Daniel	6	1
Taylor, Marke (Estate)	8	1	Clarke, William	5	8	Wilks, Thomas	3	1	Woodson, Charles, Junr	6	30
Elam, Robert	2	2	Flournoy, Gedion	1	7	Hughes, Robert	5	19	Logan, Charles	25	65
Northcut, Richard	8	4	Wingfield, Nathan	6	3	Duguid, Ann	3	19	Logwood, Edmond	6	34
Mosley, Benjamin, Senr	....	9	Moseley, Daniel	1	5						

PRINCE EDWARD COUNTY.

NAME OF HEAD OF FAMILY.	White.	Black.	NAME OF HEAD OF FAMILY.	White.	Black.	NAME OF HEAD OF FAMILY.	White.	Black.	NAME OF HEAD OF FAMILY.	White.	Black.
Booker, William	9	19	Jackson, John	7	....	Walker, David	7	20	Walker, William T	2	8
Broadway, Nicholass	5	3	Ferguson, Richard	10	10	Cauthon, William	3	2	Caldwell, John	7	2
Booker, Gedeon	1	5	Ellington, William	8	9	Cauthon, John	7	....	Parks, Joseph	13	9
Clarke, John, Senr	5	10	Poe, Samuel	5	4	Gallaher, Charles	10	....	Frayzier, James	8	....
Clarke, Thomas	4	5	Masey, Mary	9	....	Harriss, Anne	5	7	Anderson, John	6	....
Davidson, William	9	4	Savage, Richard	3	....	Caldwell, David	4	1	Martin, Robert	4	1
Moore, George	2	19	Berry, James	10	....	Dannold, William	4	6	Gibbins, John	8	....
Moore, Joseph	12	29	Gallimore, George	5	....	Dannold, John	7	9	Moore, Benjamin	1	7
Moore, Thomas	9	16	Haskins, Benjamin	10	17	Dannold, James	11	7	Baker, Caleb, jr	2	2
Mason, John	10	2	Ford, E. Dorrel	8	....	Armstrong, John	7	2	Randolph, Peyton, esqr (under Chr Rice, his overseer)	7	46
Mason, John, Junr	3	....	Rice, Benjamin	6	....	Armstrong, Thomas	3	1	Randolph, Peyton, esqr (under Sharpe Spencer, his overseer)	10	35
Watkins, Henry	6	25	Aums, John	6	....	Hays, Francis	6	....	Foster, Richard	9	13
Watkins, Thomas	2	12	Vaughn, Thomas	10	5	Chalenor, William	2	....	Watson, John	8	20
Walton, Robert	11	33	Pillar, William	6	....	Garrett, Jacob	2	11	Caldwell, Henry	7	12
Ween, Vincent	5	1	Foster, William	5	5	Harris, Lewis	8	6	Hudson, William	3	16
Walton, George	12	64	Ellington, Daniel	6	3	Wilkerson, Lovell	8	....	Mitchel, James	8	....
Washborne, John	6	....	Howerton, John	7	....	Guill, Alexander	13	....	Mitchell, John	6	....
Whitlock, John	2	4	Howerton, Grief	6	....	Webster, John	4	2	Jasup, John	6	....
Green, Thomas	10	4	Foster, Robert	9	....	Hubbard, John	11	....	Jinnings, Robert	11	....
Green, Berryman	5	8	Ligon, James	5	16	Wood, Edward	4	3	Jinnings, Elkanah	5	....
Jackson, Matthew	12	8	Howerton, Thomas	1	4	Hendeake, Ezekiel	7	5	Davis, James	3	....
Johns, Joel	8	9	Osborne, Samuel	7	1	Woodson, Daniel	4	11	Hill, Susanah	6	2
Jackson, Cain	6	4	Smith, Thomas	10	....	Woodson, Charles	4	17	Mitchell, Joseph	4	....
Scott, James	6	13	Childress, John	5	3	Woodson, Jacob	7	14	Mitchell, John	9	....
Simpson, John	4	....	Rice, William	3	....	Jinnings, Samuel	6	....	Care, Nece	8	....
Singleton, Robert	3	....	Waddill, Jacob	9	5	Jones, Thomas	4	....	Porter, Andrew	8	1
Thomason, Arnold	7	4	Rice, James	7	1	Jinnings, William (A. S.)	5	3	Taylor, Samuel	5	....
Ligon, Elizabeth	7	3	Rice, James	13	14	Armstrong, William	6	1	Matthews, Philip	8	1
Bracket, John	7	5	Chatwell, Charles	4	....	Maxey, Isel	1	....	Hill, John	8	....
West, Abraham	9	9	Estis, Abraham	6	14	Peake, Richard	5	....	Hill, William	6	4
Bauldwin, James	5	5	Marshall, Alexander	8	6	Peake, Norman	5	....	Mitchell, William	3	....
Wooton, William	9	11	Hawkins, Layborne	9	....	Ritchey, Charles	4	13	Terg, William	6	1
Davidson, Sarah	5	....	Nash, John, jr	3	17	Ritchey, Hugh	7	3	Chapman, James	6	....
Carters, William	6	4	Wray, James	8	....	Baker, Christian	2	2	McFelce, Manassah	2	....
Osborne, Thomas	9	5	Ellington, John	7	5	Caldwell, Elizabeth	5	1	Arnold, Thomas	8	3
Goode, Samuel	3	8	Patterson, Anne	3	....	Welsh, James	4	....	Hill, Mordica	4	....
Goode, Robert	11	10	Hudson, Edward	5	4	Bell, John	10	....	Fency, James	8	....
Goode, Phil	5	18	Pettus, Stephen	9	8	Gallespie, Francis	4	9	Black, James	10	....
Hawkins, Phil	10	2	Cason, Seth	12	16	Hammersley, William	6	1	Anderson, William	1	....
Watkins, Abner	3	2	Arnold, John	12	7	Davidson, William	3	2	Anderson, Micajah	1	....
Sadler, William	2	....	Andrews, John	6	3	Davidson, Mary	7	3	Penick, John	1	....
Sadler, Benjamin	5	....	Wood, James	1	9	Elliott, Robert	4	7	Venable, Elizabeth	5	20
Tucker, Joseph	5	7	Adcock, Joseph	3	1	Clarke, James	9	15	Tuggle, Thomas	3	2
Tucker, Joseph, jr	3	1	Brightwell, Charles	1	....	Gallespie, William	1	2	Thaxton, David	7	....
Farley, Jeremiah	5	4	Masey, Shadrack	5	....	Hood, James	9	....	Penick, Charles	5	7
Watkins, John	3	2	Perkins, Henry	9	....	Pucket, Peter	7	3	Simmons, Joseph	7	3
Waddell, Richard	11	5	Maxey, John	5	....	Simmons, Francis	2	7	Byrd, Williamson	13	12
Wells, Frederick	6	1	Fore, William	7	2	Bibb, Richard	5	30	Thaxton, James	6	....
Vaughn, Nicholass	7	10	Ferguson, Jethro	4	....	Price, Pugh	10	18	Fielder, John	6	....
Barnes, James	5	....	Lancaster, Nathaniel	11	9	Ashley, Joel	3	3	Clarke, John	5	....
Rice, William	9	....	Price, William	4	5	Le Grand, Peter	9	22	Fielder, Ann	2	....
Shepherd, Isaac	9	....	Foore, Joseph	5	4	Hamilton, Alexander	10	10			
Gills, William	1	3	Payne, Joseph	8	....	Hamilton, Robert	3	3			
Smith, John	6	13	Hurt, Benjamin	6	2	Hammelton, John	2	2			

PRINCE EDWARD COUNTY—Continued.

NAME OF HEAD OF FAMILY.	White.	Black.	NAME OF HEAD OF FAMILY.	White.	Black.	NAME OF HEAD OF FAMILY.	White.	Black.	NAME OF HEAD OF FAMILY.	White.	Black.
Askew, Casey	11	....	Fielder, Dennis	6	....	Halcombe, John	13	28	Price, Charles	3	6
Baldwin, William	6	....	Brightwell, Reynold	6	....	Allen, Charles	6	19	Anderson, David	1	6
Chappell, Robert	12	....	Brightwell, Barnet	2	....	Le Grand, Josiah	3	6	Robertson, Zachary	7	....
Simmons, John	13	3	Bryant, Martha	7	....	McGehee, Daniel	7	6	Peake, Robert	2	12
Meadows, Jeremiah	7	11	Sanders, John	4	....	Byrd, Phil	12	6	Peake, Charles	1	....
Sanders, David	2	....	Miller, John	8	19	Bryant, Mrs	2	....	Robinson, Isaac	5	....
Harris, Thomas	8	....	Davis, Nicholas	4	18	Martin, Robert (H. C.)	8	6	Watkins, Francis	13	34
Morain, Alexander	2	....	Davies, Elizabeth	2	13	Daniel, John	6	6	Venable, Nathaniel	10	43
Robinson, Jessee	5	....	Davies, Nicho. & Saml	5	20	Glenn, Peyton	6	8	Venable, Samuel W	5	15
Baldwin, Thomas	8	2	Taylor, James	6	2	Ewing, James	2	17			
Spencer, William	4	8	Harris, William (Estate)	....	4	Robinson, Thomas	4	....			

PRINCESS ANNE COUNTY.

UPPER PRECINCT OF WESTERN SHORE—LIST OF ERASMUS HAYNES.

NAME OF HEAD OF FAMILY.	White.	Black.
Haynes, Erasmus	7	18
Whitehurst, Joshua	8	13
Whitehurst, Caleb	5	1
Moore, Mark	7	1
Godfrey, James	4	....
Stone, John	5	2
Fentress, Joshua	6	8
Fentress, Cathorine	4	5
Simpson, William	2	1
Duncan, Mary	1	1
Temmons, Margaret	1	....
Simmons, Joel	6	11
West, William, Junr	1	3
Davis, Richard	7	....
West, William, Senr	6	8
Land, Robert	9	....
Bustin, Thomas	8	4
Land, Henry	4	....
Land, Batson	4	1
West, Thomas, Junr	9	1
West, Thomas, Senr	3	4
Fentress, Isaac	5	....
Shipp, Tully	5	....
Hardgrove, John	7	....
Fentress, Mary	3	....
Hardgrove, James	5	....
Williamson, Tully	6	....
Land, Nathaniel	8	....
Fentress, Lemuel, Junr	3	....
Whitehurst, Francis	9	2
Stone, Lemuel	10	....
Stone, William	5	....
Frizel, Willoughby	4	....
Green, Mary	3	....
Fentress, Lemuel, Senr	6	10
Fentress, Nathaniel	4	....
Land, Jeremiah	7	10
Langley, Willis	3	1
Lovett, Thomas	3	9
Lovett, William	4	....
Boush, George	3	3
Land, Thoroughgood	4	....
Murphy, Anthony	4	2
Murdin, Sarah	4	4
Langley, Bredget	1	5
Williams, Isabilla	3	2
Lovett, James	10	3
Murden, James	8	2
Lovett, Susanah	2	4
Lovett, Adam	5	4
Lovett, John	8	3
Etherige, John	9	....
Land, Rea	7	7
Land, Francis	1	1
Land, Hotatia	7	2
Land, Richard	1	3
Land, Joshua	8	2
Land, Simon	3	1
Shipp, Simon	4	1
Wright, Jeremiah	8	5
Banks, Thomas	8	8
Whitehurst, Robert	5	....
Murden, Batson	2	3
Cock, John	9	....
Godfrey, Caleb	4	....
Godfrey, Matthew	3	....
Chapple, Henry	2	....

LOWER PRECINCT OF EASTERN SHORE.

NAME OF HEAD OF FAMILY.	White.	Black.
Absalom, William	7	3
Aitcheson, Rebecca	6	21
Burkey, Jonath	10	4
Broughton, Charles	12	....
Buskey, Rebecca	2	3
Banks, Rebecca	4	7
Burgess, Lanfer	6	1
Biddle, John P.	3	9
Brown, John	5	1
Brewer, James	6	....
Butt, Beriah	8	3
Cox, Ezekl	5	7
Cornick, Henry	5	18
Cannon, Elizh	5	12

LOWER PRECINCT OF EASTERN SHORE—continued.

NAME OF HEAD OF FAMILY.	White.	Black.
Carteen, Thomas	5	1
Cavender, Henry	6	....
Cornick, Joel	7	18
Cornick, William	7	24
Chapel, Thomas	6	....
Cornick, Lemuel	6	11
Cornick, Endinm	4	5
Cornick, John	7	30
Dolby, William	4	....
Edey, Solomon	7	12
Ellegood, Mary	6	13
Fentress, John	8	1
Gisburn, Edward	7	1
Guion, Lewis	2	3
Gornto, Reuben	9	5
Henley, Wm	7	3
Holmes, William	10	1
Hill, Jesse	5	1
Jacobs, Isaac	6	3
James, Henry	7	....
Jones, Mary	5	10
James, Edward	8	21
Keeling, Henry	4	11
Keeling, Jacob	8	25
Keeling, Betty	3	15
Keeling, Adam	1	12
Keeling, Thomas	1	9
Keeling, John	4	12
Keeling, William	7	53
Keeling, William, Junr	2	7
Keeling, William (Son John)	10	10
King, Elizth	5	....
Leggit, James	7	2
Lovett, Reuben	15	2
Lamount, Lydia	1	3
Lamount, Eliza	5	7
Lovitt, John	4	14
Lamount, Cornelius	6	11
Lamount, Edwd	5	....
Mills, Southy	4	....
Mills, Ann	3	....
Maye, John	10	....
McKey, Jona	7	6
Murphy, Nathl	3	1
Moseley, William	7	....
Malbone, Daniel	....	4
Norrice, Agnes	1	11
Norrice, Thomas	8	....
Oliver, John	2	3
Pebworth, Henry	7	3
Pebworth, William	9	4
Petty, Edwd	5	5
Petty, William	4	1
Petree, John	2	1
Pallet, Mary	5	5
Pallet, Mattw	2	....
Robinson, Thomas	4	....
Robinson, Mark	4	4
Russel, Ann	4	4
Richardson, Daniel	1	5
Short, Mark	4	....
Stevens, Mary	4	....
Smith, John	3	....
Scott, Caleb	4	1
Shepherd, Smith	8	20
Scott, Ann	4	11
Smith, James	5	1
Smith, Andrew	4	....
Taner, John	6	6
Trower, Thomas	3	1
Trower, Robert	6	6
Vangover, Blazen	5	....
Weeks, Amos	3	15
Wilber, Amey	3	....
Wilkins, William	4	....
Wright, Jonathan	4	1
Wilkerson, Joseph	8	1
Whitehurst, Hillary	6	6
Woodhouse, John	2	....
Warden, Arthur	6	2
White, Joseph	12	23
Whitehurst, Reuben	6	5
Whitehurst, Drew	7	2
Woodhouse, Henry	7	12

LOWER PRECINCT OF EASTERN SHORE—continued.

NAME OF HEAD OF FAMILY.	White.	Black.
Woodhouse, Wm Deal	1	....
Walker, Thomas Reynolds	7	17
Notingham, Joseph	7	....
Keeling, Paul	3	2

PRECINCT OF BLACKWATER.

NAME OF HEAD OF FAMILY.	White.	Black.
Gibson, John, Senr	6	....
Woodard, Josier	7	1
Gibson, James	3	....
Thornington, William	5	3
Commings, Fenton	4	....
White, Cornelius	5	4
Cummings, Joshua	3	....
Sammons, John	2	....
Gibson, John, Junr	2	....
Tooley, Sarah	6	6
Etheridge, James, Junr	5	....
Cottons, Timothy	3	....
Slaughter, Hillary	4	....
Caraday, John	3	....
Canaday, Rhoda	2	....
Dougless, Solomon	4	....
Wallace, James	2	1
Woodard, Joel	7	4
Tooley, Olliff	3	2
Guggs, Martha	5	1
Corbit, Richard	2	2
Peadon, William	8	....
Reed, William	8	1
Cornis, Thomas	4	....
Plummer, George	5	....
Yelks, Mary	4	....
Gibson, Sarah	4	....
Weaver, James	6	1
Sorey, Wm, Jur	5	....
Sorey, Frances	7	....
Douge, William	5	....
Grissorn, James	5	....
Douge, Benjamin	6	....
Smith, Samuel	7	....
Brown, Thomas	6	1
Whitehurst, Samuel	4	....
Davise, Elires	8	....
Fanton, Caleb	3	1
Woodard, William	1	1
James, Elizabeth	6	....
Clay, Mary	5	....
Harress, Martha	3	....
Parr, Peter	3	....
Coats, Elizabeth	5	....
Etheridge, Andrew	7	1
Wormington, Dinah	2	....
Caton, Elezabeth	9	....
Caton, Mary	3	....
Etheridge, James, Sr	5	....
Craig, Ebneazer	5	4
Plummer, Jeremiah	4	....
Bolt, Thomas	7	....
Bolt, John	4	....
Douge, Richard	6	....
Tonge, Willis	5	....
Woodard, John	6	4
Cummings, Caleb	3	....
Banks, James	4	....
Corbit, Caleb	2	1
Elks, Solomon	5	....
Coats, Elezabeth	6	1
Dougless, Charles	6	....
Godfrey, Matthew	4	....
Shewenft, William	5	....
Sorey, William, Senr	6	....
Sorey, Andrew	5	....
Riggs, John	4	1
Deele, Mary	4	....
Riggs, James	2	1
Brown, John	2	....
Corprew, John	4	....
Gallando, Abram	3	....
Wickens, William	6	9
Ives, George	9	9
Brown, Martha	6	....
Woodard, James	4	....
Woodard, Henry	5	3
Old, Caleb	8	5

PRECINCT OF BLACKWATER—continued.

NAME OF HEAD OF FAMILY.	White.	Black.
Old, Thomas, Junr	2	5
Tooley, Betty	2	1
Purdy, John	8	....
Manning, Thomas	3	....
Weekens, John	6	11
Gnawbery, George	4	....
Corprew. George Durant	9	17
Randolph, Mary	8	....
Brown, Cortney	4	....
Humpress, John	9	....
Simmons, William, Senr	8	....
Simmons, William, Junr	4	1
Morress, Hillary	1	....
Anderson, Marshall (free negro)	....	8
Anderson, Demce (free negro)	....	6
Anderson, Nathaniel (free negro)	....	3
Bishop, Peggy	6	4
Boush, Frederick	5	14
Boush, William	1	5
Broughton, George	9	....
Barrott, Amy	4	2
Carmical, John	2	2
McClinahan, William	7	17
McClinahan, Mary	4	14
Cartwright, William	4	3
Deske, Dennis	1	....
Edwards, Richard	6	1
Ewell, William	7	....
Forrest, John	7	3
Gaskings, George	6	4
Ghiselin, John	4	9
Hague, Francis	6	....
Haynie, Abner	6	1
Harvey, Charles	4	1
Haynes, William	7	10
Huggins, David	5	....
Huggins, Sarah	6	5
Haynes, Elizabeth	3	16
Keeling, Alexander	3	....
Keeling, Robert	3	14
Lewelling, Lemuel	8	....
Lester, William	8	5
Land, Francis	4	19
Moseley, Betty	9	17
Moseley, Arther	5	1
Moseley, Edward	7	2
Moore, James	7	4
Norris, William	7	8
Pebworth, Susanah	3	....
Robinson, William	1	15
Smyth, Thomas	7	....
Stone, Simon	12	10
Thorowgood, William	10	11
Thorowgood, Thomas S.	1	5
Thorowgood, John	6	24
Thorowgood, James	2	7
Thorowgood, Lemuel	5	14
Waterson, Robert	2	....
Williamson, Joshua	2	3
Williams, Thomas	4	7
McKeel, Frances	5	....
Newton, Anne	6	14
Ramsay, Mary	6	21
Stevenson, George	1	....

LITTLE CREEK PRECINCT—LIST OF WM. NIMMO, SENIOR.

NAME OF HEAD OF FAMILY.	White.	Black.
Boush, Joice (Widow)	4	6
Brent, Haynes	6	4
Bevans, William	6	7
Collins, Henry	9	1
Collins, Frankey	7	3
Collins, Maxamilian	5	4
Campbell, Anne (Widow)	4	9
Cone, Elizabeth	6	....
Cone, James	3	1
Dudley, Anne	5	3
Denny, Frances	4	6
Ewell, Thomas	8	8
Ewell, Solomon	6	8
Frost, Frances	2	....

PRINCESS ANNE COUNTY—Continued.

NAME OF HEAD OF FAMILY.	White.	Black.	NAME OF HEAD OF FAMILY.	White.	Black.	NAME OF HEAD OF FAMILY.	White.	Black.	NAME OF HEAD OF FAMILY.	White.	Black.
LITTLE CREEK PRECINCT—LIST OF WM. NIMMO, SENIOR—continued.			EASTERN BRANCH PRECINCT—continued.			UPPER PRECINCT OF EASTERN SHORE—continued.			UPPER PRECINCT OF EASTERN SHORE—continued.		
Garreld, Elizabeth	5	....	Hopkens, Sarah	6	16	Gremstead, Lawley	6	....	Ackiss, John, Junr	5	....
Guy, George	7	6	Willoroy, Presselle	3	....	Rainey, Malachi	2	....	Salmons, Richard	8	29
Griffen, John	6	7	Nickols, Nathaniel	4	8	Frizzel, Solomon, Senr	7	....	Ackiss, John, Senr	5	29
Grindall, Elizabeth	3	....	Orsbern, Walter	4	1	Oakum, Mary	3	....	Ackiss, William	8	5
Holmes, William	3	3	Edmonds, William	5	2	Cox, John	5	....			
Haynes, Henry	6	13	Edmonds, George	3	....	Dudley, Robert, Senr	5	5	MIDDLE PRECINCT OF EASTERN SHORE.		
Hunter, Elizabeth	6	19	Taylor, James	7	2	Dudley, Robert	3	....			
Haynes, Elizabeth	2	6	Sparrow, Richard	6	3	Dudley, Charles	2	....	Eaton, James	6	2
Hunter, Jacob	1	5	McCull, John	9	2	Jackson, Elizabeth	2	7	Whitehurst, James	11	3
Hunter, John	3	7	Smith, Mary	2	3	Capps, Enock	4	....	Eaton, John	7	....
Hunter, Thomas	5	18	Toamer, Thomas	3	1	Williams, Charles	8	7	Bonny, Richard	7	....
Jones, Daniel	5	....	Williamson, Lemuel	5	1	Cornick, Amy	4	1	Garrison, Cantwell	7	....
Lawson, Anthony	9	47	Griffen, Anne	4	....	Moseley, Tully	4	7	Malbon, James	7	....
Haynes, William	4	2	Ray, Charles	5	....	Morriss, Anne	3	....	Bonny, Jonathan	8	1
Millison, Ward	2	....	Wiles, Ruben	5	3	Whitehead, John, Senr	6	13	Brown, Edward	5	5
Martin, Joshua	4	1	Lamb, Frances	3	4	Kilgore, William, Senr	6	....	Malbone, Amy	6	....
Nimmo, William, Senr	3	6	Price, Elizabeth	3	....	Fisher, Jonathan	7	4	Malbone, Jonathan	6	....
Nimmo, James	4	5	Smith, George	3	4	Ackiss, Jonathan	2	10	Moore, Tully	6	....
Oldner, Thomas	3	1	Williamson, Moses	4	1	White, Richard	4	6	Fentress, Jonathan	12	7
Pebworth, Thomas	6	1	Whitehurst, Simon	5	....	Heathe, William	8	1	Fentress, John, Senr	5	11
Powers, Pemmy	7	....	Edmonds, Able	9	....	Whitehurst, Lemuel	8	....	McClain, Betty	5	....
Powers, Joseph	1	....	Whitehurst, William	5	6	Wright, Jacob	8	....	McClain, Joab	7	3
Powers, Thomas	3	2	Brock, William	6	12	Hutchings, Wm	6	3	Brown, Betty (wife of John)	3	....
Shipp, Batson	8	....	Whitehurst, James, Junr	....	....	Capps, Dennis	5	....	Cox, William	4	....
Snale, Henry	6	1	Ward, Anne	4	1	Doudge, Tully	5	....	Cason, Solomon	4	1
Smith, Perren	6	3	Williamson, Caleb	8	....	Corbell, Josiah	3	....	Hill, Elizabeth	1	....
Smith, Charles	2	2	Williamson, Charles	6	33	Spratt, Mary	3	....	Doudge, Joab	7	....
Thorowgood, John, Junr	6	20	Williamson, George, Senr	9	7	Harrisson, Mary	4	4	Lewis, John	4	1
Valentine, John	9	11	Whitehurst, Joshua	3	....	Matthias, Charles	7	....	Lewis, Thomas	6	1
Wakefield, Lemuel	9	5	Veal, Crafford	8	....	Roberts, Jonathan	9	1	Ward, John	3	....
Whitehurst, Jesse (free negro)	....	6	Whitehurst, Elizabeth	5	....	Lawrence, Joshua	6	1	Ward, Simon	4	....
Wishart, William	3	10	Whitehurst, Thomas	3	6	Cornick, Nathan	6	1	Caleman, Charles	2	....
Wishart, Mary	8	11	Veal, Thomas	8	16	Sharwood, John	8	....	Whitehurst, Solomon, Senr	6	....
			Butt, Willis	4	2	Land, Edwd	5	....	Whitehurst, John (Son of Solomon)	7	....
EASTERN BRANCH PRECINCT.			Whitehurst, Jonathan	6	....	Doudge, Wm	7	....	Whitehurst, Solomon, Junr	6	....
Moseley, Cole Edwd Hack	5	20	Hosier, Jeremiah	8	....	Fentress, Anthony	5	....	Whitehead, Charles	6	....
Moseley, Mrs. Frances	2	20	Hosier, Samuel	2	....	Franklin, Thomas, Senr	4	....	Eaton, Michael	6	....
Moseley, Mr. Hillary	9	14	Edmonds, Mallicha	2	....	Gevin, Willis	6	....	Dyer, John, Junr	6	....
Canoway, James	8	4	Lane, Josiah	3	....	Nimmo, James	1	2	Brinson, Cornelius	4	....
Borroughs, Christopher	6	2	Murray, Matthias	6	6	Morriss, Cornelius	4	....	Simmons, Thomas	9	2
Davis, Horatio	9	1	Moore, Bagwell, Junr	3	2	Matthias, Joshua	5	....	Brock, Nathaniel	5	....
Kayes, William	12	5	Whitehurst, John, Senr	3	....	Berry, Richard	7	....	Ward, Robert, Senr	8	....
Matthias, Rheuben	7	5	Parsons, John	10	15	Moore, Abner	6	1	Gornto, William, Senr	5	1
Shipp, Josiah	3	2	Whitehurst, William, Junr	5	1	Kilgore, William, Junr	5	5	Idael, Thomas	2	2
Shipp, Jonathen	1	1	Williamson, Joshua	9	2	Kilgore, John	4	1	Otterson, Jean	6	2
Whitehurst, Sarah (free)	....	3	Whitehurst, James	6	6	Williamson, Sarah	6	....	Otterson, William	3	....
Fuller, Sarah	....	7	Whitehurst, Enock	4	16	Kinzee, Thomas	7	....	Airs, Willoughby	3	....
Murray, Isaac	2	13	Walke, Mrs Mary	5	22	Williams, William	5	....	Capps, William, Senr	5	1
Drury, Elizabeth	1	3	Walke, William	1	17	Smith, George, Senr	7	....	Capps, Morriss	4	....
Dudley, Mary	4	4	Walke, Anthony	4	72	Smith, George	4	....	Capps, Obed	2	....
Davis, Edwd	3	....	Lawrance, John	1	7	Morress, William	5	1	Capps, Frances	3	....
Davis, Samuel	4	1	Brown, Sarah	6	5	Wright, James	7	2	Whitehurst, Jonathan	7	....
Land, Caleb	4	3	Walke, Anthony, Senr	3	1	Bonny, Elizabeth	9	6	Stiring, Elizabeth	7	....
Pebworth, James	8	....	White, William	5	16	Morse, Rueben	3	....	Dickoson, Charles	2	....
Drewry, Matthias	3	7	Saulsberry, John, Junr	3	4	Griggs, George	3	....	Williams, Solomon	2	....
Matthias, Mary	7	4				Wormington, John	4	....	Fentress, William	2	....
Matthias, John	3	2	UPPER PRECINCT OF EASTERN SHORE.			Roberts, Wrencher	5	....	Capps, Moses	7	....
Barfoot, Elizabeth	5	....	Stone, John, Junr	3	....	Chapple, George	2	....	Capps, Henry, Senr	4	1
Phillips, Margaret	4	....	Whitehurst, Henry	5	....	Kelley, Harry	6	3	Dyer, Pheby	3	....
Davis, Molly	4	....	Robinson, Moses	9	....	Morse, Frances	6	1	Whitehurst, Sally	4	....
Leaversage, Molly	3	....	Mackie, William	7	....	Morris, Wm (Son of Arthur)	4	....	Davice, Aber	5	....
Jackson, Elizabeth	3	....	Whitehurst, Charles	4	....	Morriss, William, Junr	7	....	Woodhouse, Henry, Senr	11	10
Harrison, Elizabeth	7	....	Brock, John	9	....	Booth, George	4	....	Ward, Thomas	2	1
Smith, John	8	1	Stoeing, Josiah	6	....	Franklin, Thomas, Junr	5	....	Ward, Jonathan	3	1
Callaway, Elizabeth	3	1	Moore, Caleb	7	5	Booth, John	4	....	Moore, Susanna	3	....
Borroughs, Anthony	4	2	Senaca, William, Junr	4	....	Batten, William, Junr	6	....	Cavender, Reuben	4	....
Scantling, William	6	9	Green, John	3	....	Munden, Stephen	5	....	Dawley, Elizabeth	4	15
Weblen, Willoughby	3	1	Brown, Moses	4	....	Mason, Dinah	6	....	Dawley, Dennis	5	5
James, William, Junr	3	3	Berry, Willoughby	8	....	King, John	4	....	Flanagan, James	5	....
Walker, Marthe	7	1	Whitehurst, Josiah	5	....	Morse, James	3	2	Bonney, William	3	....
Greffeth, Benjamine	5	3	Williamson, Malachi	3	1	Berrey, Malachi	4	....	Hill, William	3	3
Matthias, Joshua	7	....	Whitehurst, Richard	6	....	Bisco, John	5	....	Bonney, John	6	....
Whitehurst, Peter	9	11	Senaca, John, Junr	3	....	Whitehead, John, Junr	1	3	Flanakin, Moses	6	....
Williamson, Willoughby	3	2	Dawley, Caleb	5	7	Whitehead, Jssabella	6	....	Wilbur, William	6	....
Kempe, Capt James	6	28	Wilbour, John	3	....	Bryan, John	7	....	Bonney, Edwd, Senr	2	....
Butt, Cartwright	6	3	Morse, Lazarus	6	....	Batten, James	3	....	Corrill, James	9	....
Fentress, David	8	1	Senaca, James, Senr	5	....	Etheridge, Job	6	....	Scopus, John	4	....
Ray, William	3	....	Heath, James	3	....	Etheridge, Amos	2	....	McClain, John, Junr	6	....
Matthias, Hillary	5	....	James, Jonathan	5	....	Doudle, Elizabeth	5	....	Malbone, John	4	....
Gaskings, Job	2	2	Senaca, Simon	4	....	Kelly, Thomas	3	....	Capps, Henry	5	....
Hopkins, Kesiah	5	9	Senaca, John, Senr	6	....	Smith, James	5	....	McClain, Richard	2	....
Whitehurst, William	3	3	Johnson, James	3	....	Capps, Henry	4	....	Capps, John	6	....
Fentress, Michel	6	....	Morriss, John	4	....	Creed, Mary	6	2	Dawley, Jonathan	9	2
Huchings, Mrs. Sarah	7	12	Kempe, James	7	....	Moore, Arch	9	....	Dawley, David	2	4
Matthias, John	10	11	Craft, Simon	5	....	Batten, George	7	....	Capps, James	4	....
Barwell, Barthoy	2	1	Lutland, William	3	....	Batten, Caleb	2	....	Holemes, Robert	7	2
Williamson, John	3	....	Old, Thomas	3	15	Morse, Joel	1	3	Capps, Tully	5	1
Wiggins, Frances	4	....	Smith, Henry	3	2	Nelson, Elijah	8	....	Nimmo, Johnson	9	10
Forrest, William	3	2	Salmon, Frances	4	....	Capps, William	4	....	Hartly, Sarah	5	....
Dear, Steaphen	6	....	Munden, Nathan	6	1	Capps, Edwd, Junr	3	....	Cox, Benjamin	3	....
Dudley, Daniel	4	1	Munden, Epadt	5	3	Wellins, Mary	3	....	Williamson, Jonathan	2	....
Whitehurst, Jonathan	12	22	Shipp's, John (Orpans)	....	6	Gording, William	3	....	Williamson, John	2	....
Moore, Bagwell	8	3	Capps, Edwd, Senr	8	....	Stripe, Anne	2	....	Capps, John	6	....
Russell, William	2	6	Bonny, Tully	6	....	Camell, John	3	....	Franklin, Daniel	7	....
Hancock, John	8	17	Bright, Hanson	4	....	Allen, Thomas	3	....	Woodhouse, James	3	1
Hancock, Anne	6	4	Land, Willoughby	5	3	Lawrence, Obediah	2	....	Franklin, Nathan	5	....
Whitehurst, Christopher	7	7	Grumstead, Daniel, Junr	6	....	Senaca, Averellic	6	2	Strawhan, Rachel	4	....
Whitehurst, Enock	4	....	Brown, James	2	....	Senaca, Mary	2	2	Dawley, Thomas	4	....
Hopkens, John	5	19	Gremstead, Daniel, Senr	5	....	Cox, John, Junr	6	2	Langley, Thomas	1	4
						Green, Mary	8	....			

PRINCESS ANNE COUNTY—Continued.

NAME OF HEAD OF FAMILY.	White.	Black.	NAME OF HEAD OF FAMILY.	White.	Black.	NAME OF HEAD OF FAMILY.	White.	Black.	NAME OF HEAD OF FAMILY.	White.	Black.
MIDDLE PRECINCT OF EASTERN SHORE—continued.			MIDDLE PRECINCT OF EASTERN SHORE—continued.			MIDDLE PRECINCT OF EASTERN SHORE—continued.			MIDDLE PRECINCT OF EASTERN SHORE—continued.		
Roberson, Adam, Senr	5	....	Brown, John	6	1	Dawley, Henry	6	....	Axstead, Thomas	5	....
Robinson, Adam, Junr	5	....	Caten, James	6	2	Cason, Hillary	8	....	Malborn, Solomon	7	....
Robinson, William	15	....	Caten, John	7	....	Cason, John, Senr	3	2	Whitehead, John	6	....
Snail, John	6	....	Whitehurst, James	11	3	Cason, James, Junr	4	3	Flanagan, William	3	....
Cavender, John	6	1	Legget, William	6	1	James, William, Senr	4	13	Bonney, Jeen	1	....
Cason, Moses	6	1	Matthias, Robert	2	2	James, Elizabeth	2	7	Malborn, Peter	7	....
Cason, James, Senr	8	1	Brock, William	2	3	James, Pembrook	4	7	Waterman, Jemima	12	....
Whitehurst, William	7	....	Brock, Anne	6	2	Whitehurst, Hosie	4	....	Malborn, Sarah	4	....
Whitehurst, John	6	6	Rany, John	9	....	Totewine, Isaac	3	3	Moses, Cleven	5	....
Fentress, John	10	6	Flanagan, William	5	....	Atwood, Thomas	2	4	Cavender, Thomas	5	....
Doudge, Richard	7	3	Cumberfoot, Meshaly	3	....	Atwood, William	6	....	Capps, Hillary	7	....
Whitehurst, James	7	....	Padon, Charles	10	....	Atwood, Betty	6	....	Lovett, John	7	6
Doudge, Nathan	4	....	James, John	7	6	Moore, Cason, Senr	7	3	Shipp, William, Senr	6	3
Davis, Robert	6	....	Woodhouse, John	4	8	Bonney, Ricnard	7	....	Bonney, John	8	5
Griffen, John	4	4	Harrison, Henry	6	15	Garrison, Cantwell	7	....	Dyer, Hillary	3	....
Griffen, William	4	2	King, Avarilla	2	....	Brown, John, Senr	7	....	Woodhouse, Jonathan	8	5
Cason, Cornelius, Senr	8	1	Dyer, Willoughby	5	....	Brown, Tully	7	....	Woodhouse, William	8	6
Cason, Cornelius, Junr	3	2	Dyer, John	6	....	Brown, Jonathan	1	....	Battin, William, Junr	7	....
Moore, Jacob	5	3	Barnes, Caleb	2	4	Brown, Moses	4	....	Shepherd, William	9	7
Moore, Cason	4	1	Axstead, Sarah	4	....	Henley, James	9	8	James, John	5	1
McClalin, Moses	6	....	Henly, Charles	5	6	Henley, Newdinna	2	2	Morrisset, John	6	2
McClalin, William	4	....	Cannon, Thomas	8	4	Brown, John	2	....	Gornto, John, Senr	6	2
McClalin, John	7	....	Barns, Francis	5	2	Malbone, Godfrey	4	....	Gornto, John, Junr	5	2
McClalin, William, Junr	8	....	Barns, Joshua	7	....	Barns, Kezia	5	....	Gornto, Nathaniel	4	1
Turner, John	3	....	Airs, Francis	4	....	Malbone, Evan	8	....	Rany, Thomas	8	....
Buskey, Cornelius	8	....	Spratt, Henry	8	....	Bonney, John	7	....	Roberts, Sarah	6	....
Fountain, John	7	....	Dawley, Mary	8	....	Dawley, Rhoda	7	2	Norriss, John	1	....
Hill, Tully	2	1	Dawley, Mary	2	2	Brock, Ransom	7	....			

RICHMOND COUNTY.

NAME OF HEAD OF FAMILY.	White.	Black.	NAME OF HEAD OF FAMILY.	White.	Black.	NAME OF HEAD OF FAMILY.	White.	Black.	NAME OF HEAD OF FAMILY.	White.	Black.
UPPER DISTRICT OF LUNENBURG PARISH—LIST OF MOORE BROCKENBROUGH.			UPPER DISTRICT OF LUNENBURG PARISH—LIST OF MOORE BROCKENBROUGH—continued.			UPPER DISTRICT OF LUNENBURG PARISH—LIST OF MOORE BROCKENBROUGH—continued.			LOWER PRECINCT OF LUNENBURG PARISH—LIST OF ROBERT TOMLIN—con.		
Bragg's, Moore (Family)	7	10	Hammonds, Richard	4	....	Ford's, William (Estate)	7	15	Giberne, Mr	....	29
Lee, Francis Lightfoot	8	32	Lyne, James	3	4	Annadale, Thomas	10	3	Garland, Griffin	10	20
Marks, Elias	5	1	Hall, William	9	....	Mitchell, Robert	2	22	Thrift, George	3	6
Wright, Edward	6	11	Hinson, William	6	....				Thornton, John	3	2
Kelly, James	12	13	Brockenbrough, Moore	8	44	LOWER PRECINCT OF LUNENBURG PARISH—LIST OF ROBERT TOMLIN.			Thornton, Betty	1	1
Sisson, Henry	9	12	Scates, Joseph	12	....				Pachet, William	4	....
Redman, Vincent	7	10	Willson, Joseph	10	....	Carter's, Robert Wormeley (Family)	13	156	Webster, William	2	....
Redman, Mary	6	5	Lyne, Robert	6	2	Tomlin's, Walker (Family)	5	37	Neale, Richard	4	19
Shrimser, Daniel	1	....	Bragg, Charles	7	4	Kelsick, Samuel	6	34	Callis, Robert	3	1
Franklin, Thomas	12	2	Morriss, William	9	....	Brockenbrough, John	1	24	Harford, Ann	1	....
Suttle, Bailey	5	17	Morriss, John	3	....	Hipkins, Samuel	2	13	Hendren, Priscilla	6	....
Yates, William	4	1	Nash, James	5	....	Shackelford, Richard	9	9	Raynolds, William	4	....
Carpenter, John	1	....	Mothershead, Nathaniel	6	1	Goldsby, John	7	3	Harford, H. (Orphans of)	6	....
Hart, William	1	....	Barrott, John	7	....	Barrick, Elizabeth	3	1	Tomlin, Robert	7	28
Hart, John, Senr	3	....	Willson, John	2	....	Pugh, Sarah	3	....	Raynoldses (Walker Tomlin's list)	....	9
Carpenter, William	5	....	Yeatman, William	7	3	Gill, Spencer	8	1	How, John	10	16
Carter, Mary	4	....	Jenkins, James	5	....	Brickey, Peter	4	....	Ferguson, Robert	7	....
Moore, Reuben	3	....	Newman, James	5	....	Longwith, Burges	7	....	Kelsick, Mary	7	12
Randall, George	1	1	Scutt, Thomas	5	....	Demerit, John	7	13	Ball, Williamson	8	58
Wright, John	5	16	Royals, William	6	....	Vanlandingham, James	1	10	Beale, Elizabeth	6	4
Connollee, Daniel	4	....	Jenkins, Harmon	6	....	Jordon's, Reubin (Estate)	....	8	Rust, Benjamin	4	26
Moore, Daniel	4	....	Nash, Winder	1	....	Barrick, David	10	....	Bryan, Samuel	2	....
Lee's, Esqr (Estate)	1	17	Walker, George	1	....	Carter, Robert, Esqr (No-mony)	....	11	Tayloe, Honble John, Dece'd (Estate of)	....	180
Sisson, Richard	2	....	Walker, Edmund	1	....	Northen, Peter	8	18	Beale, William, Junr	1	....
Hall, Anne	4	3	Fauntleroy, William, Senr	5	72	Weldon, John	5	1			
Sisson, John	8	6	Fauntleroy, John	....	13	Vanlandingham, Sarah	6	....	FORK OF TOLUSKEY—LIST OF JOHN SYDNOR.		
Bulger, John	4	....	Muse, Daniel	3	14	Rust, William H	6	1			
Bulger, Jane	3	2	Faucett, John	5	4	Walker's, Randall (family)	9	2	Wroe, George	3	6
Royals, Rebecca	8	....	White, Zachariah	10	3	Newman, Le Roy	10	2	Clark, William	4	2
Kelly, John	11	9	Ramey, Joshua	6	1	Nash, Edward	3	1	Roberts, James	6	....
Sanders, William, Senr	3	....	Wroe, John	2	....	Duff, Peter	6	1	Dawson, H. (Cos.)	10	1
Sanders, Almond	2	....	Thompson, Alexander	2	....	Northen, Elizabeth	8	....	Williams, Luke	4	8
Saunders, Alexander	2	....	Crash, James	1	....	Landman, William	5	....	Davis, Jobey	4	....
Mozingo, Edward, Senr	7	....	Yardley, Edmund	5	....	Eskridge, George	3	3	Thrift, John	5	1
Mozingo, Edward, Junr	3	....	Fauntleroy, Capt Moore	4	34	Headley, John	3	....	Jackson, Vincent	5	12
Sutton, William	8	....	Mayze, William	5	....	Pridham, Christopher	1	4	Clarke, George	1	1
Sandy, Mason	8	1	Collins, Thomas	2	1	Self, Presley	4	....	Haybron, George	8	1
Jenkins, Daniel	3	....	Pooley, William	7	....	Webb, James	9	....	Clarke, Thomas	2	....
Jenkins, John	3	....	Sanders, William, Junr	7	....	Purcell, John	4	5	Gupton, Caty Ann	5	....
Jones, Griffin	11	....	Eskridge, John	8	5	Purcell, Edward M	3	2	Clarke, John	1	4
Luttrel, Richard	6	2	Crewdson, William	4	....	Redman's, Solomon (family)	2	....	Garner, James	6	....
Ducan, Charity	3	2	Beckwith, Roger	4	30	How, George	5	1	Jones, John	4	7
Mothershead, John	1	....	Pratt, William	5	....	Alderson, Wm	7	3	Harrison, George	6	4
Newman, George	7	17	Lyall, John	11	3	McGuire, Mary	5	1	Jones, Ambrose	....	1
Eidson, Edward	5	2	Hall, John	2	....	Fauntleroy, Majr Moore	2	32	Proctor, Abraham	8	....
Bragg, Elizabeth	3	4	Robins, John	4	6	Brockenbrough, Thomas	1	27	Jones, William	6	1
Sandy, Mary	5	7	White, John	1	....	Weathers, George	7	3	Clarke, Rodham	7	1
McGinness, Richard	6	2	Hughs, Reubin	7	....	Billings, John	2	....	Clarke, William	2	1
Kirkham, William	4	1	Gordon, James	14	47	Goldsby, David	3	1	Clarke, Thomas	3	....
McKenny, Gerrard	4	3	Belfield, John	7	35	Franks, Henry	6	6	Dunaway, Samuel	4	13
Crash, John, Senr	5	1	Belfield, Thomas	3	10	Garland, Vincent	9	12	Clarke, Thomas, Senr	4	2
Crash, William	2	....	Barneses, Richard (Estate)	....	18	Raynolds, John	2	7	Dunaway, Samuel, Junr	1	....
Carpenter, Joseph	4	....	Brockenbrough's, Austin (Est.)	....	14	Purcell, Tobias	1	....	Dawson, David	1	....
Carter, Daniel	10	....	Marks, Edward	4	....	Ferguson, William	9	20	Martin, William	....	6
Fisher, John	7	....	Crash, Griffin	3	....	Fauntleroy, Samuel G	....	8	Brown, Ellen	6	10
Evans, Peter	4	....	Willson, Morton	....	12	Olliff, William	4	....	Harriss, Hugh	7	10
Taylor, John Fisher	10	....	Pritchett, Thomas	1	....	Lawson, Daniel	5	9	Self, Jeremiah	3	....
Alderson, Fieliff	7	....	Hinson, Jonas			Beale, Thomas	11	46	Moore, Elijah	4	....
Marks, John, Senr	7	7	Playl, William	3	....	Toombs, Edmund	6	2	Wroe, John	10	2
Bruce, William	13	2	Smith, William	8	2	Bramham, Benjamin	6	24	Clarke, Robert	3	....
Willson, Elias	3	4	Carter, Robert (Estate)	3	5	Raynolds, William (Oversr for Colo Carter)	6	2	Thornton, John, Esqr	4	....
Willson, Daniel	8	1	Hall, Robert	3	1				Littrell, William	2	....
Coats, James	4	....	Stowers, Nicholas	7	6						
Beckwith, Sir Jonathan	8	53	Nash, Solomon	3	....						
Carter, William	6	1	Turberville, George	....	10						
Carter, John	2	1									

RICHMOND COUNTY—Continued.

FORK OF TOLUSKEY—LIST OF JOHN SYDNOR—con.

NAME OF HEAD OF FAMILY.	White.	Black.
Bryant, Jonathan	6	
Moore, Garland	5	
Jesper, Robert	3	6
Lewis, Willoughby	5	1
Warmoth, Thomas	8	
Brown, Daniel	5	4
Stuckey, Job	8	
Smith, Colo John	7	67
Gathings, Ann	3	
Clarke, Robert	3	
Morgan, Andrew	9	5
Stott, Robert	11	
Garland, William	6	9
Wroe, William	2	3
Morgan, Frances	3	6
Jones, Charles	5	3
Hammock, Benjamin	9	3
Prosser, John	2	2
Claughton, Richard	6	7
Dawson, David	5	
Carter, Charles	8	51
Shurley, Peter	6	
Downman, William	2	28
Warrick, Obediah	4	
Clarke, Vincent	4	
Miskell, George	3	13
Clarke, John	4	
Deatny, Christopher	4	6
Dobyns, Thomas	8	17
Self, Jeremiah	4	
Page, John	8	2
Watts, Mary	3	
Headley, Henry	5	
Watts, Edward	5	7
Dobyns, Thomas	9	22
Brown, Daniel	5	4
Morgan, Andrew	3	4
Hammock, Robert	3	4
Dozier, Richard	10	1
Rice, Richard	4	4
Cralle, Daniel S	8	1
Hail, William	1	
Brown, Sarah C	3	
Jesper, Caty	5	6
Sydnor, Dewanna	1	13
Sydnor, Anthony	5	11
Sydnor, Giles	1	9
Sydnor, John	8	37
Whaley, William	1	1

PRECINCT OF MORATICO—LIST OF RICHARD BEALE.

NAME OF HEAD OF FAMILY.	White.	Black.
Beale, Richard	6	31
Hadon, John	5	5

PRECINCT OF MORATICO—LIST OF RICHARD BEALE—con.

NAME OF HEAD OF FAMILY.	White.	Black.
Nash, John	8	1
Ambrose, Joseph	5	26
Howard, LeRoy	5	3
Barnes, Charles	5	
Barnes, Winifred	5	9
Howard, Thomas	5	7
Lawson, Sarah	5	14
Alderson, James	7	17
Bryant, Thomas	5	
Stone, Thomas	10	10
Dale, Joseph	6	1
Dale, Alexander	6	2
Forrester, Bridget	4	7
Stonum, Mary	5	1
Forrester, William	1	4
Rout, George	4	
Downman, Rawleigh	6	39
Glascock, George	8	28
Abbleby, Richard	6	
Yerby's, John (Estate)		36
Tune, John	6	1
Thomas, John	4	
Lewis, John	6	1
Hogan, Thomas	10	3
McCarty, Thaddeus	11	23
Yerby, George	10	50
Dale, George	7	
Shurley, Joseph	2	
Deavenport, Eliza	3	8
Deavenport, Opie	4	2
Dodson, James	8	1
Moore, John	9	
Palmer, Ann	2	13
Tune, Anthony	5	4
Jackson, Thaddeus	9	6
Bryant, John	6	1
Miskell, Newman	4	9
Palmer, William	10	10
Dobyns, Edward	8	13
Prosser, Alice	9	2
Howard, Spencer	9	6
Pritchett, Rodham	9	10
McClanahan, Peter	6	2
Scurlock, George	11	1
Deavenport, Eliza	5	4
Hazard, William	9	1
Brown, Ellen	7	11
Smither, Abraham	13	7
Rice, Richard	9	6
Peachey, William	3	38
Cornelius, Josiah	6	
Flood, Elizabeth	1	59
Dale, George	6	
Cocke, John	7	2

PRECINCT OF MORATICO—LIST OF RICHARD BEALE—con.

NAME OF HEAD OF FAMILY.	White.	Black.
Tune, Caster	6	5
Headley, William	9	1
Lewis, James	8	2
Brown, Charles	6	
Douglas, William	1	5
Douglas, Rodham	10	
Aloway, Eliza	3	
Brown, Ann	5	2
Miskell, William	9	25
Tillery, Epa	8	
Popes, William (Est.)		11
Pullin, Jehu	7	1
Tune, Samuel	13	1
Stonum, William	3	11
Hazard, Henry	4	
Hazard, John	8	
Hammond, John	7	16
Jones, Edward	7	6
Luggitt's, John (Est.)		2
Webb's, John (Est.)		1
Braman, Bar	8	2
Hanks, Turner	9	2
Nash, Richard	4	1
Nash, Pitman	3	1
Phillips, Bryant	3	2
Jones, John	6	2
Newgent, Rawleigh	5	
Stott, LeRoy	12	
Bennehan, Dominick	6	3
Dobyns, Abner	7	11
Nash, George	8	2
Pope, LeRoy	8	11
Newsome, Robt	4	9
Barnes, Samuel	9	
Dodson, Alice	5	
Elmore, George	7	
Dodson, Charles	7	2
Bryant, Rawleigh	9	1
Coleman, Thomas	10	8
Hunton, Alice	14	12
Willson, John	6	
Headley, James	4	

FARNHAM DISTRICT—LIST OF JOHN SMITH.

NAME OF HEAD OF FAMILY.	White.	Black.
Dobyns, Daniel	7	9
Davis, John	8	13
Hammond, Thomas	5	3
Bunyan, Milly	7	3
Hammond, Thomas, Junr	4	1
Barber, William	10	6
Thrift, Meriman	6	
Feagins, Alexander G	4	

FARNHAM DISTRICT—LIST OF JOHN SMITH—con.

NAME OF HEAD OF FAMILY.	White.	Black.
Northen, George	8	12
Fauntleroy, Griffin	6	14
Branham, Benjamin, Jur	4	8
Yates, Mary	6	
Thornton, Betty	5	7
Barber, Charles	6	4
Samford, John A	5	3
Jesper, Thomas	9	
Cox, James	3	10
Newsom, Benjamin	5	
Inglish, William	7	1
Lightfoot, Thomas	7	2
Short, Bennedick	4	
Sisson, George	10	14
Jesper, Thomas, Jur	4	2
Jones, David	8	
Dobyns, Henry	7	6
Bailey, Charles	4	6
Gibson, Priscilla	2	6
Suggitt, Elizabeth	2	10
Packet, Richard	3	1
Efford, Zachariah	5	
Hammond, Lewis	6	1
Tillery, Job	5	
Webb, Frances	11	16
Woollard, Elizabeth	4	
Dale, Alexander	2	1
Hammock, William	2	
Hanks, John	4	
Jenkins, William	4	5
Cole, John	3	4
Downman, Rawleigh	2	8
Woollard, Samuel	10	
Jones, Sanford	6	1
McCarty, William	2	10
Bryant, Alexander, Jur	3	1
Bryant, Alexander	4	5
Hinds, Thomas	7	4
Samford, James	11	7
Williams, Jonathan	6	1
Baker, John	7	4
Williams, Betty Ann	5	20
Smith, William	8	17
Hanks, George	3	
Saunders, George	5	15
Downman, Travers	3	7
Alaway, Isaac	9	1
Woollard, Joseph	4	
Smith, John, Junr	11	25
Smith, Thomas	5	20
Smith, John	3	6
Singleton, Drucillah	6	17
Peacheys, Le Roy	7	25

SHENANDOAH COUNTY.

LIST OF ALEX'R HITE.

NAME OF HEAD OF FAMILY.	White.	Black.
Adaughthy, Jervis	6	
Acker, Henry	9	
Bushong, John, Senr	9	
Brown, Michael	6	
Bengle, Henry	6	
Bowman, John	6	
Brice, Hannah	1	
Bowman, Samuel	5	
Bratten, John	4	
Bolthias, Leonard	10	
Blend, Michael	6	
Beard, Zachariah	11	
Bitman, Nicholas	8	
Black, Peter	8	
Bowman, Peter	5	
Bley, phillip	4	
Bley, Jacob	5	
Bears, Phillip	11	
Bears, John	4	
Bush, Sarah	3	
Barbridge, Thomas	1	1
Creable, Abm, Senr	6	
Conrad, Jacob	2	
Cooper, George, (Sadler)	7	
Cooper, Capt George	6	
Cappenheafer, Susannah	7	
Capp, Christian	10	
Conn, John	4	
Camper, John	7	
Caughenhour, Jacob	11	
Campbell, Alexr	6	
Cradinger, Ulric	10	
Creable, John	10	
Creable, Abram, Junr	6	
Caplaine, Kerry	5	
Camper, Peter	10	
Dosh, Christopher	4	
Disponett, Christopher	7	
Everly, Jeremiah, Senr	4	
Doll, George	8	
Funk, Jacob	2	

LIST OF ALEX'R HITE—con.

NAME OF HEAD OF FAMILY.	White.	Black.
Funk, John	7	
Franger, Peter	8	
Funk, Henry, Jur	4	
Freeman, Charles	6	
Fleek, Christian	5	
Fleek, Peter	5	
Funkhouse, Jno	7	
Grove, Jacob	4	
Green, John	10	
Hite, Alexr	6	
Harr, Simon	7	
Hufman, Philip	6	8
Hufman, Christian	3	
Happene, Gasper	9	
Hocman, Christian	4	
Hocman, John	6	
Hocman, Peter	9	
Huddell, George, jr	11	
Huddell, David	5	
Hiser, Henry	11	
Hardwick, Fredk	1	
Holmes, William	9	
Hay, Catharina	1	
Jackson, Saml	2	
Jenkins, Saml	8	
Kendrick, Barbara	5	
Kester, Christopher	4	
Keith, Constant	7	
Keller, Henry	5	
Keller, Jacob	5	
Karshwaler, Jacob	2	
Lin——*, George	3	
Lotz, Jonas	3	
Lotz, Gasper	4	
Lampert, Christopher	10	
Lampert, Jacob	4	
Lawnn, Rudolph	2	
Lockmiller, Geo. senr	6	
Lockmiller, Geo. Junr	2	
Machir, John	1	
Machir, Alexander	11	11

LIST OF ALEX'R HITE—con.

NAME OF HEAD OF FAMILY.	White.	Black.
Maydinger, Lewis	1	
Marney, Robert	7	
Marney, James	2	
Nieberger, Christian	6	
Marcure, Lewis John	2	
Pister, Martin	2	
Porter, Saml	10	1
Posserman, Fredk, Sr	7	
Posserman, Will	3	
Posserman, Christian	5	
Russ, Joel	2	
Ravenhill, Francis	5	2
Russel, James	6	
Ruth, Michael	5	
Richards, George	3	
Reager, Michael	10	
Stover, Peter	8	
Shireman, Adam, Sr	3	
Steel, John	6	1
Smith, Peter	3	
Smith, Valentine	7	
Snider, John	2	
Sieb, Henry	12	
Stover, Jacob	8	
Stocksleger, Esther	8	
Smith, John	4	
Snapp, Margarett	8	2
Snapp, Philip	7	
Snapp, Lawrence	9	4
Stitsler, John	4	
Shaver, Danl	4	
Shue, Jabetz	7	
Shue, Joseph	4	
Speiger, Jacob	10	
Stoner, Fredk	8	2
Sivert, Jacob	7	
Sivert, Isaac	4	
Stephens, John	5	
Smilly, James	3	
Sommer, Nancy	4	
Sommer, George	3	

LIST OF ALEX'R HITE—con.

NAME OF HEAD OF FAMILY.	White.	Black.
Spoor, Henry	8	
Trout, Daniel	5	
Voegdly, George	6	
Vane, Samuel	7	
Vane, Isaac	3	2
Wilson, John	2	
Walmer, Jacob	7	
Wolf, Mary	5	
Walter, Christian	2	
Welsh, Thomas	3	
Weackman, Conrad	8	
Windle, Phillip	7	
Yost, Jacob	7	
Zea, Phillip	3	
Feltner, Adam	9	
Fultz, Joseph	3	
Froerdig, Adam	6	
Denais, John	2	
McClaniham, Robert	2	
Margrave, John	1	
Atrige, John	1	
Adougherty, Will	7	
Burner, Earherd	8	
Burner, Jacob	7	
Buck, John	8	11
Bowman, Isaac	1	8
Buck, Charles	5	13
Boothe, Will Aylett	5	11
Clem, David, Sr	4	
Clem, David, Jur	5	
Clem, Dedrick	8	
Cron, Fergus	5	
Combs, Gilbert	5	
Carrier, Henry	4	
Clem, Michel	5	
Clipple, Michall	2	
Creek, Rebeckah	2	
Colwill, Saml	10	
Dosh, Danl	4	
Dohoty, Will	9	
Coulers, John	6	

* Illegible.

SHENANDOAH COUNTY—Continued.

NAME OF HEAD OF FAMILY.	White.	Black.	NAME OF HEAD OF FAMILY.	White.	Black.	NAME OF HEAD OF FAMILY.	White.	Black.	NAME OF HEAD OF FAMILY.	White.	Black.
LIST OF ALEX'R HITE—con.			LIST OF ALEX'R HITE—con.			LIST OF ALEX'R HITE—con.			LIST OF ALEX'R HITE—con.		
Denton, John	10		Sonther, Phillip	11		Hand, Will	10	1	Lame, Adam	4	
Deloter, Lawrence	6		Supinger, John	8		Huston, John	10	1	Lacy, John	6	
Eagles, Timothy	9		Stephenson, James	9		Jenings, Will	12	1	Lame, George	4	
Franch, Henry	10		Steward, Charles	8		Johnston, Andrew	7		Musser, John	5	
Frye, Barbary	2		Sly, Henry	5		McRoy, Jas, Sr	5	2	Middleton, John	2	
Gollody, Jacob	12		Turnham, Thomas	2		McRoy, Jas, Jr	7	1	Moyre, Henry, Sr	4	
Greathouse, Will	2		Townshand, Henry	3		McCarty, Isaac	8		Moyre, Henry, Jr	3	
Greathouse, Jno	7	1	Tresler, Andrew	11		Miller, Will	8	5	Maves, John	10	
Gatewood, Phillip	7	8	William, Williams	7		McKenny, John	4		Miller, Christian	6	
Gesner, John	5		Wood, Thomas	12		Masters, James	7		Mowrer, Valle	2	
Horn, Boston	9		Windle, Jacob	4		Miller, Jas	6		Miller, Martin	3	
Heastin, Danl	7		Wilson, Archibald	5		Meginnis, Danl	3		Mowrer, Leonard	3	
Horn, George	9		Wattson, Joseph	3		McKenny, Francis	6		Mace, Henry	5	
Hysee, Jacob	10		Wattson, John	4		McDonald, Danl	3		Miller, Ulric	13	
Hunt, John	7		Wilson, Levin	3		McRoy, Robert	11		Moyley, Danl	5	
Honaker, Jacob	25		Abbitt, William	9		Mowzer, Will	6		Mowser, John	6	
Hall, Will	7		Aldor, Patty	8	1	Robinson, Will	6		Marshall, Thos	1	
Heastin, Abm	11		Bodkin, Laurence	3		Ramey, Thos	7		Messersmith, Henry	1	
Jackson, Moses	5		Bradford, David	7		Robinson, Eleanor	4		Newman, John	6	
Hannon, Jacob	5		Cooksy, John	7		Robinson, David	6		Nie, Ulric	5	
Keller, George	9		Cranford, John	9		Rice, John	10		Naile, George	6	
Lighliter, Adam	5		Conner, James	7		Smith, John	9		Orts, John	4	
Lighliter, Jacob	7		Conner, James	5		Smith, John	7		Orts, Henry	3	
Lighliter, John	6		Carter, Chandler	10		Smith, John	5		Peters, Jonas	8	
McInturf, Fredk	2		Collins, Jeophrey	8		Sellits, Will	5		Price, Will	6	
McInturf, George	7		Danial, William	4	7	Smith, Thos	12		Rodeheifer, David	7	
McInturf, Gasper	2		Grigsby, Benjamin	5		Sellers, Elijah	3		Reynolds, Joseph	4	
Miller, Geo. Henry	7		Gordon, William	8		Taylor, Lazarus	5		Rodeheifer, Saml	8	
Miller, Henry, Sr	10		Humbok, Henry	7		Taylor, John	2	3	Ruddell, Archibald	11	
Miller, Henry, Jr	3		Hurst, William	8		Tetzner, Aaron	7		Zeady, Phillip	6	
McInturf, John	4		Homes, John	8		Vanmetre, Soloman	5	1	Siering, Matthias	8	
McNacton, Peter	6		Henry, Samuel	8		Williams, Catran	4		Snap, John	7	
Mounch, Phillip	6		Huma, Thomas	4		Williams, Will	12	8	Shaver, John	5	
Murphey, Charles	7		Hopkins, John	6		Wilson, Edward	7		Strauther, Will	6	
Nicholas, Richard	7		Henry, Moses	3		Clay, Matthew	3		Stover, John	5	
O'Bannion, Jas	8		Hackney, Daniel	6	5	Anderson, John	4	1	Savage, Abm	6	1
O'Dle, Elijah	7		Jones, Thomas	9	1	Apler, John	3		Shaner, Martin	4	
O'Dell, Jeremiah	3		Jones, William	4	1	Brown, John	7		Seager, John	6	
Parkison, John	5		Jones, Francis	2		Bowman, Jacob	9	2	Utt, Henry	7	
Ramey, Thaddeus	8	4	Kelly, John	7		Busshong, John	3		Williamson, Jacob	2	
Richardson, C. Jno	7	4	Limper, John	5		Bowman, Saml	3		Wiseman, Clay	1	
Richardson, Issabel	1	3	Lambert, John	2		Bordon, Nicholas	7		Woolford, Fred	4	2
Redenhour, Henry	5		Morgan, Ezekiel	9		Black, George	3		Woolford, Soloman	5	
Redenhour, Geo	6		McCarty, Derby	3		Barnett, Will	7		Wetzel, George	6	
Redenhour, Adam	5		McCarty, Jonathan	7		Bough, Dorothy	1		Wolfenberger, John	4	
Sommerwalt, Henry	10		Adams, Susannah			Bowman, Henry	7		Wolfenberger, Fred	6	
Spangler, John	6		McKoy, Alexr	5		Barnett, Michael	7		Wolfenberger, Benjn	3	
Sibert, Moses	7		Morgan, Gilbert, Jr	5		Burner, Michael	6		Windle, Danl	6	
Teabo, Conrad	9		Morgan, Gilbert, Sr	3		Bowman, Danl	6		Yeager, Joseph	7	
Wilfong, Joseph	5		Masters, Will	6	2	Boyres, Jacob	8		Aleshite, Benedick	6	
Woollard, John	9		Morgan, Nichs	3		Clour, John	6		Aleshite, Jno Conrad	1	
Walter, Jacob	2		Meads, Nightengale	3		Caver, Jacob	4		Aleshite, Jacob	1	
Waggoner, Jacob	9		McCarty, Benjan	3		Cyvert, Francis	8		Aleshite, Henry	1	
Acker, Jacob	4		Masters, Thomas	5		Creyble, Jacob	4		Altre, Frederick	9	
Beam, Saml	7		McVay, Danial	4		Coughenour, Joseph	7		Aleshite, Conrad	5	
Beam, Jacob	6		North, Zachariah	7		Coughenour, John	4		Allen, John	10	
Beam, Reubin	4		North, Jane	4		Coughenour, Abm	2		Abel, Thamas	1	
Beam, Danl	3		Owens, William	7		Caffer, Jeremiah	9		Burner, Jacob, Sen	10	
Burnett, Elizath	4		Poker, Phillip	10		Creable, Christian	6		Beaker, Jacob	5	
Bell, John	9		Parker, John	11		Cook, John	9		Barnitt, John	5	
Baker, Hyeronemus	5		Russell, James	4		Crookshanks, John	2	1	Bullington, John	5	
Baker, George	4		Russell, John	5		Creable, John	6		Bouser, Peter	7	
Baker, Phillip	8		Rolls, Francis	3		Coughenour, Henry	11	2	Bumgamer, Chrisley	1	
Baker, Anthony	4	1	Robinson, James	6		Campbell, Rebeckh	4	2	Breeding, Jane	7	
Brodback, John	8	1	Stallions, Griffin	4		Dusting, Barbary	2		Beaker, Catharine	5	
Brodback, Adam	6		Smith, Benjamin	7		Daring, Henry	3		Bear, Jacob	5	
Crowdron, John	5		Stallions, Joseph	6		Dennis, Will	7		Blazer, Bear	1	3
Dediwick, Stephen	11		Simpson, Samuel	6		Dundon, John	4		Breeding, James	9	2
Everling, Elizabeth	2		Smith, Margaret	4		Denton, Thos	1		Beam, John	5	
Evens, William	7		Vaught, Christian	6		Delinger, John	12		Barner, Charles	4	1
Frye, John	5		Vaught, Simon	5		Finter, Conrad	6		Bailey, John	5	
Frye, Benjamin	8		Woodard, Thomas	5		Finter, Andrew	6		Conn, Michael	3	
Funkhouser, Christian	7		Johnston, George	7	1	Fetzer, Henry	13		Coleman, Jacob	3	
Funkhouse, Abm	8		Allen, Thos	10	5	Fravel, Henry	4		Cox, Jeremiah	4	
Funkerhouse, David	3		Allensworth, Phillip	7		Fravel, George	4		Combs, Soloman	4	
Funkhouser, Jacob	7		Bogus, Giles	6	3	Fetzer, Joakim	4		Combs, Job	11	
Feltner, Henry	14		Bull, Saml	5		Fetzer, George	3		Clevinger, Thos	7	
Greathouse, John	4		Bomfield, Gregory	7		Frye, Clarissa	2		Combs, Solomon	4	
Gates, Andrew	6		Barklyer, Michael	8		Grinstaff, George	6		Commer, John	6	
Hawk, Tobias	4		Curl, John	6		Hoover, Matthias	7		Dodson, John	8	
Hall, Aron	9		Cryer, Will	1		Howse, John	8		Deluney, James	4	
Hoover, Fredk	6		Coonse, Michael	13		Hoover, Balm	8		Dotson, Thomas	4	
Jemison, Robert	7		Countz, George	2		Huffman, John	7		Dodson, Samuel	4	
Keller, Joseph	5		Cain, Will	7		Harmon, Jacob	5		Fox, William	6	
Kackly, Valantine	7		Cain, Henry	2		Huffman, Ann	6		Foly, Selby	1	3
Lockmiller, John	8		Copeman, Nichs	11		Hart, Leonard	5		Flemming, William	6	
Lamby, William	4		Copeman, Andrew	7		Huffman, Christin	3		Fox, Peter	5	
Martin, John	6		Cloud, Henry	5		Harrow, David	2		Fugitt, Elizabeth	3	
Miller, George	11		Cloud, Danl	3		Hoover, Jacob	8		Fox, Allen	4	
Newall, Thomas	7	5	Carson, Simon	9	2	Hysel, Christian	4		Grove, Marks	10	
Piper, Henry	6		Cheek, Judith	3		Hysel, John	3		Greene, Jarves	6	
Piper, David	1		Cleeveland, George	9		Hommell, Eliza	1		Harding, Martin	4	
Peoples, John	5		Cleeveland, John	4		Halmich, John	6		Hugh, Ralph	4	
Price, Benjamin	8		Doctor, Martin	4		Hockman, Abm	4		Harding, Samuel	5	
Pinkly, Joseph	7		Delshaver, George	9		Houtz, Christopher	4		Heavens, John	3	
Pheasel, Michael	11		Ellzey, Thos	8		Keaner, Ulric	8		Heastant, John	4	
Pitman, Phillip	5		Funk, Henry	9		Keaner, David	5		Heastant, Jacob	11	
Rouer, Danl	5		Greenelch, Edward	8	5	Kennedy, Will	3	3	Heastant, Peter	7	
Setser, Martin	14		Hopewell, Joseph	8		Knisely, Anthony	10		Harding, Thomas	7	
Stickly, Benjamin	8		Henry, Will	12		Kibler, Phillip	3		Hust, Absolum	4	
Stickly, Jacob	8		Headly, Will	7	4	Knisely, Jacob	2		Hockman, Mary	8	
Supinger, Ulric	7		Hand, Elizabeth	6		Knisely, John	8		Hust, John	10	

SHENANDOAH COUNTY—Continued.

NAME OF HEAD OF FAMILY.	White.	Black.	NAME OF HEAD OF FAMILY.	White.	Black.	NAME OF HEAD OF FAMILY.	White.	Black.	NAME OF HEAD OF FAMILY.	White.	Black.
LIST OF ALEX'R HITE—con.			LIST OF ALEX'R HITE—con.			LIST OF ALEX'R HITE—con.			LIST OF ALEX'R HITE—con.		
Hurburger, Fred^k	9		Hancock, ——	10		Harpine, Phillip	9		Evens, Jeremiah	6	
Heplar, John	8		Harding, Nicholas	10	5	Holvah, Conrad	4		Evans Elijah	10	
Horskins, Joseph	3		Harding, Wilmouth	4	2	Holvah, John	2		Fox, Catharine	5	
Huckerson, Henry	3		Henry, Aron	4		Henton, Thos, Senr	5		Fawber, Valantine, Jr	5	
Hurst, Elijah	3		Harrel, James	9		Henton, Thos, Junr	3		Fawber, Valantine, S^r	5	
Hamp, Christly	5		Hutcheson, John	3		Halloneday, Robert	4		Fawber, Jacob	5	
Gillock, Hannah	2		Harding, Henry	6	2	Hangdon, Micha^l	1		Funkhouser, Isaac	9	
Ireland, James	8	1	Hill, George	4		Holeman, Danl	2	3	Foltz, Peter	8	
Jordon, Theodorus	10		Hankins, John	5		Holman, Jacob	9	14	Funkhouser, Christian	10	
James, Thomas	4		Harrel, Moses	11	4	Hall, James	2		Fillinger, Lewis	5	
Judge, Lettice	2		Hall, Francis	2	1	Haunsaker, Jacob	5		Glatfelter, Rudolph	9	
Jones, George	4		Jackson, James	2		Hoard, Thomas	1		Grous, Michael	8	
Job, Moses	7		Jackson, John	8		Hoop, Balsar	5		Good, William	4	
Job, Enoch	3		Keller, Abraham	6	2	Houser, Henay	9		Hudson, Richard	8	
Kiser, Charles	6		Leith, Ephraim	6		Jones, Evan	7		Hess, Abraham	6	
Kibler, Henry	6		Leith, Josia	10	2	Jones, Thomas	3		Helsley, Jacob	8	
Kiser, Andrew	2		Linch, Peter	5		Jones, William	4		Hutzel, Lewis	4	
Kiblar, Peter	6		Lashbrooks, William	9		Jones, John	8		Hoshaur, Henry	10	
Kelly, Amey	6		Leeth, James	6		Igelburger, Martin	4		Hudlow, Jacob	2	
Levisque, John	6	1	McKoy, James, Senr	3	2	Ingram, Francis	9		Keller, John	8	
Lear, John	5		Marshall, John	1		Kerick, Henry	8		Kengry, John	4	
Leath, Ebinezar	5		McKoy, Robert	4		Lewis, Mordica	6		Lindamude, Andrew	7	
McKay, Ab^m	10	2	McKoy, James, Junr	8	1	Lips, Henry	5		Lindamude, Michael	8	
Mathew, Madder	10		McKoy, Zachariah	5		Lokey, James	8		Lindamude, Christian	9	
McCoughlow, Will	5		Mathews, James	7		Moore, Thomas	4		Lonas, Leonard	9	
McDonald, John	3		McCarty, Isaac	6		Moore, Reubin	5		Messersmith, George	7	
Moody, Moses	10		Mathews, Alexander	3		Moore, Joseph	4	1	McLawlin, Michael	5	
McKoy, Jeremiah	10	1	Miller, James	6		Miller, Jacob	7		Mathias, John	7	
Nale, William	11		Miller, Peter	8		Moyers, Michael	3		Moyer, John	7	
Night, Emanuel	3		Mathews, John	6		Mowser, Michael	7		Nease, Ulric	4	
Noble, Coleman	7		Morgan, John	5		Miller, Daniel	3		Ocker, Phillip	9	
Noble, William	6		McKoy, George	7	1	McCarty, Daniel	6		Pitsenburger, Elizabeth	8	
Odell, Jonathan	9		Millar, Theophilus	7		McClusty, James	6		Poke, Adam	5	
Odell, Elizabeth	2		Netherton, Henry, S^r	2	1	Neece, Michael	6		Rencherd Jonas	9	
Odell, Ann	2		Netherton, Henry, Junr	11	6	Neece, John	4		Rumond, Henry	2	
Odell, James	10		Netherton, John	9	4	Newman, Walter	10		Rust, Valantine	7	
Odell, Leah	5	1	Nelson, William	8	2	Naff, Jacob	4		Reeder, Margaret	11	
Phraise, Samuel	10		Overall, John	8		Naff, Christian	4		Rust, Valantine, Jr	5	
Pangle, Catharine	5		Overall, William	8		Naff, John Henry	5		Rinker, George	6	
Stewart, Nathaniel	4		Pagit, John	6		Oneil, John	1		Rinker, Jacob, Senr	5	
Shaver, Jacob	9		Pagit, Reubin, S^r	2		Ord, Francis	5		Rinker Jacob, Jun	10	
Shock, Henry	7		Pagit, Theophilus	7	1	Peniwit, John	6		Ryan, Thomas	5	
Strickler, Daniel	6		Pagit, Reubin, Junr	7		Pence, Conrad	3		Sink, Jacob	3	
Strickler, Abram	8		Ragan, Charles	9	1	Reader, George	10		Seyger, Gabriel	9	
Spoon, Conrad	5		Ragan, William	4	1	Roush, Henry	5		Sink, Jacob, S^r	7	
Shank, Martin	8		Rawe, John	6	2	Roush, Phillip	10		Sivy, Mathias	10	
Stumpback, Jacob	7		Ramey, John	8	2	Roush, George	3		Stickly, Daniel	7	
Stover, Samuel	10		Snelling, Hugh	8	6	Roush, Jacob	5		Skaver, Michael	3	
Sandy, William	10		Safer, William	8		Roush, John, Senr	2		Sink, Barbara	6	
Strickler, Abraham, J^r	6		Sish, Thomas	9		Roush, John, Junr	4		Sine, Adam	4	
Skelton, John	7		Smith, John	11		Roush, Daniel	2		Smith, John	4	
Skelton, Moses	4		Thomas, William	13		Rouler, John	9		Smith, Adam	11	
Shank, Windle	3		Thomas, Joseph	1		Rambon, Jacob	8		Stout, John	7	
Smith, Nathan	5		Typton, William	8		Roush, John	7		Surber, Jacob	10	
Tyler, William	3	3	Wolf, John	8	1	Rork, David	8		Shouman, Stephen	5	
Quinn, Patrick	6		Allen, Josias	9	1	Russel, Elizabeth	4	1	Shoemaker, George	9	
Rufner, Benjamin	8		Alterfer, John	1		Roof, Jacob	7		Seyger, Conrad	8	
Strickler, Abram	6		Branner, Gaspour	7		Sievely, Catharine	9		Snider, George	9	
Rhineheart, Michael	9		Brennor, John	8	2	Slagle, John	10		Sowder, Frederick	7	
Trygler, Daniel	5		Brock, John	2	2	Stults, Peter	10		Tiesinger, Peter	6	
Wright, Isaac	8		Brock, Henry	9		Sigler, George	2		Weaver, Adam	3	
Vann, Elizabeth	8		Brock, Randolph	6		Snider, Christopher	6		Wocker, John	7	
Wood, Nehemiah	10	4	Beaver, Mathias	9		Snords (Widow)	4		Wolf, Mary	9	
Wood, John	6		Boughman, Henry	5		Seatron, Nicholus	3		Wolf, Jacob, Senr	3	
Wood, Samuel	8		Bishop, Peter	9		Seatron, John	5		Waggoner, Ulric	7	
Wiley, George	4		Brennemon, Abraham	7		Saltsman, William	5		Young, Christopher	4	
Young, Edwin	8	13	Circle, Andrew	8		Surrey, John	4		Zimmerman, John	8	
Young, Sinnitt	9	1	Circle, Michael	12		Saltsmanger, William	2		Coffelt, Elizabeth	9	
Whitson, Ruth	6	1	Clabough, Frederick	5		Stoutmoyers, Jacob	9		Miller, Elizabeth	6	
Arturbun, William	7		Cully, Jesse	6		Tully, John	6		Astrip, John	7	
Arturburn, Peter	11		Carver, John	6		Thomson, Thomas	3		Atwell, John	5	
Atwood, Gilbert	11		Carver, Martin	3		Wine, Michael	7		Alterfer, Antony	10	
Allan, Archibald	2		Call, Conrad	6		Wood, Charles	5		Branham, Graydon	5	
Atwood, John	3		Collins, John	7		Walters, Daniel	2		Branham, Richard	6	7
Allan, William	6		Cathey, William	8	8	Anthony, Wetisell	16		Brown, Thomas	8	
Blayer, William	7		Circle, George	10		Christian, Whisler	7		Bolton, William	7	
Burchhead, Abraham	5		Campbell, Charles	5		Brown, Christian	12		Brewbaker, Abram	13	
Burchhead, Eliazer	6	2	Cagey, Henry	11		Barb, Jacob	6		Bidler, Abraham	9	
Blayer, Samuel	2		Cagey, John	2		Burger, Michael	4		Baker, Phillip	2	
Bradford, John	7		Dobkin, John	4		Burgur, Henry	3		Broonback, Henry	10	
Combs, William	5		Durtt, Abraham	8		Barb, Abraham	7		Blowser, Abraham	1	
Cunningham, Rachael	8		Dobkin, Jacob	8		Brock, George	4		Boyer, Phelty	6	
Calfee, John	4		Dobkin, Reubin	4		Barb, Adam	6		Burton, John	9	
Calfee, Sarah	7		Dundon, Christly	4		Bower, Henry	5		Bellis, Henry	6	
Curl, John	7		Emry, Thomas	4		Bernherd, George	4		Boraker, Daniel	8	
Cuningham, Adam, Junr	7		Esterly, George	7		Boughman, Jacob	7		Collins, George	7	
Crume, Daniel	3		Fawcett, Benj^a	10		Barker, Peter	8		Cofman, David, Senr	5	
Combs, Nicholas	3		Fry, John	9		Bruan, Peter	1		Cofman, David, Junr	8	
Canada, Hugh	6	4	Farmer, Mathew	6		Coffman, Dorothea	3		Cofman, Martin	10	
Crume, Phillip	9		Fine, Thomas	4		Click, John, Senr	9		Counts, John	7	
Crume, Ralph	7		Fine, Vinott	6		Callander, Michael	8		Comer, Augustine	3	
Cunningham, Adam, Senr	8	2	Fine, John	6		Coffelt, George	11		Campbell, James	8	
Clevinger, Joseph	8		Funk, Peter	2		Coffman, Christopher	7		Comer, Martin	11	
Cuningham, Thomas	7		Forbes, Peter	3		Coffman, Andrew	11		Comer, Fred^k	9	
Day, Robert	3		Gordin, Charles	8		Coffelt, Christopher	7		Comer, Michael, Senr	7	
Dotion, William	2		Good, Henry	4		Delinger, Emanuel	4		Comer, Michael, Ju^r	5	
Dail, Isaac	5		Gore, Mary	4		Delinger, George	5		Cofman, John	7	
Grayham, John	13		Gore, Henry	9		Delinger, Magdalane	4		Comer, Phillip	3	
Gains, William	2		Good, Conrad	11		Dodson, Peter	7		Comer, Adam	3	
Gee, Richard	2		Gore, John	5		Dodson, John	2		Carter, William	8	
Harding, George	9	4	Good, Jacob	4		Eagle, William	1				

SHENANDOAH COUNTY—Continued.

NAME OF HEAD OF FAMILY.	White.	Black.	NAME OF HEAD OF FAMILY.	White.	Black.	NAME OF HEAD OF FAMILY.	White.	Black.	NAME OF HEAD OF FAMILY.	White.	Black.
LIST OF ALEX'R HITE—con.			LIST OF ALEX'R HITE—con.			LIST OF ALEX'R HITE—con.			LIST OF ALEX'R HITE—con.		
Cofman, Martin	8		Roodcap, George	14		Parrott, John	10		Hawkins, Benjamin	6	
Cofman, Christly	10		Rufner, Reubin	6		Parrott, Jacob	3	1	Hawkings, Joseph	8	
Davis, William	6		Rutherford, Robert	2		Parrott, Joseph	3		Kingery, Daniel	11	
Frees, John	5		Rudolph, Andrew	7		Pugh, Joseph	1	2	Keltner, Henry	7	
Fassett, Joseph	3		Robertson, John	5		Pugh, Jonathan	7		Kile, John	10	
Frimewood, Mathias	7		Rufner, Peter	9		Pence, Adam	8		Kelley, Peter	6	
Good, Gasper	10		Rufner, Emanuel	4		Pickel, Jacob	7		Moffett, Anderson	4	
Grove, Christian	11		Rukerboker, John	1		Reece, Henry	3		Matheny, Daniel	10	
Finter, Boston	3		Rukerboker, Adam	3		Rodes, Michael	3		Matheny, Joseph	6	
Finter, Mathias	7		Sparks, Austin	2		Reno, William	10		Michael, Henline	4	
George, John	2		Strickler, Jacob	13		Sunover, Henry	5		Matheny, William	6	
Grim, Jacob	3		Strickler, Joseph	10		Siver, Barnett, Jur	3		McClusty, Daniel	5	
Goring, Michael	6		Strickler, Isaac	5		Shue, Jacob	6		Milice, Elizabeth	3	
Hickman, Richard	7		Shully, Christian	4		Shue, Benjamin	4		Moore, William	6	
Heaston, John	5		Strickly, Benjamin	9		Stover, Ulric	7		McEnturf, Christopher	8	4
Harsburger, Christian	11		Smith, John	2		Stover, Danl	8		Moore, Reubin	3	
Hill, Francis	7		Spitler, Jacob	6		Sahm, Nicholas	9		Newton, Daniel	13	
Hite, Andrew	7		Spitler, Abraham	7		Spegle, Michael	5		Naff, Francis	7	
Hoke, William	8		Snider, Daniel	7		Spes, Danl	7		Miller, John	5	
Hay, Alexander	7	4	Stoneburger, Fredk	9		Stover, David	4		Moore, Jacob	10	
Hight, Daniel	8		Sowers, Henry	2		Tipton, Jno	10	4	Newton, Rebecca	1	
Huddell, Jacob	8		Sowers, Henry, Senr	3		Tipton, Saml	2		Osborn, Patiance	4	
Highmaster, Cutlip	3		Shank, John	3		Teter, Jacob	5		Ogdon, Colton	5	
Harshburger, John	10		Stoneback, Fredk	3		Witsel, Nicholas	6		Pence, Nicholas	7	
Jefferson, John	4		Sheets, George	8		Witsel, Henry	7		Penewit, Adam	3	
Kiblinger, Jacob	5		Sheets, John	4		Wever, Phillip	6		Parsons, John	7	
Kiger, Jacob	2		Snider, John	6		Wolande, Jacob	6		Penewit, John	6	
Kiblinger, Daniel	6		Sios, Andrew	5		Williamson, John	5		Painter, Jno	8	
Lourderback, John	2		Sower, Palsar	8		Windle, Augustine	6	1	Peters, Jonas	5	
Lourderback, David	5		Fyre, William	4		Winde, Augustine, Jur	4		Painter, Mathias	13	
Lourderback, Joseph	1		Taylor, John	4		Wilkins, Godphrey	6		Pence, Michael	7	
Long, Henry	1		Vincent, Joseph	9		Wisman, Nicholas	6		Penewit, Phillip	5	
Long, George	4	1	Wishett, John	1		Wisman, George	7		Pentecuf, Phillip	8	
Long, Margaret	4		Widock, John	3		Wisman, Thos	9		Passon, Thomas	5	
Long, Phillip	6	8	Wickle, Jacob	5		Windle, Stophley	4		Pleasant, Gacob	10	
Limbager, John	9		Widock, Henry	7		Windle, John	11		Peters, John	12	
Longmaker, Jacob	8		Wise, Adam	2		Westabarker, George	6		Peterson, Sarah	2	
Lusany, Laurence	1		Wise, Michael, Senr	5		Allen, Joseph	14		Richer, Christian	10	
Lionburger, Peter	5		Wolf, George	3		Bird, Abraham	13	3	Reed, Mitchel	8	
Mussulman, John	11		Zigler, George	9		Brinker, Conrad	12		Rubel, John	2	
Maggott, Christian	7		Boseman, Fredk	4		Bowman, George, jur	7		Rubel, Jacob	9	
Mauk, Daniel	10		Borden, Jacob	11		Bowman, George	7		Sheets, Barbara	2	
Maggott, Henry	5		Borden, Augustine	7		Birt, John	6		Snider, Charles	13	
Maggott, David	5		Borden, George	7		Bentley, Jacob	6		Skeen, James	3	
Maggott, Benjamin	4		Borden, Fredk	6		Bonds, John	8		Shireman, Peter	5	
Maggott, Margaret	6		Black, Martin	7		Bofman, John	3		Shireman, Barnet	5	
Newman, John	5		Bowman, David	6		Allen, Lydea	8		Sheets, Henry	5	
Newman, Thomas	6		Clime, peter	8		Bird, Mounce	18	1	Skeen, John	5	
Nun, Whartin	3		Calp, William	3		Albert, Nicholas	8		Smith, Joseph	3	
Nelson, John	3		Clime, Rinehart	2		Bishop, Peter	6		Shank, John	6	
Odell, Edward	1		Capp, Andrew	8		Burdidge, Robert	2		Smith, Isaac	4	
Overboccker, Fredk	6		Christian, Andrie	10		Burgit, Simon	11		Shutszer, Phillip	6	
Overbocker, Mary	2		Cofman, Isaac	9		Beale, Tavener	8	17	Spear, Peter	3	
Overbocker, Barbara	3		Dul, Nicholas	7		Bond, Edward	10		Stiver, Phillip	8	
Price, Anger	2		Dirting, Adam	6		Burdidge, Jno	5		Smith, Saml, Senr	9	
Price, Richard	6		Fisher, Simon	4		Carrel, Andrew	7		Smith, Saml, Junr	6	
Price, Edward, Jun	2		Fellor, John	3		Cuningham, Thomas	7		Soloman, Huddell	1	
Price, Edward	7		Hommon, Michael	11		Cesterson, William	7		Stickler, Sebastian	4	
Price, Zachariah	11		Hiser, Henry	6		Click, John	8		Smith, William	2	6
Price, Meridith	4		Huddell, Joseph	3		Counce, George	6		Shaver, Jacob, senr	12	
Price, John	8		Huddell, Henry	8		Carrell, John	5		Shaver, Jacob, Jur	6	
Price, Thomas	3		Holst, John	2		Celley, Nathan	6		Shavely, John	10	
Painter, Conrad	5		Hufman, Daniel	1		Downey, Darby	7		Taylor, Charles	11	
Pence, Daniel	7		Huddell, Daniel	1		Dobbins, Griffin	9		Conrad, Lorrey	5	
Pence, Henry	12		Hockman, Henry	7		David, Henry	7		Siple, Conrad	9	
Piper, Augustine	4	6	Kibler, John	5		Desk, Jacob	6		Turney, Danl	5	
Pibler, Lewis	5		Kibler, William	4		Dean, John	3		Turney, Peter	4	
Pibler, Christian	5		Kibler, Christian	5		Derk, John	8		Peter, Hallon	10	
Pibler, Jacob	7		Keller, George	2		David, William	8		Umphries, Elizabeth	1	
Prince, George	7		Keller, Conrad	5		Fitzmoyers, John	10		Wockker, Elias	4	
Painter, Joshua	4		Lameman, Benjamin	3		Foy, Henry	4		Weaver, George	9	
Peters, Balsar	3		Lameman, Benjamin, Jr	11		Funkhouser, Jacob	5		Weaver, George, Jun	3	
Prince, Cutlip	5		Muhlinberg, Peter	5	1	Foltz, John	9		Weatherhalt, Henry	2	
Prince, Phillip	3		Martain, Laurence	1		Giger, Adam	5		Wiatt, Jno	9	
Prince, Godphrey	4		Mock, Andrew	4		Holler, Henry	8		Waggoner, Jacob	3	
Prince, Phillip, Junr	6		Miller, Henry	7		Harrison, Burr	5		Young, Samuel	3	
Pence, Frederick	6		Mock, Jno	9		Hall, Jonathan	4	8	Lee, Perment	8	
Pence, John	8		Miley, Tobias	4		Hauton, Massa	4		Helvey, Peter	8	
Propes, Nicholas	6		North, John	9		Hallow, Peter, Junr	11		Lance, George	7	
Pence, Lewis	3		Parrott, Fredk	3		Houts, Wendle	8				
Roodcap, Peter	6		Parrott, Henry	6		Kelley, Abraham	4				

CUMBERLAND COUNTY.

NAME OF HEAD OF FAMILY.	White souls.	Dwellings.	Other buildings.	NAME OF HEAD OF FAMILY.	White souls.	Dwellings.	Other buildings.	NAME OF HEAD OF FAMILY.	White souls.	Dwellings.	Other buildings.	NAME OF HEAD OF FAMILY.	White souls.	Dwellings.	Other buildings.
Allen, William, Senr.	2	2	1	Smith, Robert	7	1	5	Meggs, Joel	4	1	3	Hubbard, Joseph	7	1	3
Arnold, Francis	10	1	7	Booker, Edward	3	1	5	Osborne, George	8	1	1	Hobson, Joanna	5	3	5
Amos, William	8			Smith, Bird	3	1	3	Richardson, Robert	4	1		Oakley, Erasmus	7	2	1
Austin, James	9	1	5	Smith, Larkin	3			Reynolds, Obadiah	6	1	4	Hobson, William	3	2	6
Anderson, Robert	11	1	9	Phillips, James	4	1	2	Richardson, Martin	9	1	5	Hobson, John	3	3	7
Anderson, William	9	1	3	Hill, Joseph (Estate)		1	5	Robinson, Jones	5	1	4	Hughes, Simon	7	2	2
Allen, Archer	9	2	11	Slaughter, John	10	1	3	Robinson, John	4	1	7	Hudson, William	10	2	2
Addams, Thomas	9	1	5	Nowel, Robert	9	1	2	Robinson, David	8	1	3	Winfree, John	4	2	3
Anderson, George	6	1	5	Bowles, John	3	1	2	Wilson, Benjamin	14	1	9	Ballew, Thoma	3	3	3
Anderson, Thomas	5	1	7	Burton, John	7	1	6	Winfree, Stephen	2	1	1	Cox, Josiah	3	1	1
Angelea, William, & David Burton	13	1	4	Nowel, John	5	1	3	Winfree, William	7	1	4	Hobson, Caleb	7	1	4
Anderson, Charles	9	1	5	Thompson, Josiah	7	2	4	White, Archeleaus	3	1	2	Hobson, William	7	2	3
Armstrong, Elisabeth	3	1	7	Mann, John	3	1	2	Wade, Henry	7	2	3	Colquit, Hezekh.	3	3	4
Asque, William	5	1		Mann, William Ford	3	1	3	Winefred, David	4	1	2	Hatcher, Sarah	7	2	5
Allen, Benjamin	9	2	3	Mann, David	2	1	1	White, John	7	1	4	Johnson, Job	8	2	3
Allen, Charles	4	1	3	Dowdy, William	11	1		Scruggs, Edward, Jun	5	1	2	Hobson, John	4	2	6
Brown, Benjamin	12	1	3	Dowdy, James	9	2	2	Scruggs, Mary	3	1	6	Booker, Richd	4	2	4
Cooke, Stephen	4	1	4	Martin, Benjamin	9	1	3	Scruggs, Drury	10	1	3	Southall, John	6	2	3
Charlton, Abram	7	2	5	Weatherford, Richd	6	2	3	Scruggs, Edward	10	1	2	Weatherford, Joseph	5	2	4
Corley, Vaul	4	2		Farmer, John	4	2	3	Scruggs, Thomas	6	1	2	Maddox, Wm	10	5	5
Corley, William	3	1		Orange, William	4	2	1	Sanderson, John	3	1	3	Bellemy, Elisha	5	2	
Charlton, John	5	1	4	Thompson, Bartlet	11	1	6	Self, William	6	1	2	Murphey, John	13		
Dickeson, David	11	1	3	Jinkings, Joseph	11	1	2	Sanderson, William	7	1	3	Flippin, Francis	10	2	1
Elliot, Richard	7	1		Davenport, William	8	1	3	Sanderson, Ann	8	1	6	Hobson, William	3	3	6
Farmer, Forrest	13	2	4	Ballow, William	7	1	3	Smith, Laurence	6	1	1	Hobson, Thoms	8	2	2
Fretwell, Richd	8	1	1	Jones, John	6	1	8	Trent, Alexander	8	4	50	Robinson, Feild, Senr	2	1	3
Fretwell, William	8	2	3	Jones, Reubin	1	1	1	Thomas, Job	10	1	4	Robinson, Feild, Junr.	6	1	
Hopkins, William	5	1	1	Jones, Harrison	3	1	3	Thomas, Phinehas	4	1	2	Wilburn, Christian	6	2	2
Holman, John	9	1	4	Dodson, John	9	1	1	Anderson, Samuel	2	1	10	Jones, Harrison	2	1	4
Hughes, Stephen	8	1	5	Bowles, Ben	4	1		Aikin, James	7	1	2	Meader, Jesse	9	2	5
Hughes, Powel	8	1	4	Doss, James	10	2	3	Allen, Daniel	9	1	10	Mosby, Jesse	7	1	
Holman, John, junr	4			Smith, Robert	7	1		Allen, William	1			Hatcher, Drury	8	1	2
Johns, Thomas, junr	7	1	3	Smith, Catherine	5	1	3	Bolling, Archd	7	1	10	Robinson, Stephen	6	1	4
Lee, John	11	1	5	Woodfin, George	6	1	3	Bradley, John	7	1	3	Fuqua, Joseph, Sn	7	4	8
Lee, Joseph	9	2	12	Orange, Joshua	5	1		Beacham, Isaac	5	1	5	Fuqua, Joseph, Junr	11	3	2
Leakes, James	9	1	2	Moore, Thomas	7	1	1	Barkiville, Jno.	1	1	6	Hudgeons, James	8	2	
Meridith, William	9	2	5	Faris, Jacob	5	1	6	Barkerville, George	4	1	3	Gentry, Simon	2	1	6
Michaux, Joseph	13	1	9	Skipwith, Henry	22	4	20	Brown, William	4	2	3	Fraser, William	6	2	2
Medore, Joel	10	1		Austin, James	9	1	5	Brown, Robert	9	1	1	Richardson, Richd	2	1	2
Neilson, Andrew	4	1	7	Anderson, Robert	11	1	9	Beck, Judith	6	1	3	Cowhan, Jacob	6	2	
Price, John	6	1	4	Anderson, William	9	1	3	Barker, Charles	4	2	6	Scruggs, Tabitha	6	3	6
Phelps, Samuel	8	1	8	Allen, Archer	9	2	11	Calland, Joseph	2	2	11	Robinson, Hezk	6	2	2
Pearce, Mary	6	2	4	Addams, Thomas	9	1	5	Cary, Archd	15	6	58	Robinson, John	4		
Richardson, Isham	7	1	7	Anderson, George	6	1	5	Cox, Francis	9	1	2	Winfree, Charles	10		
Randolph, Colo Richd	18	3	18	Brown, Robert	8	1	2	Colquit, John	9	1	7	Flippin, John	14	1	2
Russell, William	8	1	1	Bradley, William	5	1	3	Caycie, Shadrack	11	1	2	Flippin, Jacob	4	3	3
Richardson, William	5	1	6	Brown, Clement	12	1	6	Coleman, Wm	5	1	6	Carter, David	7	1	1
Ranson, Flamstead	8	1	6	Bond, Wright	4	1	3	Caldwell, Thomas	10	1	3	Walton, Robert	7		
Randolph, Beverley	2	1	8	Burton, John	6	1	1	Coleman, Patience	5	1	6	Hill, William C.	4	1	3
Sandefurs, Abram (Esta)	8	1	4	Burton, William	4	1		Coleman, Gulleelmeis	3	1	3	Moore, John	13	2	3
Sharpe, Joseph	7	1	2	Bond, William	4	1	1	Coleman, Parmenus	3			Haskins, Creed	10	2	5
Spencer, William	6	1	1	Bartee, Thomas	8	1	7	Clopton, Robert	1	1	10	Walton, Martha	2	4	4
Shapard, William	11	1	3	Baughan, Tucker	12	2	3	Coleman, Elliot	1			Minton, William	8	2	1
Tucker, St George	5	1	9	Towns, James	8	1	7	Chaffin, Joseph	8	1	4	Douglass, Robert	2	2	2
Trent, Peter Field	9	1	7	Bradley, Hezekiah	6	1	4	Daniel, John	2	1	9	Sandidge, John	4	2	1
Venable, John (Esta)	4	1	4	Bradley, Rebecca	4	1	1	Dean, Chesley	4	2	2	Nash, Thoma	2	3	5
Vanter, Samuel	10	1	2	Coleman, Thomas	6	1	1	Ellison, Garriot	4	1	6	Clarke, William	5	1	2
Webber, Phil.	8	1	8	Criddle, Ann	6	1	1	Edwards, Grissel	8	1	3	Cuningham, William	9	1	2
Wright, George	2	1	2	Cobbs, Jesse	7	1	5	Ford, John	6	1	14	Anderson, Jesse	6	1	4
Wright, Saymer	4	1	2	Clements, Edward	5	1	4	Findley, David	1			Angelea, Joseph	5	1	
Walker, William	11	3	10	Daniel, William	8	1	9	Guthery, Alexander	7	1	2	Allen, Charles	6	1	2
Williams, Matthias	6	1	4	Dunkam, John	9	1		Guthery, Henry	4	1	1	Anderson, John	6	1	3
Williams, Jane	5	1	3	Douglass, James	6	1	2	Guthery, William	7	1	5	Allen, Richd	14	1	4
Wright, Thomas	11	2	5	Doss, Joshua	10	1	2	Gadberry, Wm	7			Allen, Benjamin	9	1	2
Webber, Richd	6	2	2	Edwards, Moutre	2			Hill, John	8	1		Angelea, James	9	1	3
Williams, Roger	7	1	3	Edwards, Andrew	6	1	2	Hill, Dennit	6	1	2	Angelea, Bartlet	4	1	3
Woodson, John	10	1	6	Edwards, Archer	9	1		Hendrick, Elisabeth	4	1	9	Anderson, Rhoda	4		
Walker, William, junr.	1	1	5	Faulkner, Nicholas	8	1	2	Hendrick, Obadiah	5	1	4	Blanton, James	6	1	2
Wright, Archer	5	1	6	Faulkner, William	1			Harmon, Henry	1	1		Booker, Byrd	5	2	1
Wright, John	4	1	2	Farmer, James	8	1	3	Harrison, Precilla	5	1	14	Brown, James	3		
Walker, Warren	5	1	14	Hudgins, Holloway	2	1	3	Harrison, Cary	1		8	Brown, George	5	1	3
Walker, Thomas	1			Holland, Thomas	10	1	8	Johns, Thomas	2	1	7	Barber, Charles	7	1	1
Walker, John	3	1	1	Hubbard, Moses	6	1	5	Johns, Jesse	3	1	4	Basham, James	7	1	
Williams, Samuel	10	1	4	Hill, Elisabeth	8	1	10	Mason, Catherine	5			Brown, Davis	8	1	2
Woodson, Miller	12	1	7	Hammondre, Sarah	4	1		McRae, Christopher	9	1	8	Cox, Matthew	6	1	9
Duffie, Mary	4	1	2	Jinkings, Joseph Hull	10			Oslin, Sam	5	1	4	Corley, James	1		
Duffie, Edmond	7	1		Hudgeons, James	12	1	6	Price, John	7			Durham, James	9	1	2
Fowler, Alexander	3	1	3	Holland, Stephen	2			Sims, Mary	6	1	7	Guthery, Bernard	10	1	
Langhorne, Maurice	17	1	8	Hunibus, Henry	3			Southall, James	3	1	7	Glenn, William	1		
Carter, Theodrick	5	1	6	Hatcher, Archer	8	1	1	Swann, Ths T.	5	1	4	Gaines, Bernard	4	1	3
Hudson, John	3			Hughes, Caleb	7	2	2	Stinson, Joseph	7	1	2	Holland, Mary	6	1	9
Sims, Benjamin	4	1	3	Holloway, Samuel	13	1	6	Starkey, Joseph	5	2	2	Holland, Jonas Meder	4	1	3
Sims, John	8	1	1	Holloway, William	8	1	3	Starkey, John	1			Lee, Richd	2	1	8
Sims, Claiborne		2		Hill, Isaac	4	1	4	Trent, Peter Field	5	1	6	Lee, Charles	4	2	2
Woodson, John	5	1	7	Hammondree, John	3			Thornton, John	5	1	3	Medows, Jacob	1		
Ballew, Charles		1	2	Jefferson, John	10	1	9	Woodson, Stephen	6	2	10	Macon, Hartwell	7	1	5
Martin, Henry	14	1	3	Junior, Hugh	4	1	4	Walker, John	7	1	13	Macon, Henry	9	1	29
Griffen, John		1	3	Keeling, George	10	2	10	Williams, Nathanl	5			Pearce, Jeremiah	9	1	6
Davenport, John	13	1	3	Langhorne, Sarah	8	2	11	Wilson, Richd	9	1	9	Randolph's, John (Esta)	6	1	6
Keeble, Humphry (Estate)		1	5	Minter, John	9	1	1	Wilkins, James	1	1	4	Scruggs, Henry	2	1	6
Keeble, Walter	8	1	3	Melton, Nathan	8	1	2	Winecutt, Richd	4			Seay, John	7	1	2
Davenport, David	11	1	3	Melton, Samuel	10	1	4	Alderson, John	5	2	2	Stewart, John	2	1	3
Patterson, Nelson	4	1	3	Minter, James	6	1		Walton, Thomas	8	3	3	Thompson, John	3	1	3
Burton, Mary	6	1	3	Meaders, Jehu	13	1	7	Hatcher, John	4	1	1	Womack, Wm, Senr	1	1	3
								Flippin, Philp	5	2	1	Womack, Nathan	6	1	5

GLOUCESTER COUNTY.

NAME OF HEAD OF FAMILY.	White souls.	Dwellings.	Other buildings.
ABINGDON PARISH—LIST OF JOHN SEAWELL.			
Lewis, Warner	11	2	41
Cary, Samuel	16	3	12
Perrin, John	7	2	21
Stoakes, Christopher	3	1	2
Henderson, Francis	6	1	....
Haywood, Isaac	6	1	....
Jenkins, James	7	1	2
Jenkins, Caleb	7	1	....
Cooke, Shem	4	....	....
Stoakes, Thomas	3	1	1
Fleming, William	3	1	1
Hogg, George	4	1	....
Easter, Elizabeth	5	1	....
Burwell, Lewis (Estate of)	26	5	36
Foster, John	8	2	2
Leavit, Catherine	6	1	....
King, Francis	7	....	....
Cake, Lewis	4	1	....
Cake, Anthony	9	1	1
Haywood, Catherine	2	1	6
Thurston, Sarah	2	1	8
Shackelford, Zachariah	10	1	1
Powell, Edmund	6	1	....
Shackelford, Warner	6	1	....
Hall, Thomas	2	1	....
Jenkins, John	5	1	....
Lewis, Addison	4	1	5
Leavit, Ptolemy	5	....	....
Jerdone, Thomas	5	1	....
Shackelford, James	6	1	....
Walker, Edward	8	1	....
Cake, Jeremiah	3	1	....
Walker, Mansil	7	1	....
Mitchell, Richard	4	1	....
Hall, Beverley	5	1	1
Scott, Mary	6	1	5
Dobson, John	2	1	....
Cluverius, Benjamin	9	2	12
Tomkies, Mary	7	1	7
Dobson, Grace	3	1	1
Smith, James	5	1	1
Lewellyn, Christopher	3	1	....
Camp, Rebecca	2	1	....
Pate, Jacob	7	1	....
Harvey, John	5	1	1
Evans, Ann	4	1	....
Gardner, John	3	1	....
Dixon, James	4	1	6
Mourning, John	11	....	....
Haywood, William	9	1	2
Dudley, William	3	1	....
Mitchell, Thomas	3	1	....
Witherspoon, John	1	1	....
Powell, Thomas	9	1	2
Busbie, Edward	8	1	1
Hall, Joseph	3	1	1
Hall, Richard	3	1	3
Hall, Lewis	5	1	....
Walker, Martin	6	1	....
Pate, Obadiah	3	1	....
Belvin, William	7	1	....
Teazle, William	9	1	4
Walker, Robert	5	1	....
Walker, Spencer	5	1	1
March, John	6	1	....
Oliver, John	5	1	....
Hobday, John	7	1	5
Lewis, James	2	1	4
Lucas, William	5	1	....
Hogg, Stephen	5	1	....
Dews, Mildred	5	2	....
Vincent, John	6	1	4
Thornton, Francis	4	1	6
Hudgen, Robert	10	....	....
Raphel, Southey	6	....	....
Burton, John	5	1	....
Evans, John	4	2	....
Freeman, Thomas	4	1	1
Haywood, Richard	9	1	....
Hobday, Richard	7	1	5
Camp, John	8	1	7
Powell, Mary	5	1	1
Thompson, Charles	8	1	1
Vaughan, Elizabeth	4	1	1
Row, Hansford	9	1	8
Row, Bannister	10	1	3
Vaughan, William	5	1	6
Powell, John	8	1	....
Vaughan, John	6	1	1
Thurston, Sarah, jun	6	2	8
Stevenson, Catherine	2	....	....
Lively, Charles	2	1	2
Smith, Thomas	7	1	3
March, Richard, Junr	4	1	1
Saunders, William	5	....	....
Row, Rebecca	2	1	6
Mason, Thomas	5	1	1
Rowe, Zachariah	7	1	5

NAME OF HEAD OF FAMILY.	White souls.	Dwellings.	Other buildings.
ABINGDON PARISH—LIST OF JOHN SEAWELL—con.			
Powell, Seymour	1	1	1
Page, John (Rosewell)	21	1	6
Pepin, William	3	1	1
March, Richard, Senr	4	1	1
Crutchfield, Charles	7	1	2
Oliver, Thomas, junr	6	1	1
Oliver, Thomas, senr	2	1	5
Belvin, John	5	1	....
Rider, Solomon	4	....	....
Smith, Michael	9	1	....
Haywood, Jacob	10	1	....
Austin, Gabriel	4	1	....
Austin, John	9	1	....
Brown, Charles	9	1	....
Rider, James	3	1	....
Pointer, James	6	1	....
Davis, Richard	8	1	....
Hall, Joseph, junr	7	1	....
Hogg, Fielding	9	1	....
Hall, Thomas, junr	7	1	....
Haywood, Abraham	9	1	....
Mufie, John	5	1	....
Powers, James	5	1	....
Shackelford, Zachariah, junr	7	1	....
Jenkins, Obdh	12	2	....
Jenkins, Caleb	3	1	....
Hogg, Richard	3	1	1
Hobday, Francis	6	1	1
Moore, Edward	7	1	1
Pigg, William	3	1	1
Moore, Isaac	6	1	1
Seawell, John	7	1	6
Seawell, Elizabeth	1	....	....
Seawell, Joseph	9	1	3
Wadlington, James	5	1	2
KINGSTON PARISH—LIST OF THOMAS SMITH.			
Gwyn, Hugh	4	1	9
Addams, Ambrose	5	1	2
Hudgen, Elizabeth	5	1	3
Bragg, Benjamin	4	1	7
Robberts, Thomas	6	1	4
Sadler, Robert	8	1	3
Whiting, Thomas	6	....	....
Dawson, James	6	1	2
Hudgen, Hugh	9	1	2
Hudgen, Robert	11	1	2
Gayle, Joseph	10	1	4
Wescomb, Nicholas	7	1	5
Foster, Christopher	6	1	2
Foster, Elizabeth	6	1	3
Williams, Daniel	3	1	3
Williams, Gregory	5	1	....
Minter, Anthony	7	....	....
Williams, John	4	1	2
Wright, William	5	1	2
Buckner, William	6	1	5
Trice, James	5	....	....
Foster, George	8	1	....
Jarvis, Francis	8	1	1
Davis, Hilligan	1	1	1
Davis, Isaac	8	1	1
James, Thomas	3	1	....
Pugh, Elias	6	1	....
Pugh, William	3	1	1
Matthews, Robert	7	1	16
Dunbarr, Going	3	1	1
Smith, Peter	11	1	5
Armistead, Jno, deced (Esta of)	6	1	9
Williams, Francis	8	....	....
Hudgen, John, Senr	3	1	3
Owen, William	6	1	....
Hudgen, Anthony	7	1	2
Basset, William	8	1	2
Hudgen, William, Senr	4	1	3
Winder, Ann	7	1	3
Harris, Johanna	3	1	....
Powell, John	4	1	1
Winder, Thomas	1	1	3
Shipley, Ralph	7	1	3
Harris, Henry	2	1	3
Harris, James	7	1	....
Harris, Matthias	5	1	....
Shipley, John	4	1	1
Shipley, Joseph	7	1	1
Winder, Thomas	2	1	1
Powell, Henry	3	1	1
Winder, Edmund	2	1	....
Anderson, Edward	7	1	3
Smith, Isaac	10	1	9
Foster, Robert	22	1	7
Foster, Joel	8	1	1
Foster, John, Senr	1	1	3
Foster, Jesse	4	....	....

NAME OF HEAD OF FAMILY.	White souls.	Dwellings.	Other buildings.
KINGSTON PARISH—LIST OF THOMAS SMITH—con.			
Owen, George	7	....	....
Parsons, John	7	1	3
Hunley, Henley	5	....	....
Stuart, James	8	....	....
Weston, Thomas	10	....	....
Weston, George	4	....	....
Hurst, John, Senr	5	1	2
Ashbury, Joseph	5	1	2
Gwyn, Robert	5	1	2
Anderson, Edward, junr	2	1	....
Fitchet, Daniel	8	1	6
Hugget, Kemp	5	1	....
Jones, James	7	1	6
Billups, Joseph, junr	2	....	....
Respess, Richard	7	1	5
Respess, William	5	1	3
Anderson, John	5	1	1
Fitchet, William	4	1	3
Jarvis, Francis	5	1	2
Buckner, Samuel	1	1	1
Elliott, John, Junr	4	1	1
Wooden, George	8	1	1
Parrot, John	4	1	1
Dawson, Thomas	8	1	1
Merchant, Ann	4	1	....
Jarvis, Edward	4	1	....
Plummer, Judith	4	1	3
Tabb, Thomas	4	1	10
Smith, Thomas	4	1	19
Thomas, James	10	1	3
Dudley, Dorothy	4	1	8
Ransone, Robert	3	....	....
Dudley, George	5	1	5
Davis, Thomas	7	1	5
Soaper, William	7	1	1
Lewis, Thomas	5	1	2
Elliott, John	6	1	9
Gayle, Matthew	10	1	3
Merchant, Elisha	6	1	4
Miller, James	4	1	....
Brownley, James	7	1	1
Ripley, Andrew	4	1	1
Hobday, Richard	7	....	....
Hobday, Brookes	7	1	3
Davis, Edward	6	1	3
Davis, Elizabeth	1	1	1
Machen, Margaret	2	1	3
Machen, Mary	6	....	1
Borum, John	7	1	....
Borum, Edmund, Senr	3	1	4
Borum, Edmund, Junr	7	1	3
Booker, James	3	1	4
Whites, William	8	1	2
White, James	7	1	2
White, William	6	1	1
White, Thomas	1	....	....
White, John	2	....	....
Hayes, John	11	1	6
Ransone, Thomas	6	....	....
White, John	1	....	....
Davis, Richard H	3	1	2
Tabb, John	7	1	8
Tompkins, Hannah	4	1	4
Halls, Ann	2	1	3
Foster, Peter	5	1	3
White, Edward	7	1	1
Iveson, Abraham	6	1	5
Enos, Francis	4	1	3
Culley, Ralph	6	1	4
Cary, Robert	2	1	16
Enos, William	6	1	1
Hughes, Gabriel	8	1	13
Willis, James	3	1	2
Green, Robert	7	1	4
James, Walter	8	1	1
Read, John	5	....	....
Williams, Samuel	10	1	10
Smith, Armisteud	4	1	6
Thomas, Mark	8	1	....
Hunley, William	4	1	....
Hudgen, Humphrey, Senr	4	1	6
Hudgen, John	2	1	....
Minter, John	8	1	4
Parsons, James	4	1	1
Brookes, George	6	1	4
Tritchet, John	5	1	3
Tinsley, David	7	1	5
Blakes, Thomas	5	1	3
Keeble, Elizabeth	4	1	3
Armistead, Robert	6	1	7
Degge, William, Senr	10	1	7
Thomas, William	10	1	2
Hurst, Richard, Senr	8	1	5
Callis, James	8	1	3
Callis, William (Estate)	5	1	4
Gayle, Hunley	4	1	3
Hudgen, George, Senr	2	1	2
Hudgen, George, junr	6	1	1

NAME OF HEAD OF FAMILY.	White souls.	Dwellings.	Other buildings.
KINGSTON PARISH—LIST OF THOMAS SMITH—con.			
Cooke, Ignacious	4	1	1
Allermon, John	4	1	3
Robins, Peter	9	1	3
Owen, Edmund	2	1	....
Callis, Robert, Senr	5	1	1
Callis, Richard	7	1	3
Hayes, Mary	3	1	4
Forrest, George, Senr	4	1	5
Forrest, Thomas	5	1	1
Lewis, John	7	1	3
Forrest, Abraham	3	1	....
Forrest, Edmund	6	1	1
Forrest, John	7	1	2
Knight, Henry	8	1	6
Hayes, Thomas, Junr	2	1	4
Terrier, Philip	7	1	6
Ripley, Andrew	4	1	1
Armistead, John	5	1	2
Hudgen, James	10	1	1
Ripley, Richard	6	1	1
Gayle, John	7	1	3
Hayes, Thomas	7	1	5
Callis, Ambrose	7	1	7
Miller, Mary	2	1	8
Foster, Francis	5	1	1
Harper, James	6	1	4
Brownley, Edward	8	1	....
Hudgen, John	6	1	....
Kerr, Andrew	1	1	2
Tompkins, William	7	1	3
Lucas, William	3	....	....
Knights, Joseph	1	1	1
Davis, Joseph	8	1	4
Hudgen, Perrin	6	1	1
Foster, Josiah	7	1	5
Morris, William	8	1	4
Adams, Zachariah	7	1	3
Little, John	6	1	....
Brownley, Archibald, Sen.	5	1	2
Brownley, Archibald, Jun.	6	1	....
Brownley, James	6	1	1
Brownley, William	6	1	....
Jarvis, John	7	1	....
Brownley, John, Jun	7	1	2
Brownley, Thomas	6	1	2
Hughes, Edwd	8	1	8
Armistead, Richard	7	1	1
Hayes, Hugh	5	1	4
Lewis, Christopher	9	1	3
Lewis, Robert	7	1	2
Armistead, Dorothy	2	1	3
Bassett, Richard	6	1	4
Bassett, William, jun	5	1	4
Armistead, George	5	1	5
Minter, William	6	1	....
Brooks, Thomas	3	1	1
Samson, John	4	1	3
Hudgen, Houlder	6	1	3
Billups, Robert	8	1	4
Morris, John	10	....	....
Peed, Lewis	8	1	4
King, William	4	1	....
Atherton, Elizabeth	3	1	....
Atherton, John	6	....	....
Pallister, John	5	1	....
King, John	11	1	5
Carter, Jane	4	1	1
Armistead, Churchhill	5	1	3
Hodges, Richard	6	1	3
Hodges, William	2	1	....
Armistead, William (Este)	12	1	33
Ransone, Letitia	3	1	6
King, Joseph	5	1	2
Merchant, Ambrose	6	1	2
Miller, Francis	6	1	4
Eddin, Jno, Sen	....	2	5
Eddin, Dawson	8	1	1
Eddin, Sam	5	1	1
Glen, Duncan	8	1	3
Gwyn, Jno	5	1	1
Gwyn, Harry	3	1	2
King, Joseph	5	1	2
Lane, Ezekiel	4	1	3
Billups, Thomas	10	1	6
Jarvis, Francis	6	1	2
Davis, Humphrey	2	1	3
Owen, John	4	1	....
Christian, Martha	2	1	....
PETSWORTH PARISH—LIST OF JAMES HUBARD.			
Thornton, Presley	3	1	4
Pollard, James	6	1	3
Curtis, Ann	10	1	6
Dabney, Benjamin	3	....	9
Hall, Thomas	8	1	2
Dillard, John	7	1	3

GLOUCESTER COUNTY—Continued.

NAME OF HEAD OF FAMILY.	White souls.	Dwellings.	Other buildings.	NAME OF HEAD OF FAMILY.	White souls.	Dwellings.	Other buildings.	NAME OF HEAD OF FAMILY.	White souls.	Dwellings.	Other buildings.	NAME OF HEAD OF FAMILY.	White souls.	Dwellings.	Other buildings.
PETSWORTH PARISH—LIST OF JAMES HUBARD—continued.				**PETSWORTH PARISH—LIST OF JAMES HUBARD—continued.**				**PETSWORTH PARISH—LIST OF JAMES HUBARD—continued.**				**WARE PARISH—LIST OF MORDECAI THROCKMORTON—continued.**			
Davis, Samuel	6	1	3	Wiatt, Sarah	1	1	3	Acra, Thomas	5			Robins, William, Jun	8	1	4
Russay, James	3	1		Walker, John	5	1	2	Wilkins, Nat	1	1		Robins, William, Sen	1	1	4
Baytop, James	5	1	8	Waggoner, Elizabeth	1	1	1	Brookes, Thomas	4	1	3	Duval, William, jun	6	1	6
Shackelford, Mordᵉ	1	1	5	White, Lawrence	6	1	1	Glass, David	6	1	3	Howlet, John	5	1	10
Mason, Peleg	5			West, Mary	9	1	1	Hubard, James	4	1	20	Wadlington, Nathaniel	8	1	8
Harwood, Lucy	5	1	8	Wiatt, John	8	1	9	Robinson, Mary	4	1	6	Gregory, Mary	7	1	14
Kemp, Betty	2	1	11	Morris, William	4	1	4	Wood, Lewis	7	2	14	Tower, William	4	1	
Harwood, Susannah	1	1	2	Morris, Thomas	7	1		Lewis, Nicholas	4	1	3	Iveson, Edwards	2	1	2
Harwood, Ann	5	1	5	Mason, William	6	1	2	Spratt, Robert		1	9	Boswell, Machen	2	1	6
Thrift, William	9	1	4	Lewis, John	7			Anderson, Matthew	4	1	12	Gressit, James	3	1	4
Thornton, Meux	3	1	5	Laughlin, James	2	1	4	Glass, Thomas	3	1	1	Whiting, Beverley	7	1	7
Thornton, Sterling	2	1	12	Lewis, Thomas	5	1	2	Carney, John	3			Wilkins, Thomas	6	1	1
Taliaferro, Richard	6	1	5	Kemp, Elizabeth	11	1	7	Cooke, Thomas	3	1	4	Boswell, Thomas	4	1	9
Thrift, Thomas	4	1	1	Kemp, Mary	5	1	5	Collier, James	5	2	2	Lemmon, James	6	1	3
Sears, William	9	1	5	Keeningham, Jnᵒ	5	1	7	Blassingamie, William	7			Buckner, Frances	2		
Soles, Dawson	3			Kemp, Peter	5	1	5	Wiatt, John, Junᵣ	2	1	6	Buckner, John, Jun	1	1	2
Snow, Cuthbert	6	1		Jones, Richard	5	1	12					Buckner, Thomas	1	1	7
Shaw, Elizabeth	6	1	1	Jones, Richard, jun	3	1		**WARE PARISH—LIST OF MORDECAI THROCKMORTON.**				Tureman, William	8	1	1
Stubbs, Laurence	9	1	3	Haynes, George	7	2	2					Marable, Benjamin	3	1	4
Stubbs, Peter	5	1	2	Hope, Benjamin	5	1	1	Tomkies, Colᵒ Francis	8	1	3	Johnston, John	3	1	
Stubbs, John	9	1	3	Hall, William	3	1	6	Pryor, Christopher	9	1	9	Singleton, Isaac	8	1	6
Robinson, Ben	4	1	5	Hibble, Elizabeth	6	1	6	Baylop, Thomas	2	1	12	Browning, John	8	1	1
Robinson, Christopher	1	1	8	Hughes, Henry	4	1	3	Dawson, Thomas	6	1	3	Hall, John	4	1	7
Riley, Thomas	5	1	2	Gressit, John	5	1	4	Proctor, Richard	7	1		Fox, John			5
Royston, Richard	9	1	3	Guthrie, Richard	3	1	2	Fontaine, Revᵈ James M.	23	10		Clayton, Jasper	2	1	5
Pollard, William	3	1	2	Grymes, Phil.		1	13	Douglass, William	6	1	2	Prosser, John	5	1	1
Pollard, James				Garland, Elizabeth	1	1	11	Langford, John	9	1	2	Eanos, John	6	1	4
Padgett, John	7	1	1	Garland, Christopher	5	1	7	Buckner, John, Sen	1			Lewis, Henry	3	1	2
Pursell, Henry (Estate)	6	1	3	Guthrie, Samˡ	5	1	6	Hobday, Mary	6	1		Stubblefield, John	3	1	4
Pollard, Frances	1	1	8	Grumley, Frances	3	1	3	Tabb, Philip	17	2	32	Stubblefield, Simon	7	1	5
Pollard, Julius	6			Gressit, Thomas	1			Lutwytch, John	3			Hall, Henry, Jun	1		
Pointer, Henry	5			Hasley, Thomas	5		1	Fletcher, Nathan	8	1	4	Pointer, Mary	3	1	11
Pursell, William	2	1		Haynes, John	6	1		Fletcher, Thomas	2	1		Hall, Francis	5	1	4
Pursell, Robert	2			Groom, Mary	5			Kemp, William	9	1	4	Hall, William, jun	6	1	6
Perry, Gregory	6			Fary, Sarah	5	1	2	Davis, Reubin	6	2		Nuttall, James, jun	4	1	10
Preller, William	5	1	1	Taylor, Nat	7	1		Dunston, Almen	3			Stubblefield, Simon	3	1	3
Pursell, John	4			Freeman, James	7	1	1	Dunston, James	5		1	Green, George	6	1	4
Naughten, William	10	1	1	Davis, Richard	3	1	6	Howlet, John	2	1	2	Nuttall, George	5	1	5
Coleman, Richard	6	1	2	Douglass, Thomas	6	1	3	Wright, Thomas	7	1	2	Pointer, Michael	4	1	6
Stubbs, John S.	5	1	2	Davis, Anthony	6	1	3	Throckmorton, Susannah	3			White, William	6	1	
West, Thomas	8	1	2	Dutton, James	12	1	1	Hughes, Thomas	7			Bales, Thomas	3	1	
Preller, John	7	1	2	Duvall, William	12	1	12	Hughes, John	2	1	6	Cooke, Madˡ	5	1	5
Massey, Robert	10	1	6	Dickenson, Elizabeth	5	1	6	Debnam, Thomas	4	1	4	Kuningham, Mary	6	1	2
Morris, William		2	1	Duvall, Ann	3	1		New, John	9	1	4	Willis, Francis	11	1	12
West, Henry	4	1		Coats, Robert	6			Cooke, John	7	1	17	Dixon, John	4	1	8
Goalder, Thomas	5	1	4	Collawn, Mildred	2	1	4	Cooke, Elizabeth	4	1	5	Throckmorton, Warner	6	1	7
Currey, Richard	3	1		Booker, Lewis	6	1	11	Bellamy, Joseph	2	1	2	Throckmorton, Madˡ	7		4
Lemon, Dickson	6	1	3	Bristow, John	4			Snow, John	4			Boswell, John	2	1	6
Wright, Richard	9	1	4	Booker, John	4			Bunn, Henry	4			Robbins, John	6	1	4
Minor, Mary	4	1	7	Bentley, William	6			Lyon, Enoch	1		1	Boswell, Abraham	10	1	8
Minor, John	4	1		Burton, Henry	6	1	10	Whiting, Peter B.	7	1	7	Richardson, John	4	1	3
White, William	7	1	4	Brooking, John	6			Williams, Lewis	4	1	3	Pool, Robert	2	1	2
Buckner, Baldwin	3	1	3	Baine, Lewis	3			Booth, George		1	10	Dance, William	4	1	2
Philpots, Benjamin	9	1	4	Baker, Elizabeth	8	1	2	Eanos, Lewis	8			Baine, John	8	1	
Lemmon, Richard	8	1	5	Bentley, James	5	1	8	Urey, John	6			Davis, John	9	1	3
Lemmon, John				Brooking, Samuel	11	1	6	Griffin, John	5	1	2	Geddy, Robert	5	1	1
Minor, Benjamin	4	1		Booth, William	5	1	16	Pursell, Peter	7	1	2	Jones, John	5	1	3
Yates, Robert	7	1	12	Booth, George	8	1	18					Ransone, Augustine		1	2
Wiatt, Sarah	4	1	9	Ash, John	6	1	6					White, John	3	1	4

HAMPSHIRE COUNTY.

NAME OF HEAD OF FAMILY.	White souls.	Dwellings.	Other buildings.	NAME OF HEAD OF FAMILY.	White souls.	Dwellings.	Other buildings.	NAME OF HEAD OF FAMILY.	White souls.	Dwellings.	Other buildings.	NAME OF HEAD OF FAMILY.	White souls.	Dwellings.	Other buildings.
LIST OF JOHN WILSON.				**LIST OF JOHN WILSON—con.**				**LIST OF JOHN WILSON—con.**				**LIST OF JOHN WILSON—con.**			
Whitecotton, James	9	2		Hagler, William	5	1		Shobe, Rudy	4	1	2	Pendleton, Richard	6		
Poague, Robert	4	1	2	Weaze, Jacob	7	1	2	Peterson, Martin	8	1	2	Hier, John	6	1	2
Caplinger, Jacob	7	1	1	Wease, Adam, Junᵣ	6	1		Powers, Martin	9	2	2	Ours, Sithman	5	1	7
Algire, Michael	7	1	2	Cooper, Valentine	8	3	1	Wease, Michael	2			Boots, George	4	1	2
Mallow, Henry	4	1	1	Fisher, George	10	1	3	Carr, Conrod	7	1	1	Caterman, Daniel	5	1	2
Cann, Michael	3	1		Crites, Philip, Junᵣ	4	1	1	Miller, Michael	10			Rule, Henry	6		
Lymes, John	5	1	1	Porter, Robert	6	1	4	Thorn, Frederick	4	1		Weaze, Adam, Senᵣ	14	1	2
Toopes, John	7	1	1	Strader, Christopher	10	1	3	Crites, Jacob	7	1		Weaze, John	6	1	1
Moser, Adam	11	1	3	Henkle, Barbara	6	1	3	Peterson, Jacob	8	1	2	Weaze, Michael	3	1	
Lambert, Barnabas	7	1		Morrow, Ralph	2	1	1	Buzzard, Henry	12	1	2	Fent, George	2	1	
Carpender, Conrod	7	1		Louther, George	5	1		Hudson, John	3	1		Smith, Yokle	10	1	1
Cuningham, James	8	1	5	Ligget, Francis	5	1	2	Regar, Anthony	10	2	1	Keller, George	5	1	2
Carpender, Jacob	6	1		Crites, Philip, Senᵣ	3	1	1	Hahn, John	7			Stambough, Philip	8	1	
Harpole, Adam	5	1	1	Mace, Nicholas	9	1	3	Kuykendall, Jane	9	1	1	Dobson, ——	4	1	
Stetler, John	3	1		Hogbine, John	5	1	2	Cuningham, William	8	1	2	Brookes, Richard	2		
Borah, Charles	5	1		Shobe, Jacob	6	1	3	Cuningham, Robert	8	6	7	Coones, Lovey	3	1	
Wise, Jacob	6	1	2	Shobe, Rudy	8	1	3	Cutrack, Henry	8	1	1				
Wise, Bastian	2	1		Wirey, Robert	5	1		Rorebaugh, Henry	10	1	1	**LIST OF JOB WELTON.**			
Wise, Martin	2	1		Turner, Solomon	3			Sits, George	10	1	3				
Lightholse, John	4	1	1	Coones, Peter	5			Smith, John	4	1		Lansisko, Henry	10	1	3
Harpole, Adam, Junᵣ	3	1	2	Wilson, John	8	5	3	Shobe, Martin	8	1	3	Peck, George	6	1	1
Fultz, Philip	6	1	3	Butcher, Paul	6	1		Armintrout, Christopher	9	1	4	Horse, Peter	4	1	
Casner, John	6	1	4	Petro, Leonard	5	1		Furst, Valentine	9	1	2	Hier, Jacob	3	1	
Judy, Nicholas	6	1	3	Straley, Christian	7	1	1	Hier, Leonard, Senᵣ	5	1	4	Miller, Michael	4	1	
Judy, Martin	2	1		Mallow, Adam	6	1	3	Hier, Leonard, Junᵣ	5	1	2	Buffinberry, Peter	6	1	1
Judy, Henry	6	1	2	Caplinger, John	8	1	2	Spillman, John	7	1	3	Bonner, William	6	1	
Shields, Peter	4	1		Wise, John, Junᵣ	5	1		Horst, George	3	1	3	Shook, Jonas	6	1	1
Wise, John, Senᵣ	8	1	4	Likens, John	7	1	2	Hier, Lewis	3	1	1	Shook, Lawrence	8	1	3
Davis, Theophilus	6	1		Hagler, Bastian	9	1	3	Mace, John	6	1		Gilmore, Sarah	6	1	1
Peterson, Margaret	5	1	1	Stookey, Magdalan	4	1	1	Smith, David	7			McCave, Ross	6	1	1

HAMPSHIRE COUNTY—Continued.

NAME OF HEAD OF FAMILY.	White souls.	Dwellings.	Other buildings.
LIST OF JOB WELTON—continued.			
Gouge, Charles	12	1	....
Thixton, Thomas	7	1	1
Hudson, David	8	1	....
Woolf, John	9	1	....
Bodkin, Richard	7	1	....
Craig, David	3	1	1
Sadouskie, Samuel	9	1	1
Crow, David	2	1	2
Smith, Robert	9	1	2
Reel, David	7	1	....
Davis, Thomas	6	1	....
Stroud, Adam	10	1	....
Fleming, James	4	1	....
Hale, Daniel	6	2	....
Mace, Isaac	4	1	....
White, Ebenezer	8	1	....
Badgley, Anthony	11	2	3
Regan, Jacob	10	1	1
Scott, Benjamin, Senr	7	1	2
Eaton, Thomas	9	1	1
Eaton, Benjamin	3	1	....
Hudson, John	3	1	....
Childers, William	8	1	....
Morris, John	7	1	1
Clarke, Robert	8	1	....
Ward, George	3	1	....
Simpson, Alex^{r}	7	1	3
Ward, Sylvester	12	1	3
Welton, Jesse	9	1	2
Simpson, Jonathan	7	1	1
Scott, Alexander	6	1	1
Seymour, Richard	3	1	2
Seymour, Felix	9	1	4
Seymour, Abel	1	....	2
Seymour, George	1	....	2
Orahood, Alexander	9	1	....
Cheneworth, Jonathan	6	1	....
Huffman, Christopher	9	1	3
Hawk, Catherine	6	1	3
Howman, Sithman	5	1	2
Whitman, George	7	1	2
Robinson, John	7	1	3
Clarke, Abraham, Senr	4	1	2
Clarke, Abraham, Junr	2	1	1
Clarke, Henry	8	1	2
Scott, Benjamin, jun	7	1	1
Roby, William	3	1	1
Roby, Prior	8	1	1
Car, Henry, Senr	7	1	3
Curle, William	7	1	3
Seymour, Thomas	4	1	1
Hornback, Michael	8	1	3
Byrns, Philip	6	1	....
Jane, Joseph	7	1	....
Yazle, Jacob	4	1	....
Thomson, Jethro	8	1	....
Day, Leonard	6	1	1
Eaton, Joseph	5	1	....
Roby, Thomas	8	1	1
Smith, William	8	1	....
Carr, Michael	3	1	....
Watts, Jonathan	5	1	....
Watts, Thomas	6	1	....
Stinglee, Jacob	5	1	2
Stacey, Thomas	3	1	....
Whetstone, George	8	1	....
Richardson, Jonathan	7	1	....
Badgley, David	10	1	3
Schoonover, Benjamin	8	1	1
Sims, William	5	1	....
Everman, Michael	11	1	1
Harper, Adam	8	1	1
Mouse, Daniel	9	1	1
Judy, Margaret	8	1	1
Roy, Joseph	10	1	1
Peterson, Michael	7	1	1
Miller, Leonard	2	....	....
Borrer, Thomas	10	1	....
Clarke, John	5	1	....
Miller, George	5	1	1
Power, Valentine	10	1	3
Shill, George	3	1	....
Cubberly, James	8	1	....
Radcliff, Stephen	7	1	1
Curle, Jeremiah	10	1	....
Christie, James	4	1	....
Bean, Benjamin	6	1	2
Clarke, Watson	5	1	1
Welton, Job	11	1	5
LIST OF ABRAHAM HITE.			
Higgins, Peter	5	2	2
McNeal, John	6	1	3
Ratcliffe, Benjamin	6	1	2
Snyder, Christopher	8	1	5
Neal, Edward O	12	1	1

NAME OF HEAD OF FAMILY.	White souls.	Dwellings.	Other buildings.
LIST OF ABRAHAM HITE—continued.			
Obanion, Joseph	6	1	8
McNamarr, Joseph	9	1	....
Newill, Joseph, sen^{r}	3	1	2
Davis, Thomas	4	1	3
Newill, Joseph (Gent.)	19	1	4
Bullitt, William	8	1	3
Delonga, John	7	1	2
Hider, Adam	12	1	6
Bush, Henry	2	....	....
Extine, Leonard	1	....	....
McDavid, James	5	1	....
Yoakam, Michael	4	1	....
Gibboney, Robert	4	1	....
Tucker, Jacob	11	1	3
Talbut, Thomas	6	1	....
Carr, William	4	1	2
Reid, George	6	1	2
Yoakam, Elizabeth	5	1	2
Freeman, Rosanna	9	1	....
Reid, John	7	1	2
Reid, Elizabeth	4	1	2
Dayton, Susanah	5	1	....
Brown, Thomas	9	1	....
Wood, Ebenezer	5	1	1
Renick, William	11	1	8
Renick, John	10	1	5
Suttles, Henry	6	1	....
Batson, Mordecai	5	1	2
Shrote, Peter	7	1	....
Bradford, John	5	1	....
Delm, John	2	1	....
Green, Lewis	5	1	....
Batman, John	11	1	....
Berry, Reuben	8	1	3
Lawrence, John	10	1	2
Ashby, Jesse	7	1	1
Ashby, Peter	7	1	4
Ashby, Henry	7	1	4
Sibley, John	5	1	2
Hartley, Hugh	6	1	....
McCarny, James	4	1	1
Timmons, Samuel	11	1	3
Ashby, Stephen	10	1	5
Hardin, Evangelist	6	1	3
Carr, John	6	1	1
Pancake, John	3	1	1
Bonnett, Henry	2	1	1
Godfrey, William	5	1	2
Suffolk, John	5	1	....
Godfrey, Edward	10	1	3
Shepherd, John	9	1	2
Shepherd, James	2	1	....
Batson, Mordecai, J^{r}	5	1	2
Sage, William	11	1	1
Neale, John	8	1	1
McKenny, John	4	1	1
Roby, Peter	9	1	4
Branson, Amos	8	1	2
Vanmeter, Joseph	9	1	7
Pancake, Andrew	8	1	3
Tweey, Daniel	6	1	1
Tweey, John	2	1	....
Logan, David	5	1	3
Neale, Thomas	4	1	3
Shumate, James	8	1	1
Darling, William, j^{r}	5	1	2
Euldy, Thomas	2	1	....
Buzzard, Rhudolph	2	1	....
Darling, William	6	1	5
Dixon, John	7	1	1
Dean, Thomas	12	1	2
Moore, Conrod	5	1	3
McCarty, Thomas	6	1	5
Foley, John	9	1	2
Weidner, Jacob	6	1	1
White, Charles	4	1	....
Saturly, Samuel	7	1	....
Vanmeter, Garret	5	1	11
Vanmeter, Isaac	4	1	3
Cade, Major	12	2	1
O'Connor, Daniel	7	1	1
Parsons, James	8	1	6
Renick, Elizabeth	5	1	2
Thomas, Enoch David	9	1	2
Higgins, John	3	1	8
Blackburn, William	4	2	....
Snall, William	4	1	2
Vanmeter, Jacob	7	1	3
Bonham, Hezekiah	10	1	1
Ward, Joseph	6	1	....
Lynch, Patrick	2	1	2
McLamare, Philip	9	1	....
McLamare, John	8	1	....
Hite, Abraham	8	1	15
Likings, Richard	4	1	....
Best, Jacob	4	1	....
McNeal, Daniel	9	1	6

NAME OF HEAD OF FAMILY.	White souls.	Dwellings.	Other buildings.
LIST OF STEPHEN RUDDELL.			
Ruddell, Stephen	12	1	4
Chilcott, Eber	2	1	2
Ellis, Philip	11	1	1
Vandevander, Jacob	8	1	2
Vandevander, Peter	3	....	....
Chilcott, Joel	3	1	....
M^{c}farling, Thomas	7	1	1
Wilkins, Matthias	11	1	5
Wilkins, George	6	1	2
Homan, Jacob	8	1	2
Roby, William	4	1	....
Roberts, David, sen^{r}	6	1	2
Elswick, Thomas, sen^{r}	7	1	2
Kidner, George	7	1	3
Wise, Christopher	9	1	3
Dean, Joshua	8	1	....
Shorebaugh, David	2	....	....
Warden, William	5	1	3
Lewis, George	10	1	3
Taaffe, Elizabeth	2	1	1
Abman, John	8	1	2
Baker, Jacob	5	1	2
Viney, Stephen	3	1	2
Broughton, William	8	....	....
Baker, William	7	1	1
Pain, Evan	3	1	....
Baker, James	9	1	1
Sperry, Peter	3	1	2
Miller, Jacob	4	1	4
Denton, Thomas	8	1	....
Denton, Jane	2	1	1
Chrisman, Jacob	8	1	4
McHendry, William	10	1	1
Miller, Antony	7	1	3
Roberts, David, jun^{r}	4	1	3
Roberts, Thomas	5	1	2
Wilson, David	5	1	4
Claypole, John	13	1	3
Claypole, James	11	1	4
Claypole, Abraham	1	1	....
Osborne, Josiah	12	1	3
Nees, John M	6	1	1
Calf, James M	4	1	....
Thomas, James	7	1	3
Claypole, James, sen^{r}	1	1	3
Claypole, Jesse	7	....	....
Harrison, John	6	1	2
Harrison, Simeon	2	1	....
Chilcott, Eli	4	1	....
Baughman, Andrew	5	1	....
Pepper, Joshua, sen^{r}	5	1	1
Pepper, Joshua, Junr	5	1	....
Lowry, Adam	8	1	....
Rounsoval, Benjamin	6	1	....
Denton, Jacob	9	1	4
McBride, Francis	3	1	....
Laughland, James	5	1	....
Lowry, Samuel	2	1	1
Dixon, Thomas	8	1	....
Pugh, Jacob	8	1	3
Powell, Samuel	2	1	1
Hamilton, Henry	5	1	1
Baker, Samuel	7	1	1
Tevalt, Andrew	9	1	1
Fry, Henry	9	1	7
Sly, David	1	....	....
Tevalt, John	1	....	....
Cherry, Andrew	8	1	3
Rust, Jacob	3	1	1
Tevalt, John, sen^{r}	10	1	2
Salt, Thomas	3	1	1
Richison, William	6	1	1
Tharp, Andrew	4	1	1
Orton, Robert	11	1	3
Moore, James	13	1	4
Hughes, James	10	1	3
Hughes, Jonathan	4	1	2
Littler, Thomas	11	1	5
Wilson, Henry	8	1	1
Hunter, Thomas	3	1	....
Hennery, John	7	1	....
Young, John	4	1	....
Oldacre, Isaac	7	1	2
Steward, James	9	1	....
Steward, Joseph	1	....	....
Hawk, John	6	1	3
Ohaver, Christopher	4	1	1
Parsons, Alexander	8	5	1
Williams, Thomas	2	....	....
Swisher, Nicholas	8	1	2
Shoemaker, Peter	5	1	2
Michael, George	11	1	2
Money, Bryan	4	1	2
Wilson, William	6	1	4
Neel, Benjamin	5	1	....
Hill, Joseph	10	1	2
Stone, James	9	1	2

NAME OF HEAD OF FAMILY.	White souls.	Dwellings.	Other buildings.
LIST OF STEPHEN RUDDELL—continued.			
Hill, Daniel	2	1	1
Davis, Samuel	9	1	....
Robinson, Joel	9	1	3
Ohaver, Cornelius	4	1	....
LIST OF WILLIAM VANSE.			
Rawles, John	5	1	1
Vanse, William	11	1	6
Reuding, Reuben	3	1	....
Bruce, Charles	4	1	2
Smith, John	6	2	4
Hall, Joseph	4	1	....
Royse, Aaron	7	1	....
Tevalt, Nicholas	9	1	2
Shanton, Raymond	4	1	1
Champ, William	3	1	....
Sharpless, Joseph	6	1	....
Slater, Richard	2	....	....
Waterman, John	2	....	....
Bezley, Jesse	2	1	....
Seavers, Nicholas	8	1	4
Bond, Thomas	6	1	4
Kyger, John	7	1	2
Sinks, Jacob	10	1	....
Johnston, John	8	1	....
Bogle, James	8	1	1
Myers, Francis	10	....	....
Parker, John	3	1	4
Myers, John	2	....	....
Matthews, Jonathan	6	....	....
Wheeler, Ignatius	9	2	4
Kyger, George	9	1	1
Waterman, James	7	1	2
Barnet, Mene	5	1	....
Panter, Benjamin	7	1	1
Savage, John	6	1	1
Ravenscroft, Samuel	8	1	1
Giddens, James	6	1	....
Kite, Henry	2	1	....
Kite, Saml	3	1	....
McCarty, Edward	6	1	3
Marsh, Henry	10	3	4
Ashby, Benjamin	6	2	....
Robinson, Roger	5	1	....
Baker, John	7	1	3
Rush, Lewis	5	1	....
Moore, John	5	1	....
Ravenscroft, John	6	1	2
New, Peter	7	1	3
Ravenscroft, William	2	1	....
Miller, Henry	4	1	1
Pigman, Moses	7	1	2
Ferrand, Isaac	10	1	1
LIST OF ABRAHAM JOHNSON.			
Parker, Nathaniel	10	1	6
Emery, Edward	4	1	2
Price, Arjalor	9	2	2
Liter, Henry	8	1	2
Vandiver, William	14	1	1
Fleming, James	9	2	1
Harsman, Jacob	8	1	....
Outs, George	4	1	....
Guset, Peter	6	1	....
Pillman, Peter	11	1	1
Howell, Jonathan	4	....	....
Huffman, Henry	5	1	....
Cuningham, John	6	1	....
Neiff, Henry	10	1	2
Booker, Philip	8	1	1
Rasner, Gideon	3	1	....
Hendricks, Abraham	3	1	....
Clarke, Stephen	9	1	1
Boyce, Richard	9	1	7
Jones, Samuel	11	1	1
Hearsman, Philip	5	1	....
Beard, George	8	1	2
Spencer, John	8	1	1
Street, John	4	1	....
Burgit, Jacob	8	1	3
Hazell, Henry	8	1	2
Wise, Adam	6	1	3
Holoback, Thomas	12	1	....
Wolfe, George	8	1	1
Castleman, Lewis	8	1	4
Stagg, John	5	1	4
Caulson, Margaret	3	1	9
Taylor, George	5	1	1
Cannon, Thomas	7	1	1
Thompson, John	7	1	1
Williams, Moses	3	....	....
McBride, John	7	1	....
Beverly, John	5	....	....
Barton, Kimber	7	1	....

HAMPSHIRE COUNTY—Continued.

NAME OF HEAD OF FAMILY.	White souls.	Dwellings.	Other buildings.
LIST OF ABRAHAM JOHNSON—continued.			
Brandenburg, Matthias	12	1	1
Bonefield, Samuel	4	1	....
Wolf, David	2	1	....
Miller, Michael	7	1	3
Wayler, Michael	3	1	2
Pearsall, John	4	1	3
Duging, Patrick	3	1	....
Jones, John	10	1	2
Jones, Solomon	3	1	....
Jones, David	6	1	1
Jones, Peter	4	1	....
Beeler, Charles	5	1	3
Baiorn, Job	3	1	5
Martin, Samuel	5	1	....
Howell, William	7	1	2
Umstot, Peter	8	1	2
Parker, James	3	2	....
Cooper, Joel	11	1	1
Johnson, Okey	6	1	2
Cooper, Job	3	1	....
Kent, John	9	1	....
Burkit, Frederick	3	1	....
Parker, Benjamin	5	1	2
Totten, Ezekiel	9	1	1
Carn, Andrew	4	1	2
Titford, Isaac	3	1	....
Cooper, Thomas	10	1	1
Reasner, Jacob	10	1	3
Bogard, Jacob	5	1	2
Johnson, William	9	1	2
Johnson, William	3	1	....
Johnson, Abraham, Junr.	7	1	4
Johnson, Abraham, senr.	3	1	1
Wright, Gabriel	9	1	1
Thompson, Francis	2	1	1
Thompson, David	5	1	1
Rodgers, William	11	1	2
LIST OF MICHAEL CRESAP.			
Chapman, Luke	5	1	3
Long, Jacob	9	1	3
Farpley, James	3	1	2
Mann, Christopher	7	1	....
Bowman, Charles	4	1	....
Jacobs, John J	....	1	3
Stoddard, James	5	1	1
Dopson, William	3	1	3
Bell, William	2	1	....
Young, Henry	4	1	....
Scoot, John	9	1	1
Flarty, James	5	1	....
Roy, Abraham	3	1	1
Reeves, Austin	4	1	1
McGlolan, Daniel	2	1	2
Reeves, Benjamin	9	1	3
McGlolan, Daniel, Junr.	5	1	2
Aughney, Darby	5	1	3
Ross, Robert	9	1	....
Roy, Thomas	6	1	2
Walker, Robert	9	1	3
Donelsol, James	9	1	1
Sullivan, Jeremiah	6	1	1
Book, Anthony	3	1	1
Book, Robert	8	1	1
Spelman, Robert	4	1	1
Simmons, Henry	2	1	....
Shrodes, John	8	1	....
Hanes, Joseph	5	1	2
Rhodes, Thomas	5	1	1
Benat, Robert	6	1	1
Toselwight, William	5	1	1
Martin, James	7	1	....
Bennett, Robert	6	1	1
Hargus, William	8	1	....
Skidmer, Mary	2	1	....
Cockran, Susannah	6	1	....
Carter, Henry	10	1	2
Cole, Francis	6	1	....
Garvis, Robert	6	1	1
Murphey, James	9	1	3
Lockwood, William	4	1	2
Carruthers, George	7	1	2
Kee, Sarah	5	1	....
Ward, Stephen	8	1	....
Martin, Euriah	4	1	4
Martin, James	8	1	....
Martin, Samuel	2	1	....
Fisher, Daniel	2	1	....
Sholders, Conrad	8	1	....
Plank, Frederick	8	1	....
Mator, Philip	7	1	1
Glaze, Conrad	7	1	4
Miers, Francis	5	1	....
Glaze, Andrew	5	1	2
Made, John	2	1	1
Cresap, Michael	5	1	5

NAME OF HEAD OF FAMILY.	White souls.	Dwellings.	Other buildings.
LIST OF MARQUIS CALMES.			
Cuppy, John, Junr.	4	1	....
Blue, John, Junr.	8	1	2
Cuppy, John	5	1	2
Berry, Enoch	5	1	2
Foy, Gabriel	6	1	5
Kuykendall, Henry	6	2	1
Blue, John	12	1	2
Peterson, Peter	6	1	3
Blew, Garret	2	1	....
Corbin, David	6	1	1
Boslar, John	3	1	....
Williamson, Samuel	9	1	4
Blew, Michael	7	1	2
Corbin, William	6	1	2
Leard, Michael	5	....	....
Beatty, George	8	1	1
Beatty, Robert	4	....	....
Berry, Joel	7	1	2
Vancehock, John	5	....	....
Harness, Adam	6	1	3
Hoffman, Conrad	7	2	1
Huffman, Henry	4	1	2
Carabaugh, Peter	3	1	....
Fiddler, Jacob	1	....	....
Kuykendall, John	6	1	2
Fiddler, George	3	1	....
Atcason, William	6	1	....
Miller, Isaac	6	1	3
Bierly, John	5	....	....
Hoff, Peter	5	1	....
Popejoy, Terrence	5	1	....
Hill, Gasper	5	1	....
Ferguson, James	5	....	....
Popejoy, John	4	1	....
Ferguson, Robert	8	1	3
Parsons, Isaac	4	1	3
Means, Isaac	11	1	1
Decker, John	7	1	3
Smock, Jacob	5	1	....
Devore, David	7	1	....
Plough, Jacob	7	1	....
Plough, Alder	9	1	1
Norman, Sarah	9	2	....
Collins, Thomas	7	1	6
Woad, Thomas	6	1	....
Vanmeter, Isaac	7	1	4
Daily, William	3	1	....
Allen, David	5	1	1
Hoge, John	9	1	3
Purgit, Henry	3	1	1
Williams, Nathaniel	6	1	....
Murphey, Gabriel	2	1	....
Miller, Abraham	6	1	1
Cullins, John	3	1	....
Campbell, John	3	1	....
Hoarsman, Stophel	5	1	....
Bell, Zepheniah	11	1	1
Hodger, Reuben	2	....	....
Glaze, John	5	1	3
Norman, Benjamin	4	1	....
Kuykendall, Nathaniel	7	1	8
Parker, Job	6	1	2
Crosby, Abel	6	1	....
Etchason, Samuel	2	....	....
Campbell, John	4	1	5
Brown, Daniel	5	....	....
Barber, James	7	1	1
Casey, Nicholas	8	2	8
Forman, John, Junr.	7	2	7
Smith, William	5	1	1
Buffington, Mary	9	1	5
Buffington, David	2	1	....
Forman, William	8	1	3
Forman, John	10	1	2
Brechen, William	3	1	....
Sanders, Charles	4	1	2
McGuire, William	10	1	1
Blew, Uriah	7	1	....
Grim, Balsar	5	....	....
Harod, Ephraim	8	1	....
Buffington, Joel	8	1	1
Williams, Richard	10	1	6
Glaze, George	6	1	4
Ball, James	7	....	....
Gray, Friend	6	1	....
Kyger, Wm.	8	1	....
Miller, John Henry	8	1	....
Dew, Samuel	10	1	9
Calmes, Marquis	5	1	4
Waters, John	10	1	....
Claypole, Jeremiah	6	1	2
Hawk, Henry	8	2	2
LIST OF ELIAS POSTON.			
Engle, William	1	....	1
Williams, Thomas	5	....	1
Dever, John	11	....	4

NAME OF HEAD OF FAMILY.	White souls.	Dwellings.	Other buildings.
LIST OF ELIAS POSTON—continued.			
Thompson, John	6	....	3
Thompson, William	2	1	1
Thompson, Joseph	5	2	....
Sander, Henry	8	1	3
Parril, John	9	1	2
Chenoweth, John	5	1	1
Pritchard, Margaret	2	....	2
Hase, Thomas	2	1	....
Carlyle, William	7	....	1
Edwards, Samuel	6	1	1
Cheshire, Samuel	6	....	1
Anderson, William	5	1	2
Byrns, John	5	....	1
Lashby, William	6	....	1
Williamson, William	10	1	3
Male, Wilmore	10	....	2
Male, Wilmore, senr.	2	....	1
Blew, James	9	....	9
Hoge, John	4	....	2
Belford, Barnaba	4	1	3
Parish, Joseph	8	....	3
Parke, Andrew	4	1	4
Parke, John	3	1	....
Myers, George	8	....	2
Ogin, Peter	9	....	2
Jenkin, Evan	6	....	3
Carlin, Andrew	7	....	2
Lewis, John	4	1	....
Jenkin, Ann	7	....	4
Parke, Samuel	6	....	1
Rogers Owen	7	1	4
Hyett, James	3	....	2
Candy, Martha	8	1	1
Couden, James, Junr.	5	1	1
Couden, James, senr.	9	....	4
Morgan, William	7	....	1
Newcomb, Daniel	9	....	....
Crock, George	6	1	2
Swisher, John	11	....	1
Hawk, Isaac	10	1	2
Peters, John	7	1	....
Hardin, William	4	1	3
Huber, Jacob	14	1	1
Mckever, Paul	10	1	4
Shannon, Ruth	4	....	2
Forman, David	11	1	3
Keran, Patrick	10	....	2
Porter, Eli	4	....	2
Porter, Philip	9	....	2
Tracy, Archibald	2	1	1
Daniels, Mary	8	....	1
Pugh, Thomas	5	....	1
Lewis, David	6	....	....
Mcferson, William	1	....	1
May, John	5	1	1
Butler, Richard	7	....	1
Harris, John	8	1	1
Royce, John	2	1	1
Anderson, James	3	....	1
Maloy, James	5	....	1
Corbin, Charles	3	....	1
Sargent, James	7	1	4
Pearson, David	3	....	1
Sly, George	7	....	2
Enochs, Enoch	13	1	2
Bills, William	6	1	2
Bills, John	3	....	1
Enochs, Elizabeth	1	1	....
Slone, Daniel	8	1	1
Milslagle, Andrew	6	1	2
Milslagle, George	3	1	....
Kezoil, Michael	6	....	1
Pritchard, Rees	7	1	5
Hyett, Evan	8	1	4
Powell, Abraham	5	....	4
——, Frederick	6	....	2
Lupton, Isaac	6	....	2
Park, John	12	1	7
Ruder, Joseph	9	....	1
Lawrence, Michael	7	....	2
Jenkin, Jacob	8	1	1
Edwards, Thomas	8	1	2
Horn, George	6	....	3
Kail, George	7	1	3
Chenoweth, John	11	1	6
Devore, John	3	....	1
Nixon, George	3	2	2
Brown, John	6	1	2
Barnhouse, John	11	....	2
Shriad, Charity	4	....	1
Harris, Thomas	8	1	1
Smith, John	10	....	1
Winterton, John	8	1	1
Clutter, Jacob	12	1	....
Crawford, William	5	....	1
Bumgarner, Rudolph	8	1	3
Kale, John	4	....	1
Albin, James	3	....	1

NAME OF HEAD OF FAMILY.	White souls.	Dwellings.	Other buildings.
LIST OF ELIAS POSTON—continued.			
Emberson, Thomas	7	....	3
Milburn, William	2	....	....
Hael, Peter	7	....	2
Shanks, Joseph	5	....	2
Hubbard, John, junr.	6	1	3
Hubbard, Jacob	8	1	2
Hubbard, John	3	1	3
Arnold, John	9	1	3
Davis, Elijah	5	....	1
Arnold, Andrew	3	1	1
Slone, John	7	....	2
Haden, Webb	3	....	2
Reid, Jeremiah	9	....	3
Reid, George	8	1	2
Pugh, Robert	9	1	4
Pugh, Samuel	4	....	3
Pugh, Jesse	2	....	....
Martin, John	7	1	2
McGraw, Morris	6	....	3
Milburn, William, Junr.	6	1	2
Milburn, Joseph	6	....	1
Beall, George	6	1	2
Richards, William	5	....	1
Henderson, Sampson	3	....	1
Ritchard, John	10	....	1
Cuningham, John	7	....	1
Smith, James	8	1	4
Pugh, Bethel	9	....	2
Linegar, William	1	....	2
Emmitt, Jacob	8	....	3
Ashbrook, Levi	12	1	2
Corbin, Ann	4	1	3
Asberry, Joseph	5	1	3
Busby, John	9	....	2
Howard, Parson	6	....	2
Hogarty, John	5	....	1
Claton, Thomas	8	....	4
Posgrove, Jacob	6	....	1
Martin, George	11	....	4
Lander, Jacob	5	1	3
Carruthers, James	6	....	2
Murphy, William	5	....	2
Pugh, Jonathan	9	1	3
Pugh, Daniel	2	1	1
Fisher, Jacob	12	1	5
Kisner, Jacob	8	....	1
Hawkins, John	6	....	1
McBride, John	9	....	3
Kanada, Thomas	7	....	2
——, Elizabeth	3	....	1
Fletcher, Joseph	4	....	1
Prunty, John	6	1	5
Cheshire, Ann	3	....	1
Poston, Elias	7	1	3
Swisher, Valentine	10	1	4
Emberson, Abel	4	1	....
Shade, George	3	2	....
LIST OF SIMON TAYLOR.			
Humphreys, Ralph	5	3	2
Newell, John	3	1	....
Price, Lewellin	1	....	....
Hatheway, Eleazer	11	1	1
Miles, James	3	1	4
Taylor, John	3	1	3
Andrews, George	10	1	4
McBride, John	5	1	2
Menear, John	5	1	4
Manear, Abraham	2	....	....
Clintock, Robert M	3	1	2
Bremegen, William	3	....	....
Hambler, Adam	5	1	1
Moore, Joseph	5	1	....
Newman, Solomon	8	....	....
Johnson, John	3	1	3
Johnson, Joseph	5	1	1
Johnson, John, Junr.	3	1	1
Critton, John, senr.	9	1	3
Davis, Joseph	8	1	....
Critton, William	1	1	2
Short, Jacob	3	1	....
Taylor, Libby	6	1	2
Anderson, Henry	3	1	1
Davis, Augustus	7	1	....
Melone, John	4	1	....
Spilman, James	4	1	....
Ahrsam, John	9	1	5
Norman, George	4	1	2
Hiley, Rudolph	3	1	....
Earsam, Jacob	6	1	4
Ahrsam, Simon	2	1	1
Pankake, John	9	1	2
Ross, John	9	1	....
Combs, Thomas	8	1	1
Rodgers, Ezekiel	7	1	4
Parker, Robert	7	1	9
Blackburn, William	9	1	2
Ely, Isaac	3	1	1

HAMPSHIRE COUNTY—Continued.

NAME OF HEAD OF FAMILY.	White souls.	Dwellings.	Other buildings.
LIST OF SIMON TAYLOR—continued.			
Ely, Benjamin	8	1	2
Alexandry, Robert	5		
Williamson, Thomas	3	1	
Shrout, Samuel	3	1	
Miller, William	4	1	2
Wycoff, Peter	7	1	2
Calvin, Robert	5	1	1
Newman, Isaac	4	1	
Newman, David	3	1	
Newman, George	12	1	
Hubbs, Thomas, senr	3	1	
Lawson, Jacob	1		
Smith, David	10	1	
Long, David	9	1	
Noteman, Jane	4	1	
Stoker, John	7	1	3
Stoker, Bassar	2	1	4
Farce, Cornelius	12	1	5
Rannalls, John	6	1	
Rannalls, William	6	1	6
Taylor, Simon	5	1	10
Lions, Mary	4	1	
Maid, John	2	1	3
Newman, John	3	1	1
McDewgle, James	7	1	
Newman, John	8	1	1
Spealman, William	5	1	
Tygart, Francis	3	1	2
Critton, John Junr	6	1	2
LIST OF OKEY JOHNSON.			
Lawson, Thomas	10	1	
Slagle, Jacob	10	1	1
Critchlow, William	9		
Lawson, Moses	3	1	
Smith, Nathaniel	7	1	
Hardin, Mark	10	1	
Wilson, Mary	5	2	
Lawson, James	2		
Hougland, Cornelius	9	1	1
Collins, Elisha	6	1	
Farley, Jane	2	1	
Kimberlin, Jacob	10	1	
Stalcup, John	11	1	1
Chitton, John	4	1	1
House, John	7	1	
Deyea, Charles, Senr	2	1	
Deyea, Charles, Junr	2	1	
Martin, Edmund	8	1	
Campbell, William	4	1	1
Anderson, Thomas	9	1	1
Anderson, William	1	1	
English, William	2		
Lawson, Richard	4	1	
Frazier, Daniel	4		
Murphy, William	4	1	
Williams, George	8	1	2
Wickam, Matthew	5	1	
Dean, Daniel	4	1	
Mahon, William	9	1	3
McCarty, Charles	6	1	
Mahon, James	9	1	3
Lion, John	10	1	
Harrow, Arthur	10	1	
Goodwin, Ignatius	5	1	
Linore, John	4	1	
Johnson, Okey	9	1	3
LIST OF DAVID MITCHELL, GENT.			
Tarvin, George	11	2	3
Cracroft, Thomas	7	1	
Thomson, Jeremiah	5	1	1

NAME OF HEAD OF FAMILY.	White souls.	Dwellings.	Other buildings.
LIST OF DAVID MITCHELL, GENT.—continued.			
Throgmorton, Lewis	10	1	1
Flora, Thomas	10	1	1
Flora, Abijah	3	1	
Dickson, George	3	1	
Haff, Cornelius	6	1	2
Crisman, Comrad	4	1	
Crisman, Jacob	3	1	1
Dawson, Isaac	5	1	
Flora, William	7	1	1
Reeves, Richard	6	1	1
Matthews, Lewis	7	1	1
Dawson, Abraham	5	1	2
Jackson, William	8	1	2
Marquis, Richard	9	1	2
Benit, Thomas	4	1	
Marquis, Andrew	7	1	1
Marquis, Christopher	2	1	1
Craycraft, Joseph	8	1	2
Chrisman, Adam	6	1	
Casler, Michael	2	1	1
Smith, Richard	6	1	1
McCracken, Ovid	9	1	4
Chrisman, Philip, sr	4	1	1
Demoss, Thomas	10	1	
Largin, John	10	1	3
Weatherington, John	8	1	2
Osmun, Samuel	3	1	4
Wiggins, Philip	11	1	3
Williams, Thomas	9	1	4
Dawson, Jacob	6	1	3
McMahin, William	7	1	
Chrisman, Philip, Junr	2	1	
Martin, John	8	1	2
Ross, John	5	1	2
Wiggins, Archibald	10	1	5
Constant, John	6	1	4
McDaniel, Archibald	7	1	5
Biggerstaff, William	3	1	
Biggerstaff, William, Junr	7	1	
Sutherland, William	3	1	
Biggerstaff, John	7	1	
Hartley, John	6	1	
Robinson, John	2	1	
Haff, Luke,	5	1	3
Haines, Rudy	5	1	
Burk, Jonathan	2	1	
Williams, William	9	1	2
Morgan, John	10	1	1
Morgan, Jonathan	4	1	2
Lock, Jacob	7	1	2
Jackson, Thomas	3	1	
Morgan, Thomas	6	1	2
Swim, John	3	1	
Cunnard, James	4	1	4
Cunnard, James, Jur	5	1	2
Butcher, John	7	1	2
Lerew, Peter	10	1	4
Lerew, John	7	1	4
Lerew, Noah	3	1	6
Mitchell, David	1	1	4
LIST OF MICHAEL STUMP.			
Smith, Charles	10	1	9
Trumbo, George	8	1	3
Bible, Christian	7	1	3
Coutzman, Adam	3	2	
Reel, Nicholas	6		
Hall, Thomas	6	1	
Dickinson, Jacob	8	1	3
Cowgar, George	6	1	5
Stephenson, James	8	1	3
Rhoades, Henry	6	1	
Cochran, Simon	8	1	2
Goodwin, Solomon	2	1	

NAME OF HEAD OF FAMILY.	White souls.	Dwellings.	Other buildings.
LIST OF MICHAEL STUMP—continued.			
Morrow, James	7	1	3
Hornback, Anthony	10	1	
Lyon, Charles	4		
Nave, George	5	1	4
Nave, Jacob	4	1	1
Algire, John	3		
Marshall, Benjamin	4	1	
Moor, Anthony	8	1	1
Best, Hannah	3	1	
Algier, William	4	1	1
Algier, Hermanus	10	1	2
Row, William	6	1	
Carroll, John	5		
Nave, Henry	7	1	2
Reel, David	4	1	
Stump, Catherine	1	1	
Atchison, William	10	1	2
Brake, John	3	1	
Higgins, Robert	6	1	6
Lynch, Charles	9	1	4
Allinton, David	2	1	
Wood, Peter	5	1	
Simon, Philip	3	1	2
House, Jacob	6	1	1
Brake, Jacob, Senr	9	1	4
Simon, Leonard	4	1	
Simon, George	8	1	1
Brake, Jacob, Junr	4	1	1
Simon, Christian	6	1	
Sellers, John	5	1	
Stump, George	9	1	2
Wilson, Charles	7	1	1
Spoar, John	9	1	1
Cauffman, Adam	5	1	
Harness, Peter	7	1	1
Harness, Leonard	7	1	1
Harness, Leonard	7	1	
Regar, John	5	1	1
Rorebaugh, John	11	1	2
Shepler, Henry	6	1	
See, George	8	1	5
Shook, David	3	1	
Maus, Barnabas	3	1	
Barns, Elijah	6	1	
Scott, Joseph	5	1	
Smith, Michael	3	1	
Dasher, Christian	7	1	2
Cantrill, Christopher	8	1	
Sears, William	10	1	1
Sears, Sarah	1	1	
Stump, Leonard	6	1	3
Traiss, Jacob	8	1	1
Rudybaugh, Adam	8	1	3
Ozborn, Jeremiah	7	1	4
Lacefield, Elias	6	1	
Shook, Harman, Senr	3	1	3
Shook, Harman, Junr	3	1	
Shook, Peter	7	1	
Shook, William	13	1	
Sears, John	9	1	2
Hedger, John	7		
Nave, Michael	8	1	1
Huffman, Philip	5	1	
Cowfelt, Philip	8	1	
Cowfelt, Henry	2		
Jefferson, Luke	4	1	
Trumbo, Andrew	9	1	1
Shook, John	4	1	1
Weitmiller, John	4	1	5
Dickinson, John	3	1	
Hicks, Thomas	4	1	2
Mitcher, Nicholas	11	1	
Hays, John	2	1	
Stump, Michael	8	1	4
Tivebaugh, Daniel	8	1	2
Mitts, Adam	3	1	1

NAME OF HEAD OF FAMILY.	White souls.	Dwellings.	Other buildings.
LIST OF ABEL RANDALL.			
Cuningham, William	2	1	2
Richardson, Daniel	6	1	1
Harness, John	12	1	2
Yoakum, Jacob	9	1	1
Yoakum, Philip Paul	1	1	3
Yoakum, John	6	1	1
Harness, Michael	3	1	3
Marrs, Henry M	5	1	1
Pancake, Catherine	3	1	1
Hutton, Isaac	4	1	
Heath, Jonathan	9	2	2
Weaver, George	6	1	
Welton, David	8	1	2
Thomas, Morris	9	1	1
Hornback, Simon	13	1	2
Hornback, Samuel	7	1	2
Cutrack, Samuel	7	1	1
Hornback, James	5	1	1
Hite, Casper	8		2
Conrod, John	1	1	3
Harness, George	6	1	2
McMahen, Barnard	7	1	1
Clifford, James	7		1
Brown, John	5	1	1
Radcliff, Richard	8	1	
Longwith, Thomas	4	1	
Kimbell, Adam	2		
Steel, John	3	1	
Kimbell, John	8	1	1
Steel, Henry	7	1	1
Kimbell, Lambert	5	1	
Anderson, John	9	1	
Helmick, John	5	1	
Baker, Anthony	8	1	3
Moak, Henry	5	1	1
Sellers, Frederick	4	1	2
Westfall, John, Senr	14	1	3
Westfall, Jacob	7	1	2
Westfall, Isaac	4	1	
Inskeep, Abraham	11	1	5
Hutton, Moses	9	1	9
Harness, Michael	9	1	1
Buzzard, John	2	1	1
Miller, John	6	1	
Petty, Joseph	9	1	4
Hutton, Jacob	3	1	
Westfall, Henry	7	1	
Leonard, Martin	8	1	
Hornback, Isaac	7	1	3
Leary, Dennis	7	1	
See, Michael	9	1	2
Helmick, Jacob	8	2	
Orr, James	6	1	
Hornback, Magdalan	8	1	
Lilly, David	5	1	1
Boggard, Ezekial	8	1	2
Brink, Ursula	9	1	2
Borrer, Jacob	2	1	
Fisher, John	2	1	1
Jenny, William	6	1	2
Brown, James	5	1	
Shipley, Richard	3	1	
Fisher, Christina	4	1	1
Bonett, Samuel	10	1	1
Hoge, Moses	3	1	2
Wodrow, Andrew	3	1	3
Fisher, Adam	7	1	1
Maxwell, Robert	5	1	2
Brown, Thomas	8	1	2
Parsons, Thomas	10	1	2
Goff, Thomas	4	1	1
Miles, David	6	1	3
Randall, Abel	11	1	3

NANSEMOND COUNTY.

NAME OF HEAD OF FAMILY.	White souls.	Dwellings.	Other buildings.
CAPT. ROB'T M. RIDDICK'S DISTRICT—LIST OF JOHN RIDDICK.			
Griffin, Eli	10	3	2
Brinkly, John (of Eli)	7	3	4
Wilkins, Thomas	8	2	
Ellis, Joseph (son of Sarah)	7	1	
Ellis, Josiah	8	2	
Rabey, Kadah	6	1	1
Spivey, Joshua	8	2	7
Brinkley, Milli	7	2	1
Brinkley, Kadah	7	3	3
Lassiter, Jethro	7	1	
Lassiter, Enos	5	1	1
CAPT. ROB'T M. RIDDICK'S DISTRICT—LIST OF JOHN RIDDICK—continued.			
Ellis, Micajah	5	1	
Booth, Abraham	7	2	1
Branton, Jesse	3	1	
Rabey, Jacob	7	2	
Knight, James, Senr	4	3	5
Travathan, William	4	1	
Harrell, John (Son of Thos)	9	2	3
Harrell, Isabel	3	2	2
Ellis, William	5	1	1
Brinkley, Thomas	3	1	
Booth, Jethro	3	1	
Wilkins, James	4	1	
CAPT. ROB'T M. RIDDICK'S DISTRICT—LIST OF JOHN RIDDICK—continued.			
Branton, Jacob	6	1	
Wilkins, William (Son Thos)	3	2	
Lassiter, Abraham	7	3	
Brinkley, John (son Micl)	1	2	1
Harrell, John (Son of John)	8	2	
Griffin, Henry	10	2	3
Meltear, Thomas	4	1	
Lassiter, Robert	8	2	1
Spivey, James	3	1	1
Price, John	4	1	
Lassiter, Moses	6	2	
CAPT. ROB'T M. RIDDICK'S DISTRICT—LIST OF JOHN RIDDICK—continued.			
Peal, Jeremiah	4	1	
Lassiter, Jessey	5	3	2
Sceator, Phareby	4	1	
Ellis, Joseph (Son of Mary)	3	1	
Royce, James	4	2	2
Norfleet, Hezekiah	8	3	4
Jones, Abraham	3	1	
Ellis, James	5	1	
Griffin, Humphrey, Senr	6	3	3
Rabey, Samuel	4	2	
Parker, John	4	1	
Wilkins, Shadrick	4	1	1

NANSEMOND COUNTY—Continued.

CAPT. ROB'T M. RIDDICK'S DISTRICT—LIST OF JOHN RIDDICK—continued.

NAME OF HEAD OF FAMILY.	White souls.	Dwellings.	Other buildings.
Wilkins, Wm (Son Shad)	5	1	....
Sivils, William	4	1	....
Brinkley, Jacob	4	2	....
Franklin, Josiah	5	1	....
Franklin, Daniel	6	2	....
Brinkley, Henry	6	2	....
Brinkley, Aaron	6	1	....
Brinkley, Abraham	2	1	....
Franklin, Elanor	1	1	....
Rabey, William	4	....	....
Brinkley, David	4	1	1
Brinkley, Eli	4	1	....
Lassiter, William	7	1	....
Hufton, John	7	1	....
Spivey, George	4	3	1
Brinkley, John (Son Petr)	6	2	3
Jones, William	7	1	2
Lassiter, Daniel	8	2	6
Sumner, Jacob, Senr	5	3	3
Knight, John	8	2	2
Davies, William	5	1	....
Barr, John	6	2	4
Riddick, Daniel	3	3	4
Riddick, Solomon	9	5	4
Brothers, William	8	2	2
Brothers, Sarah	7	1	2
Riddick, John	6	4	10
Harrell, James	8	1	1
Harrell, Thomas	8	2	1

CAPT. WM. ELEY'S DISTRICT—LIST OF JEREMIAH GODWIN.

NAME OF HEAD OF FAMILY.	White souls.	Dwellings.	Other buildings.
Butler, Peter, Junr	5	1	2
Callis, George	6	1	7
Simons, John	5	1	7
Carr, Nathan	10	1	4
Archer, Stephen	9	1	1
Taylor, Jethro	6	1	3
Gay, James	10	1	2
Pierce, Matthias	2	1	3
Johnson, Wm	7	1	1
Gay, Wm	7	1	....
Butler, Peter, Senr	5	1	4
Pierce, Stephen	3	1	2
Butler, Samuel	4	1	1
Butler, John	8	....	....
McClenney, Mial	7	1	2
Johnson, Josiah	3	1	....
Taylor, Anner	4	1	3
Archer, Mary	5	1	3
Taylor, James	3	1	2
Daughtrey, John	5	1	6
Willis, Thomas	8	1	....
McClenney, Thomas	4	1	....
Holland, Alexr	4	1	....
Lawrence, George	3	1	3
Thomas, Matthew	3	1	2
Pierce, James	7	1	4
Pruden, Wm	9	1	2
Clark, Philip	8	1	2
Redman, Martin	3	1	....
Wright, Wm, Senr	8	1	....
Powel, Francis, Junr	4	1	2
Hines, Willis	2	1	2
Taylor, Pruden	4	1	....
Butler, Nathan	5	1	3
McClenney, John	6	1	4
McClenney, James	5	1	3
Pierce, David	3	1	....
Beaseby, Benja	6	1	....
Pierce, Milly	6	1	....
Parker, Jos, Junr	3	1	....
Parker, Jos, Senr	5	1	....
Copeland, John	6	1	3
Johnson, Stephen	6	1	1
Peirceen, Jethro	7	1	2
Wright, James	5	1	....
Powell, Wm	5	1	2
Norfleet, Jos	4	1	6
King, William	6	1	7
King, Eliza	1	1	2
Powell, Frances, Senr	2	1	8
Ballard, Abraham	2	1	5
Willis, Robert	8	1	4
Bishop, Henry	4	1	3
M'Clenney, Zachy	2	1	....
M'Clenney, William	9	1	8
Parker, John	6	1	2
Parker, James	7	1	1
Baker, Joseph	6	1	9
Hines, Hardy	3	1	2
Holland, Joseph	4	1	11
Villine, Prisciller	5	1	5
Ballard, Ann	4	1	6
Ashburn, John	6	1	4
Gwin, Thomas, Junr	1	....	....

CAPT. WILLIS RIDDICK'S DISTRICT—LIST OF JEREMIAH GODWIN.

NAME OF HEAD OF FAMILY.	White souls.	Dwellings.	Other buildings.
Godwin, Jeremiah	9	1	8
Cohoon, Samuel	7	1	6
Saunders, Thos	3	1	2
Sumner, William	2	1	10
Godwin, Richard W	9	1	8
Mason, Peter	5	1	5
George, Fredk	5	1	3
Nelms, George	3	1	3
Pinner, Francis	8	1	4
Wimmer, John	3	1	....
Nelms, William	8	1	1
Godwin, Saml	2	1	7
Bateman, Jethro	6	1	1
Monk, Wm	4	1	2
Richards, John	2	1	2
Elsbury, Joseph	11	1	1
Saunders, Daniel	8	1	2
Nelms, Acher	6	1	3
Marshall, Mills	7	1	3
Stakes, Leven	6	1	3
Pinner, James	4	1	2
Best, Lewis	2	1	6
Pinner, Wm	5	1	4
Lunsford, James	3	1	....
Haggard, Patience	6	1	....
Bateman, John	7	1	2
Bateman, Ann	3	1	1
Nelms, Thomas	4	1	6
Bateman, William	1	1	2
Bullock, James	4	1	4
Roberts, Esther	5	1	7
Hill, Ben	9	1	11
Nelms, Ezekiel	6	1	1
Pin, Catharine	3	1	....
Olliver, Joseph	5	1	1
Norfleet, Elisha	1	1	6
Barkley, Saml	6	1	1
Green, Thomas	5	1	4
Norfleet, Nathl	4	1	7
Norfleet, Sarah	6	1	4
Gwin, Thomas, Senr	7	1	4

CAPT. SUMNER'S, HOLLAND'S & DARDEN'S COMPANIES OF MILITIA—LIST OF ELISHA DARDEN.

NAME OF HEAD OF FAMILY.	White souls.	Dwellings.	Other buildings.
Baker, Benjamin	12	1	14
Baker, Richard	2	1	13
Riddick, Mary	6	1	6
Darden, Elisha	11	2	15
Gardner, Joshua	11	1	8
Howell, Michl	2	1	4
Howell, Edward, Senr	5	1	14
Cobb, John	9	1	6
Howel, Hopkin	6	1	4
Howel, Rebecah	5	1	6
Ballard, Willis	2	1	7
Johson, Hezekiah	5	1	2
Howel, David	7	1	4
Howel, Eley	10	1	3
Jones, David	9	1	2
Howel, Edward, Junr	....	1	8
Parker, Hardy	8	1	4
Eley, John	4	1	6
Jones, Whittey	3	1	....
Jones, Hardy	11	1	2
Parker, Kadar	8	1	5
Daughtrey, Jacob	9	1	6
Rabuck, Rawleigh	4	....	....
Rawls, Hardy	9	1	4
Holland, James (of Ro:)	6	1	4
Boyt, Timothy	6	1	2
Jones, John	5	2	6
Sumner, Denny	7	1	5
Jones, Henry	8	2	5
Jones, Thomas	4	2	4
Saunders, James	5	2	5
Saunders, John	....	1	2
Daughtrey, Robert	7	1	5
Vaughn, Charles	7	1	5
Howel, Archelaus	5	1	1
Vaughan, James	10	1	7
Wright, James	4	1	1
Howel, Stephen	4	1	4
Boyt, David	2	1	3
Phillips, Avis	1	....	....
Jukins, John, Junr	4	1	3
Journigan, William	5	1	5
Gardner, Joseph	6	1	4
Boyt, William	1	....	2
Ritter, Thomas	3	1	....
Daughtry, Lewis	10	1	6
Howel, Lyda	5	2	3
Ritter, Thomas, Senr	6	1	1
Wiggins, Willis	5	1	1
Herring, William	3	1	....

CAPT. SUMNER'S, HOLLAND'S & DARDEN'S COMPANIES OF MILITIA—LIST OF ELISHA DARDEN—con.

NAME OF HEAD OF FAMILY.	White souls.	Dwellings.	Other buildings.
Hare, Henry	8	1	4
Glover, William, Senr	5	1	5
Williams, George	3	1	7
Carr, John	10	1	11
Avis, John	4	1	1
Gardner, Henry	4	1	9
Carr, James	4	1	5
Glover, John	6	1	3
Williams, Richard	5	1	4
Birdsong, Charles	9	1	3
Williams, Jordan	5	1	4
Carr, Molley	3	1	4
Williams, John	1	1	8
Owins, Robert	3	....	....
Crosland, John	11	1	2
Darden, Robert	8	1	7
Whitfield, Ivey	5	1	4
Warren, Etheldred	7	1	6
Darden, Holland	11	1	8
Parker, Benja	4	1	....
Lawrence, Elizabeth	5	1	3
Fisher, Mary	3	1	8
Cary, Anna	2	1	8
Crosland, Edward	4	....	1
Cary, Elphiston	4	1	1
Harrel, William	6	1	1
Hart, William	8	2	11
Pibworth, Robert	6	....	....
Lawrence, Robert	6	1	8
Jones, Matthew	1	1	8
Harrel, Francis	4	1	....
Carey, Edward	9	1	3
Pope, Joel	4	....	....
Hart, Ginnet	5	1	6
Lawrence, John	5	1	13
Glover, William, Junr	3	1	....
Darden, Stephen	5	2	13
Holland, Jesse	4	1	8
Holland, William	5	1	4
Hamilton, Jno	4	1	1
Darden, Elizb	5	....	....
Harrison, Henry	5	1	....
Harrison, Anna	1	2	17
Holland, Joseph	6	1	5
Rawls, David	6	2	4
Rawls, John	11	1	6
Holland, Henry (of Jno)	9	1	3
Ballentine, Jonas	6	1	3
Flemming, Mary	2	1	3
Holland, James (of Danl)	3	1	1
Winborne, Henry	6	1	4
Everitt, John	8	1	5
Collins, Lemuel	5	1	....
Kean, Lemuel	7	1	1
Holland, John (of Solo)	1	1	2
Holland, Solomon	6	1	6
Holland, Jobe	2	1	5
Holland, James (of Jas)	6	1	9
Holland, Elisha	2	....	....
Hedgpeth, Henry	5	1	4
Holland, Henry (of Dn)	4	1	3
Holland, Titus	2	1	2
Holland, Henry (of Jos)	4	1	1
Holland, James (of Jos)	5	2	3
Holland, Jno (of Moses)	5	1	1
Holland, Absalom	7	1	1
Hedgpeth, Culbert	1	1	2
Holland, Benja	5	....	....
Holland, Joshua	7	1	1
Holland, Joseph (of Jos)	7	1	3
Norfleet, Henry	2	1	1
Holland, Danl	4	1	4
Holland, Thomas	6	1	5
Norfleet, John	7	1	7
Dulport, Joseph	4	1	....
Hookey, Joseph	2	1	5
Bigelow, Norman	1	1	3
Calvert, Christopher	....	....	2
Howel, Arthur	9	1	4
Lassiter, David	4	1	2
Holland, Brittain	1	....	....
Jinkins, Henry	1	....	....
Jinkins, Jno, Senr	2	1	6
Journigan, Hardy	10	1	3
Scoggins, James	3	1	1
Whitfield, Solo	3	1	2
Whitfield, Africa	3	1	1
Bishop, John	7	1	5
Howard, Hardy	4	1	8
Everitt, Etheldred	4	1	8
Blow, John	13	1	12
Crawford, Solomon	6	1	1
Jinkins, Willis	1	....	....
Holland, Henry, Sr	7	1	8
Hedgpeth, James	3	1	....
Fiers, William	6	1	....
Holland, David	5	1	5
Hart, John	1	1	1

LIST OF JOHN COLE.

NAME OF HEAD OF FAMILY.	White souls.	Dwellings.	Other buildings.
Duke, Ashel	6	2	2
Skinner, Eliza	5	1	5
Coles, John	8	2	4
Duke, James	12	2	3
Price, Jacob	5	1	2
Boyce, James	3	2	3
Ellis, Joseph	3	1	....
Lawrence, Rachel	8	1	1
Parker, Abraham	11	2	8
Peal, Jessey	7	1	2
Wiggins, Jessey	8	1	4
Beaman, Absolem	5	2	4
Skinner, Joseph	6	1	7
Rountree, William	8	2	2
Riddick, Jethro	7	2	4
Harrel, Thomas	6	1	1
Harrel, Jobe, Junr	5	1	1
Parker, Willis	9	3	2
Hare, Eliza	4	1	2
Harrel, Charity	7	2	3
Harrel, Lewis	8	2	1
Ross, Babel	5	1	....
Harrel, Mills	4	1	2
Rawles, Willis	1	1	....
Rawles, Ann	2	1	3
Harrel, Adam	2	2	1
Bird, Jacob, Junr	5	1	....
Folk, William	2	2	1
Tarlingtun, Leving	10	2	2
Rawles, Eliza	6	2	3
Langston, Isaac	7	2	3
Rab, John	7	2	4
Hunter, Riddick	1	1	2
Auston, Richard	8	1	3
Smith, James	7	2	....
Gomer, Rebeccah	6	1	1
Cross, Sarah	8	2	4
Cunningham, Saml	6	1	8
Cross, Hardy	10	3	4
Smith, Thomas	12	2	5
Smith, Arther	10	1	5
Cross, William	5	2	3
Goodman, James	6	2	3
Cross, Saml	4	2	2
Rawles, Cornelius	3	3	1
Savage, Calob	10	4	4
Duke, Thomas	7	2	2
King, John	7	2	2
Purvis, Tiberius	4	2	....
March, Daniel	9	2	1
March, Bernet	4	3	4
Cross, Jonathan	6	1	1
Crofford, Solomon	5	1	1
Rodgers, Drewrey	5	2	....
Haslip, Sarah	4	2	....
Russel, James	7	1	....
Russel, Mary	4	2	....
Smith, Isaac	10	1	1
Smith, Richard	2	1	4
Parker, David	6	1	....
Staples, John	8	1	1
Bird, Edmond	1	1	1
Horton, Moss	2	1	2
Coles, Mourning	6	2	6
Langston, John	6	2	3
Ease, John	7	1	5
Guing, John	7	2	1
Bird, Elisha	8	1	2
Owins, Marcum	8	1	5
Smith, John	9	2	3
Rawles, Solomon	7	2	2
Harrel, Joshua	1	1	....
Harrel, Moses	7	1	2
Acrey, Edward	5	2	4
Harrel, Silas	8	1	1
Turley, Richard	8	1	1
Barfield, Saml	4	1	1
Baker, John	3	2	1
Raby, Joel	4	....	....
Duke, James	12	2	4
Johnson, Normon	5	1	....
Banes, George	5	1	1
Draper, Thomas	6	1	2
Rawles, Arther	8	2	2
Ross, Joseph	6	1	....
Baker, James	5	2	2
Baker, Edward	8	1	1
Baker, Jonathan	4	1	1
Baker, Samuel	9	2	4
Duke, Elisha	7	2	2
Duke, Hardy	5	2	4
Parker, Jonathan	4	1	....
Harrel, Jobe, Senr	6	1	1
Harrel, Sias	4	1	1
Harrel, Noah	1	....	....
Tarlington, John	4	1	1
Griffing, James	4	2	3
Gwin, David	8	2	2

NANSEMOND COUNTY—Continued.

NAME OF HEAD OF FAMILY.	White souls.	Dwellings.	Other buildings.
LIST OF JOHN COLE—continued.			
Perry, Sarah	2	2	1
Beasley, James	3	1	....
Bird, William	6	2	2
Jones, Arther, Junr	11	2	6
Baker, Denney	8	1	2
Baker, Edward	4	2	1
Parker, Moses	7	2	1
Rabey, Henry	9	2	2
Rabey, James	9	1	....
Savage, William	4	2	2
Horton, James	5	2	2
Horton, Daniel	1	....	....
Smith, Rubin	7	2	3
Pierce, William	5	2	1
Rawls, Thos	4	2	1
Johnson, Collin	8	1	1
Rountree, John	10	1	1
Savage, William, Jur	4	1	....
Duke, Jacob	9	2	1
Jones, Micajah	9	1	3
Booth, Kadah	8	1	1
Goff, Hugh	5	2	2
Lane, Denney	4	1	....
Perce, Edward	5	1	....
Blade, Lawrence	9	1	2
Jones, Arther, Senr	8	2	2
Bird, Levey	5	2	2
Bird, Jacob	6	1	3
CAPT. HUDNAL'S & BUXTON'S COMPANIES OF MILITIA—LIST OF NATH'L BUXTON.			
Powell, John	7	1	3
Brumyer, John	7	1	2
Danby, Saml	3	1	1
Baker, William	1	....	....
Lassiter, William	3	1	2
Dardan, John	11	1	2
Moore, John	10	1	4
Pell, Joseph	6	1	6
Buxton, James	8	1	7
Minton, Martha	6	1	5
Mansfield, Mills	4	1	3
Lattemer, Wm	5	1	2
Hudnall, John	1	1	3
Jordan, Edmond	1	1	3
Jossey, Wm	4	2	4
Gumly, Isaac	2	1	2
Sanders, Robert	5	1	....
Evans, John	5	1	3

NAME OF HEAD OF FAMILY.	White souls.	Dwellings.	Other buildings.
CAPT. HUDNAL'S & BUXTON'S COMPANIES OF MILITIA—LIST OF NATH'L BUXTON—continued.			
Hargroves, Robert	3	1	7
Hargroves, John	3	1	2
Streater, Edwd	3	1	4
Baker, Denney	6	1	4
Gaskins, Josiah	5	1	4
Bridger, James	7	1	1
Jones, James	6	1	2
Pugh, John	2	1	6
Campbell, John	7	1	3
Baker, Ann	3	1	....
Smith, Margrett	3	1	....
Allmand, Thos	5	1	6
Turner, Pasco	5	1	6
Murdaugh, James	8	1	10
Slatter, Soloman	8	1	1
Pugh, Theophilus	5	....	....
Pugh, Mary	1	1	4
King, Michl	2	1	6
Conner, John	1	....	....
Osheal, David	2	1	1
Johnson, Henry	8	1	5
Casson, Eliza	4	1	2
Nelms, Saml	12	1	2
Howard, Stephen	5	1	2
Sanders, Wm	4	1	....
Shepherd, Soloman	7	1	10
Jinkins, Charles	2	1	5
Green, Henry	3	....	....
Shepherd, Lydia	5	1	4
Allmand, Eliza	5	1	....
Wakefield, Thos	4	1	3
Channel, Eliza	4	1	....
Cottrel, Charles	4	1	....
Ricks, Joseph	6	1	5
Thomson, John	4	1	1
Cowper, Mary	4	1	5
Hale, John	5	1	1
Hale, Edward	4	1	1
Jordan, Wm	4	1	5
Brewer, Josiah	3	1	....
Ash, Simon (Mulatto)	....	1	....
Jordan, Robert	6	1	10
Trotter, Eliza	4	1	6
Reams, John	3	1	....
Emerson, Arthur	6	1	6
Sturges, Wm	6	1	1
Jordan, John	2	1	6
Brown, Pharaba	2	....	....
Minton, Mills	2	1	4
Wright, Stephen	3	2	10
Wright, Miles	7	1	3
Cowper, James	4	2	4

NAME OF HEAD OF FAMILY.	White souls.	Dwellings.	Other buildings.
CAPT. HUDNAL'S & BUXTON'S COMPANIES OF MILITIA—LIST OF NATH'L BUXTON—continued.			
Powell, Ezekiel	8	1	3
Darby, Smith	3	1	4
Spencer, Abraham	7	1	3
Beaman, Jethro	3	2	4
Pierce, Ann	4	1	....
Pitt, Thos	7	1	3
Wright, Wm	6	1	8
Smith, Wm	6	1	....
Radwill, Thos	3	1	1
Rose, Margret	2	1	....
Ridgway, Thos (Mulatto)	....	1	1
Deans, John	8	1	1
Howard, Thomas	7	1	2
Cotten, Jonathan	9	1	2
Lockeart, Eliza	6	1	2
Charles, Jacob (Mulatto)	....	....	1
Lawrence, Mosses (Mulatto)	....	1	2
Mansfield, Wm	3	1	2
Homes, Wm	2	1	1
Baker, David	1	1	3
Bullard, Thos	5	1	5
Wilder, James	4	1	5
Dickson, Richd (Mulatto)	....	1	3
Marshall, Eliza	6	1	4
Clark, Lewis L	4	1	6
Hickumbotham, Wm	7	1	2
Swilivant, Judith	5	1	2
Danby, Edward	1	....	....
Cooper, Wm	10	1	1
Fulgham, Jesse	5	1	2
Powell, Mary	7	1	5
Heffeton, Thomas	7	1	....
Hefferton, John	7	1	....
Teamer, Jere (Mulatto)	....	1	4
Mitcheson, John	7	1	1
Jordan, Edmond	6	1	2
Cowper, Thos	5	1	1
Burly, Robt (Mulatto)	....	1	....
Pierce, John	4	1	....
Cumings, Geo	4	1	1
Curtis, Jona (Mulatto)	....	1	1
Wilder, James	5	1	....
Hays, Wm	9	1	4
Bullock, Thos	6	1	....
Thomas, Charles	7	1	7
Ash, Moses (Mulatto)	....	1	....
Winborn, Thos	6	1	2
Robinson, Sampson (M.)	....	1	1
Payne, James	....	1	....
Northam, Zoraba	9	1	3
Arthur, James	2	1	3

NAME OF HEAD OF FAMILY.	White souls.	Dwellings.	Other buildings.
CAPT. HUDNAL'S & BUXTON'S COMPANIES OF MILITIA—LIST OF NATH'L BUXTON—continued.			
Corbell, John	5	1	2
Wainright, Wm	7	1	....
Powell, John	7	1	3
Woodward, John	5	1	4
Stakes, Wm	8	1	3
Monro, Matthias	7	1	1
Frost, Noah	7	1	1
Aswell, Daniel	6	1	4
Deans, Willis	6	2	8
Deans, John	1	1	....
Archer, Rebecca	1	1	....
Elmore, Jos (Mulatto)	....	1	1
Young, Aaron (Mulatto)	....	1	....
Edwards, James	2	1	....
Corbell, Josiah	3	1	....
Benn, Thos	7	1	4
Aswell, James	5	1	3
Powell, Sarah	4	1	2
Dilbery, Peter	9	1	5
Creech, Charles	2	1	5
Grimes, Ann	4	....	....
Hefferton, James	5	1	....
Miars, Charity	7	1	3
Davis, John (Mulatto)	....	1	2
Ward, Jno Wyet	5	1	4
Moore, Ann	2	1	4
Deford, Sarah	2	....	....
Miars, Thos	3	1	....
Deans, John	2	1	8
Wilkinson, Mills	7	1	1
Jackson, Christo	2	1	1
Wood, William	3	1	....
Taylor, Jos	6	1	2
Deans, John	2	1	2
Deans, Martha	5	1	2
Hoffler, Saml	6	1	5
Hoffler, Thos	7	1	3
Churchwell, Sam (Mulatto)	....	1	....
White, Anthy	3	1	6
Streater, Willis	3	1	15
Graham, Mary	4	1	1
Conaway, James	1	1	3
Howard, James	3	1	3
Buxton, Nathl	5	1	4
Ash, James (Mulatto)	....	1	2
Pugh, Isaac (Mulatto)	....	1	2
Churchwill, Charles (Mulatto)	....	1	2
Roberts, Wm	2	1	10

NORTHUMBERLAND COUNTY.

NAME OF HEAD OF FAMILY.	White souls.	Dwellings.	Other buildings.
Angel, William	7	1	7
Dameron, Thomas	3	1	2
Gaskins, Thomas	7	1	21
Gaskins, Edwin	6	1	1
Kent, Daniel	3	1	3
Kent, William	13	1	4
Taylor, Dolly	2	1	....
Robuck, William	1	1	3
Mott, James	2	1	3
George, Jeduthan	4	1	....
Tarkelson, Joseph	5	1	6
Harding, Thos	2	1	1
Pinckard, Robt	6	1	7
Haydon, Thomas	7	1	2
Olliver, Benjamin	5	1	3
Sydnor, Elizabeth	8	1	7
Weaver, Joseph	....	1	1
Phillips, George	6	1	5
Jones, Judith	5	1	6
Sydnor, Frances	7	1	3
Hurst, Henry	6	1	2
Gaskins, William	4	1	....
Mott, William	3	1	3
Gaskins, Spencer	3	1	....
Pope, Josiah	4	1	....
Ball, David	13	1	12
Hughlett, Samuel	8	1	4
Ball, David, Jr	4	1	6
Ball, George, Jr	3	1	4
Hurst, Thomas	9	1	6
Hurst, William	7	1	6
Harvey, Frances S	5	1	3
Hurst, Sukey	6	1	8
Hurst, Isaac	5	1	5
Gaskins, Mary	4	1	5
Eustace, John	4	2	21
Ingram, George	12	3	13
Waddy, Margarett	3	3	4
Carters, Landon	....	1	14
Davis, William	10	....	....

NAME OF HEAD OF FAMILY.	White souls.	Dwellings.	Other buildings.
Garlington, William	3	1	3
Ball, George	3	1	8
Webb, Molly	2	1	2
Blackerby, James	5	....	....
Adams, Lott	4	1	2
Waddey, Thomas	6	1	7
Damron, Bartholimew	7	1	2
Damron, Mary	2	1	3
Hester, Moses	7	1	1
Wheeler, John	2	1	1
Waddy, Jesse	5	1	....
Astin, Agness	2	1	1
Apray, John Faldo	5	....	....
Angel, Susanah	4	1	3
Angel, Bodham	5	1	1
Adams, Lott	4	1	2
Basye, Isaac	6	1	7
Bean, George	6	1	4
Brown, John	5	1	....
Bussell, Benjamin	5	....	....
Barott, William	3	1	3
Bean, Peter	5	1	5
Barns, Henry	2	1	5
Bar, Zachariah	5	1	6
Barrott, Sarah	5	1	3
Blackerby, William	2	1	3
Brown, Sarah	7	1	....
Barrott, George	1	1	3
Cornish, John	6	1	....
Cundiff, Benjamin	7	1	6
Copedge, Charles	4	1	3
Cockrell, Peter	3	1	....
Champion, James	8	1	9
Curtice, Hillory	8	1	7
Cox, William	5	....	....
Carter, Thomas	5	1	4
Cassaty, Ann	5	1	....
Davis, Thomas	5	1	2
Dameron, Onesiphorus	3	1	4
Davenport, Opie	4	1	1

NAME OF HEAD OF FAMILY.	White souls.	Dwellings.	Other buildings.
Denney, William	4	1	5
Dudly, Sarah	4	1	1
Downman, John	9	1	....
Doolin, Elizabeth	3	1	....
Dameron, Elizabeth	5	1	1
Davenport, William	5	1	15
Everitt, Thomas	3	1	4
Easten, Ann	2	1	....
Everitt, Craven	2	1	5
Fallin, Sarah	3	1	6
Fallin, John H	2	1	6
France, Thomas	2	1	1
Fletcher, Mayse	4	1	3
Gilmore, Robert	....	1	4
Garner, Edward	2	1	2
Gaskins, Isaac	4	1	4
Garner, Moses	6	1	1
George, Nehemiah	2	1	4
Gibbions, Elizabeth	7	1	4
Gallaway, Sarah	3	1	....
Hill, Spencer	4	1	....
Harding, Hopkins	6	1	4
Hurst, Joseph	9	1	3
Hester, Joseph	8	1	2
Hanie, John	6	1	2
George, John	7	1	2
Harvey, Onesephorus	8	1	6
Haydon, Ezekiel	4	1	4
Hudnal, Richard	7	1	6
Hurst, Thomas, Junr	3	....	....
Hudnal, Ezekiel	8	1	7
Hunt, George	5	1	5
Hurst, Mary	4	1	....
James, Thomas	10	1	2
Jeffris, Joseph	7	1	1
James, William	1	....	....
Knight, Hannah	5	1	5
Kent, William	5	1	3
Kirk, George	9	1	4
Lee, Charles	13	1	15

NAME OF HEAD OF FAMILY.	White souls.	Dwellings.	Other buildings.
Lamkin, Lewis	3	1	1
Lattimore, Charles	4	1	5
Leland, Lucy	6	1	5
Lattimore, Charles	....	1	4
Lunsford, Alexander	7	1	2
Lunsford, Joseph	3	1	1
Lunsford, Tarply	3	1	1
Lunsford, Ann	4	1	....
Lunsford, Moses, Junr	6	1	1
Lansford, Moses	6	1	5
Lunsford, Lewis	2	1	4
Marsh, Gidion	5	1	2
Marsh, Matthyas	8	1	1
Moxley, Daniel	8	1	7
Moore, Jedethan	4	1	5
Marsh, Thomas	3	1	....
Marsh, Richard	9	1	2
Marsh, Wineyfret	2	1	2
Marsh, Cuthbirt	4	1	2
Marsh, Ann	6	1	3
Mott, Thomas	5	1	3
Mayse, Catharine	4	1	....
Moore, Thomas	9	1	1
Mayse, John	1	1	6
Nutt, Mosley	4	1	16
Nutt, William	9	1	7
Nutt, Richard	7	3	5
Pitman, Fortunatus	6	1	....
Pitman, Martha	5	1	1
Palmer, David	5	1	4
Payne, Richard H	3	1	4
Palmer, Elizabeth	3	1	5
Palmer, Rodhan	1	....	....
Pitman, George	2	1	3
Pitman, Isaac	1	....	....
Potts, Thomas	9	1	4
Rowand, John	5	1	7
Robertson, James	9	1	....
Rosson, William	6	1	2
Smither, Lucy	5	1	5

NORTHUMBERLAND COUNTY—Continued.

NAME OF HEAD OF FAMILY.	White souls.	Dwellings.	Other buildings.
Sullivan, James	2	1	...
Sullivan, Denis	11	1	3
Sampson, George	...	1	2
Suton, Moses	9	1	5
Sebree, John	8	1	3
Sebree, Moses, Senr.	11	1	2
Sebree, Moses, Junr.	2	1	...
Sampson, George	2	...	...
Swanson, Asa	5	1	2
Swanson, Benjamine	5	1	...
Saggas, Richard	4	1	...
Sebree, Maryann	4	1	3
Swanson, Stephen	3	1	3
Suton, James	7	1	3
Spriggs, Ann	5	1	...
Swain, Joseph	9	1	...
Snow, Spencer	3	...	...
Suton, John	6	1	2
Snow, John	7	1	7
Short, Robert	5	1	...
Talley, John	7	1	3
Marah, Taylor	6	1	5
Thomas, Joannah	6	1	...
Walker, Frances	7	1	3
Walker, Ann	1	1	2
Webb, Aaron	3	1	...
Whaley, Thomas	7	1	...
Whelor, Moses	2	1	...
Yearby, Thomas	3	1	6
Yearby, William	3	1	2
Blackwell, George	9	1	13
Blackwell, Samuel	3	1	9
Blackwell, Samuel, Junr.	3	1	8
Berry, George	3	1	2
Berry, Judith	7	1	1
Brown, Joseph	5	1	...
Beetly, John	5	1	1
Coles, William	5	1	4
Coles, Winnifred	5	1	9
Carpenter, William	...	1	...
Creddick, Thomas	1	1	...
Carpenter, James	...	1	...
Corbell, Daniel	8	1	...
Dudley, Joseph	5	1	...
Dudley, Ransom	5	1	1
Dawkins, Jesse	2	1	...
Damron, Morres	3	1	...
Edwards, Ann (Richd.)	8	1	3
Edwards, Robert	6	1	4
Evans, Mark	...	1	1
Flynt, John	10	1	1
Fallin, Elisha	7	1	3
Goff, Winnifred	4	1	3
Gootsberrough, Robert	10	1	...
Gootsberrough, William	2	...	...
Hayes, Thomas	8	1	3
Hayes, Thomas, Junr.	5	1	1
Hayes, Champion	4	1	...
Hague, Joseph	7	1	1
Jaques, William H	7	1	4
Kesterson, William	9	1	2
Keeve, John	1	1	1
McKarter, Richard	3	1	...
Kesterson, George	6	1	2
Mason, Jasias	7	1	2
Parker, Toulson	8	1	2
Pickron, John	6	1	1
Porter, Andrew	5	1	...
Popplewell, Isaac	2	1	1
Routt, Allec	4	1	4
Shepard, George	4	1	...
Sanders, Edward	6	1	...
Shepard, William	4	1	1
Shepard, Thomas	3	1	...
Tignor, James	6	1	2
Toulson, Patrick	...	1	...
Toulson, Thomas	3	1	2
Toulson, Thomas, Jr	4	1	1
Treacle, William	3	1	...
Wornom, Thomas	5	1	5
Wornom, William	7	1	4
White, Dennis	6	1	1
Webb, Isaac	8	1	2
Williams, John	7	1	1
Williams, Absolom	5	1	...
Webb, Hannah	2	1	6
White, Simon	5	1	3
Webb, John	5	1	2
Walker, Richard	2	1	...
Airs, Samuel	5	2	6
Beetley, William	4	1	2
Beetley, Jesse	5	1	...
Blundell, Seth	4	1	2
Downing, John	5	1	9
Edwards, Elles	4	...	...
Fountain, William	5	1	...
Gett, William	7	1	2
Gough, Stephen	10	1	1
Harcum, Thomas	7	1	1
Harcum, James	4	1	2
Hillman, John	5	1	...

NAME OF HEAD OF FAMILY.	White souls.	Dwellings.	Other buildings.
Haynie, William	7	1	8
Haynie, Richard	7	1	2
Haynie, David	4	1	2
Kenner, Rhodham	9	1	1
Loe, Charles	5	1	2
Lee, James	5	1	...
Moon, William	4	1	...
popplewell, Hack	3	1	...
Phillips, James	4	1	...
Corbell, John	7	2	6
Cawsey, Able	...	1	1
Tignor, George	3	1	...
Wildy, William	8	2	11
Coles, Edward	5	1	11
Williams, Elizabeth	3	1	...
Coles, Richd.	2	1	3
Downing, Sarah	6	2	14
Shearman, Ann	5	1	4
Nelms, Ebin	7	1	10
Hughlett, Yarrett	4	1	1
Betts, Thomas	4	1	4
Williams, Thos.	4	1	2
Hays, Peter	4	4	2
Harcum, Cuthbert	4	1	3
Covington, Eliza.	4	1	9
Covington, Roysten B	1	1	6
Hall, John	9	1	8
Haynie, William	5	1	6
Appleby, Norman	7	1	3
Davis, Thomas	5	1	...
Swan, Charles	2	1	2
Toulson, Thomas	4	1	4
Davis, Judith	6	1	1
Nightingale, Mathew	5	1	...
Jones, Morris	3	1	2
Doxey, Jeremiah	5	1	...
Craine, James	6	1	...
Dunaway, John	7	1	...
Williams, M. A	3	1	...
Elliston, Cuthbert	6	1	5
Maurison, Richard	9	1	3
Robertson, George	5	1	4
Palmer, Jessy	4	1	2
Pickron, John	7	1	6
Foushee, Sarah Ann	2	1	2
Nutt, Richard, Junr.	2	1	3
Nelms, William	6	1	8
Harcum, William	7	1	4
Thomas, John	4	1	3
Hughs, William	5	1	...
Gill, Sarah	5	1	3
Dudley, Molley	5	1	...
Corbell, William	6	1	2
Harcum, Ellis	8	1	3
Daughity, John	4	1	1
Ball, Richard	6	1	2
Ball, Joseph	8	1	11
Owens, Richard	4	1	...
Cottrell, John	7	1	9
Eskridge, Elizabeth	5	1	15
Haynie, John, Senr.	8	1	2
Davis, Robert	2	1	...
Rogers, John	10	2	4
Cundiff, John	5	1	3
Davis, Samuel	4	1	1
Almond, John	4	1	4
Fulcher, William	6	1	1
Sims, Jobe	5	1	5
Owens, Richd.	5	1	...
Doxey, John	3	1	2
Packquet, William	8	1	...
Elliston, Cuthbert, Junr.	1	1	...
Maurison, William	7	1	3
Owens, Richard	6	1	1
Palmor, Joseph	4	...	...
Haynie, John	3	1	1
Downing, Charles	2	2	7
Wood, Joseph	7	1	2
Edwards, Jonathan	6	1	...
Harcum, William W	4	1	...
Harcum, Elisha	3	1	5
Dougherty, John	10	2	4
Blundall, John	2	1	3
Lansdon, John	6	1	3
Dougherty, James	3	1	2
Betts, William, Junr.	5	1	1
Lansdell, Benjamin	5	1	5
Lucas, Catharine	4	1	1
Edwards, George	8	1	1
Haynie, Ann	2	1	6
Parker, William	3	...	...
Haynie, John	3	1	2
Smith, Thomas	5	1	...
Waddey, Shapleigh	17	4	4
Smither, Sarah	7	1	2
Conway, Walker	6	1	3
Crowther, Thomas	6	1	...
Hogan, John	5	1	...
Hughlett, William	6	1	6
Jones, Robert	4	1	...
Mott, Mosley	5	1	...

NAME OF HEAD OF FAMILY.	White souls.	Dwellings.	Other buildings.
Owens, William	3	1	...
Pickren, George, Junr.	4	1	...
Wilson, Natt	3	1	4
Pickren, George	6	1	5
Pickren, William	7	1	6
Lucas, Thomas	8	1	4
Nutt, Richard	6	1	2
Gill, John	6	1	3
Elliston, John S	6	1	3
Wildy, William	2	1	3
Schofield, Thomas	6	1	3
Haynie, Daniel	4	1	3
Schofield, Robert	1	1	...
Walker, George	6	1	4
Coleman, Joseph	6	1	...
Cammel, Charles	1	1	...
Lansdell, Sarah	2	1	6
Blackeby, Frances	3	1	...
Tounsand, Haynie	7	1	4
Edwards, Thomas	9	1	8
Gordon, John	9	1	14
Power, Joseph	6	1	1
Walker, William	7	1	3
Betts, Daniel	3	...	...
Crowther, John	6	1	1
Muse, Hudson	7	1	9
Muse, Daniel	6	1	6
Hudnall, Thomas	7	19	19
Haynie, Mack, Junr.	7	1	2
Ball, George	4	1	9
Butler, Mary	2	1	...
Humphreys, Joseph	6	1	5
Burton, William	10	1	2
Haynie, Henry	4	1	4
Haynie, Elisha	6	1	1
Tycer, Cornelius	4	1	1
Fosset, Pheeby	5	1	2
Leland, Ellis	2	1	...
Leland, Peter	6	1	...
Edwards, Ann	5	...	...
Litrell, John	2	1	...
Nash, John	3	1	...
Haynie, William	3	1	1
Litrell, Richard	2	1	4
Pitman, Joseph	3	...	...
Pope, Sarah	3	1	5
Williams, Rawleigh	6	1	...
Astin, George	12	1	4
Williams	3	1	...
Abby, John	6	1	5
Litrell, Moses	8	1	...
Christopher, John	6	1	5
Haynie, Mack	7	1	2
Mealy, James	7	1	4
Williams, William	8	1	1
Haynie, Richard	9	1	...
Haynie, Jedithan	3	1	2
Cralle, Kenner	2	1	2
Alexander, Rawleigh	9	1	3
Hughlett, Winter	5	3	2
Harding, Samuel	8	1	9
Langsdale, William	8	1	7
Ball, Spencer M	14	2	24
Walker, Richard	6	1	4
Rice, Isaac	8	1	6
Prosser, William	6	1	4
Smoot, Charles	6	1	4
Anderson, John	10	1	4
Haynie, John	5	1	...
Daughity, James	4	2	7
Alexander, Judith	4	...	...
Hughlett, John, Junr.	7	1	3
Walker, Thomas	6	1	5
Rice, William, Junr.	4	1	4
Rice, John	6	1	2
France, George	8	1	...
France, Sarah	2	1	1
Dawkins, Moses	4	1	1
Jones, John	3	1	1
Pullin, Leroy	5	1	3
Pullin, Nathan	2	1	5
Christopher, Henry	9	1	6
Downing, Thomas	9	11	39
Headly, Luke	5	...	...
Dawson, William	4	...	...
Bryant, Peter	3	...	...
Davis, Isaac	3	...	...
Mott, Randolph	13	1	6
Welch, Sylvester	6	1	2
Hall, Daniel	4	1	1
Hall, Josiah	9	1	2
Boush, Bennit	6	1	3
Thomas, Robert	5	1	3
Keene, Sarah	5	1	7
Thomas, Peter	7	1	6
Hughlett, John, senr.	9	1	11
Thornton, Presly	7	1	20
Yeatman, Thomas	10	...	...
Cockee, John C	8	2	42
Ball, James	6	1	10
Alexander, Jesse	7	2	10

NAME OF HEAD OF FAMILY.	White souls.	Dwellings.	Other buildings.
Betts, Jordon	6	1	1
Walker, Sarah	3	...	...
Hogan	5	...	...
Hornsby, John	10	1	3
Conway, Joseph	1	1	9
Owens, Richard	5	...	...
Blundell, Elijah	3	...	...
Corbell, Peter	2	1	2
Downing, John	6	1	10
Conway, Robert	4	1	6
Hayes, William	2	1	2
Nelms, Aaron	6	1	2
Oldham, James	4	1	5
Schofield, Henry	4	1	3
Barecroft, John	6	1	2
Edwards, Ann	4	1	4
Kenner, Mary	6	1	14
Haynie, Bridgar	9	2	9
Way, Winifred	2	1	2
Davis, Thomas	5	1	10
Winstead, John	6	1	...
Davis, John	8	...	4
Lee, Richard	...	1	5
Winstead, Samuel	9	2	1
Smith, James	2	1	...
Power, Mary	6	2	1
McAdam, Joseph	6	1	11
Oldham, William	7	1	3
Rice, William	8	1	8
Vanlandingham, Ezekiel	3	1	...
Brown, Vincent	6	1	3
Vanlandingham, Mary	3	1	3
Barecroft, Martrum	11	1	2
Blincoe, Mary	8	1	3
Griffiss, George	6	1	2
Davis, Mary	2	1	6
Simes, Ellis	6	1	...
Neale, Susanah	3	1	1
Hudnall, Joseph	5	1	7
Hudnall, George	...	1	...
Eskridge, Mary	2	1	3
Williams, Joseph	4	1	8
Routt, Richard	6	1	7
Grinstead, Grace	2	1	1
Brumley, Samuel	4	1	...
Meath, Jesse	3	1	...
Efford, Zachariah	5	1	1
Neale, John	10	1	2
Barnes, Mary	4	1	4
Beeland, Mary	7	1	...
Barecroft, Susanah	4	1	7
Stevens, John	3	1	2
Brown, Richard	7	1	...
Ashburne, George	6	1	...
Haynie, Hezekiah	5	1	4
Bryant, Jonathan	8	1	1
Sebree, William	5	2	4
Kirkham, Thomas	7	1	3
Ashburn, Thomas	9	1	3
Keene, Thomas	3	1	4
Jones, John	7	...	...
Harrison, Jesse	6	1	3
Boyall, Thomas	5	2	...
Hudson, Jeremiah	6	1	1
Jones, Thomas	5	1	12
Thomas, Thomas	6	1	...
Kemm, John	3	1	1
Edson, Joseph	8	1	...
Bryant, Robert	3	1	...
Courtney, Charnock	5	1	...
Opie, Lindsy	10	2	10
Boggess, Henry	6	1	7
Neale, Jane	5	1	11
Kenner, William	4	1	5
Hartley, William	9	1	...
Kenner, Mr. (Estate)	1	1	12
Beacham, Abraham	7	1	8
Skinner, Charles	4	1	...
Bussell, John	2	...	...
Jones, Joshua	4	1	1
Bell, Thomas	10	1	2
Thomas, James	6	1	...
McClanaham, James	4	1	2
Grenstead, Richard	8	1	3
Cammall, Price	4	1	1
Dawson, John	9	1	4
Cralle, Samuel	3	1	6
Luttrell, Leroy	2	1	3
Grenstead, John	1	...	...
Dawson, George	5	1	1
Dawson, Daniel	3	1	1
Beacham, Parker	7	1	2
Hudson, John C	12	1	4
Walker, Richard	1	...	...
Hudson, Robuck	7	1	...
Harrison, John R	5	1	2
Barecroft, Ann	2	1	...
Knott, James	1	1	3
Hale, John	6	1	2
Dugless, Edward	8	1	2
Damron, Roger	5	1	...

NORTHUMBERLAND COUNTY—Continued.

NAME OF HEAD OF FAMILY.	White souls.	Dwellings.	Other buildings.
Self, William	7	1	3
Headley, William	8	1	4
White, George	9	1	....
Brown, Jeremiah	3	1	....
Vanlandingham, Benjamin	3	1	3
Oldham, Leroy, Junr	2	1	3
Oldham, Thomas	6	1	3
Self, Mathias	9	1	4
Beacham, Daniel	3	1	2
Leader, Samuel	9	1	2
Hall, William	3	1	1
Cole, Ann	7	1	2
Beacham, Trussell	7	1	5
Lewis, John	5	1	2
Self, Margrett	6	1	4
Williams, George	1	1	1
Fulks, John	6	1	6
Lewis, William	3	1	2
Oldham, Leroy, senr	4	1	3
Lewis, William K	5	1	1
Cox, Ann	6	1	7
Lamkin, Judeth	4	1	7
Trasse, John	13	1	9

NAME OF HEAD OF FAMILY.	White souls.	Dwellings.	Other buildings.
Short, Benedick	6	1	2
Hall, Ann	8	1	....
Self, Thomas	4	1	1
Dawson, Henry	4	1	1
Cookman, Rice	9	1	4
Buttler, John	2	1	2
Lavender, John	4	1	1
Lewis, Willoby	5	1	4
Claughton, William	4	2	8
Foalks, William	2	2	....
Hall, Stephen	10	1	4
Claughton, John	5	1	4
Dale, John	6	1	....
Walker, Daniel	4	1	1
Lewis, James	3	1	3
Hall, John	3	1	1
Claughton, James	8	1	10
Hudnall, Ezekiel	3	1	3
Knott, Richard	9	1	4
Bennet, Robert	5	1	....
Hardwick, John	5	1	3
Lamkin, Ann	5	1	3
Maskell, Thomas C	6	1	....

NAME OF HEAD OF FAMILY.	White souls.	Dwellings.	Other buildings.
Jones, William	5	1	....
Larkin, Patrick	2	1	....
Clarke, Robert	3	1	1
Lewis, Jeremiah	7	1	1
Dugless, Thomas	2	1	....
Graham, William	6	1	4
Turner, John	3	1	2
Shivrall, Allin L	3	1	4
Roberts, John	3	1	1
Jones, W	10	1	8
Winstead, Frances	11	2	2
Winstead, Daniel	5	2	3
Winstead, Chloe	7	2	4
Vanlandingham, George A	8	1	4
Middleton, William	3	1	5
Eskridge, George	6	1	5
Clarke, Cha	6	1	5
Hall, Peter	6	2	2
Bearcroft, Samuel	7	1	....
Harding, William	5	1	7
Jinkins, John	4	1	....
Brumley, Daniel	5	1	4
Mortimore, James	4	1	1

NAME OF HEAD OF FAMILY.	White souls.	Dwellings.	Other buildings.
Bailess, John	4	1	3
Thomas, William	5	1	4
Oldham, William, senr	2	1	6
Ashburn, William	8	1	5
Menzies, Samuel P	4	1	6
Vanlandingham, Henry	8	1	2
Garner, Jesse	8	1	3
Garner, William P	9	1	5
Hill, George	3	1	....
France, John	4	1	....
Rice, Charles	9	1	4
Todd, Cornilious	6	1	....
Bayless, William	2	1	1
Robinson, Joseph	4	1	2
Rice, William	8	1	1
Shearley, George	2	1	....
Webb, Elizabeth	4	1	5
Dawson, William	7	1	....
Oldham, George	3	1	4
Cox, Peter	4	1	7

ROCKINGHAM COUNTY.

LIST OF MICHAEL ROROK.	White souls.	Dwellings.	Other buildings.
Grisbee, John	7	1	....
Grigsbee, Benjamin	6	....	....
Short, Saml	8	1	....
Weable, Robert	6	....	....
Kite, Phillip	6	....	....
Berry, Augustine	4	....	....
Moyer, Jacob	7	1	6
Moyer, Phillip	2	....	....
Null, John	5	1	....
Blosse, Geo	7	....	....
Snider, Gasper	3	....	....
Null, George	6	....	....
Null, Henry	9	1	1
Kite, George	7	1	....
Kite, John	8	1	....
Youly, Jacob	9	....	....
Runkle, Lewis	10	....	....
Long, Henry	7	1	....
Kite, William	8	1	....
Watson, Zachariah	5	2	2
Louderback, Joseph	3	....	....
Lee, Zachariah	3	....	....
Munger, David	4	....	....
Shulder, Matthias	6	....	....
Fulce, George	4	....	....
Oler, William	3	1	....
Oler, Henry	5	....	....
Price, Francis	3	....	....
Oler, John	6	....	....
Price, Henry	3	....	....
Kiser, Michl	10	1	1
Kiser, Felty	3	....	....
Evert, Windle	5	1	1
Loudeck, Matthias	6	....	....
Berry, Malchia	6	1	....
Fulce, John, Senr	10	1	1
Fulce, John, Junr	3	....	....
Hoard, William	9	1	....
Strickler, John	10	1	....
Toleymayer, Michl	9	....	....
Hill, Francis	5	....	....
Rutherford, Robt	5	....	....
Rorok, Michael	8	1	....
Comber, Stofley	5	1	....
Carthrea, John	10	1	7
Hannah, Joseph	3	1	2
Yarley, Benj	10	1	1
Hannah, Thomas	2	....	1
Rickle, Matthew	5	....	1
Bailes, Thomas	8	....	1
Maffort, Gasper	8	1	2
Fisher, Danl	6	....	2
Coshew, Bennoni	16	....	2
Cook, Henry	5	1	2
Hook, Robt, Senr	5	1	4
Hook, Robt, Junr	7	....	2
Hook, Wm, Senr	9	1	....
Hook, Wm, Junr	8	1	1
Morrisson, John	7	....	2
Hudlow, Andrew	8	1	2
Hook, James	6	1	1
Fisher, Abraham	3	....	1
Peslinger, Jacob	6	....	1
Scott, Jacob	6	....	1
Chapman, John	3	....	1
Lemmon, John, Junr	6	1	1
Campbell, Elizabeth	6	1	1
Beard, James	10	1	4
Miller, Leonard	2	1	1
Painter, Leonard	2	1	1

LIST OF MICHAEL ROROK—continued.	White souls.	Dwellings.	Other buildings.
Painter, George	4	....	2
Dike, Jacob	5	....	1
Dike, Henry	5	1	1
Bell, Wm	5	1	1
Smith, Henry	9	1	2
Huston, Mary	9	1	2
Kiplinger, Jacob	4	1	9
Maheffe, John	5	....	1
Whikle, Peter	8	1	2
Keller, Lewis	7	1	1
Miller, John	5	....	1
Lemmon, John	7	....	3
Kiplinger, Phillip	4	....	3
Carpenter, Barnet	8	1	2
Tanner, Michl	7	....	3
Edde, John	7	....	2
Berger, Matthias Well	12	1	1
Viah, Gidion	4	....	1
Black, Henry	3	1	2
Huston, John }	5	....	2
Ireland, Wm }			
Fanner, Michl	3	....	2
Serphes, John	3	1	2
Shire, Jacob	5	....	2
Oldorpha, Anthony	6	1	1
Davis, Thomas	5	....	1
Whitmer, Jacob	8	....	3
Trobough, Wm	10	1	1
Nicholas	1	1	2
Foutwiler, Leonard	10	1	1
Crofford, Wm	1	....	1
Baker, John	3	....	1
Snap, John	9	1	3
Fraizor, John	3	....	2
Youn, Saml, Junr	9	....	1
Cook, Jacob	6	....	1
Roadaimour, Barbary	4	....	1
Roadaimour, Jacob	3	1	1
Sherer, Michl	6	1	1
Doubt, Matthias	2	....	3
Shoulderman, John	4	1	1
Deadmour, Christan	4	....	1
Hoop, John	2	1	1
Alford, John	9	....	2
Lingerfeild, John	7	....	1
Case, Thos	5	....	1
Armstrong, Henry	5	....	2
Boswell, George	5	1	9

LIST OF JOHN FITZWATER.	White souls.	Dwellings.	Other buildings.
Bible, Adam, Senr	6	1	1
Bible, Adam, Junr	3	1	1
Berger, George	7	1	....
Baker, Michl	9	1	2
Cheryholm, Willim	11	1	2
Dove, Henry	....	....	....
Despinet, Joseph	8	1	1
Fulk, John	6	1	1
Fitzwater, John	8	1	3
Fitzwater, William	9	1	1
Humble, Cunrod	7	1	2
Harter, Henry & John	10	1	1
Hour, Godfrey	2	1	....
Harter, Adam	4	1	1
Kester, Conrod	9	1	1
Kiplinger, John, Senr	3	1	1
Keplinger, George	....	....	....
Kiplinger, Christian	10	....	....
Kiplinger, John, Junr	....	....	....

LIST OF JOHN FITZWATER—continued.	White souls.	Dwellings.	Other buildings.
Keister, Paul	6	1	1
Keister, Jacob, Senr	4	1	1
Keister, Richard & Jacob, Junr	5	1	1
Kounce, Paulser	....	....	....
Lame, Peter	8	1	1
Kunse, Christian	6	1	1
Lame, Jacob	10	1	....
Lame, Henry	6	1	....
Lame, Michael	7	1	....
Lewis, George	7	1	....
Mauk, Rudolph	10	1	1
Mauk, Daniel	3	1	1
Miller, Abraham	9	1	1
Miller, Jacob	3	1	....
Marshal, Elizabeth	6	1	1
Moyer, Michael	9	1	1
Parrot, Samuel	6	1	....
Parrot, Joseph	4	1	1
Rinehart, Adam	....	....	....
Runyon, John	9	....	....
Ruble, George	8	1	1
Ruble, John	6	1	1
Ruddle, John	7	1	2
Shoamaker, George	10	1	1
Trumbo, Jacob, Senr	5	1	2
Whetzel, Martin	3	1	1
Whetzel, Henry	....	....	....
Weatherholt Nicholas	4	1	1
Zetty, Peter	7	1	1
Zetty, Jacob	4	....	....
Henry, Kunce	3	1	....
Honnaken, Frederick	4	1	1

LIST OF JOSIAH DAVISON.	White souls.	Dwellings.	Other buildings.
Baxter, Capt George	8	1	....
Johnston, John	6	1	1
Hopkins, Capt John	10	1	1
Fedford, George, Senr	6	1	....
Fedford, George, Junr	3	1	....
Berry, Benjamin	7	1	1
Blain, John	10	1	1
Matthews, Robt	9	1	1
McClain, Ellonr (Widow)	2	1	....
Lewis, Reese	7	1	....
Vance, Wandle	7	1	....
Wright, Susanna (Widow)	2	1	....
Phillips, Samuel	6	....	....
Currey, John, Senr	7	1	7
Curry, Nichl	6	1	1
Christman, Many	4	1	1
Stover, Daniel	6	1	1
Higgins, William	8	1	....
Berry, David	12	1	....
Smith, George	7	1	....
Gordan, Thomas, Senr	5	1	1
Henton, Benjamin	3	1	1
Henton, Ebenezor	5	1	2
Gilmore, James	5	1	1
Lock, John	4	1	....
Henton, Joseph	6	1	....
Harrison, Daniel	2	1	....
Hopkins, Archd, Senr	5	1	2
Love, Ephraim	2	1	1
Williams, Owen	7	1	....
Shanklin, Elizth	7	1	....
William, David	1	....	....
Steel, John	1	....	....

LIST OF JOSIAH DAVISON—continued.	White souls.	Dwellings.	Other buildings.
Fulton, Janet (Widow)	3	1	1
Thomas, Evin	9	1	1
Matthews, Townsend	6	1	1
Ralston, William	4	1	1
Ralston, David, Senr	6	1	1
Ralston, David, Junr	3	1	....
Harrison, Jesse, Senr	8	1	1
Coffman, Jacob	6	1	1
Herdman, John, Senr	3	1	1
Herdman, John, Junr	7	1	....
Campbell, Thomas	3	1	1
Dunlap, Robert	6	1	1
Cluff, John	5	1	1
Thompson, Alexander	....	....	....
Wilson, John	1	....	....
Boyd, John	1	....	....
Mars, Charles	3	....	....
Kookhoon, James	3	1	....
Green, Francis	3	1	1
Bowan, Thomas	8	1	1
Davisson, Josiah	8	1	....
Trump, Daniel	8	1	....

LIST OF WILLIAM McDOWEL.	White souls.	Dwellings.	Other buildings.
March, Boston	12	1	1
Moor, Thomas, Junr	4	1	1
Moor, Thomas, Senr	2	1	1
Moor, John	8	....	....
Reader, Michael	....	....	....
West, Mrs	6	1	1
West, William	10	1	....
Karling, Joseph	9	1	....
Phillips, Eving	6	1	....
Phillips, James, Senr	5	1	1
Phillips, John, Junr	7	1	....
Woodley, Jacob	8	1	1
Byrd, Andrew, Junr	6	1	....
Byrd, Andw, Senr	4	1	2
Byrd, Abraham	4	1	1
Counce, Peter	11	1	1
Cumings, Moses	8	1	1
Circle, Lewis	11	1	1
Shever, John	3	1	....
Rorok, Phillimon	9	1	1
Moor, Capt Reubin	3	....	....
Gres, Jacob	10	1	1
Holsinger, Michl	8	1	1
Huling, James	4	1	1
Huling, Mr	6	1	....
Armingtrout, George	8	1	2
Lookey, John	5	1	1
Barkley, Jacob	6	1	1
Lookey, Thomas	5	1	1
Fetherhow, Michl	2	1	1
Fallowron, Knollow	6	1	1
Harrisson, Zeb	13	1	1
Bucher, James	10	1	1
McFarling, Alexander	4	1	....
Keller, Michael	2	....	....
Long, Nancy	7	....	....
Moor, Robt	3	1	....
Frailey, Daniel	8	1	1
Armstrong, Shepard	9	1	....
Pickril, William	6	1	1
Helfry, John	7	1	1
Harman, Peter	5	1	1
Barkle, Jacob	7	1	....
McDowel, William	11	1	10

ROCKINGHAM COUNTY—Continued.

LIST OF BENJA'N HARRISON.

NAME OF HEAD OF FAMILY.	White souls.	Dwellings.	Other buildings.
Harrison, Robart	1	2	2
Harrisson, Thomas, Junr.	1		
Millare, Samuel	6	1	3
Divier, James	7	1	2
Harrison, Ezekiel	6	1	2
Harrison, Robt	7	1	2
Lounsdale, Thos	5	1	1
Appler, John	6	1	2
Hicks, John	5	1	2
Honton, Jams	7		
Harrison, Josiah	5	1	2
Harrison, Nehemiah	9		
Shankling, Andw	3		
Hewit, Thos	2	1	1
Scott, Thos	4	1	3
Burges, Henry	7		1
Turner, John	2		
Lam, William	7	2	2
Guin, Patrick	8	2	1
Guin, James	6	1	
Wage, David	5		
Donaley, Charles	5		
Harrison, Benja	14	1	4
Booman, Godfrey	3		
Mansfeild, John	2		
Boshang, Jacob, Senr	10	1	2
Boshang, Jacob, Junr	3		
Love, Daniel	1	1	2
Leanaham, Dennis	6	1	2
Duck, Monanest	4		
Dicktom, Joseph	9	2	1
McClain, Charles	3		
Guin, John	3	1	1
Augabright, Adam			
Augabright, Geo			
Augabright, Martin			
Hemphill, Saml	7	1	
Cravers, Esther	9	1	3
Shanklin, Catty	6		
Ewin, Henry	10	1	4
Ewin, Wm	2	1	9
Ewin, John			
forsythe, Saml	9	1	3
Forsythe, Abram	3		
McClewer, Michl	6	1	

LIST OF CAPT. WM. HERRING.

NAME OF HEAD OF FAMILY.	White souls.	Dwellings.	Other buildings.
Butt, Adam	5	1	2
Shanklin, Andrew	4	1	
Wise, Adam	4	1	3
Magill, Alexr	2	1	1
Wolf, Andrew	2		
Bogan, Andrew	8		
Herring, Bethewel	3	1	1
Erwin, Benjamin	6	1	1
Shanklin, Edward	6	1	2
Ferrel, Edward	19		
Beard, Francis	5		
Erwin, Francis	9	1	6
Black, Frederick	9	1	1
Songer, George	4		
Harman, Henry	8		
Pace, Henry	5		
Curry, Isaiah	8	1	7
Gratton, John	9	6	8
Songer, Jacob	9	2	2
Tanner, John	12	1	1
Christian, Kinser	8		
Rowler, Conrod	2		
Magill, James	3	1	4
Magill, James, Junr	4	1	1
Devers, Jacob	2		
Roler, Peter	9	2	3
Deck, Ronamar	8	1	5
Henry, Robart	4	1	2
Erwin, Saml	6	1	1
Howard, Saml	10	2	2
Hansberger, Stephen	3	1	2
Carr's, Robt	7		
Howard, William	12		
Howard, William, Junr	4	1	2
Alford, John	10	1	1
Howard, James	12		
Venis, Christian	3		
Huffman, Valentine	7	2	2
Morris, Morris	4	1	2
Carter, Francis	5		
Herring, William	4	2	2
Poss, Nicholas	4	1	1
Butt, Windle	8	2	3
Hulby, Conrod	7	1	2

LIST OF CAPT. WM. HERRING—continued.

NAME OF HEAD OF FAMILY.	White souls.	Dwellings.	Other buildings.
Butt, John	2	1	1
Garten, Uriah	3	1	1
Murry, Barnabas	2	1	2
Huston, John	10	1	3
Erwin, Benjm & son	6	1	1
Hinds, William	3	1	1

LIST OF ISAAC HENKLE.

NAME OF HEAD OF FAMILY.	White souls.	Dwellings.	Other buildings.
Feter, George, Senr	11	1	3
Henkle, Abam	11	1	2
Johnston, Andw	7	1	2
Eberman, Jacob, Junr	5		2
Eberman, Jacob, Senr	4	1	1
Waugh, James	8		1
Cheverunt, Joseph	6		1
Elsworth, Moses, Senr	4		1
Pharis, Johnston	4		1
Henkle, Yost	6	1	3
Walker, George	11		1
Negeley, George	3		2
Harper, Jacob	10	1	2
Elsworth, Moses, Junr	2		1
Bumgardner, Godfrey	8	1	1
Bennet, Joseph	11		1
Root, Jacob	3	1	2
Teeter, Phillip	11	1	1
Summerfield, Joseph	3		1
Lambert, John	6		1
Blunt, Redding	9		2
Mitchell, John	2		1
Teeter, George, Junr	5		
Shuk, Jacob	3		
Grag, Samuel	1		
Carr, Jacob	7		3
Harper, Phillip	7	1	1
Ganday, Uriah	4		
Wood, Isaac	8		1
Teeter, Rebeckah	7	1	2
Eberman, William	1		1
Wilkenson, George	3		2
Cuningham, James	11		2
Harmes, Rihd	1		
Redman, Saml	1		
Allen, Moses	1		
Shall, John	2	1	3
Shall, Peter	5		2
Bland, Thos	5		1
Minnis, Robert	1	1	2
Henkle, Isaac	4	1	

LIST OF ANTHONY RADER.

NAME OF HEAD OF FAMILY.	White souls.	Dwellings.	Other buildings.
Ruddle, George	12	1	2
Fesel, Michael	3	1	1
Peters, John	7	1	1
Moor, John	10	1	2
Miller, David	5	1	1
Trout, Felty	9	1	1
Siples, Cunrod	10	1	1
Twotwiler, John	2		
Witman, John	5	1	1
Grass, James	6	1	
Reeves, Brewer	2	1	1
Lair, Fardinand	5	1	1
Rader, Matthias	5	1	2
Came, Nicholas	6	2	2
Surfas, Martin	4	1	
Rader, Adam	5	2	1
Knave, George	2	1	
Knave, Henry	8	1	1
Henkle, Phillip	5	1	
Stolp, Henry	3	1	1
Stolp, John	7	1	1
Talor, Peter	4	1	
Miller, Abraham	7	1	1
Miller, Jacob	2	1	1
Shutter, John	1	1	1
Andes, Andrew	8	2	2
Ritner, Jacob	5	1	2
Bare, John	7	2	2
Rips, Michl	3	1	1
Knistrick, John	9	1	1
Thomas, John	2	1	
Pup, Chrisman	2	1	1
Brion, John	9	2	1
Reader, Anthony	9	1	2
Fifer, Adam	8	2	1
Hower, Michl			
Hower, Michl	8	2	1
Trumbo, Jacob	7	1	1
Fifer, John	4		
Orback, Adam	6	1	1

LIST OF ANTHONY RADER—continued.

NAME OF HEAD OF FAMILY.	White souls.	Dwellings.	Other buildings.
Fay, Christly	5	1	
Bowman, John	5	1	1
Thomas, Benjamin	8	1	1
Coach, John	12	1	1
Roland, Richard	7	1	1
Orback, Andrew	7	1	1
Painter, Christly	10	2	1
Fulinor, Lewis	3	1	1
Shaver, George	4	1	
Mensek, John	8	1	1
Erehard, Georg	11	1	2
Holsener, Michl	8	1	
Berry, Nicholas	10	1	1
Christ, Andrew	11	1	1
Raad, Henry	5	1	1
Bowman, Benjamin	8	1	2
Bower, Laurence	9	1	
Howman, Goodlep	5	1	2
Cleck, Margaret (Widow)	6	1	
Bowman, Jacob, Junr	10	1	1
Hedreck, Charles	9	1	1
Teeter, Abraham	8	1	1
Harris, John	5	1	2
Cuntryman, Henry	8	1	1
Hersler, Woolsey	7	1	2
Coffman, Jacob	9	1	1
Lank, John	2	1	
Cherrington, Wm	7	1	1
Dunlap, Wm, Esqr	10	1	2
Lair, Matthias	5	1	2
Rife, John	3	1	2
Norton, Jacob	7	1	
Robinson, David	6	1	3
Sites, Vandle	6	1	1
Sites, Christian	5	1	1
Sites, Jno	6	1	1
Softly, Valintine	9	1	1
Masberger, John	10	1	1
ford, Michl	7	1	1
Berry, Nicholas, Junr	4	1	1
Brigs, John	6	1	
Hifft, Jacob	11	1	
Stroak, Josiah	3	1	
Brannamer, Jacob, Senr	5	2	3
Rymel, Phillip	7	1	1
Trout, George	6	1	2
Craune, Frederick	3	1	
Byan, Thomas, Senr	7	1	3
Bryan, Peter	5	1	
Bryan, John	1		
Bryan, Cornelias	4	1	
Bryan, Wm	5	1	2
Bryan, Thos, Junr	6	1	1
Bryan, Morgan	1		
Ruddle, John	2		
Vance, Handle	3	1	2
Thomas, John	12	1	4
Runnels, Jno	4	1	
Gumb, Norton	10	1	
Carsner, George	2	1	1
Shamaker, Peter	4	1	1
Sinlin, John, Senr	7	1	1
Sinlin, Jacob	4	1	2
Cring, John	8	1	3
Custard, Arnold	4	1	
Branaman, David	5	1	3
Branaman, Abraham	9	1	3
Shank, Henry	4	1	1
Whisler, Henry	8	1	3
Miller (Widow)	10	1	
Shank, Michael	7	1	1
Bunes, Laughlin	11	1	
Burnes, Jams	2	1	
Culp, Michl	3	1	
Speares, George	6	1	5
Sheffer, Nicholas	11	1	
Knave, John	2	1	
Bowman, Joseph	5	1	2
Rife, Jacob	5	1	1
Cumbaker, John	7	1	2
Crumbaker, Peter	3	1	1
Christman, Capt George	9	1	3
Green, James	9	1	1
Green, Ezekial	4	1	
Matthews, Solomon & Brumfeild in Co	50	6	7
Hank, Margaret	4	1	

LIST OF JAMES DYER.

NAME OF HEAD OF FAMILY.	White souls.	Dwellings.	Other buildings.
Blizard, John	4	1	7
Blizard, William	5	1	1

LIST OF JAMES DYER—continued.

NAME OF HEAD OF FAMILY.	White souls.	Dwellings.	Other buildings.
Gragg, William	4		1
Hoover, Laurence	6	1	1
Hoover, George	5	1	1
Hoover, Sabastian	3	1	2
Stone, Henry	8	1	3
Roleman, Christian	11	1	5
Berger, Jacob	5	1	2
Grogg, Henry	9	1	1
Swadley, Henry	6	1	2
Rexroad, Zachariah, Junr.	3	1	
Proops, Frederick	10	1	2
Galaspey, Jacob	3	1	
Props, Leonard	10	1	2
Swadley, Mark	2	1	
Props, Daniel	3	1	2
Props, Michl	2	1	1
Galaspey, Thos	3	1	2
Props, Henry	2	1	1
Hoover, Peter	9	1	1
Kester, Frederick	8	1	3
Davis, Robt	7	1	6
Havener, Frederick	8	1	2
Senate, Paterick	3	1	
Havenor, Jacob	10	1	3
Dyer, John	4	1	1
Blizard, Thomas	5	1	3
Cogar, Jacob	4	1	1
Keeper, Jacob	1	1	
Wagoner, Lewis	5	1	3
Dunkle, George	7	1	7
Gragg, Wm, Junr	6	1	
Dunkle, John	6	1	13
Fule, Lewis	1	1	
Kester, James	1	1	1
Blizard, Burton	5	1	
Morrill, Mary (Widow)	8	1	1
Dyer, Rodger	6	1	5
Dier, Mathias	13	1	1
Patton, Matthew	8	1	6
Blizard, James	2	1	1
Byrnes, John	7	1	1
Deason, John	3	1	1
Dyer, James	11	1	14

LIST OF ROBT. DAVIS.

NAME OF HEAD OF FAMILY.	White souls.	Dwellings.	Other buildings.
Friend, Jacob	10	1	2
Warpole, Nicholas	5	1	3
Warpole, John	3		
Vendevner, Jacob	6		2
Keplinger, George	8	1	1
Keplinger, Adam	3		
Harper, Jacob	11	1	1
Castel, Valintine	8		1
Michael, Nicholas	5		1
Evick, Geo	7	1	1
Evick, Francis	3		3
Bush, Jacob	4		1
Mucklewain, Thos	9	1	1
Priece, Jos	8		1
Waldrom, Geo	8		1
Vaniom, Pet	4		3
Faris, John	6		1
Collick, Thos	7		1
Coks, Thos	3		2
Richards, Saml	5		2
Hedrick, Chas	11		2
Cukhole, Andw	2		1
Skidmore, John	13	1	4
Caye, George	8		2
Davis, Jas	9		1
Springstone, Pet	6		1
Skidmore, Thos	7		1
Cayle, Gabriel	13		1
Shankling, Thos	11	1	3
Hammer, George	5	1	4
Stratton, Suriah	7		3
Bush, Leonard	7		1
Bush, Michl	5		1
Bush, Lewis	2		1
Briggs, Joseph	7		1
Skidmore, Joseph	11		3
Matthews, Lastly	3		1
Windelplack, Henry	4		1
Clishshaw, Laurence	5		1
Weaton, Benjamin	2		1
Conrod, Jacob	12		2
Clifton, William	4		1
Hole, Adam	10		2
Hole, George	4		1
Powers, Charles	5	1	

SURRY COUNTY.

LIST OF JAMES KEE AND LEMUEL COCKE.

NAME OF HEAD OF FAMILY.	White souls.	Dwellings.	Other buildings.
Avriss, John	5	1	2
Andrews, John	12	2	3
Bell, James	3		
Blunt, Richard	2	1	4
Bishop, James	8	2	2
Burges, John	2	....	....
Burgess, John	4	3	8
Bedingfield, Ann	8	1	3
Bishop, John	4	2	3
Bishop, William	3	1	1
Barker, Lemuel	4	1	2
Bishop, David	9	1	....
Bartle, Thomas	3	1	1
Barker, Lucy	2	2	....
Berriman, Nathl	8	2	3
Carseley, Michael	5	1	5
Cooper, John	6	1	2
Cooper, Frederk	4	1	2
Charity, Sally	....	1	....
Cocks, Jesse	5	2	4
Collier, John	6	1	2
Cocke, Archd	1	1	10
Cheatham, John	6	1	6
Cheatham, James	1	1	1
Cocke, Lemuel	4	1	13
Carrill, Michael	3	....	....
Dewell, Drewry	4	....	....
Dewell, Jesse	6	1	....
Dewell, Thomas	4	1	1
Dewell, Berry	8	1	....
Dewell, James	7	1	1
Davis, John	6	1	3
Davis, John, jr	2	1	....
Dowden, Thomas	1	....	....
Ellis, Benjamin	3	2	3
Emery, John	7	1	....
Emery, John, Junior	3	1	....
Emery, Howell	6	1	....
Freeland, Abram	3	....	....
Gilbert, Henry	4	1	5
Howard, Henry	4	1	3
Howard, Betty	5	1	4
Hill, Mary	1	1	6
Hill, Stirling	6	2	6
Justiss, William	3	1	1
Jordan, Margaret	4	1	....
Johnson, Levi	6	1	....
Johnson, Hartwell	5	1	....
Johnson, William	9	1	....
Jones, Nathan	4	1	12
Jones, H. (Esta)	5	1	12
Kee, James	17	2	9
McGuriman, Duncan	3	1	1
Moody, Archibd	3	1	1
Milby, William	5	1	3
Maddera, Elizabeth	5	1	2
McIntosh, Robert	6	1	6
Porter, Edward	8	1	....
Parker, Elizabeth	2	2	....
Pyland, Robert	9	1	3
Rae, James	5	1	1
Rose, John	3	1	....
Rose, William	8	2	2
Sebrele, Nathl	9	1	5
Sorsby, Stephen	11	3	6
Stiles, John	3	1	....
Steward, John	7	2	2
Sledge, Ann	4	1	4
Stephens, William	6	1	3
Thompson, William	10	1	2
Tillott, John	7	1	3
Valentine, Peter	10	1	....
Williams, James	....	1	....
Walden, Stephen	1	....	....
Warren, Joseph	9	1	2

LIST OF NATHANIEL HARRISON.

NAME OF HEAD OF FAMILY.	White souls.	Dwellings.	Other buildings.
Allen, William	9	2	35
Anthony, William	5	1	....
Buchanan, Susanna	1	1	7
Barradale, Robert	5	1	1
Belsches, James	3	1	12
Charity, David	4	1	....
Cryer, Nicholas	3	1	3
Cocke, William	2	2	9
Charity, Henry	10	1	....
Collins, William	5	1	14
Charrity, Benjamin	5	1	....
Dunlop, Archibald	3	1	13
Fletcher, Thomas	2	1	6
Grantham, Thomas	4	1	3
Grantham, Stephen	4	1	1
Harrison, Nathaniel	5	1	13
Jarratt, John	9	1	4
King, Randolph	4	1	1
Lucas, Christopher	3	2	14
Laughton, William	1	1	3
Mackie, Andrew	10	1	6
Mosing, John	5	1	1
Putney, Benjamin	9	1	6
Scott, Nicholas	11	1	....
Stewart, John	4	1	7
Sorsby, Thomas	4	1	5
Simon, Thomas	5	1	....
Stewart, James	6	1	....
Stewart, John B	3	....	....
Willison, James	6	....	....

LIST OF JOHN H. COCKE AND JOHN WATKINS.

NAME OF HEAD OF FAMILY.	White souls.	Dwellings.	Other buildings.
Andrews, William	9	1	3
Andrews, Nathl	8	1	2
Andrews, John, Sen	3	1	1
Adams, Nathl	1	1	3
Browne, William, junr	6	2	17
Bage, Thomas, Sen	2	1	4
Bartle, John, Senr	3	1	3
Badgett, John	1	1	2
Bailey, William, Senr	9	1	3
Bailey, Edward	1	....	....
Burges, Revd Henry I. (Glebes)	3	1	6
Bailey, Mary	4	1	2
Browne, William, Senr	8	2	22
Browne, Benjamin E	3	1	3
Collier, Lucy	1	1	5
Clarke, James	5	1	7
Carrile, Mary	5	1	....
Charrity, Thomas	3	1	....
Clinch, William, Senr	6	2	5
Clinch, William, junr	5	1	3
Cocke, John H	7	1	22
Cocke, Ann	7	1	8
Debereaux, David	10	1	1
Dewell, Thomas	4	1	1
Ellis, Jonathan	5	1	4
Edwards, Michael	1	....	....
Frazier, William	3	....	....
Harris, Thomas	....	....	3
Holdsworth, Rebecca	3	1	6
Hart, Joseph	5	....	....
King, Mary	4	1	2
Lane, John	9	1	2
Mosing, Henry, junr	7	1	4
Marks, John	5	1	....
Maddera, Elizabeth	5	1	2
Moody, Hannah	4	1	2
Pyland, Mary	4	1	4
Riggan, Benjamin	5	1	2
Riggan, William	8	1	1
Riggan, Jesse	6	1	....
Spratley, Thomas	3	....	....
Savidge, Joel	5	1	2
Smith, Mary	5	1	2
Smith, Michael	6	1	7
Spratley, William	6	1	4
Smith, Lucy	7	1	6
Savidge, John	3	1	3
Scammell, Thomas	6	1	4
Savidge, William	3	....	....
Thompson, William	1	....	....
Thompson, Nathaniel	1	1	....
Thompson, Ann	1	....	....
Watkins, John, jr	1	....	....
Wall, Thomas	6	1	5
Watkins, John (younger)	1	1	9
Warren, Frederick	9	1	2
Walden, Sarah	2	1	1
Walden, William	5	1	....
Watkins, John, Senr	9	1	4

LIST OF WILLIAM SPRATLEY.

NAME OF HEAD OF FAMILY.	White souls.	Dwellings.	Other buildings.
Atkinson, John	8	1	2
Andrews, David	6	1	1
Andrews, Richard	1	....	....
Atkinson, Mary	5	1	....
Atkinson, Benja	5	1	....
Atkinson, William	3	....	....
Banks, Matthew	1	1	....
Bailey, Samuel	6	1	6
Brown, John	3	2	2
Brown, Jesse	1	....	....
Bevin, George	7	1	....
Browne, Wm (To)	....	1	6
Bryant, Jesse	6	....	....
Bryant, James	6	1	....
Bailey, John	2	1	4
Bailey, Lemuel	6	1	7
Bailey, Anselm	6	1	6
Bailey, Elizabeth	4	1	7
Batts, John	10	1	2
Bell, Stephen, Senr	1	2	1
Bell, Stephen, junr	1	....	....
Bell, Benjamin	1	....	....
Bell, Ann	1	....	....
Bell, Jenny	1	....	....
Bell, Selah	1	....	....
Brown, James	9	1	....
Burges, Thomas	1	1	4
Bruce, James	9	1	....
Barham, Faith	5	1	2
Cocks, John	4	....	....
Cocks, William, Senr	7	1	3
Clarke, Ethelred	9	1	....
Cocks, Mary	4	1	3
Drury, Richard	4	1	3
Evans, Rebecca	7	1	5
Edwards, William	11	1	....
Hargrave, Hartwell	4	1	2
Hargrave, Hinckey	5	1	....
Hargrave, John	3	1	....
Hargrave, Lucy	3	1	2
Hart, Hartwell	4	1	4
Hargrave, Mary	6	1	2
Hart, Ann	4	1	1
Harriss, James	10	2	2
Harriss, Randolph	9	1	....
Holleman, Arthur	2	1	3
Holleman, Joseph, Senr	7	1	5
Holleman, Joseph, jr	6	1	....
Holleman, Wilson	4	1	2
Hargrave, Anselm	8	1	2
Holt, William	5	1	3
Holloway, Jesse	7	1	2
Holloway, Job	6	1	....
Judkins, James	4	1	5
Judkins, Samuel	8	1	1
Judkins, Jacob	6	1	4
Inman, Isham	5	1	1
Inman, Ann	1	1	1
Judkins, John	2	1	3
Judkins, John, Senr	5	1	4
Judkins, John, jr	7	1	2
Judkins, Jesse	4	1	1
Judkins, Mary	4	1	2
Kee, William	5	1	....
Kee, Robert	6	2	2
Lane, William	10	2	4
Little, Jesse	5	1	1
Little, Samuel	1	....	....
Little, Martha	2	1	2
Lane, Frederick	5	1	5
Lane, Thomas	6	1	3
Marriott, William	1	1	2
Maget, William	4	1	4
Moore, Jesse	7	1	1
Pond, Mary	5	1	1
Presson, John	8	1	6
Pleasants, Thomas	6	1	3
Pleasants, Abigail	7	1	....
Pleasants, Burwell	2	1	....
Pully, Lewis	9	1	2
Rogers, William	4	1	....
Sprattey, Benja	6	1	2
Savidge, Hartwell	3	1	....
Sharpe, Burwell	4	1	4
Spratley, William	....	1	4
Spratley, John	1	....	....
Savidge, Sarah	7	1	1
Thompson, John	5	1	3
Wilson, John	7	1	1
Wilson, Elizabeth	2	1	4
Wall, James	5	1	2
Wall, Joel	1	1	....
White, Benjamin	2	2	2
Wall, Jonathan	7	1	4
Wrenn, Thomas	6	1	3
Wrenn, John	11	1	2
Warren, Thomas	6	1	4
White, John	5	1	7
White, Henry	9	1	2

LIST OF WILLIAM HART.

NAME OF HEAD OF FAMILY.	White souls.	Dwellings.	Other buildings.
Adams, James	1	1	....
Bennett, William	10	1	1
Barham, Joseph	7	1	2
Blow, Samuel	1	2	1
Collier, Martha	3	1	2
Cocke, Richard	9	1	9
Coggin, Micajah	7	1	2
Davis, Hannah	9	1	2
Davis, Rebecca	1	1	3
Davis, Archibald	7	1	3
Faulcon, Nicholas	8	2	18
Faulcon, Jacob	11	1	14
Dekerwan, Alexander	3	1	2
Hutchings, John	4	1	6
Holt, Joseph	6	1	7
Hamlin, William	3	1	2
Holt, Thomas	8	1	....
Judkins, Martha	5	1	7
Judkins, Samuel	2	1	....
Little, John	2	....	....
Long, Mary	5	1	....
Maddera, Micajah	9	1	3
Maddera, Joel	5	1	2
Marriott, Elizabeth	2	1	4
Mitchell, William	2	1	2
Mitchell, Mary	1	1	3
Marriott, Thomas	4	2	8
Norsworthy, John	9	....	....
Pyland, Ann	6	1	....
Pettway, John	5	1	5
Pyland, Thomas	2	1	3
Pyland, John	4	1	....
Sinclair, Arthur	4	1	5
Seward, James	3	1	2
Seward, Albridgton	8	1	1
Thompson, Joel	9	1	5
Warren, John	2	1	5
Warren, John	2	1	2
Warren, Elizabeth	5	1	....
Wesson, John	2	1	4
Warren, John	5	1	4

LIST OF WILLIAM SALTER.

NAME OF HEAD OF FAMILY.	White souls.	Dwellings.	Other buildings.
Alexander, David	5	1	8
Bell, Robert	8	2	5
Bell, Benjamin	8	2	9
Bell, Micajh (Esta)	7	1	7
Bell, Jacob	5	1	1
Barlow, James	7	1	6
Brown, Edward	6	1	2
Clarke, Martha	6	2	4
Carter, William	3	1	....
Crafford, Henry	2	1	6
Crafford, Elizabeth	3	1	6
Cocks, William	4	1	5
Carter, Mourning	6	1	3
Coser, Thomas	10	1	2
Davis, James	9	2	6
Davis, Joseph	3	1	3
Derring, William	1	1	3
Edwards, Mary	7	1	2
Edwards, James	6	1	4
Foster, Richard	4	1	3
Gwaltney, Joseph	3	2	1
Gwaltney, Benjamin	6	1	....
Gwaltney, William	6	1	3
Gwaltney, John	9	2	3
Gardner, George	5	1	4
Harrison' William	7	1	2
Holloway, Lazarus	11	1	10
Hart, William	1	1	2
Ingram, Patience	6	1	4
Long, David	4	1	1
Long, Hannah	2	1	3
Mosing, Henry	7	1	7
Millington, Samuel	2	1	1
Presson, Toomer	7	1	2
Person, Mary	9	1	5
Rowell, Richard	4	1	10
Rowell, Richard, jr	4	1	4
Salter, William	4	1	10
Slade, John	7	1	3
Slade, William	8	1	1
Savidge, Mike	3	1	....
Thomas, John	9	2	....
Turner, Thomas	9	1	1
Warren, William	8	2	10
Warren, Arthur	8	1	8
Warren, Ann	8	1	4
Warren, Jesse	6	1	13
Warren, Hannah	8	1	6
Wilson, Willis	7	1	12
White, Thomas	5	1	6

LIST OF WILLIAM BOYCE AND JOSIAH WILSON.

NAME OF HEAD OF FAMILY.	White souls.	Dwellings.	Other buildings.
Adams, William	2	1	3
Barlow, James	2	1	4
Barlow, George	4	1	1
Bedgood, Samuel	1	....	....
Brown, James	8	1	2
Bradby, James A	8	2	22
Banks, Jeremiah	....	1	3
Banks, John	1	1	2
Barham, Benjamin	3	1	3
Brown, Richard D. (employed by William Wilkinson)	6	1	9
Bennett, James	2	....	....
Boyce, William	7	2	5

SURRY COUNTY—Continued.

NAME OF HEAD OF FAMILY.	White souls.	Dwellings.	Other buildings.	NAME OF HEAD OF FAMILY.	White souls.	Dwellings.	Other buildings.	NAME OF HEAD OF FAMILY.	White souls.	Dwellings.	Other buildings.	NAME OF HEAD OF FAMILY.	White souls.	Dwellings.	Other buildings.
LIST OF WILLIAM BOYCE AND JOSIAH WILSON—continued.				LIST OF WILLIAM BOYCE AND JOSIAH WILSON—continued.				LIST OF WILLIAM BOYCE AND JOSIAH WILSON—continued.				LIST OF WILLIAM BOYCE AND JOSIAH WILSON—continued.			
Crafford, Carter	4	2	11	Ellis, John	6	1	6	Little, John	3	1	...	Vaughan, William (employed by Allen Cockes ex on)	2	2	23
Colcott, Harwood	4	1	4	Gray, John	4	2	5	Newsum, Joel	1	1	4	Wills, Mary	2	1	8
Crittendon, Ephraim (employed by Wm Wilkinson)	5	1	7	Gray, Henry	7	1	1	Nelson, Ann	9	2	14	Wright, John	5	1	7
Davis, Dolphin	2	1	4	Gray, James	7	1	6	Peirce, Jeremiah	8	1	5	Wills, William	3	1	7
Dunn, William	...	2	1	Goodrich, Charles	7	1	4	Price, Copeland	3	...	...	Ward, Faithy	4	1	6
Delk, Rodwell	1	1	9	Harrison, John	4	1	4	Roberts, Joseph	...	1	1	Wilson, Samuel	...	...	...
Edwards, William (C. C.)	7	1	6	Hunnicutt, Hartwell	6	1	7	Scammell, Richard (employed by Allen Cockes ex on)	7	1	3	Waller, Benjamin	6	1	6
Edwards, Thomas S	1	...	...	Hunnicutt, Augustine	2	1	8	Skipwith, Peyton	...	1	10	Williams, Thomas	4	...	1
Edwards, Jane	4	1	...	Hunnicutt, John	4	1	3	Simpson, Ann	3	1	4	Williams, Walter	6	...	...
Edwards, Thomas	4	1	4	Holt, Archer	5	1	3	Shelley, James	3	1	1	Wright, William	3	...	...
Edwards, Lewis	3	1	2	Holt, Elizabeth	3	1	4	St George, Mary	5	1	6	Wilson, Josiah	9	1	8
Edwards, Jesse	1	...	...	Holt, William	8	2	9	Taylor, James, junr	7	1	3				
Edwards, William	3	1	...	Holt, James	3	1	2	Taylor, James	5	1	1				
Ealey, John	3	...	...	Hunnicutt, Robert	4	1	4	Verell, John	1	...	...				
				Hart, William	8	3	12								
				Holt, Ann	5	1	5								

WARWICK COUNTY.

NAME OF HEAD OF FAMILY.	White souls.	Dwellings.	Other buildings.	NAME OF HEAD OF FAMILY.	White souls.	Dwellings.	Other buildings.	NAME OF HEAD OF FAMILY.	White souls.	Dwellings.	Other buildings.	NAME OF HEAD OF FAMILY.	White souls.	Dwellings.	Other buildings.
LOWER PRECINCT.				LOWER PRECINCT—con.				UPPER PRECINCT—con.				UPPER PRECINCT—con.			
Langhorne, Wm	10	1	10	Patrick, Thos	6	1	...	Jackson, Ambrose (Overseer for J. Southall)	5	...	...	Moore, Elizabeth	4	1	1
Langhorne, John S	3	1	4	West, John	11	1	8	Mahone, Wm (Overseer for J. Southall)	8	...	...	Harrison, Richd	5	1	2
Houghton, Peter & Elizth Minson	6	1	6	Morris, John	3	1	4	Nelson, Hugh (of York County)	...	...	6	Wood, Margaret	6	1	3
Lively, Wm (on the Este of Francis Jones, Decd)	5	2	15	Lewelling, John	3	1	5	Wynne, Richd	9	1	4	Smith, James	5	1	1
Thomas, Samuel	6	1	7	Drewry, Wm	5	1	2	Noblin, Elizabeth	2	1	3	Jordan, Thos	3	1	...
Mcgregor, Wm	10	...	...	Langston, Mattw	5	1	4	Lucas, Thos	4	1	6	Gouge, Mattw	3	1	...
Allen, Hudson (Este)	...	1	7	Dawbry, Samuel	7	1	4	Smith, Wm	3	1	1	Lee, Francis	11	1	10
Mallicote, Thos	8	1	5	Burk, John	7	1	3	Gibbs, Wm, Junr	1	1	5				
Jones, David	7	1	2	Webster, Thos	1	1	2	Ambler, Jaquelin (of Henrico County)	...	1	7	STANLEY HUNDRED PRECINCT.			
Powell, Wm (Este)	5	1	4	Archer, George	10	...	...	Smith, Rd (Overseer for Jaquelin Ambler)	2	...	...	Wills, Mattw	7	1	5
Wooten, Martha	2	1	1	Rice, Judith	2	7	...	Dowsing, Everard	5	1	7	Jones, Allen	1	1	8
Amory, Thos C	10	1	1	Brown, Robt	3	1	3	Wood, Mattw	4	1	...	Haynes, Christopher	5	1	2
Tabb, Philip (Gloster County)	...	1	9	Massenburg, Josiah	6	1	4	Hansford, Elizabeth	4	1	7	Jones, Wm	5	1	10
Crandol, Richd	2	1	3	Ridley, Dorothy	3	...	...	Gibbs, John George	5	1	2	Coffin, Elizabeth	3	1	3
Haughton, Wm	9	1	8	Young, Mary	3	1	2	Harwood, Harlow	...	1	3	Bland, Samuel	9	1	2
Smith, John	5	1	7	Young, Richd	4	1	2	Charles, Martha	6	1	3	Glanville, Thos	5	1	5
Barnes, Aaron	5	...	...	McKintosh, Elizabeth	4	2	9	Gibbs, Wm	6	1	2	Noblin, Mattw	7	1	1
Crandol, John	5	1	1	Dunn, John	8	1	8	Cary, Wilson Miles	12	2	10	Wills, Miles	3	1	3
Burnham, John	6	1	5	Dunn, Hannah	4	1	4	Garrow, Sarah	5	1	1	Curtis, Edmund	4	1	5
Drewry, Anne	4	...	...	Brown, Richd	2	1	3	Gray, Samuel	5	1	3	Fox, John	1	1	1
Drewry, Johnson	7	1	1	Burgess, Wm	2	...	...	Wilkins, Thos	2	...	...	Prentis, Daniel	6	1	8
Mallicote, Wm	4	1	2	Ridley, Francis	2	1	3	Harrovison, Wm	5	1	1	Blow, Samuel	1	1	1
Pulley, Robt	3	1	3	Crandol, James	5	1	3	Lee, Wm	9	1	4				
Pierce, Peter	7	1	...	Drewry, Mattw	5	1	4	Wade, Higginson	1	1	5	MIDDLE PRECINCT.			
Mallicote, Novey	7	1	1					Haynes, Lucy B	7	1	5	Cary, Richd	10	2	11
Jones, Thos	2	1	4	UPPER PRECINCT.				Harwood, Wm	6	1	9	Aylett, Wm (Este)	...	1	2
Jones, John R	10	1	...	Harwood, Edward	13	2	17	Wood, John	11	1	1	Cary, Thos	5	1	9
Sandefur, Elizth	7	1	4	Hubbard, Matthew	8	1	5	Jones, John	2	1	...	Digges, Cole	3	1	6
Allen, Thos	4	1	1	Mallicote, Philip	5	1	2	Dudley, Rebeccah	5	1	4	Digges, Wm, senr	2	1	30
Wood, Mattw	8	1	2	Wynne, Edmund	7	1	6	Gibbs, Matthew	9	1	3	Jones, John	4	1	2
Scott, Thos	1	1	2	Whitaker, Wm (of York County)	...	1	1	Chapman, Walter	6	1	3	Henderson, Wm	7	1	...
Russell, Hinde	5	1	12	Wyld, Thos	3	1	6								
Marrow, Wm	6	1	4	Southall, James (of York County)	...	2	5								

ALBEMARLE COUNTY.

NAME OF HEAD OF FAMILY.	White souls.	Dwellings.	Other buildings.
Anderson, Barttelott	9	....	....
Barksdale, William	5	2	6
Ballard, Bland	9	2	5
Bruce, George	4	2	1
Carr, William	5	1	1
Coleman, James	9	1	3
Carter, Bernard	8	1	3
Carter, William	4	....	3
Cracks, James	9	....	....
Davis, Isaac, Jr	3	1	5
Dickerson, Thomas	10	1	12
Dickerson, John	9	2	9
Dickerson, Wm	6	....	5
Engle, Henry	2	1	....
Epperson, James	8	....	2
Estis, Elisha	5	....	5
Fielder, Francis	4	1	1
Greening, Robert	7	1	....
Greening, James	1	....	....
Gradey, Joshua	9	....	6
Golding, William, jr	3	....	13
Gooch, William	12	1	3
Huntsman, Benjamin	2	1	4
Harvey, William	6	1	....
Jefferson, Thomas, Esqr	14	6	43
Johnson, William	4	2	3
Jouett, John	9	2	4
Lamb, Richard	10	....	....
Lewis, Nicholas	8	2	23
Martin, Hudson	5	2	2
McKinzie, Alexander	5	1	6
Maupine, Zachariah	13	1	....
Maupine, Daniel	2	1	....
McCord, William	5	1	1
McCord, Samuel	5	....	....
McCullock, John	4	1	4
Mills, John	4	....	2
Mills, Wyatt	1	1	6
Mills, Lucy	4	1	9
Maupine, William	10	1	....
McKinzie, Daniel	1	....	....
Maupine, Daniel	3	1	1
Marks, Peter	9	....	....
Owens, William	5	1	5
Owens, Steward	3	....	4
Nicholas, George, Esqr	11	4	6
Philips, Stephen	7	....	1
Page, William	10	1	2
Rogers, Giles	3	1	11
Savage, John	6	1	5
Shifflett, John	4	1	3
Spencer, John	8	1	....
Stephens, John	9	1	5
Smith, Samuel	3	....	1
Tucyman, George	9	1	13
Taliaferro, Samuel	3	2	....
West, Thomas	4	1	5
Wayts, George	9	1	4
Gilmer, George	8	1	9
Meriwether, William	3	1	16
Beck, William	....	1	1
Lott, John	3	1	1
Kindred, Bartholomew	2	1	....
Fariss, William	2	1	....
Bacon, Harwood	7	1	2
Hall, Nathan	7	1	....
Sharp, Robert, Junr	10	1	4
Sharp, Robert	3	1	5
Lindsay, Reuben	12	2	8
Brush, James	2	1	2
Fisher, Patrick	4	1	....
McCoy, Daniel	2	1	....
Carver, William	11	1	1
Carver, Thomas	8	1	1
Veatch, Silas	3	1	2
Turnley, John	5	1	10
Fitch, John	9	1	4
Maurey, Mary	4	1	4
Oglesby, Jacob	12	1	5
Watts, David	11	1	3
Thorpe, Thomas	9	1	5
Wade, Nathaniel	7	....	....
Gilliam, John	11	1	4
Breadlove, Thomas	12	1	3
Hunton, John, Senr	8	1	7
Hill, Richard	5	1	....
Clark, Micajah, Senr	7	1	7
Roathwell, Claibourne	9	1	1
Robinson, John	5	1	....
Gillasby, Nathan	2	1	1
Walker, Thomas, Jr	12	3	14
Gillasby, Alexander	7	1	3
Gillasby, George	4	1	....
Beck, Jessee	8	1	2
Quarles, James	5	1	7
Wood, David	11	1	6
Carr, Micajah	5	1	5
Watson, William (estate of)	10	1	6
Henring, John	8	1	1
Ferguson, Charles	5	1	4

NAME OF HEAD OF FAMILY.	White souls.	Dwellings.	Other buildings.
Foster, Edmund	7	1	7
Roberts, Richard	1	....	....
Salmon, Thomas	7	1	5
Walker, Thomas	9	2	35
Walker, John	2	5	30
Morton, Joseph	7	1	6
Lewis, Colo Charles (estate of)	1	1	27
Bocock, Jason	8	1	1
Wansley, John	10	....	1
Taylor, James	10	....	1
Rippetoe, John, Jr	8	....	1
Stone, Thomas	12	1	6
Burbridge, Thomas	8	....	3
Hensley, William	11	....	2
Crosthwait, Isaac	11	....	7
Ballard, Thomas	7	....	2
Fowler, Samuel	5	....	2
Wills, Frederick W	12	1	4
Rippetoe, John	7	....	2
Austin, Samuel	8	1	7
Minor, James	7	1	11
Clarkson, Peter	7	1	2
Shelton, Henry	9	3	5
Dolton, William	12	1	10
Dowell, John	9	....	2
Ballard, Philip	6	1	1
Fretwell, William	9	1	6
Watts, Elijah	4	1	3
Boswell, Matthew	8	1	6
Durrett, Richard	9	2	7
Garth, John, Junr	4	1	5
Davis, Isaac	4	2	11
Watts, Jacob	6	2	6
Pritchett, John	8	....	3
Herring, David	3	....	3
Herring, James	3	....	4
Johnson, John	4	1	4
Osby, John	2	....	1
Spradling, William	5	1	2
Spradling, David	7	1	....
Ferguson, Peter	7	....	10
Dowell, Ambrose	8	1	2
Bussy, Hezekiah	5	1	4
Watts, John	5	1	5
Davis, Leonard	10	....	5
Henderson, Richard	2	....	1
Dowell, William	6	2	2
Jones, John	10	5	5
Burkett, Francis	6	....	2
Spradling, John	1	....	....
Travilliom, James	8	2	2
Lane, Dumas	10	....	3
Goldsmith, Walter	2	....	2
Rodes, Hezekiah	3	1	2
Rodes, Epaphraditus	11	1	7
Crenshaw, John	5	1	4
Davis, William	10	1	4
Allen, Isaac	5	....	5
Allen, William	3	....	4
Elliot, John	9	....	2
Elliot, John, Junr	3	....	1
Hall, William	11	....	6
Edwards, Ambrose	5	....	11
Wells, Thomas	5	1	4
Turner, John	8	1	3
Wood, William	6	1	1
Barlow, James	5	1	5
Barlow, Henry	5	1	3
Brockman, William	5	3	5
Alexander, John	7	1	1
Alexander, Hugh	7	2	1
Black, Samuel	8	1	....
Brown, Bezaleel	5	1	3
Brown, Brightberry	1	1	....
Brown, Barzillai	11	1	....
Brown, Ludlow	6	....	....
Bailey, Calem	8	1	1
Browning, Francis	6	1	....
Ballow, Solomon	5	1	2
Ballow, Peter	6	....	....
Black, William	3	1	2
Barksdale, Goodman	5	1	....
Barksdale, Jonathan	2	....	....
Birch, Samuel	4	1	2
Brooks, James	10	1	1
Brown, John	5	....	....
Brown, Robert	8	1	....
Brown, Bernard	8	1	....
Clark, Susanna	2	....	....
Clark, David	3	....	....
Clark, Benjamin	4	....	....
Cane, James	1	....	....
Colley, Zacharias	5	....	....
Craig, Thomas	7	1	2
Cleavland, Margaret	7	1	....
Collins, Thomas	8	1	....
Chenault, William	9	1	....
Craig, John	7	1	....
Davis, William	8	....	....
Davis, Francis	4	1	....

NAME OF HEAD OF FAMILY.	White souls.	Dwellings.	Other buildings.
Dollins, John	8	1	....
Douglass, Robert	3	....	....
Dean, Matthew	5	....	....
Ellis, Barttelott	9	1	....
Ewell, Maxey	9	1	....
Easton, Thomas	5	....	....
Fretwell, Alexander	8	2	....
Gilliam, John	7	1	2
Gentry, Martin	8	1	....
Gentry, Richard	2	1	2
Gentry, David	4	....	....
Gentry, Richard, jr	4	....	....
Grayson, John	4	....	....
Golden, Archibald	8	1	1
Golden, Abraham	11	....	....
Harriss, James	8	1	4
Harriss, Joell	1	....	....
Harriss, Thomas	7	1	....
Harding, Isaac	10	1	....
Harriss, Christopher	11	1	3
Holt, Joseph	9	1	2
Huleey, James P	6	2	....
Jamerson, Samuel	3	1	3
Jamerson, Samuel, jr	8	1	1
Jerman, William	7	1	....
Jerman, Thomas	3	1	3
Jamerson, Alexander	7	1	....
Johnson, Townill	6	1	....
Kerr, James	7	1	7
Kerr, Henry	7	1	....
Kerr, Samuel	9	1	....
Lewis, Isham	1	1	5
Lewis, Charles (Estate)	....	....	1
Maupine, Daniel, jr	8	1	....
Mills, Menan	2	1	1
Maupine, Daniel, Min	3	1	....
Mullins, Matthew	9	....	....
Mullins, Gabriel	8	....	....
Maupine, Cornelius	4	....	....
Musick, Ephraim	5	1	....
Musick, John	5	....	....
Musick, James	2	....	....
McWilliams, John	5	1	....
McWilliams, Hugh	4	1	....
Maupine, John, Senr	10	3	....
Maupine, Gabriel, Snr	7	1	1
McCord, Jane	5	....	....
Mullins, John	4	1	1
Maupine, Daniel (G. S.)	6	....	....
Maupine, David	1	....	....
Moore, Stephen	1	....	....
McRay, Daniel	8	....	....
McCullock, John	1	1	....
McCullock, Robert	6	1	2
Marks, John	6	1	6
Maupine, Daniel, Senr	2	2	....
Mullins, Matthew	6	1	....
Pilson, Thomas	8	....	....
Perkins, Joell	7	1	....
Ramsay, William	2	1	....
Rodes, Clifton	11	2	4
Reace, Thomas	6	....	....
Rosdels, John	7	1	....
Ray, Samuel	5	....	....
Rogers, William	8	1	....
Reid, John	8	1	....
Rawley, James	4	1	....
Rodes, John	8	2	9
Reid, Samuel	4	1	....
Reid, James	3	1	1
Sandridge, William	3	1	1
Stockton, John	7	....	....
Stockton, Thomas	5	....	....
Stockton, David	2	....	....
Snell, Philemon	7	....	....
Stockton, Dan	7	....	....
Shackleford, Roger	10	....	....
Shelton, William, Jr	8	1	8
Stockton, Jessee	3	1	....
Turk, James	5	....	....
Thurmond, Richard	5	....	....
Via, Micajah	11	....	....
Webster, Daniel	4	....	....
Woods, Wm (I. C.)	8	....	....
Wallace, Josiah	5	1	5
Woods, John	5	1	2
Woods, James	5	1	....
Woods, Richard	9	1	7
Wallace, Michael	11	1	7
Webster, Moses	8	....	....
Webster, John	3	....	....
Wingfield, Charles	....	....	4
Wray, Andrew	4	1	1
Watson, John	7	....	....
Watson, Evan	4	1	....
Wallace, William	9	1	2
Wallace, James	9	3	....
Yancey, Margarett	7	1	....
Apperson, David	5	....	5
Austin, Henry	9	1	4
Ballard, John	6	....	5

NAME OF HEAD OF FAMILY.	White souls.	Dwellings.	Other buildings.
Beckett, Humphry	5	....	2
Burruss, Thomas	10	1	7
Blackwell, Sarah	6	1	3
Beckett, Richard	2	....	4
Burruss, Charles	7	....	6
Ballard, Thomas	5	1	4
Blackwell, John	4	....	2
Burk, Henry	1	1	4
Coleman, William	3	1	4
Crosthwait, William	6	1	2
Davis, Robert	6	1	8
Davis, Lewis	9	....	4
Davis, John	6	....	3
Ferguson, William	11	1	8
Freeman, William	4	....	1
Garrison, Killey	9	....	4
Gardener, James	11	1	3
Gooch, Rowland	7	....	4
Gooch, John	6	....	2
Gaines, Richard	3	....	....
Garrison, William	8	1	4
Garth, Thomas	9	1	12
Goodman, Charles	8	1	9
Harvie, John, Esqr	2	1	14
Hammock, Robert	5	....	2
Hackett, Martin	2	1	1
Johnson, Thomas	11	1	4
Keaton, William	10	....	5
Keaton, James	7	....	3
Keaton, Hezekiah	1	....	....
Langford, Thomas	10	1	3
Langford, Jonathan	8	....	....
Lane, Edward	8	....	3
McCullock, Samuel	5	....	4
Michie, William	5	3	20
McClary, John	7	....	5
McCallow, Thomas	8	....	4
Mills, Henry	2	....	2
Miller, John	9	1	6
Norriss, William	5	....	4
Proctor, William	4	....	1
Puthuff, John	4	....	4
Rodes, David	9	1	10
Snow, Richard	5	1	5
Snow, Frost V	12	1	3
Thompson, Nelson	6	1	4
Thurmond, Philip	5	1	3
Thomas, John	7	1	10
Thompson, William	2	....	1
Woods, William (B. C.)	3	1	3
White, Conyers	10	1	6
Walton, Thompson	8	....	2
Walton, Richmond	10	....	1
Wells, John	8	....	4
Austin, William	9	1	4
Aplin, Thomas	4	....	....
Blaine, George	20	4	19
Burnett, Edmund	3	....	1
Burnett, Roland	5	....	....
Bolling, John	2	2	10
Buster, John, Senr	10	1	2
Ballard, William	3	....	....
Clark, William	4	....	....
Coles, Colo John	10	1	25
Cobbs, Thomas	3	1	5
Cocke, Capt James	7	1	8
Claybrooke, Joseph	10	1	5
Cole, William	9	1	10
Carter, Pattey	8	....	....
Drumhiller, Leonard	5	....	....
Davis, William	11	1	2
Ewbank, George	6	1	5
Ellerton, John	4	1	2
Eaves, William	6	....	....
Fitzpatrick, Thomas	12	1	10
Garland, Nathaniel	6	1	6
Gay, Samuel, Senr	4	1	1
Gentry, Moses	12	1	6
Gay, Samuel, Jr	7	....	4
Garland, James	6	2	10
Harlow, Thomas	8	1	2
Hamner, Samuel	9	2	13
Harlow, Michael	4	....	1
Jones, James, Jr	4	1	5
Key, Tandy	7	2	7
McCoy, John	1	....	3
Maxwell, Bezabel	13	1	6
Martin, Capt Thomas	10	2	14
Martin, Pleasant	7	1	3
Mooran, Elijah	10	1	1
Morriss, Hugh Rice	10	1	7
Martin, John	7	1	3
Moore, Richard	7	1	4
Mooran, William	9	1	7
Mayers, Jacob	11	....	....
Murrell, George	5	1	5
Murrell, Samuel	2	1	3
Nelson, Robert	4	2	22
Nowell, Benjamin	7	1	4
Nash, Edward	6	1	....
Old, James	4	1	9

ALBEMARLE COUNTY—Continued.

NAME OF HEAD OF FAMILY.	White souls.	Dwellings.	Other buildings.	NAME OF HEAD OF FAMILY.	White souls.	Dwellings.	Other buildings.	NAME OF HEAD OF FAMILY.	White souls.	Dwellings.	Other buildings.	NAME OF HEAD OF FAMILY.	White souls.	Dwellings.	Other buildings.
Powell, Casper	5		1	Campbell, William	2			Upton, Joseph	7	1		Dudley, George	4		1
Pemberton, Thomas	9	1	4	Gambell, Henry	10			Foileure, Josiah S	3	1		Bullen, Francis	4		
Proctor, George	8		2	Bryan, Anderson	9			Morriss, Jacob	8	1	4	Jones, Thomas	8	1	5
Page, Robert	8	1	6	Dawson, Martin	14	3	3	Lewis, John, Jr	8	1	2	Kindred, Bartholomew	3	1	
Patterson, William	6	1	3	Harriss, John	6	3	6	Thompson, Josiah	6	1		Moore, James	2		3
Runnels, James	8		1	Nicholas, Wilson C	9	3	18	Childress, John	1	1	2	Wingfield, Charles	8	1	7
Sudderth, James	6	2	11	Hopkins, James		1	3	Ward, John	10			Wingfield, Christopher	2	1	
Statham, John	6	1	4	Staples, Thomas	9	3	6	Childress, Joseph	8	1		Wingfield, William	1		
Southerlin, Joseph	7	1	5	Henderson, Wm	7	1	1	Fowls, James	3			Nowell, Spencer	10		
Toole, John	8	1	3	Hamner, Richerson	5	3	3	Jordan, John	3	1	4	Hughes, Stephen	5	1	11
Trent, Peter F		4	4	Hamner, William	2	3	10	Thomas, Michael, Jr	8	1	2	Wingfield, John	14		5
Taylor, Benjamin	3	1	1	Moon, Jacob	10	5	5	Kidd, Moses	9	1		Gordan, Alexander	1	1	2
Uptegrove, Sarah	8	1	3	Hopkins, William	12	7	8	Thomas, Michael, Sr	2	1	3	Hazbrig, Mary	5		
Via, William	2			Hamner, Henley	4	2	2	Watkins, Nathaniel	4	1		Kerrs, John	1		
Watson, William	5	2	15	Moon, Wm, Senr	5	4	4	Bell, Thomas	2	1	2	Hamner, John	2	1	4
Weatherhead, Francis	8	1	3	Lewis, John, Senr	9	5	5	Lewis, Owen	7	1	3	Benge, Martha	2		
Quick, John	7		2	Eades, John	9	1	4	Morriss, Powell	1	1	1	Harper, Castleton, Jr	9		5
Nalley, Benstil	1	1	7	Harper, Richard	5			Farrar, Perrin	9	1	4	Mitchell, Barbary	1		1
Anderson, Samuel		1	6	Kerley, Benjamin	7			Jopling, Ralph	7	1	2	Hamner, Jeremiah	7	1	6
Langford, William	10	1	3	Melton, John	6	1	1	Mooreman, Robert	8	1	5	Carter, Richard	5		2
Gilliam, John	4	1	3	Brown, Andrew	6	1	2	Bailey, Richard	9	1		Carter, Elizabeth	1		
Garrell, Lawrence	7			Hudson, Christopher	4	1	23	Thomas, Ralph	5	1		Sowell, John	9	1	2
Burger, Benjamin	2	1	9	Mansfield, Joseph	11	1		Farrar, Richard	10	1	5	Benge, Cotton	8	1	1
Burger, Joseph	5			Eubank, John, Jr	5	1		Shelton, Samuel, Senr	5	1	5	Hamner, Turner	7	1	2
Humphrys, John	3			Davenport, Richard	3	1	2	Melton, Silias	3	1	3	McQuerry, Absolam	3		
Barksdale, Samuel	1		3	Eubank, John, Senr	5	2	5	Bailey, Samuel	2	2	2	Lewis, James	4	1	4
Wood, Jessee	9	1	3	Eubank, Richard	4	1	1	Mooreman, Thomas	3	1		Humphry, David	6	1	2
Wood, William, Jr	3			Sudderth, Lawrence	6	1		Goolsley, Thomas	6	1	5	Foster, James	1		
Massie, Charles	4	1	3	Eubank, James	6	1	2	Upton, Thomas	3	1	3	Humphry, Merry	5		1
McEndree, Richard	10		1	Kinney, William	4	2	2	Baddoe, Thomas	4	1		Cobbs, Thomas	3	1	5
Carter, William	4			Tomkins, William	3	1	3	Harriss, William (B. C.)	8	1	4	Bailey, John	8	1	2
Wood, Solomon	4			Kidd, Benjamin	2	1		Anderson, Wm (England)	10	1		Bailey, Thomas	4	1	
Harlow, Nathaniel		1	2	Kidd, Jno. Norman	1	1		Tuley, Wm	5	1	4	Smith, John	4	1	3
Smith, Thomas, Jr	5	1	3	Kidd, Wm	2	1		Ball, Wm	9			Smith, James	1		1
Massie, Thomas	3	1	1	Thurmond, Philip	6	1	8	Hughes, Wm	11	2	5	Everitt, John	9		5
White, Daniel	7	1	2	Burk, John	8	1		Harriss, Wm	4	1	3	Dedman, Samuel	4		7
Fields, Robert	9	1	2	Cheatham, Peter	10	2	4	Thurmond, Wm	8	1	6	Buster, John, Jr	1	1	2
Cooke, David	8	1	1	Fortune, Wm	5			Hensley, Wm	6			Spencer, John	8	1	4
Litteral, Samuel	4			Fortune, John	7	4	13	Jopling, James	15	1	5	Buster, John, Senr	10	1	3
Durrett, Marshall	4	1	2	Scott, John	13	17	28	Haggard, Henry	6	1	8	Dedman, Dixon	1		
Rodes, Mary	3	1	12	Hensley, Samuel	6	1		Lewis, Hopkins	4	1	3	Ragland, Edmund	6		
Wood, Abner	9		3	Harriss, Benjamin	2	1	6	Henderson, John, Jr	9	1	9	Bailey, William	4	1	1
Berry, Bradley	9	1	1	Fitzpatrick, John	3	1	1	Leak, William	4		2	Spears, John	6		
Pulliam, Gideon	9	1	1	Leak, Mask	8	1	6	Bates, Robert	3	1		Harper, Castleton	2	1	
Montgomery, Francis	7	1	1	Leak, Betty	5	1	3	Spears, William, Jr	8	1	1	Olds, John	8	2	11
Ellaston, John	4	1	1	Melton, Jessee	5			Spears, Joseph	3			Haden, George	7		
Dollins, Richard	4			Tomkins, Giles	5	1	7	Spears, Wm, Senr	2		1	Radford, Edward	2		
Hays, William	5	1	1	Wharton, John	9	1	7	Gentry, Benajah	9	1	4	Copengers, Higgans	3		1
Montgomery, Matthew	6			Durham, David	8	1	3	Cleavland, Jeremiah	5	1	3	Mayberry, Justinian	8	1	3
Smith, John	5	1		Lively, John	6	2		Jones, James, Senr	4	1	10	Spears, James	8		2
Smith, Thomas, Senr	8	1	1	Copeland, Henry	9	1	3	Kennady, James	1	1	5	Henderson, Bennett	8	5	14
Smith, William	7			Martin, Shadrack	8	1		Wheeler, Benjamin D	2	2	6	Lewis, Charles L	9	5	15
Smith, John, Jr	1	1	3	Lively, Benjamin	9	1	4	Britt, Obadiah	10	1	3	Henderson, Jno., Senr	2	4	8
Burger, Nicholas	4			Hudson, Charles	5	1	3	Langford, John	2	1	3	Carter, Edward, Esqr	14	34	49
Wood, Isaac	9	1	3	Fry, John (estate of)	13	1	10	Langford, West	9	1	3	Reynolds, Wm	4	1	1
Gragg, William	5	1	1	White, Arthur	5	2	2	Langford, James	7	1	4	Reynolds, S	5	1	1
Gragg, William, Jr	5		1	Buster, Claudius	9	1	3	Wheeler, Micajah	6	1	3	Reynolds, Wm, Snr	2	1	3
Muse, Samuel	4	1	1	Cabell, Joseph, jr	3			Wood, Henry	8	1	2	Sullavin, L. B	7	1	1
Piper, John	4	1	2	Wilkinson, Jarat	8			Wheeler, Joell	7		2	Reynolds, D	5	1	1
Burger, John	4	1		Kinney, William	4	2	2	Britt, Wm	5		2	Burruss, Robert	3	1	1
Richardson, Richard	4	1	5	Squair, Andrew	4			Bullin, Joseph	5		2	Tindall, Joseph	9	1	1
Richardson, Robert	1	1	1	Hudson, John	7	1	13	Bailey, John	9	1	1	Kerley, Henry	5	1	3
Leigh, William	9	2	4	Bailey, Ann	11	1	1	Woodson, Elizabeth	1	2	3	Wingfield, Charles, Jr	10	2	10
Harlow, Elijah	5	1		Hensley, Benjamin	4	1		Woodson, Tarlton	5	1	1	Divers, George	2	3	16
Woodfork, Thomas	1		3	Irving, Charles	5	1	10	Layne, Robert	6	1	1	Morgan, Thomas	8	2	2
Martin, Sherwood			4	Napier, Champion	5	2		Shepherd, Augustine		3	6	Thomason, George	2	1	
Dollins, Presley	9		2	Kidd, Duet	9	1		Langford, Robert	10	1	6	Thurmond, John	2		
Wood, William	8	1		Mosley, Daniel	8	1	2	Wheeler, Micajah	7	1	2	Hogg, Wilbourn	5	2	2
Emberson, Henry	8	1	2	Davis, Elizabeth	4	1	2	Cartee, Edward	5			Kerley, John	5	1	1
Clark, Moses	7			Wood, Henry	5	1	4	Sheets, Samuel	7			Long, L	8		
Wood, Nelly	7	1		Gilmore, Joseph	10			Branham, Malchia	7			Gaines, Francis	5	1	
Carter, John	2	1		Nicholas, John	6	1	4	Mayo, James	8	1	1	Burruss, John	6	1	1
Guayson, William	5	1	4	Bailey, Isham	6	1	1	Mayo, Richard G	8		3	Burruss, Peter	11	1	3
Birks, John	5			Hood, James	4	1		Boan, John	5		2	Gaines, Hierom	4	1	5
Davie, Peter	1	1	4	Thomas, Joseph	9	1	1	Fry, Gabriel	5		1	Bishop, Francis	7		8
Goolsley, William, Sr	8	1	6	Melton, John, Senr	10	1	3	Hurt, John	10		2	Gaines, Humphry	3		3
Hamner, Nicholas	7	1	4	Martin, John (B. C.)	12	1	4	Dudley, George, Jr	8		1	Nemore, David	8	1	3
				Harriss, John	5	1		Chiles, Micajah	2	5	6	Lacey, Benjamin	7	1	5

AMELIA COUNTY.

NAME OF HEAD OF FAMILY.	White souls.	Dwellings.	Other buildings.	NAME OF HEAD OF FAMILY.	White souls.	Dwellings.	Other buildings.	NAME OF HEAD OF FAMILY.	White souls.	Dwellings.	Other buildings.	NAME OF HEAD OF FAMILY.	White souls.	Dwellings.	Other buildings.
Gray, William	4	1	5	Henderick, Benjamin	7	2	5	Wright, Reubin	1	2	3	Ford, William, Junr	8	3	8
Piles, Conradus	6	2	4	Booth, John	6	2	5	Foster, Thomas	6	1	2	Wingo, James	4	2	3
Jackson, John	4	1	3	Morris, Moses, junr	2	1		Chapman, John	9	3	8	Legon, Robert	9	3	3
Jackson, William	9	2	2	Butler, William	8	2	2	Wright, Thomas	4	2	4	Legon, William, Senr	7	2	2
Assilin, David	5	3	9	Pollard, Joseph	16	4	5	Bagley, James	4			Rogers, William	6	3	1
Wright, John	5	3	13	Whitworth, Abraham	9	2	3	Claibrook, Peter	9	3	5	Booker, Edward	2	2	3
Farley, Stephen	4	5	3	Lockett, John	8	2	4	Cobbs, Samuel	8	1	6	Hamm, William	3	1	2
Leagon, Thomas	8	3	6	Green, Thomas	4	2	4	Winston, William	10	1	4	Allin, Samuel	8	1	3
Hoalt, Jesse	5	2	3	Bell, John	8	2	1	Johnson, William	8	2	4	Walker, Alexander	11	1	3
Meaders, Obidiah	3	2	1	Wood, William	8	3	7	Crowder, William	11	3	9	McGehee, William	8	1	3
Morris, Zachariah	11	3	3	Hill, John	5	2	5	Hutcheson, Charles	7	1	3	Jeter, Samuel	10	3	6
Gills, John	8	3	6	Jeter, Ambrose	6	4	14	Chaffin, Joshua	9	2	7	Seay, Jacob, Junr	2	1	3
Loving, William	4	1	3	Hendrick, Zachariah	3	1	3	Hughes, John, Senr	12	5	11	Ford, Christopher	11	4	7
Burton, William	6	2	3	Pollard, William	1			Morris, Moses, Senr	11	2	2	Cocke, Stephen	11	4	7
Anderson, Paulin	1	5	16	Chappell, John	2	3	5	Legon, William, Junr	11	3	2	Cocke, John	4	3	5
Rucker, Joshua	10	1		Morris, Tabitha	5	2	1	Hurt, William	8	2	5	Cocke, Thomas	4	3	6
Weatherford, David	9			Hendrick, John	5	2	3	Farley, William	7	1	1	Batte, Thomas	8	2	3

AMELIA COUNTY—Continued.

NAME OF HEAD OF FAMILY.	White souls.	Dwellings.	Other buildings.
Thweatt, John (P. George)	5	2	3
Cress, John (Lunenburg)	1	3	6
White, Frances	8	1	3
Eckles, Thomas	10	2	4
Eckles, James	10	2	1
Bland, Mrs Judith	5	4	10
Morgan, Samuel	8		
Lock, Elizabeth	7	3	4
Crenshaw, William	6	2	3
Gunn, James	13	1	12
Gunn, Elisha	3	1	4
Bates, Abner	5	2	6
Lovsey, Richard	3	1	2
Gooch, William	8	1	3
Alpriend, Benjamin	6	2	4
Crenshaw, Sanders	5	1	
Justis, Daniel	6		
Cross, Richard	14	4	7
Morgan, Samuel	11	1	1
Farguson, Peleg	9	3	5
Jones, Repes	10	2	2
Bridgforth, Benjamin	7	4	9
Anderson, John	15	2	3
Erskine, Mrs Sarah	3	3	7
Lipscomb, Richard	2	2	2
Sydnor, Epa	3	3	5
Craddock, David	5	2	4
Hamlin, Charles	1	2	4
Booker, Edmund	3	4	12
Booker, Davis	1	2	4
Hudson, Jane	3	6	7
Mays, Daniel	7		
Gibbs, Edward	4		
Pride, John	4	9	8
Pride, Frances	2	2	7
Jackson, Philip W	2		
Sudberry, John	5		
Cobbs, John C	8	4	6
Belcher, George	2		
Hill, James	5	4	8
Worsham, William	6	2	2
Jones, Daniel	10	9	30
Royall, William	6	4	6
Baldwin, John Senr	10	2	4
Hundley, John	12	2	5
Craddock, William C	12	4	6
Craddock, Richard	10	3	6
Wingo, James	5	1	3
Vaughan, Lewis	2	2	1
Mays, Phebey	5	1	
Foster, Ann	1	1	
Foster, Richard	7	1	
Vaughan, William	7	1	
Smith, Covington	8	2	3
Scott, George	8		
Thompson, Ann	1	3	5
Ford, William	8	2	14
Walthall, Daniel	11	2	3
Truly, John	4	2	5
Webster, Anthony	9	2	2
Berry, Peter	7	7	7
Williams, Phillip, junr	7	1	1
Wily, John	5	3	14
Booker, Samuel	2	2	3
Farley, James	6	1	
Baldwin, George	9	1	4
Farley, Henry	6	1	
Farley, Mary	1	2	2
Farley, Nathaniel	6		
Angell, John	2	1	
Baldwin, Phebey	4		
Harper, John	10	4	4
Woodson, Joseph	7		
Cook, James	9	2	3
Mayes, Richard	5		
Baldwin, William	5	2	3
Hall, John	5		
Stott, James	5	2	1
Gilliam, John		3	4
Baldwin, John M	5		
Morris, James	7	2	2
Hundley, Josiah	7	6	9
Harper, Anner	5	2	4
Mitchell, James Cocke	3		
Cook, Thomas	2	1	2
Motley, Joel	6	2	3
Vaughan, Robert	8	3	5
Ward, Henry		1	5
Cook, Rains	2		
Williamson, Luelling	8	5	6
Robertson, Christopher	5	1	20
Thompson, Ann	5	1	
Blankinship, John	8	1	1
Blankinship, David	7	1	
Allin, Richard	5	1	
Stewart, Edward	1		
Archer, Peter Field		1	6
Harper, William	10	1	
Perkerson, Matthew	4	2	3
Jones, Phillip	6	2	8
Jones, John	11	4	11

NAME OF HEAD OF FAMILY.	White souls.	Dwellings.	Other buildings.
Claybrook, John	6		
Clay, Thomas	6	1	1
Marshall, John	3	2	3
Craddock, Charles	8	1	2
Jennings, Joseph, Senr	11	4	7
Oliver, James	2	3	6
Walton, Jessee	9	3	3
Bell, William	4	3	6
Roach, Millington	6	3	4
Jinnings, Captain William	8	1	1
Dunnivant, Clement	6		
Anderson, Frances	9	3	14
Townes, John, Junr	4	5	10
Jones, Richard (B.)	5	3	6
Mayes, William	4		
Branch, Benjamin		2	4
Harrison, Nathaniel (Estate of)		6	10
Ward, Matthew	7		
Walton, Sherwood	8	3	3
Atkerson, Joshua	6	2	3
Roberts, Jacob	4	2	2
Archer, Field		2	6
Childris, Robert	3		
Lockett, Abraham	9	2	1
Lockett, Benjamin	4	2	4
Vaughan, Bartholimew	8	1	2
Scott, Roger	9	1	2
Whitlow, Francis	4	1	3
Robertson, Matthew	10	2	4
Parmer, Elijah	4	1	2
Vaughan, Jane	3	1	
Smithey, Joshua	5		
Friend, Thomas (Estate of)		3	4
Jones, Peter (Sheriff)	9	3	6
Wilkinson, Joseph (Esta of)	5	2	3
Jones, Thomas	10	5	14
Holt, Richard	3		
Cocke, Stephen	9	7	14
Townes, John, Senr	7	4	8
Jackson, Frances	6	2	3
McLacklin, John	5	2	2
Dupuy, John Batte	2	3	5
Dupuy, James, Junr	4	1	1
Cabeniss, George	7	2	3
Smith, Pemberton	3	2	5
Thornton, Sterling C	8	2	5
Cashan, David	6		
Cashan, James	2		
Bruce, Alexander	8	3	6
Featherstone, Richard	8	1	2
Mitchell, Thomas	13	2	1
Beasley, John	11	3	11
Beasley, Leonard	2	1	
Devinport, Abraham	1		
Winfree, Robert	3	1	4
Lipscomb, Uriah	10	4	4
Winfree, Charles	4	1	2
Devenport, John	1		
Royall, Littleberry	3	2	7
Royall, John	7	2	8
Cabbeness, Matthew, junr	8	2	5
Vaughan, John	7	2	6
Westbrook, Phebe	5	1	2
Grigg, William	10	2	3
Williams, Bellington	6	1	2
Robertson, James	7	1	3
Chambers, Samuel	8	2	2
Farguson, Henry	4	2	4
Pryor, John, Junr	8	1	6
Clarke, Lew	4	2	3
Leonard, Frederick	6	1	
Featherstone, Burwell	6	1	
Cheatham, Archer	9	2	3
Jackson, Frances	7	2	6
Jones, Thomas F	8	1	1
Jackson, Frances, Junr	5	2	3
Beasley, Stephen	7	5	7
Beasley, Peter	3	8	4
Stanback, Peter	7	3	6
Stanback, Charles	1		
Donaty, Doctor Frances	1		
Harris, William (D.C. quater)	3	1	4
Dennis, Richard	9	3	6
Tucker, John	3	1	2
Featherstone, William	2	3	8
Featherston, Richard	8		
Thompson, Drury	7	3	6
Mann, James	12	1	4
Mann, John	1	1	4
Orsborne, Captain abnor	3	5	9
Southerland, Findal	4	1	4
Hayes, Richard	7	7	14
Ellington, Peter	7	4	4
Bass, Joseph	8	3	5
Jennings, John, Junr	6	1	2
Clarke, John	8	3	6
Hall, Bowler	11	4	9

NAME OF HEAD OF FAMILY.	White souls.	Dwellings.	Other buildings.
Hudson, Peter	6	2	7
Walker, Sarah Ann	2		
Osborne, William, Junr	11	3	6
Hausin, John	10	2	5
upuy, Bartholemew	10	3	12
Hardaway, Stith	1	2	11
Wilkerson, Revd Thomas (Estate of)	1	5	14
Steward, Charles	9	6	5
Steward, Littleberry	5	2	1
Roberson, Peter	11	3	10
Mumford, James	11	3	9
Jones, Elizabeth	7	4	9
Jones, Thomas	3	3	6
Gray, Alexander	4	1	1
Powell, Thomas	10	1	1
Short, Thomas		4	5
Robertson, John	8	2	4
Robertson, Nathaniel	5	2	7
Ramsay, Richard	3	3	3
Henderson, James	4	5	12
Byassee, John	7		
Moore, Mark	6	2	6
Birthright, Zachariah	6	2	4
Green, John	11	2	1
Porter, Susannah May	3	3	6
Porter, William May	2	1	3
Richardson, Ruler	7	2	2
Cock, John (quarter)	5	1	6
Beasley, Ambrose	3	2	2
Smith, Richard	4	2	1
Ward, Rowland, Junr	6	3	3
Gooch, John	11	2	5
Ward, Rowland	5	5	6
Brown, Laurence	2	2	3
Brown, Sarah	8	2	2
Hundley, Ann	6	3	5
Womack, Thomas	5	2	2
Fliping, Robert	4	2	
Westbrook, James	10	2	1
Jennings, Joseph	9	3	1
Jeter, Presley	3	2	3
Winn, Charles	3	4	5
Anderson, John	4	2	7
Bradshaw, Jeremiah	4	1	
Davis, James	5	1	2
Jones, Richard, Junr	11	9	11
Dod, Nick	5		
FitzGerrald, Frances	7	3	2
Craddock, Moses	9	2	3
Roberts, John	9	1	3
Davis, Asa	6	3	3
Winfree, Ann	5	2	2
Beasley, Robert	3	1	2
Elleatt, John	7	4	5
Pincham, Elizabeth	4	2	6
Roach, James	3		
Parham, Daniel	3	2	2
Fletcher, Nathan	10	6	5
Varser, Daniel	1		
Devenport, William		3	1
Tanner, Joel	4	2	4
Sherwin, Samuel	6	6	14
Cabiniss, William	1	1	
Dyson, William (for T. G. Peachy)	5	1	3
Forrest, Abraham, Senr	4	2	3
Walthall, William	9	2	6
Booker, John, Junr	8	1	8
Hutcheson, Ambrose	3		
Farmer, Frances		1	8
Borram, Richard	11	1	1
Shell, Thomas	4		
Walthall, Thomas	6	1	2
Walthall, John	3	1	5
Elam, John	5	1	
Hawtell, William	3	1	1
Forster, John	9	1	1
Dunnavant, Hodge	11	1	2
Reames, Frederick	7	1	1
Bottom, William	1	1	2
Walthall, Henry	1	1	3
Mann, Field	9	1	1
Mann, Samuel	1	1	2
Perkerson, Ralph	9	1	1
Osborne, William	2	1	5
Philips, William	1		
Bottom, John	3	1	3
Fennil, John	5	1	2
Fennil, Mary	4	1	2
Varser, Richard	9	1	2
Booker, Samuel	1	1	2
Varser, John	4	1	1
Perkerson, Isham	7	1	
Perkerson, Field	9	1	
Royall, Josh (Estate of)	13	1	9
Townes, James	3	1	4
Morgan, Simon	6	1	2
Morgan, William	5	1	1
Bott, Miles	9	1	3

NAME OF HEAD OF FAMILY.	White souls.	Dwellings.	Other buildings.
Worsham, Daniel	4	1	6
Morgan, John	4	1	
Neal, Ann	3	1	1
Mann, Cain	9	1	1
Worsham, Pheby	5	1	2
Bruniskill, Revd John	2	1	4
Tanner, Branch	8	1	9
Orsborne, Branch	1	1	3
Webster, Edward	5	1	6
Rison, Elry	4		
Webster, John	6	1	1
Webster, William	8	1	2
Dunnavant, Philip	3	1	1
Dunnavant, Nowell (Esta)		1	1
Webster, Thomas	4	1	6
Rowlett, George	9	1	2
Gibbs, William	9	1	3
Webster, Peter	11	1	2
Ford, Mary	4	1	2
Wilkerson, Anothony	1		
Hall, Ann	2	1	4
Archer, Ann	4		
Dunnavant, Abner	3	1	2
Cox, George (Estate of)	4	1	8
Wilson, Daniel	2	2	10
Fagg, John	4		
Willson, Daniel (Estate of)	3	1	11
Willson, Tom. Branch	5	1	15
Booker, William M	10	1	9
Booker, John, Senr	3	2	13
Jolly, Dudley	7		
Ragsdale, George	1	1	6
Cryor, William	1	1	10
Hood, Thomas	7	1	2
Mumford, Edward	6	1	7
Tucker, Absolam	7	1	2
Cardwell, Richard	3	1	3
Tucker, John	2	1	
Clardy, Benjamin	6	2	4
French, Robert	7	1	1
Wills, Edmund	12	1	8
Clardy, John	9	1	3
Clardy, William	5	1	2
Jones, Peter (S. house)	11	2	13
Spain, Joshua	13	1	4
Hood, Robert	13	2	1
Hood, Joel	3		
Hood, Abraham	6	1	2
Hood, Soloman	4	1	1
Hood, John	6	1	4
Tucker, Matthew	10	1	2
Thomas, David	10	1	
Thomas, Susannah	4	1	6
Atkerson, Thomas	8	3	2
Akerson, Musco	6	2	1
Asher, Henry	1	2	1
Beadle, Thomas	3	2	1
Bolton, John	6	2	
Beadle, John	10	1	4
Beadle, Augustin	8	1	
Brooks, William	1	1	
Baugh, Bartley	8	2	4
Booker, Edmund, Junr	3	3	1
Chapman, James	3	1	
Compton, Zachariah	8	1	1
Cannon, William	6	2	1
Chaffin, Stanley	11		
Deaton, George	5		
Dearran, William	7		
Dearen, Richard	5	2	1
Deaton, Levy		2	3
Dalby, John	10	1	4
Elmore, Thomas	4	2	1
Foster, Booker	8	2	3
Foster, John	3	1	
Flemming, Beverley	13	2	
Foster, William	6	1	
Farley, William	5	1	3
Foster, Claiborne	7	1	
Foster, James	8		
Foster, John	2	1	
Flemming, Samuel	2		
Green, Thomas	7	2	3
Holt, Thomas	3	2	3
Hudson, John	2	1	1
Hudson, Edward	6	1	
Holt, Shadrick	7	2	4
Hurt, William	6	2	4
Johnson, Richard	9	1	1
Johnson, Nathan	4		
Johnson, Ashley	7	1	1
Johnson, John	6	1	2
Johnson, Stephen	9	2	1
Johnson, Nicholas	8	2	1
Johnson, Garrard	10	1	1
Jackson, Aarter	10	1	2
Jackson, John	3	2	1
Jones, Hannah	7	1	
Jackson, William	5	2	3
Jones, Edward	13	3	8
Johnson, William	3		

AMELIA COUNTY—Continued.

NAME OF HEAD OF FAMILY.	White souls.	Dwellings.	Other buildings.
League, James	12	2	....
League, Aaron	8	1	....
Lovell, Charles	8	1	....
Mays, William	4	2	....
Meader, Isaac	4	....	....
Meader, Benjamin	11	2	4
McCann, John	7	....	....
Moore, William	9	1	....
Nunnally, Obediah	3	....	....
Noble, Joseph	12	1	2
Norrill, William	1	1	....
Orsborne, Thomas	5	2	1
Pride, Rawlet (Estate of)	....	2	5
Pollard, William	5	1	1
Pillow, William	7	....	....
Seay, James	12	2	2
Vaughan, Nicholas	8	1	....
Vaughan, James	9	3	2
Wright, Thomas	1	1	1
Williams, Phillip	8	3	4
Ward, William	....	1	3
White, Caleb	1	....	....
Wray, Thomas	7	1	....
Mumford, Thomas	4	1	16
Ogilby, Richard	6	1	7
Giles, William	3	1	7
Jones, Mary	2	1	3
Hobson, Thomas	....	1	3
White, John	4	1	1
Compton, Micajah	7	....	....
Compton, Elizabeth	4	1	6
Worsham, Charles	8	....	....
Crenshaw, Mary	5	1	7
Southall, William	1	1	4
Hutcheson, Drury	7	....	....
Hutcheson, William	2	1	....
Bentley, William	5	1	8
Eggleson, Judith	5	1	9
Walker, Edmund	7	1	7
Cocke, Christian	8	1	10
Scott, Sarah	3	1	5
Dunnavant, Hezekiah	8	1	....
Eggleston, Joseph	4	1	19
Eggleson, Richard	5	1	8
Moulson, Mary	2	1	5
Meade, Everard	9	1	11
Featherstone, Charles	4	1	4
Dunnavant, Abraham	7	1	....
Murray, William	1	1	5
Robertson, John	4	1	6
Royall, John, Junr	7	1	1
Royall, John, Senr	5	1	1
Robertson, George (Chestd)	6	1	3
Sadler, John	4	1	1
Baker, Jerman	6	1	2
Brackett, Benjamin	6	1	5
Brackett, Thomas	2	1	3
Brackett, Ludwell	2	1	6
Worsham, Henry	12	1	....
Archer, John	1	1	12
Williamson, Jacob	4	1	2
Hudson, Christopher	10	3	6
Eppes, Frances	7	3	10
Jones, Batt	5	2	11
Randolph, Major Peter	5	1	11
Jones, Majr Wood	2	1	6
Averton, Thomas P	4	3	5
Phillips, Richard	8	2	5
Seay, Moses	5	3	8
Hubbard, John	11	2	2
Clements, John	4	3	6
Seay, Jacob	4	3	2

NAME OF HEAD OF FAMILY.	White souls.	Dwellings.	Other buildings.
Tabb, Edward	8	3	7
Hilsman, Joseph	1	2	2
Clements, Isham	10	3	8
Utley, Jacob	7	1	2
Wingo, John	11	2	5
Ford, Milton	3	4	7
Wilson, Richard	4	....	....
Chapman, John	6	2	3
Eagle, Edward	3	1	2
Hatchell, Josiah	8	2	....
James, John	5	2	....
Wingo, Thomas	2	2	1
Seay, Lucy	2	1	....
Jones, John	2	2	6
Jenkins, James	2	....	6
Foster, John	5	1	4
Seay, Jesse	4	1	6
Seay, Gidion	8	1	3
Foster, George	7	2	4
Foster, George pollard	6	1	4
Foster, Anthony (tittle)	4	1	3
Foster, Thomas	4	4	6
Foster, William	5	2	2
Storn, Tabitha	4	2	3
Lovern, Moses	4	2	2
Harris, Benjamin	4	4	2
Booker, George	4	2	10
Booker, Efford	3	1	5
Hudson, Elizabeth	2	1	3
Foster, Anthony (Black)	8	1	....
Cox, Ann	7	2	6
Goode, Mackerness	10	3	5
Pride, Elizabeth C	6	3	5
James, William	3	2	3
Anderson, Frances	7	5	16
Forrest, Abraham, Junr	6	1	1
Cheatham, James	7	3	3
Cheatham, Archer	11	1	3
FitzGerald, William	8	3	13
Carter, Rawleigh	7	1	13
Bennett, Richard	10	1	6
Dudley, William	3	1	8
Bailey, Charles	6	1	4
Walton, Simeon	10	1	8
Bass, John	10	1	6
Anderson, Charles	13	1	7
Bagley, George	9	1	2
Borum, Edmund	10	1	1
Fawlkes, Jennings	6	1	6
Fawlkes, John, Senr	4	1	6
Fawlkes, William	5	1	2
Fawlkes, Henry	9	2	4
Fawlkes, James	3	1	....
Anderson, James	3	....	....
Boarum, Richard	4	1	3
Bagley, Dicy	8	1	1
Hubbard, Joseph	7	1	1
Fawlkes, Henry	3	1	2
Foster, Mary	8	1	4
Anderson, Elizabeth	6	1	3
Robertson, Maryann	4	1	....
Robertson, Edward	3	1	....
Foster, John	6	1	1
Knight, Charles	8	1	5
Fawlkes, Gabriel, Senr	9	1	6
Fawlkes, Gabriel, Junr	9	1	3
Richardson, Ruler	7	1	2
Leaton, Elizabeth	2	1	....
Ferguson, Susannah	6	1	3
Chandler, Claiborne	4	1	1
Fawlkes, Joseph	9	1	4
Robertson, Edword	3	1	....
Jeffress, Thomas, Senr	11	1	14

NAME OF HEAD OF FAMILY.	White souls.	Dwellings.	Other buildings.
Jeffress, Thomas, Junr	2	1	1
Zachary, Crafford	6	1	1
Bryant, John	8	1	1
Hatchell, Abraham	7	1	5
Mills, John	5	1	3
Oliver, Isaac	7	1	6
Fawlkes, John, Junr	5	1	4
Shelton, James	4	1	2
Boram, James	8	1	1
Jones, Peter (Quater)	....	1	1
Harrison, Christopher	7	1	1
Jennings, James	5	1	3
Jones, Peter (Road quater)	3	....	2
Zachary, Joshua	1	1	4
Leagon, Richard	9	1	1
Roberts, Step	7	1	2
Jones, William	5	1	15
Robertson, James	7	1	7
Jones, Peter (Road)	9	1	18
Olds, William	6	1	9
Wills, Thomas T	7	1	4
Newman, Rice	17	1	20
Clay, John	8	2	22
Scott, Majr Joseph	6	1	4
Crawley, John	5	1	9
Wills, Lou	6	1	10
Tucker, John	9	1	2
Farley, Mary	5	1	8
Tanner, Field	6	1	4
Margain, John	5	1	11
Walthall, Robert	6	1	9
Perkinson, John	4	....	....
Clay, Charles	4	1	4
Bevill, Joseph, Junr	5	1	....
Crawley, Benjamin	1	1	25
Farley, Matt	9	2	7
Bass, William, Senr	4	1	12
Murray, William	5	2	12
Ogilby, John	9	1	9
Adams, David	1	1	8
Hawkins, David	2	1	1
Talley, John	1	1	7
Talley, Jessee	....	....	6
Talley, Lodwick	....	....	3
Talley, Payton	1	1	3
Drake, William	....	....	4
Newman, Rice	2	5	9
Talley, Daniel	....	....	1
Chandler, Martin	....	....	1
Bass, William, Junr	1	5	7
Brooking, Vivion	1	6	15
Munford, Ann	....	....	6
Bass, Edward	1	11	4
Lester, Jeremiah	1	1	9
Green, William	1	5	2
Green, Thomas	1	4	3
Walthall, William	2	4	4
Robertson, George	1	3	4
League, Benjamin	....	....	3
Finney, William	1	8	7
Wilkerson, Townes	....	....	5
Coleman, John	12	2	2
Coleman, Joseph	7	1	4
Powell, Robert	9	2	3
Talley, Daniel	6	1	....
Wilkerson, Daniel	5	1	....
Murray, Daniel	7	1	....
Marshall, Robert	5	1	4
Orsborne, Joseph	4	1	9
Marshall, Mary	1	1	6
Marshall, Abraham	3	1	5
Thompson, Peter	3	1	8

NAME OF HEAD OF FAMILY.	White souls.	Dwellings.	Other buildings.
Marshall, Judith	1	1	3
Green, Abraham	8	2	14
Hardaway, Daniel	4	1	17
Booth, Phebe	9	1	5
Clements, Mrs	6	1	5
Warsham, Henry	3	1	2
Booker, Edword	14	2	14
Bradberry, James A	7	1	5
Hatton, Thomas	1	1	5
Avery, William	12	1	5
Anderson, Henry, Senr	8	3	19
Anderson, Henry, Junr	1	....	4
Cross, Charles	3	1	2
Jordan, William (Estate of)	4	1	6
Crute, Robert	4	....	....
Crenshaw, James	7	7	3
Ball, Thomas	10	2	9
Crenshaw, William, Junr	6	1	12
Wood, William	3	1	4
Pace, John	6	1	5
Farguson, Joel	8	1	1
Ussery, Thomas	3	1	....
Crallie William M	10	2	8
Dixon, William	8	1	....
Lewis, John (Estate of)	2	1	1
Thompson, Medkif	7	1	2
Wallis, Matthew	5	....	....
Irby, John	6	1	5
Crute, John	4	1	2
Waller, Major	10	1	4
Hightower, Thomas	7	1	....
Sneed, William	13	1	3
Waller, William	2	....	....
Lamkin, Peter	9	3	19
Wilkenson, Stephen	4	1	3
Bennett, Richard	3	....	....
Dawson, Christopher	6	1	8
Sturdevant, Daniel (P. George)	3	2	3
Holland, George	3	....	....
Walker, Thomas	8	1	3
Jennings, William, Senr	7	1	5
Smith, Griffin	10	1	3
Womack, Josiah	7	1	3
Crenshaw, David	3	1	3
Smith, Burwell	3	1	3
Morgan, Samuel	10	1	9
Quinn, William	2	....	1
Irby, William	8	....	1
Thomas David	2	....	....
Thomas, Joshua	4	1	2
Thomas, Samuel	8	1	4
Davis, Thomas	2	1	2
Davis, Jacob	3	1	3
Jennings, Robert	9	1	6
Jennings, Henry	3	1	3
Davis, Robert	5	1	1
Overstreet, Thomas	7	1	1
Evans, John	4	1	5
Irby, William, Junr	10	2	6
Wilkerson, Benjamin	6	2	1
Phillips, Thomas	6	1	....
Hurt, Zachariah	8	1	4
Gunn, Thomas	11	1	8
Blackley, William	7	1	6
Doswell, William	7	1	6
Evins, Ellis	2	1	4
Hurt, Absolam	6	1	7
Smith, Samuel	6	1	5
Doswell, John	1	1	10
Jordan, Samuel	5	1	6
Jordan, Thomas	6	1	3
Overton, Benjamin	7	2	3

AMHERST COUNTY.

NAME OF HEAD OF FAMILY.	White souls.	Dwellings.	Other buildings.
Allen, Samuel	6	1	1
Alford, John	3	1	5
Allen, John	8	....	....
Arrington, Samuel	4	....	....
Alford, William	10	2	3
Aron, William	5	....	....
Brabbin, Rose	6	....	....
Bethel, John	11	....	....
Bibb, John	9	2	3
Bush, John	7	2	3
Becknall, Micajah	4	2	....
Browns, James	12	1	....
Bailey Hegekiah	8	....	....
Blaine, George	8	2	2
Bibb, William	9	2	2
Burnett, James Evans	9	....	....
Ballow, Thomas	6	1	1
Cabell William	6	10	33
Cabell, Samuel Jorden	3	2	7
Cabell, William, Jun	3	3	3
Cabell, Joseph (of Buchingham County)	....	....	4
Canady, Jessee	5	....	....

NAME OF HEAD OF FAMILY.	White souls.	Dwellings.	Other buildings.
Crisp, William	11	1	3
Cabell, John (of Buckingham)	....	1	5
Carrell, Bartholomew	7	....	....
Campbell, Moses	13	1	1
Chesnall, Alexander	6	1	2
Cabell, Nicholas	13	3	21
Campbell, Ambrous	10	1	2
Dillard, Joseph	6	1	2
Dillard, James	9	1	2
Deprust, John	13	....	....
Deprust, William	2	1	1
Detterell, Richard	2	....	....
Davis, Israil	7	....	....
Edmonds, James	12	2	....
Eness, John	11	2	2
Evans, Elizabeth	6	1	....
Edmonds, Samuel	12	2	7
Edmonds, Mary	3	....	....
Edmonds, Charles	6	....	....
Freland, Mary	2	2	6
Forgason, Andrew	8	....	....
Fortune, Thomas	9	1	2

NAME OF HEAD OF FAMILY.	White souls.	Dwellings.	Other buildings.
Gregory, John	10	....	....
Golaspee, George	8	2	1
Gowen, Phillip	12	....	....
Gay, Thomas	9	....	1
Horsley, Robert	2	1	3
Horsley, John	5	1	3
Horsley, William	9	1	9
Hendrexson, Peter	5	....	....
Hawkins, Thomas	8	1	5
Henson, James	3	1	1
Hartgrove, Hezekiah	10	2	3
Helton, George	3	3	9
Hooton, Thomas	5	....	....
Harvie, Richard	8	....	....
Hollandsworth, William	4	1	....
Hollandsworth, Joseph	1	....	....
Hansborough, Hezekiah	4	1	2
Huchens, Edward	5	1	....
Johnson, Peter	3	....	....
Josling, William	5	....	....
Josling, Bengamin	3	....	....
Josling, John, Junr	9	....	....
Ludwick, Issamon	3	....	....

NAME OF HEAD OF FAMILY.	White souls.	Dwellings.	Other buildings.
Levely, Joseph	9	....	....
Young, Landrum	8	....	....
Lavender, Charles	9	....	....
Lavender, Mildred	2	....	....
Mitchell, ——	4	....	....
Megginson, Samuel	4	....	....
Mattox, Northy	4	....	....
Mays, Lige	4	....	1
Martin, Jessee	7	....	....
Mays, Joseph, Jun	3	....	1
Mays, John	11	1	1
Mills, Jessee	8	....	....
Mays, James	7	2	2
Mays, Joseph	6	2	4
Meredith, William	8	1	2
Newman, John	2	....	....
Old John (Albermarl County)	1	....	....
Powell, Benjamin	2	....	....
Pamplen, James	11	1	2
Powell, Thomas (Taylor)	4	....	....
Purves, George	6	1	4
Page, Joseph	7	....	....

AMHERST COUNTY—Continued.

NAME OF HEAD OF FAMILY.	White souls.	Dwellings.	Other buildings.
Ponton, Joel	10	...	...
Ray, Moses	6	...	...
Russle, James	5	1	...
Ray, William	6	...	...
Robertson, Arthur	11	...	...
Spencer, William	12	2	4
Staples, John	8	1	1
Stoneham, George	3	1	3
Stephens, Barnett	5	...	...
Stenchcomb, Absolam	1	...	...
Smith, Augustin	4	1	...
Stephens, James	9	1	6
Thomas, Joseph	1	...	...
Tyre, John	3	...	...
Vea, Littleberry	4	...	...
Vea, William	5	...	...
Wood, William	10	...	...
Ware, John	8	...	...
Watts, Stephen	8	1	...
Whettle, John	7	...	...
Walters, James	3	...	...
Warwick, William	3	...	...
Walton, William	8	2	6
Walton, Tilman	14	1	2
Warwick, Abraham	8	2	5
Wright, Jessee	6	...	...
Wilsher, Thomas	8	...	...
Wright, Killis	10	1	1
Wright, Menos	13	1	...
More, Benjamin	12	2	10
Lyon, Peter	8	1	2
Enecks, David	10	2	...
Hoppie, Thomas	10	...	1
Bechnal, Thomas	9	...	2
Anderson, Samuel	7	1	...
Nolly, Bennett	2	1	6
Mathews, William	8	...	1
Murrell, Corneleus	8	...	1
Lanham, Benedict	8	...	2
Turner, Teresha	3	1	6
More, William	1	...	...
Ballend, Andrew	1	...	...
Lanham, Benjamin	4	1	...
Dawson, Capt. John	12	2	8
Martin, Henry, Esq	10	1	7
Levely, Joseph	...	...	2
Wood, James	8	1	1
Conner, James	9	1	...
Mathews, Elizabeth	4	1	1
Mathews, Thomas	3	...	...
Lanham, Joseph	5	...	1
Montgomery, James	9	1	...
Tuggle, Charles	5	...	1
Montgomery, Daved, Jun.	9	1	1
Turner, James	12	4	4
Wright, John	2	1	1
Montgomery, Daved	2	1	1
Phillips, Lennard	1	...	1
Phillips, Daved	4	1	1
Phillips, Mathew	5	...	1
Fetzpattreck, William	10	...	4
Webb, Theodereck	3	...	2
Kesterson, William	5	...	1
Allen, William	3	...	1
Nash, Susanna	5	...	1
Teller, William	7	...	...
Nevel, Thomas	1	...	...
Jopling, Thomas, Jun	8	1	3
Bryan, Elizabeth	8	...	...
Kesterson, John, Jun	4	...	1
Martin, John	3	1	...
Bailey, Lucey	4	...	...
Harres, Mathew	14	2	7
Phillips, Zachereas	10	1	1
Hopkins, James	3	2	15
Horrell, Clever	3	...	...
Nevel, Colo James, decd (The Estate of)	2	1	7
Nevel, Luis	1	...	1
Thomas, Capt Corneleus, decd (The Estate of)	2	1	8
Thomas, Jessee	4	...	...
Childress, Lucey	2	1	2
Roberts, Elliot	11	2	13
Trail, Charles	9	...	...
Dickson, William	10	...	1
Blaer, Allen	5	...	...
Thomas, John	4	...	...
Key, Susanna	9	1	...
Prechard, John	7	...	1
Ward, Nathan	5	...	1
Dunnakin, Daniel	4	...	...
Trail, James	7	...	4
Patteson, Daved	10	1	14
Ditto his overseer	6	...	...
Bocock, John	4	...	...
Howard, William (Estate of)	...	1	3
Turner, Stephen	12	1	4
Harding, Edward	7	1	1
Turner, Teresha, Jun	4	1	...

NAME OF HEAD OF FAMILY.	White souls.	Dwellings.	Other buildings.
Bowman, William	13	1	2
Murrey, Richard	8	1	...
Snider, John	2	1	2
Farrar, Thomas	8	1	2
Chase, Ledea	3	...	...
Murrey, John	3	1	...
Enecks, James	3	...	1
Wist, Frances	10	1	3
Lyon, John, decd (Estate of)	1	...	1
Johnson, William	12	2	...
Levely, Joseph	7	...	2
Wade, Nathaniel	7	...	2
Jopling, Daniel	5	...	1
Bowman, William	4	...	1
Bowman, John	2	...	1
Laine, Joseph	5	...	...
Lalley, William	8	...	1
Lively, Bethel	7	...	1
West, Frances, Jun	7	...	1
Johnson, William	8	...	2
Jopling, Thomas	5	1	6
Nightingale, Mathew	7	...	1
Martin, Peter	11	...	1
Mayo, Robert	...	1	...
Forbus, William	5	...	...
Wright, Robert	15	1	4
Eads, Thomas	3	1	7
Forbus, Mary	1	1	...
Bodingham, George	1	...	...
Wood, Joseas (Land)	...	...	3
Loving, Capt. John	12	1	5
Seay, Abraham	10	1	3
Woody, George	6	...	...
Wright, William	3	1	3
Wooddy, Mary	4	...	...
Hopkins, Colo John	...	1	5
Merrean, Samuel	3	...	...
West, John	4	...	...
Wright, Andrew	5	...	2
Harloe, Nathaniel	11	1	5
Herd, John	3	1	1
Laine, Henry M. C., Jun	5	1	...
Shelton, Clough	1	1	2
Cross, Cornelius	7	...	7
Dinwedoe, Robert	6	1	3
Hundley, Nehemeah	5	1	...
Morrison, Thomas, Jun	4	1	1
Morrison, John	4	1	3
Clarke, Zachereas	5	...	1
Adams, Thomas	...	1	3
Britt, William	7	...	...
Shelton, Daved	9	1	2
Reed, Alexander	4	1	4
Anon, Benjamin	2	...	...
Lackey, Samuel	6	1	1
Beaver, Robert	11	...	2
Ewers, Thomas	9	...	5
Peasley, Hugh	9	...	1
Biggs, John	4	...	2
Biggs, Edward	9	...	1
Martin, Sarah	5	1	3
Cooper, John	4	...	1
Lobbin, John	11	...	2
Montgomery, John	9	...	...
Shannon, Thomas	12	1	1
Kyle, William	11	1	1
MCAnally, Daved	9	1	...
Craddock, Samuel	5	...	1
McCue, John	4	...	2
Witt, William	6	1	3
Wodkins, John	5	...	...
Smith, Johnson	1	...	...
Burton, Ellinor	3	1	4
Johnson, John	3	1	...
Hardie, Robert	3	1	...
Roberts, Joseph	13	1	4
Bell, Thomas	5	1	4
Wright, James	8	1	4
Bones, William	8	1	3
Henderson, John	11	1	3
Smith, Joseph	11	1	1
Simpson, William	7	1	3
Simpson, Daved	7	1	1
Harris, William	9	1	3
Harres, Lee	10	1	1
Pope, John	5	1	7
Tate, Charles	4	1	4
Denny, Samuel	9	1	2
Allin, William	8	1	3
Clarke Nathaniel	9	...	6
Hughs, Moses	10	1	5
Henderson, James	8	1	2
Henderson, Alexander	8	1	1
McLaine, Henry	3	1	1
Bailey, Phillip	9	1	...
Reed, Daved	8	1	2
McNeely, Meheal	5	1	2
Garland, James	1	1	...
Shelton, William	7	...	1
Vines, Thomas	6	...	1

NAME OF HEAD OF FAMILY.	White souls.	Dwellings.	Other buildings.
Shields, John	9	1	1
Pannell, John	2	...	1
McKnight, William	2	...	1
McKnight, John	3	...	1
Dinwedoe, Ann	2	1	1
Massy, John	1	...	...
Puckett, Jacob	9	1	1
Burnett, William	4	...	...
Crawford, John	8	...	1
Morrison, Thomas	11	1	...
Colland, Thomas	5	...	...
Phillips, James	8	...	...
Haggard, John	6	...	...
Dinwedoe, John	1	...	...
Witt, Daved	9	1	1
Witt, Littleberry	6	1	1
Dawson, Henry	6	...	1
Wilson, William	4	...	1
Bowles, James	4	...	1
Poe, Benjamin	6	1	...
Poe, John	2	...	...
Martin, Azareah	9	1	5
Bell, James	3	...	3
Bryant, Benjamin	8	...	1
Fox, Samuel	11	...	1
Crawford, Nathan	8	1	2
Carpinter, John	5	...	...
Clarke, William	3	...	1
Carpinter, Thomas	6	1	2
Small, William	5	1	1
Witt, John	7	1	1
Thusler, James	5	...	1
Witt, George	7	...	1
Sutlar, John	4	...	...
Jackson, Peter	2	...	...
Hall, John, Jun	10	...	1
Talbot, Thomas H	5	...	1
Clarke, Daved, Jun	5	...	1
Clarke, John	4	...	...
Toms, Joseph	3	...	...
Martin, Gedeon	6	...	...
Martin, Stephen	7	1	1
Murrell, John, Jun	9	...	...
Ayres, Rachel	7	1	4
Patton, Thomas	4	1	2
Burnett, Bond	6	1	...
MCLure, John	9	1	1
Ramsey, Simon	8	...	1
Henderson, Robert	7	...	1
Witt, Elijah	4	...	1
Murrell, John	5	...	...
McAlexander, James	4	1	4
McAlexander, James, Jun	4	1	1
McAlexander, John	5	...	...
Robertson, Thomas	5	1	1
Barnett, William	11	1	2
Barnett, James	3	...	...
Pratt, Thomas	5	...	...
Jopling, Josiah	11	1	4
Cheldress, Ann	5	1	2
Henderson James, Jun	7	...	1
Griffin, John	8	2	...
Diggs, John	11	1	7
Pugh, John	9	...	3
Morris, John	7	...	3
Morrison, William	3	1	2
Witt, Abner	9	1	...
Witt, Luis	3	1	...
Carpinter, Benjamin	5	1	...
Morreson, John (H. C.)	3	1	2
Lyon, William	11	1	2
Perkins, John	4	...	...
Jorden, Rueben	...	1	3
Pannell, William	3	1	3
Pannell, Benjamin	5	...	5
Poe, Virgil	4	...	...
Church, Thomas	8	...	...
Reed, Alexander, Jun	4	1	3
Coles, John	2	1	7
Cole, John	5	1	3
Bailey, John	9	1	4
Dinwedoe, William	1	...	...
Miller, William	1	...	...
Mayo, Robert	9	...	...
Woods, James	1	1	5
Daves, Peter	3	...	...
Shropshere, Samour	12	...	...
Harris, John	7	1	...
Rhodes, Charles	6	2	6
Williamson, John	7	1	4
Stone, Elijah	8	2	6
Shepherd, Augustin	7	3	6
Thurmond, John	6	1	3
Thurmond, Gutredge	5	1	4
Blaine, Epram	5	1	2
Crawford, Ann	1	1	2
Scruggs, Samuel S	3	...	...
Shelton, Samuel	...	1	...
Scruggs, John	2	...	...
Martin, Sherod	9	1	5
Statam, Charles	10	1	1

NAME OF HEAD OF FAMILY.	White souls.	Dwellings.	Other buildings.
Deprust, Langsdon	9	...	...
Deprust, Ann	7	...	1
Smith, Samuel	6	...	...
Montgomery, Joseph	3	1	...
Montgomery, John	3	1	3
Smith, Thomas	6	1	6
Oglesby, Richard	8	...	5
Clarke, Daved	8	1	1
Gilmer, John	8	1	5
Hughs, Henry	4	...	1
Littrell, James	7	1	...
Perkins, Richard	5	1	...
Arrington, William	4	...	1
Arrington, Priscilla	3	...	1
Allcock, Richard	6	1	...
Bell, Henry	5	2	1
Johnson, Bain	7	1	...
Bryant, Benjamin	10	...	1
Branham, Edward	3	...	1
Bryant, Zachereas	3	...	1
Brown, John (B. S.)	9	2	1
Bell, Samuel	5	...	1
Christain, John (B.)	8	1	3
Christain, Drury (Estate)	5	1	6
Christain, Capt. John	11	1	4
Christain, Elijah	7	1	...
Campbell, Joel	8	1	4
Campbell, Laurence	9	1	3
Campbell, Aron	7	1	...
Christain, Capt. Henry	8	1	2
Christain, Robert	10	1	6
Christain, Martha	6	1	4
Dillard, James	4	1	3
Dillard, William	9	...	1
Dehart, Aron	9	1	...
Evans, Benjamin (Mulattos 6)	...	...	1
Galwood, Ambrous	7	...	1
Gatewood, William, Jun	8	1	...
Gillinwaters, Ann	2	...	...
Gatewood, William, Sen	4	...	1
Gatewood, Richard	11	1	...
Gehe, Samuel	4	...	...
Harris, John	4	...	1
Hodges, Rachel	6	...	1
Higginbotham, Joseph	3	1	...
Hill, James	11	1	2
Higginbotham, Moses	6	1	8
Higginbotham, Capt. John	11	1	5
Higginbotham, Colo James	5	1	5
Hutcherson, John	8	...	1
Joiner, Peter	8	...	1
Johnson, John	3	...	1
London, James, Jun	8	1	1
London, Larkin	2	...	1
Lemaster, Ralph	14	...	1
Lamaster, Abraham	6	1	...
Mayo, Joseph	5	2	7
Montgomery, William	4	1	1
Pinn, Phillip	10	...	1
Phillips, John	7	2	...
Phillips, William	9	2	1
Pinn, Rawley (Mulattos 8)	...	...	1
Patterson, James	4	1	1
Rowsey, John	11	1	...
Rowsey, James	6	...	1
Spears, William	2	...	...
Strutton, John	12	1	...
Stratton, Henry	4	1	...
Tyree, Jacob	7	1	1
Turner, Henry	7	1	1
Turner, John	8	1	...
Wingfield, John	8	1	2
Wingfield, Joseas	3	1	1
Warren, John	3	1	...
Warren, Benjamin	3	...	1
Welsher, Charles	6	1	...
Walker, Joel	3	...	1
Whittle, Mathew	2	...	1
Welsher, Joseph	5	...	1
Upshaw, John	6	1	...
Kenedy, John	5	1	...
Bailey, William	3	...	...
Johns, Mary	7	...	1
Baen, Richard	5	...	1
Phillips, George	6	1	...
Gatewood, Larkin	3	1	...
Christain, John (H.)	1	1	1
Cofland, Benjamin	6	...	1
Grisham, Thomas	9	1	2
Davis, John	5	1	1
Chappell, William	8	1	...
Ham, Stephen	14	1	2
Ham, John	1	1	1
Ellis, Solomon	9	...	...
Robinson, John	12	...	...
Vigust, James	8	...	...
Rucker, Benjamin	7	1	7
Purley, Charles	5	...	...
Tinsley, John	9	1	6
North, Anthoney	2	...	...

AMHERST COUNTY—Continued.

NAME OF HEAD OF FAMILY.	White souls.	Dwellings.	Other buildings.	NAME OF HEAD OF FAMILY.	White souls.	Dwellings.	Other buildings.	NAME OF HEAD OF FAMILY.	White souls.	Dwellings.	Other buildings.	NAME OF HEAD OF FAMILY.	White souls.	Dwellings.	Other buildings.
Goodwin, Micajah	7			Bowles, Knight	8	1	13	Lewis, John, Senr	4	1		Daves, George	12		1
Goodwin, James	3			Burford, Daniel, Jun	5	1	5	Gilliam, Archelus	4			Carter, Landon	4		
Goodwin, William	3			Burford, James	3	1		Gilliam, John	3			Byass, Larkin	6		
Goodwin, John, Sen	3	1	1	Tinsley, David	11	1	2	Morriss, Thomas	5	1		Galaspie, Sherod More	6		
Goodwin, George	5	1		Rucker, John, Jun	9			Burks, Elizabeth	7	1		Whitton, John	5		
Gausney, Henry	1			Tinsley, Joshua	6	1	1	Burden, Archelus	9	1	1	Whettle, Joseph	11		
Wood, Frances	5	1	2	Pendleton, James	4	1		Payton, John	8			Wash, Benjamin	5		
Wood, Paul	6			Stewart, William	3			Edwards, Joseph	10	1		Payton, Sarah	4		
Wood, Silas	5			Rucker, Ellinor	4	1	8	Burks, Daved	10	1		Watts, Caleb	10	1	2
Wood, Jessee	3			Morton, James	6	1		Haynes, William	10	1		Watts, Thomas	3	1	1
Gillaland, Susanna	4			Rucker, Isaac, Sen	7	1	6	Eubank, Ambrous	7			Jenkins, Thomas	10	1	
Hill, John	2			Symonds, James	11	1		Tooley, James	11			Burks, John	4	1	
Smith, Reuben	4	1	3	Miles, Joseph	14			Grimes, Thomas	9			Roach, Ash Craft	9	1	
Tinsley, William, Jun	2			Harper, Edward	7	1	1	Hogg, John	11	1		Daves, Elizabeth	7	2	1
MCDaniel, George, Jun	4	1		Bibb, Martin	4	1	1	Holt, Phillip	9	1		Camden, John, Sen	4		
Street, Anthoney	4	1	3	Harrison, Reuben	9			Burks, Charles	8	1		Goodrich, John	6		
Burford, John	7	1	3	Harrison, Frankey	3	1	3	Saunders, Edward	5			Sandedge, John	9	1	
Burford, Daniel (Minor)	5	1	2	Woodroof, Daved	9	2	4	Eubank, John	8			Carter, William	4		
Alexander, James	6			Johns, Mary	7	1		Goodrich, Edmond	8		1	Tucker, Thomas	7	1	
Stennett, John	10			Pendleton, Elizabeth	8	1	1	McCulloch, Roderick	8	1	2	Barrott, Thomas		1	
Whitehead, John	14	1	1	Megann, Joseph	7	1	1	Tooley, John, Jun	10			Hartless, Henry	9	1	
Lee, William	7	1	1	Cox, Volentine	10	1	2	Waugh, Thomas	8	1	3	Coleman, Benjamin	6		
Harvie, Daniel	3	1	1	Reynolds, Charles	6	1	1	New, David	7			Ballinger, Joseph	5	3	1
Wilsher, Richard	7			Teneson, John	13	1		Williams, Frances	3			Garland, Thomas	5		
MCDaniel, John	6	1	1	Gillenwaters, Martha	5	1	1	Thomas, James	8			Martin, James	10	1	
Crews, Joseph, Sen	8	1	2	Goodwin, Joseph	13	1		Veal, Carnaby	4			Childress, John (Pedlar)	9		
Dawson, Robert D	3	1		Rickets, Thomas	9			Veal, Nathan	5			Earhart, John	6		1
Tinsley, William, Sen	6	1	6	Johnson, Thomas	6	1	3	Layne, Joseph	8			Sandedge, Benjamin	3		
Peters, William	10	1	4	Merritt, John	7	1	2	Nowlin, James	10	1		Childress, Henry	10		
Key, Martin	6			Hughs, William	8	1	3	Jarrell, Daved	5	1		Tayler, George, Sen	3	1	
Key, Rue	2			Guttrey, William	8	1		Eubank, George	7	1		Tayler, William	13		
Tineson, Jessee	3			Powell, Thomas	3	1	3	Slead, John	10			Wood, John	4		
Bonds, John	4			Mitchel, Archelus	8	1	2	Galaspie, William	6	1		Hall, William	5		
Dawson, Joseph	6	1	4	Powell, Richard	6	1		Harreson, John	11			Henderson, Nathaniel	5		
Crews, James	12	1		Trout, Henry	5	3	8	Ellis, Charles	9			Redcross, John	11		
Scott, William	8			Stovall, James	3			Rolls, Caleb	7			Higginbotham, William	7		
Baily, Samuel	9	1		Taylor, Edmond	4	1		Crawford, Daved	10	2	4	McDaniel, Argus	10		
Crittindon, John	10	1	3	Goodwin, John H	3	1		Brown, Jacob	7			Frazer, James	7		
Hannar, Robert	7	1	1	Stern, William	7			Brown, John	9		2	Hufman, Henry	6		
Tinsley, Isaac	10	1	2	Blankenship, Nowel	9	1		Davis, Moses	5	1		Ison, Charles	7		
Coleman, George	6	1	1	Blankenship, Daved	2			Milstead, Zeal	4			Hufman, Frederick	6		
Thacker, Pittis	5	1	3	Johns, Thomas	5	1	2	Milstead, Aron	5			Power, Walter	2		
Lee, George	8	1	2	McDaniel, Henry	15	1		Goodrich, Thomas	5	3		Ison, Elijah	6		
Wilson, Jonathan	6	1	3	Mahone, Daniel	9	2		Goodrich, James	4			Clarke, William	8	1	
Clements, Stephen	5			Evans, William	7	1		Pryor, Nicholas	9	1		Taylor, John	6		
Clements, William W	7	1		Jinkins, John	6			Powell, Fances	2	1		Tayler, George	8		
Clements, William, Jun	11			Waters, Frances				Roberts, John	10			Cheldress, John	5		
Pendleton, Richard	3	1	2	Gue, John	4			Veal, William	6			Cheldress, John	5		
Scott, Isaac	1			Woodroof, John	2			Sandedge, Pullim	6			Edmondson, James	3		
Shelton, Joshua	4	1	4	Mitchell, John	3	1	1	Milstead, Joseph	10			Staton, Ann	5		
Rucker, Anthoney	8	1	2	Rucker, Ambrous, Sen	13	3	11	Payton, John	8	1		Staton, Thomas	9		
Coleman, Milley	14	1	6	Plunket, Benjamin	6			Burden, Henry	7			Hartless, William	1		
Coleman, Elizabeth	9	2	2	Davis, Henry L	10	1	9	Brown, Moses	3			Tungett, Fielding	3		
Oglesbey, William	1			Davis, Nicholas			5	Carter, Edward	2			Hall, John	6		
Knight, John	6	1	3	Lucas, Thomas	5	1	3	Carter, Peter	11	1	2	Rucker, Reuben (decd)			2
Cox, Archelus	7			Watson, James	15	1	3	Wright, Isaac	10	1	4	Jervis, John	8		
Moon, William	8	1	1	Watson, Edward	8	1		Thurmond, Phillip	10	4	4	Hecks, William	6		
Padgett, Edmond	7			Bryant, William	7			Payton, William, Sen	2			Staton, Benjamin	2		
Wilcox, Thomas	6	1		Childress, Goolsbey	2			Payton, Hinry, Sen	3			Gooden, James	2		
Burford, William	5			Jones, John	5	1	3	Pope, Leroy	8	1		Hall, Moses	3		
Thurmond, Phelex	3			Gaines, Daniel	12	2	18	Routt, George	4			Hufman, Fredereck	5		
Devenport, Joseph	10			Taliaferro, Charles	9	1	4	Duncan, John	9	1	1				
Reckerson, John	5	1	1	Ellis, Josiah	15	7	4	Jones, Nicholas, Jun	3						
Shelton, Richard	7	1	4	Lewis, John F. P.	5			Whitten, Jerimeah	6						

FAIRFAX COUNTY.

LIST OF JOHN GIBSON.	White souls.	Dwellings.	Other buildings.	LIST OF JOHN GIBSON—continued.	White souls.	Dwellings.	Other buildings.	LIST OF WILLIAM PAYNE.	White souls.	Dwellings.	Other buildings.	LIST OF WILLIAM PAYNE—continued.	White souls.	Dwellings.	Other buildings.
Allison, William	8	1	3	Lay, Joseph	3			Beckwith, Marmaduke	9	1	7	Hally, James	4	2	6
Athy, Thomas	4	1		Morton, Jane	7	1	5	Buckley, John	10	1	4	Hampton, John	6	1	7
Athy, James	2			Massey, Lee	4	1	15	Bromback, John	9	1	3	Hogard, Jere	8		2
Bond, Zachariah	8			McIntosh, Louchlan	4	1		Blansett, Joseph	7	1	4	Hampton, Joseph	3	1	2
Bayley, Samuel	6	2	12	Moore, Cleon	6	1	6	Bayly, Jesse	4	1	1	Jones, John	4		1
Bussey, Hezekiah	8		3	Mills, Sarah	4		1	Clark, John	4	1	5	Jacobs, Joseph, Junr	11	1	6
Barnes, Sarah	1	1	7	McCarty, Daniel, Junr	4	1	6	Coffer, John	4	1	9	King, Benjamin	9	1	4
Boggess, Henry	8		2	McAtee, William	7			Clark, Richard	11	2	3	King, John	8		2
Barnes, Abraham	3	1	1	Mason, George, Junr	2		6	Coe, Edward	4	1	2	Kerrick, James	5		1
Boggess, Robert	6	1	4	Mason, Colo George	18	1	30	Coe, William	4	1	7	King, Hargiss	4	1	2
Cunningham, Cornelius	3			McCarty, Colo Daniel	3	1	14	Chappell, John	4	1	1	Kincheloe, Daniel	6	1	4
Cockburn, Martin	2	1	10	Pool, William	12	2	2	Dogan, Henry	7	1	2	Kincheloe, Cornelius	2	1	
Cash, William	8	1	2	Pool, Peter	4	1		Deneale, James	7	1	9	Mauzy, Peter	10	1	8
Compton, Housin	3		2	Pool, Thomas	6	1	2	Deneale, William	7	1	3	Middleton, Lutner	5	1	1
Conner, Terrence	4			Parker, Marshal	7		1	Edwards, James	9	1	2	Marshall, John	8	1	3
Cooms, Walter	4			Parker, Lawson	7	1		Edwards, William	7	1	5	Marshall, Robert	5	1	5
Evans, John	9	1		Ross, Hector	4	1	3	Edwards, Jacob	7	2	3	Nichols, George	10	1	6
Finley, Sarah Ann	5	1	5	Stone, Daniel	9	1	1	Ellzey, Lewis	8	1	12	Posey, John	9	2	4
Fairfax's, George William		1	7	Spencer, Elizabeth	4	1		Ford, Edward	14	1	8	Payne, Edward	5	1	18
Fallin, Agatha	3	1	1	Spellman, Merryman	7			Ferguson, Josiah	11	1	4	Powell, John	7	1	3
Gates, Samuel	6	1		Simpson, Gilbert	7	1	9	Gibson, John (Overseer)	6	1	6	Powell, William	4	1	4
Gibson, John	4	2	6	Triplett, William	6	1	15	Gibson, John (Overseer)	6	1	7	Payne, Sarah	6	1	1
Henderson, Alexander		1	2	Thompson, William	3	2	14	Gossom, Thomas	8	1	6	Pollard, Thomas	13	1	8
Harrison, William	8			Violett, William	3			Gill, James	9	1	3	Payne, Sanford	9	1	5
Hammilton, Dennis B	7		1	Washington, Genl Geo	30	39	21	Gosling, Robert	1	1		Philips, John	5	1	
Hereford, John, Junr	3	1	2	Washington, Lund	4	3	3	Henderson, Alexander	17	3	25	Rowland, Gilbert	8	2	2
Hutcheson, John	2	1		Washington, Lawrence	2	1	19	Harrower, Meryman	11	1	3	Russau, Henry	7	1	7
Javins, John	8	1	3	Wyley, George	9	1	4	Hollyman, William	8	1	5	Reed, Sarah	8	2	2
Lindsay, William	10	1	6	Willington, John	7	1		Hampton, John, Junr	4	1	1	Reardon, Yelverton	4	1	5

FAIRFAX COUNTY—Continued.

NAME OF HEAD OF FAMILY.	White souls.	Dwellings.	Other buildings.
LIST OF WILLIAM PAYNE—continued.			
Ryley, Peter	13	1	....
Simpson, Moses	6	1	16
Simpson, Baxter	7	1	2
Said, William	6	1	....
Simpson, William	8	1	....
Simpson, John	14	1	5
Sangster, Thomas	11	1	5
Stone, Caleb	7	2	4
Simpson, William	5	....	2
Turner, William	6	1	7
Tillett, John	10	1	5
Turner, William, Junr	3	1	1
Tillett, George	6	2	7
Tillett, John, Junr	4	1	3
Tasker, James	5	1	....
Thompson, Cornelius	11	....	3
Wilcoxon, Thomas, Junr	5	1	5
Wood, Joseph	6	1	1
Wicklif, Robert	7	1	....
Wheeler, Richard	4	1	4
West, Sarah	9	1	5
Warden, Sarah	3	1	4
Waugh, James	8	1	9
West, John	5	1	5
Williams, Joseph	8	1	4
Wren, James, Junr	7	1	2
Waugh, Tyler	9	1	2
Winn, George	....	....	1
Wagener, Peter	8	1	9
Yeoman, John	5	1	3
LIST OF RICHARD CHICHESTER.			
Ashford, Michael	4	1	4
Atcheson, Leonard	5	1	....
Ashford, John	6	....	....
Alleston, John	14	....	....
Atcheson, Clement	5	1	....
Bryan, Philip	3	....	....
Baylis, William P	10	....	1
Ballenger, Joseph	5	1	....
Barker, John	7	1	4
Baylis, Thomas	7	....	....
Barker, William, Junr	7	1	....
Barker, Moses	8	1	2
Barker, William	9	1	1
Baylis, William Cage	2	....	....
Brown, Edward	8	1	1
Beach, Charles W	12	1	1
Burton, Benjamin	3	1	....
Boggess, John	7	....	....
Bayly, Henry	5	1	....
Brookbank, Thomas	9	1	....
Clark, Josias	7	1	8
Carricoe, Abel	9	1	....
Coffer, Francis	7	1	8
Conner, Terrence	4	....	....
Church, Thomas	10	1	1
Clark, John	5	....	....
Cook, Giles	10	1	4
Conner, James	8	....	....
Chichester, Richard	10	1	11
Coulter, Peter	11	1	....
Carricoe, William	5	1	....
Compton, Zebedee	8	2	....
Dodson, Charles	11	1	....
Deevers, Gilbert	7	....	....
Dyer, Thomas	8	....	....
Donaldson, William	9	1	2
Dyer, Edward	6	1	....
Daniel, John	10	1	5
Davis, Isaac	9	1	3
Dulin, John	4	1	3
Davis, Nehemiah	4	1	5
Emmerson, Richard	7	....	....
Fowler, John	7	1	8
Fitzhugh's, William	6	1	22
Fitzhugh's, Henry (Estate)	....	3	25
Fielder, Samuel	11	1	1
Glocester, James	3	....	....
Grymes, Philip	6	1	8
Grymes, John	7	1	4
Gilpin, William	2	....	....
Garrett, Peter	4	1	....
Hall, William	6	....	....
Harris, John	4	1	1
Hornbuckle, George	4	....	....
Hornbuckle, Thomas	9	1	5
Hill, John	3	....	....
Harper, Leonard	8	....	....
Hill, Josias	3	....	....
Hunt, Priscilla	6	....	....
Hereford, John	8	2	....
Hall, Michael	6	1	4
Hornbuckle, William	6	2	4
Hornbuckle, Solomon	10	1	2
Halley, Nathaniel	7	1	7

NAME OF HEAD OF FAMILY.	White souls.	Dwellings.	Other buildings.
LIST OF RICHARD CHICHESTER—continued.			
Hammond, Jervis	3	1	2
Halley, James, Junr	13	1	3
Halley, William	2	1	9
Halley, John	....	1	2
Hunt, James	4	1	....
Halley, Richard	9	1	3
Johnson, John	8	1	1
Johnson, Walter	10	1	1
Johnson, William	3	2	1
Jacobs, Mordecai	6	1	1
Johnson, Bennett	2	1	....
Javins, Joseph	7	1	1
Johnson, Thomas	6	1	....
Johnson, Thomas	2	1	....
Jones, Thomas	6	1	....
Johnson, Lancelott	6	1	....
Johnson, William, Junr	7	1	....
Kirbey, Thomas	4	1	2
Keen, Francis	2	1	....
Kent, John	10	1	2
Keen, William	11	1	8
Kent, Jane	4	1	2
Kent, Sampson	3	1	....
Kirk, Grafton	6	1	1
Kent, Daniel	6	....	....
King, William	12	1	1
Low, James	4	1	1
Lewis, Thomas	12	1	7
Love, Thomas	6	1	....
Loyd, Mary	2	1	1
Loyd, Henry	4	....	....
Middleton, Thomas	6	....	....
Mason, George	6	1	....
McNeale, William	9	....	....
Moore, John	5	....	....
Mopley, James	7	1	2
McLoughlin, Jesse	5	....	....
Moreland, Jacob, Junr	7	....	....
Mcfarlane, John B	8	1	2
Moreland, Jacob	5	....	....
McDonald, Alexander	8	1	4
Mills, John	7	....	....
McIntosh, John	2	1	2
Noland, Charles	10	1	....
Oneale, Charles	5	....	....
Ogdon, William	10	1	....
Patterson, Susanna	1	....	....
Payne, Elizabeth	7	1	1
Powell, Joseph	6	....	....
Price, David	10	1	5
Pettit, Elizabeth	4	....	....
Potter, Edward	10	1	1
Powell, John	2	....	....
Powell, Sarah	3	....	....
Pomeroy, John	13	1	....
Regan, John	11	1	1
Rogers, William	6	1	3
Rigg, Benjamin	6	1	....
Rigg, John	8	1	2
Ryley, John	5	....	....
Rowe, John	2	1	....
Reardon, William	6	3	3
Reed, John	6	2	1
Smith, Charles	12	1	4
Simpson, Richard	7	1	1
Steel, William	7	1	....
Smitherman, William	5	1	....
Swalldo, Zephaniah	7	....	1
Smith, Samuel	5	1	5
Stone, Eli	9	1	8
Skinner, John	5	1	1
Simpson, William	9	1	2
Scrivener, Richard	10	1	....
Simpson, Aaron	4	....	2
Simpson, Susanna	4	1	6
Stone, Samuel	10	2	5
Smitherman, Samuel	8	1	1
Simpson, Thomas	8	1	1
Smith, James	11	1	2
Speake, Robert	7	1	....
Scott, John	3	1	6
Spragg, John	7	....	....
Stone, Francis	4	1	3
Solomon, James	3	1	....
Sudderth, Benjamin	7	1	1
Simpson, William	5	1	1
Simpson, George	....	1	3
Tayler, Samuel	8	1	1
Thompson, James	10	1	2
Tayler, James	8	....	....
Triplett, Sarah	7	1	2
Tayler, John	3	....	....
Tyler, William	9	1	....
Violett, Whaley	1	1	....
Vernon, John	9	2	1
Woolbright, Samuel	2	1	1
Wiser, Michael	4	1	1
Woodard, Thomas	8	1	....
Windsor, Thomas	5	1	6

NAME OF HEAD OF FAMILY.	White souls.	Dwellings.	Other buildings.
LIST OF RICHARD CHICHESTER—continued.			
West, Benjamin H	8	....	....
Warner, Joseph	7	....	....
Windsor, Thomas, Junr	6	1	1
Worthen, Edward	5	1	2
Williams, William	10	1	1
Williams, Bazel	9	1	....
Wingate, Henry	5	....	....
Ward, John	4	1	3
Weedon, Samuel	5	1	2
Worthen, Henry	2	1	1
Wiggs, Ann	4	....	....
Woolbright, Jacob	6	1	....
Washington, Edward	4	1	9
LIST OF JAMES WREN.			
Trammell, Gerrard	2	1	1
Spurling, Jeremiah	11	1	5
Moxley, Thomas	10	1	5
Sears, William	8	1	4
Barry, William	4	1	4
Fairfax, Thomas	1	1	5
Owens, John	5	2	7
Goodrick, Benjamin	9	1	2
Garrett, Henry	3	1	1
Baker, James	7	1	....
Jenkins, Daniel	6	1	5
Bradley, Daniel	5	1	3
Swink, William	13	1	3
Simpson, Joseph	9	1	5
Jenkins, Charles	5	1	....
Hodskin, Daniel	5	....	....
Scott, William	1	1	11
Gunnell, Thomas	9	1	5
Simms, William	10	1	2
Lewis, Thomas	7	1	14
Jenkins, Samuel	6	1	3
Smith, George	11	1	7
Collins, James	7	1	6
Simms, William, Junr	4	1	2
Thrift, Charles	5	1	10
Page, John	7	1	....
Thrift, Charles, Junr	6	1	2
Gullatt, Rachel	8	1	1
Henderson, William	4	1	....
Anderson, John	7	1	5
Wood, Elijah	5	1	....
Trammell, Gerrard, Junr	11	1	5
Trammell, Sampson	5	1	5
Adams, John	4	1	2
Thrift, George	6	1	6
Rooksbey, Ann	6	1	1
Ruzzey, Henry	3	1	3
Offutt, Reason	11	1	4
Trammell, Thomas	7	1	1
Blake, John	8	....	....
Davis, Allan	9	1	2
Moxley, Joab	4	1	1
Moxley, John	2	1	....
Jackson, John	10	1	7
Shortridge, John	7	1	7
Fairfax, Bryan	6	1	10
Beedle, Andrew	7	1	2
Rose, Francis	6	1	1
Burgess, Thomas	3	1	3
Burgess, Joseph	3	1	....
Bates, Edward	12	1	4
Carrington, Timothy	9	1	2
Garrett, Nicholas	10	1	6
Broadwater, Charles L	3	1	2
Thomas, David	3	1	1
Collin, William	8	1	2
Lester, John	6	....	....
Crook, James	3	1	3
McCarty, James	6	1	3
Gunnell, Henry	3	1	13
Hunter, John	8	1	5
Magruder, Thomas	1	1	6
Adams, Simon	3	1	3
Thomas, James	5	1	....
Darn, William	5	1	3
Lee, Flora	....	1	7
Wren, William	9	1	2
Sands, James	6	1	1
Payne, Annanias	10	1	2
Scott, Zacharias	4	1	....
Scott, Samuel	7	1	1
Massey, John	7	1	1
Shearwood, Thomas	5	....	....
Wray, Thomas	7	1	....
Darn, Henry	10	1	1
Gunnell, William	6	1	10
Pearson, Thomas	3	1	3
Darn, John	7	1	1
Adams, Samuel	3	1	5
Adams, Samuel, Junr	3	1	4
Hursts, John	2	1	3
Courts, John	7	1	4
Lindsay, Susanna	5	1	4

NAME OF HEAD OF FAMILY.	White souls.	Dwellings.	Other buildings.
LIST OF JAMES WREN—continued.			
Lindsay, Thomas	5	1	2
Towers, John	3	1	1
Robertson, James	10	1	1
White, Thomas	5	1	....
Tayler, Thomas	4	1	3
Craig, Charles	8	1	3
Arnold, Thomas	6	1	....
Goldup, John	6	1	4
Payne, Jacob	8	1	....
Pendall, Thomas	7	1	3
Robertson, John	7	1	....
Mattenly, John	3	1	....
Mattenly, James, Junr	2	1	....
Mattenley, James	7	1	....
Robertson, Elizabeth	1	1	1
Edwards, Elizabeth	7	1	....
Butcher, John	5	1	1
Butcher, William	3	1	....
Frizell, Mary	10	1	1
Earp, Mathew	12	1	2
Broadwater, Charles	3	2	13
Hunter, Elizabeth	2	1	2
Moody, Thomas	6	1	5
Hipkins, Lewis	4	1	5
Lee's, Henry	....	1	4
Darn, Thomas	5	....	....
Reed, Nelson	7	1	....
Poston, Francis	9	1	1
Wren, James	8	1	13
Chun, Mary	2	1	1
Turberville, John	1	1	14
Blackburn, Edward	8	1	6
Moore, Jere	12	1	4
Shepperd, John	6	1	5
Gunnell, William	11	1	1
Hurst, John	3	1	4
Gunnell, John	3	1	3
Hurst, James	12	1	2
LIST OF CHARLES LITTLE.			
Allan, Thomas	2	1	....
Williams, Edward	10	3	2
Compton, John	12	1	6
Freeman, William	5	1	....
McGinnis, Lawrence	5	1	1
Hagan, John	5	2	1
Baggett, Elizabeth	6	1	1
Darrell, Philip	6	1	3
Harper, John	7	1	4
Armstrong, John	10	1	....
Spilman, Thomas	5	1	6
Frazier, John	5	1	4
McPherson, Burges	6	1	4
Adams, Abednego	6	1	4
Reed, William	6	1	4
Slaughter, Ann	7	1	10
Boswell, Henry	3	1	....
Lewis, John	1	1	2
Little, Charles	7	1	6
Ballenger, Jacob	7	1	....
Freeman, Richard	4	1	....
Davis, John	6	1	....
Johns, John	4	1	....
Boyd, William	4	1	....
Alexander, Robert	5	1	8
Peake, Humphrey	6	1	7
Darrell, Mary	6	1	6
Lightfoot, William	9	1	3
Sanford, Richard, Junr	4	1	4
Sanford, Richard	5	1	3
Lightfoot, Samuel	6	1	3
Cox, Elizabeth	5	1	8
Moss, John	10	1	4
Dade, Baldwin	8	1	2
Tayler, Jane	5	1	....
Atkins, Thomas	2	....	....
Herbert, Thomas	5	1	4
Sanford, James	2	1	....
McKenzie, John	3	1	....
Katon, William	8	1	....
Alexander, Samuel	4	1	....
Simmonds, Thomas	5	1	1
Williams, William	4	1	1
West, Sibyl	1	....	....
West, Thomas	8	1	6
Devaughn, John	8	1	1
Williams, Ayler	8	2	1
Alton, John	4	1	2
Robertson, John	5	1	7
McLaughlan, Thomas	7	1	1
Brooke, Walter	4	1	6
Boswell, George	4	1	....
Armstrong, William	10	1	....
Halley, William	2	1	1
Lambert, Thomas	3	1	....
Allan, John	3	1	....
Cammeron, Ann	1	1	....
Ferrell, John	5	1	....

FAIRFAX COUNTY—Continued.

NAME OF HEAD OF FAMILY.	White souls.	Dwellings.	Other buildings.
LIST OF CHARLES LITTLE—continued.			
Robertson, Nanny	2	1	....
McDonald, Alexander	1	1	....
French, Penelope	4	1	3
Femister, John	5	1	....
Dow, Peter	1	1	3
Payne, Virlinda	5	1	1
Ratcliff, John	2	1	3
Summers, George	3		
Ratcliff, Richard	2	1	2
Morris, Zachariah	9	1	....
Dove, Thomas	7	1	....
Beach, Thomas	7	1	1
Curry, Charles	8	1	....
Powell, Robert	5	....	....
McLean, Samuel	3	1	....
Sanford, Robert	9	2	....
West, Roger	2	1	....
Weston, William	9	1	1
Morris, Nehemiah	8	....	....
Wright, Charles	6	....	....
LIST OF GEORGE GILPIN.			
Alexander, Charles	6	1	5
Alexander, Philip	7	1	6
Adam, Robert	5	1	4

NAME OF HEAD OF FAMILY.	White souls.	Dwellings.	Other buildings.
LIST OF GEORGE GILPIN—continued.			
Bowling, Simon	5	1	6
Bowling, William	9	1	3
Ball, Moses	5	1	2
Ball, Moses, Junr.	7	1	2
Ball, James	5	1	....
Bladen, William	11	1	1
Bolton, Sarah	4	1	....
Bushby, William	13	1	2
Burgess, Charles	6	1	....
Ballenger, Benjamin	2	1	....
Birch, Joseph	9	1	2
Bowling, Ann	5	1	3
Ballenger, Mathew	3	1	2
Chapman, George	6	1	5
Crump, William, Junr.	5	1	1
Crump, William	7	1	3
Cockerill, Joseph	7	1	5
Cockerill, Sampson	5	1	4
Davis, Edward	5	1	2
Davis, Edward, Junr.	11	1	....
Davis, John	3	1	....
Duling, Sarah	3	1	....
Duley, James	10	1	1
Daniel, Thomas	7	1	1
Dowdall, John	5	1	7
Every, John	9	1	6

NAME OF HEAD OF FAMILY.	White souls.	Dwellings.	Other buildings.
LIST OF GEORGE GILPIN—continued.			
Frazer, William	3	1	3
Gooding, William	7	1	....
Gilpin, George	12	1	5
Gates, William	3	1	....
Grafford, Thomas	4	1	....
Harding, Hall	8	1	3
Horsman, John	8	1	1
Harden, Elihue	3	1	1
Harden, Moses	8	1	....
Jones, Charles	4	1	3
Johnson, Samuel	7	2	1
Johnson, Aaron	11	1	2
Mills, John	3	1	....
Mattester, Daniel	4	1	....
Minor, Jemima	8	2	3
Mills, Daniel	7	2	2
McDougie, Robert	7	1	2
Mcfarling, Ignatius	4	1	....
Payne, John	4	1	....
Popejoy, Nathaniel	8	1	3
Pearson, Simon	9	1	1
Parsons, John	3	1	....
Payne, William	6	1	4
Powell, John	3	1	....
Richards, James	8	1	2
Rollings, John	4	1	2

NAME OF HEAD OF FAMILY.	White souls.	Dwellings.	Other buildings.
LIST OF GEORGE GILPIN—continued.			
Summers, Simon	6	1	3
Summers, John, Junr.	6	1	5
Spinks, Chandler	3	1	5
Smith, Joseph	5	1	2
Summers, Francis	15	2	3
Sebastian, Nicholas	7	1	2
Sisson, William	7	1	2
Summers, John, 3d	7	1	5
Summers, William	3	1	3
Summers, Daniel	7	....	....
Skidmore, Edward	4	1	....
Stuart, David	7	2	5
Thomas, William	5	1	....
Talbutt, Osborn	5	1	1
Thrift, Jeremiah	8	2	....
Thrift, Jeremiah, Junr	3	1	....
Thompson, William	7	1	....
Terrett, William Hy	5	1	4
Ward, Jonathan	2	1	....
Williams, Jeremiah	11	1	3
Williams, Hezekiah	3	1	2
Wiser, Henry	8	1	....
West, Margarett	4	1	1

HALIFAX COUNTY.

NAME OF HEAD OF FAMILY.	White souls.	Dwellings.	Other buildings.
LIST OF JAS. BATES.			
Street, Anthony	3	1	4
Mallicott, John	10	1	1
Eckols, Joseph	10	2	10
Adams, John	7	1	3
Eckols, Obadiah	7	....	....
Hardwick, James	6	1	3
Younger, William	7	1	3
Hurt, Philemon	6	1	6
Hurt, Moza	8	1	8
Carr, William, Senr	7	1	4
Bowman, Thomas	6	1	2
Layne, James	7	1	1
Barksdill, Peter	5	1	6
Rose, John	4	....	2
Royster, Peter	1	....	....
Montgomery, Robert	5	....	4
Crews, Redman	2	....	....
Crews, John	4	....	....
Pulin, John	7	....	....
Pulin, John, Jr	2	....	....
Crews, John	5	....	....
Minns, John	4	....	....
Richardson, John	5	....	2
Richardson, John, Senr	5	1	6
Crews, Joseph	8	....	2
Maxcy, Rachael	6	1	2
Ridgway, Thomas	8	1	....
Yates, Richard	7	....	2
Ridgway, James	9	4	....
Garrott, John	8	2	1
Garrott, Jacob	2	2	6
Roach, William	7	1	13
Rowder, Abraham	5	....	1
Pringle, Oliver	6	....	2
Martin, Jacob	6	1	1
Martin, John	6	....	1
Martin, William	4	....	3
Williams, William	5	....	2
Wyatt, John	7	1	3
Whealer, John	9	1	2
Hankla, James	10	1	6
Organ, Samuel	10	....	6
Maddison, Roger	6	2	3
Mullins, Joseph	7	....	2
Tribble, Peter	7	1	2
Tribble, James	5	....	2
Booker, Frances	7	1	12
Shields, Pleasant	5	....	....
Harper, James	6	....	2
Burchfield, John	7	1	2
Jeffries, Joseph	4	....	1
Thornton, Reuben	4	1	2
Spraggins, Thomas	7	1	9
Abney, Reuben	1	1	4
Puckett, Stephen	6	1	4
Hillard, John	5	....	3
Crews, David	8	....	2
Jones, William	6	....	....
Younger, Joseph	3	....	4
Hall, William, Jn.	5	....	5
Watkins, William	2	3	5
Brown, James	6	1	3
Gwinn, Bartlett	5	....	1
Neely, Robert	5	....	....
McCrow, Samuel	6	1	1

NAME OF HEAD OF FAMILY.	White souls.	Dwellings.	Other buildings.
LIST OF JAS. BATES—continued.			
McCrow, James	11	2	7
Backner, Avery	10	1	4
Clay, John	3	....	1
Pearman, William	4	1	4
Light, John, Jr.	8	2	7
Tucker, Edmund	6	....	7
Robertson, William	6	1	3
Carr, John	6	2	5
McGriggor, John	8	1	3
Robertson, George	5	1	5
Carr, William	9	6	7
Black, Thomas	6	1	3
Richardson, Skip	3	1	4
Richardson, Thomas	6	1	2
Crews, John	6	1	....
Fambrough, Thomas	3	....	4
Gates, William	6	1	6
Cheshlom, Adam	7	1	6
Barley, John	9	1	7
Fambrough, Andersen	5	1	3
Bass, Henry	7	1	12
Cobbs, Robert	7	....	....
Dodson, William	11	....	1
Murphy, Edward	10	....	7
Byrn, John	7	1	4
Farguson, Thomas	5	1	5
Newbill, George	2	....	3
Bates, Samuel	7	1	4
Hampton, Micajah	8	....	2
Rice, James	5	1	2
Cheatham, David	9	1	2
Rice, Joseph	4	....	3
Rice, John	2	....	1
Layne, William	2	....	2
Farmer, Frederick	5	1	3
Brown, John	11	1	12
Lax, Timothy	3	1	3
Green, William	7	....	4
Gwinn, Alman	2	1	....
Cosley, William	4	....	....
Guthrey, Travis	11	1	4
Dynnett, Elizabeth	5	3	....
Wimbesh, John	5	1	7
Crews, Peter	7	1	5
Williams, John	6	2	....
Martin, Isaac	2	....	2
Robertson, Christopher	4	1	7
Lawson, John	3	....	....
Powell, Mary	7	1	3
Royster, Nathaniel	6	1	7
Phelps, John	5	1	11
Petty, William	3	....	3
Carr, Thomas	5	1	4
Nance, William	8	1	7
Nance, Zacariah	6	1	5
Jackson, Hannah	2	1	4
Jackson, Ephraim	7	....	....
Chandler, Timothy	9	....	3
Griffin, Lewis	3	....	1
Martin, William	12	....	6
Cox, Elisha	9	....	4
Prewitt, Alexander	5	1	4
Bailey, Joseph	8	....	1
Vaughan, Thomas	5	1	3
Stone, John	5	1	4

NAME OF HEAD OF FAMILY.	White souls.	Dwellings.	Other buildings.
LIST OF JAS. BATES—continued.			
Grant, John	2	....	....
Compton, Meredith	7	2	3
Glass, William	2	....	8
Glass, John	5	1	2
Milam, Bartlett	10	1	....
Milam, Benjamin	1	1	....
Thompson, George	8	1	4
Milam, Thomas	3	....	1
Hawkins, Zachariah	10	1	3
Thompson, John	2	....	....
Bowman, Thomas	4	....	....
Bates, James	6	1	7
Bates, Daniel	3	....	1
Bates, Nathaniel	2	....	1
Vaughan, William	9	1	7
Milner, Robert D	5	....	4
Yeulle, Thomas	10	3	24
Jones, Daniel	9	1	3
Collins, Joseph	7	1	8
Rowden, John	5	1	4
Bradley, James	9	1	2
Martin, James	9	1	3
Owen, Joseph	10	1	4
Martin, John	5	....	3
Dunaway, Samuel	6	1	3
Chisum, James	12	....	7
Seemore, George	10	....	5
Skevers, James	7	2	8
Crews, Jesse	3	....	....
Vasser, William	7	2	3
Snelson, Charles	7	1	6
Scates, Thomas	10	....	5
Glass, Dudley	8	1	3
Baird, Henry	12	1	4
Kesee, John	5	1	5
Preddy, Richard	3	1	3
Glass, James	6	1	2
Weakly, Robert	5	1	6
Weakly, Thomas	2	1	4
Fambrough, Jane	....	....	....
Parker, Martha	4	....	2
Pearman, William	5	....	1
Hall, Nathaniel	10	2	3
Tucker, Robert	10	1	3
Dejernett Sarah	8	6	2
Oliver, William	13	1	11
Royall, John	8	3	6
Murphy, John	5	2	10
Royall, Richard	1	....	2
Royall, William	8	1	9
Cape, John	4	1	1
Powell, William	8	1	2
Nunally, Harbert	6	1	4
Nunally, Edward	3	1	2
Broy, William	7	1	2
Parrott, Rhodham	4	....	2
Baber, John	5	....	1
Hunt, Ambrose	7	1	4
Philips, James	6	1	2
Sloott, Solomon	9	1	4
Arnold, James	11	....	3
Corley, Thomas	11	1	4
Handcock, Benjamin	3	....	3
Handcock, Thomas	6	1	1
Gillingler, Susannah	5	2	1

NAME OF HEAD OF FAMILY.	White souls.	Dwellings.	Other buildings.
LIST OF JAS. BATES—continued.			
Corley, John	3	....	2
Spraggins, Melchesedeck	2	....	2
Kuling, Thomas	9	1	3
Scates, Margaret	6	1	2
Martin, Nathan	9	1	2
Brumfield, Major	7	2	3
Brumfield, Joseph	3	....	1
Chick, William	3	1	3
Handcock, Benjamin	3	....	1
Handcock, James	4	....	....
Hunt, Elijah	10	1	16
Clay, Caleb	7	....	3
Francis, Micajah	1	....	....
Bowman, Bibby	4	....	2
Bowman, John	7	1	4
Francis, John	1	....	....
Handcock, Thomas	7	1	2
Handcock, Joseph	8	....	2
Pitty, Davis	6	1	6
Francis, John	2	1	3
Bostick, John	1	1	4
Richardson, Thomas	1	....	....
Bostick, Moses	1	1	2
Mealer, Nicholas	5	1	....
Bostick, Absalom	1	....	....
Bostick, Billy	5	5	12
Bostick, William	4	1	3
Francis, Epraim	1	....	....
Handcock, Stephen	1	....	....
Handcock, Absalom	4	1	3
Richardson, John (Mers.)	3	1	3
Petty, Francis M.	7	2	6
Wilkerson, James	3	....	2
Petty, Frances	4	....	4
Black, William	6	1	5
Bates, William	7	1	....
Drinkard, John	8	1	2
Miles, Augustine	3	1	4
Troop, John	6	....	3
Wyatt, John	8	....	5
Vaughan, Drury	7	1	7
Barksdill, Nathaniel	5	1	9
Thomas, Thomas	4	....	6
Hodges, Thomas	9	....	3
LIST OF M. STANFIELD.			
Dickers, John	5	1	7
Turner, Ann	4	2	2
Smith, William	8	1	....
Miller, Elizabeth	4	1	3
Richeson, James	3	1	2
Irvine, John	11	3	11
Watkins, James	7	1	7
Hix, Joseph	8	....	1
Reeves, Asher	3	....	....
Turner, James	9	1	3
Goltson, Mary	4	1	2
Turner, Wm	12	....	1
Powell, Charles	10	....	3
Husk, Thomas	4	....	5
Chappel, James	4	2	2
Traylor, Edward	7	1	3
Martin, John	9	....	2
Grant, Burwell	7	1	5

HALIFAX COUNTY—Continued.

LIST OF M. STANFIELD—continued.

NAME OF HEAD OF FAMILY.	White souls.	Dwellings.	Other buildings.
Watkins, Wm	9	1	5
Salmon, John	11	1	5
Salmon, Joell	10	1	3
Chambers, John	9	1	5
Compton, John	4	1	5
Turner, Thomas	2	...	2
Wiley, George	5	...	3
Wiley, Eleanor	3	1	4
Terk, Thomas	6	...	4
True, John	8	...	1
Irvine, Mary	3	1	4
Guthrey, Thomas	7	...	3
Turner, Moses	6	...	3
Brooks, James	4	...	1
Farner, Pleasant	3	...	2
Hughs, Thomas	6	...	1
West, John	5	...	3
Garlington, Joseph	1	1	1
Gibson, Jonathan	2	...	2
Innier, Antony	1	...	3
Stanfield, Robert	10	1	6
Harriss, Judith	2	...	1
Hitt, Peter	1	1	7
Watkins, Thomas	6	2	9
Watkins, James, Senr	7	...	3
Salmon, John, Junr	6	...	1
Dixon, Edmund	8	...	3
Dickson, William	4	1	1
Pinor, John	11	...	4
Hitt, Peter	8	1	5
Oliver, Richard	8	...	2
Stanfield, Marmaduke	11	1	8

LIST OF NATH'L HUNT.

NAME OF HEAD OF FAMILY.	White souls.	Dwellings.	Other buildings.
Jordan, Benjamin	6	1	1
Hendrick, John	2	1	1
Davenport, Bedford	7	1	...
Easely, Robert	5	1	1
Parker, William	6	1	2
Neal, William	8	1	...
Parker, Daniel	5	1	3
Huddlestone, Benja	11	1	4
Daniel, William	5	1	1
Boarame, John	4	1	...
Landrum, Hawkins	8	1	2
Chappell, Robert	8	1	4
Easely, Daniel	5	2	11
Easely, Isaac	1	...	...
Johnson, Joseph	11	1	...
Madlock, John	4	...	...
Whetworth, John	3	1	2
Wood, Thomas	10	1	...
Clardy, John	3	...	...
Hendrick, Moses	8	3	3
Smith, James	8	2	5
Petty, Joseph	9	1	...
Anderson, Meady	9	1	1
Anderson, John	10	1	2
Clardy, Thomas	1	...	...
Chumley, Daniel	3	1	...
Easely, Wharhame	9	1	1
Franklin, David	6	1	...
Moore, Daniel	11	1	2
Irwin, Joshua	7	1	...
Crenshaw, Bartlett	6	3	3
Briene, Catharine	3	...	...
Bennett, Ann	5	1	1
Chumley, Grace	5	1	...
Milame, James	1	1	...
Wood, David	7	1	...
Hammon, John	3	1	...
Strange, Littleberry	9	1	...
Slaughter, John	6	1	1
Smith, Charles	9	1	...
Brady, Owin	2	1	1
Brady, Elizabeth	5	1	1
Butler, Bersheba	6	1	2
Estes, Moses, senr	2	2	...
Cox, Richard, senr	8	1	1
Hunt, Benja	5	1	...
Hunt, Nathaniel	6	1	9
Le Grand, James	11	1	6

LIST OF M'W SIMS.

NAME OF HEAD OF FAMILY.	White souls.	Dwellings.	Other buildings.
Cocks, Chasr (Estate)	6	1	9
Purcell, James	11	1	3
Stanley, John	17	1	1
Hudson, Charles	7	1	...
Vaughan, Frederick	6	1	5
Vaughan, Nicholas	6	...	...
Bolnare, Mark	10	...	...
Hudson, Peter	7	1	2
Wade, Stephen	6	1	4
Stokes, Elizabeth	3	1	...
Vasser, Nathaniel	4	1	...
Weaver, John	1	...	...

LIST OF M'W SIMS—continued.

NAME OF HEAD OF FAMILY.	White souls.	Dwellings.	Other buildings.
Frances, Nathaniel	8	1	...
Harris, James	5	1	...
Jones, Stephen	5	1	...
Jinkins, Robert	10	1	...
Parker, Frances	5	1	...
Williams, John	8	1	7
Leggon, Joseph	6	1	11
Richman, Robert	3	1	...
Asken, Daniel	7	...	...
Asken, Amos	2	...	...
Strange, Josias	4	1	...
Terrell, William	4	1	...
Terrell, William, Senr	8	1	1
Richman, Robert, Senr	5	1	1
Booker, John	6	1	3
Le Grand, Abram	7	1	2
Rose, Anne	2	2	8
Dobson, Thomas	6	1	2
Sims, Mathew	10	1	10

LIST OF JNO. COLEMAN.

NAME OF HEAD OF FAMILY.	White souls.	Dwellings.	Other buildings.
Dickson, Stephen	5	1	2
Kink, Henry	11	1	2
Kumbo, Charles	7	1	1
Smith, John	11	1	...
Easely, Daniel	5	1	...
Hall, Benjamin	10	1	3
Camp, George	5	1	1
Camp, William	5	1	1
Powell, David	7	1	1
Manner, Nathaniel	3	1	1
Echols, John	10	1	2
Watkins, Thomas	6	1	1
Owin, William	5	1	2
Roberts, Frances	1	...	...
Roberts, Daniel	1	1	2
Maskill, Mary	2	1	1
Roberts, William	1	...	1
Owin, Hatcher	1	1	3
Wood, John	5	1	2
Roberts, Moses	6	1	3
Anderson, George	5	1	...
Roberts, Jane	3	1	7
Brewis, John	8	1	4
Nelson, George	10	1	1
Wood, John, Junr	3	1	...
Roberts, Peter	5	1	3
Brewes, Michael	8	1	3
Tucker, Abraham	6	1	...
Fulkerson, John	5	1	2
Lacey, Thomas	5	1	3
Johnson, Smith	6	1	3
Lacey, Mathew	2	1	...
Jones, Reubin	4	1	3
Ragland, Reubin	6	1	...
Tuck, Thomas	9	1	...
Watkins, Susannah	5	2	6
Ashlock, John	5	1	...
Holt, Simon	13	1	4
Cole, Joseph	8	1	2
Nash, William	9	...	...
Coles, James	9	1	3
Wooding, John	6	1	1
Robbins, Thomas	9	2	3
Chandler, William	14	1	2
Compton, Caleb	8	1	...
Estes, George	4	...	...
Camp, Mary	7	1	4

LIST OF E. KING.

NAME OF HEAD OF FAMILY.	White souls.	Dwellings.	Other buildings.
King, Edmund	7	3	2
Mills, Antony	3	2	1
Terry, Moses	7	2	1
Freeman, John	8	2	2
McDonald, James	3	2	1
Chappell, James	4	2	...
Smith, Joseph	8	1	1
Osburn, Kerns	5	1	...
Smith, Joseph	5	1	...
Gent, James	2	1	1
Powell, Edward	6	1	...
Adams, William	8	1	1
Murphy, James	6	1	...
Kerby, William	6	1	...
Epps, John	2	1	3
Epps, Nathaniel	4	1	3
Lacey, Dyce	5	1	1
Dunckly, Mathew	5	1	...
Gent, William	7	1	...
Morrison, Joseph	1	1	...
Tune, Travis	12	2	3
Boman, John	4	1	...
Miller, Mark	9	1	...
Rakestraw, John	3	1	2
Echols, James	9	2	2
Cuningham, Saml	8	2	4

LIST OF E. KING—continued.

NAME OF HEAD OF FAMILY.	White souls.	Dwellings.	Other buildings.
Farmer, David	6	1	...
Farmer, Enoch	5	1	...
Sydnor, William	11	2	1
Beach, William	1	1	2
Farmer, Frederick	8	2	4
Dickson, Benja	11	2	6
Irby, Charles	7	2	1
Williams, Luke	9	1	3
Womack, Charles	9	2	3
Dickson, Thomas	9	2	7
Hunt, William	8	1	1
Hunt, Joseph	1	...	...
Taylor, James	3	...	...
Street, Antony	6	1	...
Harriss, Richard	1	...	...
Robinson, John	1	1	...
Martin, Zachariah	2	1	...
Caldwell, David	3	1	1
Langsdown, George	6	1	...
Hagood, John	7	...	...
Slourt, Agness	8	1	...
Slourt, David	4	1	...
Logan, John	2	3	...
Worthy, Richard	8	...	...
Logan, David	1	1	...
Logan, Richard	1	3	...
Hubbard, Sarah	6	2	2
Cock, Glass (Esta)	...	1	...
Moore, George	4	1	2
Shirlock, Thomas	7	1	...
Bailey, James	4	...	...
Lacey, John	7	1	1
Williams, William	1	...	...
Abbott, Benja	7	1	...
Price, William	14	...	...
Adams, Nipper	6	2	1
Adames, Joshua	9	2	2
Irby, William	1	1	1
Old, Charles	4	1	2
Gill, John	10	...	...
Hoskins, Dolly	4	2	2
Younger, Thomas	8	1	4
Ransome, Ambrose	5	...	...

LIST OF W. TERRY.

NAME OF HEAD OF FAMILY.	White souls.	Dwellings.	Other buildings.
Boyd, Wilmouth	6	1	17
Younger, William	7	1	5
Powell, William	6	1	...
Toryan, Peter	6	1	5
Winnegan, Jarrett	9	1	2
Posey, Allison	8	1	1
Beagles, Joseph	5	1	2
Lewis, Benjamin	5	1	...
Day, Thomas	2	1	3
Blackwell, James	13	1	5
Packer, Richard	11	1	1
Combs, George	10	1	2
Fitzgerrald, Chris	4	1	...
Daniel, Agness	7	1	4
Jolquet, Christianna	6	2	2
Lewis, Littleberry	5	1	...
Medlock, Zach	4	1	...
Evans, George, Senr	3	1	...
Evans, George, Junr	4	1	...
Lea, Andrew	6	1	...
Nantz, Tavner	7	1	2
Dun, Bellington	6	1	3
Thomas, Henry, Senr	8	2	3
Parker, Benajah	7	1	1
Finch, Richard	9	1	4
Parker, Mary	3	1	3
Blackwell, John	7	1	5
Holt, Peter	10	1	2
Owin, John	10	...	...
Hurt, James	2	1	1
Harrisson, Steth	2	1	1
Davenport, Thos	4	1	2
Holt, Joseph	3	1	...
Jones, Charles	9	...	...
Coles, Isaac	...	2	2
Carrington, Geo	...	1	6
Noell, Thomas	12	2	2
Bott, Conrod	11	1	...
Perry, John	1	2	...
Terry, William	8	1	4
Torry, Sarah	7	2	6
Hixs, John	...	1	2
Douglass, Alexr	8	1	1
Dixon, Anne	1	1	...
Jones, Job	7	1	...
Wall, Martha	9	1	1

LIST OF JAS. DEJERNATT.

NAME OF HEAD OF FAMILY.	White souls.	Dwellings.	Other buildings.
George, Jonadab	7	1	6
Dyernatt, James	13	1	4
Cock, Hall	7	1	3

LIST OF JAS. DEJERNATT—continued.

NAME OF HEAD OF FAMILY.	White souls.	Dwellings.	Other buildings.
Cocks, Curd	2	...	...
Ramey, John	8	2	3
Word, John	6	1	6
Jones, Ann	9	1	4
Tompkins, Samuel	6	...	6
Deves, John	6	...	3
Grant, Jasper	4	...	3
Grant, Isaac	3	...	2
Stone, Elizabeth	5	...	4
Thomas, Benjamin	7	...	2
Barber, John	7	...	4
Overton, Moses	7	1	9
Ramey, Absolam	2	1	4
Forest, Richard	8	1	3
Kelly, Jacob	7	...	...
Chattom, Joell	5	...	5
Chattom, Benja	5	...	2
Olefer, James	5	...	2
Dillion, Henry	8	1	4
Tynes, William	6	...	3
Waller, Richard	6	1	3
Bosner, Henry	6	1	...
Collins, John	10	1	4

LIST OF M. ROBERTS.

NAME OF HEAD OF FAMILY.	White souls.	Dwellings.	Other buildings.
Pheasants, John	13	1	5
Hall, John	5	...	...
Clardy, Joseph	6	1	...
Osbon, William	8	...	...
Hall, William, Senr	5	2	1
Hall, Tinton	10	1	1
Powell, William, Senr	4	2	2
Powell, John	2	...	...
Tunstall, John	4	2	2
Chandler, John	7	1	1
Chandler, Robert	7	1	4
Yeates, John	4	...	...
Thweat, William	2	1	1
Nichols, David	8	1	1
Nichols, Mary	1	1	5
Sullavent, Charles	5	1	...
Easthame, Robert	9	1	...
Carter, Jeduthen	4	1	6
Briton, William	6	1	13
Simms, O. William	5	...	3
Keene, Jeremiah	4	1	3
Clarke, Thomas	9	1	5
Cobbs, Thomas	3	1	1
Cobbs, John	1	...	1
Cobbs, James	2	...	1
Martin, Benjamin	5	...	...
Martin, Benjamin, Senr	4	1	1
Owin, William	9	...	1
Martin, John	5	...	1
Stovall, Thomas	3	1	5
Isbell, Henry	5	...	...
Burchate, Robert	1	1	3
Nichols, William	9	2	10
Rickman, John	3	1	2
Nichols, Jesse	8	1	...
Watts, Samuel	7	1	...
Shelton, Frances	4	...	...
Owin, Daker	4	...	...
Jackson, John	8	1	1
Owin, James	1	...	...
Owin, Thomas	7	1	...
Cassaday, John	5	...	...
Hundley, John	4	1	3
East, Shadrack	3	...	...
Parker, Edward	12	1	3
Cassady, William	3	1	1
Irby, Harrisson	5	1	8
Nichols, Anneritter	6	1	...
Hardwick, John	8	1	...
Le Grand, John	6	1	2
Owin, William, Senr	6	1	5
Owin, Jesse	4	1	...
Cobbs, Samuel	10	1	5
Cobbs, James	2	1	5
Owin, Elizabeth	7	1	3
Owin, Ambrose	9	1	2
Owin, Peter	2	1	3
Wright, Thomas	4	...	...
Owin, John	6	...	...
Owin, Berry	2	...	...
Frances, Vinson	5	...	...
Walters, Thomas	6	1	1
Walters, John	6	1	...
Organ, William	4	...	...
Atkins, Stephen	9	...	...
Walters, John	10	1	1
Keene, John	2	1	...
Le Grand, Betty	2	2	9
Lipscomb, Luke	6	...	...
Dejenett, Thomas	8	...	...
Lee, William	9	1	...
Pass, Thomas	3	...	...

HALIFAX COUNTY—Continued.

NAME OF HEAD OF FAMILY.	White souls.	Dwellings.	Other buildings.
LIST OF M. ROBERT—continued.			
Blackstock, Thos	7	1	3
Roberts, Betty	3	1	4
May, Agness	1	1	8
Durhame, Robert	10	1	2
McKinny, James	7	1	
Covington, Thomas	7	1	2
Watkins, Joell		1	5
Packer, William	10	1	4
Abbott, Joseph	12	1	2
Abbott, William	2		
Roberts, Michael	11	1	6
Maxy, John	3	1	4
Dickerson, Jno, Junr	6		
Dickerson, Jno, Senr	1	1	2
Maxy, William	2	1	2
Irby, Antony	3	1	4
Estes, Abraham	5		
Organ, Easter	4		
Owin, Agness	4		
Scott, William	3	1	1
Campbell, Morris	8		
LIST OF J. W. P. MARTIN.			
Kennon, Charles	5	2	3
Lewis, John, Jr	6	1	3
Taylor, Phil	5		
Waddill, Noell	6	1	2
Johnson, James	10	1	2
Hopun, Henry, Jnr	5		
Akin, Edward	7		
Caldwell, Allen	2	1	
Caldwell, John	8	1	
Tanner, Creel	2		
Wood, Joseph	2		
Smith, James	7		
Douglas, Mary	7	1	3
Maze, William	7		
Davis, William	4		
Roper, John	5		
Cearson, Thomas	4	1	
Edmund's, Sterling (Esta)	6	2	4
Walton, William	9	1	
Hamlett, William, Senr	5	2	4
Kirby, Joseph	7	2	2
Dottson, Caleb	6	1	
Chelton, Charles	8		
Hutchinson, Daniel	6	1	2
Wall, Charles	10	1	2
Hopson, Henry (little)	3	1	
Echols, Moses	13	2	2
Kent, Alexr	4		
Harbour, Talmon	1	1	3
Harbour, Noah	6	1	
Hopson, Henry, Senr	3	1	5
Hopson, Benja	3	1	1
Dickie, John, Jnr	5	1	4
Moore, Alexander	2	2	4
Seaim, Jessee	4		
Lawson, John	5	1	11
Harper, Banister	4		
Lawson (Widow)	3	3	
Carter, Mary	7	1	5
Akin, Robert	5	1	2
Hopson, Joseph	5	3	6
Akin, Joseph	7	1	
Carter, Richard (S.)	12	1	4
Dobson, Elisha	3	1	
Hedgepeth, Lemuel	7		
Russell, Absolom	2	1	
Russell, George	1	1	
Gaines, Thomas	7		
Miller, John F	4	2	1
Walton, Spencer	9	1	
Miller, Harmon	10	1	
Strange, Owin	3		
Groce, Jarrett	9	1	
Lawson, Thomas	4	1	1
Horsly, James	6	1	
King, Benja	5		
Waddill, William	6		
Santford (Widow)	1	1	3
Nobles, John	5	1	2
Beach, Thomas	1		
Owin, John	8	1	
Combs, William	3		
Martin, Wm Peters	6	2	7
Brown, Frederick	8	1	1
Wood, George	8	1	4
Moore, William	7		
Wilson, William	2	1	
Hamlet, Littleberry	2	1	1
Wall, John	9	1	3
Bates, David	8		
Waters, John	11	1	
Cheatham, Abia	3	1	
Martin, Warner	3		
Gaines, Richard	4		
Cumbo, Thomas	13		

NAME OF HEAD OF FAMILY.	White souls.	Dwellings.	Other buildings.
LIST OF J. W. P. MARTIN—continued.			
Echols, William	9	1	3
Brown, George	3		
Martin, Peter	9		
Allen, David	3	1	
Lewis, John, Senr	2	1	4
Colquet, Jonathan	6	1	4
Spradling, Jessee	3		
Colquet, Ransome	1		
Farmer, Henry, Senr	1	1	
Graves, James	5		
Haily, James	4		
Fergusson, Nimrod	7	1	
Fergusson, Isaac	5	1	
Watkins, William	9	1	2
Hamlett, William, Jnr	4	1	2
Boyd, John	9	1	2
Boyd, John, Junr	3		
Baker, Maiton	6	3	3
Countilen, Lewis	2		
Goare, Henry	1		
Fears, James	7		
Ball, John	3		
Watkins, Micajah (Esta)		1	5
Martin, John	9	1	2
Dotson, Thomas	8	1	
Wilson, Daniel	5	1	3
Jordon, William	10	1	
Harriss, William	4	1	
Stubblefield, George	8	1	1
Sullins, Nathan	11	1	2
Smith, John	5		1
Mathews, Robert	4	1	
Farmer, Henry	11	1	
Farmer, Archer	8	1	
Farmer, David	8	1	
Cocke, Henry	4		
Punkey, Stephen	10		
Moore, John	8	1	2
Dotson, Thomas	9	1	
Spradling, Charles	5		
Fallis, John	6	1	2
Lovelace, Thomas	13	1	1
Smith, Sally	9	1	
Going, Shadrack	10	1	
Going, John	4	1	
Henderson, Edward	5		
Going, David	4	1	
Huddlestone, David	10	1	1
Toler, John	8	1	
Edwards, Benja	10	1	
Evans, John	2	1	
Evans, David	5	1	1
Evans, Robert	5		
Keeling, Leonard	8		
Kendrick, Thomas	10		
Edwards, Richard	6	1	2
Harriss, Bartlett	7		
Young, James	7		
Cary, James	3	1	
LIST OF JNO. P. SMITH.			
Mise, John	4	1	
Wright, Nathan	2		
Jones, Reubin	6		
Overby, Obediah	8	1	4
Liggon, Joseph	8	1	3
Jordon, Robt (Ovr)	8	1	7
Walden, Mary	7	1	4
Hall, William	6	1	4
Hackey, John	6	1	
Jones, Richard, Jur	3	1	
Glidewell, Nast	4	1	3
Harrisson, Samuel	4		
Jones, Richard, Senr	6	1	3
Wilson, William	5	1	3
Wilson, Thomas	9		
Tally, John	9		
Glidewell, Robert	4		
Glass, Daniel	8		
Eliott, Bartlett	3		
Sizemore, John	8		
Seat, Robert	8	1	
Ovesby, Shadrack	9	1	
Pullam, John	2		
Stones, Elizabeth	2	1	
James, Joshua	3		
Eliott, Ann	7		
Arrington, John	8	1	
Arrington, Will	7		
Wright, John	5		1
Roach, David	6	1	3
Parker, Benjamin	5		
Pettypoole, William	8	2	4
Parker, Elizabeth	3		
White, Charles	8	1	1
Ballandine, William	4		
Tuck, John	11		
Griffin, John	9	1	4

NAME OF HEAD OF FAMILY.	White souls.	Dwellings.	Other buildings.
LIST OF JNO. P. SMITH—continued.			
Good, William	9		
Hill, Thomas	5		
Harrison, Presley	9		
Taley, James	4		
Hudson, Daniel	7		
Hudson, Peter	8		
Birch, Henry	4		
Hodges, William	10		
Fleming, Will	5		
Talley, Peyton	5		
Fletcher, Nicholas	5		
Wall, Robert	6	1	2
Glidewell, Robert	5		
Seaman, John	10		
Griffin, Susannah	6	1	3
Parrott, Catharine	3		
Sikes, Elizabeth	7		
Sikes, Thos Aldridge	2		
Wall, Buckner	4		
Hite, Stanly	3		
Hite, Isaac	4		
Gregory, Richard	9		1
Gregory, Smith	2	1	
Gregory, John	1	1	
Hensby, William	12		
Bunton, William P	7		
Waldrope, Luke	7		
Davis, Joseph	4		
Wall, John	5		
Sizemore, Daniel	3		
Gregory, Ambrose	3		
Arvin, William	9		
Wilborne, John	6		
Burton, Allen	7	1	1
Wilson, William, Senr	3	1	2
Wilson, Wallace	2		
Anoin, Margarett	7		
Wade, John	8	1	4
Hutchison, Robert	5		
Smith, Jno P	8	1	6
Boxby, Benja	10	1	7
Douglass, William	5	1	
LIST OF JOSEPH HAYNES.			
Throgmorton, Robert	4		
Haynes, Joseph	5	1	1
Crowder, Sterling	5		
Sammons, William	2		
Grady, John	1		
Towns, William	8		2
Billifont, John	2	1	
Comer, Thomas	8	2	4
Comer, John	8		
Stegall, William	7		
Morefield, John	9	1	1
Strange, Benjamin	6		
Morefield, Edward	3		
Strange, Jessee	5		
Strange, Julius	6	1	
Strange, Dick	4		
Enaufty, Edward	4	1	
Pride, William	8	1	4
Thompson, John	9	1	1
Clardy, Michael	8	1	3
Clay, Samuel	3		
Lencar, Thomas		1	8
Edwards, Charles	10	1	8
Throgmorton, Robt	6	1	2
Throgmorton, Josias	6	1	
Throgmorton, Will	2	1	
Hughs, John	11	1	4
Hughs, William	5		
Dennis Estate		1	2
Flinn, John	4	1	2
Mullins, William	3		
Flinn, William	2		
London, Owin	1		
Witlow, Thomas	3		
Jones, Richard	12	1	6
Towns, Henry	3	1	
Jennett, Saml	8	1	
Coles, Israel	2	8	12
Wright, Frances	1		
Scoggins, John	6	1	2
Majors, Philip	7	1	2
Faulkner, Captain	8	1	
Boyd, William	5	1	9
Fambrough, Thomas	4	1	
Legon, John	3		
Baker, Leonard	5	2	
Coles, Isaac	2	2	10
Kingston, Jno	8		
Owin, Richard	8		
LIST OF WAL. BENNETT.			
Allwood, William	7		
Ashby, Joseph	6	1	3

NAME OF HEAD OF FAMILY.	White souls.	Dwellings.	Other buildings.
LIST OF WAL. BENNETT—continued.			
Bennett, Walter	10	1	5
Bennett, William	7	1	1
Brown, James	8	1	2
Brumfield, John	9	1	2
Coles, Mildred	5	1	27
Crenshaw, Cornelius	10		
Chandler, Judea	7		2
Cooper, Job	2	1	
Cassady, James	4	1	
Claybrooke, Will	2	1	
Compton, John	8	1	
Franklin, Frank	7		
Fisher, William	4	1	
Fisher, John	4	1	
Haly, Humphrey	8	1	
Haily, Jo Eggleston	2		1
Hodge, William	7	1	
Hunt, Reubin	6		
Hunt, Molly	5	1	1
Hill, William	7	1	
Irvine, James	4		1
Lockett, Abram	1	1	1
Lax, John	8	1	
Lax, Joell	3		1
Morehead, Joseph	13	1	12
Morton, Saml	8	1	
McGinnis, James	7		4
McGinnis, Andrew	4	1	
Palmon, Elias	6	1	
Palmon, Ellisha	4	1	
Palmer, Jaffrey	10	1	
Pruitt, Byrd	4	1	
Rowlett, William	8	1	
Stevens, Jere	9	1	
Seamore, William	9	1	
Sparrow, John	7	1	
Sparrow, Thomas	7	1	
Spruebanks, Edwd	6		1
Shaw, John	7	1	1
Smallman, John	7	1	
Smallman, John, Jr	3	1	
Leasnome, Burgess	1		
Tucker, Mary	3	1	1
Thweat, Giles	8	1	5
Trainham, David	10	1	
Walker, Richard	7	1	
Wright, Billy	5		
Willard, Elizabeth	6	1	
Wootton, Nathl	5	1	
LIST OF JERE. PATE.			
Holt, Robert	3	1	
Warren, John	2	1	
Warren, James, Senr	9	1	
Brookes, John	7	1	
Payne, Robert	9	1	
Smythy, John	10	1	
Holt, Robert, Jr	4	1	1
Holt, Timothy	6	1	
Johnson, Jessee	3		
Cotman, Benja	6	1	
Warren, William	6	1	
Parrott, Elisha	5	1	
Lynk, William	9	1	1
Lynk, John	10	2	1
Johnson, Isaac	6	2	1
Garlington, Edwd	8	2	1
Brag, William	8	1	
Carmichael, John	8		
Shackleford, John	8	1	2
Adkins, William	9	2	3
Malone, Daniel	2		6
Malone, Peter	5	1	
Bracker, Richard	9	1	
Wood, William	6	1	
True, Martin	1		
Hoskins, James	4	1	3
Hitts, Alexander	4	1	
Carter, Richard (T.)	9	1	
Bale, Jeremiah	4	2	2
Pate, Mathew	2	1	
Capel, John	3	2	2
Medley, Joseph	7	1	
Muse, Hopkins	1		
Shackleford, John	1		
Lynk, Bartlett	6	1	
Traylor, William	8	1	3
Bynhame, George	5	1	2
Wyatts, Richard	5	1	
Isbell, George	8	2	2
Gordon, William	5		
Stanfield, Thos	9	2	2
Perrin, Jane	4	3	3
Waide, John	4		
Alsup, Joseph	1		
Baird, John		3	2
Lawson, Fras	8	2	1
Pullam, John	5	2	1

HALIFAX COUNTY—Continued.

NAME OF HEAD OF FAMILY.	White souls.	Dwellings.	Other buildings.
LIST OF JERE. PATE—continued.			
Collins, William	6	1	
Wills, William	2	1	
Kidd, James	5	1	
Overby, Meseck	9	1	
Sundys, Samuel	2	1	6
Faulkner, Jacob	8	1	
Palmer, Edward	9	1	1
Mc carty, Jarrard	10	1	1
Whitt, John	7	2	2
Waide, Hampton	5	2	2
Gresham, Antony	11	1	3
Watson, Chris	7	1	
Gresham, William	7	1	2
Williams, John	8		
Childres, Nicholas	8	1	1
Pickett, Henry	3	1	
Wade, John	4		
Tindall, Thos	11	1	
Watson, Steven	5	1	
Smith, Stephen	6	1	
McCarty, Joseph	2		
Boyd, Walter	1	1	6
McCran, Will	4	2	1
Wade, Edmund	1		
Edwards, Elizh	8	1	3
Thackston, Peter	4	1	
Davenport, James	1	2	2
Kent, James	3	1	
Kent, Mary	5	2	5
Kent, William	8	2	2
Nanty, Tavner	7	1	2
Evans, Ann	4	1	

NAME OF HEAD OF FAMILY.	White souls.	Dwellings.	Other buildings.
LIST OF JERE. PATE—continued.			
Ragland, John	7	1	2
Ragland, Evan, Senr	3	2	7
Thaxton, William	7	1	1
Mitchell, Charles	3	1	1
Smith, Isaac	6	1	
Butler, Joshua	9	1	
Morehead, James	1	2	
Wade, Richard	6	1	
Fontaine, Moses	10	1	6
Boyd, George	9	1	4
Pickett, Reubin	6	2	
Adams, Jno	7	1	3
Adams, Will	6	1	
Adams, Richard	5	1	
Boyd, Mary	9	1	3
Williams, William	3	1	
LIST OF THEOP'S CARTER.			
Lewis, John (Byrd)	1	2	6
Lewis, John, Senr		1	3
Robinson, James H	8		
Carson, John	7		
Dyall, James	8	1	
Nevas, Jacobos	5	1	
Carter, Theoderick	14	3	5
Lipscomb, Thomas	6	4	3
Whites, George	4		
Flagg, Robert	1	1	
Carter, Richd	9	2	2
Wyatt, Thomas	4	1	
Scott, Rachael	5	1	2

NAME OF HEAD OF FAMILY.	White souls.	Dwellings.	Other buildings.
LIST OF THEOP'S CARTER—continued.			
Turner, Champness	5	1	
Pin, David	4	1	
Farly, Hannah	7	1	1
Reynolds, John	4	1	1
Scott, Rebecca	8	1	1
Brown, John	1	1	
Brown, Lockey	4	1	
Irvine, James	3	1	
Nash, Thos	3	1	
Cromwell, William	4	1	
Carnal, Patrick	8	1	1
Mitchell, Henry	4	1	
Brandun, William	9	2	1
Brandum, Frances	13	1	1
Horsley, Richd	4	1	
Carter, William	2	1	1
Perryman, William	4	1	
Sims, Drury	6	1	
James, William	4	1	
Price, Mathew	2	2	
Stone, William	5	1	
Brooks, William	5	1	
Gray, Jno	2	1	
Dilliard, Richard	8	1	
Stanfield, Ephraim	8	1	
Chambers, Josses	4	1	1
Chappell, William	3	1	
Lee, William	8	1	
Hopson, William	6	2	5
Brown, Walter	5	1	
Towns, Caleb	7	2	1
Towne, Lucy	5	1	2

NAME OF HEAD OF FAMILY.	White souls.	Dwellings.	Other buildings.
LIST OF THEOP'S CARTER—continued.			
Foster, Ambrose	11	3	1
Brooks, *——oody	2	1	1
Williams, James	12	1	
Fletcher, James	5	1	
Taylor, William	6	1	
Brandum, John	6	1	
Brandum, Thos	6	1	3
Pullam, Joseph	9	1	2
Fanning, John	5	1	
Connelly, Geo	11	1	1
Brooks, James	7	1	1
Atkin, Shadrack	7	1	
Watkins, James	7	1	
Gray, Alexr	9	1	1
Moore, Ann	9	1	
Gray, James	7	1	
Sneed, Benjamen	7	1	
Kerby, Henry B	12	3	3
Dye, Abram	6	1	
Dye, William	9	1	
Dye, Laurence	5	1	
Owin, Richeson	6	1	2
Williamson, James	6	1	
Taylor, Charles	8	1	
Scott, Jno	7	1	3
Tinny, Susannah	2	1	
Tinny, Jno	2	1	
Coleman, James	4	2	3
Clift, Henry	7	1	
Carter, Danl	4	2	1

HARRISON COUNTY.

NAME OF HEAD OF FAMILY.	White souls.	Dwellings.	Other buildings.
Abbot, Benj	6	1	
Alexander, John	8	1	2
Burcham, Charles	8	1	
Bodkin, Charles	4	1	
Breeding, George	8	1	1
Crouch, Joseph	10	1	
Breeding, Peter	4	1	
Crouch, John, Senior	3	1	2
Crouch, John, Jnr	5	1	1
Cassity, John	8	1	1
Cassity, Peter, Jnr	6	1	
Cassity, David	5	1	1
Clem, Philip	6		
Currence, John	2	1	
Currence, Lydia	6	1	1
Currence, William	1		
Cheviler, Anthony	6		
Delay, Henry	10	1	2
Elliot, Richard	11	1	
Fornelson, Charles	7	1	1
Fornelson, Joseph	11	1	
Henderson, Robert	7	1	
Henderson, David	1		
Hamilton, William	3	1	
Hamilton, Patrick	8	1	1
Hamilton, John	9	1	
Haddan, David	5	1	1
Haddan, John	1	1	2
Harvey, John	2		
Hornbeck, Benj	4	1	1
Jones, Benj	6	1	2
Logan, Hugh	1		
Lacky, Thomas	2	1	
Lacky, James, Snr	1	1	
Lacky, James, Junior	7	1	
Mullet, Noah	5	1	
McClean, James	4	1	
McClean, Charles	6		
McDonald, Francis	7		
Moore, James	6	1	
Pettit, Ebenezer	10	1	
Parsons, Charles	8	1	
Parsons, George	7	1	
Parsons, Joseph	6	1	
Polly, John	7	1	
Riffle, Jacob	9	1	
Riffle, Eloner	7	1	
Smith, Jonathan	5	1	
Shaver, Elizabeth	4	1	1
Shaver, George	6		
Shaver, Peter	5	1	
Shaver, John	1		
Stauts, Abraham	6		
Warwick, John	6	1	2
Westfall, George, Snr	10	1	1
Crouch, Judith	5	1	
Yocum, John	6	1	1
Crouch, Jonathan	1		
Collins, Edmond	1	1	
Powell, Caleb	8		

NAME OF HEAD OF FAMILY.	White souls.	Dwellings.	Other buildings.
Prather, James	2		
Simermon, Daniel	5	1	
Rolstone, Jean	2		
Pringle, Samuel	5		
Maddox, Nathaniel	1		
Wilson, George	2		
Crouch, Hannah	3		
Gooff, Salathiel	6	1	3
Minear, David	6	1	3
Haddox, William	5	1	
Washburn, Philip	2		
Parsons, William	1	1	
Johnson, Michal	7	1	
Parsons, James		1	2
Cole, Samuel	5	1	
Gooff, James	3	1	
Cameron, Elisabeth	3	1	
Westfall, Jacob, Jur	6	1	
Westfall, Jacob, Snr	4	1	1
Wilson, John	4	1	
McHenry, Samuel	9		
Smith, William	10	1	1
Radcliff, William	10		
Bogard, Cornelius	6	1	1
Casity, William	6	1	1
Wilson, Benjamin	9	2	5
Quick, Samuel	1		
Peetro, Henry	3	1	1
Peetro, Nicholas	7	1	2
Smith, Nicholas	5	1	
Ryan, Soloman	7	1	2
Woolf, Nicholas	6	1	
Cutright, Benj	5		
Richardson, Aron	9	1	1
Levit, William	9	1	1
Smith, Anthony	4	1	
Stalnaker, Valentine	5	1	
Whitman, Matthias	7	1	
Stalnaker, Jacob, Jnr	7	1	1
Westfall, Daniel	12	1	1
Truby, Christopher	5		
Shaver, Jacob	1	1	3
Truby, John	3	1	
Philips, Thomas	10	1	1
Kittle, Abraham	10	1	
Rosecrons, Hezekiah	5	1	
Kittle, Jacob	6	1	
Wells, Phinehas	7	1	
Westfall, Cornelius	3	1	
Woolf, Jacob	3	1	
Westfall, William	13		
Booth, Daniel	8	1	
Wilson, William	4		
Fisher, Philip	5		
Springstone, Elisabeth	6	1	1
Isener, Michal	6	1	1
Westfall, George, Jnr	2		
Stalnaker, Margret	3		
Alguire, John	8		
Pickell, Jacob	11		

NAME OF HEAD OF FAMILY.	White souls.	Dwellings.	Other buildings.
Holder, Thomas	6	1	
Phillips, David	2		
Friend, Jonas	6	1	2
Vanscoy, Aron	7	1	
Donoho, Joseph	10	1	
Wilmoth, Thomas	10	1	1
West, Emond	8	1	
Stauts, Elijah	5	1	
West, Alexander	5	1	
Hacker, John	11	1	
Hughs, Ellis	6	1	
Flesher, Henry	9	1	
Hanimon, Christopher	7	1	
Hughs, Jesse	8	1	
Schoocraft, James	8		
Wagoner, John	5		
Kimolo, Peter	7	1	
Hughs, Thomas	6	1	
Sleeth, John	3	1	
Sleeth, David	2	1	
Stauts, Joseph	7	1	
Saylor, John	10	1	
Lowther, Joel	2	1	
Richards, Conrod	8	1	
McCune, Peter	2		
Stout, Daniel	5	1	2
Murhead, John	5		
Stuard, George	8		
Wilkison, Joseph	3		
Edwards, David	9	1	1
Wilkison, Samuel	6	1	
Albin, John	7	1	
Stout, Jonathan	6	2	1
Edwards, Sarah	4		
Wilkison, Joseph	4	1	1
Wilkison, Thomas	2	1	
Webb, Elisabeth	9	1	2
Webb, Thomas	5	1	
Stout, Caleb	6		
Powers, John	9	1	1
Davison, Joseph	6	1	
Thomas, Evan	5	1	
Anderson, James	5	1	3
Davis, William	7	1	
Stout, Thomas	4	1	1
Harbert, Samuel	6	1	
Ratcliff, John	7		
Moke, James	1		
Shinn, Samuel	2	1	
Bartley, Thomas	4	1	
Nutter, John	5		
Davison, Ann	7	1	
Cutright, John	6		
Smith, Aron	8	1	
Allen, Varens	3		
Roch, Jacob	9		
Wood, John	10	1	1
Powers, Margret	6	1	
Hustage, Gilbert	8	1	
Robinson, William	9	1	

NAME OF HEAD OF FAMILY.	White souls.	Dwellings.	Other buildings.
Wamsley, John	2		
Anglin, William	5	1	
Wamsley, David	5		
Robinson, Benj	1	1	
Goowin, John	3	1	
Plumber, Robert	9	1	2
Coon, Joseph	1	1	
Freeman, Edmond	8	1	
McEntire, Samuel	10	1	
McEntire, John	8	1	
Bacliss, William	6	1	
Cunningham, Thomas	5	1	
Cunningham, Edwar	7	1	
Cheney, Thomas	8	1	
Biglar Jacob	4	1	
Coon, Conrod	6	1	
Jones, Enoch	5	1	
Tucker, William	9	1	
Tucker, Nathan	1		
Hustage, Mosses	6	1	
Goodwin, John	3	1	
Thomas, Ezekiel	9		
Davis, John	2		
Owen, John	6	1	1
Owen, Owen	4		
Nutter, Matthew	5	1	3
Prunty, John	2	1	
Hess John	3		
Myars, John	2		
McCally, John	4	1	
Davisson, Obediah	4	1	
Nutter, Christopher	1		
Davisson, Josiah	3	1	
Davisson, Isaac	5	1	
Barkley, Thomas	5	1	3
Carpenter, Christopher	9	1	2
Davis, Joseph	2		
Thomas, Evan	5	1	
Davisson, Amoziah	8	1	
Johnson, William	10	1	
Shinn, Levi	8	1	1
Lambert, Jonathan	8	1	
Nutter, Thomas	7	1	2
Woolf, John	5	1	2
Haymond, William	10	1	
Davisson, Hezekiah	2	1	1
Jackson, George	8	1	3
Hastings, Joseph	2	2	3
Davisson, Daniel	7	2	4
Duvall, John Peircee	6	3	2
Washburn, Rebeca	4	1	
Duvall, Lewis	2		
Ross, Henry	6	1	
Loftburrow, John	9	1	
Beard, Samuel	9	1	
Thompson, William	9	2	
Thompson, Henery	3	1	
Woolf, Jacob	7	1	
Dave, Owen	3		
Drake, George	5		

* Illegible.

HARRISON COUNTY—Continued.

NAME OF HEAD OF FAMILY.	White souls.	Dwellings.	Other buildings.
Shinn, Benjamin	6	1	3
Shinn, Isaac	2	....	....
Coplin, Benj	5	1	2
Runyan, William	8	1	1
Runyan, John	7	1	....
Richards, George	1	....	....
Richards, Jacob	4	1	2
Hughs, Job	1	....	....
Tanner, William	3	....	....
Runyan, Elijah	4	1	....
Cain, John	9	1	....
Cain, Daniel	9	1	....
Tanner, James	1	....	....
Tanner, Edward	5	....	....
Kustard, Joseph	1	....	....
Richards, John	8	1	1
Bulger, Michal	9	1	....
Cobun, Jonathan	7	1	....
Carpenter, Nicholas	7	1	1
Williams, Bazel	5	1	1
Stackhouse, Isaac	4	....	....
Davisson, Andrew	3	1	1
Fink, Henry	8	2	1
Bosher, John	2	....	....
Casoto, John	5	1	1
Jackson, John	6	1	4
Casoto, David	3	....	....
Heagle, John	8	1	....
Runyan, Henry	6	1	1
Bush, Adam	2	....	....
Forinash, Charles	5	1	1
Jackson, Edward	3	1	1

LANCASTER COUNTY.

NAME OF HEAD OF FAMILY.	White souls.	Dwellings.	Other buildings.
Ball, James	4	3	18
Ball, James, Jur	4	1	4
Ball, Agatha	7	2	12
Bailey, Judith	10	1	6
Davenport, Rawleigh	6	1	4
Campbell, George	5	1	4
Rogers, John	9	1	4
Luckam, James	5	1	1
Stott, Richard	8	1	3
Goodridge, Richard	5	1	6
Dunaway, Thomas	6	1	4
Jones, Robert	....	1	3
Kem, Henry	2	....	....
Robinson, Jesse, Jur	9	1	6
Stott, Thomas	5	1	4
Dunaway, Samuel	5	1	2
Norris, John	6	1	7
Mitchell, Richard	4	1	10
Downman, Joseph B	....	1	30
Brumley, William	3	1	6
Brent, William	4	1	2
Brumley, Elizabeth	3	1	2
Norris, James	7	1	5
Riveer, William, Jur	2	1	2
Riveer, James	7	1	3
Robinson, William	2	....	....
Pullen, Henry	3	....	....
Stephens, Molly	3	....	....
Riveer, Johnson	8	1	3
Pullen, John	3	....	....
Pullen, William	2	....	....
Routt, Willoughby	7	1	1
Pitman, Jeduthun	3	1	4
Bell, Charles	4	1	2
Riveer, William	1	1	1
Mason, Peggy	4	1	2
Mase, Sinah	5	1	....
Bailey, Hannah	5	1	....
Norris, Elizabeth	7	1	9
Stott, Elizabeth	2	1	4
Norwood, Charles	5	....	....
Newby, John	4	1	3
Christopher, John	4	1	6
Sydnor, William	8	3	24
Stott, William (Ex on)	....	1	6
Carter, Daniel	4	....	....
Carpenter, William	5	1	4
Carpenter, John	9	....	....
Towles, Henry	8	1	4
Ewell, James	1	1	5
Newby, James	5	1	5
George, Franky	6	1	1
Myars, Matthew	3	1	6
Myars, Thomas	1	1	6
George, Daniel	5	....	....
George, William	5	1	4
Chitwood, William	4	....	....
Chonning, William	13	1	7
Chitwood, George	5	1	3
Demovel, Mrs	8	1	2
Davis, George	3	1	3
Blakemore, Edward	6	1	4
Bevans, Thomas	7	1	....
Harris, John	1	1	4
Lunceford, Rodham	7	1	4
Smith, Alice	5	1	6
Chilton, William, Jur	6	2	4
Carter, Henry	7	1	5
Chilton, William	1	1	5
Rogers, Charles	9	1	7
Harvey, Mungo	7	1	4
Garner, William	3	....	....
Smith, William	3	....	....
Coats, Rawleigh	4	1	....
Flemming, James	5	1	....
Thomas, Tarpley	5	1	....
Taylor, Ann	7	1	6
Dunaway, William	7	1	3
Gilmour, Helen	5	1	6
Norris, Martin	4	....	....
Dye, Richard	5	1	....
Biscoe, William	8	1	4
George, Nicholas	8	1	8
Faudice, Vachal	7	....	....
Neal, Presly	2	1	2
Luckam, William	4	1	....
Carter, Catharine	7	1	6
Payne, John	10	1	4
Lowry, Gavin	4	1	2
Arms, John	4	1	1
Carter, George	6	1	4
Ball, Dr William	6	1	7
Carpenter, John	3	1	4
Wiblin, William	8	1	5
Stephens, Joseph	4	1	5
Tapscott, Henry (Estate of)	6	1	10
Tapscott, Rawleigh	2	....	6
Arms, Jane	7	1	4
Chonning, John	6	1	4
Bristow, William	7	1	4
Chilton, Jesse	6	1	3
Moore, Samuel	3	1	2
Merryman, Ann	5	1	1
Doggett, Ann	2	....	....
Ball, Richard	6	2	20
Chinn, John	8	1	28
Chinn, Robt (Estate of)	....	1	7
Warren, William	8	1	5
Newby, Ozwald	7	1	4
Wilkerson, Joseph	5	1	2
Flint, Priscilla	7	1	7
Brown, Spencer	7	1	1
Robinson, James	3	1	....
Angell, Baker	2	....	....
Robinson, Epaphroditus	4	1	4
Palmer, Benjn	5	1	....
Angell, Robert	2	1	....
Robinson, George	4	....	....
Robinson, Moses	1	1	3
Robinson, Jesse	6	1	5
Clutton, John	7	1	2
Taylor, Ann	15	1	7
Mitchell, William	8	2	3
Newby, William	4	1	....
Webb, Tarpley	4	3	1
Robertson, Andrew	9	3	12
Mitchell, Richard	8	2	1
Wilkerson, John	5	....	....
Brent, William	....	1	2
Wickerson, Joseph	4	....	....
Webb, John	3	1	....
Pitman, Thomas	4	1	4
Pitman, George	2	1	6
Cundiff, Richard	9	1	7
Nutt, James	5	1	3
Leland, John	9	1	9
Montague, Lucy	4	1	11
Selden, Mary	3	2	12
Lawson, Thomas	5	1	8
Lawson, William	6	1	5
Degge, Isaac	4	1	8
Carter, Thomas	10	1	5
George, Jesse	6	1	5
Merrideth, William	8	1	4
Thrall, John	5	1	....
Mason, Mary	6	1	5
George, William	6	1	1
Berryman, John	10	1	7
Shearman, Rawleigh	7	1	1
Lawson, Mary	3	1	4
Hinton, William	4	1	7
Hinton, Elizabeth	7	....	....
Currell, Nicholas	3	1	6
Edwards, John	8	1	4
Hunton, Thomas	4	1	4
Lawson, Eppa	4	1	2
Buckan, William	5	1	3
Gaston, Anthony	4	1	3
Pollard, James	9	1	3
Hunt, John	3	1	....
Currell, George	2	1	2
Currell, Spencer	8	1	....
Currell, James	2	1	3
Lee, Charles	8	1	5
Currell, Gilbert	2	1	3
Lightburn, Henry	8	1	2
Hathaway, Lawson	8	1	4
Hunton, Thomas	5	1	5
Shearman, Martin	2	1	....
Lee, Richard	2	1	3
Lee, Thomas	5	1	2
Gaston, William	5	....	....
Moore, John	3	1	....
Cornelious, William	5	1	....
Sullivant, William	6	1	....
Corrie, David	6	1	9
Martin, William	7	1	9
Fleet, John	4	1	3
Ingram, Thomas	9	1	3
Crowder, Joshua	6	1	....
Reaves, John	8	1	2
Cornelious, William	6	....	....
Reaves, James	3	....	....
Cornelious, Samuel	5	1	....
Hill, Thomas	8	1	....
Hunt, Mary	4	1	....
Burn, Jane	3	1	....
Lawson, Henry	10	1	6
Revendge, John	8	1	....
George, Martin	6	1	2
Spilman, Joshua	8	1	....
Pullen, Thomas	....	4	....
Hinton, William	7	1	....
Campbell, Lettice	3	1	2
James, John	9	1	1
Towell, Marke	3	1	1
Brent, Judith	7	1	5
Brent, James	7	1	4
Gibson, William	8	1	4
Jones, Samuel Pawl	1	....	....
Hutchings, Sally	2	1	1
Wale, Lawson	3	1	1
Yerby, George (Richmond)	....	....	4
Stott, Eppa	5	....	....
Tapscott, Mary	2	1	3
Hammond, Sarah	9	1	2
Sullivant, John	3	1	....
Tapscott, Ezekiel	2	1	....
Watts, John	5	1	....
Elliott, Jeduthun	5	1	....
Wilder, Nathaniel	9	1	1
Norriss, William	6	1	3
Williams, Peter	7	1	2
Brent, Judith	4	1	....
Brent, Newton	5	1	4
Hutchenson, John	5	1	....
Pierciful, Eppa	1	....	....
Wilder, Jonathan	7	1	2
Pullen, Jonathan	5	1	3
Maughon, Mathias	3	1	....
Webb, Thomas	1	....	....
Doggett, William, Senr	9	1	5
Doggett, William, Jur	5	1	....
Hammond, Thomas	5	1	1
Bell, John	5	1	2
Roberts, John	4	1	1
Short, Thomas	2	1	....
Kelly, James	6	....	....
Flowers, John	6	1	3
Flowers, Lucy	3	1	....
Chilton, Henry	3	1	2
Hutchings, Learmah	6	1	1
Longwith, John	6	1	3
Pollard, Thomas	7	1	....
Yerby, George W	3	1	7
George, Judith	5	1	2
Williams, Charles	5	....	....
Longwith, Mary	2	....	....
Cox, Thomas	7	1	....
Cox, Anthony	2	....	....
Merrideth, John	4	1	3
Roberts, John	4	1	4
Miller, Stephen	9	1	....
George, Anthony	9	....	....
Wheeler, Lettice	2	1	1
Wilder, Michael	5	1	....
Schofield, Mary	5	1	....
Doggett, Elmour	1	1	4
Doggett, Maryann	4	....	....
Pinckard, Thomas	2	1	15
Kent, William	3	....	....
Kirk, William	2	1	4
Yerby, Richard	1	....	....
Cartor, George Cosotoman	3	1	39
Schofield, Natus	2	1	....
Gordon, John	1	....	....
Rellings, Mary	6	1	2
Norris, George	7	1	3
Norris, Judith	1	1	3
Hill, John, Jur	5	1	1
Palmer, Lot	6	1	1
Carter, Job	7	1	5
George, Spencer	9	1	4
Dameron, Rachel	6	1	2
Lock, Stephen	6	1	5
Simmons, James	5	1	6
George, Judith	6	1	2
Walker, Robert	4	1	1
Lunceford, Moses	....	1	2
Brent, William	10	1	6
Hubbard, Charles	5	1	4
Alford, Zachariah	6	1	....
Chilton, William	2	1	3
Miller, John	9	1	4
Hill, John	7	1	2
Palmer, Abner	7	1	4
Wormeley, John	3	1	8
Robb, Frances	4	1	5
Mctyre, Robert	8	1	....
Pinckard, Ann	3	1	1
Heath, John	4	2	4
Hill, Elizabeth	4	1	4
Yopp, William	8	1	4
Cundiff, John	7	1	5
Wilder, Jesse	2	1	1
Pierciful, Elijah	9	1	4
Kent, Edwin	8	1	1
Mctyre, John	....	1	9
George, Moses	6	1	3
Griggs, Ruth	3	1	5
Dobbs, Joseph	6	1	4
Edwards, William	8	1	4
Wallace, James	9	1	2
Carter, James	5	1	2
Yopp, Samuel, Jur	4	1	2
Kirk, James (Estate of)	4	1	7
Chilton, Stephen	5	1	1
Yerby, John	6	1	6
Doggett, John	5	1	4
Kem, Joseph	7	1	1
Kem, Thomas	8	1	7
Yopp, Samuel	4	1	4
Degges, John	7	2	7
James, Jeduthun	4	1	3
Davis, John	9	1	4
Connolly, Partrick	4	1	1
Galloway, William	5	1	2
Kelley, Lucy	5	1	1
Lewis, Margaret	1	1	1
Bean, John	10	1	4
McCarty, Colo Thad	....	1	6
Gordon, Colo James	7	2	17
Tapscott, James (Gent)	7	1	8
Garner, Thomas	12	1	2
Sullivan, Judith	7	1	2
Carter, Lucretta	3	1	1
Carter, Mary	1	1	1
Carter, Spencer	7	1	1
Horn, Elizabeth	6	1	1
Clayton, John	6	1	1
Brent, Jeduthun	5	1	3
Heath, Chloe	3	1	3
Saunders, Betty	7	1	8
Saunders, Purley	3	1	2
Riveer, John	5	1	2
Riveer, Peter	10	1	1
Haydon, Thomas	4	1	2
Hill, James	3	....	....
George, Benjam	9	1	2
Mahanes, Merredith	9	1	3
Edwards, Mary	3	1	2
Haydon, Mary	4	1	2
Haydon, William	4	....	....
Allen, John	6	1	....
Brent, George	4	1	....
Bell, Elizabeth	2	1	7
Henry, John	2	1	....
Pinckard, James	1	1	5
Conway, Edwin	7	1	12
Eustace, John (Estate of)	1	1	6

NANSEMOND COUNTY.

NAME OF HEAD OF FAMILY.	White souls.	Dwellings.	Other buildings.	NAME OF HEAD OF FAMILY.	White souls.	Dwellings.	Other buildings.	NAME OF HEAD OF FAMILY.	White souls.	Dwellings.	Other buildings.	NAME OF HEAD OF FAMILY.	White souls.	Dwellings.	Other buildings.
LIST OF JOSEPH HOLLADAY.				*LIST OF JOSEPH HOLLADAY—continued.*				*LIST OF JOSEPH HOLLADAY—continued.*				*LIST OF JOSEPH HOLLADAY—continued.*			
Godwin, Kinchen	7	1	12	Johnson, John	6	1	4	Raybourn, John	5	1	3	Corbell, John	5	1	1
Godwin, James	3	1	5	Everitt, Josiah	6	1	....	Best, Henry	1	....	2	Moore, Josiah	7	1	5
Everitt, Samuel	6	2	....	Pinner, Thos	4	1	....	Godwin, Charlotte	9	1	4	Holladay, Thos	6	1	3
Light, Jesse	7	1	....	Cowling, Eliza	2	....	....	Pitt, Edmd, Junr	4	1	4	Johnson, Thos	3	1	6
Midcalf, William	4	1	....	Rodgers, Richd	8	2	1	Godwin, Jos Mills	5	1	6	Godwin, Robert	1	1	4
Pinner, Thos	2	1	....	Powell, Wm	4	3	3	Holladay, John	1	1	5	Holladay, Joseph	9	2	15
Everitt, Willis	9	3	6	Roberts, Thomas	5	2	2	Godwin, Mills	5	1	8	Bosswell, Wm	1	1	3
Coffield, Willis	4	1	3	Eley, Mosses	4	2	2	Jordan, Wm	7	1	3	Holladay, Bruner	4	1	3
Farrow, Jacob	5	2	2	Hale, Samuel	7	2	4	Godwin, Henry	8	2	6	Godwin, Anthony	11	1	9
Cowling, Josiah	11	4	4	Milner, Thos	4	2	5	Pitt, Edmd, Senr	5	1	2	Howell, John	7	1	1
Cowling, William	5	2	2	Eley, William	5	1	7	Campbell, Thos, Senr	4	1	3	Coffield, Wm	4	1	3
Mackie, John	7	2	3	Campbell, Thos	2	1	4	Foster, Coffield	5	1	2	Wilkinson, Capt Wm	5	1	10
Pinner, Demsey	5	1	....	Godwin, Capt. Joseph	5	1	3	Mitchell, James	3	1	6	Godwin, Thos	8	2	6
Hodges, Jesse	8	2	3	Corbell, Joseph	6	1	8	Mitchell, Joseph	3	1	....	Wilkinson, Thos	8	1	2
Coffield, Mary	5	1	2	Wetherly, William	5	1	2	Pitt, Pennelope	7	1	4	Harris, Landan	1	....	....
Johnson, Nathan	6	2	6	Keely, George	6	1	2	Eley, Benja (Isle of wht)	....	1	6	Best, John	1	....	1
Cowling, Eliza	6	4	5	Pitt, Henry	4	1	1	Allmand, Aaron	4	1	5				
Haliburton, Thos	3	2	5	Godwin, Edmond	7	1	5	Powell, Benja	7	2	5				

NEW KENT COUNTY.

NAME OF HEAD OF FAMILY.	White souls.	Dwellings.	Other buildings.	NAME OF HEAD OF FAMILY.	White souls.	Dwellings.	Other buildings.	NAME OF HEAD OF FAMILY.	White souls.	Dwellings.	Other buildings.	NAME OF HEAD OF FAMILY.	White souls.	Dwellings.	Other buildings.
SAINT PETERS PARISH—LIST OF JOSEPH FOSTER.				*SAINT PETERS PARISH—LIST OF JOSEPH FOSTER—continued.*				*SAINT PETERS PARISH—LIST OF JOSEPH FOSTER—continued.*				*UPPER PRECINCT—con.*			
Clopton, William (List)	3	....	7	Crump, Sarah	3	1	4	Mitchel, Thomas	9	2	7	Martin, Elizabeth	3	2	1
Godding, David	4	1	7	Dixon, Millinton	10	1	2	Ammons, Christopher	4	1	8	Martin, Daniel	7	1	2
Crump, John	8	1	2	Dixon, Thomas	5	1	....	Daniel, Walter	6	1	3	Moss, Samuel	7	1	4
Waddill, Charles	7	1	3	Pasley, Polley	3	1	1	Clopton, William, Junr	6	1	2	Morgan, Ann	4	1	6
Hilliard, Benskin H	2	1	4	Lacy, John	5	1	5	Greens, Thos	5	1	4	Massie, Peter	3	1	6
Clark, James	4	1	2	Ross, David	3	1	2	Crump, Sarah	4	1	3	Martin, John	7	1	1
Hilliard, Ralph G	1	1	1	Furbush, Agness	2	1	....	Pears, Elisha	2	1	6	Martin, James	7	1	6
Hilliard, John	6	1	2	Baines, Thomas	1	1	3	Ladds, William	7	1	5	Martin, Robert, Jun	2	1	....
Lacy, John	2	1	2	Bailey, Park	7	....	....	Davis, Anthony	7	1	1	Martin, Robert Senr	8	1	1
Terrell, Richmond	1	1	11	Harfield, Michael	1	1	6	Claxton, Elizabeth	5	1	1	Massie, William	8	1	13
Hopkins, Walter	5	1	5	Bailey, Ann	3	1	5	Chamberlayne, Mary	1	1	5	Marsh, Aron	6	1	3
Christian, John	7	1	6	Otey, James	7	1	3	Martin, Julius	7	1	2	Poindexter, Nimrod	6	1	5
Stiff, Jacob, Senr	8	1	8	Freeman, Barnett	6	1	6	Turner, Charles	3	1	6	Pike, Richard	3	1	2
Sole, John	5	....	....	Otey, John	7	1	1	Clayton, William	6	2	9	Parke, Edmund	2	2	6
Cox, Presley	4	1	2	Bosman, James	8	1	1	Holt, Josiah	5	1	6	Penny, William	3	....	....
Sherman, Michael	2	1	7	Apperson, Richard	2	1	6					Patterson, Susanna	....	1	1
Poindexters, Jonathan	3	1	4	Howle, Thomas	10	1	3	*UPPER PRECINCT.*				Posey, John Price	4	1	13
Millet, Sarah	3	1	1	Howle, Epaphoditus	11	1	6	Adams, Peter	4	1	2	Ragland, Joel	7	1	4
Taylor, Frances	3	....	....	Graves, Richard C	12	2	23	Bassett, Burwell	....	....	8	Savage, Nathl L	14	1	16
Lindsey, Samuel	3	1	1	Parkinson, Jacob	11	1	8	Bacon, Nathaniel	1	1	....	Slauter, William	5	1	3
Bosiman, Harman	1	....	....	Crump, Bens	17	2	14	Chappel, Samuel	8	1	3	Slauter, Elias	7	1	....
Tallmans, William	5	1	10	Apperson, Samuel	4	1	15	Crump, Robert	11	1	5	Smether, John B	4	1	3
Pomfrey, William	8	1	....	Bacon, Lyddall	5	1	4	Clopton, Waldegs	9	1	7	Simco, Charles	4	1	....
Marston, John	3	1	13	Apperson, James	3	1	9	Crump, Jessee	3	1	2	Smether, Thomas	9	1	4
Wilkinson, Edward	8	....	5	Apparson, Edmund	2	1	2	Crew, Gatley	1	1	3	Slaughter, John	4	....	....
Morriss, Elizabeth	5	....	7	Lacy, William	7	1	5	Clerk, Edward G	6	1	1	Sneed, Reuben	4	1	1
Wilkins, Robert	7	....	....	Words, Charles	9	1	4	Clopton, Waldegs, Junr	6	2	3	Sneed, John	3	1	1
Pollard, Absalom	2	2	3	Crump, Billey	5	1	7	Clayton, John	7	1	....	Turner, Robert	10	1	3
Pollard, Robert	3	....	....	Meekins, Joseph	....	1	1	Chowning, Jesse	3	....	....	Thomson, John	3	1	3
Bins, Thomas	9	1	6	Mountcastle, David	7	1	2	Clopton, William H	....	1	10	Tyree, Dickey	8	1	2
Hopkins, William	4	1	7	Custis, John P. (Estate)	4	1	30	Clarke, David	4	....	....	Viak, Gideon	4	....	....
Redwood, H	4	1	7	Apperson, Richard	3	1	8	Crump, David	6	1	5	Webb, Lewis	....	1	16
Sherman, Henry D	3	1	7	Richadson, James	6	1	4	Clopton, Reuben	5	1	10	Wilkinson, Lyddall	6	1	9
Macon, William H	3	1	22	Broten, William	3	1	....	Dudley, William	6	1	6	Wilkinson, George	5	1	7
Foster, Joseph	6	1	13	Cook, William	5	1	3	Deen, Russil	4	....	....	Wilkinson, Parke	6	1	....
Bailey, John	7	1	4	Lindsey, John	4	1	....	Daniel, Ann	4	2	2	Wilsford, Mary	2	1	3
Crump, James	2	1	2	Austin, Absolem	5	1	2	Dandridge, William	4	1	6	Wilkinson, Nathaniel	5	1	7
Ragland, Jacob	3	1	3	Apperson, John	6	1	6	Ellyson, Jarrott	1	1	6	Wilkinson, Sarah	6	1	8
Moss, William	9	2	10	Richardson, Jesse	1	....	....	Ellyson, Thomas	5	1	8	Waddill, Edwin	8	1	11
Atkinson, Henry	2	1	9	Howle, Absolem	7	1	6	Ellyson, William	6	1	4	Webb, Foster	9	1	....
Clopton, William	4	4	6	Du Vall, Daniel	3	1	9	Ellyson, Gideon	10	2	3	Waddye, John	1	1	4
Jenkins, Joseph	5	....	....	Bowis, Robert	9	1	14	Ellyson, Robert	4	1	6				
Chamberlayne, William	2	1	8	Poindexter, Henry	4	1	4	Ellyott, Thomas	6	1	6	*LIST OF WILLIAM ARMISTEAD.*			
Pollard, James	4	1	1	Poindexter, George B	12	1	10	Finch, Henry	9	1	7	Armistead, William	5	1	9
Davis, James	8	1	4	Hewlett, Austin	6	1	3	Frayser, Thomas	4	2	6	Adams, John	6	1	2
Meekins, David	....	1	1	Vaughan, Stanhope	11	1	5	Finch, James	4	1	5	Auries, John	7	1	2
Cox, Charles H	5	....	....	Furbush, George	4	1	3	Griffin, Corban	8	3	37	Austin, Richard	3	1	2
Perkins, David	9	1	6	Joseph, Susanna	2	1	....	Gathright, Theodrick	5	1	6	Austin, Israel	3	1	....
Furlong, Hubbard	8	1	4	Warren, James	3	....	....	Goodman, Benja	5	1	2	Baker, George	8	1	6
Nance, James	8	1	4	Armistead, Mary	8	1	9	Gauldin, Samuel	4	1	1	Breeding, Joseph	3	1	....
Morriss, John	8	1	5	Jyne, Richard	6	1	8	Gathright, Miles	8	1	12	Blades, Joseph	4	1	4
Greens, Ithamer	4	1	3	Vaiden, Jeremiah	6	1	6	Giles, Nicholass	4	1	3	Ball, George	8	1	3
Webbs, William	3	1	3	Pearson, Charles	7	1	6	Goldwell, Temperance	1	1	....	Boswell, John	5	....	....
Martin, Susanna	4	1	3	Roper, William	4	....	....	Howle, John	6	1	3	Barkweell, Thomas	9	1	6
Humphreys, Elizabeth	3	1	3	Furbush, Hanner	4	1	....	Howle, Richard	7	1	1	Chandler, William	4	1	4
Vaughan, Bolling	4	1	1	Quiggins, James	10	1	5	Howle, Richard	5	1	6	Curle, Bennett	8	1	8
Vaughan, Lucy	5	1	3	Christian, William	4	1	6	Hill, Nathaniel	8	1	3	Claiborne, Herbert	4	1	9
Hilliard, Richard	5	1	3	Scrughs, Hanner	1	1	3	Higgins, Joseph	10	1	5	Claiborne, William	7	1	8
Baily, Samuel	8	3	7	Firth, William	7	1	8	Harriss, John	5	2	1	Crump, Richard	8	1	2
Meux, Lucy	5	1	11	Apperson, William	8	1	2	Johnson, David	8	1	....	Curle, David	3	1	4
Allen, Mathew	1	1	2	Perkins, Ann	9	1	7	Johnson, Michael	5	1	2	Cumbo, Turner	3	....	....
Burch, Samuel	8	1	2	Mountcastle, E	3	1	2	Johnson, Thomas	3	1	3	Curle, William	6	1	2
Woodward, John	6	1	2	Ammons, William	6	1	4	Kinningham, Wm	7	1	....	Day, William	3	1	1
Crump, Richard	1	....	....	Sherman, William	13	1	9	Lindsay, James	4	1	3	Dandridge, Bartholomew	12	2	35
Binns, Jeremiah	7	1	1	Neal, William	3	....	....	Meanly, William	2	1	3	Gilliam, Jane	7	2	....
Moss, James	1	1	1	Richardson, Molley	3	1	....	Mark, Samuel	2	1	3	Godding, Isham	5	1	6
Sharp, Robert	6	1	8	Furbush, Hanner	3	1	....	Mecot, Thomas	5	1	18	Gravves, Ralph	4	1	4
Poindexter, John	8	1	1	Parkinson, Jos	7	1	7								
Meekins, Criss	....	1	1	Howle, Thomas	2	....	2								

NEW KENT COUNTY—Continued.

NAME OF HEAD OF FAMILY.	White souls.	Dwellings.	Other buildings.
LIST OF WILLIAM ARMISTEAD—continued.			
Gravs, Richard	4	1	5
Gilliam, Jane	7	2	1
Holt, Amelia	4	1	....
Hix, Mary	10	1	2
Harman, John	6	1	10
Hix, John	3	....	....
Hayes, Robert	7	1	4
Harman, Keziah	4	1	2
Hilliard, William	3	1	3
Harman, William	6	1	5
Harman, Joseph	6	1	5
Heath, George	7	1	3
Jennings, William	3	1	6
Jennings, William, jr.	5	1	1
Jones, Daniel	7	1	5
Jones, Chesley	12	2	6
Ivy, Mary	2	1	1
Douglass, J } Jordone, Holt }	7	5	22
Jones, Frances	4	1	2
Langly, John	2	1	5
Langly, William	5	1	3
Mannin, John	8	1	5
Mullin, Thomas	9	1	5
Mullin, William	5	1	1
Mullin, John	4	1	2
Odell, James	6	1	5
Peasley, Susanna	5	....	....
Roper, John	11	1	5
Richardson, George	9	1	8
Ratcliffe, Thomas	2	1	3

NAME OF HEAD OF FAMILY.	White souls.	Dwellings.	Other buildings.
LIST OF WILLIAM ARMISTEAD—continued.			
Ratcliffe, Anne	6	1	5
Russell, Armistead	7	2	11
Ratcliffe, William	5	1	5
Roper, Thomas	4	1	3
Saunders, Isaac	6	1	2
Semple, James	9	2	4
Saunders, John	6	1	....
Stewart, Usley	3	1	2
Stewart, Sarah	6	1	1
Tandy, Roger	6	1	4
Taylor, Timothy	5	1	4
Timberlake, Richard	4	1	1
Tyree, Francis, Senr.	4	1	5
Tyree, Thomas	7	1	1
Taylor, John	6	1	3
Timberlake, John	5	1	5
Tyree, John	6	1	4
Vaiden, Martha	3	1	8
Volentine, John	2	1	2
Vaiden, Joseph	7	1	3
Vaiden, Jacob	4	1	4
Vaiden, Henry	8	1	7
Woodward, George	....	1	4
Woodward, Randolph	8	1	3
Woodward, Bartlet	5	1	4
Winpec, Austin	4	1	1
Warren, Edward	2	1	8
Woodward, Philemon	9	1	7
Willis, Stephen	....	....	....
Walls, Benjamian	7	1	....
Woodward, Anne	7	1	3

NAME OF HEAD OF FAMILY.	White souls.	Dwellings.	Other buildings.
LIST OF WILLIAM ARMISTEAD—continued.			
Woodward, Joseph	5	1	8
Willis, Margaret	6	1	8
LIST OF BURWELL BASSETT.			
Allen William	2	1	8
Allen, James	4	1	5
Allen, Richmond	7	1	3
Allen, Daniel	4	1	4
Armistead, Mary	3	1	6
Allen, Richard (Estate)	3	1	7
Austin, Joseph	8	1	2
Bassett, Burweell	10	2	33
Bennett, Mary	3	1	3
Bradenham, John	5	2	4
Brooker, Reba.	7	1	3
Breeding, James	4	1	1
Breeding, John	5	1	....
Breeding, Julius	2	1	1
Breeding, Elisha	4	1	2
Bosweell, John	5	1	....
Christian, Isham	7	1	7
Davies, Recd. Price	6	1	10
Dilliard, Thomas	7	1	7
Dilliard, George	5	1	8
Franks, John	4	1	8
Furbush, John	3	....	....
Furbush, Thomas	1	....	....
Fox, Lewis	1	....	....
Glaisbrook, James	5	1	....
Hervey, Charles	5	1	6

NAME OF HEAD OF FAMILY.	White souls.	Dwellings.	Other buildings.
LIST OF BURWELL BASSETT—continued.			
Hockaday, Rebah.	5	2	8
Hockaday, Edmund	7	1	4
Hockaday, James	8	1	4
James, Edward	4	1	....
Loyal, John B	2	1	1
Lacy, Henry	4	1	7
Lewis, David	6	1	7
Meridith, John	3	1	16
Moore, Benja.	7	1	5
Meremon, Thomas	9	1	1
Parish, William	5	1	3
Rissell, Armistead	2	1	6
Rawson, Thomas	3	1	7
Ratcliffe, Francis	5	1	4
Richardson, Sarah	5	1	7
Slater, William	4	1	3
Slater, John	9	1	4
Slater, William, Junr.	4	1	1
Sweeney, Mosses	6	1	1
Taylor, James	7	1	2
Tyree, James (Estate)	....	1	4
Tyree, William	8	1	3
Temple, Alex	4	1	....
Taylor, John	8	1	....
Taylor, John	5	1	5
Taylor, Richard	8	1	6
Williams, Dudley	9	1	5
Williams, David	7	2	9
Williams, James	3	1	6
Yates, John	5	1	1

NORFOLK COUNTY.

NAME OF HEAD OF FAMILY.	White souls.	Dwellings.	Other buildings.
PORTSMOUTH, SOUTH SIDE OF THE WESTERN BRANCH TO NEW MILL CREEK—LIST OF WM. KING.			
Herbert, Thomas	9	9	6
Brown, Thomas	9	1	1
Brown, Thomas, & concern	....	1	6
Matthews, James	7	2	2
Herbert, John	25	1	7
Russel, Elihu	2	1	....
Taylor, Thomas	7	1	....
Cherry, Mary	3	1	1
Wood, William	6	....	....
Culpeper, John	7	1	....
Calahan, Mary	6	....	....
Makins, Jno.	3	....	....
Owens, Joseph	7	1	2
Richardson, David	4	....	....
Owins, William	3	1	2
Porter, William	3	2	4
Burgess, Thomas	6	1	1
Griffin, Laban	7	....	....
Jollif, George	5	1	1
Cherry, Thomas	7	1	2
Stafford, Joseph	4	1	3
Bruce, Jno.	2	1	3
Hughes, Caleb	3	1	4
Smith, Wilson	2	1	....
Bruce, William M	3	1	7
Hoges, Willis	3	1	....
Buntin, Benjamin	9	1	1
Rose, Thomas	3	1	....
Bass, William	7	1	2
Makins, Elizabeth	3	....	....
Hodges, Randolph	2	1	....
Makins, Stephen	2	....	....
Carter, Benjamin	8	....	....
Ballentine, Jno.	3	....	....
Hare, Thomas	2	1	1
Johnstone, Jno.	10	2	2
Archey, Thomas	7	1	1
Boulton, Benjamin	5	1	4
Tart, Thomas	12	2	....
Culpeper, Thomas	1	1	....
Ceay, Ann	1	1	....
Culpeper, William, Junior	1	....	....
Culpepeper, Thomas	7	1	1
Culpeper, Jno., Junior	5	1	1
Culpepper, William	5	1	....
Rose, John	5	1	....
Culpeper, Henry	5	1	....
Hall, Mary Ann	1	1	4
Owins, William	7	....	....
Grant, William	2	....	....
Edwards, Cornelius	2	....	....
Etheridge, Amos	5	7	3
Cherry, Theophilus	6	1	4
Baker, William	5	....	....

NAME OF HEAD OF FAMILY.	White souls.	Dwellings.	Other buildings.
PORTSMOUTH, SOUTH SIDE OF THE WESTERN BRANCH TO NEW MILL CREEK—LIST OF WM. KING—con.			
Denby, Jonathan	3	....	....
Cherry, Faithful	3	1	1
Cherry, Jno.	9	1	2
Owens, James	6	1	3
Hare, Joseph	6	....	....
Willie, Thomas	4	1	2
Gilcot, Jno.	3	1	....
Vermillian, Francis	5	1	....
Deans, Jeremiah	7	1	4
Putnam, Benjamin	1	....	....
Richardson, Jno.	4	1	2
Tucker, William	5	1	1
Martin, James	6	1	1
Grant, Kesiah	3	1	2
Culpepper, Robert	3	1	2
Cherry, Solomon	6	1	2
Findley, James	4	1	1
Deal, James	4	1	....
Richardson, Thomas	5	1	....
Culpeper, Jno., senior	11	1	1
Cherry, Paul, Junior	9	1	....
Cherry, Paul	4	1	....
Bracket, William	3	1	2
Bracket, William, Junior	5	1	1
Moor, Matthias	4	1	1
Cherry, Jno.	6	2	....
Ballentine, Richard	8	1	....
Taylor, Elizabeth	4	1	....
Mesley, Jno.	9	1	....
Richardson, Jeremiah	4	2	....
Manning, Jno.	10	2	....
Manning, Malachi	5	1	....
Deal, David	3	....	....
Taylor, Edward	2	....	....
Richerson, William	8	2	....
Ellis, Samuel	10	1	2
Bowers, Benjamin	5	1	1
Culpeper, Sampson	6	1	2
Dyes, Peter	5	1	5
Calvert, Nathaniel	8	....	....
Dyes, Willis	5	1	2
Veale, Demsey	8	1	2
Culpeper, Robert	5	....	....
Hatton, Ann	4	1	2
Bowers, Mary	4	1	....
Powell, Samuel	5	1	1
Britton, Jno.	3	1	....
Mcdorman, Daniel	5	1	....
Mcdorman, James	5	....	....
Padro, Thomas	4	1	....
Hudson, Mary	8	....	....
Evey, Elizabeth	4	1	1
Manning, Mathew	4	1	2
Groves, Jacob	3	....	....
Stafford, Wm.	5	1	....

NAME OF HEAD OF FAMILY.	White souls.	Dwellings.	Other buildings.
PORTSMOUTH, SOUTH SIDE OF THE WESTERN BRANCH TO NEW MILL CREEK—LIST OF WM. KING—con.			
Ballentine, William	5	1	1
Henderson, James	3	....	....
Ellis, Jno., senior	7	....	....
Smith, James	3	1	....
Brown, Reubin	6	1	1
Tart, Eliza	3	1	1
Millerson, William	5	....	....
Hare, Charity	2	3	6
Bruce, Jno., senior	4	1	1
Hatton, Samuel	3	1	1
Stafford, Joseph, Junr.	8	....	....
Moor, Jno.	5	1	2
Taylor, Jno.	5	....	....
Culpeper, Annise	5	1	....
Cherry, William	5	....	....
Cherry, Luke	2	1	1
Wilkins, Mary	3	1	6
Lowe, Henry	5	1	....
Bruce, Thomas	4	1	2
Warren, Michael	11	....	....
Deans, Nathan	6	1	2
Brown, William	7	....	....
Moor, William	10	1	3
Hodges, James	10	1	3
Talbot, Jno.	10	1	5
Nichols, Susanna	2	1	1
Gibbs, Giles	1	....	....
May, Jno.	3	....	....
Graw, Thomas	3	1	1
Culpeper, Joseph	6	1	....
Spellman, William	3	....	....
Cherry, John	5	1	1
Wyat, Spivy	15	1	5
Culpeper, Robert	2	1	2
Carney, Richard	8	1	1
Lewelling, Isabell	3	1	4
Deal, Elizabeth	2	1	1
Deal, Henry	6	1	1
Green, Peter	5	1	....
Manning, Matthias	2	....	....
Cherry, Jane	4	1	....
Green, Mary	2	....	....
Williams, Lemuel	1	1	8
Heritter, Casper	5	1	1
King, William	5	....	....
Graham, Jno.	1	....	....
Kennedy, Robert	4	....	....
Gemmel, David	3	....	....
Brian, Morto	3	....	....
Jagitts, William	10	....	....
Ellis, James	7	1	....
Henry, Jno.	4	....	....
Hodges, William	3	1	....
Gemmel, Nathan	6	....	....
Wakefield, Thomas	7	1	1

NAME OF HEAD OF FAMILY.	White souls.	Dwellings.	Other buildings.
PORTSMOUTH, SOUTH SIDE OF THE WESTERN BRANCH TO NEW MILL CREEK—LIST OF WM. KING—con.			
Totterdill, Charles	8	1	1
Veale, Thomas	....	6	7
Williams, Charles	5	....	....
Ballentine, James	4	....	....
Ballentine, Joshua	....	....	....
Ellis, John	5	1	1
Ballentine, Thomas	7	1	....
Williams, Mary	4	....	....
Tart, William	8	1	2
Scott, Tenant	10	1	2
Best, Samuel	5	1	....
Cherry, Samuel	4	1	....
Plummer, Daniel	6	1	....
Plummer, William, Junior	6	1	1
Ballance, Susanna	5	2	....
Brown, James	3	1	1
Brown, Abel	8	1	2
Cherry, Matthew	6	1	1
Brown, Ivy	8	1	2
Kinder, Benjamin	4	1	2
Williams, Stephen	9	1	1
Wooldridge, Edward	8	1	3
Rutter, Jeremiah	4	1	3
Kinder, Robert	5	2	3
Millerson, Jacob	6	1	2
Burgess, Geo. W	10	3	....
Brown, Jno.	5	1	2
Wilkins, William	8	1	2
Ives, James	1	1	6
Cherry, Joseph	3	1	5
Brown, Mary	7	....	....
Cherry, Brion	8	....	....
Willey, Jno.	5	1	1
Satchwell, Emanuel	3	1	2
Cherry, Thomas, senior	1	1	1
Wilkins, Willis	1	1	3
Cherry, Jeremiah	3	1	1
Pollock, Jno.	7	1	6
Wilkins, James	2	....	....
Cherry, David	2	....	....
Ives, Robert	9	1	5
Smith, Samuel	3	1	3
Smith, George	3	....	....
Ivy, Jno.	2	1	1
Taylor, Samuel	7	1	....
Wright, Thomas	4	1	3
Reins, Powell	1	3	1
Horsefield, Israel	3	....	....
Whaley, Solomon	3	....	....
Blow, Richard	3	8	....
Dunn, Sarah	4	....	....
Fleet, Jno.	2	....	....
Luke, Isaac	5	2	3
Hall, Elizabeth	2	1	1
Herbert, Thomas, Junior	3	....	....

NORFOLK COUNTY—Continued.

PORTSMOUTH, SOUTH SIDE OF THE WESTERN BRANCH TO NEW MILL CREEK—LIST OF WM. KING—con.

NAME OF HEAD OF FAMILY.	White souls.	Dwellings.	Other buildings.
Gordon, Geo., & company	3		
Mellow, James	8	1	
Fridley, Henry	4	6	1
Andrew, Joseph	3		
Nivison, Jno	2	1	3
Robert, Ann	4	2	
Cheshure, Henry	5		
Denby, Jno	4		
Snale, Elizabeth	2		
Reveley, George	7	1	1
Healey, Martin	3	1	2
Emmons, John	3	1	
Culpeper, Willis	4	2	
Collins, Jno	4	1	2
Keeling, Thorowgood	10	2	1
Reynolds, David	5	2	2
Mushro, Jno	5		
Purdie, Ivy	4		
Porter, Ann	1	1	
Grimes, Maximilian	6	1	
Slaughter, Augustine	1	2	
Macneal, Geo. (orphan)	1	1	
Collins, Henry	7	1	
Cann, James	1	1	
Pigot, Ralph	3	1	2
Veale, Samuel	6	4	4
Conyers, Stiles	2	1	
Hoffler, Thomas	7	1	2
Skinner, William	2	1	1
Owins, Paul	5	3	3
Melo, Anthony	7		
Mushert, Christian	4		1
Pritchet, Jno	2	1	
Rawlings, Robert	7	1	1
Livingston, Ann	2		
Pritchet, William	8	1	
Bickerdick, Richard	5	1	2
Quarles, Jno	5		
Morris, Jno	7	1	6
Smith, Jno	2		
Clarkson, Thomas	4	1	
Wharton, Thomas	1	1	
Moody, Isaiah	4		
Hudson, Jno	6	1	1
Joines, Jno	7	1	3
Edwards, Thomas, senr	1	1	1
Dickinson, Thomas	5	2	
Thompson, Prudence	3	2	3
Collins, George	6	1	3
Bagnal, Nathan	3	1	2
Kidd, Jno	2	2	1
Branan, Jno	4	2	2
Timson, Thomas	5	1	
Jones, Edward	3	1	1
Pead, Nathaniel	7		
Milhado, Aaron	4	2	
Maynun, Basward	2	1	
Holmes, Joseph	5		
Elliot, Robert	6	1	3
Wood, Story	4	1	1
Gaskins, James	5	1	2
Goffegun, Laban	5	1	3
Crawl, David	3		
Dison, George	4	2	6
Hudson, Mary	5	3	2
Gole, George	1		
Guyn, John	5	2	1
Wilson, Charles	6		
Benson, Robert	4		
Hall, George Thomas		1	2
Brown, Jno, Junior	4	1	2
Crooker, William	2		
Bustin, Martha	10	1	4
Arlington, James	2		
Nestor, Richard	6	1	3
Wilson, Willis	3	1	3
Cowper, Jno	7	1	5
Dowdon, William	3		
Wilson, Goodrich	9	3	2
Brown, Frances	6	1	3
Owins, Jno	4	1	
Boyd, Alexander	5		
Grimes, William	3	1	2

NORTH SIDE OF THE WESTERN BRANCH—LIST OF CHARLES CONNER.

NAME OF HEAD OF FAMILY.	White souls.	Dwellings.	Other buildings.
Avis, John	4	1	1
Best, John	3	1	1
Best, Thomas	3	1	3
Bullock, Hannah	3	1	2
Bowers, Robert	8	2	3
Bolton, William, senr	7	1	3
Bufkin, Samuel	8	1	5
Bolton, William, Junior	4	1	1
Booker, William	4	1	3

NORTH SIDE OF THE WESTERN BRANCH—LIST OF CHARLES CONNER—con.

NAME OF HEAD OF FAMILY.	White souls.	Dwellings.	Other buildings.
Bowers, Jno	10	2	4
Beverley, Benjamin	4	1	2
Barr, Robert	3	1	
Bacon, Christian	3	2	2
Baynes, Jno	5	1	6
Bacon, Richard	8	2	2
Best, Henry	7	1	4
Buntin, Richard	6		
Conner, Charles	6	1	4
Creach, Mary	3	1	3
Carney, John	2	1	
Creech, Judith	5	1	8
Crosby, Ann	4		
Deans, Lemuel	4	1	2
Deans, Thomas	10	1	4
Deans, William, senior	3	1	3
Deans, William, Junior	5	1	8
Elks, Jno	6	1	1
Eastwood, Phœbe	7	1	
Eastwood, Samuel	5	1	2
Eastwood, Enos	4		
Etheridge, Luke	8	1	2
Eastwood, Willis	9	1	3
Eastwood, Elisha	4	1	4
Frost, Peter	4	1	1
Freeman, Judith	5	1	1
Grimes, Sarah, Junr	2	1	3
Grimes, Jno	6	1	3
Grimes, Sally	3	1	
Grimes, Sarah, senr	2	1	2
Grimes, Sarah	7	1	4
Grimes, Thomas	4	1	3
Graham, Jno	10	1	3
Harris, Thomas	8	1	3
Hatton, Eliza	8	1	8
Henderson, William	5	1	2
Hobgood, Judith	2	1	1
Hodges, William	8	1	7
Hobgood, William	5	1	4
Hoffler, William	5	1	9
Holloway, Jno	5	1	2
Isdale, Ann	5	1	
Isdale, Jno	1		1
Ives, Samuel	7	1	2
Ivy, Samuel	3		
Johnson, Benjamin	3	1	4
Jollif, John	4	1	4
Jilcut, James	5	1	1
Jollif, Jeremiah	6	1	3
King, Miles	3	1	
King, Edward	5	2	
Knott, Jno	2		
King, James, senior	6	1	2
King, James, Junior	3	1	
King, Jno	5	1	1
Love, Alexander	3	1	4
Lockhart, Jno	5	1	3
Lewelling, Jno	4	1	2
Moor, Jno	4	1	6
Manning, James	6	1	3
Moor, Edward	6	1	3
Melton, Joseph	3		
Mackie, Andrew	6	1	1
Miars, Joshua	5	1	5
Miars, David	3	1	3
Miars, Jno	3	1	
Nyall, Nicholas	3	1	5
Norcut, Thomas	4	1	2
Orton, Thomas	5	1	1
Pullin, Henry	11	1	2
Powell, Richard	8	2	4
Powell, Joseph	9	1	3
Powell, William	5	1	
Powell, Thomas	7	1	3
Powell, Thamer	2	1	5
Powell, Jeremiah	5	1	1
Pullin, Aaron	10	1	1
Reaves, Jno	8	1	1
Rose, Margaret	6	1	4
Rose, Stephen	4	1	1
Spring, Jno	4	1	
Stewart, Andrew	3	3	6
Spring, James	5	1	2
Tart, James	5	1	4
Taylor, Jno, senior	7	1	
Tart, Thomas	6	1	2
Taylor, James	4	1	1
Thompson, Henry	9	1	4
Taylor, Arthur	4	1	1
Taylor, Darkis	1	1	1
Taylor, Jno, Junior	8	1	6
Taylor, William	6	1	
Townshend, Elender	4	1	
Taylor, Richard	2		
Taylor, Thomas	6	1	2
Taylor, William	6	1	1
Watts, Demsey	9	1	3

NORTH SIDE OF THE WESTERN BRANCH—LIST OF CHARLES CONNER—con.

NAME OF HEAD OF FAMILY.	White souls.	Dwellings.	Other buildings.
Ward, Willis	6	1	1
Winget, Willis	4	1	
Ward, Godfrey	6	1	3
Williams, Joseph	7	1	
Wainright, George	4	1	1
White, Jno	5	1	2
Winget, Robert	5	1	2
Wright, Ann	8	1	7
Westcot, Fanny	4	1	3
Westcot, Samuel	3	1	2
Westcot, William	1		
Wyat, Patty	6	1	2

NORTH SIDE OF TANNERS CREEK—LIST OF JNO. WILLOUGHBY.

NAME OF HEAD OF FAMILY.	White souls.	Dwellings.	Other buildings.
Ivy, Elizabeth	2	4	4
Cooper, John	10	1	1
Creemur, James	2	1	1
Thomas, John	6	1	2
Cooper, Jno, senior	4	1	
Cooper, Arthur	3	1	1
Reads, Thomas	6	1	
Langley, James	8	1	3
Moseley, Elizabeth	4	1	9
Haynes, Christopher	5	1	3
Denby, Charles	6	1	9
Hurt, Joseph	6	1	3
Parmer, David	3	1	
Pead, Joel	4	1	
Pead, Thomas			
Pead, Lemuel			
Warmsley, Thomas	8	2	2
Dyson, Sarah	4	1	1
Talbot, Richard	6	1	5
Talbot, Mark	5	1	5
Guy, Bailey	5	1	4
Langley, William	6	1	2
Cone, Willis	3	1	
Bartee, Isaac	3	1	3
Denby, William	2	1	1
Denby, Lemuel	5	1	3
Grant, John	6	1	
Williams, Jno, Junior	6	1	
Harvey, Alexander	5	1	2
Cone, James	3	1	
Oast, James	4	1	
Talbot, Mary	9	1	7
Drayton, Lewis	5	1	
Cooper, Jonathan	7	1	1
Bashaw, Thomas	7	1	
Jones, James	7	1	
Haynes, Edward	5	1	1
Mason, William	2	1	
Barret, Elizabeth	6	1	
Warren, William	7	1	2
Grant, Ann	4	1	
Buckley, Francis	6	1	
Williams, Robert	5	1	
Bartee, Samuel	4	1	
Langley, Moses	3	1	
Arnold, Moses	2	1	
Golsbery, Elizabeth	2	1	
Grant, James	8	1	
Boush, Robert	2	1	2
Read, John	7	1	2
Boush, Charles	6	1	
Cooper, Rhoda	5	1	
Jordan, John	10	1	
Godfrey, Daniel	7	1	1
Williams, William	3	1	
Burgess, Jno	10	1	
Willoughby, Jno	12	1	7
Snail, Christopher	4	1	2
McCloud, James	3	1	
Snail, Henry	5	1	
Talbot, Solo. B	4	1	7
Tarrant, Francis	4	1	

DISTRICT FROM THE GREAT BRIDGE TO EDMUND'S BRIDGE AND TO NEW MILL CREEK—LIST OF D. SANFORD.

NAME OF HEAD OF FAMILY.	White souls.	Dwellings.	Other buildings.
Jollif, James	6	2	10
Armstrong, Jno	1	1	1
Hodges, Martha	6	1	1
Stevens, Warrington	3	1	
Griffin, Luke	6	1	
Watson, William	4	1	
Owens, Jno	4	1	1
Thompson, Theophilus	4	1	1
Curling, James	9	1	
Webb, James, senior	4	2	4

DISTRICT FROM THE GREAT BRIDGE TO EDMUND'S BRIDGE AND TO NEW MILL CREEK—LIST OF D. SANFORD—con.

NAME OF HEAD OF FAMILY.	White souls.	Dwellings.	Other buildings.
Webb, James, Junior	3	1	4
Nicholson, Thomas	5	1	4
Nicholson, Wm, senior	5	1	4
Bressie, Thomas	6	1	4
Sikes, Solomon	3	1	1
Gammon, Josiah	10	1	2
Williams, Thomas	10		
Sikes, Josiah	5		
Bell, Jno	4		
Hodges, Charles	6	1	3
Poole, Robert	7	1	1
Smith, William	5	2	11
Sanford, Daniel	2		
Hodges, Solomon	7	1	4
Gammon, Richard	7	1	2
Foreman, Elizabeth	1	1	5
Shirley, Jno	9	1	2
Savells, Daniel	7	2	3
Sikes, Caleb	6	1	1
Hodges, Thomas	7	1	1
Bagnall, James	6	1	1
Foreman, Alexander	5	1	2
Bressie, William	5	1	1
Hanbury, James	5	1	
Stewart, Charles	5	1	1
Ferebee, Charles	8	1	3
Denby, Edward	3		
Ballentine, Jno	7	1	2
Hodges, Stephen	8	1	6
Shipwash, Thomas	9	1	1
Bailey, William, senior	2	1	
Barber, Willis	7	1	2
McBride, Duncan	3	1	
Armstrong, Bennet	10	2	5
Ballentine, Jacob	4	1	1
Stewart, Jno	8	1	4
Truss, Mary	3	1	4
Cavenaugh, Sarah	1	1	1
Gammon, Joel	11	1	3
Lane, Josiah	3	1	
Hodges, Daniel	4	1	1
Curling, Arthur	5	1	
Culpeper, Thomas	1		2
Hodges, James	6		
Reed, Jno	6	1	1
Hodges, Caleb	3		
Creekmore, Edward	5	1	
Caine, Richard	4	1	1
Sevills, James	4		
Manning, Honour	1	2	
Shipwash, Willis	7	1	1
Hodges, Anne	1	1	3
Evans, Jno	2		
Curling, Joseph	7	1	1
Hodges, Mason	7	1	7
Hall, George	6		
Wood, Timothy	4	1	
Curling, Dorothy	8	1	2
Butt, Wilson	11	1	8
Savills, Taylor	7	1	1
Shipwash, Ambros	5	1	2
Bell, Alexander	3	1	4
Southerland, Thomas	10	1	6
Manning, Thomas	3		
Shipwash, Jno	3	1	1
Etheridge, Elijah	6	1	3
Hanbury, Thomas	6	1	3
Maund, Marcum	3	1	3
Waller, Robert	4	2	7
Smith, Richard	4	1	3
Sanford, Sarah	5	1	2
Maund, Matthew	3	1	3
Shipwash, Elizabeth	4	1	
Miller, Mary	2	1	1
Roach, Jamima	4	1	
Nicholson, John	8	1	3
Nicholson, William, Junr	5	1	2
Nicholson, Stephen	5	1	
Pierce, William	2	1	
Bailey, James	5		
Hodges, Jno	3	1	2
Creekmore, Thomas	3	1	
Creekmore, Mary	6	1	
Miller, Mary, senior	3	1	
Bailey, Martha	5	1	

DISTRICT FROM THE BOROUGH OF NORFOLK TO WILLIS CARES AND TO PRINCESS ANNE, INCLUDING THE SOUTH SIDE OF TANNER'S CREEK—LIST OF MATTHEW GODFREY.

NAME OF HEAD OF FAMILY.	White souls.	Dwellings.	Other buildings.
Archdeacon, Parnel	4	1	1
Archer, James	5		
Boggess, Susanna	5		

NORFOLK COUNTY—Continued.

DISTRICT FROM THE BOROUGH OF NORFOLK TO WILLIS CARES AND TO PRINCESS ANNE, INCLUDING THE SOUTH SIDE OF TANNER'S CREEK—LIST OF MATTHEW GODFREY—con.

NAME OF HEAD OF FAMILY.	White souls.	Dwellings.	Other buildings.
Boush, Catherine	5	1	5
Baynes, Jno.	7		
Burgess, Jno.	2		
Bailey, Isaac	6	1	
Cooper, Arthur	4	1	
Colley, William	8	1	5
Cooper, William, senior	3	2	5
Colley, Bridget	5	1	
Cratchet, Thomas	7	1	
Conner, Jno.	5		
Christian, Matthias	4	5	2
Care, Jno.	1	1	2
Colley, Francis	3	1	1
Dison, Manor	4	1	1
Dunn, Samuel	4	1	
Denby, Samuel	6		
Davis, James	6	1	2
Ewell, Jesse	5		
Edy, Solomon	6		
Godfrey, James	3	1	6
Guy, Jno.	9	1	1
Guy, James	5		
Goaff, John	7		
Guthery, Alexander	3		
Godfrey, Elizabeth	1	1	2
Godfrey, Charles	3		
Godfrey, Matthew	4	2	7
Hutchings, Eliza	3		
Hutchings, Jno.	7		
James, Christopher	2	1	
James, Thomas	4	1	
James, Jno.	10	3	2
Jackson, Jno.	4		
Ingram, Wm.	4	1	3
Langley, Lemuel	8	2	3
Lewelling, Abel	10	1	1
Leitch, David	5	1	
Lee, Jane	4	1	4
Lowry, Thomas	5	2	1
Lambert, Solomon	3	1	
McVie, Matthew	4		
Mason, John	8		
Morris, Thomas	3		
Marley, Maximilian	11	1	1
Millerson, William	4	1	
Murphy, Susanna	2		
Murphy, Nathaniel	5		
Marley, William	6	1	
Millerson, Lemuel	5	1	
Millerson, Joshua	9	1	
Maxnox, Jamima	8	1	
Martin, James Green	3	1	4
Nicholson, William	5	1	2
Oldner, Thomas	1		
Oldner, George	16	1	6
Peyton, Joshua	4		
Righton, Millerson	4		
Robinson, Tully	4	2	1
Roberts, Lemuel	7	1	5
Ramsay, Mary	6		
Riddel, Eliza	2		
Rogers, William	2		
Shore, George	4	1	1
Shelton, Alice	5	1	1
Stroud, Honour	2	1	1
Shipp, Samuel	4		
Singleton, Ann	5		
Simmons, Sampson	3		
Talbot, Elizabeth	2	2	4
Thorowgood, Frances	2		
Thelaball, Prudence	2		
Taylor, William	3		
Thorowgood, Mary	6		
Terry, Thomas	2		
Tabb, Augustine	4	2	4
Thomas, Frances	1	1	4
Vesey, Joseph	2	1	1
Williams, Jno.	4		
Warren, Jno.	5	1	1
Williamson, James	4	1	1
Williamson, Eliza	6	1	2
Wilder, Samuel	4		
Willoughby, Mary	1	1	1
Weddle, Jno.	5		
Wilder, Edward	6		
Wells, Henry	5		
Wills, Ann	1	1	1
Warren, James	4		

DISTRICT FROM THE FERRY POINT TO THE GREAT BRIDGE—LIST OF THOMAS NASH.

NAME OF HEAD OF FAMILY.	White souls.	Dwellings.	Other buildings.
Smallwood, Jno.	4	1	1
Etheridge, Maxey	9	1	3

DISTRICT FROM THE FERRY POINT TO THE GREAT BRIDGE—LIST OF THOMAS NASH—con.

NAME OF HEAD OF FAMILY.	White souls.	Dwellings.	Other buildings.
Nichols, Isaiah	7	1	12
Macoy, Jno.	4	1	2
Murden, Robert	7	1	4
Macoy, Josiah	10	1	4
Allman, Edmund	4	1	6
McClenahan, William		1	6
Pebworth, James	7		
Etheridge, Abel	6	1	3
Etheridge, Tho. W	8	1	3
Etheridge, Argil	6	1	4
Ballentine, Paul	7	1	4
Herbert, Caleb	7	1	7
Cooper, Hillery	3		
Bartee, Ardre	4	1	4
Whitehurst, Jno.	6	1	3
Cotton, Abram B	7		
Macoy, Thomas	7	1	1
Matthias, Joshua	7	1	7
Butt, Peter	6	1	9
Jamieson, Henry	4	1	3
Jamieson, Standley	2	1	3
Sparrow, Richard	10	1	7
Tucker, Jno.	2	1	2
Smallwood, Anne	2	1	2
Etheridge, Reubin	6		
Barrington, Lemuel	5	1	3
Murden, Jno., senior	2	1	3
Murden, Jno., Junior	7	2	9
Griggs, William	4		
Manning, David	9	1	3
Ballentine, Lemuel	5	1	1
Murden, Edward	5		
Halstead, Simon	6	1	3
Butt, William	6	1	4
Cuthrell, Garvin	5	1	2
Cuthrell, James	5	1	1
Sikes, Trim	9	1	2
Edwards, Peter	9	1	5
Portlock, William	5	1	4
Whitehurst, Richard	8	1	2
Whitehurst, William	5	1	1
Tatem, James	4	1	
Tatem, Nathaniel	5	1	4
Cuthrell, Daniel	11	1	3
Harris, Samuel	3	1	2
Cuthrell, William	8	1	3
Etheridge, Thomas	3		
Cherry, Caleb	7	1	1
Ross, Jno.	2	1	
Nash, Jno.	8	1	7
Nash, Dinah	2	1	7
Portlock, Willis	9		
Sikes, Lot	9	1	
Macoy, Enos	3	1	3
Caton, William	4	1	2
Fentriss, William	2	1	2
Macoy, Richard	5		
Jones, Jno.	6	1	2
Fentriss, Geo., senior	7	1	6
Etheridge, Edward, senior	3	1	5
Lee, Thomas	2		
Fentriss, George, Junior	9	1	3
Fentriss, Lancaster	7	1	4
Portlock, Matthew	5	1	3
Macoy, Caleb	6	1	2
Macoy, Joshua, senior	9	3	5
Sikes, Mary	4		
Dobbs, Kedar	5		
Macoy, Joshua, Junior	4		
Hebdon, Seth	8	2	7
Macoy, Maxey	5		
Macoy, William	2		
Macoy, Charles	1		
Herbert, Jennet	4	2	4
Ballentine, David	2	1	3
Ballentine, William	5	1	3
Godfrey, George	2	1	
Bartee, Mary	1	1	1
Herbert, Reubin	8	1	3
Whitehurst, Edward	5	1	2
Butt, Henry	9	1	5
Portlock, Lemuel	7	1	3
Butt, Samuel	8	1	2
Odean, Charles	8	1	11
Etheridge, Enock, senior	6	1	10
Holstead, Matt	2		
Portlock, Annis	1	1	5
Drewry, Jno.	3	1	5
Barrington, Sarah	5	1	5
Butt, Cartwright	5	1	3
Butt, Willis	4	1	2
Jarvis, Robert	8	1	3
Bartee, Thomas	6	1	7
Herbert, James	7	1	3
Mayle, Lydia	6	1	2

DISTRICT FROM THE FERRY POINT TO THE GREAT BRIDGE—LIST OF THOMAS NASH—con.

NAME OF HEAD OF FAMILY.	White souls.	Dwellings.	Other buildings.
Hodges, Courtney	2	1	5
Hodges, Joseph	5	1	
Dawes, Abram	5	1	2
Carson, Andrew, Junior	4	1	4
Butt, Eppe	12	1	5
Macoy, Willis	4	1	3
Stokes, Jonathan	7	1	6
Matthias, Robertson	6	1	1
Jones, Jesse	5		
Butt, Malta	7	1	5
Butt, Amy	6		
Whiddon, Jno.	5	5	10
Smith, George	5		
Robertson, Moses		1	4
Rudder, Charles, Junior	2	1	
Harper, Edward	10		
Portlock, Jno.	7	2	12
Nash, Thomas, senior	10	1	3
Sparrow, Mary	5	2	1
Etheridge, Lemuel	1	2	7
Butt, Lemuel	6	1	3
Armistead, Thomas	4	1	5
Boush, Mary	5		

DISTRICT FROM EDMUND'S HILL TO PRINCESS ANNE AND CAROLINA LINES AS FAR AS THE NORTHWEST RIVER—LIST OF MALACHI WILSON.

NAME OF HEAD OF FAMILY.	White souls.	Dwellings.	Other buildings.
Bartee, Lemuel	4	1	4
Bartee, Letishia	4	1	3
Woodard, Henry	5	1	2
Wilkins, Robert	4	1	10
Holstead, Matthew	8	1	9
Holstead, Samuel	3	1	4
Wilson, William, junior	1	1	11
Butt, Ann	5	1	4
Godfrey, Matthew	3	1	
Edmonds, Isaac	7	1	1
Wilkins, Francis	4	1	7
Sevills, Absolam	6	1	4
Foreman, Jacob	8	1	1
Bailey, James	5	1	
Fulford, Matthew	1	1	10
Peadon, William	6	1	3
Woodard, Charles	2		
Butt, Nathaniel, senior	8	1	6
Bulley, Jno.	4	1	3
Taylor, Jno.	2	1	4
Parsons, Abijah	4	1	2
Ferebee, Benjamin	1		
Fulford, Levy	6	1	3
Mansfield, Edmund	11	1	1
Randolph, Thomas	3	1	4
Smith, Samuel	3	1	4
Stewart, James	7	1	2
Sherley, Daniel	5	1	2
Taylor, Thomas	5	1	1
Stewart, Maximilian	4	1	3
Toomer, Charles	3		
Sikes, Joseph	7	1	2
Sikes, Willis	4	1	2
Grimes, Mercer	9	1	7
Creekmur, Benjamin	8	1	3
Woodard, Thomas	4	1	3
Leak, Willis	4	1	1
Halstead, Thomas	7	1	7
Smith, Jesse	5	1	2
Foreman, James	7	1	7
Smith, Samuel, senior	5	1	4
Evans, Matthew	5	1	
Butt, Robert	8	1	5
Dailey, Zadock	6	1	
Grimes, Israel	5	1	4
Hall, Edmund, senior	3	2	2
Davis, Isaac	6	1	4
Corbell, Josiah	7		
Old, Kedar	6	1	11
Wallace, Samuel	9	1	9
Graves, Jno.	8		
Miller, Nathaniel	10	1	4
Ballance, Isaiah	1		
Creekmur, Lydia	3	1	
Hodges, Joshua	10		
Foreman, Ivy	4		
Woodard, Caleb	10	1	3
White, Caleb	1	1	3
White, Mary	5	1	1
Miller, Mason	4	1	
Wallace, Kedar	4	1	
Wallace, Mary	1	1	1
Halstead, Simon	12	1	5
Simmons, Jno.	3	1	2

DISTRICT FROM EDMUND'S HILL TO PRINCESS ANNE AND CAROLINA LINES AS FAR AS THE NORTHWEST RIVER—LIST OF MALACHI WILSON—continued.

NAME OF HEAD OF FAMILY.	White souls.	Dwellings.	Other buildings.
Miller, Simon	3		
Kilgore, Jno.	3		
Lane, Gisbon	5	1	6
Smith, Butler	5	1	5
Hodges, Daniel	5	1	
Savells, Jno.	6	1	2
Jones, Jno., senior	7		
Jones, John	6	1	4
Manning, Ann	5	1	2
Foreman, William	8	1	3
Hodges, Mary	3	1	4
Miller, Patrick	5	1	3
Holstead, Elizabeth	5	1	1
Wiles, Anthony	8	1	
Miller, Solomon	6		
Miller, Matthias	10	1	4
Hodges, Benjamin	4	1	1
Williams, Abiah	5	1	1
Holstead, Smith	11	1	6
Hollowell, Henry	3	1	3
Fentriss, William	5	1	
Hollowell, Benjamin	4	1	3
Silvester, Dorcus	8	4	9
Jeffery, Aaron	5		
Footil, William	10	1	
Grimes, Alexander	9	2	5
Ballance, Henry	5		
Suggs, Moses	3	1	2
Manning, Elizabeth	3	1	2
Sikes, Jeremiah	5	1	7
Miller, George	6		
Poyner, James	3	1	2
Bright, William	6	1	5
Bright, Jobel	3	1	2
Dickens, Jno.	5	1	
Miller, Benjamin	5	1	6
Riggs, Jno.	5		
Smith, Jno.	4	2	3
Corprew, George D		2	3
Wormington, Jno.	5		
Sikes, Thomas	4	1	1
Smith, Solomon	9	1	10
Wilson, James, senior	7	1	5
Morris, James	6	1	2
Manning, Penelope	8	1	1
Fulford, Josiah	5		
Halstead, Henry	9	1	5
Murden, Maximilian	10	1	5
Parsons, Thomas	9	1	5
Wilson, William, senior	6	1	3
Wilson, Simon	6	1	8
Williams, Sarah	1	1	2
Miller, William	1	1	2
Hanbury, Job	5	1	2
Wilson, Malachi, senior	7	1	13
Grimes, Charles	7	1	5
Butt, Simon	3	1	4
Butt, Samuel	8	1	6
Parsons, Willis	4	1	1
Miller, Aaron	5	1	1
Fentriss, James	5	1	3
Butt, Benjamin	8	2	6
Hall, Thomas	5	1	
Gammon, Meriot	5		
Smith, Henry	10	1	3
Holt, James	3	2	7
Wilkins, Malachi	7	1	7
Ballance, Richard	3	1	1
Creekmur, Caleb	5	1	
Banks, Thomas	3	1	
Randolph, William	4	1	3
Pinkerton, Sarah	5	1	4
Hall, Edmund	5		
Wilson, James	8	1	4
Creekmur, Robert	5	1	
Hodges, Jno., Junior	9	2	7
Lockhart, Jno.	4	1	1
Creekmur, David	5	1	1
Parsons, William	4	1	1
Willey, William	6	1	7
Warden, William	9	1	8
Smith, Jno.	6	1	3
West, Daniel	6	1	1
Williamson, Lydia	5	1	1
Halstead, Latimer	3		
Mansfield, Robert	6	1	2
Smith, George	2	1	5
Randolph, Argent	6	1	1
Parker, Thomas	4	1	2
Godfrey, Solomon	3	1	2
Smith, Elizabeth	5	1	1
Ball, Willis	6	1	2
Bartee, William	3	1	3
Miller, Matthias	6	1	2
Wallace, William, Junior	4	1	2

NORFOLK COUNTY—Continued.

DISTRICT FROM EDMUND'S HILL TO PRINCESS ANNE AND CAROLINA LINES AS FAR AS THE NORTHWEST RIVER—LIST OF MALACHI WILSON—continued.

NAME OF HEAD OF FAMILY.	White souls.	Dwellings.	Other buildings.
Wallace, Thomas	5	1	1
Wallace, William, senior	4	1	4
Whites, Sarah	5	1	3
Wilson, Josiah	5	1	8
Wilson, Lemuel		1	1
Corprew, Jno.	11	1	8
Corprew, Jno. Junior	1	1	4
Murden, Jeremiah	3	1	4
Wormington, Abraham	10	6	15
Wilson, John	2		
Curling, Daniel	10	1	3
Godfrey, Jesse	10	1	6
Corprew, Thomas	8		
Fulford, Joseph	8	1	7
Wilson, Marget	4	1	8
Butt, Josiah	5	1	11
Ross, Mary	4	1	4
Butt, Nathaniel	7	1	6
Wilson, Charles	2	1	3
Wilson, Malachi, Junior	11	1	18
Sikes, Walter	4	1	2
Baxter, Jno	5	1	2
Wilson, Grace	1	1	2
West, Henry	7		
Casteen, Jeremiah	5	1	2
Weston, Benjamin	5	1	1
Fentriss, James, Junior	11	1	3

DISTRICT FROM EDMUND'S HILL TO PRINCESS ANNE AND CAROLINA LINES AS FAR AS THE NORTHWEST RIVER—LIST OF MALACHI WILSON—continued.

NAME OF HEAD OF FAMILY.	White souls.	Dwellings.	Other buildings.
Meggs, Robert	7	1	2
Whitehurst, Arthur	5	1	2
Sikes, Josiah	10	1	3
Murden, William	6	1	10
Wallace, Roger	4		

DISTRICT FROM THE NORTHWEST RIVER TO THE CAROLINA LINE—LIST OF WILLIAM HALL.

NAME OF HEAD OF FAMILY.	White souls.	Dwellings.	Other buildings.
Hall, William	12	2	10
Nosay, Thomas	3	1	3
Parsons, Willoughby	2	1	
Leak, Jno.			
Warren, Annis	2	1	1
Jones, Edward	5	1	
Williams, Phœbe	3	1	5
McPherson, Ann	4	1	
Ballance, Moses	5	1	2
Ballance, Elizabeth	1	1	
Warren, William	5	1	4
Randolph, Josiah	4	1	5
Etheridge, Henry	4	1	2
Happer, William	9	1	23
Happer, Mary	8	1	21
Creekmur, Wright	5	1	1

DISTRICT FROM THE NORTHWEST RIVER TO THE CAROLINA LINE—LIST OF WILLIAM HALL—continued.

NAME OF HEAD OF FAMILY.	White souls.	Dwellings.	Other buildings.
Creekmur, Eli	3	1	
Creekmur, George	4	1	
Wilson, Caleb	7	1	7
Butt, Malachi	6	1	3
Miller, Bateman	7	1	6
Butt, John	4	1	1
McPherson, Daniel, senr.	7	1	2
Etheridge, Malachi	6	1	
West, John, senior	5	1	
Wilson, Henry	10	2	15
Hanbury, Thomas, Junr.	5	1	2
Creekmur, Thomas, Junr.	3	1	4
McPherson, Courtney	6	1	2
Creekmur, Absolam	3	1	
Pierce, Ignatus	4	1	4
Etheridge, Mathias	8	1	3
Culpeper, Henry	3	1	
Macpherson, Jno., Junr	5	1	
Linch, Solomon	6	1	1
Cooper, Joseph	6	1	3
McPherson, William	3	1	
McPherson, Willis	3	1	
Ballance, Mordecai	8	1	2
McPherson, Jno., senr	3	1	
Wilkins, James	1	1	1
Williams, Edward	9	1	1
Prescot, Jno	8	1	4

DISTRICT FROM THE NORTHWEST RIVER TO THE CAROLINA LINE—LIST OF WILLIAM HALL—continued.

NAME OF HEAD OF FAMILY.	White souls.	Dwellings.	Other buildings.
McPherson, Daniel, Jr	7	1	1
Whitehurst, John	1		
Ballance, Henry	5	1	
Cherry, Lemuel	4	1	1
Etheridge, Richard	8	1	1
Williams, Sarah	7	1	1
Waller, John	2		
Noray, Daniel	5	1	5
Creekmur, Peter	7	1	4
Creekmur, Nicholas	5	1	9
Wilkins, William	7	1	7
Etheridge, Robert	6	1	
Creekmur, Edmund	7	1	2
Creekmur, Willis	7	1	1
Creekmur, David	6	1	1
Woodard, Nicholas	3	1	5
Creekmur, Edward	5	1	3
Creekmur, Affiah	4	1	2
Deford, John	3	1	3
Creekmur, Joel	3	1	
Grimes, John	7	1	3
Grimes, James	2	1	4
Creekmur Solomon	5	1	1
Creekmur, Joseph	1	1	

ORANGE COUNTY.

LIST OF JEREMIAH WHITE.

NAME OF HEAD OF FAMILY.	White souls.	Dwellings.	Other buildings.
Ham, Samuel, Junr	6	1	1
Ham, Samuel	5	1	1
Gear, Nathl	11	1	1
Riddell, Lewis	2	1	1
Shackleford, Henry	7	1	1
Haney, John	4		
Shackleford, Edmund	7	1	2
Riddell, James	9	1	2
Haney, James	2		
Powell, Jannett	1	1	1
Goodall, John, Junr	1	1	
Harvey, Thomas	4		
Earley, James	4	1	4
Davis, Thomas	3	1	2
Shifflet, William	13		
Collier, Martin	7		
Ham, Joseph	2		
Goodall, James	4		1
Goodall, John	9	1	2
Lamb, William	7		
Lamb, John	9		
Haney, Susannah	3		
Bruce, Elizabeth	7	1	
Lamb, John, Junr	2		
Lamb, Mary	5		
Shifflet, John	5		
Snow, John	3	1	
Rogers, William	9		
Ansill, Edward	7	1	
Williams, John	5		
Duglass, Margaret	2		
Davis, William	3	1	1
Machal, John	1	1	3
Gibbs, Churchill	5	1	2
Estis, Samuel	6	2	
Ogg, John	4	1	2
Lamb, Thomas	8		
Golding, Robert	7		
Earley, Theadoshea	3	1	3
White, Richard	3	1	
White, Jeremiah	11	1	6
Morris, William	8		
Morris, Thomas	4		
Morris, Richard	7		
Morris, William	7		
Snow, Thomas	11		
Davis, Lewis	11	1	
Cave, John	2		
Simands, Joell	4		
Meadows, Francis	4		
Ogg, Alexander	7	1	
White, Jeremiah	2		
White, John	6		
Marshall, Richard	5		
Marshall, Martin	6		
Smith, William	8		
Cave, William	11	1	
Lane, Edward	5		
Shifflet, Bland	4		

LIST OF BENJA. GRYMES.

NAME OF HEAD OF FAMILY.	White souls.	Dwellings.	Other buildings.
Grymes, Benjamin	6	1	8
Spotswood, John	9	1	6
Jones, Churchill		1	
Gordon, James	13	1	2
Smith, Jesse	9		
Bledsoe, George	3	2	2
Bledsoe, George, Junr	8		
Webb, Richard Cn	7	1	2
Perry, Peirce	8	1	3
Atkins, Alice	6		
Breedlove, Madison	2	1	1
Wood, James	9	2	2
Jones, James	3	1	3
Bledsoe, Moses	5	3	4
Hawkins, Elisha	3	1	
Hawkins, William	2	1	3
Morris, John	3		
Morris, Thomas	5	1	1
Jennings, Luke	3	1	
Head, Benjamn	3	2	
Head, Francis	3		
Webb, John Cn	9		
Landrum, Thomas	7	1	
Richards, Ambrose	5		
Jones, John	1		
Richards, Philimon	5	1	
Robinson, John	10	1	
Davis, Daniel	7	1	5
Prale, Daniel	6		
Gaines, Robert	10	1	2
Woolford, John	5		
Leathers, Nicholas	10		
Jones, Francis	4	1	
Hawkins, Reuben	6	1	
Overton, Obediah	7	1	
Overton, George	6		
Almon, John	5		
Hanson, Francis	4		
Parmor, William	4	1	
Parish, Joseph	9	1	1
Cook, George	7		
Perry, John	6		
Pigg, Mourning	6		
Perry, William	3		
Jones, Thomas	4	1	5
Falconer, Thomas	7	1	2
Sulivan, William	7		
Oaks, Major	11	1	
Singleton, Daniel	1	1	5
Lancastor, John	8	1	2
Beckham, Henry	7		
Sisson, William	11		
Martin, Henry	5	1	4
Rumsey, Thomas	6		
Rumsey, Richard	6		
Strother, William	3	1	2
Row, Edmond	8	1	3
Dilion, Andrew	2	1	

LIST OF BENJA. GRYMES—continued.

NAME OF HEAD OF FAMILY.	White souls.	Dwellings.	Other buildings.
Row, Thomas	8		
Johnson, Thomas	9		
Rawson, Joseph	5	2	1
Jones, Elijah	8		
Rawson, Thomas	9		
Bledsoe, John	2		
Clark, Patreck	4		
Clark, Sarah	4		
Johnson, Isaac	2		
Collins, Richard	4		

LIST OF THOMAS BARBOUR.

NAME OF HEAD OF FAMILY.	White souls.	Dwellings.	Other buildings.
Barbour, Thomas	7	2	20
Brockman, William	8	1	3
Cave, Belfield	6	1	2
Cock, Robert	3	1	1
Collins, George	5	1	
Connolly, James	8	1	3
Connolly, Stephen	6	1	
Dollins, William	2	1	1
Dollins, John	4	1	5
Ehart, Adam	6	1	1
Franklyn, John	2	1	
Farney, Thomas	6	1	3
Farney, Edward	4	1	2
Griffith, David	11	1	5
Galloway, John	6	1	2
Gholson, John	4	3	1
Garr, Lewis	2	1	3
Harvey, John	12	1	1
Hammand, Charles	7	1	4
Haskew, John	3	1	2
Henderson, Alexander	6		
Jarrell, James	4	1	
Johnson, Benjamin	5	2	20
Johnson, Martin	7	1	4
Lucas, William	6	1	8
Lucas, John	12	1	3
Miligan, William	7	1	4
Mace, Henry	3		
Ogby, Robert	6	1	3
Payne, Richard	8	1	4
Patterson, Joseph	6	1	3
Patterson, John	7	1	4
Snell, John	6	1	2
Smith, Thomas	3	1	4
Sebree, Richard, Junr	8	1	1
Sebree, William	5	1	1
Tillery, George	6	1	
Williams, John	7	1	5
Weathers, Francis	4		1
White, John	10	1	6
White, Jeremiah, Junr	4	1	3
White, Henry	6	1	5
White, Galand	3	1	1
Wood, James	10	1	3
Wood, Hopefull	9	1	3

LIST OF THOMAS BELL.

NAME OF HEAD OF FAMILY.	White souls.	Dwellings.	Other buildings.
Atkins, John	9	1	3
Allen, James	1	1	5
Boston, John	4	1	1
Bell, Thomas	10	1	10
Boston, James	10	1	3
Clark, James	3	2	5
Clark, John	3	1	
Collins, Benjamin	1	1	
Collins, Nicholas	4	1	2
Dade, Francis	4	1	3
Finnell, John	7	1	2
Grace, George	4	1	2
Hansford, Ben	9	1	1
Hawkins, James	5	1	7
Hawkins, Ben	7	1	6
Lee, John	9	1	1
McNeil, Patrick	6	1	5
Proctor, George	6	2	11
Petty, George	10	1	4
Porter, Abner	9	1	9
Ransdell, Sansford	1	1	2
Samuel, John	8	1	10
Sleet, Phil	4	1	6
Stocks, Thomas	4	1	5
Sylvio, Robert	9	1	2
Thompson, Samuel	5	2	2
Taliaferro, Lawrence	23	4	16
Vaughan, James	7	1	
Willis, John	6	2	7
Willis, Lewis	1	3	19
Willis, Moses	2	1	

LIST OF CATLETT CONWAY.

NAME OF HEAD OF FAMILY.	White souls.	Dwellings.	Other buildings.
Abell, Caleb	5	1	1
Abell, Ephraim	3	1	
Abell, Richard	5	1	1
Beckham, Henry	7	1	3
Bruce, Charles	9	1	9
Bradley, Benjamin	5	1	
Burrage, Edward	7	1	
Bledsoe, John	1	1	3
Bradley, Robert	6	1	
Coghill, Zachy	8	1	
Chism, George	4	1	
Cook, John	7	1	2
Chism, John	9	2	3
Cockburn, Robert	6	1	2
Dawson, John	12	1	3
Foster, Thomas	6	1	1
Falconer, George	4		
Gibson, John	2	1	2
Graves, Richard	10	1	6
Griffe, Benjamin	6	1	2
George, Catherine	6	1	2
Hughs, Francis	9		
Hilman, Joseph	9	1	1
Hunter, Sarah	1	2	5

ORANGE COUNTY—Continued.

LIST OF CATLETT CONWAY—continued.

Name of head of family.	White souls.	Dwellings.	Other buildings.
Johnson, Thomas	9	1	3
Lancastor, William	7	1	....
Mothershead, Nathaniel	4	1	2
Mothershead, Mary	6	1	2
Morrison, Thomas	6	1	1
Morrison, John	3	1	1
Martin, Benjamin	6	2	3
Morton, William	8	3	20
Pannill, William	11	1	12
Rumsey, Richard	8	1	....
Robb, James	8	1	8
Sanders, James	5	1	2
Sanders, Nathaniel	10	1	4
Straughn, John	2	1	1
Shadrack, Job	7	1	2
Summers, Thomas	6	1	3
Stubblefield, George	4	1	....
Scott, George	3	1	....
Tinder, James	11	1	....
Thornton, Daniel	5	1	....
Thornton, James	3	1	....
Wharton, George	6	1	1
Welch, Thomas	4	1	4
Weatherspoon, Susannah	6	1	....
Wharton, John	1	....	....
Watts, Aaron	6	1	....
York, John	7	1	....
Adams, John	4	1	....
Adams, Benjamin	1	1	4
Barrett, David	5	....	....
Broaddus, James	8	1	....
Conner, John	4	1	....
Coleman, James	10	1	4
Chandler, Robert	8	1	....
Collins, John	11	1	....
Conway, Catlett	9	1	8
Doling, Thomas	7	1	....
Dedman, John	8	1	....
Fisher, Nicholas	4	1	....
Fisher, William	3	....	....
Haley, Benjamin	7	1	8
Herndon, James	8	1	3
Hiatt, Stephen	6	1	....
Hiatt, Benjamin	5	1	3
Homes, John	3	1	....
Herndon, John	4	1	....
Hiatt, William	9	1	....
Hiatt, John	2	1	....
Jones, Morton	8	1	....
Lancastor, Richard	6	1	....
Lancastor, John	8	1	1
Lancastor, Robert	6	1	3
Lancastor, Robert, Junr	5	1	1
Lindsay, Adam	5	1	5
Lee, William	9	1	....
Massingberd, George	1	1	2
McNeal, Archabald	4	1	....
Mooney, William	7	1	2
Marshall, Thomas	6	1	....
Pecher, William	11	1	2
Proctor, Uriah	5	1	....
Proctor, John	9	1	2
Peirce, Francis	3	1	....
Peirce, Isaac	3	1	1
Reynolds, Joseph	5	1	....
Rice, William	1	1	3
Reynolds, William	8	1	2
Southerland, Kenneth	5	1	....
Spice, William	3	1	....
Smith, Stephen	3	1	2
Smithers, Robert	6	1	....
Thomas, Rowland	10	1	5
Taliaferro, William	2	1	10
Wright, William	8	1	3
Wright, John	8	1	1
Wright, John, Junr	2	1	2

LIST OF ANDREW SHEPHERD.

Name of head of family.	White souls.	Dwellings.	Other buildings.
Bourn, Henry	8	1	3
Bourn, William	6	1	2
Beckham, James	11	1	8
Bramham, Spencer	9	1	2
Bohan, John	5	....	....
Bryant, Thomas	7	1	2
Booth, John	9	1	....
Cartie, William	4	2	7
Clark, John	10	1	7
Campbells, Rosanna	8	1	5
Davis, Thomas	2	1	4
Dodd, John	6	1	1
George, Catherine	6	1	5
Gillett, Laurence	4	1	4
Gillett, Thomas	3	1	....
Goodlett, Adam	12	1	6
Herring, William	6	1	1
Humphreys, William	5	1	....
Jones, George	11	1	4

LIST OF ANDREW SHEPHERD—continued.

Name of head of family.	White souls.	Dwellings.	Other buildings.
Jones, Hugh	3	1	....
Jameson, Margaret	2	1	5
Jameson, William	4	1	3
Ish, Christian	5	1	4
Kendall, John	8	1	3
Lantor, Thomas	7	2	1
Morton, Richard	7	1	2
Moore, Francis	2	2	10
Moore, Lucy	11	1	2
Moore, Reuben	8	....	....
Minor, Jeremiah	10	1	3
Mallory, Uriel	9	1	10
Newman, Alexander	9	1	8
Newman, Thomas	6	1	....
Porter, Charles	16	1	17
Price, Joseph	3	1	2
Petty, James	5	....	....
Ransdell, John	8	1	1
Ransdell, William	11	1	3
Robertson's, William (Place)	....	1	1
Spencer, Joseph	11	1	8
Sleet, James	9	....	....
Shepherd, Andrew	8	1	12
Terrell, John	9	1	2
Thornton, James	9	1	1
Thornton, Daniel	13	1	2
Twisdale, William	5	....	....
Thomas, Joseph	8	1	8
Waugh, Alexander	3	1	17
Willis, John, Junr	2	....	....
Wood, Absalom	5	1	1

LIST OF WILLIAM MOORE.

Name of head of family.	White souls.	Dwellings.	Other buildings.
Burrus, Thomas	5	1	8
Tandy, Henry	13	1	9
Herndon, Zachariah	8	1	7
Atkins, John, Junr	4	1	2
Quisenberry, Aaron	8	1	7
Bell, Thomas	7	1	6
Smith, Ann	4	1	2
Page, John	5	1	1
Chiles, Malacha	3	1	....
Gaston, Uriah	7	1	2
Morton, George	9	1	7
Head, Isaac	6	....	....
Harrison, Henry	6	....	....
Burrus, Mary	9	1	2
Chandler, Jeremiah	9	1	....
Brockman, Lewis	6	1	5
Morton, Elijah	4	1	4
Terrell, William	9	2	3
Pollock, William	10	1	7
Atkins, James	6	1	2
Harris, Thomas	5	1	3
Cave, Benjamin	3	1	1
Bickers, John	10	1	4
Brockman, Samuel, Jr	9	2	4
Dear, Charles	4	1	2
Arnold, Elisha	6	1	2
Homes, Alexander	3	1	2
Woolfolk, Thomas	6	1	3
Bell, Joseph	10	1	7
Landrum, Thomas	7	1	4
Stevens, John	5	2	7
Perry, Moses	3	1	2
Lindsay, Caleb	1	1	3
Daniel, James	8	1	4
Cooper, James	13	1	1
Graves, Isaac	8	1	9
Vass, Vincent	4	1	6
Smith, James	10	1	3
Smith, Mary	2	1	3
Oaks, John	10	1	3
Oaks, Isaac	4	1	2
Henderson, John	2	1	15
Mills, Nathaniel	8	1	7
Daniel, Vivian	7	1	4
Vivian, John	2	1	6
Wright, John	7	1	3
Atkins, William	6	1	2
Atkins, James, Junr	6	1	....
Atkins, Edward	5	1	1
Edmondson, Patty	6	1	2
Bledsoe, John	5	1	4
Bowen, John	7	1	....
Bledsoe, Aaron	12	1	5
Thomas, Robert	9	1	4
Quisenberry, John	7	1	4
Quisenberry, William	6	1	2
Groom, John	6	1	5
Boling, Thornberry	3	1	1
Long, Ann	3	1	1
Manspail, Michael	7	1	....
Atkins, Benjamin	4	1	2
Bledsoe, Miller	3	1	2
Boling, John	11	1	4

LIST OF WILLIAM MOORE—continued.

Name of head of family.	White souls.	Dwellings.	Other buildings.
Nelson, James	5	1	2
Cook, Thomas	7	1	2
Bullock, Richard	11	1	1
Landrum, Reuben	9	1	5
Duncan, Joseph	8	1	6
Brockman, Samuel	4	1	15
Richards, William	2	1	4
Richards, William, Jr	9	1	3
Brockman, John	9	1	4
Brockman, William	4	....	....
Quisenberry, Aaron, Junr	4	1	4
Quisenberry, Moses	9	1	4
Williams, Jacob	10	1	4
Embree, John	3	1	7
Bradley, William	10	1	3
Bradley, Richard	3	1	2
Chiles, Fanny	6	1	4
Alcock, John	7	1	5
Atkins, John	11	1	5
Harris, Lindsay	6	1	2
Coleman, James	6	1	3
May, Thomas	8	1	....
Groom, William	11	1	3
Moore, William	8	1	16
Clayton, Henry	8	....	....
Yager, Elisha	4	....	....
Payne, William	8	1	8
Payne, Thomas	10	1	6
Payne, George	7	1	6
Lindsay, William	2	1	1
Gaines, James	6	1	5
Smith, Absalom	4	1	1
Chiles, Henry	8	1	3
Daniel, William	2	1	....
Bickers, Nicholas	4	1	1

LIST OF WILLIAM BELL.

Name of head of family.	White souls.	Dwellings.	Other buildings.
Bell, William	1	1	1
Burton, May, junr	6	2	4
Payne, John	11	1	2
Ahart, Jacob	4	1	....
Rains, Richard	4	....	....
Beasley, James, junr	4	1	1
Chapman, Joseph	4	1	1
Cofer, James	12	....	....
Stapp, Joshua	9	1	2
Carril, John	6	1	2
Head, Benjamin	6	1	3
Burton, May	4	2	4
Tomlinson, John	4	....	....
Brooke, John	...	2	2
Snell, John, junr	11	1	3
Stapp, Achilles	4	1	....
Golding, Robert	9	1	1
Estes, William	10	2	12
Burton, William	2	1	1
Burton, James	5	1	1
Davis, Joseph	9	1	2
Gully, Enoch	4	1	....
Gully, Richard	4	....	....
Davis, Matthew	2	1	3
Rucker, Peter	4	1	2
Beasley, James	4	1	3
Bruce, Mordecai	4	....	....
Bruce, David	7	1	1
Marshall, Merryman	6	....	....
Stodghill, Joel	5	....	....
Night, Barnard	1	....	....
Beadles, Dilly	2	1	5
King, Sabret	1	....	....
Oliver, Tabitha	4	1	....
Dohony, Thomas	10	1	5
Wayt, James	12	1	3
Dohony, James	6	1	....
Sanford, Robert	9	1	1
Herring, Thomas	7	1	2
Lucas, William, junr	5	....	....
Connoly, James	7	1	2
Ballard, Marman	6	1	..
Ballard, Philip	5	1	1
Ballard, Philip, junr	2	1	....
Head, Benjamin, junr	2	1	....
Burton, John	8	2	1
Hunton, John	1	1	2
Ogg, John	4	1	6
Stapp, Thomas	4	1	1
Cox, Sarah	7	1	10
Rogers, John	8	1	5
Golding, William	7	1	13
Rogers, William	9	1	2
Mallory, Nathan	10	1	4
Meadows, Francis	6	....	2
Pritt, Edward	7	1	2
James, Mildred	3	1	2
Buckner, William	11	1	5
Pearson, Robert	5	1	2

LIST OF JAMES MADISON.

Name of head of family.	White souls.	Dwellings.	Other buildings.
Bell, Mary	8	2	10
Bowes, John	5	....	....
Adkins, John	4	....	....
Bickers, Joseph	10	1	2
Burnley, Garland	5	1	7
Beale, William	1	1	14
Brown, Anne	6	1	....
Brown, William	5	2	2
Baylor, John	....	3	19
Boston, Youill	7	....	....
Chew, Martha	3	1	2
Coleman, Thomas	9	1	6
Edwards, William	8	1	2
Finnell, Thomas	7	....	2
Clark, Joseph	7	....	....
Coleman, James	4	....	....
Goodin, John	2	....	1
Gilbert, Thomas	4	....	....
Graves, John	2	1	3
Graves, Samuel	3	1	4
Hancock, William	6	1	....
Ingram, William	3	....	....
Leathers, John	13	1	2
Mountague, John	10	1	6
Mozingo, Spence	7	....	2
Mallory, Thomas	13	1	3
Madison, James	8	4	32
Newman, George	5	....	....
Newman, William	9	....	....
Noel, John	4	1	....
Porter, Benjamin	4	1	11
Smith, Jeremiah	8	1	2
Sutton, William	9	1	5
Sanford, Pierce	9	2	6
Stevenson, Thomas	10	1	6
Taylor, George	....	1	7
Taylor, Erasmus	7	1	11
Taylor, Charles	4	1	10
Taylor, James	7	1	7
Taylor, Hubbard	4	2	21
Terrill, Robert	3	3	6
Taliaferro, Francis	5	1	15
Taliaferro, Hay	2	1	13
Willis, Lewis	5	1	5
Winslow, Benjamin	9	1	8
Winslow, Harry	5	1	5
Wood, Joseph	3	1	4
Watson, Samuel	8	1	2

LIST OF ZACH BURNLEY.

Name of head of family.	White souls.	Dwellings.	Other buildings.
Fortson, Thomas	9	1	1
Key, Simon	9	1	....
McClemorick, Robert	7	1	....
Beadles, John	5	1	....
Breeding, Abner	9	1	....
Miller, Robert	10	1	3
Plunkett, Jesse	8	1	2
Collins, William	8	1	1
Eddins, Joseph	3	1	4
Crowe, Daniel	6	1	....
Shifflett, Elizabeth	5	1	....
Powell, Thomas	9	1	....
Duncomb, James	9	1	....
Furnish, Samuel	6	1	....
Kalker, Charles	7	1	....
Pickett, Mace	5	1	1
Begils, Joel	2	1	....
Niting, Thomas	5	1	....
Page, John	7	1	2
Bush, James	5	1	....
Kendal, John	7	1	1
Bryant, Edward	5	1	....
Furnish, Eliza	3	1	....
Walker, Thomas	7	1	....
Taylor, William	2	1	....
Walker, Thomas, jur	2	1	....
Powell, Benjamin	7	1	....
Powell, Frank	8	1	....
Powell, Mary	5	1	....
Thirman, Elisha	3	1	....
Fitchgaritt, Thos	12	1	....
Rogers, Ann	5	1	....
Taylor, James (son of Charles)	8	1	....
Taylor, Charles	9	....	....
Cocar, Jacob	8	1	....
Taylor, James	6	1	....
Anderson, Jacob	1	....	....
Samson, John	5	1	....
Wornor, John	11	1	....
Simson, James	10	1	2
Thornton, George	6	1	1
White, John	4	1	4
White, Thomas	8	1	....
Scott, William	2	1	2
Hawkins, Jehu	6	1	3
Foster, Anthony	10	1	....

ORANGE COUNTY—Continued.

NAME OF HEAD OF FAMILY.	White souls.	Dwellings.	Other buildings.
LIST OF ZACH BURNLEY—continued.			
Head, James	5	2	4
Furnish, Jacob	3	1	....
Jones, William	7	1	....
Coopwood, Ben	5	1	....
Page, John, Junr	3	1	....
LIST OF JOHNY SCOTT.			
Buckner, Jane	5	1	1
Taylor, Zachary	5	1	9
Deering, Robert	12	1	....
Deering, Thomas	5	1	....
Lee, John	10	1	8
Douglass, John	7	1	10

NAME OF HEAD OF FAMILY.	White souls.	Dwellings.	Other buildings.
LIST OF JOHNY SCOTT—continued.			
Maury, Walker	....	2	8
Tomlinson, William	6	1	....
Taylor, Alexander	8	1	2
Smith, Samuel	9	2	3
Mallory, Roger	11	1	2
Grymes, Ludwell	6	1	7
White, Jonathan	5	1	2
Bush, Francis	7	1	2
Gaines, Richard	3	1	2
Darnold, Abraham	7	1	4
Davis, Joseph	8	1	3
Boswell, John	16	2	16
Webb, Wm Crittendon	9	1	12
Marr, Alexander	8	1	4

NAME OF HEAD OF FAMILY.	White souls.	Dwellings.	Other buildings.
LIST OF JOHNY SCOTT—continued.			
Davis, Jonathan	8	1	3
Jones, Thomas	10	1	14
Young, William	7	1	8
Young, John	6	1	4
Willis, John	....	1	3
Craig, Elijah	7	1	6
Burton, Edmond	6	1	....
Newman, James	9	1	9
Cowherd, Jonathon	9	1	6
Merry, Prettyman	11	1	6
Hamilton, John Tayloe	8	1	10
Fleet, Henry	7	1	8
Bell, John	5	1	7
Daniel, John	2	2	4

NAME OF HEAD OF FAMILY.	White souls.	Dwellings.	Other buildings.
LIST OF JOHNY SCOTT—continued.			
Madison, Ambrose	4	1	7
Martin, Ann	1	1	4
Eve, Ann	6	1	....
Hawkins, John	7	1	3
Eastin, Elizabeth	5	1	4
Eastin, John	1	1	2
Hill, David	12	1	3
Morriss, John	7	1	2
Joseph, Moses	7	1	2
Clasby, David	12	1	4
Smith, Rice	3	1	5
Scott, Johnny	4	1	7
Lisk, Martin	6	1	....

PITTSYLVANIA COUNTY.

NAME OF HEAD OF FAMILY.	White souls.	Dwellings.	Other buildings.
Johnson, John	3	1	4
Todd, Richd	4	1	3
Varon, William	5	1	2
Rowland, Simon	5	1	4
Telonurs, Edward	7	1	4
George, John	10	1	6
Dunning, William	4	1	7
Watlington, John	5	1	12
Banott, John, jr	8	1	2
Tunstall, Thomas, jr	3	1	4
Tunstall, Thomas	4	1	8
Allen, William, jr	7	1	3
Banott, Richard	5	1	1
Banott, John	2	1	1
Lester, William	5	....	....
George, James	5	1	6
Rowland, Jesse	5	1	....
Stone, Joshua	9	1	6
Womack, William	....	1	6
Willard, Beaverly	7	....	....
Sanders, Daniel	7	1	1
Doss, William	10	1	5
Nowling, James	1	....	....
Short, Joshua	5	1	4
Lattamore, Samuel	8	1	7
Ham, Sarah	3	1	3
Seph, Thomas	2	....	....
Jones, William	2	1	....
Robinson, Samuel	11	1	5
Mitchell, Michael	2	1	....
Coody, Redmon	2	....	....
Terrell, Richard	6	....	....
Redmon, John	4	....	....
Childress, Moses	8	1	....
Short, Jael	8	1	2
Crinshaw, Nathaniel	....	1	8
Colley, Bartlett	6	....	....
Craddock, John	8	1	6
Farris, Joseph, Senr	10	1	2
Anderson, Richard	8	1	6
Douglass, John	5	....	....
Clark, Joseph	5	1	1
Perkins, John	5	1	1
Martin, Joseph	7	1	2
Mchaney, Cornelius	9	1	10
Davis, Thomas	4	1	4
Jenkins, Daniel	12	1	1
Mitchell, James	8	1	6
Lankfand, Benjamin	9	1	6
Vaughan, Thomas	4	1	3
Vaughan, William	3	1	2
Morgan, Haynes	4	1	5
Bettenton, William	11	1	4
Allen, George	6	1	4
Allen, William	5	1	6
Ballinger, John	3	1	2
Ballinger, Benjamin	3	1	2
Hall, Moses	6	1	3
Henderson, James	3	1	2
Snider, Henny	11	1	4
Keezee, Charles	10	1	5
Burkley, John	1	1	7
Anderson, James	5	1	4
Dove, Joseph	5	1	....
Hodges, Jesse	4	1	2
Keezee, Jeremiah	6	1	4
Burkley, James	5	1	9
Ramey, Presley	4	1	....
Chisinhall, John	4	....	....
Ramey, Absalom	3	1	3
Alexander, William	6	1	3
Wire, John	5	1	2
Wire,, Bazalich	4	1	4
Farguson, Joseph	12	....	2
Fearn, Thomas	2	1	6
Binian, Wm., jr	3	1	3
Payne, Robert	10	1	6
Warsham, John	4	1	8

NAME OF HEAD OF FAMILY.	White souls.	Dwellings.	Other buildings.
Wynne, Matthew	6	2	3
Travers, Wm	14	1	6
Stilwell, Jacob, jr	3	1	3
Bynum, Samuel	9	1	3
McLane, John	8	....	2
Spoolman, Frederick	5	1	2
Rose, Francis	3	....	1
Sparks, Matthew	5	....	1
Whitley, Richd	4	....	1
Ardin, Richard	7	....	2
Duncan, William	12	....	3
Stone, John, Senr	3	....	1
Lay, David, Junr	7	1	....
Scott, Bardale	5	....	1
Vandavour, John	6	....	1
McDaniel, James	13	1	3
Lay, David, Senr	12	1	2
Lay, John, jr	8	....	3
Tombling, Joseph	9	....	3
Billings, Easten	7	....	2
Lumkins, Joseph	8	1	2
Lumkins, George	8	1	2
Norton, Nelley	6	....	1
Norton, Jacob	5	....	1
Williamson, Thomas	3	....	1
Artin, William, Jur	11	1	3
Bolling, John	7	....	....
May, John	6	....	2
Garrott, Henry	4	....	1
Southerland, George, Senr	7	1	3
Wilson, John	12	1	11
Connar, William	7	....	2
Mickleberry, Henry	11	1	3
Coleman, William	11	....	2
O'Daniel, Michael	5	....	2
Wynne, Robert	11	1	2
Benion, William, Senr	4	1	3
Ramsey, James	9	....	1
Tombling, Jasper	4	....	2
Wilson, Peter	7	1	5
Wright, Thomas	6	....	1
Yates, Elizabeth	3	1	4
Pistole, Thomas	7	1	2
Warsham, Thomas	4	....	3
Southerland, Thomas	2	....	2
Pistole, Abraham	3	....	1
Pistole, Charles	3	....	1
Falling, Edmund	10	1	2
Dix, Larkin	7	....	3
Wynne, Matthew	5	....	....
Barry, John	5	....	2
Marthaley, William	6	....	2
Witcher, William	5	2	15
Witcher, John	4	....	1
Witcher, William, jr	3	....	1
Taylor, John	3	....	1
Mitchell, James	8	1	2
Witcher, James	5	....	1
Hudson, John P	5	....	1
Polley, David	1	1	1
Standley, Isaac	3	....	2
Standley, Joseph	3	....	1
Adams, Nathaniel	7	1	....
Henson, William	5	....	2
Thompson, William	8	1	3
Dalton Timothy	4	....	....
Dalton, Samuel	5	....	....
Dalton, John	7	....	....
Bennett, Thomas	9	1	3
Bennett, Richard	7	1	3
Hensley, John	1	....	2
Marlow, George	6	....	1
Polley, David, jr	1	....	....
Herndon, George	6	2	38
Robinson, Joseph	8	1	2
Smith, William	7	....	2
Hudson, John	12	....	1
Smith, William	4	....	4

NAME OF HEAD OF FAMILY.	White souls.	Dwellings.	Other buildings.
Hensley, Benjamin	7	....	....
Atkins, William	5	....	1
Cook, Harmon	6	2	4
Atkins, Jesse	6	1	1
Bennett, James	6	....	2
Cook, John	5	....	....
Tarrants, Benjamin	10	1	4
Snow, Mark	2	....	1
Wright, John	1	....	....
Razor, Paul	6	....	2
Turley, John, jr	3	....	....
Dalton, James	9	1	2
Goad, Charles	7	1	2
Croff, Henry	7	....	1
Young, Archd	4	....	2
Turley, John, Senr	4	....	2
Goad, Wm	10	....	2
Hammack, John	3	....	1
Goad, John	4	....	1
Young, Wm	8	....	8
Lovell, Daniel	7	1	8
Nowling, Bryant W	14	1	3
Barger, Jacob	7	1	3
Razar, Abraham	2	....	1
Laws, Joseph	6	1	1
Parker, Wm	8	1	3
Young, Melton	1	....	1
Witcher, Daniel	10	....	2
Dalton, David	9	....	1
Delosher, Leanard	6	....	2
Vaughan, Hundley	7	....	2
Clarke, Frances	11	1	4
Razar, Anthony	8	....	....
Phillips, Jonathan	9	1	2
Downing, James	4	....	3
Swiney, Moses	6	....	....
Smith, Booker	2	1	10
Watson, John	10	1	3
Townsend, Thomas	8	....	1
Wade, Peyton	2	....	2
Ward, Jeremiah	10	....	....
Kreek, Killian	10	....	4
Wheale, Nottley	6	....	4
Hodges, Nephe	4	1	3
Watson, Wm	9	....	1
Watson, John	3	1	2
Hankins, Daniel	1	2	2
Morton, Joseph	12	3	2
Alsup, John	7	....	....
Riger, Jacob	8	....	2
Gibson, Thomas	1	....	....
Austin, Joseph	12	1	1
Conington, Edward	8	1	....
Brewer, James	5	1	1
Kendrick, Thomas	4	1	....
Rawlins, Henry	6	1	....
Thomas, Jonathan	9	1	....
Elliott, William	5	1	....
Harget, Thomas	3	....	....
Bleakley, James	8	1	....
Bleakley, John	3	1	....
Prenett, Richd	7	1	....
Biggers, James	8	1	....
Brown, John	1	....	....
Clift, Thomas	11	1	....
Littrell, Daniel	3	....	....
Johns, Thomas	6	1	....
Oliver, Wm	9	1	....
McGeehee, James	2	1	....
Mattaney, Richd	4	1	....
Goad, Thomas	3	1	....
Hankins, William	10	1	....
Bayes, William	5	1	....
Wells, Matthew	4	1	1
Dalton, James	3	1	....
Pearson, John	5	1	....
Hankins, Dinnah	4	1	....
Fuller, Arthur	6	2	....

NAME OF HEAD OF FAMILY.	White souls.	Dwellings.	Other buildings.
Warren, John	10	1	....
Fuller, Brittin	3	1	....
Johnson, Daniel	8	1	....
Lawrance, Henry	4	1	....
Smith, John	3	1	....
Cooley, Jacob	7	1	....
Vincent, William	1	1	....
Hill, Rozell	4	1	....
Fuller, Zachariah	5	1	....
Ross, David	4	1	....
Lang, John	3	1	....
Lang, Edward	12	1	2
Warren, Henry	8	1	....
Biswell, John	6	1	2
Wallis, Richd	9	1	....
Dyer, William	6	....	....
Barr, David	3	1	....
Dyer, Isaac	3	1	....
Roan, Anne	5	1	....
Beck, Wm	8	1	....
Devin, Wm	6	1	....
Tuggle, Lodowick	11	1	7
Smith, George	4	....	3
Jefferson, Peter F	13	1	9
Gilbert, Michael	7	....	5
Justice, William	10	1	6
Henry, Francis	6	1	6
King, Joseph	9	....	4
Bobbett, John	7	1	3
Ramsey, Thomas	12	1	3
Atkins, Henry	2	....	2
Ball, John	11	....	5
Whiteworth, John	9	....	....
Campbell, John	5	1	3
Terry, Thomas, Senr	8	1	10
Terry, Thomas, jr	3	....	....
Dalton, Solomon	3	....	....
Irvin, Wm	1	1	5
Minzie, John	7	....	....
Leprad, Benjamin	7	....	7
Hundley, Caleb	7	1	4
Breeding, John	10	1	3
Black, Thomas	10	1	11
Ramsey, Thomas, jr	3	....	3
Burdett, Humphrey	7	....	3
Bell, James	5	....	....
Dear, Joseph	3	....	1
Blair, Wm	8	....	3
Calland, Samuel	....	1	7
Lucas, Wm	7	....	....
Dyer, Joseph	6	....	2
Dyer, George	6	....	3
Peak, William	8	....	2
Wright, James	3	....	....
Kimings, James	7	....	....
Pearson, Sherwood	8	....	6
Shockley, James	2	....	3
Martin, Isaac	7	1	2
Moody, Blanks	7	1	3
Lester, Thomas	11	1	5
Vaughan, John	9	1	4
Vaughan, Thomas, jr	5	1	2
Vaughan, Thomas	4	1	2
Alford, William	....	....	4
Collins, Thomas	4	1	1
Ward, John, jr	1	1	5
Doe, Leonard	6	....	....
Hunt, Gilbert	1	1	3
Parriott, Curties	5	1	3
Fieldes, Anne	3	....	....
Terrell, Benjamin	5	1	....
Bone, Henry	2	....	....
Clements, Isaac	9	1	5
Vest, Wm	8	....	1
East, Thomas	8	1	4
East, John	3	....	1
Pattey, Jesse	12	2	4
Bruce, Daniel	2	....	....

NAME OF HEAD OF FAMILY.	White souls.	Dwellings.	Other buildings.	NAME OF HEAD OF FAMILY.	White souls.	Dwellings.	Other buildings.	NAME OF HEAD OF FAMILY.	White souls.	Dwellings.	Other buildings.	NAME OF HEAD OF FAMILY.	White souls.	Dwellings.	Other buildings.
Powell, Keziah	2			Westbrook, Henry	6		1	McGuffand, Nathl	4		5	Hill, Thomas	11	1	
Bruce, Robert	11	1	11	Ragsdale, Frederick	3		1	Church, Jonathan	10		7	Hill, Joseph	2		1
Doss, James	5	1	4	Wright, George	2		1	Sparks, Thomas	6		2	Ashlock, Maryann	6		1
Doss, James, jr	7		2	Price, Thomas	10		1	Perkins, Constant	3	2	11	Owen, Joshua	11		1
Vest, William	2			Orr, Robert	9	1		Miller, Peter	2			Slayton, William	4		1
Adams, Charles L	3	1	5	Lackey, Thomas	7	1		Gains, Edwd	9		2	Burch, John	4	1	1
Foster, Benja	1			Martin, John	8	1		Asher, Nathan	8		4	Ragsland, Gedeon	10	1	4
West, Joseph	7	1	3	Summers, William	8		1	Elliott, Jonathan	6			Madding, John	9		1
West, George	5	1	2	Weatherford, John	8		1	Gamman, Harris	5		6	Clapton, Robert	4	1	2
West, Owen	3	1		Dyer, John	10	1	1	Nelson, John	10		4	Mann, Jesse	4	1	
West, Joseph, jr	4	1		Emmerson, John	8		1	Still, John	7		6	Dodson, Fortune	3		1
Templeton, Robert	7	1	2	Slayton, James	3		1	quinn, Joseph	10		2	Pond, John	6		1
Kelley, John	4	1	2	Johnson, James	8	1	3	Price, Wm	1	1	6	Sherley, Elisha	6		1
Webb, Edmd	4	1	2	Shelton, Armstead	9		1	Oakes, Charles	5		4	Slayton, Daniel	7		1
Ballinger, Benjamin	3	1		Parks, John	12	1	2	Weatherford, Harding	5		1	Colley, James	5		1
Patrick, John F.	8	1	12	Brim, Elijah	3		1	Clark, Joseph	1			Walker, Samuel	2		1
Gilbert, Perton	6	1	3	Stratton, William	2		1	Pulliam, Drury	6		3	Hanks, Moses	7	1	
Pemberton, John	5	1	1	Echolls, Jeremiah	3		1	Davis, John	8		2	Hill, Reubin	2		1
Pemberton, Joseph	5	1	1	Duncan, Jesse	3		2	Davis, Wm	8		4	Bennett, John	6		1
Pemberton, Wm	4	1	1	Prosize, George	6		2	Davis, Geo	8		4	Lee, Alexr	5		1
Luck, Sarah	7	2	2	Beckles, Edmund	9		1	Rigg, Peter	3			Bennett, Thomas	5		1
Baber, James	2	1		Adams, Absalom	7	1		Pyatt, Joseph	3		1	McDaniel, Rhoderick	5		1
Johnson, David	6	1	1	Nuckles, Josiah	2		1	Browner, Wm	4		2	Dodson, David	9	1	1
Check, Wm	9	1	3	Burton, Elijah	8		1	Scott, John	3			Gardner, Heath	5		1
Hubbard, Elizabeth	8	1	3	Prenett, Joseph	5		1	Duncan, John	3		1	Walters, Elijah	5		1
Burton, Edward	4		3	Holder, Susanna	4		1	Harris, Geo. Fuller	10	1	4	Walters, Robert	8	1	1
Check, Richd	4		1	Terry, Wm	9		1	Bullington, Robert	6	1	5	Walters, Robert, jr	7		1
Mchaney, Terry	4			Williams, Joseph T.	5		1	Lansford, Isham	6	1	5	Walters, Wm	7		1
Kearsey, Thomas	6		2	Collier, John	7	1	3	Lansford, Henry	6		5	Madding, Wm	9		2
Brown, Henry	8		4	Keezee, Jesse	7	1	2	Mitchell, Wm	6		2	McMenday, James	9	1	1
Sanders, Daniel	1			Bennett, Micajah	6	1		Vance, Clement	1		1	Harris, John	7		1
Hunt, David	3	1	8	Green, William	5			Wilson, Ignatious	7		5	Mading, Champness	2		1
Morris, Ambrose	9	1	4	Parker, John	9	1	1	Jones, George	6		1	Herring, Wm	8	1	1
Dejarnett, George	2			Smith, Ralph	2	1	13	Farrar, Richd	6		4	Tannar, Matthew	7	1	1
Kendrick, Obediah	3	1	5	Smith, William	5	1	2	Shares, David	4		2	Tanner, Matthew, jr	4		1
Kendrick, Nathl	3	1	5	Dalton, John	10	1	9	Norton, Ellenor	8		5	Hendrick, John H.	9		3
Thurman, Richd	10	1	5	Bennett, William	5	1	1	Norton, Wilson	1			Dickerson, Obediah	6		1
Muse, John	3	1	5	Radford, Jonathan	10		1	Roberson, Thomas	6		3	Terry, Henry	5		
Davis, Sarah	1	1	2	Clements, Susannah	3	1	11	Jenkins, Philip	6	1	4	Terry, David	11	1	4
Walker, Susannah	4			Abston, Joshua	7	1	7	Oakes, Wm	7		3	McLotherlin, Charles	6		1
Doss, John	7	1	1	Farmer, Thomas	9	1	2	Oakes, James	9		5	Terry, Thomas	3		1
Gaves, John	7		2	Abston, John	1			Brimm, Richd	6			Chaney, Joseph	2		1
Meade, James	5	1	1	Mullings, Michael	3			Cummins, Jonathan	10		1	Adkins, John	9		1
Adams, Elkannah	6	1	1	Evens, William	9	1	7	Hampton, Wm	2			Chaney, Jacob	9		1
Walsond, Benjamin	6	1	4	Brown, Robert	3		1	Owen, John	6	2	2	Dodson, Joshua	7		1
Davis, William	8	1	1	Brown, James	5		1	Hampton, John	6			Slate, Samuel	13		2
Bradley, Daniel	2		1	Thurman, Allen	3			Conn, John	1		2	Davis, Thomas	5		
Adams, John, jr	7	1		Baber, Wm	10	1	4	Harris, Joseph	7		2	Allen, James	5		
Pigg, Wm	8			Patterson, Littleberry	11	1	7	Southerland, Wm	7		2	Simpson, Jeremiah	4		1
Pendleton, Philip	10	1		Allen, David	6	1	2	Brown, John	7		2	Lewis, Charles	6		3
Voding, Burrell	10	1		Handy, John	3			Watkins, Isaiah	9		6	Simpson, Rachael	2		1
Adams, Morning	6	1	4	Strange, John	6		1	Dodson, Daniel	9		4	Simpson, Avassnus	3		2
Adams, Allen	6	1	1	Smith, Francis	7		3	Sullivant, Daniel	5		2	Hamlin, Wm	12		2
Mabery, Braxton	6	1	1	Walding, John	6	1	4	Ware, John	1		7	Barrott, Peter	4		
Meade, Mary	2		1	Walding, Richard	4	2	1	Lewis, Samuel	6		4	Anderson, Matthew	3		1
Ragsdale, John	7	1		Shockley, Thomas	5		1	Brawner, John	5		1	Hardey, Wm	8		1
Carter, Jesse	8	1	1	Ward, Henry		1	5	Harris, David	9		3	Hardey, Benja	11		2
Chambers, Thomas	9		1	Bennett, Thomas	8		2	Briscoe, John	6	1	8	Holloway, James	10		2
Nelson, Basdale	7		1	Ward, William	6	1	6	Southerland, Jesse	9		2	Flipping, Joseph	5	1	2
Nelson, Wm	3		1	Snow, Thomas	4			Warren, Edward	7	1	5	Bennett, Wm	5		1
Nelson, James	4		1	Harrison, William	10	1	13	Nance, Wm	3			Russell, Wm	11		2
Ricketts, Wm	7		1	Perkins, Col Peter	13	1	3	Inglish, Wm	3			Russell, Moses	3		1
Hutchings, Ann	6		1	Perkins, Hardin	5	1	3	Cornwall, Stephen	3		4	Wilson, John	11		2
Hutchings, Christopher	4	1	3	Thornton, Presley	12		4	Brown, Samuel	6		1	Murrah, Nathaniel	8		2
Chattin, John	9		1	Vinceent, Moses	4		5	Parker, Elijah	4			Walters, Thomas	8	1	1
Short, Wm	9	1	2	Sutton, Wm	7		4	Oneale, Hugh	2		1	Terry, John	3		3
Stokes, Silvanus	6	1	2	McMillian, John	6		1	Trayham, Nehemiah	10		3	Walker, Catherine	4	1	5
Stokes, Allen	2		1	Tucker, Lewes	5		4	Stone Street, Butler	5		3	Shaw, Thomas	9	1	1
Hall, Henry	6		1	Gwyne, Homes	7		4	White, Jeremiah	10	2	5	Linthicum, Thomas	4	1	1
Prosize, Wm	8		1	Wadlow, Wm	2		6	Wisdom, Francis	3	1	6	Linthicum, Thomas, jr	7		2
Pigg, Ann	2	1	7	Watson, Wm	5		3	Williams, Robert	11	2	10	Duff, Laurance	4		1
Pigg, Hezekiah	7	1	4	Barnard, Zadock	7		3	Kirby, John	4		3	Lawless, Michael	3		1
Hutchings, Moses	4		1	Adams, Sylvester	7	1	6	Kirby, Francis	5		3	Hendrick, Micah	3		1
Richards, Joseph	10	1	1	Adams, George	6	1	3	Burgess, Thomas	10		3	Clarke, Wm	2	1	1
Campbell, Abraham	11	1	1	Watson, Nathan	8		7	Terry, Ben	11	1	3	Crane, James	7		1
Campbell, Henry	3		1	Still, Tho	7		6	Stratton, Thomas	3		3	Morton, Joseph	8	1	4
Ragsdale, Daniel	5		1	Elliott, Jonathan	8	1	1	Stratton, Ben	3		1	Shields, Samuel	9	1	1
Adams, Thomas	5		1	Burton, Nancy	5		5	Hodnett, Mary	8		3	Grisham, Thomas	7		1
Denney, John	5		1	Barkshere, Henry	5			Wright, John	3		3	Shields, William	9	1	1
Shoemaker, Linsey	9	1		Morton, John	10		3	Hardin, Henry	5		1	Burnett, Henry	7	3	6
Willis, Wm	7	1	3	Scott, Simon	10		1	Davison, Abraham	5		1	McDaniel, Randolph	3		2
Hughes, Joseph	6		1	Cahal, Edwd	10		3	Shelton, George	3		1	Cuningham, Thomas	9	1	2
Davis, John	7		1	Conn, Jos	7	1	20	Shelton, Mark	7		1	Sparks, Matthew	11		1
Easley, Pirant	3	1	1	Elliott, James	5		3	Handey, George	4		4	Baggesly, John	9	1	1
Allen, John	5	1		Merricks, John	8	1	7	Handey, George, jr	7		3	Harris, John	3		1
Moyers, George	10	1		Dean, Jacob	9	1	4	Holder, Daniel	4		2	Fulton, John	4	2	2
Carter, Thomas (the Elder)	11		2	Perkins, Nicholas	10	2	6	Lewis, Charles, jr	3		1	Frezel, Nathan	8		1
Allen, Welcom	3		1	Smith, Capt Tho	3	1	8	Kelley, Hugh	5	1	2	Cuningham, Joseph	9	1	1
Meade, Thomas	3		1	Poor, Adam	10		2	Walker, Wm	3	1	1	Sheilds, Thomas	2	1	2
Easley, Wm	13	1		Finn, Richard	7		1	Creel, John	9	1	6	Dear, George	5		1
Welch, Joshua	9	1	1	Watts, Richd	11		2	Hughes, Rebecke	11		2	Roberson, John	4		1
Adams, John, Senr	5	1	6	Norton, Nehemiah	6	1	3	Chelton, John	5		2	Sparks, Martha	1		1
Parks, William	4		1	Kennett, Geo	2		1	Madding, Thomas	6		2	Smith, Martha	10	1	2
Richards, Joseph	4			Norton, Jacob	5		2	Donelson, James	6	1	1	Garner, James	6	1	3
Lancy, William	7		1	Norton, Thomas	8		3	Morris, Samuel	8	1	1	Read, Wm	8		1
Watson, Thomas	8	1	2	Roberson, James	9		2	Ingrum, Wm	7		2	Sheilds, Joseph	6	1	3
Watson, John	3		1	White, Benjamin	4	1	2	Dodson, Wm	5		1	Burnett, Gilbert	5		3
Jones, Elisha	3		1	Prewett, John	7	1	3	Dodson, Rawley	3		1	Deason, Enock	6		
Hardy, Thomas	10	1	3	Cook, Edwd	7		2	Dodson, Jesse	8		1	Cox, James	7		2
Warsham, Jeremiah	9		1	Hammonds, Edwin	6		2	Chelton, Thomas	6	1	2	Burnett, James	9		2
Ferguson, Josiah	5		1	Williams, Charles	7		4	Chelton, Wm	5	1	1	Shackleford, Henry	3		1

PITTSYLVANIA COUNTY—Continued.

NAME OF HEAD OF FAMILY.	White souls.	Dwellings.	Other buildings.
Boaz, Thomas	10	1	4
Shields, John	9	1	3
Alsup, Joseph	5	....	3
Boaz, Shadrick	5	1	2
Boaz, James	4	1	3
Cox, James	5	1	1
Denton, James	7	....	2
Robinson, Wm	7	....	1
McCollough, Barnett	7	....	2
Mosley, Samuel	4	1	2
Nash, Arthur	4	....	2
Hewlett, Martin	4	....	2
Fulton, James	7	1	3
Shields, John	4	....	1
Young, George	5	1	1
Young, James	8	....	1
McMillian, Stephen	6	....	1
McMillian, Joseph	2	....	....
McMillian, Abraham	5	....	....
Cunay, James	7	....	....
Young, John	6	1	2
Cunay, John	3	....	....
Nash, John	10	....	2
Nash, Jebel	4	....	2
Grooms, Zachariah	7	1	1
Sparks, Thomas	3	....	1
Williams, Thomas	4	....	1
Sparks, Leand	4	....	1
Roberson, Jesse	8	1	5
Megehee, Matthew	4	....	1
Douglass, Thomas	8	....	1
Popejoy, Edward	8	....	1
Cantrill, Joshua	6	1	1
Winsbish, John	8	1	18
Jones, Thomas	5	2	5
McDaniel, Clement	5	2	5
Baker, James	4	....	5
Blanks, Henry	6	1	3
Brooks, Samuel	9	....	2
Watkins, John	5	1	2
Coleman, Stephen	12	3	4
Watkins, Ben	4	....	1
James, Thomas	10	....	4
Worthy, Thomas	1	....	6
Mayes, Mattox	4	....	3
Mayes, Margeret	7	....	1
Walrond, William	9	3	3
Stewart, John	5	....	3
Stewart, Martha	9	2	3
Nash, John	8	....	2
Johnson, Archd	9	1	3
Brown, John	4	1	4
Walker, John	3	....	3
Barksdale, Hickerson	4	....	4
Barksdale, Beaverley	5	2	3
Gray, James	5	1	5
Mottley, Daniel	4	1	6
Yates, John	4	1	1
Walker, Charles	8	....	3
Ryburn, William	7	....	4
Irby, John	3	1	5
Owen, John	9	....	4
Neal, Stephen	3	1	7
Brawner, Benja	5	1	6
Bayne, Richd	4	2	5
Terry, Joseph	9	2	5

NAME OF HEAD OF FAMILY.	White souls.	Dwellings.	Other buildings.
Crafford, David	3	....	1
Ellington, Enoch Ward	4	1	1
Ellington, Jeremiah	....	....	....
Payne, Reuben	7	1	6
Payne, Edmd	1	....	3
Fitzgarald, Edmd	6	....	4
Payne, Philemon	1	1	....
Jones, William	6	1	3
Hutchinson, Walter	3	....	....
Right, James	3	....	....
Ford, Richd	9	....	3
Hammonds, John	5	....	3
Hammonds, George	3	....	1
Buckley, John	....	....	2
Hopwood, William	5	....	4
Bucknall, Francis	2	....	2
Farthing, Richard	10	2	4
Griffeth, William	4	1	1
Bates, Daniel	2	....	1
Blackburn, James	4	....	2
Hames, Wm	8	....	6
Yates, Stephen	9	1	5
Hammack, John	5	....	....
Parsons, John	6	....	2
Pickrel, Henry	4	....	4
Neal, John	3	....	2
Taylor, James	10	1	2
Medcalf, Joseph	5	....	4
Cammeron, Uriah	8	....	....
Hoskins, Thomas	8	2	4
Medcalf, John	3	....	2
Ivey, Francis	5	1	3
Burks, James	7	1	3
Shelton, Spencer	8	....	1
Roach, Gedeon	5	1	2
Parsons, Saml	3	1	4
Boatman, Robert	3	....	1
Roach, Thomas	3	....	....
Shelton, Ben	8	1	2
Pace, Williamson	2	....	....
Pace, Spencer	3	....	....
Parsons, Joseph	9	1	5
Adams, Nathan	8	....	2
Taylor, James	9	1	4
Thacker, Jos	8	....	2
Griffeth, Jonathan	4	....	1
Murphey, George	7	....	2
Willis, Major	3	....	5
Hodges, John	4	2	5
Hendrick, Obediah	5	....	2
Caldwell, Seth	7	....	1
Portor, William	6	....	1
Mottley, Joseph	8	3	5
Kay, Henry	3	1	1
Burton, James	10	1	....
Burton, John	1	....	....
Burton, William	4	....	2
Parsons, William	4	....	4
Hall, John	3	....	2
Thacker, Nathan	8	....	5
Tanner, Thomas	2	....	4
Tanner, David	4	1	4
Lackey, Alexander	3	....	2
Parish, Abraham	3	1	5
Shelton, Crispin	3	1	17
Shelton, Abraham	12	1	13

NAME OF HEAD OF FAMILY.	White souls.	Dwellings.	Other buildings.
Shelton, Vincent	6	1	5
Bruce, James	3	1	5
Nicholes, Jacob	11	1	2
Brown, James	7	....	3
Crenshaw, Joseph	4	1	4
Payne, William	8	1	5
Lewis, Zachariah	3	....	2
Goodman, William	6	....	6
Moore, Thomas	7	....	2
Thompson, John	3	....	5
Willis, Sterling	4	....	4
Keatt, John	8	1	4
Barber, David	10	....	1
Shelton, Beaverly	7	1	6
Willis, Sherwood	6	....	1
Burton, William	7	....	1
Lewis, Charles, jr	3	1	3
Hust, Moses	11	....	8
Musteen, Jesse	9	1	3
Mayes, Joseph	10	....	2
King, James	9	....	2
Mitchell, Henry	10	1	2
Irby, Peter	8	1	7
Shelton, Joel	2	....	3
Foster, Robert	8	....	2
Musteen, Avery	4	....	....
Shelton, Daniel	10	1	6
Clarke, William	5	1	2
Martin, John, Senr	6	....	2
Mustain, Thomas	4	1	4
Lewis, Charles	7	1	4
Pace, William	7	1	7
Davis, Thomas	11	1	3
Sullivan, Frederick	7	1	2
Shelton, John	8	1	11
Payne, Thomas	5	1	6
Tucker, Robert	5	....	4
Tucker, William	10	1	8
Shelton, Gabriel	12	1	9
McBryant, John	7	....	5
Irby, Francis	7	1	4
Walter, John	7	....	5
Irby, David	....	....	2
Griggory, William	4	1	5
Keatt, William	6	1	2
Keatt, Charles	4	....	3
Parsons, George	6	....	2
Parsons, John, jr	2	....	1
Shelton, Ben	5	....	4
Overton, John	4	....	1
Hamblett, Rachel	4	....	....
Atkins, Joseph	9	....	3
Atkins, James	7	....	1
Atkins, Moses	4	....	1
Aron, Abraham	10	1	3
Burdit, Wm	9	1	3
Calland, Saml	6	1	4
Collins, Daniel	9	....	....
Devin, Wm., jr	6	....	4
Dyer, James	9	....	1
Dear, James	5	1	5
Dear, Joseph	3	1	....
Hughes, Samuel	8	1	1
Jenkins, Wm	6	....	4
Kerby, John	6	1	5
Lawson, Wm	1	....	....

NAME OF HEAD OF FAMILY.	White souls.	Dwellings.	Other buildings.
Maples, Joseph	8	....	2
Mitchell, James	7	....	6
Oliver, Mary	8	....	5
Oakes, Daniel	5	....	1
Pearson, Richd	4	....	....
Reynalds, Hugh	4	1	2
Reynalds, Joseph	5	....	2
Roberts, William	3	1	2
Russell, William	4	....	....
Smith, Peyton	9	1	12
Swinney, Joseph	2	....	....
Swinney, John	9	....	2
Swinney, Moses	2	....	2
Walker, Elisha	7	....	4
Whitsel, John	3	....	1
Ray, David	4	....	2
Hodges, Thomas	6	....	3
Hopper, Luther	3	1	2
Swinney, James S	7	....	1
Lewis, Colo John	4	2	19
Thrasher, Ben	1	1	6
Wilkinson, Thomas	7	1	6
Woody, James	4	....	3
Cole, Tunas	7	....	1
Shackleford, John	7	....	1
Dodson, Roley	1	....	....
Lawless, James	3	....	1
Anglin, John	10	....	5
Thomas, Wm	9	1	12
Burgess, Edward	10	1	3
Prewett, Saml	7	....	3
Stamps, John	9	....	3
Burgess, Ben	3	....	2
Durrett, Wm	8	....	6
Richards, Gabriel	10	1	4
Ball, John	8	....	2
Harrison, William	6	....	7
Cook, George, jr	3	....	2
Cook, George	6	....	2
But, Zachariah	5	1	....
Slayton, Joseph	10	....	2
Owen, Uriah	4	....	2
Hall, Joseph	6	....	2
Hall, John, jr	4	....	1
Hall, John, Senr	6	....	2
Scott, Nimrod	6	1	2
Scott, John	4	....	1
Seal, Solomon	5	....	2
Seal, James	4	....	2
Seal, Wm	4	....	1
Seal, Zachariah	6	....	1
Scott, Robert	7	....	2
Hammack, Maryan	8	....	5
Watkins, John	7	1	5
Neighbour, Wm	5	....	1
Johnson, John	7	1	2
Richardson, Wm	10	....	5
Hill, Jonathan	11	....	5
Walters, Robert	8	1	7
Walters, Clement	3	....	2
Walker, John	6	1	3
Dix, James	2	1	3
Warfe, Thomas	7	....	....
Going, Suffiah	12	....	5

PRINCE EDWARD COUNTY.

NAME OF HEAD OF FAMILY.	White souls.	Dwellings.	Other buildings.
Bassett, Nathl	6	1	5
Porter, William	7	2	8
Sunderman, John	13	2	1
Graham, Thomas	10	1	5
Graham, Samuel	7	1	3
Graham, James	8	1	2
Read, Joseph	10	1	6
Read, Moses	6	1	3
Baker, Douglas	2	1	7
Graham, James, Jur	3	1	....
Read, Robert	10	1	3
Scott, William	6	1	3
Porter, Hugh	9	1	4
Baldwin, William	4	1	8
Baldwin, William, Jur	3	1	4
Baldwin, Thomas	6	1	5
Morrison, James	1	1	3
Moore, John	8	1	2
Baker, Samuel	11	1	10
Baker, Andrew	7	1	9
Rathall, James	2	....	2
Hamilton, Robert	4	1	2
Franklin, Benja	11	1	3
Morgan, Thomas	10	1	5
Moore, Benja	3	1	3
Selvy, Charles	7	1	....
Huston, William	7	....	....
Hill, John	9	1	3
Cunningham, Saml	9	1	3

NAME OF HEAD OF FAMILY.	White souls.	Dwellings.	Other buildings.
Hamilton, John	2	1	2
Thompson, John	6	1	1
Black, Robert	7	1	4
Black, John	5	1	3
Mash, Zophar	6	1	3
Smith, John	5	1	....
Baker, Caleb	3	1	2
Petters, Stephen	10	1	11
Lankester, Nathl	11	1	7
Hubbard, John	11	1	2
Fore, William	7	1	7
Price, William	5	1	5
Daniel, William	5	1	5
Armstrong, Thomas	3	1	7
Armstrong, William	7	1	5
Cheadle, John	....	1	7
Jennings, William	6	....	....
Pane, Joseph	8	1	3
Wilkerson, Lovel	8	1	3
Daverson, John	5	1	3
Daverson, William	3	1	....
Cook, John	7	1	7
Caldwell, David	5	1	8
Armstrong, John	8	1	8
Caldwell, James	4	1	5
Daniel, James	13	1	7
Daniel, John	7	1	6
Fore, Joseph	7	1	6
Maxey, Elizabeth	5	1	1

NAME OF HEAD OF FAMILY.	White souls.	Dwellings.	Other buildings.
Maxey, Shadrick	6	1	1
Maxey, Joel	2	....	1
Grisham, Lawrence	6	....	....
Young, Elizabeth	8	1	7
Cason, Seth	10	1	10
Yorkshire, Thomas	3	....	....
Davis, William	11	1	3
Hays, William	10	1	3
McDermonroe, Bryant	8	1	2
Womack, Massanello	7	1	7
Mitchel, John, Senr	8	1	4
Mitchel, John, Junr	7	1	4
Mitchel, William	3	1	....
Jennings, Robert	12	2	4
Mitchel, James	9	1	5
Davis, George, Senr	8	1	....
Pryor, Harris	10	1	2
Jennings, Elkanah	5	1	3
Davis, George, Junr	2	....	....
Arnold, William	4	1	6
Hill, John	10	1	4
Wooldridge, Simon	7	1	3
Chapman, James	7	1	3
Pearce, David	6	1	2
Zachery, Bartholomew	4	1	4
Tyree, William	7	1	7
Swinney, Moses	7	1	3
Gray, Charles	8	1	4
Hill, William (Bloreek)	3	1	2

NAME OF HEAD OF FAMILY.	White souls.	Dwellings.	Other buildings.
Mann, Fargus	6	1	2
Mann, James	2	1	....
Mann, John	7	1	1
Walker, William	10	1	2
Hill, Susannah	7	1	4
Davis, James	2	1	3
Porter, Andrew	10	1	10
Sweeney, Moses	7	1	4
Jemerson, Robert	4	1	3
Arnold, John	13	2	12
Walker, David	8	1	10
Andrews, John	7	1	6
Harris, Ann	5	1	7
Weakley, James	10	1	2
Hill, William, Senr	6	1	6
Womack, Masanello	....	1	1
Forsythe, James	11	1	4
Watkins, Rhoda	5	1	6
Woodson, Charles	5	1	5
Woodson, Daniel	5	1	6
Woodson, Jacob	6	1	7
Gibson, Thomas	7	1	7
Inge, Ambrose	2	....	....
Hardwick, Jeremiah	12	1	1
Chandler, Ambraham	10	1	1
Matthews, Phillip	5	1	6
Harriss, Elizabeth	9	1	5
Webster, John	2	1	6
McDewel, James	6	1	4

PRINCE EDWARD COUNTY—Continued.

Name of head of family.	White souls.	Dwellings.	Other buildings.	Name of head of family.	White souls.	Dwellings.	Other buildings.	Name of head of family.	White souls.	Dwellings.	Other buildings.	Name of head of family.	White souls.	Dwellings.	Other buildings.
Coffee, Susannah	3	1	4	Chambers, Josiah	5	1	5	Brown, Mary	2	1	2	Hamblen, Eliza	9	1	9
Dabney, John	8	1	6	Gaulding, Jesse	6	1	2	Brown, Jesse	4	1	1	Mason, Peter	3		
Jesuph, John	7	1		Gaulding, Willm	2	1	1	Bell, George	8	1	3	Mason, Benja	7	1	1
Bird, Philemon	11	1	4	Gaulding, Alexr	8	2	4	Cary, Harwood	2	1	3	Baldwin, Wm	3	1	1
Penick, Charles	6	1	1	Green, Thomas, Senr	8	1	3	Crain, John	10	1		Dejernatt, Jno T	10	1	4
Chappell, Robert	11	1		Hamblett, David	3	1	5	Cardwell, John	7	1	1	Dunnivant, Wm	3	1	2
Chappell, Jesse	2			Hudson, Susannah	4	1	5	Carter, Wm	8	1	4	Ellington, Hezekiah	5	1	2
Ewing, James	2	1	10	Hudson, Willm	2	1	5	Calhoon, Adam	7	1	2	Owen, Wm	4	1	
Ewing, Saml	3			Holcombe, Phila	6	2	8	Dickson, John	9			Holt, Plunkett	8	1	
Hurt, Benjamin	7	1	5	Jones, Henry	6	1		Dupey, John	3	1	3	Holt, Robt	4	1	
Hurt, Obadiah	2	1	3	Johnston, Peter, Senr	5	1	12	Fears, James	5	1	4	Palmore, Tho	3	1	
Hammersley, Wm	6	1	1	Le Grand, Alexr	12	1	6	Flournoy, Tho	10	1	8	Chandler, Thos	6	1	
Foster, Richd	10	1	4	Lee, Willm (for Richd Randolph)	8	2	10	Fowlkes, Daniel	10	1	1	Harrison, Mary	4	1	4
Estes, Abraham	5	2	4	Lawson, Genl Robt	5	1	6	Gillaspie, George	3	1	1	Hall, William	2	1	1
Foster, Robt	8	2	3	League, Joshua	1			Gillaspie, David	1		1	Fielder, Dennis	6	1	
Marshall, Alexander	7	2	5	Morton, John, senr	10	1	9	Goode, Samuel	9	1	3	Fielder, John	6	1	
Holt, David	9	1	1	Morton, John, junr	7	1	1	Holloway, John	10			Thackston, David	7	1	
Nash, John, Junr	4			Morton, Richd	7	1	3	Hudson, Charles	3	1	2	Thackston, James	4	1	
Armes, John	6	1	1	Morton, James (Stewd)	35	1	4	Lunderman, John	3	1	2	Simmons, Joseph	5	1	
Childers, John, Jur		1	4	Morrow, John	3	1	4	McRoy, James	9	1	4	Peck, Richard	4	1	1
Sadler, Thomas	8			McCargo, John	8	2	5	McCune, Robert	2	1	1	Simmons, John	10	1	2
Hutcherson, John	3			Mettauer, Joseph	2	1	2	Morton, Thomas	4	1	1	Clarke, John	4	1	
Childers, William	2	1		McFall, Danl	4	1	1	Morton, Joseph	3	1	1	Fielder, Ann	5	1	2
Childers, John	4	1	2	Overstreet, John	12	2	2	Martin, John	5	1	5	Peck, Robert	2	2	8
Childers, Reps	7	1	4	Penick, Willm	13	1	6	Martin, Robert	9	1	4	Peck, Charles	1		
Mitchell, John	12	1	4	Price, Jerusha	6	1	13	Meadows, Terry	7	1		Robinson, Thomas	4		
Mitchell, William	4	1	3	Penick, Jeremiah	14	1	3	Meadows, James	6			Anderson, Micajah	1		
Jackson, Obadiah	5	1		Richie, Hugh	7	1	4	Morton, Peyton	3	1		Cunningham, John	1		
Vaughn, Nicholas	8	1	2	Richie, Chs	8	1	5	McGehee, John	3	1	7	Price, Charles	4	1	6
Walker, George	5	2	8	Richie, Jane	6	1		Nelson, Ambrose	6	1	2	Robinson, Zachariah	3	1	
Collier, Charles	3			Rice, Saml	7	1		Nelson, Humphrey	1	1	2	Brightwell, Renard	9	1	
Watkins, John	3	1		Redd, Thos	11	1	4	Nelson, Gearrard	4	1	2	Harris, Elizabeth	5	1	
Foster, William	8	1	2	Roberts, Henry	4	1		Purnall, William	4	1		Robinson, Isaac	4	1	1
Watkins, Abner	5	1	1	Smith, Martin	6	1	3	Pig, Henry	7	1	2	Robinson, Jesse	5	1	
Watkins, Ann	1	1	4	Smith, George	4	1	5	Price, Bird	7	1	7	Bird, Williamson	13	1	4
Tucker, Joseph	5	1	4	Scott, Col Thos	3	1	6	Price, William	8	1	7	Venable, Abraham	4	1	5
Tucker, Joseph, Junr	4	1		Smith, John B	10	1	4	Ransome, Robert	10	1	1	Sanders, Robert	1		
Hurt, James	10	1	2	Sydney, Hampden (Trustees)		2	9	Russell, Joseph	4	1	1	Tyree, David	8		
Ligon, James	2	1	9	Smith, Francis	4	1	3	Ritchie, Jane	5	1	1	Bryant, Martha	10	1	
Armes, Akin	3			Tuggle, Thos	4	1		Stromb, Christian	11	1	1	Venable, Elizabeth	5	1	17
Deshasor, John	7			Tanner, Archd	8	1		Thackston, Jas	5	1	5	Baldwin, Thomas	5	1	4
Price, Benjamin	6			Venable, Saml W	5	1	9	Tuggle, John	5			Sanders, John	4	1	
Osborne, Samuel	10			Venable, Nathl	13	2	13	Thackston, Ben	4	1	1	Baldwin, William	7	1	
Waddill, Jacob	10	1	2	Watson, John, senr	4	2	5	Truman, Joseph	6	1	4	Miller, John	10	1	3
Brockes, Charles	5			Watson, John, junr	8	1	6	Womack, William	11	1	1	Watson, John	8	3	7
Drinkard, Francis	9			Watson, Saml	11	1	1	Weaver, More	5	1		Askew, Casey	11	1	
Osborne, Thomas	9	1	3	Womack, William	11	1	1	Watkins, Henry	6	1	8	Woodson, Tarleton	4	1	1
Smith, John	7	1	8	Watson, Joseph	3	1		Quarter, Da	1	1	2	Glenn, Peyton	8	1	3
Goode, Robert	13	1	9	Watkins, Francis	13	1	12	Allen, Charles	10	2	7	Venable, Robert	1	1	1
Walthall, Chr	9	1	6	Gilcrist, John	7	1	3	Anderson, Jordan	1	1	2	Martin, Robert	8	1	6
Goode, Samuel	3	1	4	Ewing, William	8	1	2	Holt, Phenkett	11	1	3	Simmons, Charles	3		
Ray, Henry	2			Ewing, Sarl	3	1		Holt, Robert	4	1		Venable, Charles	7	1	6
Shepherd, Isaac	9	1	6	McTaggot, Phillip	9	1	3	Jackson, Matthew	13	1	5	Venable, Nathl			5
Farley, Jeremiah	6	1	3	Gollihor, Chs	11	1		Ligon, Elizabeth	12	1	3	Taylor, Samuel	9	1	4
Sadler, Benja	6	2	3	Welch, James	3	1	5	Ligon, William	6	1	1	Randolph, Peyton (Est Spr Creek)	2	1	18
Jackson, John	7	1	2	Davidson, Mary	6	2		Moore, Joseph	26	3	26	Markham, Arthur		1	1
Lewis, David	6	1	1	Simmons, Frances	3			Moore, George	8	2	19	Holland, Sarah	4	1	
Gills, Wm	2	1	2	Bibb, William	8	1	20	McGehee, Jacob	6	1	3	Kerr (Widow)	8	1	
Lockett, Stephen	9	1	7	Parker, Joseph	12	2	4	Redd, George	11	3	6	Rice, James	9	2	1
Pow, Saml	2	1	2	Caldwell, Eliza	4	1	1	Scott, Joseph	6	1	6	Brackett, John	7	1	3
Rice, Matthew	6	2	1	Le Grand, Peter	9	2	10	Thomason, Arnold	8	1	2	Baldwin, James	6		
Lewelling, Jesse	8	1		Caldwell, John (W.)	8	1	2	Wade, Philemon	8	1	5	Burks, Richd	7	2	5
Lewelling, Anderson	3			Anderson, David	2	1		Watkins, Thomas	5	1	4	Broadway, Nicholas	4		
Lewelling, Wm	4	1		Hill, William	5	1		Walton, George	19	2	15	Booker, George	5	1	8
Page, Samuel	7			Martin, Ester	4	1	1	Walton, Jesse Hughes	1	1	5	Branch, Mattw	7	1	5
Howerton, John	8	1	2	Bibb, Richd	7	2	13	Watson, Jesse	1	1	2	Brooks, Isaac	6	1	
Haskins, Benja	10	1	8	Scott, Jno	8	1	5	Wood, James	6	1	1	Clarke, Thos, senr	3	1	2
Haskins, Thos	8	1	4	Walker, Wm Townes	3	1	6	Winn, Richard	5	1	5	Clarke, John, jur	3	1	1
Ellington, John	7	1	3	Caldwell, Henry	8	1	2	Jackson, Wm	8	1	2	Cunningham, Esther	4	1	1
Ellington, Davd	8	1	4	Gillispie, Frakee	3	1	5	Palmore, Wm	4	1		Clarke, John, Senr	5	1	2
Ellington, Daniel	7	1	5	Bell, John	8	1	1	Smith, Henry	10	1	2	Clarke, Thomas, jur	5	1	2
Ellington, Jesse	8	1	3	Gibbins, John	9	1	1	Dejernatt, Christn	6	1	5	Dickenson, Henry	3	1	4
Ferguson, Richd	10	1	4	Anderson, John	8	1		Wiltcher, Henry	6	1		Davison, Sarah	5		
Vaughn, Thomas	12	1	6	Dean, Richd	1	1	1	Johnson, Henry	6	1	1	Fraser, John	5		
Le Neve, John	7	1		Baker, Caleb	12	1	4	Brooks, Joel	8	1		Fielder, Bartlett	5		
Jackson, Thos	7	1	3	Elliott, Robt	4	1	3	Palmore, Reuben	8	1	1	Fraser, Alexr	5	1	3
Nash, John, Esqr	6	7	21	Ritchie, Chs	5	1	3	Mason, Joseph, jur	1	1	3	Foster, George	6	1	3
Jackson, Mark	5	2		Clarke, Capt Jas	9	1	6	Burks, George	8	1		Foster, Abraham	4	1	2
Jackson, Wm	4	2		Adams, Wm Robt	7	2		Calticote, Jno	5	1	1	Fugua, Giles	8	1	
Howerton, Thomas	6	1	1	Gillaspie, Wm	1	1	1	Hudson, Wm	6	1	2	Freeman, Gaulthup	3		
Ward, Joseph	6	2	3	Spencer, Sharpe (own property)	12	2	2	Hudson, Jno	6	1	2	Harper, James	9	1	4
Ellington, Wm	9	1	2	Randolph, Peyton (Estate under Sharpe Spencer)		2	6	Hudson, Thos	5	1	3	Jackson, Joel	6	1	6
Berry, Joseph	11	1		Davis, Nichs	6	1	3	Griffen, Wm	8	1	3	Johns, Joel	15	1	2
Wells, Frederick	7	1		Davis, Eliza	2	1	3	Young, Stephen	10	1		Jackson, Thos	6		
Hawkins, Phil	8	1	1	Davis, Saml	3	1	1	Morris, Ann	6	1	4	Keeling, Wm	3		
Rice, Joseph	9	2		McSwine, Jno	2			Furguson, Jacob	2			Ligon, Wm	5	1	6
Jones, Richd		1	7	McSwine, Saml	3	1		Rowlett, McRoss	8	1	2	Ligon, John	1		
Barnes, James	4			Arbuckle, Saml	6	1	1	Jennings, James	5	1	1	Morton, Josiah	4		
Hawkins, Laban	2	1	2	Atkins, Joseph	2	1	1	Perkinson, Jno	10	1	4	Morton, Thomas, senr	3	1	
Cheatham, Bethene	2	1		Archdeacon, Edwd	11	1	2	Geers, Thos	7	1	1	Morton, Saml	10	1	2
McRobert, Archd	8	1	13	Booker, Mary	6	1	8	Penix, Thos	8	1	2	Morton, Thomas, Junr	10		
Allen, James, Senr	2	1	6	Booker, Gideon	4	1	1	Penix, Jno, jur	3	1		Owen, Jesse	12	1	6
Allen, James, Junr	9	1	4	Biggar, John	6	1	3	Penix, Jno	6	1	3	Pulliam, George	7	1	6
Bauldwin, John	10	1	3	Biggar, James	6	1		Brooks, Thos	6	1	1	Rutledge, John	11	1	
Barnett, John	2	1		Bowers, Nicholas	1	1	1	Dupey, Stephen	5	1	1	Rutledge, Thos	10		
Bohanan, Henry	10	1	4	Bibb, James	10	1	3	Wiltcher, John	7	1	1	Rutledge, Richd	6		
Brightwell, Barnard	3	1						Burks, Jno	8	1	1	Rutledge, Joseph	10	1	2
Cunningham, Josiah	11	1	2					Neal, Stephen	10	1	1	Richards, John	8	1	3
Chaffin, Isham	4	1	1									Rowlett, John	8	1	2
Carter, Saml	2	1	7									Rudd, John	3	1	2
Carter, Milley	9	1	7												

PRINCE EDWARD COUNTY—Continued.

NAME OF HEAD OF FAMILY.	White souls.	Dwellings.	Other buildings.
Rice, Francis	9	1	8
Raines, John	4	1	....
Scott, James	9	4	10
Scott, Rice	6	1	7
Turner, Robert	10	1	1
Turner, James	5	....	....
Wade, James	4	2	6
Wade, Elezabeth	6	1	....
Wood, John	7	1	....
Wood, Joseph	13	1	....
Wood, Stephen	4	....	....
Harte, Mary	3	1	....
Whitcoorth, William	7	1	2
Leigh, John	11	1	4
Burton, Saml	5	1	....
Blanton, Richd	9	4	3
Bowman, John S	7	1	....
McDermon, Dudley	9	....	....
McGehee, Jacob	4	1	14
McGehee, Wm	9	1	8
Love, Saml	4	....	....
Gowing, Thos	7	1	....
Harrison, Benja	4	1	3
Slythe, Richard	6	....	....
Lewelling, Danl	4	1	1
Green, Berry	7	1	4
Green, Thos	1	1	6
Blanton, Joshua	14	1	5
Wootten, Wm	10	1	7

PRINCESS ANNE COUNTY.

UPPER PRECINCT OF THE WESTERN SHORE—LIST OF PETER SINGLETON.

NAME OF HEAD OF FAMILY.	White souls.	Dwellings.	Other buildings.
Bustin, Thomas	6	1	2
Cock, Jno	6	1	5
Davis, Richard	2	1	2
Etherage, John	8	1	3
Fentress, Catharine	4	1	4
Frizel, Willoughby	4	1	3
Fentress, Lemuel, Junr	4	1	3
Fentress, Nathaniel	5	1	....
Fentress, Lemuel, senr	2	1	9
Fentress, Mary	3	1	....
Fentress, Isaac	6	1	1
Fentress, Joshua	8	1	5
Godfrey, James	5	1	1
Green, Mary	3	1	1
Hughson, Benjamin	1	....	....
Haynes, Erasmus	4	2	10
Hargrove, James	9	1	1
Land, Richard	1	1	4
Land, Horatio	7	1	4
Land, Batson	4	1	1
Land, Joshua	8	1	7
Lovitt, John	9	1	2
Land, Henry	4	1	....
Lovitt, Susanna	1	1	6
Land, Jeremiah	7	2	10
Land, Thorowgood	3	1	1
Land, Ree	7	2	13
Lovitt, Thomas, senr	6	1	6
Lovitt, William	6	1	2
Lovitt, Lancaster	3	1	1
Moore, Bagwell, senr	8	1	3
Murden, James	9	1	3
Moore, Mark	8	1	1
Murden, Sarah	5	1	5
Murphey, Anthony	4	1	3
Murden, Batson	2	1	3
Murden, Jeremiah	6	1	1
Shipp, Simon	5	1	3
Shipp, Tully	7	1	1
Simmons, Joel	6	1	5
Stone, William	4	1	2
Stone, Martha	7	1	6
Singleton, Peter	9	1	19
Whitehurst, Robert	6	1	1
Whitehurst, Amy	2	1	1
West, Amy	1	1	6
West, William, senr	5	1	4
Whitehurst, Francis	9	1	3
West, William, Junr	2	1	7
Whitehurst, Joshua	7	1	7
Whitehurst, Caleb	6	1	1
Wright, Jeremiah	7	1	3
Whitehurst, Elizabeth	4	1	....
Widgen, Isaac	5	....	....
West, Thomas	8	1	5

EASTERN BRANCH PRECINCT—LIST OF WILLIAM WHITE.

NAME OF HEAD OF FAMILY.	White souls.	Dwellings.	Other buildings.
Boroughs, Christopher	6	1	2
Burley, Robert	5	1	2
Brown, Sarah	6	1	1
Carraway, James	6	1	4
Carraway, John	7	1	....
Carmichael, John	2	....	....
Cottle, William	6	1	1
Callaway, Elizabeth	3	1	1
Davis, Rachel	2	1	3
Davis, Edward	2	1	2
Dennel, Edward	3	1	....
Dudley, Mary	4	1	6
Davis, Horatio	7	1	2
Drury, Matthias	4	1	4
Dudley, Daniel	1	....	....
Edgar, Mary	5	1	1
Edmonds, Nathaniel	1	1	....
Edmonds, Malachi	3	....	....
Edmonds, George	4	1	....
Edmonds, William	5	1	5
Edmonds, Abel	9	1	6
Fentress, Mary	3	1	....
Fentress, Dinah	2	1	1

EASTERN BRANCH PRECINCT—LIST OF WILLIAM WHITE—continued.

NAME OF HEAD OF FAMILY.	White souls.	Dwellings.	Other buildings.
Fentress, David	4	1	2
Fentress, Michael	6	1	2
Forrest, William	5	1	3
Griffith, Benjamin	4	1	3
Godfrey, Matthew	7	1	7
Godfrey, Patience	2	1	2
Griffin, Anne	3	....	....
Gauteer, Nicholas	2	....	1
Hartgrove, John	7	1	1
Hosier, Jeremiah	7	....	....
Hosier, Samuel	3	....	....
Hancock, Anne	6	1	5
Hancock, John	7	2	13
Hopkins, John	6	1	5
Hopkins, Joshua	5	1	3
Hopkins, Sarah	6	1	11
Hoggard, Nathaniel	3	2	9
Hill, William	6	2	10
Jamieson, Neil	4	1	9
Keeling, Robert	2	1	2
Kays, Robert	2	....	1
Kempe, Thomas	5	1	6
Keeling, John	6	....	....
Land, Caleb	5	1	6
Lamb, James	4	1	3
Moore, Bagwell, Junr	2	1	1
Matthias, Reuben	6	1	3
Matthias, John, senr	10	1	3
Matthias, Hillary	6	1	1
Matthias, John, Junr	2	1	2
Matthias, Henry	3	....	....
Matthias, Joshua	5	1	1
Morfits, Henry P	3	1	2
Matthias, Henry	3	....	....
Moseley, Francis	1	1	6
Moseley, Edward Hack	4	1	5
McClenahan, William	9	2	13
Moseley, Hillary	10	2	16
Murray, John	7	1	8
Murray, Isaac	3	1	8
Nicholas, Nathaniel	4	1	4
Cast, George	2	1	1
Park, Jonathan	1	1	2
Parsons, John	10	1	3
Peek, William	6	2	....
Robinson, William	....	....	....
Robinson, Mary	....	....	....
Russell, William	5	1	2
Robinson, Tully	....	....	3
Selden, Mary	6	1	6
Smith, Margaret	3	1	2
Shipp, Josiah	4	1	6
Shipp, Jonathan	1	1	....
Smith, John	10	1	3
Scantling, William	2	1	7
Statha, James	8	1	1
Sparrow, Richard	....	1	3
Salusbury, John, senr	4	1	....
Salusbury, John S	3	1	1
Tomer, Thomas	3	....	....
Taylor, James	6	1	1
Valentine, Jacob	3	2	7
Williamson, Joshua	5	1	3
Williamson, Caleb	9	1	4
Whitehurst, Christopher	8	1	6
Wiggins, Frances	4	....	....
Williamson, Willoughby	3	1	3
Whitehurst, Elizabeth	4	1	1
Whitehurst, William	4	1	6
Whitehurst, Jonathan, senr	6	1	3
Whitehurst, Thomas	4	1	6
Wiles, Reuben	6	1	4
Whitehurst, Simon	6	1	2
Ward, Anne	4	....	....
Williamson, George, Junr	8	1	1
Williamson, George, senr	7	1	4
Williamson, William	4	1	1
Willeroy, Lydia	3	2	2
Willeroy, Abraham	1	1	....
Willeroy, Priscilla	3	....	....
Whitehurst, Enoch	5	1	7
Williams, Isaac	1	....	1
Whitehurst, Enoch, Junr	5	1	1

EASTERN BRANCH PRECINCT—LIST OF WILLIAM WHITE—continued.

NAME OF HEAD OF FAMILY.	White souls.	Dwellings.	Other buildings.
Williamson, Moses	3	1	2
Whitehurst, Joshua	3	1	1
Whitehurst, Nathaniel	2	1	....
Whitehurst, William, Junr	4	1	2
Whitehurst, James, senr	7	1	4
Wiles, William	1	1	6
Weblin, Willoughby	3	1	1
Waddy, James	8	1	1
Walke, Anthony	12	4	36
Whitehurst, Wm (son of Lemuel)	3	1	4
Williamson, Charles	6	1	8
White, William	7	1	7
Brownlie, John	1	1	1
Black, William	....	....	....
Bearfoot, Elizabeth	....	....	....
Harrison, Frances	....	....	....
Henley, John	3	1	3
McCaul, Archibald	3	....	....
McCaul, John	7	1	2
Butt, Beriah	9	1	3

LOWER PRECINCT OF THE WESTERN SHORE—LIST OF FRANCIS LAND.

NAME OF HEAD OF FAMILY.	White souls.	Dwellings.	Other buildings.
Boush, Frederick	4	1	6
Benthall, Harrison	7	1	4
Broughton, George	9	....	....
Boush, George	3	....	....
Barrott, Amey	4	1	....
Bromley, Augustine	4	1	....
Benthall, William	8	2	4
Brown, John (blacksmith)	7	....	....
Bishop, Peggy	5	1	4
Brock, William	6	2	7
Cox, Zekiel	5	1	5
Coppedge, Augustine	8	1	6
Cartwright, William	4	....	....
Davis, Obedience	4	1	....
Dear, Sophia	4	....	....
Edwards, Richards	6	1	4
Ewell, William	7	1	....
Forrest, John	6	1	4
Ghieslin, John	8	1	5
Gasking, George	7	1	8
Huggins, Sarah	5	1	6
Haynes, Abner	6	....	....
Huggins, David	4	1	....
Hardison, Oliff	8	1	....
Hauge, Francis	6	....	....
Haynes, William	6	1	6
Haynes, Elizabeth	3	1	3
Haynes (the Orphans of William)	....	1	5
Lewelling, Frances	5	1	3
Land, Simon	4	1	....
Land, Francis	3	....	9
Moseley, Charles	4	1	4
Moseley, Betty	7	1	9
Moseley, Elizabeth	5	1	6
McKeel, Frances	5	....	....
Moseley, Edward	8	....	....
Moseley, Arthur	5	1	1
Moore, James	6	1	4
Norriss, William	5	....	....
Nicholson, Charles	3	1	4
Pebworth, William	8	1	3
Pebworth, Henry	7	1	5
Rosson, Joseph	4	....	....
Stone, Simon	12	1	6
Smyth, Charles	3	1	2
Smyth, Anne	5	....	....
Thorowgood, John	8	3	18
Thorowgood, James	2	1	3
Thorowgood, Lemuel	5	4	15
Thorowgood, William	8	1	5
Walke, Mary	....	1	4
Whitehurst, Drew	8	1	2
Williamson, Joshua	2	1	3
Walke, William	3	1	4
Williams, Sarah	2	....	3
Williams, Thomas	4	1	4

LOWER PRECINCT OF THE WESTERN SHORE—LIST OF FRANCIS LAND—con.

NAME OF HEAD OF FAMILY.	White souls.	Dwellings.	Other buildings.
Warden, Arthur	6	1	2
Waterson, Robert	2	....	....
Whitehurst, Samuel	3	1	3
Whitehurst, Jonathan	11	1	14

LITTLE CREEK PRECINCT—LIST OF JOHN THOROWGOOD.

NAME OF HEAD OF FAMILY.	White souls.	Dwellings.	Other buildings.
Bevan, William	5	1	2
Brent, Haynes	8	1	2
Boush, Joice	4	1	5
Collins, Henry	8	1	2
Collins, Frances	4	1	2
Collins, Maximilian	5	1	1
Cone, Hillary	5	1	3
Cowper, John	4	1	3
Ewell, Thomas	7	1	3
Ewell, Solomon	4	1	2
Floyd, John	8	1	1
Griffin, John	5	1	1
Haynes, Henry	5	1	10
Guy, George	6	1	2
Griffin, John	6	1	1
Hunter, Jacob	1	1	3
Hunter, John	3	1	3
Hudgen, George	8	1	2
Hunter, Elizabeth	7	1	15
Hunter, Thomas	4	2	13
Holmes, Mary	6	1	2
Harvey, John	4	1	2
Holmes, William	1	1	2
Jones, Daniel	4	1	....
Jamieson, George	5	1	4
Kilgore, David	2	1	4
Lester, William	9	2	2
Lawson, Anthony	9	3	13
Mason, Obadiah	7	1	6
Moore, James	6	1	8
Main, William	4	1	1
Martin, Joshua	5	1	1
Millerson, Ward	4	1	....
Pebworth, Thomas	9	1	2
Park, Jonathan	2	....	....
Power's, Pembroke	4	1	1
Powers, Francis	4	1	1
Petre, John	6	1	....
Smyth, Robinson	7	1	2
Smyth, Perrin	7	1	5
Story, John	2	1	1
Thorowgood, Thomas	1	....	....
Thorowgood, John	4	1	6
Wishart, Mary	2	1	10
Wilkins, John	7	1	8
Wakefield, Anne	9	1	2
Ward, Benjamin	3	1	....
Wishart, Mary	5	1	8
Denny, Frances	3	1	2

BLACK WATER PRECINCT—LIST OF GEORGE D. CORPREW.

NAME OF HEAD OF FAMILY.	White souls.	Dwellings.	Other buildings.
Craig, Ebenezer	4	1	5
Randolph, Giles	5	1	....
Cannaday, John	4	1	....
Fenton, Caleb, senr	5	1	3
Fenton, Caleb, Junr	2	1	1
James, Elizabeth	6	1	2
Collins, John	5	1	1
Riggs, James	2	1	1
Doudge, John	4	1	....
Elks, Solomon	6	1	....
Douglass, Charles	5	1	....
White, Cornelius	6	1	3
Reed, William	9	1	10
Doudge, William	5	1	3
Doudge, Willis	5	1	....
Corbett, Caleb	2	1	1
Cummings, Caleb	4	1	3
Griggs, Martha	4	1	....
Plummer, George	5	1	2
Nickolds, Martha	3	1	1

PRINCESS ANNE COUNTY—Continued.

BLACK WATER PRECINCT—LIST OF GEORGE D. CORPREW—continued.

NAME OF HEAD OF FAMILY.	White souls.	Dwellings.	Other buildings.
Wallace, James	4	1	2
Wickens, Elizabeth	6	1	6
Sorey, Anne	4	1	3
Sorey, Caleb	3	....	....
Gisbourn, John, Junr	2	1	3
Cummings, Benjn	2	....	....
Thorrington, William	6	1	3
Shewcraft, William	5	1	2
Padon, William	8	1	3
Humphrey's, John	10	1	2
Coates, Betty	6	1	....
Gisbourn, John, senr	6	1	2
Etheredge, Andrew	6	1	4
Butt, Josiah	....	1	4
Boult, John	6	1	2
Coates, Elizabeth	5	1	2
Boult, Elizabeth	6	1	2
Old, Caleb	8	1	8
Etheredge, James, Senr	7	1	1
Etheredge, Joshua	6	1	....
Hodges, Thomas	6	....	....
Ives, George	8	1	7
Davis, Elias	8	....	....
Sorey, William	10	1	9
Sorey, Kedar	3	....	....
Grisson, James	4	....	....
Randolph, Mary	3	1	2
Tooley, Sarah	6	1	5
Woodard, John	6	2	7
Corbett, Richard	1	1	2
Wickens, William	7	1	8
Cummings, Fenton	4	1	1
Cannon, Lovey	4	1	....
Woodard, William	5	1	4
Tooley, Betty	3	1	1
Phillips, Elanor	5	1	4
Douglass, Solomon	4	1	....
Berry, Malachi	5	....	....
Godfrey, Sarah	2	1	3
Wilson, John	....	1	....
Wormington, Abraham	....	1	16
Gnawberry, George	4	....	....
Woodard, James	4	1	1
Woodard, Joel	7	1	4
Malbourn, Malachi	3	....	....
Woodard, Henry	4	1	5
Weaver, James	6	1	2
Simmons, William, senr	6	1	1
Simmons, William, Junr	5	1	2
Parr, Peter	3	1	....
Woodard, Josiah	6	1	3
Etheredge, Frances	2	1	....
Caton, Betty	3	1	....
Sikes, Levi	7	1	....
Gallando, Abraham	3	1	1
Corprew, John	4	....	....
Whitehurst, Samuel	3	1	....
Chay, Mary	3	1	1
Chay, Ezekiel	1	....	....
Old, Thomas, Junr	3	1	4
Purdy, Abia	7	1	....
Sorey, Anne	4	1	2
Sorey, James	1	1	2
Corprew, George D	9	1	11

MIDDLE PRECINCT OF THE EASTERN SHORE—LIST OF CASON MOORE.

NAME OF HEAD OF FAMILY.	White souls.	Dwellings.	Other buildings.
Brown, John, senr	4	2	4
Capps, Tully	5	1	1
Isdale, Thomas	2	1	....
Henly, John, senr	2	1	3
Shipp, William	7	1	3
Lovitt, Sarah	7	1	6
Fountain, John	6	1	3
McClalin, William, senr	3	1	6
McClalin, John, senr	8	1	5
McClalin, William, Junr	8	1	6
Henley, Nowdinna	2	1	5
McClalin, Richard, senr	4	1	3
Dyer, Hillary	4	....	....
Dawley, Jonathan	2	1	1
Dyer, John	5	1	2
Whitehurst, Solomon	7	1	3
Stivin, Elizabeth	6	1	5
Brinson, Cornelius	3	1	1
Malbone, Peter	6	1	3
Malbone, Sarah	4	1	2
Whitehurst, William	7	1	5
Malbone, James	8	1	5
Whitchard, John	6	1	5
James, William, Junr	4	1	3
Wright, Jonathan	4	1	3
Holmes, Robert	7	1	5
Brown, Moses	5	1	....
Capp, William	5	1	4

MIDDLE PRECINCT OF THE EASTERN SHORE—LIST OF CASON MOORE—con.

NAME OF HEAD OF FAMILY.	White souls.	Dwellings.	Other buildings.
Capps, Hillary	7	1	1
Dawley, Dennis	6	1	7
Dawley, Elizabeth	5	1	6
Flanagan, James	5	1	....
Rany, Malachi	3	1	3
Whitehurst, Jonathan	8	1	2
Garrisson, Cantwell	7	1	3
Bonney, Jonathan	8	1	6
Brock, Nathaniel	5	1	3
Simmons, Thomas	7	1	7
Brock, Moses	1	....	3
Dyer, Pheby	2	1	2
Doudge, Joab	6	1	4
Wilbour, William	5	....	....
Cason, James, senr	7	1	6
Eaton, Michael	6	1	1
Bonney, Edward, Junr	3	1	....
Eaton, James	7	1	6
Moore, Cason, senr	6	1	8
Cox, William	5	1	....
Land, Edward	5	1	1
Land, Willoughby	5	1	3
Franklin, Moses	1	....	....
Franklin, Daniel	2	1	2
Robinson, William	14	1	9
Stivin, Robert	3	....	....
Padon, Charles	10	1	4
Otterson, William	4	1	1
Flanagan, Moses	6	1	2
Otterson, Jane	6	1	4
Dawley, David	5	1	1
Whitehurst, Jeremiah	3	1	....
Eaton, Michael	7	1	....
Whitehurst, Jno (son Solomon)	4	1	4
Rany, Thomas	8	1	4
Griffin, William	2	1	5
Brown, Edward	3	1	2
Brown, Jonathan	3	....	....
Franklin, Daniel, Junr	2	....	....
Fentress, Letisha	5	1	9
Cox, John	5	1	1
Capps, Jno (son of Thorowgood)	6	1	1
Davis, Abner	5	1	1
Waterman, Charles	1	....	....
Bonney, Edward, senr	2	2	9
Bonney, John	7	1	....
Roberts, Sarah	7	2	2
Bonney, William	3	1	....
Bonney, Thomas	6	2	5
Gornto, William, senr	6	1	4
Barns, Francis	5	1	3
Barns, Joshua	7	1	2
Snail, John	5	1	2
Henley, Charles	8	1	3
Griffin, John	5	1	9
Flanagan, William	3	1	....
Gornto, John	3	1	10
Gornto, John, Junr	6	1	6
Carrill, David	5	....	....
Spratt, Henry	7	1	....
Hill, William	3	1	1
Carrill, Martha	7	1	3
Airs, Willoughby	3	1	1
Lewis, Elizabeth	3	1	2
Snail, Henry	2	....	....
Whitehead, Charles	7	1	1
Capps, Obediah	3	1	1
Shepherd, William	10	1	7
Kays, William	10	1	9
Capps, William, senr	1	1	1
Brown, Smith	3	....	....
Rany, John	4	1	1
Ward, Robert	1	1	1
Dyer, Willoughby	5	1	1
Dyer, John, Junr	5	1	2
Woodhouse, Francis	7	1	4
Moore, Henry	5	1	1
Ward, Thomas	1	1	4
Ward, Jonathan	3	1	2
Woodhouse, Jonathan, Junr	2	1	2
Fentress, Jonathan	11	1	8
James, John, Junr	6	1	13
Woodhouse, John	4	1	3
James, Pembrook	3	1	3
James, Thomas	1	....	2
James, William, senr	2	1	11
James, Elizabeth	2	1	7
James, John, senr	7	1	3
Henley, James	9	1	8
Lamount, Joshua	2	1	2
Malbone, Solomon	7	1	1
McClalin, Moses, Junr	3	....	....
Cason, John, Junr	2	1	8
Stone, Thomas	1	1	2

MIDDLE PRECINCT OF THE EASTERN SHORE—LIST OF CASON MOORE—con.

NAME OF HEAD OF FAMILY.	White souls.	Dwellings.	Other buildings.
Creed, Dennis	6	1	2
Creed, John	8	1	3
Henley, Cornelius	2	....	....
Battin, William, Junr	13	1	....
Morrisset, John	5	1	4
Moore, William	3	1	1
Moore, Jacob	3	1	4
Moore, Cason, Junr	4	1	1
Cason, Hillary	8	1	3
Whitehurst, Thomas	4	1	1
Harrison, Henry, senr	6	1	6
Salusbury, Newman	1	....	....
Brown, John, senr	7	1	8
Brown, Tully	8	1	2
Langley, Willis	2	1	2
Gornto, Nathaniel	3	1	2
Brown, John, senr	6	1	1
Bonney, Jane	1	1	3
Fentress, John	11	1	10
Doudge, Richard	6	1	2
Doudge, Nathan	3	1	....
Atwood, Thomas	4	1	6
Atwood, Betty	6	1	6
Atwood, William	7	....	....
Capps, John (son of John)	5	1	2
Whitehurst, Solomon, senr	6	1	5
Woodhouse, Frances	8	1	3
Nimmo, Anne	7	1	7
Whitehurst, John	5	1	4
Whitehurst, Henry	2	....	....
Whitehurst, James	6	1	3
Whitehurst, Hoses	1	1	....
Cason, Cornelius, senr	8	1	2
Flanikin, Phillip	8	....	....
Cason, Cornelius, Junr	4	1	5
Moore, Tully	7	1	5
Cason, James, Junr	4	1	5
Cason, Solomon	5	1	1
Bonney, Richard, senr	5	1	5
Cason, Moses	7	1	3
Bonney, John, Junr (son of John)	7	1	4
Dougde, Reuben	6	1	3
Freeman, Moses	4	1	3
McClalin, Joab	7	1	2
Dawley, Mary	1	1	1
McClalin, Moses	7	1	4
Hill, Tully	4	1	4
Sharwood, Isaac	4	1	....
Malbone, Godfrey	5	1	2
Whitehurst, Reuben	2	1	....
Hartley, Charles	3	1	2
Whitehurst, James	11	1	6
Capps, Moses	7	1	2
Cox, Benjamin	3	....	....
Gunter, Charles	3	....	....
Williamson, Jonathan	3	1	....
Williamson, John	2	1	....
Avis, Francis	6	1	....
Dawley, Henry	5	1	1
Brock, Ransom	8	1	6
Capps, Dennis	4	1	2
Capps, Henry	5	1	2
McClalin, Elizabeth	6	....	....
Bonney, John	14	1	7
Dawley, Thomas	4	1	1
Eaton, John	6	1	2
Brock, Anne	4	....	....
Brock, William	2	2	4
Ward, John	5	1	2
Franklin, Nathan	5	1	2
Hill, Joseph	3	1	....
Capps, Morris	3	1	2
McClalin, Elisabeth	5	1	3
Capps, Henry, senr	4	1	4
Scopus, John	8	1	....
Ward, Mary	6	....	....

LOWER PRECINCT OF THE EASTERN SHORE—LIST OF CAPT. LEMUEL CORNICK.

NAME OF HEAD OF FAMILY.	White souls.	Dwellings.	Other buildings.
Absalom, William	8	2	4
Aitchason, Rebecca			
Biddle, John P	5	1	5
Brinson, Mary	3	1	....
Benthall, Caleb	9	1	....
Brewer, James	6	1	3
Burgess, Lanfar	5	1	3
Brickhouse, Hezekiah	10	1	3
Boush, William	1	....	2
Buskey, Jonathan	10	2	3
Broughton, Charles	8	....	....
Cary, William	6	1	3
Casteen, Thomas	5	1	2
Cannon, Elizabeth	3	1	8

LOWER PRECINCT OF THE EASTERN SHORE—LIST OF CAPT. LEMUEL CORNICK—continued.

NAME OF HEAD OF FAMILY.	White souls.	Dwellings.	Other buildings.
Chapple, Thomas	6	1	1
Cannon, Edward	6	1	4
Cannon, Thomas	9	1	5
Cary, Isaac	5	1	5
Cavendar, Henry	4	1	1
Chapple, John	1	....	....
Cornick, Joel	7	3	8
Cornick, William	8	2	17
Cornick, Horatio	6	1	8
Cornick, Dim	5	1	3
Cornick, John	6	1	14
Cornick, Henry	2	1	6
Cornick, Lemuel	6	1	11
Cavendar, William	4	1	....
Cox, George	7	1	2
Fentress, John	6	1	1
Finkley, James	4	....	....
Guion, Lewis	8	1	4
Gornto, Reuben	8	1	9
Gisbourn, Mary	4	1	1
Holmes, William	12	1	2
Henley, William	4	1	3
Hill, Jesse	4	1	4
Hudging, Thomas	6	1	1
Jones, Enoch	4	1	5
James, Ann	7	4	12
James, Henry	5	1	2
Keeling, Robert	5	1	3
Keeling, William, senr	5	3	23
Keeling, William, Junr	5	....	2
Keeling, Jacob	8	2	10
Keeling, William (son of John)	11	1	4
Keeling, Betty	2	1	10
Keeling, Adam	1	1	10
Keeling, Henry	2	1	6
Keeling, Thomas	1	1	5
Keeling, Paul	3	1	3
Lovitt, John (son of Lancaster)	5	1	9
Land, James	7	1	4
Lamount, Lydia	1	1	1
Lamount, Cornelius	7	1	6
Leggett, James	6	1	4
Lovitt, John	6	1	1
Lovitt, Reuben	11	1	6
Lamount, Edward	5	....	....
Mills, Southey	3	....	....
Mackey, Jonathan	7	1	3
Moore, Joshua	3	....	....
Maye, John	7	1	2
Nicholson, John	4	....	....
Nottingham, Joseph	7	1	1
Norris, Thomas	7	1	1
Oliver, John	5	1	2
Petty, Edward	6	1	6
Petty, William	4	1	1
Pallet, Matthew	6	1	4
Robinson, Thomas	2	1	2
Robinson, Mark	4	1	4
Russell, Ann	4	1	2
Shepherd, Smith	9	1	9
Scott, Ann	4	1	2
Scott, Ann	4	1	6
Smith, James	6	1	2
Scott, Caleb	4	....	....
Smith, Andrew	1	1	3
Smith, John	3	1	3
Scott Henry	1	....	....
Stevens, Robert	4	1	....
Tainor, John	8	1	4
Trower, Thomas	3	1	2
Trower, Robert	7	1	5
Vangover, Blazon	5	1	5
Walker, Thomas R	6	2	8
Walker, Thomas	2	2	5
Whitehurst, Hillary	6	1	4
Weakes, Amos	5	1	6
White, Rebecca	9	1	11
Wilkinson, Joseph	8	....	....
Woodhouse, Henry	2	2	12
Wilbour, Margaret	3	1	....
Woodhouse, William D	1	1	3
Whitehurst, Reuben	4	1	4
Whitehurst, Hillary	1	....	....
Wilkins, William	3	1	....
Wilkins, Solomon	5	2	6
Wilkins, William, senr	4	1	....
Woodhouse, Mary	3	1	4
Woodhouse, John	2	1	4
Woodhouse, Josiah	1	....	....

UPPER PRECINCT OF THE EASTERN SHORE—LIST OF COLO JNO ACKISS.

NAME OF HEAD OF FAMILY.	White souls.	Dwellings.	Other buildings.
Ackiss, Jonathan	3	1	4
Heath, James	5	1	2

PRINCESS ANNE COUNTY—Continued.

NAME OF HEAD OF FAMILY.	White souls.	Dwellings.	Other buildings.
UPPER PRECINCT OF THE EASTERN SHORE—LIST OF COLo JNo ACKISS—continued.			
Brown, James	3	1	1
Oakem, Nathan	1	1	2
Ward, Caleb	10	1	5
Wellins, Mary	4	1	....
Whitehead, John, senr	4	1	10
Lawrence, Joshua	7	1	5
Whitehurst, Charles	4	1	3
Brock, Elias	3	1	....
Brock, John	8	1	1
Williamson, Thomas	3	1	1
Williamson, Malachi	4	1	6
Williamson, Natt	2	1	1
Munden, William	3	1	1
Hutchings, William	7	1	5
Old, Capt Thomas	4	1	11
Lane, Solomon	9	1	5
Woodland, William	8	1	3
Moore, Abner	5	1	2
Salmons, Henry	4	1	2
Berry, Jesse	2	1	5
Capps, Jonathan	2	....	....
Styring, Josiah	7	1	6
Barnes, Tully	8	1	5
Corbett, Joel	4	1	....
Berry, Willoughby	6	2	2
Kilgore, William, Junr	6	1	5
Kilgore, John	3	1	3
Woodland, John	7	1	1
Morris, Anne	4	1	2
Cox, John	4	1	1
King, James	4	1	1
King, Jeremiah	4	1	....
King, John	5	1	1
Whitehead, Isabella	5	1	2
Whitehurst, Henry	5	1	6
Creed, Mary	6	1	3
Booth, George	3	1	1
Booth, John	6	1	1

NAME OF HEAD OF FAMILY.	White souls.	Dwellings.	Other buildings.
UPPER PRECINCT OF THE EASTERN SHORE—LIST OF COLo JNo ACKISS—continued.			
Whitehead, John, Junr	3	1	2
Dawley, Caleb	7	1	5
Kinzee, Henry	8	2	1
Purdy, John	5	1	1
Grimstead, Rawley	6	1	2
Grimstead, Thomas	2	1	1
Whitehurst, Richard	6	1	4
Corbell, Malachi	3	....	....
Martin, Moses	6	1	1
Fountain, Henry	3	1	....
Moore, Caleb	8	1	3
Smith, James	4	1	1
Wright, Jacob	8	1	5
James, Charles	4	1	....
Cornish, Amy	3	1	2
Wright, Thomas	4	1	6
Robinson, Moses	8	1	5
Morse, Francis	5	1	4
Kelley, Harry	4	2	7
Brown, Moses	4	1	4
Morse, Lazarus	5	1	4
Kelley, Thomas	5	1	....
Whitehurst, Lemuel	8	2	2
Moseley, Tully	6	1	6
Cason, John	8	1	7
Hill, Peter	9	1	....
Frizzle, Solomon	7	1	4
Franklin, Thomas, senr	2	1	3
Gwin, Joseph	5	1	1
Matthias, Charles	5	1	2
Matthias, Joshua	5	1	1
Kinzee, Thomas	7	1	2
Sikes, Elias	7	1	....
Munden, Venus	3	1	5
James, Jonathan	4	1	3
Oram, John	2	1	....
Allen, Thomas	2	1	....
Chappell, George	3	2	2

NAME OF HEAD OF FAMILY.	White souls.	Dwellings.	Other buildings.
UPPER PRECINCT OF THE EASTERN SHORE—LIST OF COLo JNo ACKISS—continued.			
Morse, Archibald	8	2	2
Morriss, William, senr	7	1	8
Morriss, James	7	1	1
Holstead, Mary	6	1	....
Morriss, Cornelius	3	1	1
Salmons, William	8	1	2
Nimmo, James	2	1	1
Williams, Arthur	2	....	....
Gwin, Willis	5	1	....
Capps, Edward	5	1	....
Williams, Solomon	2	1	....
Morriss, William (son An)	4	1	4
Seneca, Malachi	3	1	....
Morriss, Hillary	1	1	1
Stripes, Anne	1	1	1
Williams, William	5	1	2
Morriss, John	4	1	3
Seneca, Averilla	4	1	4
Doudge, Tully	6	1	1
Payne, Elizabeth	6	1	1
Payne, Enoch	3	1	....
Roberts, Wrencher	5	1	2
Gording, William	4	1	....
Rutland, William	2	1	2
Morse, James	4	1	6
Mason, Jonathan	4	1	2
Ackiss, John, Junr	6	1	1
Smith, Henry	3	1	....
Malbone, Jonathan	8	1	3
Hill, Joshua	5	1	....
Fisher, Jonathan	6	1	6
Jones, Willoughby	3	1	....
Senecca, William	5	1	....
Senecca, John	5	1	....
Senecca, James	5	1	2
Senecca, Simon	6	1	....
Batten, George	6	1	3
Senecca, John, senr	6	1	2

NAME OF HEAD OF FAMILY.	White souls.	Dwellings.	Other buildings.
UPPER PRECINCT OF THE EASTERN SHORE—LIST OF COLo JNo ACKISS—continued.			
Williamson, Sarah	5	1	3
Stone, John	5	1	2
Grimstead, Daniel	6	1	3
Bonney, Tully	5	1	1
Morriss, Josiah	10	1	3
Willoughby, Thomas	8	1	3
Smyth, George	4	1	....
Barnes, Absalom	4	1	3
Dudley, Robert, senr	6	1	4
Dudley, Robert	3	1	....
Shortztraizte, John	1	1	2
Franklin, Thomas	5	1	....
Idlelott, Caleb	8	1	1
Cammell, John	6	1	4
Capps, William	3	1	....
Green, Nathan	1	....	....
Heath, Elizabeth	4	2	2
Morriss, William, Junr	5	1	4
Williams, Charles	7	1	1
Jackson, Elizabeth	2	1	2
Ackiss, William	7	1	4
Wright, James	7	1	4
Kempe, James	7	1	....
Smyth, George	5	1	....
Smyth, Charles	3	....	....
Cormick, Nathan	7	1	2
Batten, James	3	....	....
Bonney, Elizabeth	9	1	7
Fentress, William	3	1	1
Ackiss, John, senr	5	2	13
Ackiss, Francis	1	1	6
Styring, George	4	1	1
Capps, Edward	9	1	2
Craft, Simon	6	1	2
Wilbur, John	5	1	1
Flanikin, William	4	1	2
Spann, John	4	1	5

SHENANDOAH COUNTY.

NAME OF HEAD OF FAMILY.	White souls.	Dwellings.	Other buildings.
LIST OF ABRAHAM KELLER.			
Allen, John	9	1	3
Allen, William	2	1	2
Allen, James	6	....	....
Bailey, John	4	....	....
Bailey, John, Junr	3	....	....
Breding, Spencer	10	1	....
Beack, John	2	....	....
Cunningham, Adam	9	2	3
Clevenger, Thomas	8	1	1
Catlet, Charles	3	1	....
Day, Robert	5	....	....
Dothon, Thos	4	1	....
Dothon, Thos, Junr	4	....	....
Greyham, John	12	1	....
Green, James	7	....	....
Green, John	3	....	....
Horner, Isaac	4	....	....
Harding, Samuel	3	....	....
Hurst, Elijah	4	....	....
Harrel, James	1	1	1
Jobe, Moses	7	1	....
Jobe, Enuch	6	1	1
Jox, William	7	....	....
Jaris, Samuel	10	1	....
Ireland, James	1	1	1
Jollis, Jacob	12	1	1
Linch, Peter	6	....	....
Lewesuce, John	6	1	....
Leeth, Ephraim, Junr	4	....	....
Mathewes, James	7	1	....
Matocks, Mathew	9	1	....
Madox, Scofield	6	1	....
More, Jonothan	7	1	....
McKoy, Jeremiah	11	1	1
Millar, Peter	8	2	1
McKulley, Wm	4	1	....
McDaniel, John	2	....	....
Moody, Moses	9	1	2
Millar, Jacob	3	1	....
Mathewes, John	6	2	1
McKoy, George	7	1	2
Noble, Coleman	9	....	....
Noble, Wm	6	....	....
Night, Amannuel	3	....	....
Odle, Jonithen	9	1	....
Odle, James	8	1	....
Overall, John	10	2	3
Puling, George	12	1	....
Pagit, Reubin	3	1	....
Reagan, Charles, Senr	7	....	....

NAME OF HEAD OF FAMILY.	White souls.	Dwellings.	Other buildings.
LIST OF ABRAHAM KELLER—continued.			
Reagan, Charles, Junr	2	....	....
Summery, Samuel	7	1	....
Safer, William	7	1	....
Sandy, Wm	10	....	....
Sulton, Moses	5	....	....
Typton, William	9	....	....
Vaughon, Elizabeth	8	1	....
Whitson, Jeremiah	2	1	....
Wiley, George	5	1	....
Whitson, John	9	1	....
Wood, John	6	....	....
Wood, Wm	3	1	....
Whitson, Ruth	6	1	1
Wood, John	1	....	....
Young, Sinnit	10	1	....
LIST OF ABRAHAM BIRD.			
Allen, Jackson	8	1	5
Allen, Lidia	9	1	6
Allen, Reubin	1	1	1
Bird, Abraham	12	1	4
Bird, Nounce	7	1	4
Brannamam, Daniel	4	1	1
Brinker, Conrod	11	1	3
Beale, Taverner	8	1	11
Coil, John	12	1	3
Crider, George	3	1	1
Dobbins, Griffith	10	1	1
Filsmoyers, John	10	2	3
Funkhouser, Jacob	6	2	2
Graybil, George	3	1	....
Giger, Adam	7	1	1
Harrison, Burr	....	1	9
Kingary, Daniel	11	1	3
Kingary, Soloman	1	1	2
Longacre, Jacob	6	1	1
Moore, John	6	3	10
Moffitt, Anderson	6	1	2
Miller, John	3	....	....
Moore, Jacob	9	1	3
Moore, Reubin	3	1	2
Moore, Reubin, Senr	4	1	3
Moore, William	6	2	4
Mathany, Joseph	8	1	1
Neff, John	12	1	2
Neff, Francis	7	1	3
Ozburn, Rachel	4	1	....
Penewit, John	2	1	4
Penewit, Jacob	4	1	1

NAME OF HEAD OF FAMILY.	White souls.	Dwellings.	Other buildings.
LIST OF ABRAHAM BIRD—continued.			
Penewit, Philip	6	1	....
Penewit, Adam	4	1	3
Runnion, Barefoot	4	1	2
Russell, James	8	1	2
Soltsman, William	3	1	....
Skeen, James	4	1	2
Taylor, Christn Charles	5	....	....
Taylor, Charles	8	1	2
Young, Samuel	3	1	2
Weaver, George	9	1	2
LIST OF EDWIN YOUNG.			
Ailshite, Jno Conrod	2	....	1
Alter, Frederick	9	....	....
Ailshite, Benedick	6	....	....
Ailshite, Conrod	6	....	....
Ailshite, Jacob	3	....	....
Bullington, Jno	5	....	....
Bloser, Abm	2	....	....
Beam, Jno	5	....	....
Beaver, Jno	3	1	1
Bumgarner, Peter	1	1	1
Bumgarner, David	1	....	....
Burner, Joseph	3	1	1
Beaker, Philip	2	....	....
Bumgarner, Christn	1	1	....
Breeding, James, Senr	9	1	1
Beever, Cunrod	1	....	....
Beever, Christian	3	....	....
Barnett, Jno	5	....	....
Beever, Abm	2	....	....
Cook, Henry	4	....	....
Cox, Jeremiah	5	1	....
Countz, George	4	....	....
Combs, Job	13	1	1
Campbell, James	8	1	1
Countz, Jacob	2	....	....
Countz, Jno	6	1	1
Combs, Soloman	5	....	....
Cofman, Martin	8	2	1
Cofman, David	7	1	2
Cofman, Christly	9	1	1
Cofman, Martin (on the halks bill)	7	1	2
Dasher, Danl	3	....	....
Dotson, Saml	3	1	....
Foley, Selby	1	....	....
Fox, Peter	3	1	....
Flemming, William	7	....	....

NAME OF HEAD OF FAMILY.	White souls.	Dwellings.	Other buildings.
LIST OF EDWIN YOUNG—continued.			
Frees, Jno	6	....	....
Grover, Six Barnard	2	....	....
Grover, Marks	10	1	1
Hapler, Jno	8	....	....
Harshbarger, Isaac	3	1	4
Hawkins, Joseph	4	....	....
Humback, Henry	9	2	6
Hockman, Mary	9	1	....
Hastans, Jacob	9	1	1
Harshbarger, Christn	11	1	1
Heaston, Jacob, Junr	4	1	....
Heaston, Jno	3	....	....
Husk, Aboslem	7	....	....
Hoke, William	9	....	....
Haubers, Peter	5	....	....
Hashbarger, Fredk	10	....	....
Humphrey, Jno	8	....	....
Harshbarger, Jno	8	1	3
Hite, Andrew	6	1	1
James, George	11	2	6
Jones, Mary	4	....	....
Judge, Michl	4	....	....
Kibber, Henry	6	1	2
Kiser, Andrew	3	1	1
Kiser, Charles	6	1	....
Kiblinger, Peter	6	....	....
Leeth, Ebenezer	5	2	3
Lear, Jno	5	1	2
Mauk, Henry	10	....	....
Neal, Jno	2	1	....
Num, Wharton	3	....	1
Nelson, Jno	3	....	....
Orback, Rudolph	6	....	....
Pangle, Catharine	4	....	....
Rufner, Peter	10	....	....
Rufner, Mary	3	....	....
Roadcap, Isaac	2	1	....
Roadcap, Peter	6	1	1
Rufner, Benja	7	1	2
Rufner, Joseph	10	1	2
Stuart, Natha	4	1	2
Shock, Henry	7	....	2
Shanks, Martin	9	1	2
Sowers, Fredk	3	....	....
Stump, Jacob	9	1	4
Shank, Windle	3	....	....
Sheetz, Michl	5	....	....
Stickler, Danl	6	1	1
Stickler, Isaac	6	1	1
Stickler, Abm, Junr	8	1	2

NAME OF HEAD OF FAMILY.	White souls.	Dwellings.	Other buildings.	NAME OF HEAD OF FAMILY.	White souls.	Dwellings.	Other buildings.	NAME OF HEAD OF FAMILY.	White souls.	Dwellings.	Other buildings.	NAME OF HEAD OF FAMILY.	White souls.	Dwellings.	Other buildings.
LIST OF EDWIN YOUNG— continued.				**LIST OF EVAN JONES— continued.**				**LIST OF EVAN JONES— continued.**				**LIST OF RICH'D BRANHAM— continued.**			
Sisk, Thos	7			Cunningham, Arabela	6	1		Taylor, Charles	4			Boswill, Jonathan	7	1	1
Sumpback, Fredᵏ	4			Durst, Abraham	6	1	2	Wood, Charel	7	1	1	Boyer, Pholy	6		2
Smith, William	12	1		Durst, Daniel	3	1		Witsel, Anthony	11	1	3	Baker, Jacob	7	1	1
Tyler, Willᵐ	4	1		Deen, John	5	1	1	Wever, George	3			Baker, Henry	2		2
Taylor, Jnᵒ	3	1		Dundore, Chrisley	5	1	1	Walters, Daniel	11	1	1	Ballace, Henry	6		2
Varnhouser, Jacob	10	1	1	Easterly, George	7	1	1	Will, Andrew	3			Branham, Richᵈ	6		
Varner, Philip	7	1	3	Emmery, Thomas	5	1	1	Wine, Michael	9	1	1	Blawser, Peter	8		2
Vincent, Joseph	7	1	1	Evey, Andrew	6	1	1	Zircle, Michael	12	1		Boroker, Daniel	6		2
Underwood, George	1	1	1	Farmer, Mathew	5	1						Bumgarner, Michael	2		1
Wright, Isaac Simson	8			Taber, Peter	5	1	1	**LIST OF ALEXANDER HITE.**				Bair, Jacob	8		2
Young, Edwin	7	1	2	Fine, John	6	1						Comer, John	5	1	1
Zisler, George	11			Funk, Peter	5	1	2	Adoughuthey, William	7	1	1	Crim, Jacob	2		2
				Faber, Vollentine	4	1	2	Adoughuthey, Jervices	6	1	1	Coomer, Michael	6	1	2
LIST OF THOMAS ALLEN.				Frout, Frederick	6	1	2	Blent, Michael	5	1	2	Cofman, David	7	1	2
Allensworth, John	2	1	3	Fawcett, Benjam	10	1	1	Balthias, Leonard	11	1	1	Coomer, Philip	3		1
Allensworth, Philip	9	1	3	Fry, Henry	4	1	1	Bowman, Samuel	5	1	1	Coomer, Augustine	3		2
Allen, Thomas	10	1	4	Fauber, Jacob	7	1		Brumfield, John	2			Coomer, Martin	12	2	1
Bogges, Giles	8	1	2	Goore, Henry	8	1	1	Blass, John	2			Coomer, Adam	3	1	1
Branson, Lionle	4	1	1	Gore, Mary	4	1		Bowman, Peter	4	1	1	Coomer, Frederick	10	1	2
Carter, Chanler	5	1		Gore, John	4	1		Bushong, John, Senʳ	7			Cofman, David	6	1	2
Cleveland, George	7	1	1	Good, Jacob	5	1		Backing, Mathias	2			Crump, George	11		
Cain, Joshua	6	1		Good, Peter	6	1		Coper, George (Saddler)	6			Decker, Adam	8		2
Cain, Henry	2	1	2	Garver, Martin	3	1		Cooper, George (Shoemaker)	7	1	1	Davis, Jonathan	3		
Cloud, William	8	1	2	Garver, Samuel	8	1	1					Finter, Mathias	5		1
Cloud, Daniel	3	1	2	Good, Henry	6	1		Conrad, Jacob	3			Finter, Frederick	2		
Cloud, Henry	4	1	1	Garve, John	8	1	1	Crowdson, John	6			Frimoode, Mathias	4	1	1
Carson, Simon	9	1	7	Holeman, Mary	6	1	1	Creable, Abraham	4	1	2	Grove, Christian	12	1	1
Coffman, Andrew	8	1		Hupp, Polser	8	1	1	Dosh, Christopher	3	1	1	Going, Michael	7		2
Coffman, Nicholas	10	1		Houser, Henry	9	1	3	Deboe, John Conrad	8	1		Harris, William	1		
Cleveland, John	5	1		Hannegan, Michael	3	1		Eberly, Jeremiah, Senʳ	3	1	1	Hite, John	1		
Evisten, Francis	2	1	1	Haugh, Tobias	5			Eberly, Jeremiah, Junʳ	7	1	1	Harris, James	4	1	1
Martin, Doctor	4	1	1	Holvah, John	3			Funkhouser, Christian	7	1	1	Hite, Daniel	8		2
Elsy, Thomas	9	1		Holvah, George	2			Feltner, Henry	10	1	2	Hay, Alexander	6	1	2
Funk, Henry	7	1	5	Harpine, Philip	9	1	3	Feassel, Michael, Senʳ	6	1		Hite, Abraham	8		2
Galmon, John	2	1		Henton, Thoˢ, Junʳ	5	1		Faegdly, George	6	2	3	Howbert, Nicholas	4		2
Halle, Peter	7	1	1	Henton, Thoˢ, Senʳ	6	1	1	Funk, Jacob	7	1	2	Hopewood, Wᵐ	1		
Hopewell, Joseph	9	1	1	Jones, Evan	7	1	1	Funk, Henry, Junʳ	5	1	2	Judy, Jacob	7		1
Hery, Aaron	12	1		Jones, Thomas	4	1		Funk, Catharine (widow)	6	1	1	Killinger, Jacob	6		2
Hand, William	11	1		Ingrum, Francis	8	1	2	Feltner, Jacob	7	1	1	Linbark, Peter	7	1	2
Hand, Robert	7	1	1	Jones, John	8	1		Gross, William	3			Lung, George	4	1	3
Hand, Thomas	2			Jones, William	6	1	1	Hockman, Abraham	2	1	1	Linonbark, John	7	1	2
Houghn, John	10	1		Kingry, Michael	3	1	1	Hunter, William	4			Lung, Philip	9	2	3
Headly, William	7	1	2	Keltnor, Henry	9	1	2	Huffman, Philip	8	2	2	Maggott, Margrett	4	2	2
Jennings, William	11	2	2	Lokely, James	10	1	1	Harr, Simon	5	1	1	Maggott, David	6		
Jones, Thomas	7	1		Lips, Henry	6	1		Harr, John	3			Maggott, Benjᵃ	1		
Jones, William	4	1		Lewis, Mordicai	7	1		Hite, Alexander	6	1	1	Maggott, John	2		1
Jones, Frank	2	1		Miller, Daniel	4			Hahn, Henry	4			Mits, John	3		1
Jones, George	2	1		MᶜCarty, James	5	1		Karshwaylar, Catherine	3	1		Maggott, Henry	6		2
Johnston, Andrew	8	1		Miller, Jacob	10	1	1	Klippble, Henry	5	1	2	McGince, John	2		1
Masterson, Thomas	7	1		Mowerer, Michael	9	1		Kister, Christopher	3	1	1	Maggott, Christian	8	1	2
MᶜDniel, Molle	5	1		Moor, Joseph	9	1	3	Launn, Rudolph	2	1		Mussleman, John	10	1	1
MᶜKay, Robert	8	1	2	Neaff, Christley	4	1		Lamput, Christopher	8	1	1	Nowman, John	6		2
Miller, James	7	1	2	Naff, Jacob	7	1	1	Lamput, Tobias	2			Newman, Thos	7	1	1
Mercer, William	7	1	1	Naff, Abraham	3	1	3	Lamput, Jacob	4	1		Ofinbacker, Frederick	6		1
Miller, William	8	1	5	Newman, Walter	9	1	1	Lotz, Jonas	3	1		Ofenbacker, John	3		2
Reynolds, Thomas	6	1		Nuse, John	4	1		Lotz, Gasper	4			Painter, Joseph	1		
Settles, William	5	1		Neace, Michael	7	2	3	Lockmiller, George, Senʳ	5	1	1	Painter, Conrod	4	1	3
Smith, Thomas	10	1	2	Orock, David	9	2	1	Miller, Henry	9	1	1	Painter, Joshua	3		1
Smith, John (on passage creek)	9	1	2	Penneybacker, Derick	64	1	3	MᶜClaningham, Robert	4	1		Pence, Lewis	3	1	1
Smith, Henry	4	1		Polsel, Peter	8	1	2	Marcuro, John	2	1		Pence, Barbey	5	1	1
Smith, John (Cabimur)	5	1	1	Poniwit, John	6	1		Machir, Alexander, Esqʳ	13	6	11	Pibler, Lewis	7	1	1
Robertson, William (Tyl)	12	1	2	Peters, Abraham	2	1		Niebenger, Christian, Senʳ	7	1		Pibler, Jacob	6		2
Taylor, Lazarus	4	1	2	Pence, Conrad	4	1	1	Pister, Martin	2	1	1	Pibler, Francis	3		2
Wilson, Edward	8	1	1	Pence, Michael	8	1	2	Ravenhill, Francis	6	2	1	Pibler, Christian	6	1	2
Wey, Edward	8	1		Seyters, John	13	1	2	Richardson, John C	7	1	1	Pence, Henry	14		2
				Rinehart, Lewis	7	1		Richardson, Samuel	3	1	1	Pence, Frederick	7		1
LIST OF EVAN JONES.				Roof, Jacob	8	1	2	Reager, Michael	10	2	2	Piper, Augustine	4	1	2
Allen, Josias	10	1	3	Russel, Mary	1			Smith, Daniel	4			Prince, George	8	1	2
Antrom, John	5	1	1	Russee, Elizabeth	1			Smith, Valentine	5	1	4	Pence, John	8	1	2
Albrite, Laronee	2			Roush, John	6	1	2	Smith, Peter	3	1	1	Proper, Nichoˢ	7		1
Branaman, Abraham	7	1		Roush, Daniel	2			Still, John	6	1		Prince, Cutlip	5		2
Brongman, John	7	1		Roush, John	3	1		Sherman, Adam, Senʳ	5	2	1	Prince, Philip	3	1	
Broam, Henry	5	1	2	Roush, Henry	5	1		Schnider, John	2	1	1	Prince, Goodfrie	5		2
Broks, John	4	1	1	Roush, John, Senʳ	3	1		Seib, Henry	10			Prince, Philip, Junʳ	7		2
Brock, John	4	1	1	Roler, John	11	1	1	Stoner, Frederick	7	2	4	Richebaker, John	1	1	2
Blesing, Jacob	8			Readen, George	10	2	2	Snapp, Margaret	2	2	2	Richebaker, Adam	1		2
Beck, John	5			Roush, Philip	10	1	1	Snapp, Peter	4		2	Roods, Joseph	2		2
Briner, Gagbour	7	1	2	Roush, George	4			Stover, Christian (Son of P.)	6	2	4	Rufner, Reubin	5	1	2
Bowers, Christian	12	1	1	Roush, Jacob	5	2	3	Stover, Peter	7	1	4	Roodcap, George	13	1	2
Brit, John	5	1	1	Sircle, George	11	1	2	Stover, Christian	1			Roodcap, Isaac	2	1	1
Brock, Roudolph	6	1		Seahorn, Nicholas	3	1		Stover, Jacob	9	1	3	Robinson, John	4		2
Brock, Henry	10	1	1	States, Mary	2	1		Trout, Daniel	7	1		Sower, Polser	4		3
Brennor, John	8	1	1	Selsor, Henry	10	1	1	Walter, Daniel	3	1		Spitler, Jacob	7	1	1
Cathy, William, Senʳ	5	1	2	Stickler, Samuel	5	1	1	Watson, Joseph, Esqʳ	3	2	1	Sites, Andrew	2	1	1
Cathy, William, Junʳ	11	1	6	Surrey, John	3	1		Yost, Jacob	7	1	1	Spitler, Abraham	7	1	2
Campbell, Charles	6	1	3	Seickel, Jacob	4	1	2	Zeah, Philip	3	1	1	Sparks, Augustine	2		
Caggey, John	3	1		Sinder, Christopher	7							Snider, John	6		1
Caggey, Henry	11	1	2	Stults, Peter	3			**LIST OF RICH'D BRANHAM.**				Shulling, Christian	3		1
Caggey, Roudolph	8	1		Stotson, Jacob	11	1	2					Stonebarger, Frederick	10		1
Click, John	6	1	2	Siverly, Peter	2	1		Atwill, John	5		2	Sheets, John	5		2
Coolle, Conrad	5	1	1	Siverly, Christian	8	1	3	Ammon, Peter	1			Snider, Daniel	6		2
Caruy, Josey	7	1	1	Shaven, Jacob	11	2	1	Beever, Michael	3	1	1	Sommers, Philip	8		3
Caruy, Cutlip	2			Sirile, Andrew	9	1	5	Branham, Gaydon	5			Shaver, Jacob	8	1	1
Cook, Adam	8	1	1	Shaver, Jacob	5	1		Brewbaker, Abraham	10	2	2	Sowers, Henry	2	1	2
				Shaver, Frederick	3			Brewbaker, Abraham, Junʳ	4			Stickler, Benjᵃ	6		2
				Thomson, David	4							Wice, Michael, Senʳ	5	1	2

SHENANDOAH COUNTY—Continued.

LIST OF RICH'D BRANHAM—continued.

NAME OF HEAD OF FAMILY.	White souls.	Dwellings.	Other buildings.
Whidack, Henry	9	1	2
Wickle, Jacob	5	....	2
Widrick, John	4	....	2
Wise, Michael, Junr	3	....	2
Wishart, John	4	....	1
Wooff, Jacob	5	1	....
Williams, Samuel	1	....	....

LIST OF JACOB RINKER.

NAME OF HEAD OF FAMILY.	White souls.	Dwellings.	Other buildings.
Acker, Philip	8	....	1
Bower, Christian	12	1	....
Baughman, Jacob	7	1	1
Bernhard, George	5	....	....
Boyer, Margaret (widow)	7	....	....
Burger, Michael	4	....	....
Berger, Henry	3	....	....
Burkhard, Simon	10	1	....
Baker, Peter	8	....	....
Barb, Abraham	8	....	....
Barb, Adam	7	1	1
Barb, Jacob	6	....	....
Bower, Henry	5	....	....
Coffelt, Christian	8	1	....
Callender, Michael	6	....	....
Coffelt, Valentine	7	....	1
Coffelt, George	10	1	1
Click, John, Senr	7	1	1
Cofman, Augustine	5	1	1
Cofman, Daniel	4	....	....
Cofman, Andrew	6	1	1
Cofman, George	1	1	1
Crous, Michael	8	1	1
Dellinger, George	5	....	....
Dellinger, Emanuel	5	....	....
Dodson, Peter	8	....	....
Dellinger, Magdaline	3	1	1
Dytch, George	1	....	....
Foltz, Joshua	5	....	....
Funkhouser, Christian	9	1	1
Funkhouser, Abraham	7	....	....
Frocshouser, John	2	....	....
Foltz, Peter	7	....	....
Fauber, Valentine, Junr	5	....	1
Fox, Catharine (widow)	4	1	1
Fry, John	8	....	....
Good, William	11	1	1
Glatfelter, Rudolph	7	....	....
Henly, Michael	4	1	2
Hess, Abraham	7	....	....
Helsley, Jacob	7	....	1
Hudson, Thomas	2	....	....
Hoshaur, Peter	2	....	....
Hoshaur, Henry	10	....	....
Haller, Peter, Senr	11	1	1
Haller, Henry	5	....	1
Houts, Windle	2	1	1
Kingry, John	4	....	....
Keller, John	9	1	1
Knertzer, Balzar	1	....	....
Lindamude, Andrew	8	....	1
Lindamude, John	2	....	....
Lindamude, George Henry	3	....	....
Lindamude, Michael	8	....	....
Lindamude, Christopher	11	....	1
Lonas, Leonard	9	....	....
Lonas, George	5	....	....
Miller, George	5	....	....
Messersmith, George	4	....	....
Mathias, John	7	1	1
Moyer, George	8	1	....
Miller, John (Saddler)	7	....	1
Nease, Ubrick	5	....	....
Pitzenberger, Elizabeth	6	....	....
Poke, Adam	6	1	....
Rust, Valentine, Senr	7	....	....
Rodenheffer, Anthony	2	....	....
Ryan, Thomas	6	....	....
Rust, Abraham	2	....	....
Rinker, George	7	....	1
Rinehard, Jonas	9	....	1
Rust, Valentine, Junr	6	....	....
Rinker, Jacob, Senr	8	1	3
Richard, Christian	9	1	1
Rinker, Jacob, Junr	10	1	1
Seyger, Cunrod	7	....	....
Shouman, Stephen	5	....	....
Shoemaker, Mary (Widow)	8	....	....
Sink, Jacob	3	....	....
Seyger, John	7	....	....
Siron, Nathaniel	7	....	....
Smith, Adam	11	....	....
Spitler, John	6	....	....
Sink, Godlove	8	1	1
Shaver, Michael	3	....	....
Shaver, Christian	2	....	....

LIST OF JACOB RINKER—continued.

NAME OF HEAD OF FAMILY.	White souls.	Dwellings.	Other buildings.
Sivy, Mathias	10	....	....
Stout, John	8	....	....
Surber, Jacob	10	....	....
Sine, Adam	5	....	....
Seyger, Gabriel	10	1	1
Smith, John	4	....	....
Stegeler, Sebastian	4	1	1
Stickly, Daniel	8	1	1
Tiesinger, Peter	7	....	....
Woolf, Mary (widow)	7	1	....
Woolf, Jacob, Senr	2	....	....
Wocker, John	7	1	1
Weaver, Adam	3	....	....
Waggoner, Ubrick	6	....	1
Young, Christopher	5	1	....
Zimmerman, John	7	....	....

LIST OF WILLIAM A. BOOTH.

NAME OF HEAD OF FAMILY.	White souls.	Dwellings.	Other buildings.
Booth, William A	6	1	5
Beam, Reubin	4	1	2
Beam, Samuel	10	1	5
Bell, John	11	1	4
Baker, Philpeter	8	1	1
Baker, Anthony	7	1	1
Baker, George	10	1	2
Brewback, Jacob	7	1	2
Beam, Jacob	7	2	1
Barr, Christian	2	....	....
Barr, Philip	5	1	1
Croutson, John	10	2	6
Cesner, John	5	1	1
Cronk, John	4	1	1
Colvill, Samuel	4	1	3
Colvill, John	3	1	....
Fizle, John	4	1	1
Frye, Benja	9	1	5
Frye, John	7	1	2
Funkhouser, Jacob	8	1	6
Hover, Frederick	9	1	3
Jameson, Robt	9	1	5
Keeler, Joseph	4	1	1
Kiger, George	7	....	....
Lind, George	4	1	1
Lockmaler, John	7	1	2
Linn, Jacob	6	1	....
Miller, George	12	2	3
Newill, Thomas	11	1	3
Newill, Thomas	8	1	2
Piper, Henry	7	1	1
Piper, Davis	3	1	....
Peoples, John	6	1	3
Pingley, Joseph	9	1	2
Pitman, Philip	6	1	3
Pence, Adam	6	1	....
Rower, Daniel	4	1	2
Sunner, Philip	9	1	4
Setser, John	2	1	1
Stenson, William	9	1	3
Stickley, Benja	10	1	2
Setser, Martin	12	1	3
Stickley, Jacob	7	1	1
Suppenger, Ubrick	6	1	3
Suppenger, John	8	1	3
Townsin, Henry	7	1	1
Tidwick, Stephen	12	1	2
Wilson, Archd	9	1	8
Willy, Henry	5	1	....
Windle, Jacob	9	1	2
Waggner, Jacob	7	1	1
Wood, Thomas	5	1	....
Watson, John	5	1	1

LIST OF SAMUEL PORTER.

NAME OF HEAD OF FAMILY.	White souls.	Dwellings.	Other buildings.
Bosserman, Christian	5	1	1
Bly, Philip	3	2	2
Bly, George	4	....	....
Bly, Jacob	5	....	....
Black, Martin	7	1	1
Baird, Zechariah	4	1	1
Baird, Martin	5	2	1
Baird, Christle	3	1	....
Black, Peter	9	1	1
Black, Martin	6	1	1
Buck, John, Esqr	8	1	6
Buck, Charles	8	1	8
Cop, Christian	9	1	1
Crisel, Nicholas	5	1	....
Campell, Alexander	5	1	3
Coplin, Kerry	6	....	....
Coughener, Jacob	12	1	1
Cline, Peter	2	1	1
Disponent, Christopher	8	1	2
Evans, Jeremiah	7	1	....
Eaker, Henry	10	1	1
Flick, Peter	6	1	....

LIST OF SAMUEL PORTER—continued.

NAME OF HEAD OF FAMILY.	White souls.	Dwellings.	Other buildings.
Flood, Berry	4	....	....
Fryman, Charles	8	1	....
Gaspenger, Ubrick	10	1	1
Grim, John	3	1	1
Grabell, Christian	6	1	1
Grabell, John	3	1	....
Grim, Jacob	5	1	....
Gatewood, Philip	5	1	6
Harbock, Peter	9	1	1
Hogman, John	5	1	1
Huddle, David	6	1	....
Hiser, Henry	11	1	1
Hudle, George	11	1	2
Hogman, Christopher	2	1	....
Hauserfleck, Henry	3	....	....
Hogman, Peter	7	1	1
Headly, William	7	1	3
Holms, William	9	1	2
Jinkins, Samuel	8	1	1
Jickson, Samuel	2	1	....
Keller, Henry	6	1	2
Keller, Jacob	6	1	1
Lockmiller, George	3	1	1
Merny, Robert	6	1	1
Pier, John	5	1	....
Pier, Philip	12	2	1
Pitman, Nicholas	8	1	1
Porter, Samuel	7	1	3
Posserman, Frederick	5	1	1
Russell, James	8	1	2
Rute, Michael	5	1	....
Richards, George	4	1	1
Russell, Joseph	6	2	1
Reece, Joel	12	1	1
Snapp, Philip	7	1	1
Snapp, George	5	1	1
Sibert, Barnet	3	1	....
Snare, Henry	3	1	1
Shever, Daniel	4	1	1
Sibert, Jacob	3	....	....
Summer, Andrew	4	1	1
Spiker, Jacob	9	1	1
Sunner, John	3	1	....
Strother, William	8	2	4
Sibert, Adam	1	1	....
Snapp, Lawrence	10	1	2
Shua, Joseph	10	....	2
Smith, John	5	1	....
Smily, James	3	1	1
Vance, Isaac	3	....	....
Vance, Samuel	6	2	5
Windle, Capt Philip	9	1	1
Wilson, John	4	1	1

LIST OF JOHN ANDERSON.

NAME OF HEAD OF FAMILY.	White souls.	Dwellings.	Other buildings.
Albert, Nicholas	7	1	2
Albert, Jacob	3	1	....
Albert, John	6	1	2
Arts, John	5	....	....
Bowman, John	7	1	1
Brewbaker, Abraham	3	....	....
Bird, Abraham	15	2	4
Bond, John	7	1	2
Bowman, Benja	2	1	1
Bowman, George	8	....	....
Countz, George	9	1	2
Clous, Adam	3	....	....
Dundore, John	5	....	....
Dorony, Darby	9	1	2
Denter, Mathis	13	1	3
David, Henry	9	1	1
Evans, Elijah	11	1	3
Evans, Samuel	7	1	....
Emshwelbs, Jacob	4	1	2
Funk, Peter	5	1	1
Gallehon, Edward	4	....	....
Hawkins, Joseph	9	1	2
Holeman, Christian	9	1	1
Hallow, Peter	12	1	2
Hank, John	6	1	4
Huddle, John	1	1	....
Helvy, Peter	6	....	....
Huffman, Christian	4	1	1
Hall, Joseph	4	1	....
Hower, Henry	9	1	2
Jueltz, John	8	1	1
Cunningham, Thomas	6	1	1
Lee, Peetmount	8	....	....
Lonce, George	4	1	2
Lonce, Jacob	3	....	....
Lowery, Conrod	5	....	....
Manthany, Joseph	7	1	....
Mackinturff, Christopher	10	1	....
Megol, James	3	....	....
Mathony, Daniel	10	2	1
Nuland, Daniel, Junr	8	1	1

LIST OF JOHN ANDERSON—continued.

NAME OF HEAD OF FAMILY.	White souls.	Dwellings.	Other buildings.
Nisely, Jacob	6	....	1
Parsons, Thomas	6	....	....
Parsons, John	6	....	....
Pennecof, Philip	9	....	....
Pence, Nicholas	7	1	1
Reed, Mitchel	8	1	1
Beyby, Jacob	9	....	....
Russell, James	8	1	2
Reacomb, Jacob	5	1	....
Smith, Joseph	4	1	1
Stover, John	3	2	3
Sparks, Peter	4	1	....
Shank, John	7	....	....
Smith, Samuel	5	1	1
Shetser, Philip	7	1	....
Smith, William	2	1	2
Sheetz, Barbary	3	1	3
Sheetz, Henry	6	....	....
Stouder, Frederick	8	....	....
Stickler, Saml	5	1	1
Turney, Daniel	6	1	1
Turney, Peter	3	1	1
Wiatt, Edward	6	1	....
Wiatt, John	9	1	1
Waterhold, Henry	3	1	....

LIST OF JOSEPH PUGH.

NAME OF HEAD OF FAMILY.	White souls.	Dwellings.	Other buildings.
Anderson, John	7	1	1
Bowman, Henry	8	1	1
Borden, Nicholas	6	1	1
Bonn, Daniel	1	....	....
Boush, Debault	5	1	....
Bushong, John	4	1	1
Bowman, Jacob	10	2	1
Berner, Michael	10	3	5
Barnet, William	7	1	....
Bough, Dorety	3	1	1
Bruner, John	2	....	....
Brown, John	7	2	3
Bowman, John	3	1	1
Crable, Cristine	8	1	2
Coakanhour, Joseph	6	1	1
Coakanhour, Abraham	3	1	1
Cokinhour, John	5	1	1
Clour, George	4	....	....
Crable, Jacob	7	1	1
Crookshanks, John	3	2	1
Dennis, William	8	1	1
Dillinger, John	11	1	3
Daring, Henry	6	....	....
Feater, Jacob	5	....	....
Fetzer, George	3	1	2
Fetzer, Henry	5	....	....
Fetzer, Joaham	5	....	....
Frevel, George	5	1	....
Frevel, Henry	12	1	1
Finter, Conrad	4	....	....
Finter, Henry	5	1	1
Geyer, John	3	1	1
Granstuff, George	7	1	1
Huver, John	4	....	....
Huver, Jacob	4	1	1
Hise, Christian	5	....	1
Hise, John	4	1	1
Hufman, Daniel	7	1	1
Huffman, Ann	2	1	....
Hart, Lanard	5	1	1
Hover, Polser	10	1	1
Hokman, Henry	7	1	1
Hufman, Christley	5	1	1
Huddle, Soloman	2	1	....
Helmick, John	6	1	....
Haws, John	8	1	1
Kener, Ubrick	9	1	2
Kibler, Christian	5	1	2
Keffer, Jeremiah	9	1	1
Kenar, Ann	3	....	....
Kennady, William	3	2	4
Kibler, John	6	1	1
Kibler, Philip	4	1	....
Kelp, William	3	1	2
Kener, David	7	1	1
Kerkehiser, Leonard	7	1	....
Lacey, John	6	....	....
Leman, David	7	1	1
Messer, John	5	1	1
Miller, Christian	7	1	2
Miers, Henry	4	1	1
Mavis, George	10	1	1
Miller, Ulrick	9	....	....
Miller, Peter	8	....	....
Machir, John	....	1	2
Mace, Henry	6	....	....
Miller, Martin	4	1	....
Mathery, Joseph	8	1	1

SHENANDOAH COUNTY—Continued.

LIST OF JOSEPH PUGH—continued.

NAME OF HEAD OF FAMILY.	White souls.	Dwellings.	Other buildings.
Milly, Daniel	6	1	1
Milley, Tobias	4	....	....
Moirs, Henry	4	....	....
Moirer, Valentine	4	1	....
Mawer, John	5	1	1
Nisely, Jacob	3	....	1
Nisely, Anthony	9	1	....
Nogle, George	6	1	....
Nisely, Anthony	10	....	....
Nisely, John	9	2	2
Ott, Henry	6	1	2
Ortz, Henry	4	1	1
Ogdon, Joshua	4	....	....
Pugh, Joseph	8	6	6
Price, William	7	....	....
Ready, Augustine	2	1	1
Beady, Barnet	2	1	1
Ready, Philip	6	1	1
Riddle, Abraham	13	1	2
Rinzer, Andrew	7	....	....
Rodeheffer, David	5	1	1
Rodeheffer, Samuel	8	1	1
Rife, Christian	12	....	....
Saring, Mathias	10	2	2
Shiner, Martin	5	1	2
Sine, John	7	....	....
Savage, Abraham	6	1	1
Sockin, Tobias	6	1	1
Williams, John	3	....	....
Woolfard, Frederick	6	2	3
Wakeman, Conrod	7	....	....
Wiseman, Nicholas	6	1	1
Wiseman, George	9	1	1
Wetz, Nicholas	6	1	1
Wolfenberger, John	7	....	....
Weaver, Philip	7	....	....
Witsel, George	7	1	1
Wolfenberger, John	6	1	1
Wolfenberger, Peter	8	....	....
Wolfenberger, Benja	3	....	....
Wood, George	3	1	2
Yarger, Joseph	5	1	2
Wiseman, Thomas	9	1	1

LIST OF JOHN NETHERTON.

NAME OF HEAD OF FAMILY.	White souls.	Dwellings.	Other buildings.
Atwood, John	5	1	....
Allen, Moses	3	1	....
Allen, William	5	1	3
Arterbon, William	9	....	....
Atwood, James	2	....	....
Atwood, Gilbert	6	1	1
Arterbern, Peter	13	1	....
Berkhead, Abraham	8	1	....
Cunningham, Adam	8	1	....
Crume, Philip	7	1	3
Comes, William	6	1	....
Crume, Daniel	3	1	....
Calfee, John	4	1	2
Crume, Jesse	4	1	....
Curl, John	8	1	1
Dale, Isaac	6	1	....
Edwards, John	5	....	....
Gant, William	2	....	....
Gee, Richard	2	1	....

LIST OF JOHN NETHERTON—continued.

NAME OF HEAD OF FAMILY.	White souls.	Dwellings.	Other buildings.
Hall, William	8	1	....
Hurst, William	9	1	....
Harding, Wilmot	3	1	....
Harding, John	3	1	....
Harding, Henry, Senr	7	1	2
Hash, John	8	1	....
Hutchison, John	9	2	....
Harding, Nicholas	8	2	5
Harding, Henry, Junr	3	....	....
Harding, George	7	1	....
Handisck, John	11	1	....
Leeth, James	5	1	....
McCay, Robert	5	1	....
McCay, James, Senr	2	1	2
McCay, James, Junr	10	1	1
Netherton, Henry, Senr	2	1	2
Netherton, Henry, Junr	12	1	1
Netherton, John	10	1	1
Pagett, Reubin, Senr	3	1	1
Perry, Samuel	9	1	1
Pagget, Theophelus	8	1	....
Pagget, Reubin, Junr	8	2	1
Parker, John	11	1	....
Quinn, Patrick	6	1	....
Roy, John	7	1	....
Ramey, John	8	1	1
Roy, James	7	....	....
Rogers, James	1	....	....
Smith, John	9	1	....
Sollars, William	6	1	....
Wilson, Robert	4	1	....

LIST OF JOHN HUTCHIRSON.

NAME OF HEAD OF FAMILY.	White souls.	Dwellings.	Other buildings.
Albert, William	9	1	....
Bodkin, Lawrence	2	1	....
Bently, John	4	1	....
Cable, Henry	3	1	....
Collins, Jessey	1	....	....
Crawford, John	8	1	....
Crocksey, John	8	1	....
Conner, James	6	1	....
Daniel, William	6	1	1
Dilshaver, George	11	1	1
Gordin, William	6	1	....
Hakney, Daniel	8	1	1
Henry, Moses	4	1	1
Humbock, Henry	4	1	....
Holms, James	4	1	....
Humes, Thomas	16	1	1
Jonson, Thomas	10	1	1
Lashbrooke, William	10	1	....
McCarty, Derby	2	1	....
Morgan, Gilbert	5	1	....
Morgan, Nicholas	4	1	....
Morgan, Jonas	7	1	....
Morgan, John	6	1	....
North, Zacheriah	5	1	....
Owens, William	6	1	....
Poker, Philip	11	1	....
Russell, Robert	2	1	....
Ramey, Thomas	7	1	....
Russell, James	5	1	....
Russell, John	5	1	....
Roles, Francis	3	1	....

LIST OF JOHN HUTCHIRSON—continued.

NAME OF HEAD OF FAMILY.	White souls.	Dwellings.	Other buildings.
Stallings, Griffin	5	1	....
Simson, Samuel	7	1	....
Tibbs, Capt Duskin	5	1	1
Thomas, William	13	1	....
Vaught, Christian	8	1	....
Vaught, Simon	7	1	....
Wilson, William	6	1	....
Woodward, Thos	5	1	....
Willis, Edmand	8	1	....

LIST OF MICHAEL SPEAGLE.

NAME OF HEAD OF FAMILY.	White souls.	Dwellings.	Other buildings.
Andrick, Christian	10	1	3
Bosserman, William	4	1	2
Bowman, David	7	1	1
Bitlor, Abraham	9	1	3
Boserman, Frederick	5	1	2
Brown, Michael	6	....	....
Brock, Henry	4	....	....
Bordin, Frederick	6	1	1
Bordin, Augustine	7	1	1
Cap, Andrew	9	1	2
Conrod, John	6	....	....
Cofman, Jacob	2	1	1
Cofman, Isaac	8	1	1
Cline, Peter	4	....	....
Derting, Adam	6	1	1
Dull, Frederick	2	1	....
Dull, Nicholas	6	1	1
Dull, George	9	....	....
Franker, Peter	5	1	1
Gefeller, John	7	1	1
Gragwer, George	6	....	....
Gefeller, Adam	8	1	1
Hockman, Benjaman	3	1	1
Hamarr, Michael	11	1	1
Holtz, John	2	....	....
Huddle, Henry	8	1	2
Huddle, Daniel	1	1	....
Huddle, Jacob	4	1	1
Huddle, Daniel	3	....	....
Hapner, Chasper	8	....	....
Hiser, Henry	5	1	2
Hufman, John	10	1	4
Jacob, Francis	14	1	1
Innepnet, Jacob	6	1	1
Keller, George	3	....	....
Keller, Conrod	6	1	1
Layman, Benjaman, Junr	3	1	1
Layman, Isaac	2	....	....
Layman, John	5	1	1
Layman, Benja, Senr	10	1	2
Miller, Marck	6	1	2
Martin, Lawrence	9	1	2
Metzer, Henry	1	....	....
Mauck, John	8	2	5
Parrot, Frederick	2	1	1
Parrot, Henry	5	1	1
Parrot, Jacob	3	1	1
Pickle, Jacob	4	1	1
Rush, Henry	4	....	....
Rodes, Michael	5	1	1
Stover, Albrick	8	1	3
Stover, David	6	1	2
Stover, Daniel	8	....	....

LIST OF MICHAEL SPEAGLE—continued.

NAME OF HEAD OF FAMILY.	White souls.	Dwellings.	Other buildings.
Shoe, Benja	6	1	....
Speice, Daniel	5	....	....
Speagle, Michl	6	1	2
Same, Nicholas	9	1	1
Windle, Peter	4	....	....
Windle, Augustine, Senr	4	1	2
Windle, Augustine, Junr	4	1	....
Windle, Valentine	2	1	3
Windle, Christopher	4	1	2
Wollande, Jacob	7	....	....
Windle, John	10	1	2
Westenberger, George	7	1	2

LIST OF GEORGE KELLER.

NAME OF HEAD OF FAMILY.	White souls.	Dwellings.	Other buildings.
Bomer, Erhard	7	1	2
Bomer, Jacob	8	1	1
Combs, Job	13	1	2
Combs, Soloman	5	1	....
Combs, Gilbert	4	1	1
Cron, Fergus	5	2	1
Conner, Moses	5	1	1
Combs, Nicholas	4	1	....
Dendon, John	11	1	2
Dellador, Lavenus	7	1	1
Egle, Temotheus	10	1	....
Frantz, Henry	9	1	1
Gallode, Jacob	11	1	3
Giveds, Henry	5	1	....
Grig, Rebecca	7	1	1
Hiser, Jacob	8	1	3
Honn, George	8	1	1
Honn, Sebastian	9	1	1
Krebeell, Abraham	7	1	1
Klem, David	5	1	1
Klem, Decdareck	10	1	1
Klem, David	4	1	I
Keller, George	8	1	4
Klem, Michael	4	1	1
Keller, John	7	1	3
Letchliter, Jacob	8	1	2
Lechliter, John	7	1	1
Lechliter, Adam	5	1	1
Migendorffer, Casper	4	1	1
Migendorffer, Frederick	5	1	1
Migendorffer, George	7	1	1
Miller, Henry	3	1	....
Muncts, Philip	7	1	1
Nigols, Richard	6	1	2
Odelle, Elige	8	1	2
Odelle, Jeremiah	4	1	1
Obenein, James	8	1	....
Omiller, George	7	1	2
Pridy, Samuel	4	1	1
Peogosen, John	5	1	1
Rudennaner, George	6	1	1
Rudennaner, Henry	6	1	1
Rudennaner, Adam	6	1	1
Senber, Moses	8	1	1
Spengler, John	7	1	....
Shocoer, Ludweg	10	1	1
Walter, Henry	8	1	1
Wollerd, John	9	2	1
Sumwalt, Henry	11	1	2

STAFFORD COUNTY.

NAME OF HEAD OF FAMILY.	White souls.	Dwellings.	Other buildings.
Tyler, Tho. E. S.	5	1	3
Adie, William	4	1	3
Ashby, Sarah	10	1	1
Adie, Benjamin	1	1	2
Ally, Nathan Barton	4	1	1
Burroughs, George	5	1	1
Battoe, William	3	1	1
Battoe, James	5	1	1
Bridwell, John	5	1	2
Bridwell, Abraham	10	1	1
Banister, Nathan	10	1	....
Botts, Joseph	11	1	3
Botts, Aaron	9	1	3
Botts, William	9	1	3
Botts, John	7	1	6
Bridwell, George	4	1	....
Brint, William	5	1	10
Burroughs, Bazill	7	1	....
Bridwell, William, Senr	10	1	4
Bridwell, Moses	12	1	1
Bridwell, Benjamin	7	1	....
Brent, Anne	4	1	13
Brent, George	1	1	8
Brent, Robert	3	....	....
Bell, Jonathan	5	1	1
Bell, George	4	1	2
Bell, Elijah	5	1	1

NAME OF HEAD OF FAMILY.	White souls.	Dwellings.	Other buildings.
Bell, George, Junr	5	1	....
Butler, John	1	1	....
Butler, Sally	1	1	....
Cloe, James	8	1	2
Cooke, John	2	1	4
Carter, Katherin	1	1	....
Combs, Joseph	3	1	2
Carmy, Joshua	9	1	1
Clifton, Henry	10	1	1
Carter, Harris	6	1	3
Carter, James	7	1	2
Carter, Jedediah	1	....	....
Carter, John	....	1	2
Davis, John	8	1	....
Dent, Bradly	9	1	1
Dillion, John	4	1	1
Dawson, William	7	1	....
Dent, Arthur	....	....	....
Edwards, Haden	5	1	12
Edwards, William	4	1	....
Ellis, Rhodam	....	....	....
Edwards, Baker	....	1	1
Fugate, Gerrard	5	1	....
Fristoe, John	3	1	1
Franklin, John	6	1	1
Ford, James	7	1	3
Fristoe, William	8	1	5

NAME OF HEAD OF FAMILY.	White souls.	Dwellings.	Other buildings.
Fristoe, Richard	7	1	3
Ford, John	7	1	4
Fugate, Jeremiah	3	1	1
French, William	7	1	1
Groves, William	5	1	1
Groves, Samuel	8	1	1
Grigory, Walter	7	1	1
Garison, Moses	6	1	1
Garrison, Aaron	5	1	5
Gregsby, John	3	1	....
Garrard, William	6	1	6
Hughs, Virginia	3	1	1
Hardy, John	2	1	7
Hoar, John	7	1	3
Hoar, Elias	7	1	....
Hewitt, Richard	2	1	4
Harding, Thomas	5	1	2
Hardin, John S	9	1	3
Harwood, William	9	1	2
Harding, George	6	1	....
Humes, John	3	1	1
Jordan, Joseph	10	1	1
Lunsford, Jane	4	1	....
Lusher, John	4	1	....
Lunsford, Moses	3	1	1
Hoor, William	7	1	1
Mountjoy, Allen	9	1	1

NAME OF HEAD OF FAMILY.	White souls.	Dwellings.	Other buildings.
Million, Benjamn	10	1	1
Million, Robert	9	1	3
Moncure, Anne	7	1	3
Mason, Will. Ab	....	....	....
Lettuce, Massey	7	1	....
Mason, Thompson	7	1	5
Mountjoy, Thomas	9	1	1
Nash, Phillip	7	1	....
Pattin, John	4	1	....
Porter, Calvert	8	1	3
Porter, Charles	8	1	2
Ralls, Jesse	4	1	1
Routt, William	2	1	1
Ralls, Mary Ann	2	1	....
Richards, William	3	1	1
Ratcliff, John	5	1	4
Richards, William, Senr	7	1	....
Sims, Richard, Senr	9	1	....
Stone, Joseph	7	1	5
Shelton, Wilson	8	1	....
Shelton, William	6	1	3
Starke, John	4	1	4
Stuart, Charles	8	1	4
Smith, John	13	1	3
Smiddy, Benjamin	3	1	....
Hardin, John Scot	....	....	....
Hardin, Thomas	....	....	....

STAFFORD COUNTY—Continued.

NAME OF HEAD OF FAMILY.	White souls.	Dwellings.	Other buildings.	NAME OF HEAD OF FAMILY.	White souls.	Dwellings.	Other buildings.	NAME OF HEAD OF FAMILY.	White souls.	Dwellings.	Other buildings.	NAME OF HEAD OF FAMILY.	White souls.	Dwellings.	Other buildings.
Schacklit, Benjamin	7	1	1	Potes, William	6	1	1	Wallis, Nathan	3	1	...	Chapman, Phillip	5	...	2
Taylor, William	9	1	7	Latham, John	3	1	1	Mountjoy, William	6	1	3	Latham, John	7	1	2
Tolson, Hannah	5	1	3	Waters, John	9	1	4	Mauzy, William	7	1	1	Sharpe, Thomas	5	1	...
Starke, William	1	1	1	Knight, Peter, Senr	7	1	5	Mauzy, Peter	7	1	...	Sharpe, Thomas, Junr	6	1	...
Stone, Hawkin	6	1	2	Knight, Peter, Junr	2	1	1	Kendal, William	10	1	...	Hord, Peter, Junr	9	1	3
Stone, Wm B.	4	1	2	Knight, Christopher	1	1	1	Lowry, James	5	1	1	Loggie, Alexander	4	1	...
West, William	8	1	3	Willott, Ben	8	1	...	Weeks, William	5	1	1	Bates, Thomas	3	1	...
Waters, John	3	1	...	Washington, Bailey	5	1	11	West, William	3	1	...	Taylor, Zachariah	3	...	...
Wegington, Sarah	3	1	1	Byram, William	3	1	1	Phillips, William	2	1	...	Sooter, John	8	1	...
Warren, John	8	1	2	Aitcheson, Nathan	3	1	3	Dickerson, William	2	1	...	Hord, James, Senr	5	1	5
Wells, George	10	1	6	Kendall, Charles	6	1	2	Foushee, Francis	5	1	2	Massey, Thomas	5	1	2
Williams, Nathaniel	8	1	...	Cummins, William	5	1	1	Abbet, George	2	1	...	Ellerton, Robert	11	1	3
Williams, Margaret	7	1	3	Latham, Charles	6	1	...	Siler, Jane	2	1	...	Jackson, Rosomond	9	1	1
Williams, George	12	1	4	Eaton, William	13	1	...	Berry, Richard	8	1	...	Horton, William	7	1	...
Waters, Mark	...	...	...	Stark, Jeremiah	8	1	...	Thatcher, Joshua	5	1	1	Carter, Robert W. (Quarter)	8	1	1
Wells, Elizabeth	1	1	2	Stark, William	1	...	...	Gollohorn, William	5	1	...	Stone, Joseph	9	...	...
Waters, William	5	1	2	Green, Robert	8	1	1	Benear, Dedrick	3	1	...	Jett, William	11	2	...
Wright, Thomas	7	1	2	Bronaugh, Mary A.	8	1	1	Snoxall, Edward	4	1	...	Spence, William	4	1	2
Drummon, Andrew	6	1	1	Bridges, James	7	1	...	Hiden, Lucy	1	1	...	Heffernon, Martin	10	...	...
Strother, Anthony	5	1	6	Kendall, John	8	1	6	Porch, Esom	5	1	...	Lunsford, Johana	6	1	2
Payton, Ann	7	1	5	Aitcheson, Amos	9	1	...	Fritter, John	2	1	...	Martin, Samuel	10	1	...
Gates, Aaron	5	1	1	Ralls, Charles	6	1	3	Mountjoy, John	5	1	2	Crop, James, Senr	2	1	6
Clark, Ann	3	1	1	Eustace, Isaac	4	1	5	Waller, William	7	1	2	Hord, Rohodam	10	1	5
Leach, Benjamin	15	1	2	Shelton, William, Senr	2	1	2	Finch, John	4	1	...	James, George	2	1	...
Swillivan, Darby	6	1	1	Shelton, George	6	1	...	McKinsey, Edward	2	1	...	Taylor, Jesse	3	1	...
Swillivan, Daniel	7	1	2	Miflin, Charles	7	1	1	Brown, R. Travers	6	1	1	Walker, Solomon	4	...	...
Henson, Elijah	9	1	3	Foxworthy, Phil	6	1	...	McDaniel, Hugh	5	1	...	Palmer, Ranleigh	9	...	...
Snelling, Enoch	5	1	4	Ryley, Burley	3	1	1	Grigsby, Elisha	4	1	...	Conner, John	8	1	...
Lembrick, Frances	13	1	2	Harding, Cuthbert	2	1	1	Jones, William	4	1	...	West, John	2	1	...
Jett, Frances	10	1	4	Brown, Joseph	9	1	4	Snoxall, Ann	2	1	...	Young, William	6	1	...
Curtice, George	7	1	2	Bridwell, Simson	3	1	...	Latham, Jemima	5	1	1	Jackson, Robert	5	1	2
White, George	6	1	...	Golahorn, Solomon	5	1	...	Markham, John	8	1	1	Martin, Daniel	8	...	...
Washington, Genl George	6	1	10	Innis, William	8	2	2	Waller, Barshaba	1	1	1	Leitch, James	1	1	1
Cox, George	4	1	2	Patten, William	3	1	...	Ross, William, Junr	6	1	1	Turner, Absolam	13	2	...
Chambers, John	5	1	1	Bredwell, George	4	1	1	Kincher, Mary	2	1	1	Burgess, Rubin	10	1	1
Brown, James	8	1	1	Jameson, Alexander	5	1	...	Hay, Thomas	8	1	...	Fant, John	8	1	1
Kenyon, James	8	1	6	Hansbrough, Peter	3	1	1	Withers, John	8	1	5	Stringfellow, James	11	1	...
Snellings, John	5	1	1	Harding, William	8	1	2	Lowry, Robert	2	...	...	Turner, James	8	1	3
Green, Jesse	5	1	1	McIntire, Henry	2	1	...	Lee, Thomas Ludwell	1	1	2	Mellet, John	6	1	1
Curtice, John	7	1	6	Tolson, Elizabith	11	1	5	Payne, Francis	2	1	...	Hill, Leonard	9	...	...
Alexander, Phil T.	2	1	7	Bredwell, Jacob	6	1	...	Bowlen, Benjamin	4	1	...	Hughs, Micajah	5	1	...
Fines, Patrick	5	1	4	Mason, Richard	8	1	2	Rogers, Reuben	3	1	...	Monro, Daniel	7	1	...
Wellford, Doctr Robert	9	1	8	Potes, Richard	1	...	...	Davis, William	4	1	...	Mountjoy, George	4	1	1
Curtice, Richard	4	1	1	Waters, Charles	2	1	...	Brown, John	4	1	3	Weeks, George	9	...	...
Downman, Rawlegh	3	1	9	Abbot, John	7	1	...	Dougless, Archibeld	2	1	...	Roach, Robert	8	1	3
McGuire, Richard	6	1	...	Carter, John, Senr	3	1	...	Suddoth, Thoms	4	1	...	Burchard, James	3	...	...
Possey, Colo Thomas	2	1	8	Byram, George	7	1	...	Bedgel, John	8	1	...	Courtney, John	7	1	...
Casson, Thomas	2	1	7	Green, Robert	8	1	...	Hudson, Margaret	3	1	...	Stribling, Elizabeth	3	1	...
Robertson, Thomas	12	1	...	Primm, John	5	1	2	Stuart, James	6	1	...	Ballard, Thomas	2	1	2
Curtis, Theodoshe	3	1	...	Pritchard, Ben	1	1	6	Ficklen, Anthony	4	1	2	White, George	8	1	1
Alexander, William	5	1	9	Aitcheson, Amos	10	1	...	Ficklen, Benjamin	7	1	2	West, Edward	9	1	3
Brown, William	9	1	2	McDaniel, Polly	3	1	2	Jones, Gabriel	5	1	2	Hudson, David	3	1	...
Lembrick, William	7	1	3	Bridwell, William	12	1	...	Benson, Enoch	4	1	2	Timmons, John	4	1	...
Stone, William	3	1	...	Lawless, John	7	1	...	Mountjoy, William	6	1	3	Brown, James	8	...	...
Bruce, William	8	1	3	Combs, John	4	1	5	Mercer, John F.	2	1	8	West, Edward, Junr	4	1	...
Snellenge, William	6	1	2	Raiby, Joseph	7	1	1	Habern, David	3	1	...	Hall, Hanah	4	1	...
Curtice, William	6	1	2	Peyton, John R.	6	1	4	Taylor, Richard	4	1	2	Humphrys, William	8	1	2
Butler, William	8	1	2	Mountjoy, Thomas	3	2	6	Crop, John	8	1	5	Arrosmith, Thomas	8	1	...
Shelton, William	8	1	...	Peyton, Valentine	2	1	...	Crop, James, Junr	6	1	3	Kirk, Jesse	3	1	3
Fitzhugh, William (Chath'm)	5	1	27	Ball, Benjamin	9	1	...	Hopwood, John	9	1	2	Graves, William	8	1	...
Porch, Thomas	4	1	6	Mountjoy, John, Senr	2	1	3	Adam, John	4	1	...	Graves, Benjamin	5	1	...
Gallehew, Solomon	6	1	...	Threlkeld, Elijah	5	1	5	Thompson, Zacariah	4	1	1	Turner, Griffin	12	1	1
Thornton, Thomas	8	1	5	Norman, George	6	1	2	Hord, Kollis	9	1	3	Wood, William	10	2	1
Fitzhugh, Thomas	5	1	6	Daniel, Travers	10	2	5	Pullen, Jedediah	8	1	4	Arrasmith, Richard	1	...	...
Ratcliff, Richard	4	1	3	Daniel, Sarah	2	1	5	Briggs, David	6	1	5	Conyers, John	10	...	...
Reley, Jessey	7	1	...	Chinn, Susanna	7	1	1	Burgess, William	4	...	...	Foster, Seth	7	1	...
Ryley, Nicolas	1	1	...	Chinn, Joseph	2	1	...	Brock, Benjamin	6	1	...	Smith, John	7	1	...
Franklin, Joseph	3	2	2	Reads, Daniel	7	1	...	Garrard, Daniel	8	1	1	Oliver, John	7	1	...
Stark, Hanah	5	1	4	Nilson, William	6	1	...	Berry, Anthony	6	1	1	Maddox, Lazrus	10	1	2
Franklin, Reuben	4	1	...	Gollerhorn, John	11	1	...	Stribling, Joseph	1	1	...	Scooler, Thomas	7	1	...
Dorson, John	8	1	2	Davis, Charles	7	1	...	Strother, Thomas	6	1	3	Burton, Rachel	9	...	...
Franklin, William	6	1	1	Berry, William	4	1	...	Sharpe, Lincifield	2	1	...	Carter, Joseph	3	1	...
Latham, Snowdwell	5	1	2	Shilket, John	4	1	1	Pilcher, Mason	6	1	5	Massey, Toliver	4	...	...
Duffee, Leonard	7	1	...	Threlkeld, George	2	1	2	Stone, Jesse	8	1	...	Bolling, Samuel	5	...	...
Chiverall, John	5	1	2	Stuart, Elizabeth	6	1	...	Smith, Samuel	9	1	3	Tate, William	4	...	...
Peyton, Elizabeth	9	2	11	Walker, Mary	8	1	2	Paton, James	9	1	4	Hord, Jesse	9	1	3
Garrison, George	12	1	...	Seddon, Thomas	3	1	2	Gregg, John	3	1	...	Allen, Mary	6	1	4
Harding, Charles	9	1	2	Taylor, Richard	2	1	...	Hord, Peter	4	1	4	Moore, Edward	10	1	1
Cooper, Jesse	5	2	1	Ralls, William	5	1	3	Honey, William	4	1	...	Morson, Arthur	6	1	10
Cooper, Joseph	3	1	1	Deckarson, Edward	10	1	1	Latham, Franklyn	8	1	1	Fant, George	9	...	...
Fristoe, John	9	1	14	Ball, John	8	1	...	Jones, Charles	7	1	...	White, Thomas	7	1	...
Garrison, John	10	2	2	Bell, Mary	4	1	1	Martin, Charles	1	...	...	Webb, Aaron	11	1	...
Combs, Cuthbert	11	1	1	Redish, Burdit	9	1	...	Bolling, Thomas	4	1	1	Lawson, Gavin	4	1	4
Wilson, William	9	1	...	Lunsford, John	5	1	...	Sooter, Andrew	6	1	2				
Cummins, Asa	11	1	2	Hedgman, John	5	1	3	Bolling, James	10	2	...				
				Mauzy, John	1	1	2	Skenker, Thomas	1	2	4				

GREENBRIER COUNTY.[1]

Acres, Simon.
Adams, George.
Alderson, George.
Alderson, Jno.
Alderson, Thos.
Allen, James.
Alexander, Hugh.
Alexander, Jas.
Allison, Elizebeth.
Anderson, Jno.
Anderson, Jno.
Anglin, Edrin.
Anglin, Isaac.
Arbuckle, Jno.
Arbuckle, Wm.
Archer, Jno.
Archer, Sampson.
Armstrong, James.
Armstrong, Robt.
Bailey, Jno.
Bailey, Wm.
Bails, Eden.
Bails, Jos.
Bails, Thos.
Baily, Jas.
Baker, Ebram.
Balentine, Hugh.
Balentine, Thos.
Balinger, Isaac.
Barns, Adam.
Barrett, Edward.
Bartlet, Nicholas.
Bartley, Lazarus.
Bartley, Nicho.
Baxter, Gorman, Jr.
Beard, Jno.
Belew, Lead.
Bellow, Jno.
Benick, Wm, Senr.
Benson, Levon.
Bert, Francis.
Best, Fran.
Biard, Thos.
Bicket, Thos.
Bird, Thos.
Black, James.
Black, Jos.
Black, Saml.
Blackburn, George.
Blair, Jno Neal.
Blair, Thos.
Blair, Wm.
Blake, George.
Blake, Jno.
Blake, Sam.
Blake, Theos.
Blake, Wm.
Blaken, Abigail.
Blankenship, Jno.
Blankenship, Lodawick.
Blann, Jesse.
Blann, Robt.
Blann, Robt.
Blann, Robt, Sen.
Blanton, Wm.
Blanton, Wm.
Bodkin, Jno (Augta).
Boggs, Ezekial.
Boggs, Francis, Junr.
Boggs, Francis, Sen.
Boggs, James, Jur.
Boggs, James, Senr.
Boggs, Sam.
Boggs, Wm.
Boiling, Jno.
Booten, Lewis.
Booten, Reubin.
Booten, Wm.
Bostick, Moses.
Bowen, Antony.
Bowyer, Adam.
Bowyer, Mich.
Boyd, Pat.
Bradshaw, James.
Bradshaw, Thos.
Brahen, Jam.
Braken, Abigal.
Breeden, Elijah.
Breton, Wallace.
Briger, Mary.
Brindly, Jas.
Brindley, Jas, Ju.
Brinkley, Jno.
Brisco, George.
Brookes, Thos.
Brooks, Thos.
Brown, Jno.
Brown, Saml.
Brown, Wm.
Bryan, Chrit.
Buck, Charles.
Buckly, Joshua.
Burbridge, Roland.
Burdet, Jno.
Burdict, Archd.
Butcher, Jno.
Butler, James.
Butler, Jno.
Butler, Peter.
Byrns, Isaac.
Byrnside, James.

Byrnside, Jno.
Cail, Jno.
Cairns, Allex.
Cairns, Jno.
Cairns, Jno.
Cairns, Thos.
Caldwell, Saml.
Callison, James.
Callison, Jno.
Callison, Wm.
Campbell, Joseph.
Campbell, Saml.
Canterbery, Fno.
Canterberry, Jno.
Cantly, Jno.
Caperton, Hugh.
Caperton, Jno.
Carraway, Thos.
Carry, Henry.
Carslile, David.
Carslile, Jno.
Casebolt, Henry.
Casebolt, John.
Casteel, Joseph.
Cavindish, Wm H.
Ceatley, Fran.
Chambers, James.
Chambers, Jno.
Chambers, Robt.
Chapman, Jacob.
Charlton, Thos.
Childers, Henry.
Childers, Mosby.
Childers, Reubin.
Christie, James.
Christie, Jas.
Christie, Julias.
Christle, Wm.
Christy, James.
Chritie, James.
Chrity, Julias.
Clark, Allex.
Clark, James.
Clark, Jno.
Claypole, David.
Claypole, James.
Claypole, Joseph.
Cledenan, Co.
Clendenan, Allex.
Clendenan, George.
Clendenan, Robt.
Clendenan, Wm.
Clerk, Jno.
Cochron, Patrick.
Cockron, Thos.
Cockron, Thos.
Collins, James.
Combes, Wm.
Conner, Angel.
Conner, Jno.
Conrod, George.
Conrod, Katha.
Constantine, Pat.
Cook, Dan.
Cook, Valentine.
Cooke, Jno.
Cooke, Stephen.
Cooper, Abner.
Cooper, Leanard.
Cooper, Phil.
Cooper, Simon.
Cooper, Spencer.
Cooper, Thos.
Cooper, Wm.
Corder, Jno.
Cornwell, Edward.
Cottle, Wm.
Cowtricks, ——.
Craig, Robt.
Craig, Wm.
Craig, Wm.
Crain, Wm.
Crawford, Wm.
Creed, Matthew.
Cristle, Wm.
Cullers, Matthias.
Culton, Joseph.
Cummins, Jno.
Curry, Jno.
Curry, Joseph.
Curry, Robt.
Cutlip, David.
Cutlip, George.
Dahub, Christ.
Danosdal, Caleb.
Danosdal, Cornelus.
Davidson, Wm.
Davis, Aron.
Davis, Danial.
Davis, Jacob.
Davis, James.
Davis, Jno.
Davis, Pat.
Davis, Thos.
Davis, Walter.
Davis, Wm.
Day, Jno.
Day, Nat., Senr.
Dempsey, Jas.
Dew, Robt.
Dickson, George.

Dickson, Jno.
Dickson, Joseph.
Dickson, Pat.
Dickson, Richd.
Dinyard, George.
Dinyard, Jno.
Dinyard, Stephen.
Dinyard, Wm.
Dixon, George.
Dixon, Patrick.
Dixon, Richd.
Dodrige, Wm.
Donally, Andw.
Donelly, James.
Doran, Jacob.
Dougherty, Geo.
Drinen (Widdow).
Drody, Wm.
Duet, Ebram.
Duglas, Henry.
Dunan, Serah.
Dunbar, Jno, Jun.
Dunbar, Jno, Sen.
Dunbar, Sam.
Dunn, Jno.
Dunn, Wm.
Dunwiddy, Jas.
Dunwiddy, Thos.
Dunwiddy, Wm.
Dunwiddy, Wm, Sen.
Dyche, James.
Dyer, Jno.
Edger, Thos.
Edmiston, Jas.
Edmiston, Thos.
Edmondson, James.
Edmondson, Tho.
Edmonson, James.
Edwards, Joseph.
Eiken, Jno.
Eiken, Wm.
Ekers, Simon.
Elliot, Wm.
Elliott, Wm.
Ellis, Jno.
Ellis, Owen.
Ellis, Thos.
Ellison, Elezebeth.
Ellison, Esau.
Ellison, James, Junr.
Ellison, James, Senr.
Ellison, Jno.
Ellison, Joseph.
Ellison, Rot.
Elmbough, Peter.
Ermison, James.
Erwin, Andw.
Erwin, Jno.
Erwin, Robt.
Erwin, Williams.
Estle, Bond.
Estle, Wallace.
Ethel, Joseph.
Evans, Jno.
Ewin, Andr.
Ewin, Elijah.
Ewin, James.
Ewin, John (L. B.).
Ewin, Jno, Jur.
Ewin, Jno, Senr.
Ewin, Joseph.
Ewin, Joshua.
Ewin, Saml.
Ewin, Williams.
Ewin, Wm.
Ewing, John.
Ewing, John, Junr.
Ewing, Joshua.
Ewing, Wm.
Fackett, Jno.
Fargy, Hugh.
Farley, Fran.
Farley, Jno.
farley, Matt.
Farley, Matt.
Fincher, Francis.
Fincher, Wm.
Finton, Jno.
Fisher, Isaac.
Fitzpatrick, Jas.
flathers, Edwd.
fleming, James.
Fleming, Wm.
Fleming, Wm.
flinn, James.
Flinn, Jno.
flinn, Jno.
ford, Fran.
Fosster, John.
Foster, James.
foster, Robt.
Foy, Jno.
freind, Charles.
freind, Ebram.
frogg, Wm.
Fryor, Jno.
fullerton, Wm, Ju.
Fullorton, Wm.
fulton, Thos.
Fumster, Wm.
Gardner, Jno.

Garret, Barkley.
Gartin, Elijah.
Gatliff, Martha.
George, Wm.
Gibson, Jno.
Gilkison, Jno.
Gillaspy, Thos.
Gillelan, Wm.
Gillilan, James.
Gillilan, Nathan.
Gillilan, Saml.
Gillilan, Wm.
Glass, Capt.
Glass, Jno.
Glass, Wm.
Goff, Jno.
Graham, James.
Graham, Wm.
Gratton, Charles.
Gratton, David.
Gratton, Thos.
Gray, George.
Gray, Jno.
Gray, Saml.
Green, Garrett.
Green, Hary.
Green, Henry.
Greer, Stephen.
Griffin, Gordin.
Griffit, Jno.
Griffith, Wm.
Griffits, Thos.
Griffits, Wm.
Grigson, Jno.
Growmore, Fred.
Gullet, Jno.
Gully, Thos.
Gwin, James.
Gwin, Jno.
Gwin, Matt.
Gwin, Saml.
Hacket, Nelson.
Hall, Jno.
Hall, Edward.
Hall, Jno.
Hall, Moses, Jur.
Hall, Moses, Senr.
Ham, Jno.
Ham, Joseph.
Hamilton, Allex.
Hamilton, Andw.
Hamilton, Jno.
Hamilton, Thos.
Hamilton, Wm.
Hamilton, Wm.
Hamrick, Ben.
Handley, Archd.
Handley, James.
Handley, Jno.
Hanna, David.
Hanna, David.
Hanna, James, Ju.
Hanna, James, Senr.
Hanna, Jno.
Hanna, Joseph.
Hanna, Wm.
Hardy, Jno.
Harra, Danl, Junr.
Harriman, Shederick.
Harris, Christ.
Harris, Jno.
Harris, Robt.
Harvy, Nichs.
Hayns, James.
Hayns, Joseph.
Hedrick, Henry.
Hempenstall, Ebram, Jun.
Hempenstall, Ebram, Sr.
Hempenstall, Isaac.
Henderson, James.
Henderson, Jno.
Hickenbottom, Jos.
Hickenbottom, Moses.
Hicks, Richd.
Hicks, Wm.
Hill, Richd.
Hinchman, Wm.
Hirons, Joseph.
Hirons, Sally.
Hirons, Saml.
Hogan, Wm.
Holms, Richard.
Holms, Richd.
Holshopple, Henry.
Hopple, George.
Hosiah, Allex.
Howard, Charles.
Howard, James.
Howard, Robt.
Howard, Saml.
Howe, Edwd.
Huff, Saml.
Huggard, James.
Huggard, Jas, Jun.
Huggard, Jos.
Huggard, Wm.
Hughes, Wm.
Hughs, George.

Hughs, thos.
Hughs, Wm.
Humphreys, Saml.
Humphris, David.
Humphris, James.
Humphris, Jno.
Humphris, Jos.
Humpris, Richd.
Humphris, Saml.
Hunter, Henry.
Hunter, Wm.
Huston, Jno.
Hutcheson, George.
Hutcheson, Jno, Junr.
Hutcheson, Jno, Sen.
Hutcheson, Wm.
Hyde, Charles.
Hyns, Charles.
James, David.
James, Ellison.
Jamison, David.
Jamison, Jno.
Jamison, Saml.
Jamison, Wm.
Jarrett, David.
Jarrett, James.
Jarrett, Jesse.
Jarrett, Owen.
Jeffers, Jno.
Jinkins, Amos.
Jinkins, Jacob.
Jinkins, Jno.
John, Jadgills.
Johnson, Wm.
Johnston, Arwalker.
Johnston, Barney.
Johnston, Ben.
Johnston, David.
Johnston, Edward.
Johnston, James.
Johnston, Jno.
Johnston, John.
Johnston, Richd.
Johnston, Robt.
Johnston, Wm.
Johnston, Wm.
Jones, Berryman.
Jones, Foster.
Jones, George W.
Jones, James.
Jones, Jno.
Jones, John.
jones, Mosias.
jones, Peter.
Jones, Stephen.
jones, Thos.
Jones, Wm.
Jones, Wm.
Jorden, James.
Jordon, James.
Kairns, Jas.
Kairns, John.
Kairns, Thos.
Keaney, John.
Keany, Jno.
Keany, Michl.
Keany, thos.
Keenan, Edward.
Keenan, Patrick.
Keirns, Allex.
Keirns, James.
Keirns, Jno.
Kelly, James.
Kenaman, Henry.
Kenedy, James.
Keney, David.
Kenifax, Wm.
Kenison, Charles.
Kenison, David.
Kenison, Edward.
Kenison, Jacob.
Kenison, Nat.
Kennard, Thos.
Kenny, Jno.
Kently, Jno.
Kently, Jno, Jun.
Keny, Jno.
Kincaid, Andw.
Kincaid, George.
Kincaid, Hugh.
Kincaid, James.
Kincaid, Jno.
Kincaid, Jno.
Kincaid, Marget.
Kincaid, Saml.
Kincaid, Saml.
Kincaid, thos.
Kincaid, thos.
Kinder, Peter.
Kiney, Michel.
King, George.
King, Jno.
King, Robt.
Kippers, Jno.
Kirkpatrick, Roger.
Kishinger, Andw.
Kishinger, Jacob.
Kishinger, Mathias.

Kitchen, James.
Knox, Jas.
Knox, Robt.
Kyzer, Martin.
Lakins, Jno.
Lakins, Peter.
Larkin, James.
Laverty, Wm.
Lawyers, Jno.
Leach, Wm.
Leacy, James.
Leacy, Mark.
Leacy, Wm, Junr.
Leacy, Wm, Senr.
Legg, Thos.
Levels (Widow).
Levesy, Thos.
Lewis, Ben.
Lewis, George.
Lewis, Hezekiah.
Lewis, James.
Lewis, Jno, Junr.
Lewis, Jno, Senr.
Lewis, Saml.
Lewis, Wilson.
Lindsey, Jane.
Lindsey, Jno.
Lindsey, Kat.
Littlenage, Jno.
Lockhart, Jacob.
Lockhart, James.
Lockridge, John.
Lockridge, Wm.
Logan, Saml.
Logan, Wm.
long, Paul.
long, Wm.
Louderback, David.
Low, Livi.
Low, Zedock.
Lowens, Jno.
Ludington, Esau.
Lynch, Jno.
Lynch, John.
McCanless, Jno.
McCanless, Wm.
McCay, David.
McCay, James.
McCay, Jane.
McCay, Serah.
McCay, Wm.
McClintock, Joseph.
McClung, Charles.
McClung, James.
McClung, Joseph.
McClung, Saml.
McClung, thos.
McClure, Arthur.
McCue, Charles.
McCue, Jno.
McDanald, Henry.
McDanald, Henry J.
McDanald, Henry S.
McDanald, James.
McDanald, Jno.
McDavid, Pat.
McDowel, Archd.
McDowel, Danl.
McDowel, Hanson.
McDowel, Joshua.
McDowel, Wm.
McDowel, Wm.
Mcfarrin, Andw.
Mcfarrin, Jno.
McGaraugh, Saml.
McGlamory, Matt.
McKinsy, Keneth.
McMillian, Jno.
McMullen, Danl.
McMullen, Jno.
McNeal, Jno.
McNeal, Thos.
McNutt, Frances.
McNutt, Jno.
McNutt, Jno.
McWilliams, Hugh.
Maddy, Wm.
Magort, David.
Maiden, Isaac.
Malahan, George.
Man, Adam.
Man, Jacob, Jur.
Man, Jacob, Senr.
Mason, James.
Mason, Wm.
Masse, Jacob.
Masse, Jephta.
Masters, Stephen.
Matthews, Adonijah.
Matthews, Archer.
Matthews, Richd.
Matthews, Richard.
Matthews, Richd, Ju.
Maupin, Mosias.
Maze, James.
Meadows, Arris.
Meadows, Isreal.
Meady, Jno.
Meady, Wm.

[1] Name taken from county tax lists.

GREENBRIER COUNTY—Continued.

Meredith, Bradly.
Meritt, Lerose.
Miller, ——.
Miller, Brice.
Miller, David.
Miller, Hugh.
Miller, Jacob..
Miller, Jacob, Junr.
Miller, James.
Miller, Jno.
Miller, Jno, Junr.
Miller, Jno, Senr.
Miller, Jno Ewin.
Miller, Joseph.
Miller, West.
Miller, W^m.
Milone, Ebram.
Milstead, John.
Mitchel, Allex.
Mitchel, Robt.
Moore, Saml.
Morison, James.
Morris, Calas.
Morris, Jno.
Morris, Leanard.
Morris, W^m, Jur.
Morris, W^m, Senr.
Morrow, James, Ju.
Morrow, Ja^s, Sen.
Morrow, Saml.
Morrow, Saml.
Morrow, W^m.
Mulhollan, Hugh.
Mullen, Rich^d.
Murdock, David.
Murdock, James.
Murdock, Ja^s.
Murphy, Pat.
Murry, W^m.
Murry, W^m.
Myans, W^m.
Nailer, Stephen.
Neal, Jno.
Nesbitt, James.
Newhouse, Henry.
Nichol, Isaac.
Nichol, Robt.
Nicholas, Th^o.
Nicholas, Th^o, Jun.
Nichols, Andw.
Nichols, Isaac.
Nichols, Joseph.
Nichols, Robt.
Nichols, tho^s.
Nichols, Thos, J.
Norcut, Jno.
Nosler, Boston.
Null, George.
Oahub, Chrit.
Offall, Jno.
Oharra, Charles.

O'Harra, Danial, Jur.
O'Harra, Danl, Senr.
O'Harra, James.
O'Harra, Jno.
O'Harra, W^m.
O'Heltree, Elizabeth.
Oldham, W^m.
ONeal, Jno.
Owens, George.
Ozburn, Jno, Ju.
Ozburn, Jno, Senr.
Page, James.
Parker, Joseph.
Parks, George.
Pasons, James.
Patterson, James.
Patterson, Jo^s.
Patterson, Matt.
Patton, Jno.
Paul, Daniel.
Paul, Hugh.
Paul, Isaac.
Payn, Charles.
Peck, George.
Peck, Saml.
Pemberton, Edward.
Penvey, Danl.
Perry, Danial.
Perry, Jno.
Perry, Swift.
Persons, Ann.
Persons, George.
Persons, James.
Pettyjohn, James.
Pettyjohn, Moleston.
Pettyjohn, Peter.
Phillips, Robt.
Pine, James.
Piper, Jno.
Pirkins, Eli.
Pirkins, Henry.
Pirkins, James.
Pirkins, Ja^s.
Poage, W^m.
Poltan, Isaac.
Price, Arch.
Price, Elezebeth.
Price, Jacob.
Price, Saml.
Price, W^m.
Price, W^m.
Price, W^m, Junr.
Pursell, Jno.
Ralston, David.
Ralston, David.
Ralston, Elizabeth,
Ralston, Ja^s.
Ralston, Jno.
Ramsay, Saml.
Reah, Robt.
Realy, Thos.

Reanys, Mich^l (Est.).
Reburn, Henry.
Reburn, Jno.
Redmon, Thos.
Reid, Allex.
Reid, Ben.
Reid, James.
Reid, Jno.
Reid, Robt.
Reiff, Ebram.
Reiff, Jacob J.
Reiff, Jacob, Junr.
Reiff, Jacob, Senr.
Reiff, Joseph.
Reily, Jno.
Renick, Robt.
Renick, W^m.
Richard, Josiah, Senr.
Richards, David.
Richards, Elijah.
Richards, James.
Richards, Josiah.
Richey, Jno.
Richmond, W^m.
Riffle, Abrm.
Riney, Mich.
Ritchey, David.
Ritchey, Robt.
River, Jno Jones.
River, Jno Williams.
Roach, Jonathan.
Robinson, Jno.
Robinson, W^m.
Robuck, Ja^s.
Rodgers, Chesly.
Rodgers, David.
Rodgers, James.
Rodgers, Jno.
Rodgers, Jno, Jun.
Roe, W^m.
Ross, Charles.
Rucker, Jame.
Rucker, Wyatt.
Russell, Jno.
Ruth, Joseph.
Salms, Saml.
Salsburry, W^m.
Sample, Moses.
Sawyers, Jno.
Scaggs, Jno.
Scaggs, Rich^d.
Scaggs, Thos.
Scarborough, David.
Scarborough, Isaac.
Scarborough, Ja^s.
Scarborough, Robt.
Scarborough, W^m.
Scarce, David.
Scott, Ja^s.
Scott, Jo^s.
Seott, W^m.

Sea, George.
Sea, Jno.
Sea, Mich.
Sewel, James.
Shanklin, Jno.
Shanklin, Robt.
Shanks, W^m.
Shannon, W^m.
Sharp, Jno.
Shock, Antony.
Shoemaker, Jno.
Shoemaker, Peter.
Shoemaker, Simon.
Shoemate, Danl.
Sholz, Henry.
Shook, Jno.
Simpson, Joseph.
Slatery, Patrick.
Smith, And^w.
Smith, Danl.
Smith, James.
Smith, Jno.
Smith, John.
Smith, Man.
Smith, Martin.
Smith, Stephen.
Smith, Thos.
Snediger, Chrit.
Snediger, Isaac.
Snodgrass, James.
Sonethers, Arch^d.
Sowards, Isaac, Jun.
Sowards, Isaac, Sen.
Sowards, Thos.
Spencer, Thos, Junr.
Spencer, Thos, Sen.
Steffy, Jno.
Stepenson, Jno.
Stephens, George.
Stephens, James.
Stephens, Ja^s, Jun.
Stephens, Jno.
Stephens, Jno.
Stephenson, Allex.
Stephenson, David.
Stephenson, James.
Stephenson, James, Senr.
Stephenson, Robt.
Stiff, Jno.
Stiffy, John.
Strother, Ben.
Stroud, James.
Stuart, George.
Stuart, James.
Stuart, Jno.
Stuart, W^m.
Sturgill, Jno.
Sturgin, Jno.
Sulavan, Phil.
Sulavan, Sim.
Sulavan, timothy.

Sutton, Joseph.
Swobe, George.
Swobe, Jno.
Swobe, Joseph.
Swobe, Mich.
Swsher, Phil.
tackett, Jno.
tackett, Nimrod.
Tayler, Danial.
tharp, Jno.
tharp, Joshua.
Therp, Jno.
thomas, David.
Thompson, John.
thornton, George.
tillory, Jno.
tincher, Francis.
Tincher, Samuel.
tincher, W^m.
tompson, James.
tompson, Ja^s.
tompson, Jno.
tompson, Robt.
Trasewell, Ederias.
trimble, David.
trimble, Thos.
trotter, James.
Tuckweller, Jno.
turpin, Aron.
turpin, Martin.
Turpin, Miriam.
turpin, Moses.
tylar, Isaac.
Urkhart, W^m.
Vahub, Christ.
Vanbebber, Jno.
Vanbebber, Peter.
Vanbebber, Peter, Jun.
Vanbibber, Peter J.
Vanosdal, Calab.
Varner, W^m.
Vest, George.
Viney, Jno.
Vinyard, George.
Vinyard, Jno.
Vinyard, W^m.
Waddle, Allex.
Walker, Jno.
Wallace, Jno.
Wallace, Joseph.
Wallace, Moses.
Wallace, W^m.
Walton, Ja^s.
Walton, Jno, Ju.
Walton, Jno, Senr.
Ward, Ben.
Ward, W^m.
Waring, Jacob.
Warnick, James.
Watts, James.
Welch, Allex.

West, Isaac. .
West, Littleton.
West, Luke.
West, Sam.
West, W^m.
Whealen, Jno.
Whealy, George.
Wheeler, Joseph.
Whitman, Rich^d.
Wigleblack, Henry.
Wiley, Jno.
Wiley, Robt, Jur.
Wiley, Robt, Sen.
Wiley, W^m.
Williams, David.
Williams, James.
Williams, Jno.
Williams, Jno.
Williams, Jno, Ju.
Williams, Jno, Sr.
Williams, Joseph.
Williams, Rich^d.
Williams, Sam.
Williams, Thos.
Williams, W^m.
Williams, W^m.
Willis, Henry.
Willis, James.
Willis, Jno.
Wilson, Allex.
Wilson, And^w.
Wilson, And^w.
Wilson, Danl.
Wilson, James.
Wilsonⁱ Jno.
Wilson, Jno.
Wilson, Moses.
Wilson, Richard.
Wilson, Sampson.
Wilson, W^m.
Wilson, W^m.
Windsor, Jonathan.
Wood, Baily.
Woodfin, Nich^s.
Woodfin, Saml.
Woods, And^w.
Wooten, Jno.
Workman, Danl.
Wright, Thos.
Wyatt, Edward, Jr.
Wyatt, Edward, Sr.
Wyatt, Jesse.
Wyatt, Thos.
Wyatt, W^m.
Wyatt, W^m.
Wymor, Fred.
Yates, Ralph.
Yokem, Conrod.
Yokim, George.
Young, Robt.
Young, W^m.

A list of the inhabitants and property in the city of Richmond: 1782.

WARDSHIP No. 1.

NAME.	Age.	Occupation.	Time of residence.	Lots improved and their numbers.	Slaves tithable.	Slaves not tithable.	Cattle.	Horses.	Mares.	Colts.	Mules.	Wheels.	Billiard tables.	Miscellaneous.
Bowles, Elijah	31	Wagoner		1; 519		1	2	6	1					
Bowles, Mary (wife)	22													
Bowles, Claiborne (son)	Infant.													
Maxxie, Pater	32	Chairmaker		2; 517, 518	1	2	3							
Maxxie, Mary (wife)	26													
Maxxie, John	7													
Maxxie, Somner														
Maxxie, Elizabeth														
Maxxie, Mary	2													
Bryan, John	24	Chairmaker												
McLin, Han	30			1; 498, 479	1		2							
McLin, Peggy	14													
McLin, Milley	18													
McLin, Lucretia	40													
Smith, Edw	35	Labourer												
5 free mulattoes														
Bryan, John	59	Sadler		2; 627, 628		2	2	1						
Bryan, Obidence (wife)														
Bryan, Simkin	22	ditto												
Bryan, Sylla	20													
Bryan, Benjamin	14													
Bryan, Wilson	11													
Murphy, John	22	Chairmaker				1		1						
Murphy, Sarah (wife)	18													
Wilson, Peter	57	Waggoner	5 months	Bryan's stable										
Wilson, Elizabeth (wife)	35													
Wilson, Peter	5													
Wilson, Alexander	1													
Swinton, James	25	Blacksmith		1; 645	1		1	4						1 waggon.
Swinton, Elizabeth (wife)	30													
Swinton, Elizabeth	8													
Swinton, James	5													
Swinton, Ann	3													
Gunn, John (apprentice)	13													
Ann	20													
Mourning, Katy	18													
Thomas, James	50													
Thomas, Mary	15													
Thomas, Jefro	11													
Thomas, William	9													
Thomas, Olive	6													
Lots 529 occupied by soldiers and thier Wives among them Peggy Lee a free mulatto.														
Downer, Joseph	21	Nailer		1; 643				1						
Downer, Hester (wife)	21													
Mouring, Sarah	16													
Pierce, Widow	35													
Pierce, Jimmy	6													
Salmonds, Jacob	23	Waggoner												
Graves, Ralph	57	Ditto	6 months	1; 568	1	1		5						1 waggon.
Minns, Robin	19	Ditto						8						2 waggons.
Dobie, Samuel	52	Chymist		1; 530	1	2								
Dobie, Ann (wife)	40													
Evans, Ann (neice)	12													
Smedly, Robert	30	Rope maker		1; 428										
Smedly, Ann (Wife)	23													
Smedly, John (Son)	7													
Barker, James	27	Tailor		1; 429		1								
Barker, Ann (Wife)	23													
Barker, Frances (Daughter)	6													
Barker, Thomas (Son)	1													
Ford, Milton	24	Carpenter		1; 472, ½ 479	7		4	5						1 waggon.
Morris, Fain	20													
Daniel, Henry	19	Journeyman	3 months											
Eggleston, Mat	18				7		4	5						1 waggon.
Eggleston, Rich	16													
Ferguson, Robt	15													
Tate, Lenar	45	Carpenter		1; 458		1		1						
Tate, Lucy	46													
Tate, Mary (Daughter)	19													
Currie, John	4	Orphan												
Hawkins, John	30	Carpenter	4 months		6	9								
Hawkins, Elizabeth (Wife)	26													
Hawkins, Mary (Daughter)	3													
Wylly, Alex	32	Shop keeper		1; 474	2	4	1	2				2		3 goats.
Wylly, Dorothy (Wife)	27													
Wylly, William (Son)	1													
Wylly, Polly (Daughter)	2													

A list of the inhabitants and property in the city of Richmond: 1782—Continued.

WARDSHIP No. 1—Continued.

NAME.	Age.	Occupation.	Time of residence.	Lots improved and their numbers.	Slaves titha-ble.	Slaves not titha-ble.	Cat-tle.	Horses.	Mares.	Colts.	Mules.	Wheels.	Billiard tables.	Miscella-neous.
Hoy, Ann	16													
Miller, Dabney	32	Planter		2; 461, 462	4	3	1	4				2		1 waggon.
Miller, Sarah (Wife)	26													
Miller, Ann	8													
Miller, Mary	6													
Miller, John	4													
Miller, Beckey	3													
Miller, Betsey	1													
Miller, Barley	15													
Miller, Armis	9													
Miller, Nathl	22	Waggoner						9						
Johnson, Will	60	Inn Holder	3 months		9	5	2	4						
Johnson, Ann (Wife)	46													
Johnson, Frances	20													
Johnson, Martha	23													
Johnson, Sam	15													
Johnson, Meriwether	13													
Johnson, John	10													
Johnson, Susanna	8													
Johnson, Mary	5													
Clayton, Cath	15													
Gordon, Jona	17	Bar Keeper												
Booker belonging to Mrs Watson & 5 negroes left by Squire Boon to secure a debt viz:—2 tithables & 3 not tithable.														
Anderson, Henry	24	Mason		1; 537	5			1						
Jones, David	33	Taylor		1; 554		1								
Jones, Levina (Wife)	18													
Jones, John ⎱children														
Jones Sarah ⎰														
Ambler, J	40			1; 592	7	2								
Ambler, Rebecca (Wife)	36													
Ambler, Elizabeth	17													
Ambler, Mary	16													
Ambler, Ann	9													
Ambler, Lucy	6													
Mary Lucas, a free mulatto, hireling, her son 6 years old & her daughter an infant, 3 cows, 5 horses, 4 weels, & 1 waggon.														
Total, 107					44	35	21	57	1			8		8 wag-gons, 3 goats.

WARDSHIP No. 2.

NAME.	Age.	Occupation.	Time of residence.	Lots improved and their numbers.	Slaves titha-ble.	Slaves not titha-ble.	Cat-tle.	Horses.	Mares.	Colts.	Mules.	Wheels.	Billiard tables.	Miscella-neous.
Adams, Richard	56	Merchant		8, 9	8	10	8	3				6		
Adams, Elizabeth	45													
Adams, Thomas Bowler	22													
Adams, Richard	21													
Adams, William														
Adams, John	8													
Adams, Samuel	6													
Adams, Tabitha	24													
Adams, Elizzbeth Griffin	23													
Adams, Ann	18													
Adams, Sarah	16													
Adams, Ailcea	13													
Free mulattoes or negroes in lot or rear of residence; Brazilde Romo, Hannah, his wife, a tithable, and Grace, a tithable; 1 horse, 1 mare; tenant to Mr. Adams. Lease for 10 years, 18 months residence. P. Humphrey Baine, Nancy Baine; 1 horse; tenant to Mr. Borum; were there 12 months. Negro permitted to hire themselves; Rachael belonging to John Gun, Junr.														
Armistead, William	28	Merchant			4	3		2				2		
Armistead, Sucanna	20													
Armistead, Ann	1													
Free mulatto Bridget Anderson; tenant in Crouch Tenement.														
Armistead, Isaac	30	Ship Carpenter.			3		1							
Free mulatto, Peter Robertson; name not given belonging to Isaac Armistead.														
Beckley, John	26	Atto. at law			4	2								
Craig, Adam	22									1			2		
Hay, Charles	18														
Free mulatto Kate Robertson, 26; Nancy, a slave tithable or hire; 1 horse. Tenant to Charles Lewis.														

A list of the inhabitants and property in the city of Richmond: 1782—Continued.

WARDSHIP No. 2—Continued.

NAME.	Age.	Occupation.	Time of residence.	Lots improved and their numbers.	Slaves tithable.	Slaves not tithable.	Cattle.	Horses.	Mares.	Colts.	Mules.	Wheels.	Billiard tables.	Miscellaneous.
Boush, John	32	Auditor			1	1			1			2		
Boush, Ann	26													
Nell, negro, permitted to hire; belonging to John Boush.														
Bridgwater, James	23	Waterman	3 months				2							
Bridgwater, Elizabeth	28													
Swine, Mary	54													
Stanhope, William	8													
Stanhope, Polly	6													
Bridgwater, Daniel	27	Waggoner	3 months				1	4						
Bennet, James	30	Sippling			1	2	2	1						
Bennet, Rebecca	29													
Bennet, Nathaniel	14													
Bennet, William	13													
Bennet, Nancy	12													
Bennet, Polly	10													
Bennet, Lucy	8													
Bennet, James	7													
Bennet, Susanna	5													
Bennet, William	45						1		1					
Bennet, Ann	29													
Bennet, Polly	14													
Bennet, Nancy	12													
Bennet, Sally	9													
Bennet, Jonnie	6													
Bennet, William	5													
Bennet, Barlary	3													
Borum, William	24	Ship Carp						1						
Clark, John	36	Cabinet Maker.			1			1						
Thompson, Molly	28													
Roberts, Charles	14													
Thompson, William	10													
Crouch, John	23	Storekeeper			5	3								
Drummond, James	25	Shoe Maker	5 weeks											
Ferguson, Charles Edward	30	Watch Maker												
Ferguson, Sally	21													
Ferguson, Polly	3													
Franklin, William	27	Cooper					1							
Franklin, Lucy	27													
Franklin, Elizabeth	9													
Franklin, Delphia	6													
Franklin, William	4													
Humphreys, Joshua	39	Watch Maker			3			1	1					1 ordinary license.
Humphries, Anne	36													
Humphreys, David	12													
Humphries, Elijah	10													
Humphreys, Mary	7													
Humphreys, Charles	6													
Humphries, Parry	4													
Humphries, Joshua	8													
Redding, Emelia	18													
Hill, Judy	9													
Hubbard, Sarah	40	Washer & Sunps trips.	4 weeks											
Hubbard, Betsy	19													
Hubbard, Pattie	15													
Montgomery, Alexander	28	Joiner	7 months		1	1								
Montgomery, Margaret	25													
Montgomery, Jannet	4													
Montgomery, Peggy	1½													
Newman, Edward	27	Joiner	10 months						1					
Newman, Anne	64													
Adams, Tabitha	20													
Perry, William	25									1					
Perry, Sarah	24													
Rose, William	48	Keeper O. Jail												
Rose, Mary	48													
Rose, Polly	17													
Rose, Thomas	14													
Rose, Peyton	6													
Roper, John	35	Ordy Keeper			2	1	8	4	1					1 ordinary license.
Roper, Elizabeth	30													
Clarkston, Mary	18													
Clarkston, Matthew	16													
Clarkston, Davis	13													
Craddock, Robert	16													
Tankard, Stephen	50	Ordy Keeper			8	7	5	1						1 ordinary license.
Tankard, Martha	45													
Tankard, Peggy	17													
Tankard, John	16													

A list of the inhabitants and property in the city of Richmond: 1782—Continued.

WARDSHIP No. 2—Continued.

NAME.	Age.	Occupation.	Time of residence.	Lots improved and their numbers.	Slaves tithable.	Slaves not tithable.	Cattle.	Horses.	Mares.	Colts.	Mules.	Wheels.	Billiard tables.	Miscellaneous.
Taylor, Mary..............	23				1									
Williams, Lecrutia.........														
Tucker, Valentine..........	46	Shoe Maker ..	1 week....		1									
Edwards, Thomas..........	20	Typler.......												
Total, 100.............					43	30	33	23	4			12		

WARDSHIP No. 3.

NAME.	Age.	Occupation.	Time of residence.	Lots improved and their numbers.	Slaves tithable.	Slaves not tithable.	Cattle.	Horses.	Mares.	Colts.	Mules.	Wheels.	Billiard tables.	Miscellaneous.
Mitchell, Rob...........	36			A; 2 lots, C. & F., belonging to Nicholas B. Seabrook; 1 lot # 63 belonging to John Orr; 2 lots no. 99 & 100 John Hague.	3	4	3	5	1			4		1 waggon.
Mitchell, Judith.............	36													
Hughs, Judith....	14													
Hughes Hester....	10													
Mitchell, William...........	2													
Mitchell, Sally...........	4													
Free mulattoes:														
Patterson, Anne........	50													
Patterson, Rice........	20													
In a house of Geo. Picketts on lot No. D.														
Free negro:														
Bettie. Lives with Miles Taylor lot No. 17.	29													
Hired negroes:														
Lucy Macklin. In a house of Mr. Eges. She belongs to Mr. Neumans, dancing master in King William. Friday, a wench belonging to estate of Isham Allen and living at Doctor Browns.														
Archer, Thomas.............	30	Merchant....		D; Square 4, lots Nos. 63 & 64, 77 & 78, owners not known.	1	2								
Roberts, Alexander M.......	40													
Gauf, Effy........	35													
Gauf, Judy.....	18													
Gauf, Sally.....	20													
Rent the lot of Samuel Mitchell No. 32.														
Hired negroe:														
James. In a house on lot No. 1, a carpenter belonging to Mr. Armistead.														
Barr, Richard.............	30	Shoemaker...		Square 4, lots #91 & 92, 105 & 106 Rchd. Adams; 3 lots No. 62, 75 & 76, owners not known.	1									
Barr, Elizabeth.............	27													
Toplift, Throthy..........	17													
Burnet, Thomas...........	9													
Burnett, William..........	8													
Gauf, Molly.............	25													
Rents house of Mr. Ege.														
Hired negro:														
Richard. In a house on lot No. 1, a carpenter to Edward Harris of James City county.														
Pickett, Geo.................	30	Merchant....		D; Square 4, lots No. 89 & 90, 103 & 104, owners unknown.	2	1		1	1			2		
Blackwell, Thomas..........	30													
Sal...................	10													
Lives with Mr. Samuel Ege (black) Free born.														
Hired negro:														
Stephen. A laborer belonging to estate Josea Pleasants.														
Brown, John.................	30	Clerk........		3 lots #88, 102 & 101, owners unknown.										
Whitlock, William..........	21													

A list of the inhabitants and property in the city of Richmond: 1782—Continued.

WARDSHIP No. 3—Continued.

NAME.	Age.	Occupation.	Time of residence.	Lots improved and their numbers.	Slaves tithable.	Slaves not tithable.	Cattle.	Horses.	Mares.	Colts.	Mules.	Wheels.	Billiard tables.	Miscellaneous.
Lambert, David	28	Merchant		2; No. B & 59				1						
Norman, James	50													
Norman, Mol	34													
Norman, Pleasant	7													
Norman, John	5													
Norman, Betsy	2													
Scott, Abnegal	14													
Scott, Elec	11													
Part of lot No. 71 the above property.														
Halkit, Thomas	39	Butcher	6 months	No. 59; 2 lots 99 & 100, Jno. Hague.										
Halkit, Lucy	50													
Younghusband, Isaac	55	Merchant		1 lot No. O, John Rose; 3 lots No. 2, 15, 16.	1	1								
Graves, Francis	36	Merchant	7 months	No. 16; 1 lot No. O, owner unknown.				1						
Harwood, John, Jun	17			Land of Richd Adams.										
Craton, William	39	Wages												
Craton, Mary	40													
Craton, Hanah	8													
Craton, Nell	6													
Craton, Polly	15													
Rawlings, Rob	35	Sadler		No. 29; 2 lots L & M, owner unknown; 1 lot No. 71, Mary Warwick; 1 lot part of Nos. H & K John Clapton.	2	1	2	1						
Rawlings, Sarah	28													
Rawlings, Ben	12													
Rawlings, Moses	10													
Rawlings, Betsey	7													
Rawlings, John	2													
Gunn, John	18	No business												
Geoghegan, Anthony	54	Barber		No. 29; 1 lot No. 8 a lumber house on same, the property of Thomas N. Randolph.	2	2								
Geoghegan Martha	45													
Lyon, Mary	68													
Geoghegan, Molly	8													
Rowland, Tach	37	Merchant	11 months	No. 17; 1 lot No. 101, William White.	5	2	5	4	1	1		2		
Rowland, Peggy	28													
Rowland, James	5													
Rowland, Frances	3													
Rowland, Peggy	1													
Hare, Kitty	17													
Hare, James	14													
Hare, Nancy	10													
Taylor, Miles	23	Sadler	15 months	No. 57	1									
Taylor, John	20													
Taylor, James	18													
Clay, James	22	Merchant	18 months	2; No. 31 & 48	1			1						
Beal, John	24	Merchant	9 months					1						
Brown, Rob	54	Doctor		3; Nos. 3, 4, 18	4	3		1						
Edge, Dorthy	58													
Edge, Jacob	28	Silversmith		2; No. 3 & 47	2	4		3						
Edge, Sally	19			No. 50										
Edge, Nancy	17													
Valentine, Sally	9													
Catlet, John	18													
Barker, William	25	Taylor	2 years	1; No. 86	1									
Barker, Elizabeth	20													
Pedley, Thomas	24	Barber	18 months	Part No. 9	1									
Pedley, Polly	20													
Thomas, Catrien	60													
Thomas, Jacob, Jun	24	Barber	16 months	Part No. 19	1									
Thomas, Jacob, Sen	52	Barber												
Thomas, Nancy	18													
Stewart, Samuel	30	Carpenter	6 months											
Isaac, Isaiah	35	Merchant		3; No. 34 & 48		1	1	2						
Cohn, Jacob	35	Ditto	18 months											
Mardecai, Jacob	20	ditto	3 Ditto											
Isaac, Mary	53													
Sian, Ann	12													

A list of the inhabitants and property in the city of Richmond: 1782—Continued.

WARDSHIP No. 3—Continued.

NAME.	Age.	Occupation.	Time of residence.	Lots improved and their numbers.	Slaves tithable.	Slaves not tithable.	Cattle.	Horses.	Mares.	Colts.	Mules.	Wheels.	Billiard tables.	Miscellaneous.
Edge, Samuel	24	Inspector of flour.		No. 321 & 46	2	1	2	7						1 wagon.
Edge, Elizabeth	30													
Hutchings, Martha	19													
Rysal, Nancy	9													
Edge, Jacob, Jun	5													
Edge, Betsey	3													
Edge, Molly	1													
Orr, John	57	Taylor		2; No. 35 & 49	6	2	3							
Orr, Eliz	60													
Orr, Nancy	25													
Underwood, Martha	18													
Underwood, James	14													
Lawson, Philip	15													
Burton, John	19													
Sikes, James	23													
Parke, Jonathan	29	Tanner		1; No. 82	6			3						
Dempsey, Thomas	29	Ditto												
Harper, John	25	Ditto												
Valentine, Edwd	19	Ditto												
Galt, Gabriel	33	Tavern Keeper		5; No. 30, 44, 60, 74, & 43.	7	1	10	4						1 ordinary license.
Galt, Elizabeth	32													
Galt, Martha	20													
Galt, Betsey	19													
Hutchings, Dolly	19													
Galt, Wm	10													
Galt, Karel	14													
Galt, Elizabeth	4													
Bowler, Richard	21	Bar Keeper												
Mantonia, John	40	Gardner												
Molly	30	Washer												
Sherer, Samuel	25	Chairmaker		2; No. 5 & 519	4	4	3	1						
Sherer, Hanna	18													
Sherer	39													
Sherer, Salley	17													
Bayley, Betsey	19													
Blades, Wm	18													
Slate, James	32	Taylor	18 months	½ Lot #6 of S. Sherer.	2	1								
Slate, Kitty	26													
Slate, Geo	4													
Slate, Mary	2													
Pearman, John	16													
Warrington, Rebeccah	14													
Sennos, Thomas	14													
Harwood, Wm	17													
Skinner, Richard	25	Taylor	18 months	Part No. 6										
Skinner, Mary	20													
Jones, John	29													
Puryear, Ruben	22													
Hutchins, James	50	Joiner		Part No. 20										
Richardson, William	25	Silver Smith		No. 87	1	1	3	2						
Richardson, George	21	Ditto												
Richardson, John	60	Joiner												
Richardson, Abigal	45													
Richardson, Frances	19													
Richardson, Peggy	17													
Jeffs, Susanna	17													
Jeffs, Mary	17													
Moss, Samuel	16	Apprentice												
Davenport, Geo	18	Ditto												
Crenshaw, Nathenal	19	Hireling												
Didde, Archibald	14	Apprentice												
Liggon, John	40	Cooper		2; No. G. & I	2		2	4	1					
Allegre, Jane, Sen	42	Mantua Maker		Part No. H. & K.	1	2	2							
Allegre, Jane, Jun	18	Ditto												
Allegre, Sophia	16	Ditto												
Allegre, William	14													
Warrick, Mary	40	Sempstress		3; No. 58 & 12										
Warrick, Jane	20													
Warrick, James	20													
Warrick, Tabitha	14													
Warrick, William	12													
Warrick, John	9													
Smith, Francis	34	Merchant		Part No. 20										
Omohundro, Thomas	28	School Master	18 months	Part No. H										
Sheerman, Robert	27	Joiner	9 Months	Part No. ½										
Sheerman, Mary	27													
Combes, Richard	47	Shoemaker												
Sheerman, John	2													
Sheerman, Jane	1													
Todd, Geo	41	Merchant		2; No. 21 & Y			2	4	1	1			6	1 ordinary license.

A list of the inhabitants and property in the city of Richmond: 1782—Continued.

WARDSHIP No. 3—Continued.

NAME.	Age.	Occupation.	Time of residence.	Lots improved and their numbers.	Slaves tithable.	Slaves not tithable.	Cattle.	Horses.	Mares.	Colts.	Mules.	Wheels.	Billiard tables.	Miscellaneous.
Todd, Elizabeth	23													
Todd, William	12													
Todd, Rob	1													
Patton, Geo	23	Commissary	12 Mon	On Part 21										
Powers, Richard	27	Barber	24 Do	On Part 21		1			1					1 ordinary license.
Powers, Eleanor	29													
Cookeson, Mary	7													
Cookeson, Samuel	5													
Whitlow, Hayes	31	Shoemaker	8 Months	No. 21										
Whitlow, Sarah	24													
Whitlow, Elizabeth	9													
Whitlow, Aaron	7													
Whitlow, Moses	4													
Whitlow, Daniel	3													
Fisher, Joseph	48	Pedler	13 Months											
Fisher, Nancy	29													
Kerson, William	40	Cooper	9 Mo				1							
Kerson, Elizabeth	32													
Kerson, William	8													
Kerson, Susanna	10													
Barret, John	34	Merchant		Part No. 34 & 48	4	3	2	1	1					
Barret, Mary	32													
Barret, Mary Jun	7													
Barrett, Charles	5													
Barret, Elizabeth	3													
Barret, John L	1													
Oglervey, Elizabeth	34	S. Mistress		Lot 34 & 49	4	4	2	1						
Oglervey, Mary	8													
Oglervey, James	6													
Oglervey, Peter	4													
Oglervey, Elizabeth	15													
Prentice, William	20	Printer		Lot No. 36										
Nicholson, Thomas	24	Ditto				1			2					
Prind, William A	16	Ditto												
Boyd, Rob	30	Merchant		1; No. 36	4	4	1	1						
Boyd, Martha	24													
Boyd, William	3													
Boyd, Martha	1													
Cowley, Abraham	17													
White, William	27													
Liper, Andrew	31	Doctor	24 Mo	On No. 36	2	2		1						
Castle, Joseph	26		4 Do					1						
Roper, Jese	36	Merchant		1; No. 61	4	5	3		1					
Roper, Docia	35													
Cocke, Docher	18													
Roper, Eldridge	12													
Lord, Dresham	29	Potter	9 Mo											
Robinson, John	28	Ditto	9 Ditto											
Pate, Matthew	27	S Maker	24 Ditto	No. 57 T. Colders.	1	1		1	2					
Pate, Elizzbeth	23													
Pate, Nancy	5													
White, Nancy	10													
Total, 205					76	61	49	51	11	2		14	1	

WARDSHIP No. 4.

NAME.	Age.	Occupation.	Time of residence.	Lots improved and their numbers.	Slaves tithable.	Slaves not tithable.	Cattle.	Horses.	Mares.	Colts.	Mules.	Wheels.	Billiard tables.	Miscellaneous.
Harvey, John	33	State Register	7 mo	1; 601	5	6	1	2				4		
Harvey, Margeret	25													
Harvey, Gabriella	10													
Harvey, Amelia	8													
Lewis, Robert	18													
Robertson, Colin	25													
McKeand, John	40	Merchant	19½ years	1	4	6	4	2						
McKeand, Elizabeth	31													
McKeand, Elizabeth Carter	9													
McKeand, Jeannett	7													
McKeand, Priscilla	5													
McKeand, John	2													
McKeand, Willis	1													
Kennon, Judith	10													
One hired negro of Mr. Watson Free Mulattoe Turkey Smith and four other wenches in kitchen adjoining auditor's office.														
Irvin, Charles	35	Merchant	2 years		1			3						
Baine, Robert	30													
Rose, Alexandria	27													
Gordan, Fleming	18													
Buchanan, James	45	Merchant	25 years											
Buchanan, Alexandria	30													

A list of inhabitants and property in the city of Richmond: 1782—Continued.

WARDSHIP No. 4—Continued.

NAME.	Age.	Occupation.	Time of residence.	Lots improved and their numbers.	Slaves tithable.	Slaves not tithable.	Cattle.	Horses.	Mares.	Colts.	Mules.	Wheels.	Billiard tables.	Miscellaneous.
Price, John White	19													
Hayes, James	23	Printer	2 years		1			1						
Hayes, John	22													
Hunter, Miles	25													
Simmon, William	25													
Webb, Foster	22	Treasurer	2 Ditto		1									
Free negro Kate, her husband and one young wench.														
Lyon, W.	35	Ditto	Ditto		1									
Nelson, Alex	30	Merchant	6 months					1	1					
Hired negro Davy, Mrs. Mills York.														
Heron, James	28													
Car, James	17													
Skipwith, Fuller	19													
Oldham, William	23	Planter	6 months			1		2						1 ordinary license.
Coulter, Alex	22	Saddler	2 weeks											
Nicholson, George	24	Merchant	7 months		1			1	1					
Nicholson, Andrew	19													
Heath, Henry	18													
Younghusband, Isaac	18													
Ross, Davis & Co.		Merchants												
Pennock, William	30	Ditto	7 months		3	3	2	3				4		
Pennock, Anne	21													
Vandeval, David	21													
Lewis, Robert	18													
Punter, Henry	23													
Currie, James	25	Physician	12 years		3	1		2						
Hay, William	33	Merchant	3 Ditto		3	5	1							
Hay, Elizabeth	28													
Hay, John	6													
Simmons, James	21													
Smith, W.	18													
Crouch, Richard	50	Smith	7 years		2	2	3	6						
Crouch, Elizabeth	42													
Crouch, John	22													
Crouch, Richard	18													
Crouch, Stephen	16													
Crouch, Elizabeth	12													
Crouch, Robert	5													
Crouch, Polly	2													
Hired negro George of William Burtons, tender at the warehouse.														
Harrison, Benjamin	54	Governor	1 year		7	9	2	1	2					
Harrison, Sady	52													
Bassett, Miss	18													
Harrison, Sattey	13													
Harrison, Benjiman	30	Merchant	4 months		1	1		2						
Denholm, Archibold	25													
Cormick, M.	33													
Formicola, Lerafino	39	Taver Keeper	19 months		10	7	3	3				6		
Formicola, William	28													
Formicola, Eva	2													
Radcliffe, Thomas	23													
Brown, John	45													
Stewart & Hopkins	21	Merchants	3 months		1			3				2		
Cox & Higgans	21	Ditto	6 months		1			3						
Thruston, Charles	17													
Hogg, Richard	37	Tavern Keeper	11 years		10	8	5	7				2		1 ordinary license.
Younghusband, William	37													
Younghusband, Bettsey	11													
Younghusband, Mary	4													
Brown, Nancy	35													
Williams, James	21													
Anderson, James	42	Smith	10 months		1	2								
Anderson, Hannah	41													
Anderson, Billy	15													
Anderson, James	7													
Anderson, Henry	4													
Anderson, Robert	9 mos.													
Apprentices 9.														
Banks, Henry	21	Merchant	2 years		1			1				4		
Banks, Hunter & Co.		Merchants	2 Ditto		1			1				4		
Foushee, William	31	Physician	5 Ditto		6		2	3				6		
Foushee, Mrs.	25													
Foushee, John	6													
Foushee, Nancy	3													
Foushee, Charlotte	6 mos.													
Free negro Thomas Jacob														

A list of the inhabitants and property in the city of Richmond: 1782—Continued.

WARDSHIP No. 4—Continued.

NAME.	Age.	Occupation.	Time of residence.	Lots improved and their numbers.	Slaves tithable.	Slaves not tithable.	Cattle.	Horses.	Mares.	Colts.	Mules.	Wheels.	Billiard tables.	Miscellaneous.
Ramsey, James............	20													
Smith, Wm................	20													
Jones, Samuel.............	27	Boarding-house.	5 months .		2	1	4		1					
Jones, Mary..............	25													
Maxwell, Capt...........														
Hunter, James...........	35	Merchant......	7 months .											
Hunter, Mary Anne......	34													
Hunter, John.............	4													
Hunter, Adam............	1													
Kem, William.............	50													
Capt. Young gives in one negro hired of Colo. Davies refuses to given in his property in a house adjoining J. Hunter's. Mr. Abbey Peggy McLin her daughter and a child also Mr. Tewer a Soldier, works in the laboratory, his wife and child one horse. Also in the adjoining house assembly house Mr. Jones, a child, and a negro girl. Also in J. Hunters, Mrs. Roades, Molley Tye, and four children. Also in Mrs. Streaker's 8 children, four orphan children (Barkers). Three heard of cattle one mare belonging to her eldest son who is lame.														
Total, 151					66	54	30	46	4		2	28		

INDEX.[1]

---

[1] No attempt has been made in this publication to correct mistakes in spelling made by the assistants, and the names have been reproduced as they appear upon the state lists.